SCRIPTURE STUDY

FOR LATTER-DAY SAINT FAMILIES

THE NEW TESTAMENT

SCRIPTURE STUDY

FOR LATTER-DAY SAINT FAMILIES

THE NEW TESTAMENT

Dennis H. Leavitt and Richard O. Christensen
with
Bruce L. Andreason, Randall C. Bird, John Bushman, Dean E. Garner, Lynn H. Hatch,
Nihla W. Judd, and Todd A. Knowles

DESERET
BOOK

SALT LAKE CITY, UTAH

© 2006 Dennis H. Leavitt, Richard O. Christensen, Bruce L. Andreason, Randall C. Bird, John Bushman, Dean E. Garner, Lynn H. Hatch, Nihla W. Judd, Todd A. Knowles

Library of Congress Cataloging-in-Publication Data

Leavitt, Dennis H.
  Scripture study for Latter-day Saint families : the New Testament / Dennis H. Leavitt, Richard O. Christensen ; with Bruce L. Andreason . . . [et al.].
      p. cm.
  Includes bibliographical references and index.
  ISBN-10 1-59038-585-3 (pbk.)
  ISBN-13 978-1-59038-585-2 (pbk.)
  1. Jesus Christ—Mormon interpretations. 2. Bible. N.T.—Criticism, interpretation, etc. 3. Mormon families—Religious life. I. Christensen, Richard O. II. Andreason, Bruce L. III. Title.
  BX8643.J4L42 2006
  225.071—dc22   2006014460

Printed in the United States of America
Publishers Printing, Salt Lake City, UT

10   9   8   7   6   5   4

CONTENTS

CONTENTS

INTRODUCTION

Paul spoke of Timothy in the New Testament, saying "that from a child thou hast known the holy scriptures." (2 Timothy 3:15.) Timothy's knowledge and faith are impressive and cause us to consider where his faith and expertise came from. His mother and grandmother seem to have played a key role, as suggested in 2 Timothy 1:5. Certainly, the home is the place where children receive the most important teaching. (See also Alma 56:47.)

In modern revelation, the Lord declared, "I have commanded you to bring up your children in light and truth." (D&C 93:40.) In February 1999, the First Presidency sent a letter to Church members throughout the world, giving the following instruction: "We call upon parents to devote their best efforts to the teaching and rearing of their children in gospel principles which will keep them close to the Church. The home is the basis of a righteous life, and no other instrumentality can take its place or fulfill its essential functions in carrying forward this God-given responsibility." (First Presidency letter, Feb. 11, 1999.)

One of the best ways to fulfill this responsibility is through family scripture study. "Just as the best meals are home cooked," Elder M. Russell Ballard explained, "the most nourishing gospel instruction takes place at home." (*Ensign,* May 1996, 81.) Elder Howard W. Hunter testified, "Families are greatly blessed when wise fathers and mothers bring their children about them, read from the pages of the scriptural library together, and then discuss freely the beautiful stories and thoughts according to the understanding of all." (*Ensign,* Nov. 1979, 64.)

This book is the third in a series designed to help Latter-day Saint families enhance teaching moments while studying the scriptures together. The first book provided resources for studying the Book of Mormon, the "keystone" of our religion. The second book provided ideas to use in studying the Doctrine and Covenants, which President Ezra Taft Benson called the "capstone" of our religion. (See *Ensign,* May 1987, 83.) This third book in the series will help your family take a more in-depth look at the great teachings of the New Testament.

"In the New Testament and its four Gospels, each with its unique emphasis, the portrait of the living and mortal Messiah is painted powerfully. All of it was . . . for the primary purpose described by John: 'But these are written, that ye might believe that Jesus is the Christ, the Son of God; and that believing ye might have life through his name.' (John 20:31.)" (Neal A. Maxwell, *Ensign,* Dec. 1986, 21–23.)

WHAT YOU WILL FIND IN THIS BOOK

Every effort has been made to make this book simple to use, even for children. As you thumb through it, you will notice that it follows the New Testament sequentially.

You will find many helpful and exciting tools in this book: object lessons, activities, scripture insights, prophetic statements, discussion questions, stories, and many other learning aids. They are provided to help your family unlock the scriptures and deepen their testimonies. You will find yourselves having enjoyable and inspirational experiences with the scriptures in your family.

HOW TO USE THIS BOOK

It is important to note that this is a resource book. Do not feel obligated to use every lesson. Think of the book as a buffet of scripture-teaching ideas from which you may pick and choose as part of your daily scripture diet. Simply review the material for the chapter or verses you are studying and, with the aid of the Spirit, select those teaching ideas you feel will be most helpful to your family. Help your children use this book so they will be able to teach the family also.

Each chapter is divided into shorter scripture blocks that have a unifying message or theme. The scripture is listed first and is followed by a simple question or statement. The question or statement gives you an idea of the topics discussed in that particular section. As you read these questions and statements, you can quickly find a topic your family might need to consider.

You will also see icons, or small pictures. These icons are quick visual prompts to let you know what kind of teaching ideas you might use with that chapter. Though many lessons use more than one teaching approach, the icon identifies the major approach for that set of verses. The icons you will find are explained below.

This is the activity icon. It lets you know your family will be actively involved during the lesson. The activity might be drawing pictures, creating projects, taking a quiz, or making a list. Some activities might be more involved than others and may require preparation in advance.

This is the insight icon. It lets you know that questions, cross-references, side-by-side comparisons, or other teaching devices will be used to lead your family to find insights in the scriptures.

This is the object lesson icon. Simple objects or experiments can draw the mind to see spiritual parallels in the scriptures. We have attempted to keep the object lessons simple so they can be used with children of various ages.

This is the quotation icon. It identifies teaching suggestions that use quotations, usually from General Authorities, to help us understand a doctrine or scriptural concept or help us apply important principles in our lives.

This is the story icon. It points to a story used to help teach a block of scripture.

Sometimes the story is a personal one told by a family member. Sometimes you will find a case study that develops a situation for which answers can be found in the scriptures. You may even find a story told by a General Authority. Sometimes the story simply inspires you to do better.

This is the writing and scripture marking icon. It identifies activities designed to allow your family to write their impressions and feelings in a journal or other book. Pondering and expressing thoughts in writing helps to make gospel principles and doctrines part of our thinking and actions. Marking the scriptures personalizes them so family members can remember what was important to them.

HELPING YOUR FAMILY BECOME STUDENTS OF THE SCRIPTURES

This book assumes each family member will have his or her own copy of the Latter-day Saint editions of the scriptures and a journal. All references to the Bible Dictionary, Topical Guide, Maps and Index of Place-Names (called Gazetteer in pre-1999 copies of the Bible), and Appendix are to the LDS edition of the King James Version of the Bible.

The teaching ideas invite everyone to participate in scripture study. There will be a lot of searching in the pages of your scriptures. Often you will be asked to look for things in a block of scripture that you might mark, list, or discuss. As you study in this manner, your scriptures will become a handbook for life. On subsequent visits to these scripture pages, they will be marked or have marginal notes that will remind family members of principles learned before.

Do not be afraid to slow down as you study. Elder Henry B. Eyring taught, "We may be nourished more by pondering a few words, allowing the Holy Ghost to make them treasures to us, than to pass quickly and superficially over whole chapters of scripture." (*Ensign,* Nov. 1997, 84.) Elder D. Todd Christofferson explained, "For the gospel to be written in your heart, you need to know what it is and grow to understand it more fully. That means you will study it. When I say 'study,' I mean something more than reading. It is a good thing sometimes to read a book of scripture within a set period of time to get an overall sense of its message, but *for conversion, you should care more about the amount of time you spend in the scriptures than about the amount you read in that time.* I see you sometimes reading a few verses, stopping to ponder them, carefully reading the verses again, and as you think about what they mean, praying for understanding, asking questions in your mind, waiting for spiritual impressions, and writing down the impressions and insights that come so you can remember and learn more. Studying in this way, you may not read a lot of chapters or verses in a half hour, but you will be giving place in your heart for the word of God, and He will be speaking to you." (*Ensign,* May 2004, 11; emphasis added.)

You might also find the following suggestions helpful:

- When possible have a set time for scripture study: each morning, at dinnertime, or each night.
- Make sure everyone has scriptures, marking pens or pencils, and a journal.
- Begin with prayer and invite the Spirit.
- Adapt teaching ideas to the different ages and learning levels of family members.
- When you come across difficult words, be sure to stop and define them.

YOU CAN REAP BLESSINGS

Imagine what might happen as a result of studying the scriptures together as a family. What value might there be in an increased understanding of the scriptures? What would it mean to young and old alike to be comfortable and conversant with the scriptures? Elder Neal A. Maxwell taught, "The igniting in our youth of a love for the holy scriptures is to ignite a fire that will probably never be extinguished. After all, our youth can take their scriptures and their understanding thereof with them long after parents, bishops, and advisers, of necessity, are left behind." (*Ensign,* Apr. 1985, 10.) Notice these promises given by President Ezra Taft Benson: "When individual members and families immerse themselves in the scriptures regularly and consistently . . . testimonies will increase. Commitment will be strengthened. Families will be fortified. Personal revelation will flow." (*Ensign,* May 1986, 81.)

We hope you find this book useful. We hope it will bless you and your family. It is our wish that you might find some keys to unlocking the scriptures and feasting upon the words of Christ. (See 2 Nephi 31:20.) We feel the following counsel from the Lord has application to family scripture study: "Wherefore be not weary in well-doing, for ye are laying the foundation of a great work. And out of small things proceedeth that which is great." (D&C 64:33.)

MATTHEW

The first four books in the New Testament are known as the Gospels, and each gives an account of the earthly ministry of our Lord Jesus Christ. "The four Gospels are not so much biographies as they are testimonies. They do not reveal a day-by-day story of the life of Jesus; rather, they tell who Jesus was, what he said, what he did, and why it was important." (Bible Dictionary, "Gospels," 683.) The Joseph Smith Translation changes the title of each Gospel to "The Testimony of St. Matthew," or St Mark, or St. Luke, or St. John. (See footnotes for Matthew Title; Mark Title; Luke Title; John Title.)

Matthew lived in Capernaum and was a publican, or tax collector, by profession. He was one of Jesus' Twelve Apostles and saw firsthand much of what he wrote. "It appears . . . that Matthew was written to persuade the Jews that Jesus is the promised Messiah. To do so, he cites several Old Testament prophecies and speaks repeatedly of Jesus as the Son of David, thus emphasizing his royal lineage." (Bible Dictionary, "Gospels," 683.) Matthew was the only Gospel writer to tell about the visit of the wise men, a star in the East, the holy family's escape to Egypt, and Herod's slaying of the infants. (See Matthew 2:1–16.)

MATTHEW 1: CHRIST IS BORN

Matthew 1:1–17
Why did Matthew list Jesus' genealogy?

Ask your family to scan Matthew 1:1–17 and find the names of individuals they recognize and know something about. Have family members take turns sharing what they found. Ask family members who have received a patriarchal blessing if they are related to any of the individuals on the list (for example, Abraham, Isaac, or Jacob). Have them tell what it means to them to share common ancestors with the Savior. Ask:

- How many generations can you count in these verses? (42.)
- How many generations of our family genealogy can we identify?
- What do these verses suggest about how important genealogy was to the Jews at the time of Christ?

- How can we show that family history or genealogy is important to us?
- Who are the two ancestors of Jesus that Matthew focuses on? (Abraham and David.)
- Why do you think Matthew emphasized that Jesus descended from Abraham and David?

To help answer that last question, share this insight from Elder James E. Talmage: "Matthew's account is that of the royal lineage, . . .

"Had Judah been a free and independent nation, ruled by her rightful sovereign [king], Joseph the carpenter would have been her crowned king; and his lawful successor to the throne would have been Jesus of Nazareth, the King of the Jews." (*Jesus the Christ,* 86–87.) Ask:

- How does Joseph's royal lineage change what you think of him?
- In Matthew 1:16, what did Matthew call the Savior? (Invite family members to read and mark Matthew 1:16, footnote *e.*)
- Why do you think Matthew tied the name

"Jesus" and the title "Christ" together? (Jesus is the "Anointed One," thus testifying to the Jews that He is the Messiah.)

Tell your family that though the Jews in general did not recognize Joseph's or Jesus' royal lineage, Matthew testified of Jesus Christ's position as the "Anointed One," the Son of God.

Matthew 1:18–25
Joseph's dilemma

Read Matthew 1:18 with your family and ask them to point out any words or phrases they do not understand. (The footnotes may be helpful in answering their questions.) If someone mentions the word *espoused,* have a family member read the following: "Betrothal, or espousal, in that time was in some respects as binding as the marriage vow, . . . yet an espousal was but an engagement to marry, not a marriage." (Talmage, *Jesus the Christ,* 84.)

Ask your family how Joseph's love for Mary was tested when he learned that Mary was "with child." How do you think you would have felt if you had been in Joseph's place? Read together Matthew 1:19 and find out what Joseph decided to do. Ask:

- What do you think the phrase "minded to put her away privily" means?
- How does footnote 19*b* help us to understand this phrase?
- What does this teach us about Joseph?

Point out that under Jewish law, Joseph could have accused Mary of breaking their engagement and brought her to public trial. Such a trial would have humiliated Mary and may have resulted in a death sentence. Joseph kindly decided to release her from the marriage contract as privately as the law allowed. Before that occurred, however, something happened to change Joseph's mind. Read Matthew 1:20–25 together. Ask:

- What did the Lord do to help Joseph understand and accept Mary's condition?
- Which Old Testament prophet had prophesied about a virgin giving birth to a son who would be called Emmanuel? (See Matthew 1:23, footnote *a.*)

- What does *Emmanuel* mean? (See Bible Dictionary, "Immanuel," 706.)
- What does the name "Jesus" mean? (See Bible Dictionary, "Jesus," 713.)
- What was Joseph's response to the dream?

Give each family member a sheet of paper or have them use their scripture journals. Have them write a characteristic of Joseph they admire and how having that characteristic might help them when they are faced with a difficult dilemma.

MATTHEW 2: "WHERE IS HE THAT IS BORN KING OF THE JEWS?"

Matthew 2:1–11
Where did the wise men find Jesus?

 Invite family members to show with their fingers how many wise men came to see Jesus. Show a picture of the wise men with King Herod (such as *Gospel Art Kit,* no. 203, or *Ensign,* Dec. 1997, 44). Ask why they think most people believe there were three. Have your family look for how many wise men are mentioned as you study Matthew 2.

Read together Matthew 2:1–11 and discuss the following questions:

- Where was Jesus born and who was the king of Judea? (Verse 1.)
- Who were the wise men looking for? (See Matthew 2:2, footnote *a.* The wise men were not seeking just a "king" but the "Messiah.")
- Why were Herod and "all Jerusalem with him" troubled? (Herod was a jealous king and didn't want anyone else, not even a son, to take his throne.)
- Why do you think Herod *really* wanted to know where and when this "King of the Jews" was born? (See verse 16.)
- How did the wise men find Jesus?
- Where did the wise men find Jesus? (Invite family members to mark the words *house* and *young child.*)

Ask family members if they noticed the words *manger* or *baby* or any mention of the number of wise men. What does this tell us about the Christmas story as it is told year after year? Share the following statements by Elder Bruce R. McConkie:

"There came from unnamed eastern lands . . . an unspecified number of wise men. Whether they were two, three, or twenty in number is a matter of pure speculation." (*Doctrinal New Testament Commentary,* 1:102–3.)

"It appears from Matthew's account . . . that . . . the wise men came two or three years after the birth of our Lord. It was a 'young child,' not a baby, they were seeking; he was found in a 'house,' not a manger; and Herod 'sent forth, and slew all the children that were in Bethlehem, and in all the coasts thereof, from two years old and under.'" (*Mormon Doctrine,* 230.)

Invite family members to look once more at Matthew 2:10–11 and mark phrases that show how the wise men felt about finding the young child. Have family members record in their journals how they would have felt if they had been the ones who found the child Jesus.

Conclude by singing verse 2 of "Stars Were Gleaming," 37 and/or verse 4 of "The Nativity Song." (*Children's Songbook,* 52–53.)

MATTHEW 3: JESUS IS BAPTIZED BY JOHN THE BAPTIST

Matthew 3:1–6
Who am I?

Come to scripture study dressed in shorts, a towel (wrapped around your waist), and bare feet, saying, "Prepare ye the way of the Lord." Also bring a container of honey and a picture of grasshoppers placed on a plate. Ask your family to scan Matthew 3:1–6 and find answers to the following questions:

- Who am I?
- Why do you think I'm dressed this way?
- How do you like my diet?
- What is my mission?

Invite a family member to read the first paragraph of the entry for "John the Baptist" in the Bible Dictionary, page 714. Ask your family what they learned about John's mission.

Take turns reading Matthew 3:2–6 again. Ask:

- What message did John teach the Jews?
- Why did he teach them this message?
- How is this message similar to the one being taught by missionaries today?
- How will this message help "prepare . . . the way of the Lord" in our day?

Discuss ways your family can also prepare for the coming of the Lord and set goals to become more prepared.

Matthew 3:7–12
Who were the Pharisees and Sadducees?

Invite someone to read Matthew 3:7. Ask family members what two groups of people were watching John the Baptist baptize in the River Jordan. After your family identifies each group, ask them who they think the Pharisees and Sadducees are. Read key phrases from the Bible Dictionary that describe each group (see Bible Dictionary, "Pharisees," 750; "Sadducees," 767) and ask family members to listen for differences between them.

Have children draw pictures of fruit, stones, a viper (snake), a winnowing fan (see picture below), an axe, and a tree.

Ask family members to match the objects with the verses in Matthew 3:7–10, 12. The information below might help your family understand some difficult phrases.

"Generation of vipers." A viper is a snake. The spiritual poison of the Pharisees and Sadducees was as dangerous as the venom of poisonous snakes.

"Fruits meet for repentance." This phrase can also be translated as "fruits worthy of repentance."

(Matthew 3:8, footnote *a*.) In other words, these "fruits" are things people can do to show they are trying to repent. Elder Neal A. Maxwell taught, "A turning unto God brings forth appropriate works 'meet for repentance' (Acts 26:20)." (*Not My Will, but Thine*, 68.)

"God is able of these stones to raise up children." Elder James E. Talmage wrote: "[The Jews] held that the posterity [children] of Abraham had an assured place in the kingdom of the expected Messiah, and that no proselyte [convert] from among the Gentiles could possibly attain the rank and distinction of which the 'children' were sure. John's forceful assertion [statement] that God could raise up, from the stones on the river bank, children to Abraham, meant to those who heard that even the lowest of the human family might be preferred before themselves unless they repented and reformed." (*Jesus the Christ*, 123.)

"Axe is laid unto the root of the trees." Elder James E. Talmage said: "[The Pharisees' and Sadducees'] time of wordy profession [useless talk] had passed; fruits were demanded . . . ; the ax was ready, aye, at the very root of the tree; and every tree that produced not good fruit was to be hewn [cut] down and cast into the fire." (*Jesus the Christ*, 123.) One day, these religious leaders who lacked true spirituality would be cut down and destroyed.

"Whose fan is in his hand, and he will thoroughly purge his floor." A winnowing fan is a large wooden fork used to throw the grain in the air so the wind will carry the chaff (the dry, inedible husk) away. The heavier seed falls to the ground and can be gathered up. Elder Bruce R. McConkie wrote: "Jesus . . . has taken the winnowing fan of judgment in his hand to blow the chaff from the wheat. . . . The eternal harvest has begun and shall not cease until the threshing floor of the world is thoroughly purged [cleaned], with every straw of chaff blown away, leaving only the wheat to be garnered [stored] into a heavenly granary. And the chaff he will burn with fire unquenchable!" (*Mortal Messiah*, 2:381–82.)

Have one family member read Matthew 3:8–12, while the others mark what they think are key points of John's teachings to the Pharisees and Sadducees. Have them share their key points with the family. Be sure to note the significant helps in the footnotes, including the Joseph Smith Translation of Matthew 3:38–40. Ask:

- How would you summarize John's message to the religious leaders among the Jews?
- How did John let them know that he was not the Messiah?
- How does knowing about the weakened spiritual state of Jewish religious leaders help us see the need for the coming of the Messiah?
- What kind of baptism was John performing?
- What does it mean to be "baptized with fire?"

Invite family members to think about what attitudes or actions in their own lives Jesus would want them to get rid of before He comes again. Encourage them to write in their journals one thing they will do to make their lives more acceptable to the Lord.

Matthew 3:13–17

Was Jesus baptized for the same reasons we are?

Fold a blank piece of paper in half. Open it again and on one side write the title "Jesus" and on the other "Us." Read together 2 Nephi 31:12–13 and look for reasons why we need to be baptized. Have one person record the answers under the heading "Us." Then read 2 Nephi 31:6–9 and Matthew 3:15 as a family. Have someone record under the heading "Jesus" the reasons that Jesus was baptized. Compare the lists and discuss why some of the reasons we need to be baptized are different from the reasons Jesus was baptized.

Share the following by Elder Bruce R. McConkie: "Nephi gives four reasons as to how our Lord fulfilled all righteousness in being baptized: (1) He humbled himself before the Father; (2) He covenanted to be obedient and keep the Father's commandments; (3) He had to be baptized to gain admission to the celestial kingdom; and (4) He set an example for all men to follow. (2 Ne. 31:4–11.) To fulfil all righteousness is to perform every ordinance, keep every commandment, and do every act necessary to the attainment of eternal life." (*Doctrinal New Testament Commentary,* 1:123.)

Show a picture of Christ being baptized by John the Baptist. (See *Gospel Art Kit,* no. 208.) Have your family look closely at the picture as another family member reads Matthew 3:13–17. Have them identify the members of the Godhead that were present during this event. Ask:

- Which verse indicates that Heavenly Father was there? (Verse 17.)
- Which verse indicates that the Holy Ghost was there? (Verse 16.)
- To what did John compare the Holy Ghost?

You may need to help your family understand the relationship between the Holy Ghost and a dove by sharing the following statement from President Joseph Fielding Smith: "The Holy Ghost is a personage, and is in the form of a personage. It does not confine itself to the *form* of the dove, but in *sign* of the dove. The Holy Ghost cannot be transformed into a dove; but the sign of a dove was given to John to signify the truth of the deed, as the dove is an emblem or token of truth and innocence." (*Answers to Gospel Questions,* 1:77.)

Share your testimony of the importance of baptism.

MATTHEW 4: JESUS RESISTS TEMPTATIONS

Matthew 4:1–11
How do we resist temptations?

Assign family members to read aloud, as if they were one of the following individuals in Matthew 4:1–11 (including the JST changes in the footnotes): Matthew (the narrator), Jesus, and Satan. Tell them to read dramatically, using the tone of voice they think might have been used by that individual in this story.

As this reader's theater is performed, invite all family members to think about what this event teaches us about Satan and about resisting temptation. After the reader's theater, have family members share their thoughts, insights, and questions. As part of this discussion, consider doing the following:

- Ask: What did Jesus do to resist temptation? After noting that Jesus responded to each temptation by quoting scriptures and separating Himself from Satan, invite family members to tell how a passage of scripture has helped them in a time of temptation. Also make a list of some common temptations and have family members use the Topical Guide to find scriptures that would be appropriate to use in resisting that temptation.
- Share the following statement from President David O. McKay about Jesus' temptations: "Classify them, and you will find that under one of those three nearly every given temptation that makes you and me spotted, ever so little maybe, comes to us as (1) a temptation of the appetite or passion; (2) a yielding to the pride and fashion or vanity of those alienated from the things of God; or (3) a desire for the riches of the world, or power among men." (*Gospel Ideals,* 154.) Make a list of common temptations today that fit in each of those three categories. Talk about how important it is to resist those temptations and why. Share ideas of how you and your family can resist the temptations of Satan.

Matthew 4:11–12
Help from the Savior

Have family members read Matthew 4:11–12 to themselves. Then have them read Joseph Smith Translation Matthew 4:11 in footnote 11a of the LDS edition of the Bible and look for what insight it provides to Matthew 4:11–12. Ask:

- What does this small insight teach us about the Savior?
- What are some ways Jesus has sent relief to you in times of need?

Read together Mosiah 24:14–15 and Alma 36:3 for additional testimonies of this principle.

Matthew 4:13–16
Where are these places?

Have one family member read Isaiah 9:2 aloud while the rest of the family looks for a phrase in Matthew 4:12–16 that is similar. Talk about reasons Matthew may have quoted Isaiah in this instance.

Explain to your family that at the time of Isaiah the lands of Zebulon and Naphtali (the lands close to the Sea of Galilee) were on the main road to Egypt from the lands northeast of Israel. It was the first place attacked by armies from the East, and the people who lived there often experienced much bloodshed and trouble. It was known as a region of death. Furthermore, it was a land of great physical "darkness," because of the abundance of black-colored stone in the ground (basalt). At the time of Jesus it was a land in spiritual darkness as well. But, as Isaiah promised, at the time of Matthew it became the main residence of Jesus, who brought light and hope to this land of darkness and death.

Invite family members to give examples of how they have personally received the light and hope Jesus offers. Also discuss how the Savior's light has not only affected people in the Holy Land of Israel, but also people throughout the world.

Matthew 4:17–22
Following the Savior

Read Matthew 4:17–22 together and invite family members to tell how important they think nets were in the story. Ask:

- Why do you think these men "straightway" left their nets?
- According to verses 23–24, what did these men eventually see Jesus do?
- How do you imagine it might have felt to be one of these early disciples?

Show them a picture of a net similar to those used for fishing in New Testament times. (See *Gospel Art Kit,* nos. 209 or 210.)

Distribute to each family member a few strips of paper and a marker to write with. As you read the following statement by Elder Joseph B. Wirthlin, have family members write on strips of paper the different activities that may be considered "nets" today.

" 'If the Savior were to call you today, would you be just as willing to leave your nets and follow Him?' I am confident that many would.

"But for some, it may not be such an easy decision. . . .

"Nets come in many sizes and shapes. The nets that Peter, Andrew, James, and John left were tangible objects—tools that helped them earn a living.

"We sometimes think of these four men as modest fishermen who did not sacrifice much when they left their nets to follow the Savior. To the contrary, . . . Peter, Andrew, James, and John were partners in a prosperous business. . . .

"Nets are generally defined as devices for capturing something. In a more narrow but more important sense, we might define a net as anything that entices or prevents us from following the call of Jesus Christ, the Son of the living God.

"Nets in this context can be our work, our hobbies, our pleasures, and, above all else, our temptations and sins. In short, a net can be anything that pulls us away from our relationship with our Heavenly Father or from His restored Church.

"Let me give you a modern example. A computer can be a useful and indispensable tool. But if we allow it to devour our time with vain, unproductive, and sometimes destructive pursuits, it becomes an entangling net.

"It is impossible to list the many nets that can ensnare us and keep us from following the Savior. But if we are sincere in our desire to follow Him, we must straightway leave the world's entangling nets and follow Him. . . .

" . . . I do not suggest that the road will be easy. But I will give you my witness that those who, in faith, leave their nets and follow the Savior will experience happiness beyond their ability to comprehend. . . .

"We have nets that must be tended and nets that must be mended. But when the Master of ocean, earth, and sky calls to us, 'Follow me,' we should leave the entangling, worldly nets behind and follow His footsteps." (*Ensign,* May 2002, 15, 17.)

Ask your family the following:

- According to Elder Wirthlin, what are some "nets" we deal with today?
- Why is it difficult for some of us to leave our "nets" behind?

- What can you do to get rid of entangling "nets" in your life?

Attach the strips of paper made by family members to the picture of the net you displayed. Put the picture in a place in your home where it will remind the family of the call to more fully follow the Savior. *1-4-15*

MATTHEW 5: JESUS BEGINS THE SERMON ON THE MOUNT

Matthew 5:1–12
How do we come unto Christ?

Ask your family to read Matthew 5:1–12 and find the most common word used in those verses. Afterwards have them look at footnote 3a in the LDS edition of the Bible for answers to the following questions:

- What does "blessed" mean?
- Why is this group of verses called the Beatitudes?
- What do you think is the main message of these verses?

Invite your family to read "Beatitudes" on page 620 of the Bible Dictionary. Then ask, What do you think the sentence "Rather than being isolated statements, the Beatitudes are interrelated and progressive in their arrangement" means?

Show your family some stairs in the house. If your house does not have stairs, use a ladder or draw stairs on a piece of paper. Divide your family into groups and assign verses 3–12 evenly among the groups. Tell each group to read their assigned verses and especially look for insights in the footnotes. Then have them write a short summary (four or five words at the most) of each verse on a half sheet of paper and place their paper where it would belong on the stair steps. Then have each group read their verses and share what they found in the footnotes that helps with understanding the verses.

Notice that these steps can show how one turns from sin to righteousness. To help family members better understand this, do the following together:

1. Identify a common sin.

2. Give an example of what a person would feel and do if he or she were "poor in spirit" regarding that sin.
3. Continue identifying feelings and actions a person might experience for each of the remaining steps.

Matthew 5:13–16
Why is Jesus calling us salt and light?

 Show your family a saltshaker and have one of them read Matthew 5:13 aloud. Ask:

- Why do you think the Savior refers to His followers as salt?
- What are some common uses for salt?

Uses for Salt	Example	Spiritual Application
Flavoring	Salt enhances the flavor of food.	We should enhance the lives of others we associate with.
Preservative		
Antiseptic		

- How could we apply the uses for salt to the things Jesus expects us to do?

Fill in and expand the accompanying chart during your discussion of the preceding questions:

Explain that salt does not spoil over time. Salt can only lose its savor by being contaminated by something else. Mix some dirt in your salt and discuss why contaminated salt would not be useful for cooking or as an antiseptic. Ask:

- How could our lives become contaminated? (By mixing with the evil or dirty influences in the world.)
- What are some common "contaminations" many people struggle with today?
- Why would being contaminated with sin harm our abilities to help others?

Encourage your family to stay clean and pure from evil influences so they do not "lose [their] savor."

Show your family a flashlight and read together Matthew 5:14–16. Have your family work through and discuss the examples and spiritual application of light in their lives. Make a chart about the uses of light, just like you made for the uses of salt.

Matthew 5:17–20
Did Jesus destroy the law of Moses?

 Show your family a seed and discuss these questions:

- Is a seed alive?
- When a seed sprouts into a plant, does the seed die or start a new life?

Ask your family to look for comparisons with the seed and the law of Moses as they read Matthew 5:17–19.

Have family members turn to "Law of Moses" in the Bible Dictionary (722–23). Invite half of the family to read the first paragraph and the other half to read the third paragraph. Have each group prepare and share the three most important things they think the family should learn from those paragraphs about the law of Moses.

Ask your family:

- What did Jesus want the Jews to know about the law of Moses?
- What do you think Jesus means when He says that not "one jot or one tittle" shall pass away from the law? (Not even the smallest portion will be ignored in the fulfillment of the law of Moses.) To illustrate this, show your family a picture of a jot and tittle. You can find this symbol next to the word *JOD* preceding verse 73 of Psalm 119.

Explain that examples of Christ's greater law of righteousness is found in Matthew 5:21–48 and is discussed in the activity below.

The jot is the tenth letter in the Hebrew alphabet and is also the smallest letter. The tittle is the small mark, or point, on the upper left edge of the jot and on other letters as well. These could be compared to the dot on an i or the cross mark through a t in our writing.

Matthew 5:21–48
The law of Christ leads to perfection

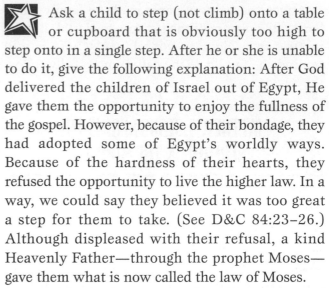 Ask a child to step (not climb) onto a table or cupboard that is obviously too high to step onto in a single step. After he or she is unable to do it, give the following explanation: After God delivered the children of Israel out of Egypt, He gave them the opportunity to enjoy the fullness of the gospel. However, because of their bondage, they had adopted some of Egypt's worldly ways. Because of the hardness of their hearts, they refused the opportunity to live the higher law. In a way, we could say they believed it was too great a step for them to take. (See D&C 84:23–26.) Although displeased with their refusal, a kind Heavenly Father—through the prophet Moses—gave them what is now called the law of Moses.

Now place a chair next to the table or cupboard and have the child step onto the chair and then onto the table or cupboard. Explain that the chair is like the law of Moses. It prepared them to later be able to step higher and live the fulness of the gospel.

Make a chart like the one on the following page and fill it in as you study together Matthew 5:21–48. (Note also the footnotes, especially the JST changes, as you study.) As family members take turns reading verses from the law of Moses column, have them identify (1) the subject of the law, (2) the associated higher law that Christ gave from the scriptures, and then have them (3) give a modern example of how a person could live that higher law today.

After completing the chart, ask some of the following questions:

- Which of these higher laws do you think is most difficult to obey?
- Why is it important to strive to live Christ's higher law?
- What would 1 Nephi 3:7; Moroni 10:32–33; and Matthew 11:28–30 teach us about Christ and His willingness to help us follow a higher law?
- Which of these laws do you think our family ought to focus on now and why?

Law of Moses	Law of Christ	Example
Verse 21 _____	→ Verses 22–26 _____	_____
Verse 27 _____	→ Verses 28–30 _____	_____
Verse 31 _____	→ Verse 32 _____	_____
Verse 33 _____	→ Verses 34–37 _____	_____
Verse 38 _____	→ Verses 39–42 _____	_____
Verse 43 _____	→ Verses 44–47 _____	_____

Matthew 5:20, 48

How righteous do you need to become to make it to heaven?

Discuss the following question with your family: Do you believe it is possible to become perfect? Why or why not? Read Matthew 5:48; 3 Nephi 27:19; and Doctrine and Covenants 1:31 and ask:

- According to these verses, what does the Lord expect from each of us?
- How can we attain that level of righteousness?
- Do you think it is possible to never make a mistake? Why or why not?
- What must we do whenever we fall short of perfection?

Have family members read Moroni 10:32–33. Ask them what it teaches about how perfection is attained. Testify that as we try our best to keep our covenants and humbly follow the Savior—seeking to live the higher law of righteousness of the heart, God grants us His Spirit that cleanses us, forgives us, and prepares us to live this great higher law spoken of in Matthew 5 and ultimately become perfect through Christ's perfection and righteousness.

Share the following statement from Elder Dallin H. Oaks:

"The Final Judgment is not just an evaluation of a sum total of good and evil acts—what we have *done.* It is an acknowledgment of the final effect of our acts and thoughts—what we have *become.* It is not enough for anyone just to go through the motions. The commandments, ordinances, and covenants of the gospel are not a list of deposits required to be made in some heavenly account. The gospel of Jesus Christ is a plan that shows us how to become what our Heavenly Father desires us to become." (*Ensign,* Nov. 2000, 32.)

MATTHEW 6: JESUS CONTINUES THE SERMON ON THE MOUNT

Matthew 6:1–18

Being righteous in secret

If the children in your family are young, play a quick game of hide-and-seek. If your family is older have them remember playing hide-and-seek as a child. Ask family members to share some reasons they wouldn't want others to tell where they were hiding.

Ask a family member to define the word *secret* and list some reasons, events, or times when they would want a secret kept. Have your family look for what the Lord wants us to keep secret as you read together Matthew 6:1–4. (If they need help defining the word *alms,* have someone read aloud Matthew 6:1, footnote *b,* and discuss what it means.) Ask:

- Why might Heavenly Father want our alms, or righteous acts, to be kept secret?
- How do you feel when you secretly do good things for others?
- What are some other advantages of doing good

things in secret instead of telling others what you did?

- What problems might occur if we brag about our good works?
- What examples can you think of when someone served in secret?

Read verses 16–18 with your family and look for how being righteous in secret applies to fasting. What reasons did the Savior give for fasting in "secret"?

Write each family member's name on individual pieces of paper. Fold the papers and place them in a container and have each family member draw a name from that container, while being careful to keep it secret. Invite each family member to secretly serve during the upcoming week the person whose name they drew. Ask them to think about how they feel as they give this service, and talk about it as a family when the week has concluded.

Matthew 6:5–15
How can we improve our prayers?

Ask members of your family to share their testimony of prayer and some reasons why they love to pray. Discuss some of the following questions with your family:

- How might our prayers become more meaningful?
- What are some things we should pray for?
- When do you think it is appropriate to pray?
- Where are some proper places to pray?

Read Matthew 6:5–8 together and talk about the Savior's teachings about prayer. Ask:

- What are some of the Savior's main ideas in these verses?
- What does the phrase "vain repetitions" mean? (*Vain* means "worthless or meaningless." *Repetition* means "to repeat.")
- Why do you think it is important to be thoughtful and sincere when we pray?

Explain that Matthew 6:9–15 contains the Lord's Prayer, and it shows us the proper pattern for prayer, not the exact words we should use when praying. Have a family member read Matthew 6:9–15 and identify the pattern the Lord described.

Share the following statement by President James E. Faust:

"*First,* prayer is a humble acknowledgement that God is our Father and that the Lord Jesus Christ is our Savior and Redeemer. *Second,* it is a sincere confession of sin and transgression and a request for forgiveness. *Third,* it is recognition that we need help beyond our own ability. *Fourth,* it is an opportunity to express thanksgiving and gratitude to our Creator. It is important that we frequently say: 'We thank Thee . . . ,' 'We acknowledge before Thee . . . ,' 'We are grateful unto Thee . . .' *Fifth,* it is a privilege to ask Deity for specific blessings." (*Ensign,* May 2002, 59–60; emphasis added.)

Ask each family member to match the verses from Matthew 6:9–13 with each of the five things President Faust mentioned. Share your testimony of prayer and invite your family to follow the Lord's pattern in their personal prayers.

Matthew 6:19–23
Heavenly treasures

Place a set of scriptures in a gift bag (or tie a bow around them) and hide them in a room. Tell your family you have a "hidden treasure" and ask them to find it. Ask the person who finds the "treasure" to read Mathew 6:19–21. Ask:

- According to Matthew 6:19–21, what are the two kinds of treasure the Savior speaks about?
- In which of these categories does scripture study belong? Why?
- What are some other examples of heavenly treasures?
- What are some examples of "treasures upon earth?"
- Why is it dangerous to mainly focus our efforts on gaining earthly treasures?

Read Matthew 6:22–23 and consider sharing some experiences where you have gained more "light" by having your eye single to heavenly treasures rather than to earthly treasures.

Matthew 6:24–33
What should we seek first?

Show your family a picture of the Savior, some money, and an article of clothing. Ask your family to think about how they would rank these three items in importance. Have a family member read Matthew 6:24 and then discuss the following questions:

- What is mammon? (See footnote 24*e*.)
- How can worldly possessions get in the way of gaining a strong testimony?
- How might the Savior rank these three items in importance?

Tell your family that as a resurrected being the Savior gave a sermon similar to the one recorded in Matthew 5–7. He gave it to the Nephites in the Americas. Have your family compare 3 Nephi 13:25 with Matthew 6:25 and find who the Savior was specifically speaking to in 3 Nephi. (The Twelve.) Read Matthew 6:25–32 together and make a list of those things the Twelve were commanded not to worry about.

Explain to your family that riches can be used for good if we seek God first. Ask a family member to read Jacob 2:18–19 and Matthew 6:33 (include footnote 33*a*). Share your feelings regarding putting God first and how that priority has blessed your life.

MATTHEW 7: JESUS CONCLUDES THE SERMON ON THE MOUNT

Matthew 7:1–5

Is it ever okay to judge?

Share the following story with your family: "Lara and Todd had been told repeatedly not to leave their bicycles in the driveway. One day their father came home to find both bikes in the driveway. He confronted Todd first. 'Todd,' he said, 'I just found Lara's bike in the driveway. What should I do?'

"You should ground her for a week, like you told us you would,' Todd answered.

"Later, the father asked Lara: 'I just found Todd's bicycle in the driveway. What should I do?'

"Give him another chance; he'll remember next time,' Lara responded.

"The father then called both children together and had them read Matthew 7:1–2."

Have a family member read Matthew 7:1–2 aloud. Then ask your family what they think the

father did next, based on those verses. Share the rest of the story:

"When they finished reading these verses, he said: 'Todd, you are grounded for one week. Lara, I'll consider this a warning if you'll go out and move the bike right now.'" (Story adapted from *Duties and Blessings of the Priesthood,* 129.)

Discuss these questions as a family:

- What do you think is the basic message of Matthew 7:1–2?
- What idea from these verses caused the father to give Lara and Todd different punishments?

Read together the Joseph Smith Translation of Matthew 7:1 (see footnote 1*a*) and Moroni 7:14–18. Ask:

- How does the Joseph Smith Translation change Matthew 7:1?
- What is righteous judgment?
- What are the dangers of judging unrighteously?
- How can you make sure you judge righteously?

Have your family read together Matthew 7:3–5 looking for some added insights about judging others. Ask them to particularly notice footnotes *b* and *c* to verse 3 as they read. Show your family a 2-by-4 piece of wood to illustrate a beam and a small sliver or speck of sawdust (or a picture of these things) to illustrate a mote. Discuss these questions:

- Why is it sometimes easier to see faults in others than to see our own faults?
- Why are we usually more willing to point out another person's faults than our own?
- What are some "beams" in your life that can get in the way of judging others more righteously?
- What must you do to cast the "beams" out of your own eye?

Ask family members to scan Matthew 7:4–5 and find what Jesus calls people who unrighteously correct others. Invite family members to better follow the Savior's counsel in the coming week.

Matthew 7:6
Do not cast pearls before swine

Show your family a picture of an expensive watch or piece of jewelry. Talk about why it would be inappropriate to give that jewelry to the family dog, or any other animal, for a toy. What would an animal do with jewelry? Ask your family to read Matthew 7:6. Ask:

- What does it say swine (pigs) will do to pearls?
- What does it mean to "trample them under their feet"?
- What other valuable thing is mentioned in that verse that tells us that Jesus is not talking about real pigs or real pearls? ("That which is holy.")
- What "holy" things, as valuable as pearls, do you think Jesus is talking about?

To help answer that last question, have your family read the Joseph Smith Translation additions to this verse. (See JST Matthew 7:9–11 in the Bible Appendix.) Ask:

- What other word is used to describe these holy things? (Mysteries.)
- What other word is used for the dogs and swine? (The world.)
- What do you think the "mysteries" are and why can the world not know them?

To help answer that question, share the following: "There are, however, certain 'mysteries' that are held in reserve for those whose hearts are right and whose faith is full (3 Ne. 26:9–11; Ether 4:7). The Prophet Joseph Smith taught that the mysteries can only be revealed to men of faith, for the moment you teach these sacred secrets to those of fallible faith, 'they will be the first to stone you and put you to death' (*[Teachings of the Prophet Joseph Smith]*, 309)." (Brewster, *Doctrine and Covenants Encyclopedia*, 374.)

Share with your family experiences you have had sharing the gospel with others and how you could tell who was likely to listen with respect and who was not.

Matthew 7:7–11
Will He answer?

 Write the letters *A, S,* and *K* vertically on a piece of paper.

Show your family the paper and tell them each letter is the first letter of a word that is part of a formula Jesus gave for us to follow when we want answers or need direction in our lives. Have your family study Matthew 7:7 and figure out what the three words are. Once they have discovered the three words, read Matthew 7:7–11 as a family and have one family member summarize the main message. Ask the following questions:

- Why do you think Jesus uses all three words?
- How would you describe the amount of effort required to *ask* compared to the effort required to *seek* and to *knock?*
- What do you think Jesus is trying to teach us by giving us this *ask and seek and knock* formula?

Share the following about prayer:

"As soon as we learn the true relationship in which we stand toward God (namely, God is our Father, and we are his children), then at once prayer becomes natural and instinctive on our part (Matt. 7:7–11). Many of the so-called difficulties about prayer arise from forgetting this relationship. Prayer is the act by which the will of the Father and the will of the child are brought into correspondence with each other. The object of prayer is not to change the will of God, but to secure for ourselves and for others blessings that God is already willing to grant, but that are made conditional on our asking for them. Blessings require some work or effort on our part before we can obtain them. Prayer is a form of work and is the appointed means for obtaining the highest of all blessings." (Bible Dictionary, "Prayer," 752–53.) Discuss the following questions:

- What do you learn in Matthew 7:11 that helps you want to pray to Heavenly Father?
- What could you do to more diligently seek Heavenly Father's help?
- What have been some of your favorite experiences with prayer?

Matthew 7:12
The Golden Rule

Share the following statement with your family. President Gordon B. Hinckley said, "If only each of us would reflect occasionally on that Christ-given mandate and make an effort to observe it, this would be a different world. There would be greater happiness in our homes; there would be kinder feelings among our associates; there would be much less of litigation and a greater effort to compose differences. There would be a new measure of love and appreciation and respect.

"There would be more generous hearts, more thoughtful consideration and concern, and a greater desire to spread the gospel of peace and to advance the work of salvation among the children of men." (*Ensign*, Dec. 1991, 4.)

Tell family members the following to help them remember the scripture reference for the Golden Rule: We should live this principle seven days a week, twelve months of the year. (Matthew 7:12.) Testify of the importance of living the Golden Rule, and encourage family members to always do so.

Matthew 7:13–14, 21–23
Who can enter the kingdom of heaven?

Give each family member a pencil, a straight edge or ruler, and a piece of paper. Ask them to draw a horizontal line and label it "Straight Line." Ask them to draw another straight line parallel to the first about one-half inch (two centimeters) apart. Label the space between the two lines "Narrow Way." Then ask them to draw a strait gate at the left end of the two lines. If they seem confused about drawing a strait gate, have a family member read aloud Matthew 7:13–14. Ask, "What is the difference between the word *straight* (spell it) and the word *strait* (spell it)?" If they need help, have them look at the alternate Greek translation for the word *strait* in Matthew 7:13, footnote *a*. Ask:

- What would a "strait gate" be? (A narrow gate like on a narrow way. Have them write "Strait Gate" on their paper.)
- How do these verses describe the way to destruction?
- How do the scriptures describe the way to eternal life?

- Why would the way to eternal life be more narrow than the way to destruction? (See 1 Nephi 15:34–36.)

Tell your family that in Matthew 7:21–23 Jesus provided further explanation concerning who can enter the kingdom of heaven. Read these verses together as a family. Ask, "Besides believing in Jesus as our Lord and Savior, what else is required?" (*Doing* His will.) Tell your family the phrase "I never knew you" in verse 23 is changed in the Joseph Smith Translation to "Ye never knew me" (*Joseph Smith's "New Translation" of the Bible*, Matthew 7:33, 252; or *LDS Collector's Library*, JST Matthew 7:33.) Ask:

- Why is it essential that we know Jesus Christ? (See John 17:3.)
- How does doing His will help us know Him? (See Mosiah 5:10–13.)
- How well do you feel you know the Lord?
- What could you do to get to know Him better?

Matthew 7:15–20
The test of a prophet

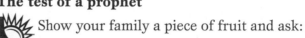

Show your family a piece of fruit and ask:

- How can you tell if a fruit tree is a good tree or a bad tree?
- Have you ever tasted a sour orange or a bitter apple?
- What good would a tree be that grew bad fruit?

Read Matthew 7:15–20 together as a family and look for what Jesus compared to a fruit tree. Ask:

- How can we tell if a person is a false prophet or a true prophet?
- What other words could you use in place of "fruits" in these verses? (Works, acts, or accomplishments.)
- How useful is a person whose works or advice are bad?

Have a family member read verses 16–20 aloud, substituting the word *works* each time the word *fruits* occurs. Show a picture of the current prophet and make a list of some his "fruits." Share your love for him and your testimony of his calling, authority, and power.

Matthew 7:24–29
The wise man and the foolish man

For this object lesson you will need some moist sand that will conform to the shape of a cup. Turn a cup of moist sand upside down on a plate (like building a sand castle) and then stand a small object on top of the sand. (You could use a coin, pen cap, small plastic toy, etc.) Give a volunteer a squirt gun or squirt bottle and have them squirt the sand without hitting the object on top. See how long it takes to erode the foundation of sand and make the object topple. Ask for another volunteer, only this time, instead of using sand, place a solid rock on the plate with the same object on top of it. The same rules apply. They can squirt the foundation but not the object on top.

Read Matthew 7:24–27 as a family. Ask:

- What did the foolish man use for the foundation of his house?
- What did the wise man use for his foundation? You may want to have the family sing "The Wise Man and the Foolish Man." (*Children's Songbook,* 281.)
- How does this parable apply to us?
- According to Helaman 5:12, who is the "rock" on which we should build?
- How are the Savior's teachings and life similar to a rock foundation?

1:7~15

MATTHEW 8: THE SAVIOR'S HEALING TOUCH

Matthew 8:1–33
Faith-filled miracles

Show your family a picture of the Savior's hands. (See *Gospel Art Kit,* nos. 211, 213, 215, or 234.) While showing the picture, read them the following statement from Elder Howard W. Hunter: "Whatever Jesus lays his hands upon lives. If Jesus lays his hands upon a marriage, it lives. If he is allowed to lay his hands on the family, it lives." (*Ensign,* Nov. 1979, 65.)

Talk about the following questions:

- Why do you think the Savior's touch is so powerful?
- What is your favorite scriptural example of the Savior touching and miraculously healing someone?
- What are some modern miracles that have occurred because of Jesus Christ's power?
- What does a person need to do in order to receive a miracle?

To help answer that last question, share the following: "Miracles were and are a response to faith, and its best encouragement. They were never wrought without prayer, felt need, and faith." (Bible Dictionary, "Miracles," 732–33.)

Make a chart similar to the one below. Assign family members the verses listed and have them identify the miracle that occurred and evidence that those who received the miracle had faith.

Verses	Miracle	Evidence of faith
Matthew 8:1–4		
Matthew 8:5–13		
Matthew 8:14–15		
Matthew 8:16–17		
Matthew 8:23–27		
Matthew 8:28–33		

Ask your family members to share what they learned about the role of faith in receiving miracles. You might like to read the first two paragraphs in the entry "Faith" in the Bible Dictionary, pages 669–70, to your family.

Have your family look again at the chart you made and notice the variety of the miracles Jesus performed. What does this chapter teach us about the power of the Savior? (He has power over all things: diseases, the weather, devils, etc.) Share your testimony of the power Jesus Christ has to bless us in all things and why we can safely have faith in Him.

Matthew 8:23–27
How strong was the faith of Jesus' disciples?

 Ask each family member to rate their faith on a scale of 1–10 and then ask each one to share why they chose that rating. Invite family members to share examples of their faith and some positive experiences that have resulted.

Show your family a picture of the Savior. (See *Gospel Art Kit,* no. 214.) Have a family member read aloud Matthew 8:23–27. Ask:

- What part of that story most impresses you?
- Why was Jesus able to still the storm but the disciples were not?
- What evidence can you find that shows the current level of the disciples' faith?
- What do you think the disciples could have done if they had greater faith?

Share the following:

"Jesus, now awake, before he arises from the wooden bench whereon he lay, says to those who sought his help: 'Why are ye fearful, O ye of little faith?' After the storm is quelled, he will say to them again: 'Where is your faith?' From this we need not suppose they were without faith. Their very importunings [persistent pleadings] bore witness of their assurance that this man, whom they followed as the Messiah, could do whatever must be done to prevent disaster. Their lack of faith—as with all of us—was one of degree; had they believed with that fervor that might have been the case, they of themselves could have stilled the storm, without arousing their weary Lord from his needed rest." (McConkie, *Mortal Messiah,* 2:276–77.)

Ask family members:

- What challenges or trials do you face that are like the storm in this story?
- How are we sometimes like the disciples when these "storms" arise in our lives?
- How do you show the Savior that you have faith that He can help you with your trials?
- What could you do to increase your faith in the Lord?

Matthew 8:28–34
Even the devils know Jesus is the Son of God

 Show your family the following diagram and discuss the following questions:

- What have you been taught about your premortal life?

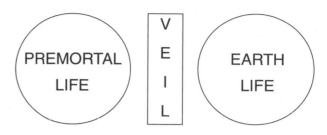

- According to Doctrine and Covenants 29:36–37, who else was there with us?
- Why was the devil "cast out" of the premortal life?
- According to 2 Nephi 2:17–18, what does the devil now seek?
- Why can't you remember your premortal life?

Now read Matthew 8:28–34 as a family. Discuss the following questions:

- What does this teach you about Satan's followers?
- What did these devils know about Jesus?
- Where did they get that knowledge?

To help with the last question, read Matthias F. Cowley's statement to your family,

"It is probable, from some references in the Scriptures, that if our spirits were sent here unembodied [without bodies], the remembrance of the past would come with us. At least, this was doubtless the case with Lucifer and his rebel host. . . .

"It is not probable that these evil spirits knew Jesus because of a testimony from above, while all Judea failed to recognize in Him the Messiah, the Savior of the world. Many likely knew Him because they had been associated and acquainted with Him before the world was." (Cowley, *Talks on Doctrine,* 118–19.)

Testify to your family that it is not adequate just to know Jesus. We must exercise faith in Him and follow His teachings.

MATTHEW 9: JESUS HEALS MANY

Matthew 9:1–38
What common reason is there for the healings performed by Jesus?

 Tell family members they will be given verses to read that discuss healings.

(Depending on the age of your family, you may need to have some older family members read the verses while younger ones draw pictures of what is happening.) Have your family look for details such as the following as they read:

- People involved
- Location of healing
- Situation of person needing healing
- What Jesus did and said
- Why the healing occurred (if mentioned)

Make a chart like the one below but leave the Healing column blank. Assign each family member to study one or more sets of verses. When all are finished, have them tell what happened in the verses they read and record it on the chart. Remind them to use the footnotes and other study helps.

Verses	Healing	Why the miracle occurred
Matthew 9:1–8	Healing of palsy	
Matthew 9:18–19, 23–26	Raising one from the dead	
Matthew 9:20–22	Healing an issue of blood	
Matthew 9:27–31	Healing the blind	
Matthew 9:32–34	Healing a man possessed	
Matthew 9:35	Healing every sickness and disease	

After everyone has given their report, have a family member reread Matthew 9:2, 22, 29 aloud. Ask:

- What is the stated reason for these miracles?
- What evidences of faith did you find in the other healings?
- Whose faith was involved in the raising of the young girl from the dead?
- What reason do we have to believe that faith was involved in the other healings as well?

To help answer that last question, have your family write Ether 12:12–19 in the margin next to Matthew 9:22. Go to Ether 12:12–19 and read it together. Ask:

- What power is involved in all miracles?
- In whom should our faith be centered?
- How can we increase our faith?

Share the following from Elder Bruce R. McConkie: "Faith is a gift of God bestowed as a reward for personal righteousness. It is always given when righteousness is present, and the greater the measure of obedience to God's laws the greater will be the endowment of faith." (*Mormon Doctrine*, 264.)

Read Matthew 9:10–13 together and ask:

- What does Jesus Christ refer to Himself as?
- What kind of a physician is Jesus?
- How can exercising our faith help the Physician (Jesus) heal us?

Share your testimony of the power that Christ has to heal us and the need for us to exercise our faith in that healing process.

MATTHEW 10: JESUS SENDS FORTH THE TWELVE APOSTLES

Matthew 10:1–4
Who are the Twelve Apostles?

Ask your family to name as many of the current Apostles as they can. (The May and November editions of the *Ensign* include the names and pictures of the First Presidency and Quorum of the Twelve Apostles.) Ask family members to share ways that the calling and responsibility of these fifteen men differs from other callings in the Church. (See D&C 107:22–24.) Share the following statement by Elder James E. Talmage:

"The title 'Apostle' is . . . one of special significance and sanctity. . . . [It] is the English equivalent of the Greek *apostolos,* indicating a messenger, an ambassador, or literally 'one who is sent.' It signifies that he who is rightly so called, speaks and acts not of himself, but as the representative of a higher power whence [where] his commission issued." (*Jesus the Christ*, 228–29, note 2; see also Bible Dictionary, 612.)

While someone reads aloud Matthew 10:1–4, have the rest of the family look for the names of the Apostles Jesus chose during His mortal ministry. Invite family members to tell what they know about any of the names listed. (If you know little or nothing about these men, see the entry for each in the Bible Dictionary.) You may want to point out other times these Twelve are listed in the New Testament. (See Mark 3:16–19; Luke 6:14–16; and Acts 1:13. Note that there are some slight differences in their names. For example, Peter was also known as "Simon bar-jona," meaning "Simon, son of Jonah.")

If you can, share an experience where you felt the power of the calling of an Apostle. Also, invite family members to tell something they remember about any one of the Apostles and/or tell about an experience of meeting or hearing from one of them.

Matthew 10:5–42

Counsel for those called to full-time service of the Lord

Tell your family that when full-time missionaries are called they are given a small handbook with important counsel to help direct them during their mission. (If you have a missionary handbook, show it to your family.)

Explain that Matthew 10 contains Jesus' counsel to His twelve Apostles just before they were sent out to preach the gospel full time.

Divide your family into two groups. Give each group some paper and pencils. Assign them to create a missionary handbook with Jesus' counsel organized in the following sections: "What You Should Do," "How You Should Do It," "Warnings," and "Promises." Have each group write these four section titles on their paper.

Then have one group search Matthew 10:5–22 and the other group search Matthew 10:23–42. Ask each group to assign a person to list Jesus' counsel, in his/her own words, under the appropriate section title in their handbook.

After completing their handbook, have each group share what they wrote for each section and discuss ways it applies to full-time missionary service and/or any other kinds of service in the Lord's kingdom today.

MATTHEW 11: JESUS TESTIFIES OF JOHN THE BAPTIST

Matthew 11:1–6

Did John the Baptist doubt Jesus?

 Invite a family member to read Matthew 11:1–3. Ask:

- Why would John have his disciples ask if Jesus was the Messiah?
- Didn't he already know Him?
- What ordinance had John performed for Jesus that all people must have to enter the kingdom of heaven? (Baptism.)

Share the following: "Any inference that the Baptist was uncertain or doubtful in his own mind, as to the identity and mission of the Master, is totally unwarranted. In reality, the imprisoned . . . forerunner of our Lord was using this means to persuade his disciples to forsake him and follow Jesus. . . .

"This act of sending his disciples to Jesus was in effect a final great testimony on John's part that Jesus was the Lamb of God, for the Baptist knew that his disciples, seeing the Master personally and hearing his teachings, could not help but follow the greater light." (McConkie, *Doctrinal New Testament Commentary,* 1:261–62.)

Have a family member read Matthew 11:4–6 and ask:

- What evidences did the disciples find that Jesus is the Christ?
- What evidences do we have today that Jesus is the Christ?

Invite family members to share how they have come to know the Lord or how He has blessed them.

Matthew 11:7–13

Why was John the Baptist considered great?

 Have your family make a list of things that make a person popular in the eyes of the world. Read Matthew 11:7–11 and ask:

- Why do you think John attracted so much attention?

- What drew people to listen to John even though he did not preach in a nice synagogue or wear nice clothes?
- What did Jesus say about John in verse 11?

To help identify why John was such a great prophet, divide the following references among family members. Have them read the assigned verses and report what those verses say about John's greatness.

- 1 Nephi 10:7–10 (The forerunner of the Messiah.)
- Matthew 3:13–17 (The one chosen to baptize the Son of God.)
- Doctrine and Covenants 13 (The angel chosen to bring the Aaronic Priesthood back to the earth in this dispensation.)

Invite someone to reread Matthew 11:11. Ask:

- What does the Lord consider great?
- What do we learn from the Savior about being both the "least" and the "greatest" among our associates?
- How would you finish this statement? "To be truly great I must _____."

Matthew 11:28–30
How can we lighten our heavy burdens?

Have the strongest member of the family hold his or her arm straight out, lock the elbow, and place a weight (such as a large book) in the hand. Ask this person how long he or she might be able to hold up the weight. While he or she is holding the weight, have another family member read Matthew 11:28–30. Ask:

- How can Jesus give us rest from our burdens?
- According to Isaiah 53:4, what would the Savior do to lighten our burdens?

Invite a shorter member of the family to stand near the one holding the weight. Allow the one with the weight to rest the burden on the assistant's shoulder. Ask the person holding the burden how long he or she could continue to carry the weight now. Let them sit down and then ask: How was the heavy burden made light?

Ask your family to list some things that may seem to be a burden that we are asked to bear. Some of their answers may include:

- Church callings
- Service
- Home or visiting teaching
- Family scripture study
- Family home evening
- Prayer
- Sabbath day observance
- Word of Wisdom
- Tithing
- Honesty

Ask:

- Why are these burdens not always easy to bear?
- How can they make life much easier to bear in the long run?
- Why does Jesus want us to bear these burdens? (To help us grow and bring us happiness.)
- What are some burdens Satan and the world would have us bear? (For example, addictions, grudges, dishonesty, pride, or guilt.)
- Why would Satan want us to bear these burdens? (To damn us, or stop our progression and bring us misery.)
- In what ways are the Lord's burdens much lighter in comparison to Satan's burdens?

Testify to your family that the Lord's burdens will help us avoid Satan's burdens and will bring joy and satisfaction.

MATTHEW 12: JESUS RESPONDS TO OPPOSITION

Matthew 12:1–13
What is the purpose of the Sabbath?

Have each family member write down three things they think are appropriate to do on the Sabbath and three things they feel are inappropriate to do. When they are finished, invite them to share what they wrote. Ask:

- Does everyone agree with what has been listed?
- How can we as a family decide what is

appropriate or inappropriate to do on the Sabbath day? (Note: Listen to all suggestions without making any judgments.)

Invite your family to look for help in answering this question as they study Matthew 12. Remind them that at the time of Christ religious leaders had added their own complicated rules to the law of Moses. For example, plucking and eating of corn (grain) was considered work and therefore unlawful on the Sabbath.

Take turns reading aloud Matthew 12:1–13 and look for things on the Pharisees' "list" that should or shouldn't be done on the Sabbath. Also look for a clue given by Jesus about how to decide what is appropriate or inappropriate to do on the Sabbath. Ask:

- What would the Pharisees' Sabbath list look like?
- What do you learn from the Savior's teachings and example?
- How can we know what is appropriate or inappropriate to do on the Sabbath day?

Invite each family member to highlight the words "it is lawful to do well on the sabbath days" in Matthew 12:12. Encourage your family to seek the Spirit of the Lord to help them decide how to "do well" on Sundays.

Matthew 12:14–21
The long-suffering of Jesus

Show your family a stem, a weed, or a small plant that is already slightly bent. Tell them you have decided to impress them with your strength. Break the plant in half before their very eyes. Of course, this is not a very impressive feat. Explain that the prophet Isaiah used a similar example to prophesy of a very impressive part of Jesus' character. Have a family member read Matthew 12:17–21 where Matthew quotes Isaiah. (A "bruised reed" is a damaged plant stalk; a "smoking flax" is a candlewick whose flame has gone out.)

Then, read together Matthew 12:14–16 and find what Jesus did to fulfill Isaiah's prophecy. Ask:

- What were the Pharisees planning to do? (To destroy Jesus by catching Him breaking the law of Moses; see Matthew 12:1–13.)
- Because Jesus knew what the Pharisees were planning, what did He do?
- How are the sick and afflicted like a "bruised" plant or a "smoking" wick?
- How do these healings show Jesus' compassion?
- How was that a fulfillment of Isaiah's prophecy? (See verses 15–16.)

Point out in verse 20 the phrase "judgment unto victory." Discuss the circumstances under which the "judgment" is a "victory." (For example, when Satan and his followers can no longer afflict us, or when the righteous are saved in God's presence.) Read together 1 Nephi 1:20 and highlight the "tender mercies of the Lord." Invite family members to share how the Savior has shown His "tender mercies" to them.

Matthew 12:22–30
A divided family will fall

Ask your family how they would respond to the accusation that members of The Church of Jesus Christ of Latter-day Saints are not Christians. Read aloud with your family Matthew 12:22–26 and ask:

- What did the Pharisees accuse the Savior of doing?
- Why do you think they did this?
- How did Jesus respond to this accusation?
- How might this account help us know how to respond to our accusers?

Invite your family to write Moroni 7:16–17 in the margin next to Matthew 12:25–26. Have someone read Moroni 7:16–17 and ask your family how this counsel in the Book of Mormon helps us know what is of God and what is not.

Matthew 12:31–32
Speaking against the Holy Ghost

Write this question where your family can all see it: "Are there any sins that God will not forgive?" Have them silently read Matthew 13:31–32 (including footnote 31a) and look for an answer to this question. Read the following statement by the Prophet Joseph Smith:

"'What must a man do to commit the unpardonable sin?' He must receive the Holy Ghost, have the heavens opened unto him, and know God, and then sin against him. After a man has sinned against the Holy Ghost, there is no repentance for him." (*Teachings of the Prophet Joseph Smith*, 358.)

Ask:

- What do you think it means to have "the heavens opened unto [you]"?
- Why might it be difficult for most people to commit the unpardonable sin?
- How does knowing that all sins can be forgiven except the sin against the Holy Ghost make you feel about the Atonement of Jesus Christ?

Read with your family the first phrase of Matthew 12:31, including footnote 31*a*. Discuss how always receiving the Lord and repenting can help ensure that your family never needs to worry about committing the unpardonable sin.

Matthew 12:33–37
Trees and their fruit

Hold up two different kinds of fruit (for example, an apple and an orange). Ask your family to tell what kind of tree each fruit came from. Ask: Do we get apples from an orange tree? Why not? Take turns reading Matthew 12:33–37. Discuss some or all of the following questions:

- What two kinds of fruit are mentioned in these verses? (Good and corrupt [bad].)
- Is it possible to tell if a person is good or bad by what they say or do?
- How can we tell what kind of a tree we are? (By our fruits.)
- What kind of a tree do you want to be? (Note the description in Isaiah 61:3.)
- How important is the heart in determining what kind of fruit we will have?
- How can changing our hearts improve what we say and do? (Changing our hearts will automatically change our actions.)

Encourage your family to pray for the kind of heart that will bear the fruits they truly desire.

Matthew 12:38–42
The problem with seeking signs

Give your family a copy of the accompanying chart (or a sheet of paper on which each one can draw the chart). Have them silently read the verses and fill in the chart. (Have a parent or older siblings help young children.)

Scripture Reference	Messenger	Who was the audience and how did they respond?
Matt. 12:38–40		
Matt. 12:41		
Matt. 12:42		

When they are finished, discuss the following questions:

- Who were the three messengers in these verses? (Jesus, Jonas [Jonah], Solomon.)
- Who were their audiences? (Scribes and Pharisees, "men of Nineveh," "queen of the south.")
- How was the way the scribes and Pharisees responded to Jesus different from the way the other two responded?
- How did "sign seeking" get in the way of the Pharisees' ability to hear and accept Jesus' message of salvation?
- What sign, or proof, did Jesus say they would get?
- In what way was the life of the prophet Jonas (Jonah) a sign of the mission of Jesus Christ? (See Matthew 12:40 and Jonah 1:17; Jesus would be three days in the tomb and come out alive, thus proving He is the Savior.)
- Are there people today as stubborn and unbelieving as the Pharisees?
- In what ways do we seek signs in our own day?

Testify that it is more important that we live by faith and not see amazing signs than to satisfy our curiosity and miss the message of salvation.

MATTHEW 13: "HE SPAKE MANY THINGS UNTO THEM IN PARABLES"

Matthew 13:1–17

Why did Jesus speak in parables?

Have one family member find and report the meaning of *parable* in a common dictionary and another report on what he/she learned from the second paragraph under the entry for parable in the Bible Dictionary, page 741. (*Parable* literally means "to set side by side.")

Have family members read Matthew 13:11–17 and look for why Jesus spoke in parables. Invite family members to tell what they think Jesus meant when He said, "They seeing see not; and hearing they hear not." (Verse 13.) Share this explanation from the Prophet Joseph Smith:

"The multitude . . . received not His saying . . . because they were not willing to see with their eyes, and hear with their ears; not because they could not, and were not privileged to see and hear, but because their hearts were full of iniquity and abominations [evil]. . . . The very reason why the multitude . . . did not receive an explanation upon His parables, was because of unbelief." (*Teachings of the Prophet Joseph Smith,* 96–97.)

Have a family member read the first paragraph in the Bible Dictionary entry for "parable," page 740. Based on what you have learned about Jesus' purpose for teaching in parables, discuss as a family ways you can develop "eyes to see" and "ears to hear" to apply Jesus' parables.

Matthew 13:3–8, 18–23

The parable of the sower

Prepare four cups or bowls with different kinds of soil. In one cup, make sure the soil is well packed and hard. In another cup, put rocks and gravel. The third cup or bowl should be filled with soil that is full of thorns or weeds. The last cup should be filled with good, fertile soil. Show the four bowls or cups to your family, along with some seeds, and ask what is likely to happen to seeds planted in each of the four types of soil.

Ask a family member to read aloud Matthew

13:3–8. Have another family member point to which kind of soil (in the cups) is being referred to as the verses are read. You might need to explain that a *sower* is a person who plants seeds; the *way side* is like a path or road; *fowls* are birds.

Ask your family what spiritual message they think Jesus is teaching in this parable. After they give their responses, tell them that Jesus explains the parable of the sower in Matthew 13:18–23. Read those verses together as a family and ask:

- What does the seed represent? (Word of God; see verse 19.)
- Who would the "sower" be that plants the word of God? ([provide answer]).
- What does the soil represent? (The condition of our heart; see verse 19.)
- What does the "way side" represent? (People who hear the word but do not understand or do not want to understand; see verse 19.)
- What do the "stony places" represent? (People who hear and receive the word but do not allow it to take root; see verses 20–21.)
- What do the "thorny places" represent? (People who hear the word but get caught up in worldly cares and riches; see verse 22.)
- What does the "good ground" represent? (People who hear the word, understand it, and do righteous works; see verse 23.)
- What needs to happen to each type of soil so that it is better able to grow seeds? (For example, how would we make the "way side" into ground that can grow "good fruit"? How about the stony ground?)
- What do we call the changes that need to happen in our hearts? (Repentance.)

Leave the soils and the seeds someplace in the house where everyone will see them. Tell your family that when they see the different soils to remember that they can determine the condition of their hearts. Challenge them to prepare their "soil" for the truths the Lord would plant there.

Matthew 13:24–30, 36–43

The wheat and the tares

 Have your family search Matthew 13:24–30 and find the main objects spoken of in the parable. List them on a sheet of paper. Your list should look similar to the first column below.

Elements of the Parable	Interpretations
Sower	Jesus Christ
Good seed (wheat)	Followers of Jesus
Field	World
Enemy	Satan
Tares (weeds)	Followers of Satan
Reapers	Angels
Harvest	Jesus' Second Coming

After you have made the list in the first column, have your family see if they can determine what each object represents. Tell your family Jesus gave the interpretation of this parable to His disciples in Matthew 13:36–43 and also to the Prophet Joseph Smith in Doctrine and Covenants 86:1–7. Have some family members read the verses in Matthew while the rest read those in the Doctrine and Covenants. As family members share interpretations write their responses in the second column. Their interpretations should be similar to those in the chart above. Ask:

- Why does the sower not allow his servants to immediately remove the tares? (See Matthew 13:28–29; D&C 86:6.)
- According to footnote *b* for Matthew 13:30 what new insight can be learned about the order of the gathering and the burning? (Notice that this agrees with what is taught in D&C 86:7.)
- What do you think the Savior would have us know from this parable, and how could we apply it to situations faced by members of our family?

Matthew 13:31–33, 44–50
Small parables about the kingdom of God

To help your family understand and remember these parables from Matthew 13, you may want to show them the following objects:

- A mustard seed. (If you do not have a mustard seed, you could show some ground pepper, which is similar in size to a black mustard seed.) See verses 31–32.

- Two different loaves of bread or similar items (one made with yeast and one without). See verse 33.
- Something that represents a "treasure." See verse 44.
- Some pearls. See verses 45–46.
- A net. See verses 47–48.

Have one family member read aloud Matthew 13:31–32. Ask:

- What is remarkable about the mustard plant? (It grows so large from such a small seed.)
- How is the Church like the mustard seed?

Tell your family that in addition to saying this parable "is given to represent the Church as it shall come forth in the last days," the Prophet Joseph Smith also compared the mustard seed to the Book of Mormon: "Let us take the Book of Mormon, which a man took and hid in his field, securing it by his faith, to spring up in the last days, or in due time; let us behold it coming forth out of the ground, which is indeed accounted the least of all seeds, but behold it branching forth, yea, even towering, with lofty branches, and God-like majesty, until it, like the mustard seed, becomes the greatest of all herbs. And it is truth, and it has sprouted and come forth out of the earth, and righteousness begins to look down from heaven, and God is sending down His powers, gifts and angels, to lodge in the branches thereof." (*Teachings of the Prophet Joseph Smith*, 98.)

Before reading the next parable, explain that leaven is an ingredient, such as yeast, that causes bread to rise. Have another family member read Matthew 13:33. Ask:

- Which do you prefer, bread made with leaven or without? Why?
- How does leaven make the bread better?
- How are Church members, and our family, a leavening influence that makes the world better?

Have family members silently read Matthew 13:44–46, looking for what else Jesus compared the Church to in these two short parables. Ask:

- How is the Church like a hidden treasure or a costly pearl?

- What would you be willing to sacrifice or do to obtain the treasure of the gospel?

Finally, have another family member read Matthew 13:47–50. Ask:

- What does it mean to be gathered into the net?
- What does the gathering of the "good into vessels" and casting the bad away represent?
- What does this teach us about the Church and the members?

Share the following statement by Elder Carl B. Pratt of the Seventy:

"I have seen all kinds of people brought into the Church by the gospel net—men, women, and children of all races, cultures, education levels, and economic circumstances. My experience has taught me that while nearly all new converts join the Church with good intentions, they, like the rest of us, are not perfect. It is not enough to be baptized into the true Church. Baptism is merely the gate to the 'strait and narrow path which leads to eternal life' (2 Ne. 31:18). Striving to stay on the path, never giving up, pressing 'forward with a steadfastness in Christ, having a perfect brightness of hope' (2 Ne. 31:20) are what enable us to be among the good who will be gathered into vessels." (*Ensign*, Jan. 2003, 63.)

Ask your family what they can do to stay true and faithful in the gospel and help others to do the same.

MATTHEW 14: HORRIBLE HEROD AND MIGHTY MIRACLES

Matthew 14:1–12
Herod orders the death of John the Baptist

Ask your family if they have ever made a promise that they were sorry for later. Read together Matthew 14:1–12 and have your family look for a promise that later brought sorrow. Discuss the following questions:

- What unwise promise was made and who made it? (See verses 6–10. If you would like more information about Herod the tetrarch, also called Herod Antipas, see Bible Dictionary, "Herod," 700–701, and "Tetrarch," 784.)

- Why was Herod sorry that he had to kill John the Baptist? (Verse 5.)
- Why was John in prison and why did Herodias want him killed? (Verses 3–4; see also Bible Dictionary, "Herodias," 702.)
- What verses indicate that Herod's conscience was really bothering him? (Verses 1–2.)
- Why do you think Herod thought Jesus was John the Baptist come back from the dead? (See Talmage, *Jesus the Christ*, 331–32.)
- What does this story teach us about the effects of sin on our peace and even on our imagination? (See Proverbs 28:1.)

Have your family picture in their minds Herod sitting on his throne and John the Baptist locked up in prison. Ask:

- Do you suppose that Herod was glad he was the king and not in John's situation?
- If he were asked to trade places with John, do you think he would have agreed?
- Where do you think John is now? (See D&C 13 for an example.)
- Where do you think Herod is now?
- Do you think Herod wishes he could trade places with John now?

Read together Doctrine and Covenants 121:7–8 and discuss what principle we can learn from the story of the beheading of John?

Matthew 14:14–21
"They did all eat, and were filled"

Place enough slices of bread in a basket or bowl for only half the number of people in your family. Pass the basket around, inviting everyone to eat until they are full. Read together Matthew 14:14–21 and ask your family what the bread has to do with these verses. (Pictures of reenactments of this event can be found in the *Ensign*, Mar. 1999, 11, and *Ensign*, Mar. 1995, 31.) Ask:

- Why do you think the people stayed with the Savior though they were hungry and obviously had no food?
- What do you think Jesus was trying to teach when He suggested that the disciples feed the

multitude instead of sending them away to the village to buy "victuals" (food).

- How many people were in the multitude? (Verse 21.)
- How much bread and fish do you think it would take to feed that many people?
- What would you do if you had more people show up for dinner than you had food for?
- What did Jesus do about feeding more people than He had enough food for? (Verse 19.)
- What does this tell us about the Savior's power?
- What does this tell us about the depth of the Savior's love?

Write this statement where your family can see it: "If Jesus Christ can feed over 5,000 with just five loaves and two fishes, then He can help me with _____." Invite your family to write that sentence in their personal journals and finish it privately with some challenge they would like the Savior's help on. Then encourage them to pray in faith for help in overcoming their problem.

Matthew 14:22–33
"Bid me come unto thee on the water"

Hand each family member a piece of paper and a pencil and have them write down a good thing they would like to do, or ought to do, but are afraid to try. Have them fold their paper so no one can see it. Next, fill a bucket with water and place it in front of your family. Invite someone to stand on top of the water. Make sure they understand that you are not asking them to stand in the bucket but on top of the water. Ask them if they know anyone who can stand on water. Take turns reading Matthew 14:22–33, looking for two individuals who did walk on water. Discuss some or all of the following questions:

- What do you think it must have been like to be on a boat in the middle of a stormy night and see someone walking toward you on the water?
- When the disciples cried out "for fear," what did Jesus do to comfort them? (Verses 26–29.)
- Why do you think Peter wanted to try walking to Jesus? (Verse 28.)

- Why do you think the Savior invited him to come out on the water? (Verse 29.)
- Why did Peter begin to sink? (Verses 30–31.)
- What are some ways a person may take his/her eyes off the Savior today?

Have your family open their papers and invite some to share what they wrote. For each person, discuss any of the following questions you think are appropriate:

- How is what you wrote on your paper like Peter walking on the water?
- Did Jesus want Peter to be able to walk on the water?
- Would Jesus want you to be able to do what you wrote? (If it is a good thing, yes.)
- What does Peter show us we can do when we are afraid?

Share your testimony with your family of the Savior's power to help us do things we might not be able to do by ourselves. Conclude by singing "Come unto Him." (*Hymns,* no. 114.)

Matthew 14:34–36
How would you like to be made "perfectly whole"?

Tell everyone to look up the word *Gennesaret* in the Bible Dictionary. (Do not give the page number.) The prize for the first one to find the dictionary entry is to read the information to the rest of the family. Invite your family to learn more about what happened in Gennesaret by silently reading Matthew 14:34–36. Ask:

- What do you think the following phrase means: "men . . . had knowledge of him"? (See footnote 35*a*.)
- Why would recognizing Jesus cause them to bring "all that were diseased" to Him? (Verse 35.)
- Where do you think the idea to "touch the hem of his garment" might have come from? (Read together the cross-reference listed in footnote 36*a*.)

Share the following story about the Prophet Joseph Smith with your family: "After healing the sick in Montrose, all the company followed Joseph to the bank of the river, where he was going to take the boat to return home. While waiting for the boat, a man from the West, who had seen that the sick and dying were healed, asked Joseph if he would not go to his house and heal two of his children who were very sick. They were twins and were three months old. Joseph told the man he could not go, but he would send some one to heal them. He told Elder Woodruff to go with the man and heal his children. At the same time he took from his pocket a silk bandanna handkerchief, and gave to Brother Woodruff, telling him to wipe the faces of the children with it, and they should be healed. . . . Elder Woodruff did as he was commanded, and the children were healed." (Smith, *History of the Church,* 4:4–5.)

Ask:

- Do you think that the hem of the garment or a handkerchief has the power to heal?
- Then by what power were these people healed? (Faith.)
- What other types of healing do we need besides from sicknesses? (For example, sorrow, sin, or anger.)
- How has your faith brought healing in your life or in the life of someone close to you?

Share the following from Elder James E. Talmage with your family: faith is "a living, inspiring confidence in God, and an acceptance of His will as our law, and of His words as our guide, in life. Faith in God is possible only as we come to know that He exists, and moreover, that He is a Being of worthy character and attributes." (*Articles of Faith,* 100.)

MATTHEW 15: JESUS AMAZES AND CONFUSES THE SCRIBES AND PHARISEES WITH PARABLES AND MIRACLES

Matthew 15:1–20

What makes us unclean?

Read or sing the third verse and chorus of "Truth Reflects upon Our Senses." (*Hymns,* no. 273.) Ask your family members what they think is being taught in this verse. Help them understand that sometimes our own shortcomings (beams) are bigger than the shortcomings (motes)

of those around us, even though we may think otherwise.

Take turns reading Matthew 15:1–6 and explain to your family that the commandments, like "Honour thy father and mother," were written in the law of Moses, but the "tradition of the elders" were rules added to the law by uninspired Jewish teachers. Two examples of these traditions are found in these verses.

1. Before eating, the Jews felt it was necessary to wash their hands twice, "the 'second water' being necessary to wash away the 'first water,' which had become defiled [unclean] by contact with the 'common' hands." (Talmage, *Jesus the Christ,* 366.)

2. To understand the second tradition, read Mark 7:11 and ask your family to identify an unfamiliar word. Read the definition of *Corban* in the Bible Dictionary, page 650. Make sure your family understands that the Pharisees used this vow of dedicating property to God as a way to legally escape the responsibility of supporting their parents and still retain the use of their property.

Have your family look again at the words they read in the hymn. Ask:

- How do these verses relate to the third verse of this hymn?
- Who would you say had the greater shortcomings, the disciples of Christ who didn't wash their hands or the scribes who didn't honor their fathers or mothers? Why?

Read Matthew 15:7–9 together and share the following explanation: The Jewish teachers "held that [strict obedience to] the traditions of the elders was more important than observance of the law itself; and Jesus in His counter-question put their cherished traditions as in direct conflict with the commandment of God. Adding to their [embarrassment], He cited the prophecy of Isaiah, and applied to them whom He designated hypocrites, the prophet's words: 'Well hath Esaias prophesied of you hypocrites, as it is written, This people honoureth me with their lips, but their heart is far from me. Howbeit in vain do they worship me, teaching for doctrines the commandments of men.'" (Talmage, *Jesus the Christ,* 351.)

Ask:

- What did Jesus call the traditions that the

Pharisees and scribes thought were so important? (Commandments of men.)

- Can you think of any beliefs people have today that are the "commandments of men" and not truths from God?

Read together Matthew 15:10–20 and ask:

- How did the Pharisees feel about what Jesus said? Why?
- How does 1 Nephi 16:2 help explain why they were offended?
- According to Matthew 15:18–20, what makes a person unclean?
- What are some things that make people spiritually unclean today?

Matthew 15:21–28

What caused Jesus to heal a gentile woman's daughter?

Bring a state road map to scripture study. Give the map to a member of your family and have that person locate your state capital. Ask:

- How did you find the capital?
- How would someone who didn't live in the state find the capital?

Have your family look on the top and sides of the map and find the number and letter coordinates to the state capitol. Explain that many maps have similar coordinates, even the maps in the scriptures. Invite your family to turn to the map section called Maps and Index of Place-Names (called Gazetteer in pre-1999 copies of the Bible) and find the cities Sidon and Tyre. Looking at Map 11 (Map 14 in pre-1999 Bible maps), ask your family what they notice about the location of these two cities. Help them see that Jesus was outside the boundaries of Israel. Turn to Matthew 15 and read with your family verses 21–28. Ask:

- Where was Jesus traveling at this time? (Verse 21.)
- What nationality was the woman? (Verse 22.)
- According to verse 24, who was the Savior sent to at this time?
- Why did Jesus have compassion on this non-Israelite woman? (Verse 28.)
- What does this teach us about how we should

treat good people in the world that are not of our faith?

If anyone is troubled by the Savior's words in verse 26, share the following statement from Elder James E. Talmage: "The words [in verse 26], harsh as they may sound to us, were understood by her in the spirit of the Lord's intent. The original term here translated 'dogs' connoted, as the narrative shows, not the vagrant [stray] and despised curs elsewhere spoken of in the Bible as typical of a degraded state, or of positive badness, but literally the 'little dogs' or domestic pets, such as were allowed in the house and under the table. Certainly the woman took no offense at the comparison." (*Jesus the Christ,* 355.)

Discuss ways the Savior both tested and rewarded this woman's faith. Invite your family members to share a time when they successfully went through a test of their faith.

MATTHEW 16: "THOU ART THE CHRIST"

Matthew 16:1–12
Signs

Have your family imagine that the following message appeared in the sky in such a way that the entire world could clearly see it during their daylight hours: "The Church of Jesus Christ of Latter-day Saints Is My True Church." Ask them: What would you think? What would be the responses of the people of the world?

While one family member reads aloud Matthew 16:1–4, have the rest of the family look for what the Pharisees and Sadducees wanted from Jesus and how Jesus responded to their request. Discuss answers to the following questions:

- What did Jesus seem to be saying to the Pharisees and Sadducees about signs in verses 2–3?
- What evidences had Jesus given them already of who He is?
- What other sign did Jesus promise to give to the "wicked and adulterous generation"?
  You may need to review Jonah's story in Jonah 1:15–2:10; Matthew 12:39–41; and Elder

Bruce R. McConkie's insight that just as "Jonah of old spent three days and three nights in the belly of a whale, so shall the Son of Man spend a like period in an earthly tomb." And just "as the whale vomited Jonah from the blackness of a living tomb, so Jesus comes forth in a newness of life from a grave that cannot hold him. It is that the Son of Man—the Son of God—burst the bands of death, became the firstfruits of them that sleep, and ever liveth in immortal glory. The resurrection proves that Jesus is the Messiah; it is the sign, given of God, to all men of the truth and divinity of his work." (*Mortal Messiah*, 2:224.)

- Do all people recognize all signs?
- What signs do you generally pay attention to? Why?

Invite family members to tell about a time when they saw a "sign" that provided evidence to them that God lives.

Matthew 16:13–20

The power of personal testimony

 Write the following on a poster or paper large enough for everyone in the family to see:

"_____ is the great strength of the Church." (President Gordon B. Hinckley.)

Have family members guess what word goes in the blank. (The word is *testimony;* see Hinckley, *Ensign,* May 1998, 69.) Invite them to read to themselves Matthew 16:13–18 and look for how Jesus taught this truth about testimony to his disciples.

After everyone has had a chance to read these verses, discuss:

- Where did Jesus say strong testimonies come from? (Verse 17.)
- What did Jesus tell Peter about the power of a testimony gained by revelation? (Verse 18.)

Share with your family the following statement from President Marion G. Romney (then a member of the First Presidency) about obtaining and strengthening a testimony:

"How do you get a testimony? I think that Jesus gave the answer as well or better than it has ever been given. [He taught] . . . 'My doctrine is not mine, but his that sent me. If any man will do his will, he shall know of the doctrine, whether it be of God, or whether I speak of myself.' (John 7:15–17.). . . .

"It is obvious that the first step toward getting a testimony is to learn the will of the Father. This can be done by studying the word of God and by obeying his commandments as they are learned. Study the scriptures. Study the teachings of the prophets. . . . Learn and obey the will of God.

"There is no shortcut to a testimony. There are not two ways; there is only one way. . . .

"Everyone who sincerely prays with real desire to know the truth concerning what he has learned about the gospel will receive a witness in his mind and in his heart, by the Holy Ghost, as the Lord promised to Oliver. And, as the Lord said, this witness shall dwell in his heart. It shall dwell in his heart forever if he retains his faith by repenting of his sins, by being baptized, by receiving the gift of the Holy Ghost by the laying on of hands, and by continuing to obey the principles of the gospel to the end of his mortal life." (*New Era,* May 1976, 12.)

Invite family members to share their testimony—including how their testimony has helped them "prevail" against "the gates of hell." (Matthew 16:18.) Provide time for family members to write their testimony in their journals along with what they will do to obtain and/or strengthen this testimony.

Matthew 16:19

"The keys of the kingdom of heaven"

 Show your family a key or set of keys and have them describe some uses for keys. You might ask:

- If I had a powerful and expensive car, but did not have the keys, what value would the car be to me?
- If I had a safe containing many valuable possessions but no way to lock it, how safe would the possessions really be?

While one family member reads aloud Matthew 16:19, have the rest of the family look for what

Jesus promised Peter. To clarify the meaning of the keys of the kingdom, share with your family these statements from two of the Brethren:

"We use the word *keys* in a symbolic way. Here the keys of priesthood authority represent the limits of the power extended from beyond the veil to mortal man to act in the name of God upon the earth." (Boyd K. Packer, *Ensign,* Feb. 1995, 34.)

"To be efficacious and valid, every act in the Church must be performed under the authority of the keys at the appropriate time and place, and in the proper manner and order. The authority and power to direct all of the labors of the kingdom of God on earth constitute the keys of the priesthood. Those who possess them have the right to preside over and direct the affairs of the Church in their jurisdiction." (James E. Faust, *Ensign,* Nov. 1994, 73.)

"In the Church we hold sufficient authority to perform all of the ordinances necessary to redeem and to exalt the whole human family. And, because we have the keys to the sealing power, what we bind in proper order here will be bound in heaven. . . . With that authority we can baptize and bless, we can endow and seal, and the Lord will honor our commitments." (Boyd K. Packer, *Ensign,* Feb. 1995, 36.)

Ask your family to name the men who hold the keys of the kingdom today. Reinforce the idea that only the president of the Church holds and is able to exercise all the priesthood keys for the salvation of mankind. You could reinforce this idea by studying Doctrine and Covenants 81:1–2; 107:18, 21–22.

Matthew 16:21–28
The cost of discipleship

Make a poster like the following to display to your family:

Have your family suggest the cost for the last item by reading Matthew 16:24–27. Remind them to check the footnotes for help from the Joseph Smith Translation.

After writing suggestions on the poster, have them give responses to the questions in verse 26. Then ask:

- Is the cost we wrote on the poster really worth it? Why?

Activity	Cost
To learn from and play like a master pianist	$50/hour
To learn from and play like a golf pro	$60/hour
To learn how to swim well from a certified teacher	$10/half-hour
To receive training to become a doctor	$30,000/year
To follow Jesus and become His disciple	??????

- How does verse 27 provide an answer for why it's worth it?

Write the following sentence on your poster: "If I gain the things of the world but lose my soul, I have _____." Invite your family to suggest how they would complete that sentence. Encourage family members to write that sentence in their journals and identify one specific thing they could do during the upcoming week to "take up [Jesus'] cross."

MATTHEW 17: THE MOUNT OF TRANSFIGURATION

Matthew 17:1–13
What happened on the Mount of Transfiguration?

Tell your family they are going to be interviewed for a pretend news broadcast. You will be the reporter, and they will answer some questions about the Mount of Transfiguration for a special report. Assign each family member one or more of the following questions and allow some time to research and prepare an answer for the interview. When they are ready, bring your family onto the "news set" and "interview" them together. Have each family member read Matthew 17:1–13 along with the additional references or quotations listed by their particular questions:

- What does it mean to be transfigured? ("Transfiguration is a special change in appearance and nature which is wrought upon a person or thing by the power of God. This divine transformation is from a lower to a higher state; it results in a more exalted, impressive, and glorious condition." [McConkie,

Mormon Doctrine, 803.] See also 3 Nephi 28:7–8, 38–39.)

- Why were Peter, James, and John taken "apart" from the other Apostles on the Mount of Transfiguration? "The plain fact is that Peter, James, and John were the First Presidency of the Church in their day." (McConkie, *Doctrinal New Testament Commentary,* 1:402.)
- Who else was on the mount besides the three Apostles and Jesus? (Read Bible Dictionary, "Transfiguration, Mount of," 786, second paragraph.)
- Name some other occasions when the Father has introduced His Son. (See footnote *c* to Matthew 17:5.)
- Why did this event need to happen? (Read the first paragraph of the Bible Dictionary, "Transfiguration, Mount of," 786.)
- In modern Church history, when did a similar event happen? (Read the third paragraph of "Transfiguration, Mount of," in the Bible Dictionary, 786.)

When you have finished the interviews, talk with your family about how important it is that God calls prophets and Apostles in our day, just as He did in New Testament times.

Matthew 17:14–21
What is required to work miracles?

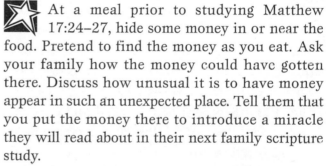 Show your family the accompanying picture and ask them to consider what these tiny seeds have to do with Matthew 17:14–21. Read the passage together as a family.

When you are finished reading, allow family members to share what they learned. Ask:

- What is required in order to have the power to perform a miracle?
- By using the image of a mustard seed, what

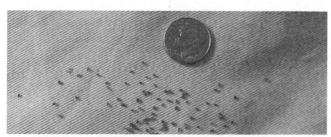

A mustard seed is about the size of a speck of pepper.

was Jesus telling the disciples about how much faith they had?

- What are ways you can increase your faith? (Verse 21.)
- Why do you think prayer and fasting are sometimes required?
- What are some problems you have faced in which prayer and fasting helped?
- According to Romans 10:17, what is another way to increase your faith?

Share the following explanation from Elder Bruce R. McConkie: "Faith is a gift of God bestowed as a reward for personal righteousness. It is always given when righteousness is present, and the greater the measure of obedience to God's laws the greater will be the endowment of faith." (*Mormon Doctrine,* 264.) Challenge your family to experiment with fasting and prayer when they are dealing with difficult decisions or problems.

Matthew 17:24–27
Jesus teaches who He is by means of a miracle

At a meal prior to studying Matthew 17:24–27, hide some money in or near the food. Pretend to find the money as you eat. Ask your family how the money could have gotten there. Discuss how unusual it is to have money appear in such an unexpected place. Tell them that you put the money there to introduce a miracle they will read about in their next family scripture study.

Bring the money to your family scripture study and have the family read Matthew 17:24–27 silently and report what the money has to do with these verses. Share Elder Bruce R. McConkie's explanation of these verses: "[This tax] consisted of an annual payment of a half shekel . . . levied upon all males twenty years of age and older for the maintenance of the temple. As originally announced by Moses, it was an offering whereby men made an atonement for their sins; that is, the payment was in the nature of a sacrifice designed to accompany prayers beseeching [asking] forgiveness from personal sins. (Ex. 30:11–16.) Jesus, of course, was without sin and needed to offer no such supplication." (*Doctrinal New Testament Commentary,* 1:412.)

Ask:

- Why would Peter need to pay this tax? (He had sins and needed forgiveness.)
- Why was Jesus not obligated to pay this tax?
- Why did Jesus pay the tax anyway? (Verse 27.)
- What lesson do you think Jesus was teaching Peter by providing the money through a miracle instead of just letting Peter pay it?
- What difference does it make to you to know that Jesus was without sin?

MATTHEW 18: BECOMING WORTHY TO INHERIT THE CELESTIAL KINGDOM

Matthew 18:1–10

"Who is the greatest in the kingdom of heaven?"

 Ask a child to sit, or place a picture of a child, on a chair in the middle of the room. Have the other family members write down five qualities they think are most impressive about children. Have everyone share their answers, then compare your lists to Mosiah 3:19.

Read Matthew 18:1 together and find the question the disciples asked Jesus. Have a family member read Matthew 18:2–10. Ask:

- Why do you think Jesus answered the way He did?
- According to verses 6 and 10, what did Jesus never want to happen to children?
- Why do you think it is important to never offend little children?

Have your family look at the Joseph Smith Translation changes in Matthew 18:9, footnote *a,* and Matthew 18:11, footnote *c.* What do those additions help us better understand about children?

Invite your family to think of ways they can become more childlike, especially considering the five qualities they listed initially.

Matthew 18:11–14

What would you search harder for: lost money or a lost soul?

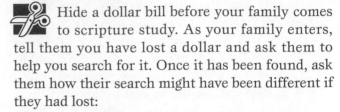 Hide a dollar bill before your family comes to scripture study. As your family enters, tell them you have lost a dollar and ask them to help you search for it. Once it has been found, ask them how their search might have been different if they had lost:

- $1,000
- $10,000
- A family pet
- A child in your family

Have a family member read Matthew 18:11–14. Ask your family to contrast finding lost money or a lost pet to finding a lost soul.

Read together Doctrine and Covenants 18:11–16 and discuss what more we learn about helping those who are lost. As a family, think about someone you might be able to help bring back to the fold and talk about ways that you could help that person.

Matthew 18:15–35

How should you respond when someone sins against you?

Ask family members to think of a time when someone hurt their feelings or another person's sins hurt them in some way. You might ask for someone to share their experience and then ask:

- How did you handle yourself in this situation?
- What did you do to overcome any hard or unforgiving feelings you had?

Invite your family to silently read Matthew 18:15–22. As they do, ask them to mark any teachings they find that give advice about responding when others sin against us. When everyone has finished, take turns sharing what each person discovered.

Read the following statement from President Spencer W. Kimball to your family: "Until seventy times seven! That seems very difficult indeed for us mortals, and yet there are still harder things to do. When they have repented and come on their knees to ask forgiveness, most of us can forgive, but the

Lord has required that we shall even forgive them if they do not repent nor ask forgiveness of us." (Conference Report, Oct. 1949, 129–30.)

Read the following story told by President Thomas S. Monson:

"An elderly man disclosed at the funeral of his brother, with whom he had shared, from early manhood, a small, one-room cabin near Canisteo, New York, that following a quarrel, they had divided the room in half with a chalk line and neither had crossed the line or spoken a word to the other since that day—62 years before." (*Ensign*, May 2002, 20.) Ask:

- Why is this such a tragedy?
- If someone offends you, what does the Lord expect of you?
- Why do you think it is important to forgive others?

Explain to your family that you are going to act out the parable told in Matthew 18:23–35. Assign family members the following parts: narrator, king, unmerciful servant, fellowservant.

As your narrator reads the verses, have the other assigned family members act out their parts. You may want to use the accompanying explanations and questions to help your family better understand the story.

Narrator: Read Matthew 18:23–25, as the king and unmerciful servant act out their parts. Following this activity, explain to your family that a talent is a very large sum of money. (See Bible Dictionary, "Money," 734.) The Savior purposely used 10,000 talents in this parable because it was an amount of money impossible to repay. It would represent millions (maybe billions) of dollars in our currency.

Narrator: Read Matthew 18:26–27 as the king and unmerciful servant perform what is being read. Following the reading, talk about how the servant might feel after being forgiven of such a huge debt. Ask:

- In what ways does the king remind you of the Savior?
- How does this servant's debt compare to the indebtedness you have to the Savior?
- How should we feel when we are forgiven? Why?

Narrator: Read Matthew 18:28–30 as the unmerciful servant and the fellowservant act out their parts. Read footnote 28*a* to your family and ask:

- How much would that represent in our currency?
- How does this debt compare to the 10,000 talents?
- How does this part of the story make you feel about the unmerciful servant?
- Why is it wrong for him to be so unforgiving?

Narrator: Read Matthew 18:31–35 as the king and unmerciful servant perform what is being read. After the reading, give the following statement by Elder Bruce R. McConkie: "Thus, in effect, the king was saying: 'I have cancelled your million dollar obligation to me and yet you demand from your fellow servant the one thin dime he owes you.'" (*Doctrinal New Testament Commentary,* 1:430.) Ask:

- Why do you think the king was justified?
- How do you think the Savior would react to us if we are unwilling to forgive others? Why?

Have a family member read Doctrine and Covenants 64:9–11 and discuss the following questions with your family:

- How are we sometimes like the servant who wouldn't forgive his fellow servant?
- How is our debt to Heavenly Father impossible to repay without the help of the Savior?
- Why do we have the greater sin if we don't forgive?
- How have you felt when you have forgiven another?
- How have you felt when another has forgiven you?

MATTHEW 19: WHAT MUST I DO TO HAVE ETERNAL LIFE?

Matthew 19:1–12
Marriage and divorce

 Share this experience related by Emma Rae McKay, wife of President David O. McKay:

"Last summer on reaching Los Angeles, we decided to have our car washed. . . .

"As I was watching the last part of the operation from a bench, to my surprise a tiny voice at my elbow said, 'I guess that man over there loves you.'

"I turned and saw a beautiful little curly-haired child with great brown eyes who looked to be about seven years of age.

"'What did you say?' I asked.

"'I said, I guess that man over there loves you.'

"'Oh, yes, he loves me; he is my husband. But why do you ask?'

"A tender smile lighted up his face and his voice softened as he said, 'Cuz, the way he smiled at you. Do you know I'd give anything in this world if my pop would smile at my mom that way.'

"'Oh, I'm sorry if he doesn't.'

"'I guess you're not going to get a divorce,' he [said].

"'No, of course not; we've been married over fifty years. Why do you ask that?'

"'Cuz everybody gets a divorce around here. My pop is getting a divorce from my mom, and I love my pop and I love my mom. . . .'

"His voice broke, and tears welled up in his eyes, but he was too much of a little man to let them fall.

"'Oh, I'm sorry to hear that!'

"And then he came very close and whispered confidentially into my ear, 'You'd better hurry out of this place or you'll get a divorce, too!'" (*The Savior, the Priesthood, and You,* 207–8.)

Have a family member read Matthew 19:1–3 and look for the question the Pharisees asked Jesus as they tried to trap Him. (See also footnote 3*a*.) Explain to your family that at the time of Christ divorce was a fiercely debated topic. Have family members take turns reading Matthew 19:4–9. Then ask:

- What did Jesus teach regarding the relationship between "male and female"? (Marriage partners should not be divided or separated; see footnote 6*b*.)

- Why do you think the Lord wants families to stay together?

Read the first and seventh paragraphs from "The Family: A Proclamation to the World" (*Ensign,* Nov. 1995, 101; or see the appendix of this book.)

Ask family members how they feel about those messages from the First Presidency.

To help explain verse 9, share the following from Elder Bruce R. McConkie: "Divorce is not part of the gospel plan no matter what kind of marriage is involved. But because men in practice do not always live in harmony with gospel standards, the Lord permits divorce for one reason or another, depending on the spiritual stability of the people involved. . . . Under the most perfect conditions there would be no divorce permitted except where sex sin was involved. In this day divorces are permitted in accordance with civil statutes, and the divorced persons are permitted by the Church to marry again without the stain of immorality which under a higher system would attend such a course." (*Doctrinal New Testament Commentary,* 1:547.)

Matthew 19:16–30
"What lack I yet?"

⭐ Invite family members to bring one of their most prized possessions to scripture study, and share the following story from Elder Robert L. Backman:

"In Africa, the natives have a unique, effective way to capture monkeys. They lop the top off a coconut, remove the meat, and leave a hole in the top of the coconut large enough for the monkey to put his paw in. Then they anchor the coconut to the ground with some peanuts in it. When the natives leave, the monkeys, smelling those delicious peanuts, approach the coconuts, see the peanuts in them, put their paws in to grasp the nuts, and attempt to remove the nuts—but find that the hole is too small for their doubled-up fists. The natives return with gunny sacks and pick up the monkeys—clawing, biting, screaming—but they won't drop the peanuts to save their lives.

"Do you know anyone who is caught in a monkey trap, where the things that matter the most are at the mercy of those things that matter the least?" (*Ensign,* Nov. 1980, 42.)

Have your family answer the final question posed by Elder Backman and then ask: How does his question apply to the monkey trap? What lessons should we learn from the trapped monkeys?

Read together Matthew 19:16–22 and have your family look for how the young man in the story is like the monkey in the trap. Ask:

- What did Jesus say the rich young man should do to receive eternal life?
- On a scale of 1–10, how obedient had this young man been up to this point?
- What did Jesus ask of him that he could not obey?
- Why do you think the Lord asked the young man to give up all his possessions?
- What was Jesus offering him in place of his wealth?
- How is that like the monkey in the trap?
- How can Jesus' instructions to the young man apply to us?

Invite family members to show the prized possession they brought to scripture study. Ask:

- If the Lord asked you to give it up, could you?
- Why would it be difficult?
- Why would it be worth it?

Tell your family that Jesus answers that last question in Matthew 19:23–30. Read those verses together and have your family point out verses that give us reasons for putting God first. Share this statement from President Joseph F. Smith: "No man can obtain the gift of eternal life unless he is willing to sacrifice all earthly things in order to obtain it." (*Gospel Doctrine*, 261.)

Matthew 19:23–26

Is money the root of all evil?

Hold up a needle and tell your family that Jesus uses a needle to teach an important lesson in Matthew 19:23–26. Have a family member read those verses aloud, including the Joseph Smith Translation in footnote 26*a*. Ask:

- What did Jesus teach about the relationship between having riches and being able to enter the kingdom of God?
- What additional information does 1 Timothy 6:10 add?
- What is the difference between saying, 'Money is the root of all evil' and 'The love of money is the root of all evil'?

Share this insight from President Joseph F. Smith: "God is not a respecter of persons. The rich man may enter into the kingdom of heaven as freely as the poor, if he will bring his heart and affections into subjection to the law of God and to the principle of truth; if he will place his affections upon God, his heart upon the truth, and his soul upon the accomplishment of God's purposes, and not fix his affections and his hopes upon the things of the world." (*Gospel Doctrine*, 260–61.)

Read Jacob 2:17–19 aloud and share your testimony of the importance of placing God first, above all worldly possessions.

MATTHEW 20: JESUS TELLS OF "LABORERS" AND OF HIS LABORS

Matthew 20:1–19

The rewards for serving in God's kingdom

Tell your family that all day today will be spent "cleaning the house," and those who participate will earn the same reward. No one will finish until bedtime, but each person will be given a different starting time. Some will begin in the morning, some in the afternoon, and some in the evening. Ask your family how they feel about this arrangement and what thoughts they might have if they are chosen to begin in the morning instead of the afternoon or evening.

Take turns reading Matthew 20:1–16 and discuss these questions:

- What does Matthew 20:1 say this parable is about? (The kingdom of heaven.)
- Who is the householder? (The Lord.)
- How much money does each laborer hired in the early morning earn?
- How much do the laborers receive who begin work at the third hour? The sixth hour? The eleventh hour?
- What is the reason that the laborers were "idle" at the eleventh hour? (Verses 6–7.)
- What phrase in the parable indicates that the householder will be fair to all laborers?
- Is it fair to give all laborers one penny, even

though some worked for only one hour? Why or why not?

- What comfort or message do you think converts to the Church find in this parable?
- What message does the parable have for those who have been in the Church all of their lives?

The following statement may help your family understand this difficult parable better:

"One application of this parable is that those called to Christ's service in the latter-days will inherit equally with Adam and Abraham, though those ancient prophets have long since gone to their exaltation." (McConkie, *Mormon Doctrine,* 219.)

Matthew 20:20–28
Who is the greatest?

 Have a mother respond to the following questions:

- What are some of your greatest hopes and desires for your children?
- How important is it to you that your children return to heaven and why?

Read together Matthew 20:20–24 and ask:

- What did the mother of James and John desire for her two sons?
- Why do you think the other Apostles resented her request?
- What did they learn about what is really involved in sitting close to Jesus in His kingdom?
- When have you felt close to the Savior? What were you doing? What does that teach you about what will help you be close to Him in eternity?

To illustrate what Jesus was saying in Matthew 20:22, offer one of your children a cup of water and a cup of vinegar to drink. Ask them why they chose the water and talk about their reaction to the vinegar. Invite family members to read Matthew 20:22 again and relate it to the experience they have just viewed. Ask them what they think is represented by "the cup" Jesus would drink of and "the baptism" that He is baptized with. Have someone read

3 Nephi 27:27 and ask how it might relate to what Jesus was teaching in these verses in Matthew 20.

Read together Matthew 20:25–28 and ask:

- What do Jesus' teachings help us understand about what will make us great?
- Think about people you know that you think are truly great in the kingdom of God. How have these teachings of Jesus been true for them?

You may want to give everyone in your family some time to write in their journals some thoughts about where they want to be in eternity and how they might apply these teachings of Jesus.

Matthew 20:29–34
"Have mercy on us, O Lord, thou Son of David"

Blindfold each family member and read aloud to them Matthew 20:29–34. While they remain blindfolded, have them respond to the following questions:

- What did the two blind men know about Jesus even though they could not see?
- How could they, in their sightless condition, know who He was?
- Why do you think the "multitude rebuked" the blind men who were asking for help?
- What difficulties would come from being blind?

Testify to your family that like physical blindness there is also spiritual blindness. Have your family remove their blindfolds and show them the picture of Jesus healing a blind man. (See *Gospel Art Kit,* no. 213.)

Talk about these questions:

- What are some other types of "blindness" people may suffer from?
- What are some ways the Lord has helped you to "see"?
- How have you responded to the blessings you have received from Him?

Consider singing a hymn about gratitude to conclude, such as "Because I Have Been Given Much." (*Hymns,* no. 219.)

MATTHEW 21: JESUS' TRIUMPHAL ENTRY

Matthew 21:1–11
Why did Jesus ride triumphantly into Jerusalem on a donkey?

Obtain a long piece of cloth such as a towel and roll it up. As your family comes to scripture study, roll out the cloth in the door way or hall for your family to walk in on. Ask:

- What does the phrase "roll out the red carpet" mean?
- Who usually gets this special treatment?
- How would royalty or other rich and famous people travel as part of the "red carpet treatment"? (Private jets, limousines, or other fancy cars, etc.)

Tell your family that kings were treated a little differently in ancient Israel. Have your family take turns reading Matthew 21:1–11 and look for how Israel honored royalty. Discuss the following questions:

- How did Jesus travel to Jerusalem for His triumphal entrance? (Verses 2–7.)
- Why was it prophesied that the Messiah would ride a donkey into Jerusalem? (See Zechariah 9:9 and the following quotation.)

"There was nothing in any sense degrading in the idea of riding on a donkey, as might perhaps be inferred from Zechariah 9:9. . . . It was the sign of the peaceful mission of Christ. Kings, high priests, judges, and the richest people of ancient and modern times have ridden on donkeys." (*New Unger's Bible Dictionary*, "Donkey," 69.)

- What were the people shouting as Jesus came into Jerusalem?
- What does *Hosanna* mean? (See "Hosanna" in the Bible Dictionary, 704–5.)
- What message was Jesus sending by the way He entered Jerusalem?

"Every detail of this unique episode joined in testifying of the identity of the central figure in the picture. It was as though Jesus had said: 'Many times I have told you in plain words and by necessary implication that I am the Messiah. My disciples also bear the same witness. Now I come unto you as the King of Israel in the very way that the prophet of old said I would; and your participation in this event is itself a witness that I am he who should come to redeem my people.'" (McConkie, *Doctrinal New Testament Commentary*, 1:577–78.)

- How does it make you feel to know Jesus can save you?
- What do you think you would feel like doing to show your respect for the Savior when He comes again?

Matthew 21:12–16
What is the purpose of the temple?

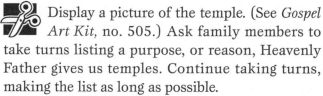 Display a picture of the temple. (See *Gospel Art Kit*, no. 505.) Ask family members to take turns listing a purpose, or reason, Heavenly Father gives us temples. Continue taking turns, making the list as long as possible.

Explain that the story of Jesus cleansing the temple is found in Matthew 21:12–16. Read those verses together and ask:

- What did Jesus do first when He came to the temple?
- What did He do after the temple was cleansed? (He healed people.)
- What principle is the Lord teaching us about what we must do to receive the blessings of the temple?
- What can we do to keep the temple clean and holy?

Read together Doctrine and Covenants 109:20–21 and talk about what more those verses teach about this principle. Invite an endowed member of your family to share his or her feelings about the healing they have felt by attending the temple.

Matthew 21:23–27
Jesus answers a question with a question

 Ask your family members if they remember their baptism. Have a few share their memories. Ask:

- Who were some of the people present?
- Why did you want to be baptized?

- Who baptized you?
- Why did you ask that person to baptize you?
- Where did the person get the authority to baptize you?

Show your family a copy of a priesthood line of authority and read through it with them. Explain what a line of authority means. Read together Matthew 21:23–27 and ask:

- What did the chief priest and elders want from Jesus?
- What did Jesus do instead of showing them His line of authority?
- Jesus obviously has the authority, so why do you think He answered them with a question?
- Have you ever refused to answer someone who didn't want an answer but really only wanted to argue?

Read Article of Faith 5 and share your testimony of the importance of authority, particularly the authority that Jesus Christ possesses.

Matthew 21:28–32
Why is it important to do what we are asked?

Share this modern parable with your family: Before I leave for work, I ask you (point to your oldest child) to clean your room, and you say no. I then turn to you (your next oldest child) and say clean your room, and you say OK. After I leave for work, the oldest child repents and cleans the room, but the second never does. Ask: Which child did the will of the parent? Take turns reading Matthew 21:28–32 and ask:

- Who did Jesus say would enter into the kingdom of heaven before the Pharisee? (See verse 32.)
- What is a publican and what is a harlot? (See page 755 of your Bible Dictionary for the definition of a publican. A harlot was a woman who was paid to break the law of chastity.)
- Why would publicans or harlots enter the kingdom of heaven before the Pharisees, if their actions were so detested by the Jews?
- How is a Pharisee like the second son in the parable? (Pharisees outwardly promised to

serve the people, the Lord's vineyard, but they really only cared about themselves.)

- How are the harlots and the publicans like the first son in the parable? (Verse 32.)

Write the following sentence where your family can see it, but leave the parentheses empty:

"It is what I *(become)* that will get me into heaven, not what I *(pretend to be)*."

Ask your family how they would fill in the blanks to express the principle Jesus taught in this parable. (Any words that express the same idea are acceptable.) Display this statement of principle where all can be reminded of it.

Matthew 21:33–46
The parable of the wicked husbandman

Tell your family that in today's scripture study they are going to analyze a parable. (If needed, turn to page 740 in the Bible Dictionary and read the definition of *parable*.)

Draw a line down the middle of a sheet of paper from top to bottom. On the top of the left-hand column write *Parable* and on the top of the right-hand column write *Interpretation*. As you read together Matthew 21:33–46, have a family member write the main parts of the parable in the left-hand column.

Parable	Interpretation
Householder	God
Vineyard	The earth
Husbandmen	Priests and Teachers of Israel
Far country	A distant heaven
Other servants	Prophets of Israel
His son (the householder's son)	Jesus
Miserably destroys the wicked men	Destruction of Jerusalem in A.D. 70 by Titus
New husbandmen	New leaders of Christ's Church and the Gentiles who accept the gospel

(Adapted from McConkie, *Doctrinal New Testament Commentary,* 1:593–94.)

After you have identified each element of the parable, ask your family what the symbols or events represent.

After you have discovered the message of this parable, ask:

- How did the "chief priests and Pharisees" react to this parable? (See verses 45–46.)
- How did the "multitude" feel about Jesus' teachings?
- Why do you think the people accepted Jesus and the leaders wanted to get rid of Him? (See 1 Nephi 16:1–2.)

As a summary, ask your family to write down a principle of truth we can learn from this story for our day.

MATTHEW 22: QUESTIONS FROM PHARISEES AND SADDUCEES

Matthew 22:1–14

Many are called, but few are chosen

Have family members name some events for which they were given special invitations. Ask, Which of these events were you most excited to attend? Why?

Read together Matthew 22:1–10. Ask:

- Why did the people invited to attend the marriage feast refuse the invitation? (See Matthew 22:3, footnote *a*.)
- How are the reactions of the people in verses 5–6 of this parable similar to ways some people today respond to the gospel message?

To help your family understand the symbolism of this wedding feast, have them look up the references listed in footnote *b* for Matthew 22:2 and report what they learn. Read to them Doctrine and Covenants 58:6–11 and discuss it as well. Ask:

- What do you think the wedding feast in this parable symbolizes? (The Second Coming.)
- According to Matthew 22:3, who actually did the inviting and how is this like our day? (See D&C 1:2–4, 14.)

Have a family member read Matthew 22:11–14 and then share the following explanation:

"The interpretation of much of the parable is [as follows:] The king is God; the son is Christ; the place of the wedding feast is the kingdom of heaven; those bidden to the feast are those to whom the message of the gospel is taken; the servants are obviously the prophets who had been rejected and killed by those of their own nation; . . . After their rejection by Israel, the servants went to the gentile nations, preaching to all, the righteous and unrighteous alike. What is not immediately evident is why a particular dress is so necessary for the wedding feast and why the punishment (the endless woe of outer darkness) is appropriate for one not properly dressed.

"It was well known to the Savior's audience that one had to be suitably dressed to appear before a king. The apparel of the guest was a reflection of respect for the host. . . . It appears evident that people brought in from the highways of the earth would have neither time nor means to procure wedding garments. The king had obviously supplied his guests from his own wardrobe. All had been invited to clothe themselves in the garments of royalty. The man cast out had chosen to trust in his own dress rather than that provided by the king. By interpretation, he had chosen to join the true worshipers, that is the church or kingdom of God, yet he had not chosen to dress as the others had dressed. He was not one with them. He desired the full blessings of the kingdom, but on his own terms, not those of the king. . . .

"All who are to feast in the heavenly kingdom must be properly clothed. They must be wearing the garments of purity and holiness, garments made white through 'the blood of the Lamb' (Revelation 7:14)." (McConkie, *Gospel Symbolism*, 132–33.)

Matthew 22:15–22

God and Caesar

The account in Matthew 22:15–22 will make more sense to your family if they understand the meaning of *Pharisees, Herodians, Caesar,* and *tribute.* Assign various family members to look up these terms in the Bible Dictionary and/or a regular dictionary and report what they learn. As they report, you may want to draw attention to the following ideas:

- The Pharisees believed it was their religious duty to separate themselves from worldly governments and become a religious government to the Jews.
- The Herodians supported the Roman government because Rome granted them the right to be rulers over the Jews.
- Caesar was the ruler of Rome.
- Tribute refers to taxes paid to the Roman government.

With these ideas in mind, read together Matthew 22:15–22. Ask:

- Why could the questions asked of Jesus in verse 17 be a way to possibly "entangle" Him?
- How did Jesus' answer keep Him from being entangled?
- What do you think Jesus meant by His statement in verse 21?
- What is our duty to our governments? (See D&C 134:1, 5; Articles of Faith 1:12.) Share with your family the following from Elder Howard W. Hunter: "In the present day of unrest, the question might appropriately be asked, what do we owe to Caesar?. . . . We owe allegiance, respect, and honor. . . . We must pay tribute to sustain the government." (Conference Report, Apr. 1968, 65.)
- What things are we to render to God?

Discuss as a family what difference it would make if we could always remember that we—and every person we meet—is "stamped" with the image of God.

Matthew 22:23–33
Marriage and the Resurrection

 Show your family a picture of the temple. Ask:

- Why does the Lord have us build temples?
- What are some ordinances that can only be performed in temples?
- What blessing can come to our family in the temple?

To help answer those questions, share the following statement from President Gordon B. Hinckley:

"Every temple that this Church has built has in effect stood as a monument to our belief in the immortality of the human soul, that this phase of mortal life through which we pass is part of a continuous upward climb, so to speak, and that as certain as there is life here, there will be life there. That is our firm belief. It comes about through the Atonement of the Savior, and the temple becomes, as I have indicated, the bridge from this life to the next. The temple is concerned with things of immortality. We wouldn't have to build a temple for marriages if we didn't believe in the eternity of the family. We build it so the family may be eternal." (*Ensign,* Apr. 2002, 4.)

Invite someone to read aloud Matthew 22:23–28. Ask:

- What do we learn about the beliefs of the Sadducees? (See Bible Dictionary, "Sadducee," for more information.)
- How do the beliefs of the Sadducees make their question to Jesus seem strange?
- Do you think they really wanted to know the answer to the question? Why or why not?

Read together the answer Jesus gave to the Sadducees in Matthew 22:29–32. Ask:

- What two truths did Jesus say the Sadducees needed to understand?
- What did Jesus mean in verse 30? (See D&C 132:15–17 for an explanation.)

Tell your family that while working on the translation of this part of the New Testament, the Prophet Joseph Smith said he learned that "man in this life must marry in view of eternity, otherwise they must remain as angels, or be single in heaven." (*History of the Church,* 6:442.) Share your testimony that now is the time to prepare for the marriage covenant that can be received only in the temple.

Matthew 22:34–40
What are the greatest commandments?

Beginning with the youngest person in the family and working towards the oldest, have each family member name one or two commandments of God. Appoint one person to be a scribe and write on a piece of paper or poster the responses of the family. Show the whole list to the family and ask: Which of these commandments is the most important on this list? For each suggestion given, invite that family member to explain why he or she thinks that commandment is most important.

Explain that Jesus was asked a similar question. Read together Matthew 22:34–40 and have family members look for and mark the commandments Jesus said were most important. Ask: Why do you think that the "first and great commandment" is first? Share with them the following from President Ezra Taft Benson:

"Why did God put the first commandment first? Because He knew that if we truly loved Him we would want to keep all of His other commandments. . . .

"We must put God in the forefront of everything else in our lives. He must come first. . . .

"When we put God first, all other things fall into their proper place or drop out of our lives." (*Ensign,* May 1988, 4.)

Invite family members to give examples from the scriptures or your own family history of people who put God first and explain how it brought great power to their lives.

MATTHEW 23: JESUS REPROVES THE SCRIBES AND PHARISEES

Matthew 23:1–35
Who am I?

Before family scripture study, prepare a "Who Am I?" game by writing on a sheet of paper the verses and characteristics listed in the chart below and cover it with another sheet of paper, or you could just use the accompanying chart. Begin the game by revealing the characteristics listed in the right-hand column one by one and have your family guess the kind of person each describes.

As soon as the word *hypocrite* is guessed, show the rest of the list to see if each characteristic

Verses in Matthew 23	Who Am I?
a. 4	I claim to follow ancient prophets but find fault with living prophets.
b. 5	I try to make it seem too difficult to be able to go to heaven.
c. 5	I love to be called by respected titles.
d. 6	I go to extreme lengths to live minor commandments but often neglect the most important principles of the gospel.
e. 7–10	I like to make my prayers long so people will think I am very righteous.
f. 12	I make my religious objects bigger so people will notice how spiritual I am.
g. 13	I like to build myself up in other's eyes.
h. 14	I like to sit on the stand at church so I will be noticed.
i. 23–24	I will only do good things if people are watching.
j. 25–28	Outward righteousness is more important than inward righteousness.
k. 29–35	I ask others to do things that I am not willing to do myself.

describes a hypocrite. (If no one guesses correctly, review the verses as described until someone discovers the right word.) As a family, review the verses in the first column and match them with the characteristics. Write the letter next to the sentence that best describes what is said in the verse(s). Ask:

- Why do you think Jesus spoke so strongly against hypocrisy?
- In what ways can hypocrisy affect our spirituality today?
- What can you do to better avoid hyppocrisy?

Matthew 23:25–26
Pick your cup

Get two cups that you can't see through, one that is old and worn and one that is new and nicer. Make some mud and smear it on the inside of the nicer cup. Show your family the outside of the cups and a jug of milk and ask them which cup they would choose to drink from. Then show them the inside and ask them which cup they would prefer now. Invite them to talk about why they chose the ordinary cup over the nicer cup. Read together Matthew 23:25–26 and discuss the following questions:

- Who in these verses is like the nicer cup? Why?
- What does the mud represent?
- Which cup is potentially the most dangerous? (The one that looks clean outside but really isn't.)
- What kind of people are potentially the most dangerous?
- Why would some people care more about what they look like on the outside than what they are really like on the inside?

Invite your family to think of some people they know that the world would think are very ordinary but who are really wonderful and Christlike people on the inside. Read together 1 Samuel 16:7 and then decide as a family how to finish the following sentence.

"What I am on the _____ is more important than what I look like on the _____."

Matthew 23:37–39
How does the Savior love us?

 Ask the children in the family the following questions:

- Have you ever wanted to sleep near a parent or sibling when scared? Why?
- Why does this make you feel safer?

Have your family silently read Matthew 23:37–39 and look for ways these verses relate to the questions. Tell your family that during a storm or when danger is near a mother hen allows her young chicks to hide under her wings for safety. Discuss the following questions:

- Why do you think Jesus compared Himself to a hen gathering her chicks?
- Do you think the hen would be able to fight off a hawk or a fox?
- If the hen cannot scare away the fox, how will she protect her chicks?
- How is this like what Jesus Christ did for us?
- What does this teach about the Savior's love?

- Where can the Savior's children gather for safety today?
- What can happen when we refuse to gather to the safe places the Savior has provided?

Read together Doctrine and Covenants 115:5–6 and discuss how your family can find safety in dangerous times.

MATTHEW 24: JESUS FORETELLS HIS SECOND COMING

Matthew 24:1–51
Signs warn us of what's ahead

Place a tree or plant (real or artificial) in the middle of the room. Ask your family how they can tell when winter is coming by what happens to many trees and plants? Explain that just as there are signs that let us know winter is coming, there are signs that let us know the Second Coming of Jesus Christ is near. Give each family member two or three pieces of scratch paper. Have them search Matthew 24 for signs of Jesus' Second Coming and write down a sign on each piece of paper. After everyone has finished writing, have each family member put their papers on the tree and tell what signs they wrote down.

Ask your family to describe the kinds of feelings they have about some of the signs. Read together Matthew 24:6 and ask:

- What are some synonyms (words with similar meanings) for the word *troubled?*
- What other synonym do you find in footnote 6*b?*
- Why do you think the Lord would ask us not to be frightened with all the horrible things that will happen?
- How can we overcome fear as the signs of the times are fulfilled?

After some discussion, have your family read Doctrine and Covenants 38:30 and write that reference next to Matthew 24:6. Ask again what we can do to not be afraid during these times. Discuss ways your family can be prepared both spiritually and materially. Testify to your family that the signs of the Savior's Second Coming are given to help us be ready for that great day.

Matthew 24:2–3, 5–20, 21–55
Two important questions are answered

Show your family a picture of the Salt Lake Temple. Ask them if they believe it will ever be destroyed. Read Matthew 24:2 to your family. Explain that some of the stones used to build the temple in Jerusalem were 67.5 feet long, 7.5 feet high, and 9 feet wide. Ask your family why, considering the time in which they lived, it would have been hard for people to believe that their temple could be destroyed.

Have each family member silently read verse 3 and find two questions that the disciples asked of the Savior. Write the questions on a sheet of paper and place it where all can see it. Tell your family that these two questions are best answered in Joseph Smith's inspired translation of Matthew 24 found in the Pearl of Great Price. Divide your family into two groups and have them search for answers to these two questions by using the information listed below:

- Group 1—Answer the first question by searching Joseph Smith–Matthew 1:5–20.
- Group 2—Answer the second question by searching Joseph Smith–Matthew 1:21–55.

Once they have had time to search for an answer invite each group to share what they found.

Explain to your family that although many Jews did not believe their great city and temple could be destroyed, the Lord's prophecies were fulfilled in A.D. 70. The Jews revolted against the Romans in A.D. 66, and four years later the Romans destroyed the entire city. Those who listened to the Savior and fled into the mountains were spared. Those who did not heed this counsel were either killed or taken captive and scattered.

As a family discuss teachings given by the living prophet that will help you prepare for the Savior's Second Coming and avoid destruction.

Matthew 24:36–51
Why won't He just tell us?

Invite your family to tell of a time when they were given a pop quiz and ask:

- How do you prepare for a surprise quiz?
- Why do teachers sometimes give a pop quiz?
- What spiritual "pop quizzes" might we have to face?
- How can we always be prepared for them?

Have a family member read aloud Matthew 24:36 and ask:

- Who knows when the Second Coming will be?
- Why won't Heavenly Father just tell us?
- How does this encourage the Lord's children to always be prepared for His coming?

Take turns reading Matthew 24:37–51 and ask your family to look for, and make a list of, ways they can always be prepared. Share with your family your feelings about preparing, day-by-day, for the eternal "pop quiz."

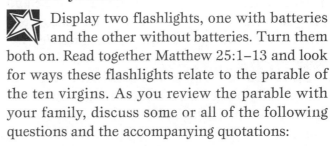

MATTHEW 25: HOW TO PREPARE FOR THE SECOND COMING

Matthew 25:1–13
"I know you not"

Display two flashlights, one with batteries and the other without batteries. Turn them both on. Read together Matthew 25:1–13 and look for ways these flashlights relate to the parable of the ten virgins. As you review the parable with your family, discuss some or all of the following questions and the accompanying quotations:

- Who do the virgins and the bridegroom represent? (Verses 1–2; see also statement no. 1 below.)
- Why were the foolish virgins unprepared? (Verse 3.)
- What does the oil represent? (Verses 3–4; see also statement no. 2 below.)
- How might one get this oil in their lamps? (See statement no. 3 below.)
- Why do you think the bridegroom (Savior) chooses to come at midnight? (Verse 6; see also statement no. 4 below.)
- If the wise virgins represent faithful members of the Church, why didn't they share their oil

with the foolish virgins? (Verses 8–9; see statement no. 5 below.)

- Why do you think the Savior shut the door on the foolish virgins? (Verses 10–12; see also statement no. 6 below.)

Statement 1: "These ten virgins were members of the Church. The bridegroom was the Lord Jesus Christ." (Kimball, *Teachings of Spencer W. Kimball*, 183.)

Statement 2: "The oil-filled lamps are symbolic of the Holy Spirit which lights the way before the saints." (McConkie, *Doctrinal New Testament Commentary*, 1:684; see also D&C 45:56–59.)

Statement 3: "Those who have got oil in their lamps, are [those] who live their religion, pay their tithing, pay their debts, keep the commandments of God, and do not blaspheme [curse] his name; . . . those that will be valiant in the testimony of Jesus Christ." (Wilford Woodruff, *Journal of Discourses*, 21:126.)

Statement 4: "At midnight! Precisely at the darkest hour, when least expected, the bridegroom came. . . . But when the cry sounds, there is no time for preparation. . . . those without lamps or oil are left in darkness. . . . In the daytime, wise and unwise seemed alike; midnight is the time of test and judgment." (Kimball, *Faith Precedes the Miracle*, 255.)

Statement 5: "The refusal of the wise virgins to give of their oil at such a critical time must not be regarded as uncharitable; the circumstance typifies the fact that in the day of judgment every soul must answer for himself; there is no way by which the righteousness of one can be credited to another's account." (Talmage, *Jesus the Christ*, 579.)

Statement 6: "[The foolish virgins] had been so careless, that all the Spirit of God—which may be compared to the oil that gives brightness to the lamps—had gone out of them, and their lamps would not burn. . . . But they afterwards arrived and begged to be admitted. . . . What is the reply? 'I know you not.' Why? Because they have apostatized; they have lost the oil out of their lamps; they failed to be prepared for the coming of the Savior." (Orson Pratt, *Journal of Discourses*, 21:278–79.)

Read again Matthew 25:13 and discuss as a family ways you can fill your lamps with oil. Share the following from President Spencer W. Kimball:

"In the parable, oil can be purchased at the market. In our lives the oil of preparedness is accumulated drop by drop in righteous living. Attendance at sacrament meetings adds oil to our lamps, drop by drop over years. Fasting, family prayer, home teaching, control of bodily appetites, preaching the gospel, studying the scriptures—each act of dedication and obedience is a drop added to our store. Deeds of kindness, payment of offerings and tithes, chaste thoughts and actions, marriage in the covenant for eternity—these, too, contribute importantly to the oil with which we can at midnight refuel our exhausted lamps. Midnight is so late for those who have procrastinated." (*Faith Precedes the Miracle*, 256.)

Matthew 25:14–30
How can we develop our talents?

Have each family member list his or her talents on a sheet of paper. (Parents or older children can help younger ones.) Then have them write what they are doing to improve upon them. Take the lists and hide them. As you read aloud Matthew 25:14–30, ask the following questions:

- According to this parable, what did the three different individuals do with the talents given them? (Verses 16–18.)
- Why do you think one chose to bury his talent? (Verses 24–25.)
- How did the lord respond to his servants? (Verses 21, 23, 26–30.)
- Why was the one servant scolded when he didn't lose anything?
- In what ways do we tend to "bury" our talents?
- Why do you think it is important to continue to grow spiritually?

Divide the following references among your family and have them read them aloud: Doctrine and Covenants 4:2; 58:27; 60:13; 64:33–34. As you read each one, discuss what those verses teach us about being better than we are. Return the hidden lists of talents and encourage everyone to record in their journals how they will develop and improve upon their talents.

Matthew 25:31–46

Are you a sheep or a goat?

 Hand each member of your family a sheet of paper, crayons, colored pencils, or markers. Invite some to draw a sheep and others to draw a goat. Display a picture of the Savior. Take turns reading Matthew 25:31–33 and have family members place their pictures on the left or right hand of Jesus according to what is said in the verses (goats on Jesus' left hand and sheep on His right).

Write Matthew 25:35–40 beneath a drawing of a sheep and Matthew 25:42–45 beneath a drawing of a goat. Have those family members who made drawings of sheep read Matthew 25:35–40 and list on their paper words and phrases that describe the things "sheep" do. Have those who made drawings of goats read Matthew 25:42–45 and list on their paper words and phrases that describe the things "goats" fail to do.

Ask a family member who drew a sheep to read aloud Matthew 25:34 and then draw a crown on their sheep. Have another family member who drew a goat read aloud Matthew 25:41 and 46 and then remove all of the goat drawings from the left-hand side of the Savior. Share the following insight from Elder Bruce R. McConkie:

"This is the day of judgment for the saints of the Most High. For them the judgment is set and the books are opened. Their eternal destiny is to be determined on the basis of their earthly works. This is the great day of division in the Church, the sheep being divided from the goats, the one group going to the right hand of honor, the other to the left hand of disgrace. It is the story of the ten virgins all over again—five wise, five foolish—half of whom entered the house and sat at the marriage feast and half of whom were locked out because they never knew the Bridegroom." (*Mortal Messiah,* 3:473–74.)

Ask:

- What acts of service have you seen in our home that are similar to those performed by the sheep in these verses?
- How do acts of service help the server come to know the Savior?
- How do acts of service help the one who is served come to know the Savior?

MATTHEW 26: THE LAST SUPPER AND GETHSEMANE

Before studying this chapter it may be helpful to identify some locations on a map. Write the following places on slips of paper and hand one to each family member: *House of Caiaphas, Road to Bethany, Upper Room, Mount of Olives,* and *Gethsemane.* Tell family members their challenge is to find each place on a map in the back of their Bibles. (In post-1999 copies of the Bible, use Map 12, entitled "Jerusalem at the Time of Jesus." In pre-1999 copies, use Map 17, entitled "Jerusalem in Jesus' Time.") Have each person locate the assigned place on a map and show it to the rest of the family. Refer to the map(s) as you study the chapter.

Matthew 26:1–13

An honored guest

Have your family imagine that a very special guest is visiting in your home. Ask, How would you show respect and honor to a special guest in our home? Then have one part of your family read Matthew 26:1–5 and the other Matthew 26:6–13 and discuss how the people in their verses might treat Jesus if He were a guest in their house. Discuss some or all of the following questions:

- What did Jesus tell His disciples would soon happen to Him? (Verse 2.)
- Who assembled together and where were they gathered? (Verse 3.)
- What were the chief priests, scribes, and elders plotting to do? (Verse 4.)
- In contrast, whose house did Jesus visit in Bethany? (Verse 6.)
- What does this teach us about what was important to Jesus compared to what was important to the chief priests and elders?
- What did the woman do to show how she felt about the Savior? (Verse 7.)

Share this insight from Elder James E. Talmage: "To anoint the head of a guest with ordinary oil was to do him honor; to anoint his feet also was to show unusual and signal [special] regard; but the anointing of head and feet with spikenard, and in such abundance, was an act of reverential homage rarely rendered even to kings." (*Jesus the Christ,* 512.) Ask:

- What was the reaction of some of Jesus' disciples to this woman's display of adoration? (Verses 8–9.)
- What was Jesus' response to the criticism? (Verses 10–13.)
- What kind of things can we do to show our honor and respect for Heavenly Father and His Son Jesus Christ?

Matthew 26:17–29

The Last Supper

Show your family a picture of the Last Supper (such as *Gospel Art Kit,* no. 225). Have a family member read Matthew 26:17–19 aloud. Ask:

- What do we often call this particular celebration of the Passover? (The Last Supper.)
- Can you give two reasons why it is called the Last Supper? (Not only was it the last meal of the Savior in mortality but it was the final divinely approved celebration of the feast of the Passover.)

Explain to your family that for nearly 1,500 years—ever since Moses' day when the destroying angel passed over the firstborn of the children of Israel while slaying the firstborn of the Egyptians—the Israelites had celebrated the Passover as a sign of their gratitude and to help them remember their escape from Egypt. Also, the lamb, which was sacrificed as part of the Passover meal, helped them look forward to the ultimate sacrifice of the Messiah. (See Bible Dictionary, "Feasts," 672.)

Invite family members to search Matthew 26:20–25 for answers to the following questions:

- How did the Twelve respond when Jesus said one of them would betray Him? (Verse 22.)
- What insight can you gain from their response? (Rather than pointing at someone else, each one wondered if he were the offender.)
- When problems arise, do we seek to blame others first or look to ourselves for what we might have done wrong?

- Who was the last of the Twelve to ask, "Is it I"? (Verse 25.) Why?
- What was Jesus' response to Judas's question? (Verse 25.)
- What do you think "thou hast said" means?

Read Matthew 26:26–29 as a family. Point out and mark the Joseph Smith Translation changes found in footnotes 26*b* and 28*a*. Be sure to read aloud each change and discuss how it clarifies the meaning of each passage. Ask:

- What purpose does Jesus give for the sacrament?
- Why is it important to remember the sacrifice of our Savior?
- How does remembering what Jesus did for us influence the choices we make each day?

Share this teaching from President Joseph Fielding Smith: "In my judgment the sacrament meeting is the *most sacred,* the *most holy,* of all the meetings of the Church. When I reflect upon the gathering of the Savior and his apostles on that memorable night when he introduced the sacrament, when I think of that solemn occasion, my heart is filled with wonderment and my feelings are touched. I consider that gathering one of the most solemn and wonderful since the beginning of time." (*Doctrines of Salvation,* 2:340.)

Ask your family to think back to the last time they partook of the sacrament. Ask:

- What kind of feelings did you have?
- What can you do to make that ordinance more meaningful, sacred, and holy?

Matthew 26:30

What is your favorite hymn?

 Read Matthew 26:30 and ask:

- What did Jesus and the Apostles do before going to Gethsemane?
- Why do you think they sang a hymn?
- In what way might this hymn have been a source of strength at this time?
- How have the hymns of the Church blessed your life?

Have family members identify their favorite

sacrament hymn and tell why it is their favorite. Sing together as a family the selected hymns.

Matthew 26:31–46
Gethsemane

Share the following statement with your family: "President Ezra Taft Benson said that what transpired in the Garden of Gethsemane 'was the greatest single act of love in recorded history.'" (*Church News,* May 27, 1995, 14.) Write the following question where all can see it: "How was the Atonement the greatest act of love?" Ask family members to ponder that question as they take turns reading Matthew 26:36–46. Then ask them what they learned.

When finished, tell your family that other scriptures give added insights into what took place in Gethsemane. Invite family members to write the following references in the margin of their scriptures: Luke 22:39–44; Doctrine and Covenants 19:16–19; Mosiah 3:7; Alma 7:11–13; and Isaiah 53:3–5. Have family members take turns reading aloud some or all of the references. Share the following quotations:

Elder James E. Talmage: "Christ's agony in the garden is unfathomable by the finite mind [cannot be understood by mortal man], both as to intensity and cause. . . . He struggled and groaned under a burden such as no other being who has lived on earth might even conceive as possible. It was not physical pain, nor mental anguish alone, that caused Him to suffer such torture as to produce an extrusion of blood from every pore; but a spiritual agony of soul such as only God was capable of experiencing. No other man, however great his powers of physical or mental endurance, could have suffered so; for his human organism would have succumbed, and . . . produced unconsciousness and welcome oblivion. In that hour of anguish Christ met and overcame all the horrors that Satan, 'the prince of this world,' could inflict. . . . In some manner, actual and terribly real though to man incomprehensible, the Savior took upon Himself the burden of the sins of mankind from Adam to the end of the world." (*Jesus the Christ,* 613.) Ask:

- Why was Jesus willing to suffer so much? (See John 15:13.)

- How does it make you feel to know Jesus did this for you and me?
- How can you show your love and gratitude in return?

Share your feelings about the Atonement and allow time for other family members to share their feelings.

Matthew 26:47–75
Betrayal and Arrest

Tell your family that answers to the following questions come from Matthew 26:47–75. Read each question aloud and have family members scan the verses to find the answers.

1. After the Savior had finished praying in the Garden of Gethsemane, who appeared with a great multitude? (Verse 47.)

2. What was the sign Judas gave so they would know whom to take? (Verse 48.)

3. When Judas kissed Jesus, what did Jesus say to him? (Verse 50.)

4. When the Apostles saw what was about to happen, what did one of them do? (Verse 51.)

5. After telling Peter to put away the sword, what does Jesus say His Father would do for Him if He asked? (Verse 53.)

6. What did Jesus say to the multitude that had come to take Him? (Verse 55.)

7. As Jesus was being led away, what did all the disciples do? (Verse 56.)

8. Where was Jesus taken for trial? (Verse 57.)

9. What kind of witnesses did the chief priests, elders, and council gather to testify against Jesus? (Verses 59–60.)

10. How did Jesus respond when the high priest demanded, "Tell us whether thou be the Christ, the Son of God"? (Verses 63–64.)

11. What crime was Jesus then accused of by the high priest? (Verse 65.)

12. What was the penalty for such a crime? (Verse 66.)

13. What did they then do to mock Jesus? (Verses 67–68.)

14. How did Peter answer when he was accused of being with Jesus? (Verses 69–74.)

15. How many times did Peter deny that he knew Jesus? (Verses 70–74.)

16. What happened immediately after his third denial? (Verse 74.)

17. When Peter remembered what Jesus had told him earlier, what did Peter do? (Verse 75.)

Discuss as a family how each of the following people may have felt about their part in the Savior's final night: Judas, chief priests and elders of the people, and Peter. Ask: How would you have felt if you had been any one of these individuals? Share the following insight from President Gordon B. Hinckley:

"My heart goes out to Peter. So many of us are so much like him. We pledge our loyalty; we affirm our determination to be of good courage; we declare, sometimes even publicly, that come what may we will do the right thing, that we will stand for the right cause, that we will be true to ourselves and to others.

"Then the pressures begin to build. Sometimes these are social pressures. Sometimes they are personal appetites. Sometimes they are false ambitions. There is a weakening of the will. There is a softening of discipline. There is capitulation. And then there is remorse, followed by self-accusation and bitter tears of regret. . . .

"If there be those throughout the Church who by word or act have denied the faith, I pray that you may draw comfort and resolution from the example of Peter, who, though he had walked daily with Jesus, in an hour of extremity momentarily denied the Lord and also the testimony which he carried in his own heart. But he rose above this and became a mighty defender and a powerful advocate. So, too, there is a way for any person to turn about and add his or her strength and faith to the strength and faith of others in building the kingdom of God." (*Ensign*, Mar. 1995, 2, 4, 6.)

MATTHEW 27: THE CRUCIFIXION OF JESUS

Matthew 27:1–14
The price of betrayal

 Tell or read to your family the following short story: A young man who had just graduated from high school got a job at a jewelry store. One day the young man found a $6,000 diamond in his pocket when he got home—one that he had shown to a customer and forgotten about. The next day, with great embarrassment, he told the owner what he had done and expected to be fired. Instead the owner said, "I'm not worried about it at all. I can tell that your desire to serve a mission is worth more than $6,000—much more; more than I have in my whole store." This was the first time the young man had ever looked at it that way. From then on, he put a "price tag" on temptation. When faced with temptation, he would say to himself: "Am I really willing to sell eternal blessings for what I would gain by submitting to this temptation?" Then have the family read Matthew 27:1–10. (See also Matthew 26:14–16.) Ask:

- For what price was Judas willing to "sell" his eternal happiness?
- After he realized what he had done, how much do you think he would have been willing to pay to undo what he had done?
- How can we tell that the chief priests felt guilty as well?
- How do you think we can avoid making such regrettable decisions?

Share with your family the following statement on the significance of thirty pieces of silver:

"They could have said one piece of silver or a thousand. Judas had not come to haggle but to betray. What amount, then, should they set? With devilish cunning they chose that sum which in their law was the fixed price of a slave." (McConkie, *Doctrinal New Testament Commentary,* 1:702; see also Exodus 21:32.)

Ask your family:

- What did Judas do when he could no longer undo the betrayal? (Read Matthew 27:5*a*.)
- What did the chief priest do with the thirty pieces of silver? (Verses 7–8.)
- Are there things in your life that you wish you could take back?
- How do we take back the things that we have done wrong?

Matthew 27:15–25
The decision to crucify Jesus

 Read the following quotation to your family:

"In a school yard game, young boys sometimes form a circle, and one hits another on the shoulder and says, 'Pass it on.' The one who receives the blow obediently transmits it to the next in line and says, 'Pass it on.' The third recipient promptly punches a fourth, and each in succession thereafter, by 'passing it on,' tries to rid himself of his pain, and the responsibility for it, by inflicting it on another.

"Many of us are like these schoolboys. Perhaps without realizing it, as adults we continue to play the same childish game and risk far more than a bruised shoulder in the process. Let me explain what I mean.

"Unwillingness to accept the responsibility for and consequences of one's actions is an all too common condition in today's world." (F. Burton Howard, *Ensign,* May 1991, 12–13.)

Ask:

- Why do you think that some people have a hard time taking responsibility?
- How might you help a friend who struggles with this problem?

Tell your family to look for this problem as you study Matthew 27:15–25. On a sheet of paper write the name *Barabbas.* Ask your family to identify who this person is as you read together Matthew 27:15–22. When you have finished reading, ask:

- What do you think *Barabbas* means? (The Hebrew word *bar* means "son of" and *abba* means "father," so the name means, literally, "son of the father.")
- Why is this name significant in this story? (By name, Barabbas was *a* "son of the father," but Jesus was *the* "Son of the Father." One guilty "son of the father" was released so an innocent "Son of the Father" could be crucified.)

Invite a family member to read Matthew 27:23–25. Ask:

- After the release of Barabbas, what did the Jews want?

- What did Pilate want?
- Why did Pilate do and say what he did?
- Who accepted responsibility for what was about to happen?
- Do you think Pilate has any responsibility for what happened? Why? (See verse 19.)
- In what ways are we sometimes tempted to act as Pilate did?

Pilate may have thought he had escaped guilt by passing the responsibility of Jesus' execution on to the Jews. Share the following:

"But Pilate was guilty, and guilt is cowardice, and cowardice is weakness. His own past cruelties, recoiling in kind on his own head, forced him to crush the impulse of pity, and to add to his many cruelties another more heinous [terrible] still." (McConkie, *Mortal Messiah,* 4:185–86.)

Matthew 27:26–33
Why did Jesus allow Himself to be scourged and spat upon?

Ask family members: Have you ever witnessed someone "take a beating" that person didn't deserve? How did it make you feel? Have each family member read Matthew 27:26–33 to themselves. When they finish, ask the following questions:

- After releasing Barabbas, what did Pilate do to Jesus? (Verse 26; *scourged* means whipped with a multistrand leather whip that has pieces of glass or pottery shards in the end to gouge and scratch.)
- After stripping Jesus of His outer clothing, what did the Romans put on Him? (Verse 28.)
- What was placed on His head and in His hand? (Verse 29; read with your family the footnotes 29*a* and 29*b* for further clarification.)
- After the crown of thorns was placed and the staff given, what did the soldiers do to Jesus? (Verse 30.)
- When Jesus couldn't carry the cross any further, who was chosen to carry it? (Verse 32.)
- What was the name of the place where Jesus was crucified? (Verse 33. See "Golgotha" in the Bible Dictionary, page 682.)

Jesus was beaten with a scourge.

- Why do you think Jesus allowed all these things to happen to Him without resisting?
- What do you think gave Him the strength to suffer such injustices?

Read as a family 1 Nephi 19:9 and Hebrews 12:2 and look for answers to these last two questions. Invite family members to share their thoughts about the character of the Savior and how His "taking the beating" has benefited them in their lives.

Matthew 27:34–66
Why did Jesus have to be crucified?

Display a picture of Jesus on the cross. (See *Gospel Art Kit,* no. 230.) Write on a sheet of paper the phrases listed below and cut them into strips. Lay them on the floor or tape them somewhere so that all family members can see them while you read.

- Jesus was given vinegar and gall to drink. (Verse 34.)
- The Roman solders divided His garments among themselves. (Verse 35.)
- Jesus trusted in God. (Verse 43.)
- "My God, my God, why hast thou forsaken me?" (Verse 46.)

- The earth did quake and the rocks rent. (Verse 51.)
- Joseph of Arimathaea put the body of Jesus in his new tomb. (Verses 59–60.)

Also write on a sheet of paper the following references: Psalm 69:21; Psalm 22:18; Psalm 22:8; Psalm 22:1; Moses 7:56; and Isaiah 53:9. Cut them into strips. Divide these strips among family members and ask them to look up their scripture and carefully read it.

As you take turns reading Matthew 27:34–66, invite family members to match their scripture reference with one of the events related to the death and burial of Jesus. When finished, ask the following questions:

- Why do you think Old Testament writers wrote about these events thousands of years before they took place?
- In what way does this testify of how important the Savior is to all mankind?
- What impressed you most as you read about Jesus' Crucifixion?

Show a picture of Jesus' Crucifixion and share the following from Elder Melvin J. Ballard:

"In that moment when [Heavenly Father] might have saved his Son, I thank him and praise him that he did not fail us, for he had not only the love of his Son in mind, but he had love for us, and I rejoice that he did not interfere, and that his love for us made it possible for him to endure to look upon the sufferings of his Son and give him finally to us, our Savior and our Redeemer. For without him, without his sacrifice, we would have been buried in the earth, and there our bodies would have remained and we would never have come glorified into his presence. And so this is what it cost, in part, for our Father in heaven to give the gift of his Son unto men." (*Improvement Era,* Oct. 1919, 1030–31.)

Sing or read the words of the hymn, "Upon the Cross of Calvary." (*Hymns,* no. 184.) Share your feelings about the Savior.

MATTHEW 28: THE RESURRECTION OF JESUS

Matthew 28:1–20
Witnesses of the Resurrection

Invite family members to tell about a time when someone gave them some really great news. Have them describe what they were doing, what the news was, and what they did after they heard the news.

As you read together Matthew 28:1–15, stop every time people in these verses are given some news. Read enough to find out how they responded to that news. Invite family members to tell how they think they would have responded to the news had they been in each particular situation. Ask, How important is this news? Share with your family the following statement by President Howard W. Hunter:

"The doctrine of the Resurrection is the single most fundamental and crucial doctrine in the Christian religion. It cannot be overemphasized, nor can it be disregarded. . . .

" . . . He *was* the Son of God, the Son of our immortal Father in Heaven, and his triumph over physical and spiritual death is the good news every Christian tongue should speak." (*Ensign,* May 1986, 16.)

Ask: Who helps us know the reality of Jesus Christ's Resurrection in our day? (See D&C 18:26–28; 76:22–24; and 107:23–24 for help.)

Read together Matthew 28:16–20 and ask:

- Who was Jesus speaking to?
- What did He tell them to do?
- How do you think the experiences recorded in Matthew 28 will help them do this?

Share the following statement of the Prophet Joseph Smith with your family:

"The fundamental principles of our religion are the testimony of the Apostles and Prophets, concerning Jesus Christ, that He died, was buried, and rose again the third day, and ascended into heaven; and all other things which pertain to our religion are only appendages [additions] to it." (*Teachings of the Prophet Joseph Smith,* 121.)

Invite family members to tell how their testimony of the Resurrection has affected their life or how a latter-day prophet's testimony of Christ has strengthened them.

Matthew 28:19–20
"Go ye into all the world"

Show your family a map of the world. Have them identify the places where family, friends, and people from your ward and stake have served missions. Using the most recent May *Ensign* magazine, which reports the April general conference of the Church, identify the number of missions and the number of missionaries serving in the world. (A current Deseret News *Church Almanac* will list all the missions of the Church.)

Have a family member read Matthew 28:19–20. Ask:

- How many nations did Jesus say His disciples were to go to?
- What were they to do there?
- How close are we to accomplishing that great charge?
- Is it really possible to go into every nation?

To help answer that question, read 1 Nephi 3:7 with your family and the following from President Spencer W. Kimball:

"We have hardly scratched the surface, though we have opened up a number of missions for proselyting and many, many good people have accepted the truth. We are sure the Lord is conscious, as we are, of the great world outspread before us which is without the gospel. Relatively small groups huddle in scattered areas in the world, and as we attempt to go into the new nations and cultures, we come to locked doors, but know of a surety that the Lord would never command us to do something for which he would not prepare the way." (*Teachings of Spencer W. Kimball,* 586.)

Point out the explanations given in Matthew 28, footnotes 19*a* and 20*a,* in the LDS edition of the Bible. Ask, What do these footnotes add to our understanding of what Jesus meant when He commanded His disciples to teach? Who are we to teach? Why?

Ask your family what it will take on our part to help accomplish the Savior's command in Matthew

28:19–20. Share with them the following counsel from Elder M. Russell Ballard:

"Please allow me to suggest three simple things that we can do to assist in this divinely commissioned responsibility.

"First, we should exercise our faith and pray individually and as families, asking for help in finding ways to share the restored gospel of Jesus Christ. Ask the Lord to open the way. Prayerfully set a date with your family to have someone in your home for the missionaries to teach. Remember, brothers and sisters, this is the Lord's Church. Let Him guide you through constant prayer. With a prayer in your heart, talk to everyone you can. Don't prejudge. Don't withhold the good news from anyone. Talk to everyone, and trust in the promised power of the Spirit to give you the words you should say. Let them make the decision to accept or reject your invitation. Over time, the Lord will put into your path those who are seeking the truth. He is the Good Shepherd. He knows His sheep, and they will know His voice, spoken through you, and they will follow Him (see John 10). . . .

"Second, leaders must lead by example. The Spirit will prompt and guide you in finding those interested in our message. Your personal worthiness will give you the courage and the spiritual power to inspire your members to actively help the missionaries. . . .

"Third, member missionary work does not require the development of strategies or gimmicks. It does require faith—real faith and trust in the Lord. It also requires genuine love. The first great commandment is to 'love the Lord thy God with all thy heart, and with all thy soul, and with all thy mind. . . . The second is like unto it, Thou shalt love thy neighbour as thyself' (Matthew 22:37, 39)." (*Ensign,* May 2003, 38–39.)

Discuss as a family ways you can implement the counsel of the Savior and the suggestions of Elder Ballard. Invite them to look at what the Savior promised in Matthew 28:20 as we seek to fulfill this great commission and discuss what it should mean to us as we move forward in applying it.

MARK

Mark's testament is the shortest of the four Gospels. "Mark has the least amount of unique material, being only about 7 percent exclusive." (Bible Dictionary, "Gospels," 683.) Mark mentions most events the other three Gospel writers mention but in less detail. He focuses on what Jesus Christ did more than on what He said. The Bible Dictionary states: "[Mark's] object is to describe our Lord as the incarnate Son of God, living and acting among men. The Gospel contains a living picture of a living Man. Energy and humility are the characteristics of his portrait." ("Mark," 728.) Mark provides many helpful explanations in his text, and it appears this Gospel was written to a non-Jewish audience.

MARK 1: JESUS BEGINS HIS MINISTRY

Mark 1:1–45
How do you see it?

Give each family member a piece of paper divided into six equal parts. Assign each family member one of the clusters of verses on the following page. Have them read those verses and draw that story in six pictures, as if it were a comic strip. Take turns having each person show his or her picture while telling the story to the family. As each person finishes teaching his or her part, discuss some of the accompanying questions.

Mark 1:1–11
The baptism of fire

Show your family a match (representing fire) and some water. Ask them to read Mark 1:1–11 (especially notice footnote 8a) and find the person best represented by fire and the person best represented by water in this story. Share the following statements by Elder Bruce R. McConkie:

"Baptism is for the remission of sins; it is the ordinance, ordained of God, to cleanse a human soul. Baptism is in water and of the Spirit and is preceded by repentance. The actual cleansing of the soul comes when the Holy Ghost is received. The Holy Ghost is a sanctifier whose divine commission is to burn dross and evil out of a human soul as though by fire, thus giving rise to the expression *baptism of fire,* which is the baptism of the Spirit. Forgiveness is assured when the contrite soul receives the Holy Spirit, because the Spirit will not dwell in an unclean tabernacle." (*New Witness for the Articles of Faith,* 239; see also Moroni 6:4.)

"After baptism in water, legal administrators lay their hands upon a repentant person and say: 'Receive the Holy Ghost.' This gives him the gift of the Holy Ghost, which is the right to the constant companionship of that member of the Godhead based on faithfulness. Either then or later, depending upon the individual's personal worthiness, the Holy Ghost comes. The baptized person becomes a new creature. He is baptized with fire, sin and evil are burned out of his soul, and he is born again." (*New Witness for the Articles of Faith,* 291.)

Discuss the following questions and share your testimony of the importance of baptism and confirmation in The Church of Jesus Christ of Latter-day Saints:

• What blessings have come to you because of your baptism?

Clusters of Verses	Questions to Discuss
Mark 1:1–8	• Why do you think John felt he was not worthy even to untie Jesus' shoes?
	• How does the baptism of fire differ from the baptism of water?
Mark 1:9–13	• What verses show that all three members of the Godhead (Heavenly Father, Jesus Christ, and the Holy Ghost) were present at Jesus' baptism?
	• What verse best shows that Jesus Christ was baptized by immersion, meaning being placed completely under the water?
	• According to Romans 6:4–5, what is one symbolic meaning of being immersed in water when we are baptized? How does Mark 1, footnote 12a, help you better understand that verse?
	• Who ministered to (cared for) Jesus in the wilderness?
Mark 1:14–20	• How does footnote 15c help you better understand that verse?
	• How quickly did the fishermen follow Jesus and why?
	• What do you think it means to become "fishers of men"?
Mark 1:21–28	• In what verse were people astonished and why?
	• In verse 24, what did the unclean spirit know that others did not?
	• Who has greater power, Jesus Christ or evil spirits?
	• How could knowing the greatness of Jesus Christ's power help you in your life?
Mark 1:29–39	• What do you learn about Jesus' power in these verses?
	• Who did Jesus lift up physically in this story? (Verse 31.)
	• How does Jesus lift people up spiritually in our day?
Mark 1:40–45	• How did the leper show his faith to be healed?
	• Why did Jesus ask the healed leper to show himself to the priests? (Verse 44.)

• Why is it important to have the Holy Ghost?
• When has the Holy Ghost guided you?

MARK 2: THE LORD TEACHES AND WORKS MIRACLES

Mark 2:1–12

How determined are you to be healed?

Share the following story with your family: "In 1968 a marathon runner by the name of John Stephen Akhwari represented Tanzania in an international competition. A little over an hour after [the winner] had crossed the finish line, John Stephen Akhwari . . . approached the stadium, the last man to complete the journey. [Though suffering from fatigue, leg cramps, dehydration, and disorientation,] a voice called from within to go on,

and so he went on. Afterwards, it was written, 'Today we have seen a young African runner who symbolizes the finest in human spirit, a performance that gives meaning to the word *courage.*' . . . When asked why he would complete a race he could never win, Akhwari replied, 'My country did not send me 5,000 miles to *start* the race; my country sent me to *finish* the race.'" (Robert D. Hales, *Ensign,* May 1998, 76.)

Talk about some of these questions:

• What character trait of John Akhwari most impresses you?
• What do you think about his determination?
• Why does determination make such a difference in a person's life?

Take your family into a small room, like a hall closet, and try to squeeze everyone in. Then have a family member read Mark 2:1–3 and ask what occurred at the home where Jesus was staying.

(You may need to point out footnote 3*a* and explain that "sick of the palsy" means being paralyzed, and "borne of four" means carried by four people.)

Have your family read silently Mark 2:4–12 and then ask them the following questions:

- How did the four people carrying the paralyzed man show their determination and faith? (Verse 4.)
- What question did Jesus ask the scribes? (Verse 9.)
- What did Jesus then say to the paralyzed man? (Verse 11.)
- What would you have thought if you were one of the people inside the house?
- What message do you think Jesus was teaching about who He is? (Verse 10.)
- What part do you think the faith and determination of the man and those that carried him played in his being healed?
- Is there any blessing you need that is as important to you as healing was to the man in the story?
- What does this story teach us about how we can receive these great blessings from the Lord?

Write the following statement where all can see it and invite your family to finish it from what they learned in this story: "If I want the blessings from the Lord that are most important to me, I must _____."

Mark 2:13–17
Who is your physician?

Ask your family to tell who your family physician is and what he does for your family. Then, as a family, take turns reading Mark 2:15–17 and discuss the following questions as you read.

- What is Jesus doing and who is with Him? (Verse 15.)
- What did the scribes and Pharisees not like about what Jesus was doing? (Verse 16.)
- How is Jesus like a physician? (Verse 17.)
- Why was it important that He spend time with the publicans and sinners?

- Do you think it is more important to be physically healthy or spiritually healthy? Why?
- How does Christ heal people spiritually?

As a family, share experiences of having felt the Savior's healing power and then read the following from Elder Jeffrey R. Holland: "To those who feel they have somehow forfeited their place at the table of the Lord, we say again with the Prophet Joseph Smith that God has 'a forgiving disposition.' . . .

"Now, if you feel too spiritually maimed to come to the feast, please realize that the Church is not a monastery for perfect people, though all of us ought to be striving on the road to godliness. No, at least one aspect of the Church is more like a hospital or an aid station, provided for those who are ill and want to get well." (*Ensign*, Nov. 1997, 65–66.)

Share your testimony of the Savior's love and power to heal that you have experienced in your own life.

Mark 2:18–22
Out with the old, in with the new

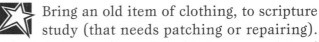 Bring an old item of clothing, to scripture study (that needs patching or repairing). Also bring a new item of clothing you can pretend to use as a patch. Show the old clothing item to your family and the new article of clothing and pretend that you are going to cut it up to patch the old clothes. Ask your family how they feel about using someone's new clothes to patch the old item of clothing.

Have a family member read Mark 2:18–22. Ask :

- Who is the bridegroom? (Jesus Christ.)
- What do you think Christ meant by teaching these people about sewing new cloth on old garments (or items of clothing), or putting new wine in old bottles?

To help your family with the last question, you might share the following statement by Elder James E. Talmage: "In such wise did our Lord proclaim the newness and completeness of His gospel. It was in no sense a patching up of Judaism. He had not come to mend old and torn garments; the cloth He provided was new, and to sew it on the old would be but to tear afresh the threadbare fabric and leave a more unsightly rent than at first. . . . The gospel

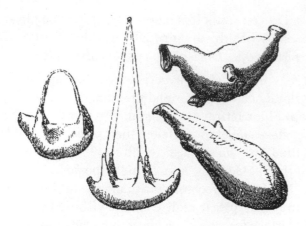

In New Testament times wine was often stored in "bottles" made of animal skins. The leather becomes brittle with age, making it unsuitable for storing wine for a long time because it could leak more easily.

taught by Christ was a new revelation, superseding the past, and marking the fulfilment of the law; . . . it embodied a new and an everlasting covenant." (*Jesus the Christ*, 196–97.)

With the following questions, summarize what they have learned:

- Why do you think Jesus did not come to patch up worn-out Judaism?
- How does this also help explain why the Lord called the boy Joseph Smith to restore the gospel instead of repairing or patching up the churches that already existed?

Mark 2:23–28
The Sabbath was made for man

Have a family member read Mark 2:23–24. Ask why the Jewish leaders were upset. (Reading the third paragraph in the Bible Dictionary under "Sabbath," 765, may help your family better understand this story.) Read Mark 2:27 and ask how Jesus responded to their criticism. Tell your family that since Jesus is the Jehovah of the Old Testament who made the Sabbath, He was also the Lord of the Sabbath in the New Testament. Ask:

- What do you think the Savior means when He says the Sabbath was made for man?
- How can you show your love for the Savior on the Sabbath day?

Read the following statement by President Gordon B. Hinckley to your family and discuss what it means:

"I mention the Sabbath day. The Sabbath of the Lord is becoming the play day of the people. It is a day of golf and football on television, of buying and selling in our stores and markets. Are we moving to [the mainstream] as some observers believe? In this I fear we are. . . .

"Our strength for the future, our resolution to grow the Church across the world, will be weakened if we violate the will of the Lord in this important matter. He has so very clearly spoken anciently and again in modern revelation. We cannot disregard with impunity that which He has said." (*Ensign*, Nov. 1997, 69.)

Invite your family to read Doctrine and Covenants 59:9–14 and also refer to *True to the Faith, a Gospel Reference*, the entry for "Sabbath" on pages 145–47 to see how the Lord desires us to worship on His holy day. Set some family goals about how you can better worship the Lord on His holy day.

MARK 3: JESUS HEALS ON THE SABBATH DAY AND CALLS TWELVE APOSTLES

Mark 3:1–6
Is it lawful to do good on the Sabbath?

Present the following case study to your family: On your way to sacrament meeting you see a car full of children pulled off the street. The mother is standing nearby and looks concerned. You notice one car tire is flat. If you stop to help, you'll be late for sacrament meeting. Ask: What would you do?

After discussing the possibilities, read together Mark 3:1–6 and ask:

- What were the Pharisees trying to get Jesus to do? (See also footnote 2*a*.)
- What was their attitude about the Sabbath?
- How would you answer the Savior's question in verse 4?
- What do you think is the purpose of the

Sabbath? (See D&C 59:12–16 for additional help.)

- What lesson do you think we should learn from this story?
- What can we do to improve our Sabbath worship?

The following statement may help in your family discussion:

"Observance of the Sabbath is an indication of the depth of our conversion. Our observance or nonobservance of the Sabbath is an unerring measure of our attitude toward the Lord personally and toward his suffering in Gethsemane, his death on the cross, and his resurrection from the dead. It is a sign of whether we are Christians in very deed, or whether our conversion is so shallow that commemoration of his atoning sacrifice means little or nothing to us." (Mark E. Petersen, *Ensign,* May 1975, 49.)

Mark 3:7–21
What are some duties of an Apostle?

Show your family a picture of each member of the Quorum of the Twelve Apostles and First Presidency, but do not show their names. (These pictures can be found in a recent May or November *Ensign.)* Let each family member see how many of these men they can name.

Explain that Jesus also called Twelve Apostles when He was on earth. Have your family try to name as many of Jesus' original Twelve Apostles as they can. Ask each family member to silently read Mark 3:16–21 and mark the names of the original Twelve Apostles.

Discuss the following questions:

- According to Mark 3:13–15, what did Jesus ask these men to do?
- According to the Bible Dictionary ("Apostle," 612), what is the principal responsibility of an Apostle?
- How do Apostles witness that Jesus is the Christ today?
- What messages do you remember from the Apostles in the last conference?

Invite family members to share feelings, testimonies, or personal experiences they may have had with today's Apostles.

Mark 3:28–30
Can all sins be forgiven?

Have family members mark footnote *a* for Mark 3:28 and turn to the Joseph Smith Translation of Mark 3:21–25 in the Appendix of the Bible (804). Take turns reading the verses aloud. Discuss the following questions as you read:

- What must we do if we want forgiveness of sin?
- What sin is unpardonable?
- What is blasphemy against the Holy Ghost?

To help answer that question, share this statement by Elder Bruce R. McConkie: "*Blasphemy* consists in either or both of the following: 1. Speaking irreverently, evilly, abusively, or scurrilously against God or sacred things; or 2. Speaking profanely or *falsely* about Deity. . . . Blasphemy against the Holy Ghost—which is falsely denying Christ after receiving a perfect revelation of him from the Holy Ghost—is the unpardonable sin." (*Mormon Doctrine,* 90–91.)

Mark 3:31–35
Who belongs to the family of Jesus?

Display a camera and tell your family to suppose you wanted to take a family photograph. Discuss these questions:

- How many members are in our family?
- Besides our immediate family, who are some others you would consider "family"?
- What other families could you be considered a part of?
- How would you feel about being a part of the family of Jesus?

Explain that we are all God's children, Jesus included, and in that sense we are all brothers and sisters. In addition, Jesus taught what we must do to be considered His brother or sister. Read Mark 3:31–35 together and find the requirements to belong to Jesus' family.

Give family members time to ponder how well they are following these requirements. Ask each person to make a sign listing one goal they can improve upon this week. If possible, take each person's picture holding their sign and place the picture in a place where they can see it often.

MARK 4: "HE TAUGHT THEM MANY THINGS BY PARABLES"

Before teaching this chapter, consider reviewing the teaching idea from Matthew 13:1–17 on why Jesus taught in parables

Mark 4:3–9, 14–20
Sowers, seeds, and soil

 Prepare the following four bowls and show them to your family:

- An empty bowl.
- A bowl filled with rocks.
- A bowl filled with dirt and weeds.
- A bowl filled with good soil.

Read Mark 4:3 with your family and explain that a sower is someone who plants seeds. Show your family a packet of seeds and have them explain which of the four bowls they would prefer to plant a seed in and why. Share ideas about why some soil is better than other soil for growing food.

Prepare four pieces of paper (one with each of the following references listed) and divide them among your family:

- Mark 4:3–4, 13–15.
- Mark 4:3, 5–6, 13, 16–17.
- Mark 4:3, 7, 13, 18–19.
- Mark 4:3, 8, 13, 20.

Ask family members to study their assigned references and then place the piece of paper into the bowl which those verses best describe. When each group is finished, ask someone from each group to share answers to the following questions:

- What is it about your particular soil that makes it hard or easy for a seed to grow?
- What kind of people do you think this particular type of soil represents?
- How would you describe the heart of a person represented by this soil?

- If your heart were like this soil, what do you think you could do to change it?

Encourage family members to let the gospel sink deep into their hearts so they can bless the lives of others.

Mark 4:21–25
Gospel light—How much will you get?

 Light a candle and ask your family members which of the following three places would be the best place to display it and why:

- under a barrel or basket?
- under a bed?
- on a candlestick?

Then read Mark 4:21–22 as a family and ask:

- Where does Jesus indicate is the best place to put a candle? (See also Luke 8:16.)
- How are Jesus' teachings like a candle?
- What does Jesus promise to do with the truths He brought? (See Mark 4:22.)
- Since Jesus promises to reveal His truths to us, what should we do if there are some truths of the gospel we do not know or questions we do not yet have answers for?

To help answer that question, read together Mark 4:23–25 and ask:

- What do you think the word *hear* means in these verses? (Read also James 1:22.)
- What then must we do to receive more light or revelation from God?
- How much light can I receive? (Read also D&C 50:24–25.)
- What will happen if I do not want any more light from God? (Read also Alma 12:10.)

Encourage your family to write the cross-references listed above next to verses 23–25 in Mark 4. Invite your family to identify the principle taught in these verses and share with your family your testimony of how obedience invites more light and truth.

Mark 4:26–32
How is a tiny seed like the kingdom of God?

 Read or sing together verse 2 of "Come, Ye Thankful People." (*Hymns,* no. 94.) Also read together Mark 4:26–32 and ask your family to find phrases in the song which match those verses in Mark. Ask your family to share some possible interpretations for this parable and then share these words from Elder James E. Talmage:

"The sower . . . implants the seed of the gospel in the hearts of men, knowing not what the issue [fruit] shall be. Passing on to similar or other ministry elsewhere, attending to his appointed duties in other fields, he, with faith and hope, leaves with God the result of his planting. In the harvest of souls converted through his labor, he is enriched and made to rejoice. . . . It is of perennial value, as truly applicable today as when first spoken. Let the seed be sown, even though the sower be straightway called to other fields or other duties; in the gladsome harvest he shall find his recompense [reward]." (*Jesus the Christ,* 289–90.)

Distribute to family members a variety of seeds (including a mustard seed if you have one) and some paper cups filled with soil. Write Mark 4:32 on the cups. Draw attention to the smallness of the mustard seed and then invite them to plant seeds in their cups.

If you have mustard seeds, place one of them in the palm of the hand of each family member. To help your family understand why the Savior chose the mustard seed, share this information from Elder Talmage with them: "The wild mustard . . . reaches in semitropical lands the height of a horse and its rider. . . . Those who heard the parable evidently understood the contrast between size of seed and that of the fully developed plant . . . This plant obviously was chosen by the Lord, not on account of its absolute magnitude, but because it . . . was recognized to be, a striking instance of increase from very small to very great." (*Jesus the Christ,* 302.)

Ask your family how the kingdom of God (verse 30) is like the mustard seed they are holding in their hands. Share the following statement from the Prophet Joseph Smith:

"The Standard of Truth has been erected; no unhallowed hand can stop the work from progressing; persecutions may rage, mobs may combine, armies may assemble, calumny may defame, but the truth of God will go forth boldly, nobly, and independent, till it has penetrated every continent, visited every clime, swept every country, and sounded in every ear, till the purposes of God shall be accomplished, and the Great Jehovah shall say the work is done." (*History of the Church,* 4:540.)

Mark 4:35–41
Faith vs. Fear

Bring a pillow to scripture study. Assign family members the following parts: Jesus, the wind, and His disciples in the ship. Have them act out Mark 4:35–41 as you read aloud to your family. Then discuss these questions:

- How much water was in the ship? (Verse 37.)
- Where was the Savior, and what was He doing? (Verse 38.)
- Why do you think the Savior could sleep through such a storm?
- What emotion were the disciples experiencing? (Verses 40–41.)
- What do you think you would have felt if you had been there?
- What quality did the Savior accuse the disciples of lacking? (Verse 40.)

Tell your family that hymn number 105, "Master, the Tempest Is Raging," was written about this experience. Share this information from Elder Howard W. Hunter with your family:

"None of us would like to think that we have *no* faith, but I suppose the Lord's gentle rebuke here is largely deserved. . . . Certainly it should be no surprise that he could command a few elements acting up on the Sea of Galilee. And our faith should remind us that he can calm the troubled waters of our lives. . . .

"Peace was on the lips and in the heart of the Savior no matter how fiercely the tempest was raging. May it so be with us—in our own hearts, in our own homes." (*Ensign,* Nov. 1984, 33–35.)

Share an experience of how faith in the Savior has helped you through a storm in your life and ask your family what they can do to exercise faith in Him.

MARK 5: MIGHTY MIRACLES OF JESUS

Mark 5:1–20
Jesus has power over evil spirits

Have your family read 1 Nephi 19:23 and ask: What did Nephi say he would do so that the scriptures would provide more "profit and learning" for his family? Explain that "likening" the scriptures can be as simple as saying, "How does this apply to me?" But often it requires searching for details that make the comparisons and application more powerful. Appoint a family member to be a scribe. Have the scribe write on a sheet of paper the details found by family members as you study Mark 5:1–20.

Invite a family member to read Mark 5:1–2 and identify who Jesus met. Have the scribe write "man with unclean spirit" at the top of the paper. As your family takes turns reading verses 3–9, have the scribe list information discovered about this man (such as he dwelt among the tombs; he couldn't be restrained by fetters and chains; nothing seemed to be able to control him; he harmed himself; he knew who Jesus was, but the presence of Jesus tormented him; there were "many" unclean spirits in him). Have them look at the list and ask:

- What are some ways the man with an unclean spirit can be compared to people in sin? (For example, sin harms the sinner, but he or she often doesn't want to change.)
- What do these things teach us about what happens to those who choose to sin?
- What did Jesus command in verse 8?

Read together verses 10–20 looking for what happened when Jesus commanded the evil spirits to depart. Ask:

- What does this story teach about Jesus' power over evil spirits?
- According to verse 19, what else do we learn about Jesus?
- How could we use this story to encourage someone whose life has been deeply affected by addiction and other sins?

Testify that obedience to God can keep us from the captivity of Satan. Also share your testimony of the power of God over evil—as powerful, tempting, or alluring as it might be.

Questions may arise about evil spirits being cast into swine and why local Jews were afraid. Explain that the scriptures do not give a reason as to why Jesus cast evil spirits into swine. Some things might give us insight, however. (1) Swine, or pigs, were unclean animals to the Jews. The fact that these Jews were raising swine says something about how much they lived their religion. Jesus may have allowed this to happen to teach them to conform their lives to what they knew to be true—that disobedience leads to death. (2) Their fear may be an acknowledgement of their guilt in this matter. (3) It is also significant to note that evil spirits are so desperate to receive a body that they are willing to take a swine's body rather than have none at all.

Mark 5:21–43
Receiving power from the Savior

Divide your family into two groups. Tell them that Mark 5:21–43 tells the story of two individuals who experienced the Savior's miraculous power. Assign one group to look for Jairus's experience and the other group to look for the experience of "a certain woman, which had an issue of blood." (Verse 25.) Have them read the story in their group and look for the following:

- What problem or challenge the individual had.
- Everything this person did in preparation to receive the power of the Savior.
- What the Savior said to him or her.
- What the miracle teaches us about the Savior.

After each group has had time to talk about what they learned from Mark 5, have them decide what kinds of things their person would say to your family about the Savior's power. Then ask each group to choose a person to represent Jairus and the "woman with the issue of blood." Have the family members playing Jairus and the woman speak to the family as if they are that person and share their testimony about meeting the Savior and receiving His miraculous power. When they have finished, talk about how the things they learned from these two stories might apply to your family and others you love.

MARK 6: JESUS MINISTERS IN GALILEE

Mark 6:1–6

Why was Jesus not accepted in His hometown?

Have your family turn to the map section in the back of their Bibles, and using the Maps and Index of Place–Names (or Gazetteer in pre-1999 copies of the Bible), have them locate a map where Nazareth can be found and turn to that map. (If you have an edition of the Bible with photographs, look at the photo of Nazareth and read about some of the events that happened there.) Remind family members that this was Jesus' hometown.

Read Mark 6:1–6 aloud and ask:

- What do you learn about His family in these verses?
- Where did He go and what did He do? (Verse 2.)
- Where should we be on the Sabbath?
- Why were they offended by His message? (Verses 3–4.)
- What kept them from receiving the mighty miracles that Jesus performed in other villages? (Verses 5–6.) To help answer this question, read the following from Elder Neal A. Maxwell:

"It was His 'own country.' This time, however, listeners were astonished instead of enraged. What happened next, however, is both illuminating and discouraging: He was rejected not because of *what* He said or *how* He said it—rather, because of *who* He was perceived to be: 'Is not this the carpenter, the son of Mary?' Then came Jesus' well-known lamentation: 'A prophet is not without honour, but in his own country, and among his own kin, and in his own house.'

"In short, 'they were offended at him.' . . . Think upon it! They were His neighbors and had some awareness of at least some of His mighty works—yet all this was dismissed because He was a local individual.

"Satan's stratagems are apparent: If one cannot face truth, then he can merely dismiss it by stereotyping the source. Dismiss the message because of the lowly messengers." (*Even As I Am,* 84–85.)

Discuss some of the following questions:

- How many members of the Church today do you know who have callings to teach?
- How many of them are our neighbors or friends?
- How would you feel if their teachings were rejected just because they were familiar to us and didn't come from far away?
- What can we learn through the bad examples of the people of Nazareth in this story?

Mark 6:7–13

What do missionaries need to serve a mission?

On a sheet of paper, have your family list all the physical items a missionary might need to serve a mission. Have a family member read Mark 6:7–13 and compare these teachings to the list your family made. Ask:

- Why do you think there is such a difference in missionary preparation from New Testament time and today?
- What is *scrip?* (As a family, turn to page 770 in the Bible Dictionary and read the definition of *scrip.*)
- What kind of things did the Twelve Apostles do as missionaries? (Verses 11–13.)
- What kind of activities are missionaries involved in today?
- How can we be better missionaries? (More help for this question can be found in the teaching idea for Matthew 28:19–20.)

Mark 6:14–32

Herod kills John the Baptist

Make word strips with one of the following names on each, or show their pictures: Joseph Smith (*Gospel Art Kit,* no. 401), Hyrum Smith (*Ensign,* Dec. 2005, 8), Abinadi (*Gospel Art Kit,* no. 308), and John the Baptist (*Gospel Art Kit,* no. 207).

Discuss the following questions:

- What do these men have in common? (One thing is that they are martyrs.)
- What is a martyr? (A person killed for his or her beliefs.)

- What other martyrs can you think of?
- What blessing awaits those who give their lives for the truth?

Share the following statement about Abinadi: "He died a martyr and went to a martyr's reward—exaltation." (Kimball, *Faith Precedes the Miracle,* 99.)

As a family, take turns reading Mark 6:14–32 and discover the events that lead to the death of John the Baptist. Discuss the following questions:

- Why did Herodias, Herod's wife, dislike John? (Verses 17–18.)
- Why didn't Herod want to kill John? (Verse 20; see footnote *b* for further clarification.)
- What promise did Herod make to the daughter of Herodias? (Verse 23.)
- What did the daughter of Herodias ask for? (Verse 25.)
- How did Herod feel about the request of the daughter of Herodias? (Verse 26.)
- Can you think of a time when you promised to do something and later regretted it?
- What do we need to do in order to exercise good judgment when making promises?

Share your gratitude for those who have sacrificed their lives for the gospel's sake and encourage family members to always stand up for their beliefs, even when they may be persecuted or ridiculed.

Mark 6:33–44

How could Jesus feed 5,000 people?

 Ask your family what it costs to take one person out for a meal. Have your family read Mark 6:44 and ask: How many men did Jesus feed? Have your scribe multiply the cost of the meal by 5,000 to come up with the cost to feed 5,000 people for one meal. Have your family take turns reading Mark 6:33–44 and discuss the following questions as you read:

- What did the disciples want Jesus to do? (Verse 36.)
- What did Jesus suggest they do?
- How much money did the disciples think it

would take to buy bread for the people? (Verse 37.)
- A penny is about a day's wages. (See footnote 37*a.*) How much money would that be in our day?
- What did Jesus do instead of buying food?
- Why do you think Jesus was able to perform this great miracle for these people? (See Mark 6:5–6.) Remind your family of the statement by Elder Bruce R. McConkie: "Where there is faith, there will be signs, miracles, and gifts of the Spirit." (*Doctrinal New Testament Commentary,* 1:322.)

Mark 6:45–56

Jesus walks on water

Have your family close their eyes as you read Mark 6:47–51 aloud. While you read, have them use their imagination to visualize as many details as possible of this stormy night. When you are finished, have everyone open their eyes and discuss the following questions about what they imagined:

- What were the disciples doing? (Verse 45.)
- What was the sea like? (Verse 48.)
- What did Jesus look like as He came toward the boat? (Verse 49.)
- What were the waves doing?
- How did the disciples show their faith in Jesus after they landed? (Verses 54–56.)
- What was Jesus able to do for the people because of their faith? (Verse 56.)
- What can Jesus do for us besides calming storms and healing sicknesses?

Invite your family to write in their journals about a "storm" or an "illness" they are facing in their lives that they would like some help with. Then invite them to write down one thing they will do to increase their faith so that Jesus can better help them with their needs. Share your testimony of the Savior's power to help us with all our problems.

MARK 7: JESUS TEACHES ABOUT TRADITIONS

Mark 7:1–13
When are traditions good or bad?

 Ask each family member to name their favorite family tradition. Ask:

- Is it good or bad to have traditions? Why?
- In what kinds of situations might a tradition be a bad thing?

Invite your family to look for what Jesus said about traditions as you read together Mark 7:1–13. Pause to discuss the questions below that deal with verse 5 and verses 9–13:

- Verse 5. What were Jesus' disciples accused of not doing? Where did this rule come from? What does the phrase "tradition of the elders" mean? (Elder Bruce R. McConkie explained that the traditions of the elders "were added to the Mosaic law by the scribes and teachers over the years. These traditions were actually and formally deemed to be more important and have greater binding force than the law itself. Among them, as supposed guards against ceremonial uncleanness, were the ritualistic washings which Jesus and his disciples had ignored." (*Doctrinal New Testament Commentary,* 1:366.)
- Verses 9–13. Ask your family to identify an unfamiliar word in verse 11. Invite a family member to look up the word *Corban* in the Bible Dictionary (page 650) and explain to the rest of the family what the word means. Ask, Which of the Ten Commandments did this tradition cause people to break?

If possible, ask a returned missionary in your family if they ever met a person who had no interest in the gospel message because he/she was born into a particular religion and intended to die in that religion. Ask what this has to do with good or bad traditions. Share the following statement by Elder Donald L. Hallstrom:

"Uplifting traditions play a significant role in leading us toward the things of the Spirit. Those that promote love for Deity and unity in families and among people are especially important. . . .

"Unwanted traditions are those which lead us away from performing holy ordinances and keeping sacred covenants. Our guide should be the doctrine taught by the scriptures and the prophets. Traditions which devalue marriage and family, abase women or do not recognize the majesty of their God-given roles, honor temporal success more than spiritual, or teach that reliance upon God is a weakness of character, all lead us away from eternal truths.

"Of all the traditions we should cultivate within ourselves and our families, a 'tradition of righteousness' should be preeminent. Hallmarks of this tradition are an unwavering love for God and His Only Begotten Son, respect for prophets and priesthood power, a constant seeking of the Holy Spirit, and the discipline of discipleship which transforms believing into doing. A tradition of righteousness sets a pattern for living which draws children closer to parents, and both closer to God, and elevates obedience from a burden to a blessing." (*Ensign,* Nov. 2000, 28.)

As a family make a list of the positive traditions your family has and how those traditions help support righteous goals.

Mark 7:14–23
What defiles a man?

 Bring a plate of cookies or other treats to scripture study and place it on the table. Also bring a bowl of mud or something similar. When the family has gathered, ask if anyone wants a cookie. Then cover your hand with mud, pick up a cookie with your muddy hand, and offer it to anyone who wants one. Discuss the following questions:

- Why are you reluctant to take the cookie offered with a dirty hand?
- What could happen to you if you ate a cookie with dirt on it? (It could make you sick.)
- How would you feel if I offered you a cookie with my clean hand?

Remind your family that Jesus had just scolded the Pharisees for defining righteousness as keeping traditions of outer cleanliness while at the same time ignoring the true commandments of God that bring inner righteousness. (See Mark 7:1–13.)

Invite your family to keep the cookie illustration in mind as you study together Mark 7:14–23. Assign a family member to read aloud Mark 7:14–15 and ask:

- According to the Joseph Smith Translation (see footnote 15a), what was Jesus referring to when He spoke of things that go into us and things that come out of us?
- What does the word *defile* mean? (It means to make unholy or unrighteous.)
- Pick up a cookie with your muddy hand again and ask: So according to what Jesus taught, eating food without washing might make you sick but what would it not do? (It would not make you unrighteous.)

Read together Mark 7:16–23 and discuss the following questions as you read:

- Why aren't you defiled or made unrighteous by the food you eat? (Verses 18–19.)
- Does that mean we can take into our bodies anything we want? (No, Jesus was talking about food, not things we know are bad for us.)
- What did Jesus say will "defile" us or make us unrighteous? (The sins we commit; see verses 22–23.)
- Where does Jesus say these evil acts actually begin? (In the thoughts of our heart; see verses 20–21.)
- What are some activities or ideas that some people today set their hearts on that lead to breaking the commandments of God? (For example, wearing immodest fashions, seeing inappropriate movies or TV, making lots of money, etc.)
- What kinds of things should we bring into our hearts that will help us keep the commandments of God?

Share your testimony with your family of the eternal peace and joy that comes from following the Lord rather than the traditions of the world.

Mark 7:31–37
Jesus heals a deaf mute

 Ask your family to imagine that they cannot hear or speak. Have each one share what they think the most difficult part of their daily life would be if they were deaf. How does a person with these problems communicate?

Tell your family that Jesus met a man who had these problems. Read together Mark 7:31–37 and ask your family to imagine how the man felt and what he understood as Jesus healed him. Ask:

- What did Jesus do to the man's ears and tongue?
- What do you think the man understood about what Jesus was doing?

To help answer these questions, consider sharing the following insight from Elder Bruce R. McConkie: "He spit and placed his own saliva on the man's tongue. Such was a practice commonly believed by the Rabbis and the Jews to have healing virtue; it thus encouraged the man to believe—or, rather, increased his faith—that his tongue would be loosed and his fluency restored." (*Mortal Messiah,* 3:15.)

- How does the fact that the man allowed Jesus to do those things show his faith?
- How are people today, who refuse to listen to the words of the Lord, like a deaf man?
- How are people who refuse to pray or share their testimonies with others like a man who cannot talk?
- What kinds of things does the Lord do to try to "touch" people who do not hear or refuse to (or fear to) speak?
- The man who could not hear had to allow the Lord to touch him in order to be healed. What must a person do who will not hear in order to be healed?

MARK 8: JESUS HEALS BOTH PHYSICAL AND SPIRITUAL BLINDNESS

Mark 8:1–9
He will have compassion on you

 Place some fruit before your family and have them imagine they have not eaten for days. Ask them if this fruit was all they had to eat, what problems might arise? Have family members take turns reading Mark 8:1–9. Ask:

- How many days had the people been with Jesus? (Verse 2.)
- What feelings did Jesus have for them? (Verse 2.)
- How much food did the disciples have with them? (Verse 5.)
- How much did they offer to the Savior? (All they had.)
- What did Jesus do after obtaining the seven loaves and few fishes? (Verses 6–7.)
- What do we learn in this account about the Savior's ability to magnify the little we give to provide for many?
- In what ways has He shown compassion for you?

Write the following sentence where all can see it:

"If I offer to the Savior all I have, then _____."

Invite your family to finish the sentence so that it expresses the principle taught in this marvelous miracle. (For example, "He will make me equal to whatever challenge I face.")

Mark 8:14–21
What does "beware the leaven of the Pharisees" mean?

Before you begin this lesson, gather the following items: napkins, yeast, a glass of warm water, a small spoon. Have family members open their Bibles to Mark 8:14–21 and set them nearby so they can read while keeping their hands free.

Give each person a napkin and have them cup one hand and hold it over the napkin. Pour a spoonful of warm water in each cupped hand. Explain that the water represents the Savior's teachings. Just as water is clear and will sustain physical life, the Savior's teachings are clear and will sustain eternal life. Now add a pinch of yeast to the water in each family member's hand. Ask them to watch what happens over the next few minutes. Read together Mark 8:14–21 and ask:

- What did the Savior warn His disciples about? (Verse 15.)

- What did they think He was referring to? (Bread; see verse 16.)
- What did Jesus remind them of that showed He didn't need more bread? (Verses 17–21.)

Explain to your family that *leaven* is an ancient word for yeast and that yeast is used to make bread rise. Have them look at the mixture of yeast and water in their hands. Ask:

- What did the yeast do to the water at first? (Clouded it.)
- How would you explain the "leaven of the Pharisees"? (The false teachings of the Pharisees.)
- How are false teachings similar to yeast or leaven? (It is mostly a gas and makes bread seem like more than it is. It quickly goes bad.)
- Why would the Savior warn His disciples about it?
- What are some latter-day teachings that might be considered "leaven" that we should beware of?

Mark 8:22–33
Why did Jesus heal this blind man in stages?

Read together Mark 8:22–26 and have your family think about how this miracle compares to healings they are aware of today. Discuss the following questions:

- How is this healing different from others we have read about in the scriptures?
- Why do you think some people are healed immediately and others gradually?
- How does this compare to the healings you are aware of?
- Are most people healed immediately or over time?

Read the following statement by Elder Bruce R. McConkie to your family:

"This miracle is unique; it is the only recorded instance in which Jesus healed a person by stages. It may be that our Lord followed this course to strengthen the weak but growing faith of the blind man. It would appear that the successive instances of physical contact with Jesus had the effect of adding hope, assurance, and faith to the sightless one. . . .

"Certainly the manner in which this healing took place teaches that men should seek the Lord's healing grace with all their strength and faith. . . . Men also are often healed of their spiritual maladies by degrees, step by step as they get their lives in harmony with the plans and purposes of Deity." (*Doctrinal New Testament Commentary,* 1:379–80.)

Discuss the following questions:

- How can healing that comes in stages actually build faith and testimony?
- What might happen if we were always healed the instant we prayed for it?
- What happens to our relationship with our Heavenly Father when we must pray for help over an extended period of time?
- What could happen to a person who gets angry when God does not grant his or her wishes immediately?
- Why do your parents sometimes not give you what you want immediately? Or not at all?

Share your testimony of how much Heavenly Father loves His children and will do what is best for them even if it takes a longer time.

Mark 8:34–38
How do we take up the cross and follow Jesus?

Read Mark 8:34–35 and ask your family what they think the Savior meant when He told His disciples that in order to find their lives they would have to lose them.

Ask your family these questions:

- What do you think it means to lose your life for the Lord?
- In what ways can you lose yourself for the Lord without dying?
- Would the Lord expect teenagers to be willing to give their all?
- Which do you think would be easier: to die for the Lord or live for the Lord? Why?

Ask your family if they have ever felt overwhelmed trying to lose themselves for the Lord. Share the following story about Gordon B. Hinckley as a young missionary:

"I was not well and I got a little discouraged and I wrote home to my father and said, 'I am just wasting your money and my time. I think I might as well come home and do vicarious baptisms.'

"He wrote me back a very short letter in which he said, . . . 'I have only one suggestion: forget yourself and go to work.' About the same day I received that letter, we were reading in the scriptures and I read these great words: 'He that findeth his life shall lose it: and he that loseth his life for my sake shall find it' (Matt. 10:39). Between my father's letter and that statement, I made a resolution which changed my whole attitude and outlook on life, and everything that has happened to me since then that is good I can trace back to that decision." (*Ensign,* July 1997, 74.)

Read again Mark 8:34–35. Invite your family to write in their journals ways they can lose their lives in the service of others. Share your own testimony of the joy that comes from losing yourself in selfless service.

MARK 9: TRANSFIGURATION, FASTING, AND PRAYER

Mark 9:1–10
Transfigured

Invite your family to look for answers to the following questions as they read Mark 9:2–10:

- Who did Jesus take with Him and where did they go? (Verse 2.)
- Who was transfigured? (Joseph Smith taught that Peter, James, and John were also "transfigured before him"; see *Teachings of the Prophet Joseph Smith,* 158.)
- What does it mean to be transfigured? (Share this definition from Elder Bruce R. McConkie: "Transfiguration is a special change in appearance and nature which is wrought upon a person or thing by the power of God. This divine transformation is from a lower to a higher state; it results in a more exalted, impressive and glorious condition." [*Mormon Doctrine,* 803.])
- Who else appeared? (Verses 4–5.)

- What did the voice out of the cloud say? (Verse 7.)
- As they came down from the mount, what did Jesus request of Peter, James, and John? (Verse 9.)

Help your family learn additional insights by reading together the three paragraphs under "Transfiguration, Mount of," in the Bible Dictionary, page 786. Ask:

- What happened on the Mount of Transfiguration that made it such an important event?
- What difference does this event make to our family today?

Mark 9:11–29
"Why could not we cast him out?"

 Do an activity with your family that involves things that go together, or pairs. As you say the first word or show the first item, have your family fill in the blank with the name of the second item.

"Salt and _____" (pepper)
"Table and _____" (chairs)
"Husband and _____" (wife)
"Shoes and _____" (socks)

Tell your family that Jesus demonstrated the power of "pairing" two important principles. Have your family look for the important pair as they read Mark 9:14–29. Ask:

- After Jesus had cast out the evil spirit, what did His disciples ask privately?
- What was Jesus' response?
- How does prayer make fasting more meaningful?
- How does fasting make prayer more meaningful?

Share the following statement:

"Throughout the scriptures the term *fasting* is usually combined with prayer. 'Ye shall continue in prayer and fasting from this time forth' is the Lord's counsel (D&C 88:76). Fasting without prayer is just going hungry for 24 hours. But fasting combined with prayer brings increased spiritual power. . . .

"Let us begin our fasts with prayer. This could be kneeling at the table as we finish the meal with which we begin the fast. That prayer should be a natural thing as we speak to our Heavenly Father concerning the purpose of our fast and plead with Him for His help in accomplishing our goals. Likewise, let us end our fasts with prayer. We could very appropriately kneel at the table before we sit down to consume the meal with which we break our fast. We would thank the Lord for His help during the fast and for what we have felt and learned from the fast.

"In addition to a beginning and ending prayer, we should seek the Lord often in personal prayer throughout the fast." (Carl B. Pratt, *Ensign*, Nov. 2004, 47–48.)

Ask family members if they have had an experience with fasting and prayer they would be willing to share. Invite the family to unite in fasting and prayer next fast Sunday.

Mark 9:38–50
What evil do I need to cut out?

Ask the following questions:

- What body parts are mentioned in Mark 9:43, 45, and 47?
- If you had to choose, would you rather lose a hand, a foot, or an eye? Why?
- What message do you think Jesus is trying to get across in these verses?

Share the following statement by Elder James E. Talmage:

"[Jesus] urged the overcoming of evil propensities [tendencies] whatever the sacrifice. As it is better that a man undergo surgical treatment though he lose thereby a hand, a foot, or an eye, than that his whole body be involved and his life forfeited [given away], so it is commended that he cut off, tear away, or root out from his soul the passions of evil, which, if suffered to remain, shall surely bring him under condemnation." (*Jesus the Christ,* 388.)

Invite family members to consider their own lives and determine if there are things that ought to be cut off, torn away, or rooted out of their lives to bring them more in harmony with Christ's teachings.

MARK 10: JESUS TEACHES ETERNAL PRINCIPLES

Mark 10:1–12

Why was Jesus asked about divorce?

 Display a picture of a temple. Read together Mark 10:1–4 and ask:

- What question did the Pharisees ask Jesus?
- Why did they ask this question? (Verse 2.)
- How was this question "tempting" Jesus?

To help answer these questions, share the following statement from Elder James E. Talmage:

"Among the questions of the day fiercely debated between the great rival [Jewish] schools of Hillel and Shammai, no one was more so than that of divorce. The school of Hillel contended that a man had a right to divorce his wife for any cause he might assign, if it were no more than his having ceased to love her, or his having seen one he liked better, or her having cooked a dinner badly. The school of Shammai, on the contrary, held that divorce could be issued only for the crime of adultery, and offences against chastity. If it were possible to get Jesus to pronounce in favor of either school, the hostility of the other would be roused." (*Jesus the Christ,* 483–84.)

Ask:

- What might have happened if Jesus had sided with one school over the other?
- What did Jesus teach that went beyond the earthly ideas of both schools? (See verses 6–9.)
- What does this teach us about the importance of making our marriages and families loving and strong?

Invite a family member to read the following from "The Family: A Proclamation to the World": "The divine plan of happiness enables family relationships to be perpetuated [continued] beyond the grave. Sacred ordinances and covenants available in holy temples make it possible for individuals to return to the presence of God and for families to be united eternally." (*Ensign,* Nov. 1995, 101; or see the appendix of this book.)

Ask:

- According to God's plan, how long are marriage and family relationships supposed to last?
- Where can we go to obtain the ordinances that make those eternal relationships possible?
- How can we help ensure that our family is an eternal one?

Mark 10:13–16

How can we become more Christlike?

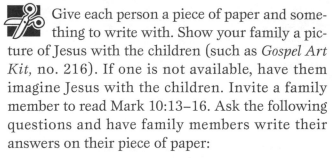 Give each person a piece of paper and something to write with. Show your family a picture of Jesus with the children (such as *Gospel Art Kit,* no. 216). If one is not available, have them imagine Jesus with the children. Invite a family member to read Mark 10:13–16. Ask the following questions and have family members write their answers on their piece of paper:

- How does Jesus feel about little children?
- What qualities do little children have that are an example of what we must be like to obtain the kingdom of heaven?

When they are finished, invite family members to share what they have written. Read together Mosiah 3:19 and ask:

- What qualities does King Benjamin mention that are not on your list?
- What characteristics do some people have that are *childish,* instead of *childlike,* that we should avoid?

Make a list of ways your family can become more childlike and talk about ways your family can develop these childlike qualities. You may want to post these qualities where they can be seen often.

Mark 10:17–31

What lack I yet?

 Take turns reading Mark 10:17–30 and discuss the following questions:

- Why do you think the Savior required something of this young man that seemed impossible for him to do? (Verse 21.)
- What do you find in these verses that seems impossible to do? (Verse 25.)
- How did the disciples feel about the Savior's comparison? (Verse 26.)

- What was Peter's concern? (Verse 28.)
- What did the Lord promise those who are willing to give their all for the kingdom of God? (Verse 30.)
- How can we accomplish the things that Jesus has asked of us, even when they seem overwhelming? (Note the JST changes in footnote 27a.)

Mark 10:32–45
Who will be the greatest in the kingdom of God?

Invite your family to name some of the greatest people they know. Ask them what they think makes them great. Have your family scan Mark 10:32–45 and look for Jesus' teachings on what it takes to be great. You might find it helpful to discuss the following questions:

- What did James and John ask Jesus to grant unto them? (Verses 35–37.)
- How did the Savior answer their request? (Verse 40.)
- What kind of person does Jesus consider to be "great"? (Verses 43–44.)
- In what way was Jesus the best example? (Verse 45; see also verses 32–34.)

Share the following insight from Elder Bruce R. McConkie: "Jesus . . . teaches them how greatness in God's kingdom is gained. It is not the position occupied, but the service rendered; not the office held, but the call magnified; not the rank enjoyed, but the labors performed; not the pre-eminent station attained, but the spiritual diligence exhibited; not where one sits with reference to the King, but the love and obedience shown forth to him." (*Doctrinal New Testament Commentary,* 1:565.)

Write the following sentence where your family can see it. "If I want to be great in the Lord's eyes I will _____." Ask family members how they would complete this statement. Discuss ways that all family members could better serve others.

Mark 10:46–52
How were the blind able to see?

Blindfold a family member and take him or her into another room. Tell the blindfolded person that the rest of the family is going to move to a different room and his or her job is to find them, blindfolded. Have another family member walk closely by the blindfolded person to prevent injury. Instruct the rest of the family to be as quiet as possible. When the blindfolded person finds the rest of the family, discuss the following questions:

- What was it like to blindly look for the family?
- What kinds of obstacles did you run into?
- What do you think it would be like to live without being able to see?

Read Mark 10:46–52 as a family and ask:

- What was Bartimaeus doing when Jesus passed by? (Verse 46.)
- When Bartimaeus heard that Jesus was near, what did he do? (Verses 47–48.)
- What did Bartimaeus do when Jesus called him? (Verse 50.)
- Why was Bartimaeus able to receive this great miracle? (Verse 52.)
- Why is it important that we, like Bartimaeus, come when Jesus calls?
- What are some ways we can come unto Jesus when we cannot see Him?
- Do you think spiritual eyes or physical eyes are more important in order for us to follow Jesus today? Why?

Discuss how prayer, family home evening, and scripture study help improve our spiritual sight.

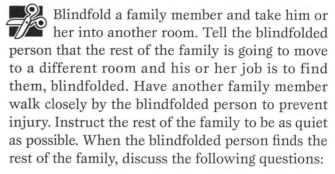

MARK 11: JESUS RETURNS TO JERUSALEM FOR THE LAST TIME

Mark 11:1–10
A colt, clothing, and tree branches

Ask family members to share different ways people around the world show honor and respect to royalty (for example, rolling out a red or purple carpet, bowing before kings or queens, etc.). Read together Zechariah 9:9 and ask:

- Who do you think is the "King" in this prophecy?
- What do you find unusual about the manner in which this king shall come?

Display the picture of Jesus' triumphal entry. (See *Gospel Art Kit,* no. 223, or *Ensign,* Apr. 1987, 8.) Ask your family to describe what they see. Then have your family silently read Mark 11:1–10. Ask:

- Why do you think Jesus was able to tell His disciples precisely where they could find a colt? (Verse 2.)
- Why does Jesus enter Jerusalem on a colt? (Verse 7.)
- What did the people do that demonstrated they believed He was the King? (Verse 8.)
- How is the prophecy in Zechariah 9:9 fulfilled in Mark 11:7–10?

Tell your family that this event is known as the Triumphal Entry. Share the following insight from Harold B. Lee: "My text is taken from the 'Hosanna shout' which sounded from the multitude who jubilantly acclaimed Jesus, the lowly Nazarene, as He rode triumphantly into Jerusalem . . . on a colt. . . . As the animal upon which He rode had been designated in their literature as the ancient symbol of Jewish royalty (Zechariah 9:9) and their acquaintanceship with the might of His messianic power impressed the appropriateness of His kingly right to such an entry, they cast their garments before Him and cast palm branches and other foliage in His path as though carpeting the way of a king." (*Stand Ye in Holy Places,* 39.) Ask:

- How did the believing Jews show that Jesus was their King of kings?
- When Jesus comes again, how can we show the Savior that He is our King of kings? (See D&C 88:104; Mosiah 27:31.)

Mark 11:12–14, 20–26
Figs and faith

Show your family the picture of the fig tree and explain that fruit forms on a fig tree before the leaves do. Invite a family member to read aloud Mark 11:12–14. Ask:

- When Jesus saw the fig tree with leaves, what did He assume? (That there would be figs to eat.)
- How long did Jesus say it would be until men could eat figs of this tree again?
- Why do you think Jesus cursed this tree?

Ask another family member to read aloud the entry about fig trees in the Bible Dictionary, page 674, and ask:

- What did the fruitless fig tree symbolize or represent? (Spiritually fruitless Israel.)
- From this account, what consequences will come to those who are spiritually fruitless like this fig tree?
- What do you think we can do to avoid being spiritually fruitless?

Take turns reading Mark 11:20–26 and have your family look for answers to that question. Then ask:

- What did Jesus' disciples notice about the fig tree the next day?
- How does faith influence our ability to be spiritually fruitful?
- What effect can doubt have on our faith? (See Matthew 21:21.)
- What can we do so that our prayers have more power in our lives?
- In order to be forgiven of our sins, what is required? (Verses 25–26.)

Have family members write the following sentence in a journal and finish it in their own words:

"I will increase my 'spiritual fruit' and enjoy its power in my life by_____."

Mark 11:15–19
His holy, holy house

Explain to your family that in the temple Church members are required to wear special white clothing. If a member does not own this clothing, they can rent it in many temples for a minimal cost. Ask your family how they would feel if they went to the temple, were charged a high price to rent their temple clothing, and then watched a temple worker put some of the money in his or her pocket.

Read together Mark 11:15–19 and ask:

- What did Jesus *do* that demonstrated His feelings about what He found in the temple at Jerusalem? (Verses 15–16.)
- How would you describe His reaction?
- Why do you think this experience both angered and caused fear among the scribes and chief priests? (Verse 18.)
- What can we learn from this account about holy places and how we should treat them?

Share the following statement by President Gordon B. Hinckley:

"Cultivate a spirit of reverence always in the House of the Lord. I regret to say that we have so little of it in our meetinghouses. There is little of it even in the homes of the people. The temple is the one place to which our people go, many of them carrying very heavy burdens, and feel a quiet and wonderful spirit of communion with our Father in Heaven." (*Teachings of Gordon B. Hinckley,* 558.)

Talk about things you can do as a family to keep the Lord's houses holy.

Mark 11:27–33
Scribes and chief priests try to challenge Jesus' authority

Ask your family if they know anyone who answers questions with a question and how they feel when that occurs. Have someone read aloud Mark 11:27–33 and ask:

- Who answered questions with a question in this account?

- In what way did answering a question with a question give the Savior control of the situation?
- What does this teach you about the Savior's wisdom and leadership?

MARK 12: RELIGIOUS LEADERS CONFRONT JESUS

Mark 12:1–44
The "High-Low" Game

To prepare this game, which reviews all of Mark 12, fill a small cup or jar with a favorite candy or cereal. Count the exact amount of candy or cereal pieces and keep that number a secret.

Ask family members to take turns reading as you study Mark 12:1–44 and explain that when you finish you will ask questions about the material. By answering questions, everyone will have a chance to win the jar of candy, which can then be shared with the entire family.

Ask the questions below, one at a time. When a family member answers a question correctly, let that person guess the actual number of candy pieces in the jar. After they have guessed, tell them whether their guess is "too high" or "too low." Continue to ask questions and play the game until someone has guessed the correct amount and wins the candy.

Questions:

- Who did the man send to the vineyard? (Verses 2–4, 6.)
- Did the husbandmen know that this really was the owner's son? (Verse 7.)
- Who could the servants represent? (God's servants, the prophets.)
- Who could the owner's son represent? (Jesus Christ, the Son of God.)
- What event does verse 8 represent? (The Crucifixion of Jesus.)
- The Pharisees brought a penny to Jesus to trick Him. Whose image was on the coin? (Verse 16.)
- Which religious group in Jesus' day did not believe in the Resurrection? (Verse 18.)

- How many brothers did the woman in the parable marry? (Verse 22.)
- What did Jesus say was the first (or most important) commandment? (Verses 29–30.)

Mark 12:28–34
What commandment is the most important?

 Ask family members the difference between doing something with your "whole heart" and doing something "halfheartedly." Have family members share some examples of doing an activity with your "whole heart."

Read Mark 12:28–34 together and ask:

- What is the first commandment?
- Why do you think it is important to love God with all your heart, soul, mind, and strength?
- What can you do to increase your love for Heavenly Father?

Share the following statement from C. S. Lewis and discuss how it applies to these verses:

"Imagine yourself as a living house. God comes in to rebuild that house. At first, perhaps, you can understand what He is doing. He is getting the drains right and stopping the leaks in the roof and so on: you knew those jobs needed doing and so you are not surprised. But presently he starts knocking the house about in a way that hurts abominably and does not seem to make sense. What on earth is He up to? The explanation is that He is building quite a different house from the one you thought of—throwing out a new wing here, putting on an extra floor there, running up towers, making courtyards. You thought you were going to be made into a decent little cottage: but He is building a palace." (*Mere Christianity*, 174.)

Mark 12:41–44
How does God measure the value of our offerings?

 Invite a family member to read Mark 12:41–44 and ask:

- Do you think the amount of money we donate to the Church is important? Why or why not?
- What can we learn in this story about our contributions?

- Do you think the rich people in this story had to sacrifice to make their donations?
- Why do you think the widow's contribution was so impressive?
- What does our financial capacity have to do with how much we should give?
- Besides tithing, in what other ways can we financially help build the kingdom of God?

Share what Elder Joe J. Christensen of the Presidency of the Seventy has taught: "In addition to paying an honest tithing, we should be generous in assisting the poor. How much should we give? I appreciate the thought of C. S. Lewis on this subject. He said: 'I am afraid the only safe rule is to give more than we can spare. . . . If our charities do not at all pinch or hamper us, . . . they are too small. There ought to be things we should like to do and cannot do because our charitable expenditure excludes them' (*Mere Christianity* (1952) 67)." (*Ensign*, May 1999, 11.)

Encourage your family to evaluate their donations and to consider making a plan to be more generous in your tithes and offerings.

MARK 13: SIGNS AND CALAMITIES PRECEDING CHRIST'S SECOND COMING

Mark 13:1–37
Two questions for the Savior

Ask your family to tell of the biggest or most impressive building they have ever seen. Discuss how much effort went into building such a building. Show your family a picture of Herod's Temple. (See *Gospel Art Kit,* no. 118.) Share some impressive details about the building using the Bible Dictionary, "Temple of Herod," 781.

Read Mark 13:1–2. Ask: What did Jesus say would happen to that great building? If you heard Jesus say that, what would you want to know? Read verses 3–4. What did *they* want to know?

Assign a family member to read aloud Mark 13:5–9. Ask: How does Jesus respond to their questions? Invite your family to notice the words "take heed" used by the Savior in verses 5 and 9. Ask:

- What do you think it means to "take heed"? (Watch and be ready.)
- What are some ways we could "take heed" of the Savior today? (Follow the prophet's counsel, obey the commandments, listen to our priesthood leaders.)
- How well are you personally "taking heed" of the Lord?
- What could you do better?

Ask your family if they look forward to or are afraid of the Second Coming of Jesus Christ and ask them to explain why. Read the following statement by Elder Neal A. Maxwell concerning the last days: "Only those in the process of becoming the men and women of Christ will be able to keep their spiritual balance. . . . may we 'walk by faith' and, if necessary, even on our knees!" (*Ensign*, May 1992, 39.)

Note: The clearest account of the Savior's teachings in Mark 13 is found in Joseph Smith–Matthew. See teaching ideas for Matthew 24.

MARK 14: THE LAST DAY BEFORE JESUS' DEATH

Mark 14:1–11
What do you value?

Invite your family to turn to Matthew 22:42 and find the question asked there. ("What think ye of Christ?") Then have them turn to Mark 14:1–11 and look for how the people mentioned in this story might have answered that question. After reading these verses together, ask your family to explain what they think the following people thought of Jesus Christ:

- The chief priests and scribes.
- The woman with the ointment of spikenard.
- "Some that had indignation."
- Judas Iscariot.

Regarding the woman with the ointment, you may want to share with your family the following: "To anoint the head of a guest with ordinary oil was to do him honor; to anoint his feet also was to show unusual and signal regard; but the anointing of head and feet with spikenard, and in such abundance, was an act of reverential homage rarely rendered even to kings. Mary's act was an expression of adoration; it was the fragrant outwelling of a heart overflowing with worship and affection." (Talmage, *Jesus the Christ,* 512.)

- Why do you think their responses are different?
- How do the actions and attitudes of these ancient people compare to actions and attitudes some people have toward Christ today?

Share with your family the following teaching of President David O. McKay: "What you sincerely in your heart think of Christ will determine what you are, will largely determine what your acts will be. No person can study this divine personality, can accept his teachings without becoming conscious of an uplifting and refining influence within himself. In fact, every individual may experience the operation of the most potent force that can affect humanity." (*Cherished Experiences,* 24.)

Ask:

- How have you seen President McKay's statement to be true?
- What things have increased your appreciation, adoration, and love for the Savior?
- How has your understanding of Him affected decisions you make?
- How might your life be different if you did not know that Jesus is your Savior?

Share with your family, or invite members of your family to share, feelings about the Savior that are like those expressed by the actions of the woman in Mark 14:3–9.

Mark 14:12–72
What would they say to us?

Remind your family that although they are reading the "Testimony of Mark," his record comes from the stories of dozens of real individuals who also saw and heard Jesus. Tell your family that they will each be assigned to represent one of these witnesses found in Mark 14:12–72 for the purpose of helping us all better understand the last day of the Savior's life.

Assign family members to be one of the following people:

- One of the two disciples. (Verses 12–16.)

- One of the Twelve—but not Peter, James, or John. (Verses 17–26, including JST Mark 14:20–25 in the Bible Appendix.)
- Peter. (Verses 27–31, 53–72.)
- James or John. (Verses 32–45.)
- A young man (Verses 46–52.)

Have family members read the verses especially assigned to them and perhaps a little before and a little after their assigned verses to completely understand the story line. As they read, have them imagine what it would have been like to be the person they represent and be prepared to tell the rest of the family what that person saw and heard.

When they have finished reading, invite each person to retell the story that is written and tell what they think that person would say to us, if they had the chance, regarding what they learned about Jesus from their experience, or anything else (such as how they felt about their experience, what they learned from it, how it affected them after the events of this night, and so forth).

You may want to use this activity as a reminder for family members to record in their journals the important things that they see and hear relative to the Lord's work.

Mark 14:32–42
Jesus in Gethsemane

Share with your family the testimony of Elder Bruce R. McConkie, that the "atonement is the most transcendent event that ever has or ever will occur from Creation's dawn through all the ages of a never-ending eternity.

"It is the supreme act of goodness and grace that only a god could perform. Through it, all of the terms and conditions of the Father's eternal plan of salvation became operative.

"Through it are brought to pass the immortality and eternal life of man. Through it, all men are saved from death, hell, the devil, and endless torment.

"And through it, all who believe and obey the glorious gospel of God, all who are true and faithful and overcome the world, all who suffer for Christ and his word, all who are chastened and scourged in the Cause of him whose we are—all shall become as their Maker and sit with him on his throne and reign with him forever in everlasting glory." (*Ensign,* May 1985, 9.)

Tell your family that because of the significance of the Atonement, it is good to carefully read the few, small accounts we have of what happened. Mark 14:32–42 is one of those accounts. As you read it together, invite family members to share what impresses them about this account. For example, ask them to choose words they think have special significance, or specific things that happen that they think are amazing, and then share their thoughts. You might read the following to them to help in your discussion:

"Amid the awful suffering at Gethsemane, He was, wrote Mark, 'sore amazed' and 'very heavy' (Mark 14:33), meaning 'astonished,' 'awestruck,' 'depressed,' 'dejected.' It was so much worse than the keenest of intellects could have imagined! Then came His anguished 'Abba cry,' the cry of a child in distress for His Father: 'And he said, Abba, Father, all things are possible unto thee; take away this cup from me: nevertheless not what I will, but what thou wilt' (Mark 14:36)." (Neal A. Maxwell, *That Ye May Believe,* 207.)

"I am a father, inadequate to be sure, but I cannot comprehend the burden it must have been for God in His heaven to witness the deep suffering and Crucifixion of His Beloved Son in such a manner. His every impulse and instinct *must* have been to stop it, to send angels to intervene—but He did not intervene. He endured what He saw because it was the only way that a saving, vicarious payment could be made for the sins of all His other children from Adam and Eve to the end of the world. I am eternally grateful for a perfect Father and His perfect Son, neither of whom shrank from the bitter cup nor forsook the rest of us who are imperfect, who fall short and stumble, who too often miss the mark." (Jeffrey R. Holland, *Ensign,* May 1999, 14.)

MARK 15: THE CRUCIFIXION AND BURIAL OF JESUS

Mark 15:1–15
Christ or Barabbas?

Ask your family the following questions:

- Have you ever been persuaded to do something you really did not want to do? Why?
- After you did it, how did you feel?

Explain to your family that a man named Pilate was sent by the Roman government to be the governor in Jerusalem. As such, he had legal power to put Jesus to death—power the Jewish leaders did not have. As you read together Mark 15:1–15, invite family members to pay special attention to what Pilate says and does and to imagine what he was thinking at the time. After reading, ask the following questions:

- What caused Pilate to marvel? (Verses 3–5.)
- Who was Barabbas and what crimes was he guilty of? (Verse 7 and Bible Dictionary, 619.)
- What word is used in verse 10 to describe why the chief priests had delivered Jesus?
- Why do you think the chief priests were able to get the people to demand that Barabbas be released instead of Jesus?
- After the crowd had cried out to crucify Jesus, what question did Pilate ask? (Verse 14.)
- What phrase is used in verse 15 to tell why Pilate delivered Jesus to be scourged and crucified?
- In what ways have you been tempted to please others instead of God, or in what ways do you think people your age worry about what others think more than what is right?
- What do you think gives a person strength to stand up against the direction the crowd wants them to go?

Share your testimony of the eternal value of always striving to please God rather than man.

Mark 15:16–47
The Crucifixion

 Write the following words or phrases on separate slips of paper, number them, and put them in a cup or a bowl.

1. purple	7. sixth hour
2. mocked	8. ninth hour
3. Simon, a Cyrenian	9. vinegar
4. Golgotha	10. veil
5. casting lots	11. centurion
6. third hour	12. Mary Magdalene

13. superscription	15. Joseph of Arimathaea
14. transgressors	

Have family members take turns drawing out the slips of paper until they are gone. Tell your family you will give them a few minutes to read and study Mark 15:16–47, looking for what their words or phrases have to do with the Crucifixion of Jesus. After they have had time to complete their study, have them report in numerical order. After all fifteen topics have been reported on, invite family members to share what impressed them as they read and talked about this event.

MARK 16: THE RESURRECTED LORD

Mark 16:1–8
What happened at the Savior's sepulchre (tomb)?

Assign family members one of the following parts:

- Mary Magdalene.
- Mary, the mother of James.
- Salome.
- Angel (known as a "young man" in this chapter).
- Narrator.

Designate a place to be "the garden tomb." Have the narrator tell or read the story from Mark 16:1–8, while those assigned act out their parts. When you have finished, turn to page 765 in the Bible Dictionary and read the third full paragraph under the heading of "Sabbath" that begins "After the ascension. . . ." Discuss the following questions:

- On what day of the week did the women visit the tomb? (Verse 2.)
- On what day of the week did the Jews observe the Sabbath day? (The seventh day; verses 1–2.)
- Why was the Sabbath day changed to Sunday?
- What might you think and feel if you had the experience these three women did?
- Do you think people need to go to that garden tomb in order to gain a testimony of the Resurrection? Why or why not?

• What difference does it make to you that Jesus rose from the dead? (See 2 Nephi 9:6–9.)

You may want to read with your family some other scriptures about Resurrection. (See 1 Corinthians 15:22; Alma 11:43–44; Alma 40:23–26, for example.) Share your testimony of the Resurrection and invite your family to express their feelings about the Resurrection.

Mark 16:9–20
Would you believe the testimony of witnesses?

Ask your family to define the word *witness.* (One who has a personal knowledge of something.) Ask your family to silently read Mark 16:9–14 and identify the people who witnessed the resurrected Lord. Ask:

• How did other people respond to the witnesses' testimonies?
• Why do you think no one seemed to believe that the witnesses had seen the Savior?
• Do you think you would have believed them? Why or why not?

Read Doctrine and Covenants 107:23 aloud and ask your family to identify the responsibility listed for the Twelve Apostles today. (To be special witnesses of the name of Christ in all the world.) Discuss these questions:

• How does this responsibility compare to the responsibility given Christ's disciples in Mark 16:15–18?
• According to Mark 16:19–20, how well did the disciples follow Christ's command?
• What do the Apostles today do to preach the gospel and bear witness of the name of Christ throughout the world?

Explain that each of us can know that Jesus is the Christ by the power of the Holy Ghost. We should each have firm testimonies of the Resurrection. When we do, we should follow the counsel of the Savior and share that testimony with others. Have someone read what Elder Henry B. Eyring has said:

"All of us who are under the baptismal covenant have promised to offer the gospel to others. . . .

"Pray for the chance to encounter people who sense there could be something better in their lives. Pray to know what you should do to help them. Your prayers will be answered. You will meet people prepared by the Lord. You will find yourself feeling and saying things beyond your past experience." (*Ensign,* May 2003, 29, 32.)

Share your testimony about the importance of doing missionary work and ask if there are any of your friends and neighbors with whom you could share the gospel.

LUKE

Luke was "born of gentile parents, and practiced medicine. He may have become a believer before our Lord's ascension, but there is no evidence of this." (Bible Dictionary, "Luke," 726.) He was not one of the original Twelve Apostles, but his Gospel "offers his readers a polished literary account of the ministry of Jesus, presenting Jesus as the universal Savior of both Jews and gentiles. He dwells extensively on Jesus' teachings and his doings. Luke is favorable toward the gentiles and also gives more stories involving women than do the other records." (Bible Dictionary, "Gospels," 683.) A Gentile himself, Luke served a mission to the Gentiles with Paul. His Gospel testifies that the gospel is for everyone: Jew and Gentile, men and women, rich and poor. As you study Luke's testimony and Gospel, look for stories that have personal significance in your life.

LUKE 1: ANGELIC VISITS TO ZACHARIAS AND MARY

Luke 1:1–38
One angel, two visits

Ask family members to list as many angelic visitations to mortals as they can. Also have them share some of the reasons those visitations occurred. If no one mentions Gabriel, have one person turn to the Bible Dictionary, 676, and read the information to the rest of the family about Gabriel.

Divide your family into two groups. Ask one group to gather together and read aloud to each other Luke 1:1–25 and the other group Luke 1:1–4, 26–38. When they have finished, have them briefly share the story with the other group. Then give each group a piece of paper. Put Zacharias's name at the top of one and Mary's name at the top of the other.

Compare the visits Gabriel made to Zacharias and to Mary by asking the following questions. Have one member of each team record the answers on their paper. When you have finished, allow a person from each group to share their answers and

talk about what they feel is the most important part of this angelic visitation.

- What kind of people were Zacharias and Mary? (Luke 1:5–9, 27–28.)
- How did Zacharias and Mary feel about their angelic visitation? (Luke 1:12, 29.)
- What was Gabriel's message to Zacharias and to Mary? (Luke 1:13–17, 30–33.)
- What questions did Zacharias and Mary ask? (Luke 1:18, 34.)
- How were Zacharias's and Mary's questions answered? (Luke 1:19–20, 35–37.)
- Why was Zacharias punished for his reaction and Mary rewarded for hers? (Verse 20.)

Discuss with your family how hard it might have been to believe the miracles the angel promised Zacharias and Mary. Ask them how they think they might have reacted and what would have helped them be as faithful as Mary. Share your testimony of the miraculous nature of Jesus' birth and why we can have faith in Him.

Luke 1:39–75
Before His birth, John bears witness of the Savior

Have someone read Mosiah 18:9 aloud. Ask your family to describe someone they know who "stands as a witness" of Jesus Christ.

Divide your family into three groups with the following reading assignments:

- Luke 1:39–45.
- Luke 1:46–56.
- Luke 1:57–75.

Explain that they are to do the following:

- Find and report on any individuals in their verses who stand as witnesses of Jesus Christ.
- Find how they do it "at all times, and in all things, and in all places."
- Find by what power they were able to testify. (Verses 41 and 67.)
- Tell how you feel when you have been filled with the Holy Ghost.
- Tell what you can do to bear witness of Jesus Christ "at all times."
- Tell what example you have seen of someone standing as a witness of Christ.

Encourage your family to strengthen their resolve to stand for truth and righteousness in all circumstances.

Luke 1:76–80

What was John born to do?

Ask the members of your family who have patriarchal blessings if there are statements in their blessings that identify responsibilities they have been given from God. Have some family members share some of those sacred responsibilities. Explain that in a similar way, John the Baptist was called by God to do a great work.

Assign half of your family to read Luke 1:76–80 and the other half to read about John the Baptist in the Bible Dictionary, 714–15. Have them make a list of some of John's earthly responsibilities and report.

If family members are uncertain of responsibilities in their patriarchal blessings, encourage them to reread their blessings and then contemplate what they need to be doing to accomplish their responsibilities.

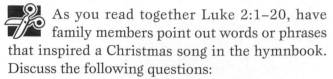

LUKE 2: THE SAVIOR'S BIRTH AND CHILDHOOD

Luke 2:1–20

The Christmas story

As you read together Luke 2:1–20, have family members point out words or phrases that inspired a Christmas song in the hymnbook. Discuss the following questions:

- Why do you think there are so many hymns and songs written about Christmas?
- What is so significant about the event described in these verses?

Invite each family member to share at least one way they have experienced "great joy" (Luke 2:10) because of Jesus. Read Luke 2:17 again, noting what the shepherds did after they saw the baby in the manger. Ask:

- What are some ways we can—like the angels and the shepherds—help others to know of the joy and peace Jesus offers?
- How can we better help people to know that He is our "Saviour, which is Christ the Lord"?

Luke 2:21–39

Special events in Jesus' infancy

Share with your family the stories and/or meanings associated with the naming of the children in your family (including what you know about your own name). Have a family member read Luke 2:21. Ask:

- How did Jesus get His name?
- What does the name mean? (See "Jesus" in the Bible Dictionary, 713.)

Ask your family to name some of the family and Church traditions associated with new babies in our day. Have someone look up Leviticus 12:2–3, 6–8 and report on what was associated with new babies under the law of Moses. Read together Luke 2:22–24 and identify how Mary and Joseph were attempting to do all that was required under the law of Moses.

Divide your family into two groups: males and females. Have the males read Luke 2:25–35 about Simeon and the females read Luke 2:36–39 about Anna. Have each group write six questions that can be answered in those verses—one question that begins with each of the following words: *Who, What, When, Where, Why,* and *How.* Then exchange papers and let the other group find the answers in the verses. When the groups have finished, invite family members to tell one thing that impressed them about either Simeon or Anna or one thing that impressed them about what they said to Joseph, Mary, and Jesus. Ask, What do we learn about Jesus from what these two great people said?

Luke 2:40–52
The childhood of Jesus

Sing or read the words to the song "Jesus Once Was a Little Child." (*Children's Songbook,* 55.) Ask your family what they know about Jesus when He was a child. Have a family member read Luke 2:40, noting that this is all we know from the scriptures concerning His life between infancy and twelve years old. Share the following with your family:

"As a babe he began to grow, normally and naturally, and there was nothing supernatural about it. He learned to crawl, to walk, to run. He spoke his first word, cut his first tooth, took his first step—the same as other children do. He learned to speak; he played with toys like those of his brothers and sisters; and he played with them and with the neighbor children. He went to sleep at night and he awoke with the morning light. He took exercise, and his muscles were strong because he used them. . . .

"It seems perfectly clear that our Lord grew mentally and spiritually on the same basis that he developed physically. In each case he obeyed the laws of experience and of learning, and the rewards flowed to him. . . .

"'He labored and studied and struggled; he treasured up words of light and truth; he pondered the scriptures—all under the influence of the Holy Spirit of God, which came to him without measure and without limit, because he was clean and pure

and upright.'" (McConkie, *Mortal Messiah,* 1:368–69, 71.)

As a family, read the story in Luke 2:41–51. Be sure to read footnote 46c and note the difference it makes to the meaning of the story. Ask your family:

- What does this story teach about Jesus' learning by the time He was twelve years old?
- What does it teach us about His desires?
- Even though Jesus knew that one day He must "be about [His] Father's business" (verse 49), according to verse 51, what did He do as He continued to grow up? (He was subject to His earthly parents.)

Share with your family the following:

"Sometimes you might feel that your parents and leaders respond like Mary and Joseph did. After Jesus answered by asking His important question about His Father's business, Luke records, 'They understood not the saying which he spake unto them.'

"Nevertheless, please pay close attention to what Jesus did! It is an example for what we must do if we are really to fulfill our duty to God. [quotes Luke 2:51–52.]

"You must remember that your duty to God is very clearly linked to your duties to your own family members, particularly your parents. It is not only in being properly subject or submissive to God, but also to parents and priesthood leaders, that we can truly fulfill our duty to God." (Cecil O. Samuelson Jr., *Ensign,* Nov. 2001, 43.)

Have someone read Luke 2:52 and have the rest of the family look for four ways Jesus grew. As each of these areas is identified, write them on a sheet of paper. (Wisdom, stature, in favor with God, in favor with man.)

Ask your family what they think each of these categories of growth represent. For each of these four categories, invite family members to suggest specific ways they might also "increase." Invite family members to write these goals down where they will remember and act upon them.

LUKE 3: JOHN THE BAPTIST PREACHES AND CHRIST'S LINEAGE IS GIVEN

Luke 3:1–14
What kind of fruit are you producing?

Show your family a piece of fruit. As family members take turns reading Luke 3:1–8, ask them to identify what the fruit has to do with John the Baptist's teachings. Invite your family to describe "fruits [actions] worthy of repentance" (for example, recognize the sin, feel sorrow, confess, restore what was lost, forsake or never commit the sin again).

Read together Luke 3:9–14 and mark other things John the Baptist said people can do to show that they have these "fruits." It might be helpful to ask the following questions:

- What did John tell the publicans (tax collectors)? (Verses 12–13.)
- What did John tell the soldiers? (Verse 14.)
- What did John tell the people? (Verses 10–11.)
- What do you think he would tell a car mechanic or schoolteacher?
- What do you think he would tell a student?
- What do you think he would tell a son or daughter?

Make a list of the answers to these questions and discuss ways your family can apply them. Invite family members to record in their journals one thing they will do in the next week to be more faithful.

Luke 3:15–20
How do you feel about someone else's shoes?

Before family scripture study, make sure the second oldest child has his or her shoes on. Then ask the oldest child if he or she would please kneel and take off the shoes of the second oldest child. If he or she resists, say that it is just part of the lesson. Ask:

- How did you feel about kneeling and taking off the shoes of your little brother or sister?
- How might doing a kind service like this show another person how you feel about them?

Have the oldest child read Luke 3:15–18 and ask the second oldest to explain what John the Baptist was saying about Jesus. Ask:

- What character traits was John the Baptist showing? (For example, humility and love.)
- What can we learn from his example?
- Why was John willing to honor Jesus?
- How did this bear witness of his Master?
- What can we do to show the Savior how we feel about Him?

Luke 3:21–22
Proof of the Godhead

Explain to your family that some Christian religions believe that the Father, the Son, and the Holy Spirit are all the same person. Have family members silently read Luke 3:21–22 and look for evidence that the Father, the Son, and the Holy Spirit are separate beings. Have family members point out in their scriptures where they find evidence of each member of the Godhead.

LUKE 4: JESUS IS TEMPTED OF THE DEVIL AND DECLARES HIS DIVINE SONSHIP

Luke 4:1–13
Jesus understands our temptations

Invite your family to name some of the temptations people are faced with today. Ask them if they can think of a time when Jesus was tempted. Have your family turn to Luke 4 and read verses 1–2 (include the JST in footnote 2a). Ask:

- Who came to Jesus after He had fasted forty days?
- Verses 1–2 almost make it sound like Jesus went for the purpose of being tempted. How does the Joseph Smith Translation footnote correct that misunderstanding? (The devil came after Jesus had fasted forty days.)
- Why do you think Satan chose to come then?

Have your family search Luke 4:3–13 and mark the verses where Satan tempts Jesus (see verses 3, 7, 9). Ask a family member to read the following from Elder David O. McKay about these three temptations:

"Now nearly every temptation that comes to you and me comes in one of those forms. Classify them, and you will find that under one of those three [temptations] nearly every given temptation that makes you and me spotted, ever so little maybe, comes to us as (1) a temptation of the appetite; (2) a yielding to the pride and fashion and vanity of those alienated [separated] from the things of God; or (3) a gratifying of the passion, or a desire for the riches of the world, or power among men." (Conference Report, Oct. 1911, 59.)

Write each of the three types of temptations on separate sheets of paper as follows: *Appetite; Pride, Fashion, and Vanity; Riches and Power.* Assign different family members to hold each sign. As a family, discuss modern temptations that are similar to those Jesus suffered. Ask:

- In what ways do you think Jesus can understand our temptations?
- Why can knowing this help us turn to the Savior when we struggle with temptation?

Have your family write 1 Corinthians 10:13 next to Luke 4:1–13. Turn to 1 Corinthians 10:13 and invite someone to read it. Ask a different family member how it makes him or her feel to know that Jesus will not allow us to be tempted more than we can handle.

Luke 4:14–32

Dare to share

As you take turns reading verses from Luke 4:14–21, have a family member tell in his or her own words what Jesus did. Once finished, divide family members into two groups. Have one group read Luke 4:22–24 and the other group read Luke 4:28–31. Help each group explain to the other group what they read. Then discuss the following questions:

- How did the multitude respond to Jesus' announcement that He was the Son of God? (Verse 28.)
- Why do you think they had a hard time believing Him? (Verses 22–24.)

- What did the people of Nazareth try to do to Jesus? (Verse 29.)
- Why do you think Satan inspires some people to fight so hard against the truth?
- Why is it important for the truth to be told regardless of the efforts of others to stop it?
- How do you think Satan feels when you decide not to share what you know with others?

Invite one or more members of your family to share a time they were able to bear their testimonies and how they felt afterward.

Luke 4:33–44

Can we receive miracles at the hands of Jesus Christ today?

 Have your family search Luke 4:33–44 and mark each miracle that Jesus performed. Allow each person the opportunity to share one of the miracles they marked. Invite your family to record in their journals their answers to the following questions:

- Why do you think Jesus spent so much time laying His hands on the people to heal them?
- How would you have felt if you had seen Jesus perform one of those miracles?
- What challenges do you face in your life that you would like the Savior to "lay his hands upon"?
- In what ways can Jesus perform miracles today even though He is not physically in our midst?

To help answer that question, have family members write D&C 36:2 in the margin next to Luke 4:40. Read together Doctrine and Covenants 36:2 and ask:

- According to this verse, what is happening when a blessing is given by a worthy priesthood holder?
- What does this teach us about what the priesthood really is?

Have your family members think of a time when they had hands laid upon their heads and were healed by the power of the priesthood. Invite volunteers to share their thoughts. Share your own testimony that through the priesthood and power of faith miracles still happen.

LUKE 5: FISHING, HEALING, AND FORGIVING

Luke 5:1–11
Fishing for what?

Make a simple fishing pole by tying a string to a stick and attaching a paper clip or piece of tape to the end of the string for a hook. Cut out paper fish and a small silhouette of a person (maybe a family member). Have each child dangle the string over the edge of a sofa or a chair so they cannot see the end of the string. Attach one of the paper fish to the paper clip or tape and let the child pull it out. (If you do not have young children in your family, have family members tell of a time they went fishing.)

Tell your family they are going to learn about a fishing experience in the scriptures. Read together Luke 5:1–9. Ask:

- What was the name of the lake where this fishing experience took place? (Verse 1.)
- What is another name for the lake? (See "Gennesaret" in the Bible Dictionary, 679.)
- Why did Jesus get into a ship? (Verse 3.)
- What did Jesus tell Simon to do? (Verse 4.)
- What was Simon's response? (Verse 5.)
- How many fish did they catch? (Verses 6–7.)

Ask for a volunteer to try fishing again. This time when they dangle the string, instead of attaching a fish, attach the silhouette of a person and have them pull it out (or show the silhouette). Have a family member read aloud Luke 5:10–11. Ask:

- What do you think Jesus meant when He said, "Henceforth thou shalt catch men"? (Verse 10.)
- What does this teach us is most important to Jesus?
- Why should missionary work also be important to us? (See D&C 18:10–16.)
- What did Peter, James, and John do to show their faith in Jesus? (Verse 11.)

Explain to your family that one way you can show your faith in Jesus Christ and "catch men" is to do missionary work.

Luke 5:12–26
The blessings of faith

 Read Luke 5:12–17 together as a family. Ask:

- What disease did this man have?
- How did the man show his great faith in Jesus? (He did not ask if Jesus *could* heal him, he said, "If thou wilt, thou canst make me clean.")
- What blessing did the man receive because of his faith? (Verse 13.)

Share this insight about leprosy: "Scarcely is there a more loathsome, defiling, and hopeless disease than leprosy. Even to this day it remains incurable except through divine intercession." (McConkie, *Doctrinal New Testament Commentary*, 1:173.)

Have a family member read Luke 5:16. Ask:

- What did Jesus do shortly after healing the leper?
- How does this show Jesus' faith in His Father in Heaven?
- What blessings have you received from regular, faithful prayer?

Have your family search Luke 5:18–26 and look for another demonstration of faith. Ask the following questions:

- Who does "their" refer to in verse 20?
- How did they demonstrate their faith? (Verse 19.)
- What great blessing did the man receive because of their faith? (Verse 25.)

Tell your family that you would like them to compare the stories of the man healed of leprosy and the man cured of palsy that they just read about. Ask:

- What did Jesus first tell the paralyzed man? (Verses 20–24.)
- From what Jesus said there, what great blessing can come from faith besides healing?
- What do you think Jesus was trying to teach them about His forgiving the man's sins?

- Who did the leper trust to remove his disease? (See verse 12.)
- From what we just read, who can we trust to also remove our sins?
- What does Jesus require of us before He will take away our sins? (See Mosiah 26:29.)

Invite your family to record privately in their journals one thing they will do (or stop doing) that will help them receive forgiveness from the Lord.

Luke 5:27–39

What would you be willing to give up?

Tell your family you would like to have them listen for similarities between two verses. Have one family member read aloud Luke 5:28 and then another read Luke 5:11. Ask:

- What similarities did you notice?
- Who is "he" in verse 28? (See verse 27; explain that Levi is also known as Matthew [see Matthew 9:9].)
- Who are "they" in verse 11?
- What were Matthew, Peter, James, and John willing to give up to follow Jesus? (Explain that here they were called to be disciples, or followers, of Jesus and later they would be ordained Apostles or special witnesses of Christ.)
- Why do you think they wanted to be disciples of Jesus Christ more than they wanted their occupations?

Ask your family to name some of their most prized possessions and also some of the things they dream of having in this life. Ask one family member to be a scribe and write all the responses on a piece of paper. Then read together Doctrine and Covenants 76:50–59 and have your family find all the blessings promised to the righteous. Have your scribe write all these in a second list. Then discuss the two lists with the following questions:

- What has the Lord promised those who go to the celestial kingdom?
- How does that compare with the things this world has to offer?

Share with your family your testimony of the blessings and joy that come from being willing to put God first.

LUKE 6: THE SABBATH, THE TWELVE, AND THE SERMON

Luke 6:1–11, 17–19

What is good to do on the Sabbath?

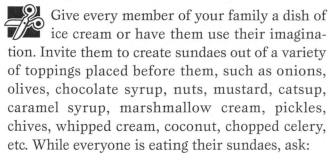 Give every member of your family a dish of ice cream or have them use their imagination. Invite them to create sundaes out of a variety of toppings placed before them, such as onions, olives, chocolate syrup, nuts, mustard, catsup, caramel syrup, marshmallow cream, pickles, chives, whipped cream, coconut, chopped celery, etc. While everyone is eating their sundaes, ask:

- Why did you choose the toppings you put on your ice cream?
- Why did you choose to leave other toppings off?
- What would you say to someone who thought there was absolutely only one right way to make a sundae?
- Is it OK that one prefers chocolate and another prefers caramel?

Read together Luke 6:1–11. Have your family notice what Jesus chose to do on the Sabbath. Ask:

- Do you agree that what Jesus did on the Sabbath was good? Why?
- What are some other good things Jesus could have done but are not mentioned?
- How did the Pharisees feel about what Jesus did?
- Why were they so angry?
- How is choosing what you think is right for the Sabbath different from choosing what you want on your ice cream? (We have been given some guidelines on what is right to do on the Sabbath.)
- What are some choices you can make about what to do on the Sabbath? (There are many good things we can choose to do.)
- What do you think Jesus was trying to teach those people?

Read this statement by Spencer W. Kimball: "People frequently wonder where to draw the line: what is worthy and what is unworthy to do upon the Sabbath. But if one loves the Lord with all his heart, might, mind, and strength; if one can put away selfishness and curb desire; if one can measure each Sabbath activity by the yardstick of worshipfulness; if one is honest with his Lord and with himself; if one offers a 'broken heart and a contrite spirit,' it is quite unlikely that there will be Sabbath breaking in that person's life." (*Ensign,* Apr. 2001, 50.)

Ask your family:

- How might using the "yardstick of worshipfulness" show love for Heavenly Father and Jesus on the Sabbath day?
- What have you found that best helps you keep the Sabbath a holy day?

Have family members write in their journals how they can also "do good" on the Sabbath.

Luke 6:12–16

Jesus calls the Twelve

Ask your family: If you had to choose the Twelve Apostles from among all the people you know in the Church in your area, who would you choose and why? After discussing their suggestions, have everyone silently read Luke 6:12–16. Ask:

- How did Jesus choose his Twelve Apostles?
- Why do you think He put so much time, thought, and prayer into choosing these men?

Cut out pictures of the current Twelve Apostles and First Presidency from a conference issue of the *Ensign* (May or November) and glue them on 3x5 cards. Write the Apostles' names on the reverse side of the cards. Invite your family to try and name the First Presidency and the Twelve. If they cannot, hold up the cards to see if they can name them using the pictures. Finally, invite them to share things they know about each of these fifteen men or ways they have been inspired by them.

Luke 6:20–49

Luke's version of Jesus' Sermon on the Mount

Prepare five pieces of paper, each with one of the five references, topics, and questions listed in the accompanying chart. Divide the sheets

Reference	Topic/Question
1. Luke 6:20–23	1. Topic: Why do you think the Savior blessed the poor, the hungry, those who weep, the hated, the rejected, the reproached, and those who are falsely accused for the Savior's sake? What blessings are promised to them? Notice that the four "blesseds" are paralleled by four "woes."
2. Luke 6:24–26	2. Topic: Why does the Savior pronounce woes upon the rich, the full, those who laugh, and those who are well spoken of in public? What consequences will come to them?
3. Luke 6:27–31, 35–38	3. Topic: Why would the Lord give counsel which sounds like it could turn the doer into a door mat? What qualities might we develop by doing these things? What blessings are promised?
4. Luke 6:32–34, 40–42, 46	4. Topic: Find the questions the Savior asks and invite members of your family to answer them.
5. Luke 6:39–40, 43–45, 47–49	5. Topic: Find the three parables the Savior teaches and talk about their meaning with the family. How can we avoid spiritual blindness? How can knowing that good fruit cannot come from a corrupt tree help us to avoid evil? What blessings come to us when we build our lives on a strong foundation?

of paper among family members and tell them to be prepared to share what they learn with the rest of the family. Encourage them to use the Bible footnotes to help them understand difficult parts.

When family members have had time to study their assigned scripture references, allow them to share and discuss their topics.

LUKE 7: JESUS MINISTERS IN GALILEE

Luke 7:1–10

How can the healing powers of the Savior work in your life?

Share the following story of the Saints when they arrived in the Nauvoo area after being driven out of Missouri.

"After healing the sick in Montrose, all the company followed Joseph to the bank of the river, where he was going to take the boat to return home. While waiting for the boat, a man from the West, who had seen that the sick and dying were healed, asked Joseph if he would not go to his house and heal two of his children who were very sick. They were twins and were three months old. Joseph told the man he could not go, but he would send some one to heal them. He told Elder Woodruff to go with the man and heal his children. At the same time he took from his pocket a silk bandanna handkerchief, and gave to Brother Woodruff, telling him to wipe the faces of the children with it, and they should be healed. . . . Elder Woodruff did as he was commanded, and the children were healed." (*History of the Church,* 4:4–5.)

Invite your family to read Luke 7:1–3 and look for similarities between the two accounts. Ask:

- What similarities do you see between these two stories?
- What is a centurion and how does this explain why he sent Jewish leaders to make this special request of the Savior? (See "Centurion," in the Bible Dictionary, 632.)

Read together the rest of the story in Luke 7:4–10. Ask:

- According to the Jewish leaders, what kind of a man was this centurion? (Verses 4–5.)
- Why did Jesus say of this man that He had "not found so great faith, no, not in Israel"? (Verses 6–9.)
- What can we learn from this centurion about how to build our faith so that we can enjoy the Lord's healing power?

Share with your family (or invite someone else to share) a time in your life when you were blessed by the Savior's healing power.

Luke 7:11–18

The Savior's compassion

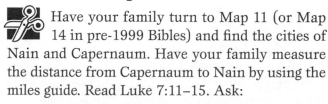 Have your family turn to Map 11 (or Map 14 in pre-1999 Bibles) and find the cities of Nain and Capernaum. Have your family measure the distance from Capernaum to Nain by using the miles guide. Read Luke 7:11–15. Ask:

- Approximately how many miles did Jesus walk to get to Nain from Capernaum? (About 25 miles.)
- What did Jesus find when He arrived in Nain? (Verses 12–13.)
- After such a long journey, how difficult do you think it would have been to be interested in an unknown family's funeral procession?
- What word describes Jesus' feelings on this occasion and what did it lead Him to do? (Compassion; see verses 13–15.)

Have a family member look up in a dictionary the word *compassion* and read it to the family. Ask your family how compassion for one another might lead to other kinds of healing in the family (forgiving one another, being kind when someone else is angry, etc.). As a family, discuss ways you can develop more compassion for each other.

Luke 7:19–35

Why is John "much more than a prophet"?

Have your family search Luke 7:19–35 for information about John the Baptist. They may want to mark the things that impress them most. Ask:

- What words or phrases did you find that indicate how Jesus felt about John the Baptist?

- Since John was such a great prophet, why do you think he sent two disciples to ask Jesus if He was the promised Messiah? (John wasn't asking for himself. He wanted his two disciples to find out that Jesus was the Messiah.)
- What was John assigned to do that no other prophet was asked to do? (See verse 27.)
- In your opinion, how do these things show that John is "much more than a prophet"?

To help answer that question, share the following reasons given by Joseph Smith:

"First. He was entrusted with a divine mission of preparing the way before the face of the Lord. Whoever had such a trust committed to him before or since? No man.

"Secondly. He was entrusted with the important mission, and it was required at his hands, to baptize the Son of Man. . . .

"Thirdly. John, at that time, was the only legal administrator [priesthood leader] in the affairs of the kingdom there was then on earth, and holding the keys of power and these three reasons constitute him the greatest prophet born of a woman." (*Teachings of the Prophet Joseph Smith,* 275–76.)

Explain that John the Baptist was called in the premortal world to prepare the way for the first coming of the Lord Jesus Christ. Discuss ways the prophets today are preparing the Saints for the Second Coming of the Lord. Testify of the importance of John's role and the role of our prophet today.

Luke 7:36–50
Why is the burden of sin so heavy?

Bring two objects to scripture study, one heavy, the other light. Have two family members stand and give one the heavy object and the other the light object. Instruct them to hold the object straight out, away from their side, keeping their arms stiff. As the one holding the heavy object begins to falter, ask both if they would like some help. Ask two other family members to help support the arms of those holding the objects. Ask the following questions:

- Who needed more help? Why?
- Which of you was the most grateful for the help?

Have your family silently read Luke 7:36–50, looking for parallels to the object lesson. Invite your family to share what they find or discuss the following questions:

- How is this object lesson similar to the repentant woman and Simon the Pharisee?
- How is the parable in verses 41–42 also similar?
- What could the heavy and light objects represent? (Verse 47.)
- How is sin like a heavy burden?
- What does it feel like when the burden of sin is lifted?
- Who is the only One who can forgive sin?
- How would you explain the reaction of the other dinner guests when Jesus forgave the sins of the woman? (Verse 49.)
- Who do you think was happier about their experience with Jesus that night, Simon or the woman?

Testify of the Savior's power to forgive sin and of the joy that comes from being forgiven as we sincerely repent.

LUKE 8: JESUS TEACHES AND PERFORMS MIRACLES

Luke 8:1–56
Training His disciples

While one family member reads aloud Luke 8:1–3, invite the rest of the family to note who went with Jesus as He journeyed from place to place. Ask: Why do you think He had this large group travel with Him? Assign family members one or more of the following seven blocks of verses: Luke 8:4–15, 16–21, 22–25, 26–40, 41–42, 43–48, and 49–56. Have them read the verses, considering what Jesus' disciples might have learned from being there to observe what He said and did. Tell them to imagine they were one of the disciples there at the time of the events in Luke 8 and that they have returned at the end of these events to talk about what they have learned. Invite each person to give their report—not only of what happened (i.e., what they observed and heard), but also what they learned from their experiences that would help them "bear . . . the burdens of the . . . kingdom" and "witness of his name" after He was no longer in mortality.

After their reports, remind your family that although we do not have the opportunity to learn from watching Jesus teach and minister to people in our day, we do have His faithful servants who serve as general and local authorities.

LUKE 9: JESUS FEEDS, HEALS, AND TEACHES

Luke 9:1–62

Tic-tac-toe

Play a tic-tac-toe type game with Luke 9. Because of length, the true/false statements below are divided so verses 1–27 can be read and the game played on one day and then verses 28–62 can be read and played on another day. Get a piece of paper and make a large tic-tac-toe grid. Read the verses for that day and divide the family into two teams with one person acting as the game host to read the statements and mark the tic-tac-toe paper. When a question is asked, the teams may not look down in their scriptures for the answer. After an answer is given, read the indicated verse(s) together to decide if the statement was true or false and why. Flip a coin to see which group goes first. If the team answers the statement correctly, they get their symbol in the square. If the team is wrong, the square goes to the other team. Turns are rotated between teams whether or not they answer the question correctly. If one team is not able to get 3 in a row, then the team with 5 squares wins. Periodically ask questions like, What is the lesson here for us? or Why is this important to know? Also, take the opportunity to discuss any questions that arise during the game.

True / False Statements for Luke 9:1–27

- Before sending the Twelve forth to preach, Jesus gave them power and authority over all devils and to heal the sick. (Verses 1–2.)
- Jesus told the Twelve not to take a coat with them on their missionary journey. (Verse 3.)
- Jesus said to stay in people's houses. (Verse 4.)

- Herod was worried because people said Jesus was John the Baptist risen from the dead. (Verse 7.)
- The disciples wanted Jesus to feed the people. (Verses 12–13.)
- Jesus blessed the food before He had them eat. (Verse 16.)
- Jesus fed about 4,000 men. (Verse 14.)
- Some people thought Jesus was the prophet Elias returned to the earth. (Verse 19.)
- James was the Apostle who declared Jesus was the Christ. (Verse 20.)
- Jesus taught that the best way to save your life was to be very careful. (Verses 24–25.)

True/False Statements for Luke 9:28–62

- Jesus took Peter, James, and John up into the mountain to pray. (Verses 28–29.)
- The cloud that came over Peter, James, and John made them scared. (Verse 34.)
- The disciples could not heal the child with a devil in him. (Verse 40.)
- The disciples were discussing who had the best pair of sandals. (Verse 46.)
- Jesus taught it was best to forbid someone from casting out devils in Jesus' name if they did not follow Jesus around. (Verses 49–50.)
- The Samaritans did not receive Jesus and His disciples because they were just passing through on their way to Jerusalem, which offended them. (Verses 52–53.)
- Jesus was going to call fire down from heaven to destroy the Samaritan village. (Verses 54–56.)
- Family matters were the reason most did not want to immediately follow Jesus. (Verses 57–62.)

Luke 9:51–56

What are your feelings towards those who reject you?

Ask your family if anyone has had the experience of trying to make friends with someone and being rejected. Discuss with your family how that feels and what they felt like doing to the person who rejected them. Then read together Luke 9:51–56. Ask:

- How was Jesus treated by the people of the Samaritan village?
- What did the disciples want to do to them?
- Why did Jesus rebuke His disciples?
- What does this teach us about the personality of God?
- How should we feel about people who are not nice to us?

Luke 9:57–62
Where are your priorities?

 Put the following words on strips of paper:

- Car
- Children
- God
- Hobbies
- House
- Job
- Spouse
- Television

Mix them up and have your family members put them in order from most important to least important. Read Luke 9:57–62 together. Ask:

- What three things was Jesus asking His disciples to prioritize? (God, comforts, and family.)
- Do you know of any person who has had to make a similar decision? (You may need to explain that often new converts are forced to choose between their beliefs and their relationships with family members who don't believe the gospel.)
- How was Abraham asked to choose between family and the Lord? (When he was asked to sacrifice his son Isaac.) Show an illustration of Abraham offering his son Isaac. (See *Gospel Art Kit,* no. 105.)

Share the following statement from President Ezra Taft Benson:

"When we put God first, all other things fall into their proper place or drop out of our lives. Our love of the Lord will govern the claims for our affection, the demands on our time, the interests we pursue, and the order of our priorities.

"We should put God ahead of *everyone else* in our lives." (*Ensign,* May 1988, 4–5.)

Share your testimony that when we make God the first priority in our lives, we end up loving our family more than ever.

LUKE 10: THE SEVENTY CALLED AND TEACHINGS ABOUT GOOD NEIGHBORS

Luke 10:1–20
Whose voice are you following?

Ask for a volunteer to take off his or her shoes and be blindfolded. Ask him or her to pick another family member whom they trust. Place the blindfolded person on one side of the room and the person he or she chose on the other. Put some obstacles on the floor between them. Explain to the family that the trusted person is going to tell the blindfolded person where to step so he or she can make it safely across the room. While they are doing this, have everyone else in the family try to mislead the blindfolded person by giving instructions that will cause him or her to step on the obstacles. When the family member has made it safely across the room, discuss the following questions:

- How did the blindfolded person know which voice to listen to?
- How is this activity like earth life? (In our life's journey, there are sources we can turn to for direction.)
- Who are some groups of people whose voices you trust? (Parents, priesthood leaders, General Authorities.)
- According to Luke 10:1, whom did the Savior call to assist in His work?
- Who are some of the Seventies that assist the Savior today? (You can find their pictures in the center section of a May or November *Ensign.*)

Have a family member read Luke 10:13–16 (include footnotes 16*a* and 16*c*) and describe what these verses teach about following the counsel of the Seventy or other Church leaders. Have your family write D&C 1:38 in the margin next to verse 16. Turn to it and read it to your family. Ask a family member how listening to the direction of the General Authorities helps us avoid obstacles in our lives. Ask family members to share a time when the counsel given by a General Authority blessed their life.

Ask your family to silently study Luke 10:1–12, 17–20 and create a list of what the Seventy were called to do. Share your testimony of the important work the Seventy participate in today and encourage family members to listen to and follow their teachings.

Luke 10:25–37
Who is your neighbor?

Ask each family member to write down on a piece of paper as many of their neighbors as they can. Have each one share their list and ask them why they stopped their list where they did. Talk about how far away a person can live and still be a neighbor.

Tell your family that Jesus talked about this same question. Have your family read Luke 10:25 together and identify the question the lawyer asked. Have a family member read aloud Luke 10:26–28 and find the response to the question. Read verse 29 to your family and ask someone why the lawyer wanted to know who his neighbor was. (He didn't want to love everybody.)

Have your family take turns reading a verse from Luke 10:30–37. After reading the parable of the Good Samaritan, ask:

- What two people passed by and didn't help? (A priest and a Levite; verses 31–32.)
- Why do you think these religious leaders did not offer to help?
- Who stopped to help? (A Samaritan; verse 33.)
- How did the Jews and the Samaritans feel about each other? (See Bible Dictionary, "Samaritans," 768.)
- How did the Samaritan act in a Christlike manner?
- Which one would you rather have as a neighbor?
- What can you do to be a better neighbor?

Have your family reread Luke 10:34–35 and identify what the Samaritan did to help. Ask:

- How did he go the extra mile?
- What does this teach us about what we should do when we see a neighbor in need?

Share your feelings with your family about being a "neighbor" and challenge them to look for opportunities to be a good "neighbor." You may want to follow up tomorrow with your family and ask them what experiences they had.

Luke 10:38–42
How do my actions show what is important to me?

Show a picture of Mary and Martha to your family. (See *Gospel Art Kit,* no. 219.) Invite family members to tell you what they see. Read aloud Luke 10:38–42. Ask a family member to explain the story in his/her own words. Read the following statement by Elder Bruce R. McConkie to your family:

"From Martha's housewifely complaint and Jesus' mild reproof, we learn the principle that, though temporal food is essential to life, once a reasonable amount has been acquired, then spiritual matters should take precedence. Bread is essential to life, but man is not to live by bread alone. Food, clothing, and shelter are essential to mortal existence, but once these have been gained in reasonable degree, there is only 'one thing' needful—and that is to partake of the spiritual food spread on the gospel table." (*Doctrinal New Testament Commentary,* 1:473.)

Ask:

- What did Mary do that was commendable?
- How do you feel about what Martha was doing?
- What "one thing is needful"?
- What examples can you think of where people today act more like Martha and not enough like Mary?
- What can you do to better serve the Lord?

Bear your testimony or share an experience of the value of placing spiritual priorities in their proper place.

LUKE 11: PRAYER, DEVILS, LIGHT AND HYPOCRISY

Luke 11:1–41, 52–54
Insights from the Savior

 Write the following words or phrases on separate slips of paper:

- Pray
- Bread
- House divided
- Sign of Jonah (See Bible Dictionary, "Jonah," 716.)
- Candle
- Cup and platter
- Key

Have your family play a game with these words (similar to *Pictionary*). One family member will look at the word or phrase on one of the slips of paper without showing it to the others. That family member will then get others to guess the word or phrase by drawing pictures or clues. When someone guesses the correct word or phrase being depicted in the drawing, read together as a family the verses in Luke 11 given below and discuss how they relate to the word or phrase. Have family members take turns drawing the clues.

Pray—Luke 11:1–4.

- What do you learn about prayer after reading how the Lord prayed?
- Why do you think the Savior prayed?
- Why did He teach us to pray?
- What could you do to better follow this pattern in your personal prayers?

Bread—Luke 11:5–13.

- What do these verses teach about our Father in Heaven's willingness to give good gifts when we ask in faith? (See the JST changes in footnote 5*a*.)
- Why do you think He is so willing to answer your prayers?
- How does it make you feel to know that Heavenly Father wants to treat you as His friend if you just ask?
- Why would it be important then to pray regularly and sincerely?

House divided—Luke 11:14–23.

- By what power were some of the people claiming Jesus was able to cast out evil spirits?
- What was Jesus' response?
- What can happen to kingdoms and houses that are divided?

- How could what Jesus said apply to our family?
- What one thing could we work on to increase family unity?

Sign of Jonah—Luke 11:29–32.

- What is the sign of Jonas (Jonah)? How does it relate to Christ?

Share this insight from Elder Bruce R. McConkie: "Jonah's burial in and coming forth from the 'great fish' (Jonah 1:15–17; 2) symbolizes the death, burial and resurrection of Christ. . . . By repenting and believing Jonah, wicked Nineveh was saved; by repenting and believing Christ, the wicked Jews could have freed themselves from sin. And the miracle of the resurrection, symbolized by the sign of Jonas, stands as a witness against them that they rejected their God." (*Doctrinal New Testament Commentary,* 1:278.)

Candle—Luke 11:33–36.

- According to Luke 11:33, why do men light candles?
- How can we live our lives to be like a candle?
- What should we do with the gospel light?

Cup and platter—Luke 11:37–41.

- At what did the Pharisees marvel?
- What did Jesus teach about inward and outward cleanliness? (See the JST, footnote 41*a*.)
- What does the Savior say we can do to keep our "inward part" clean?

Key—Luke 11:52–54.

- What is Jesus accusing the lawyers of doing? (See JST, footnote 52*c*.)

Share with your family this explanation from Elder Bruce R. McConkie: "The devil wages war against the scriptures. He hates them, perverts their plain meanings, and destroys them when he can. He entices those who heed his temptings to delete and discard, to change and corrupt, to alter and amend, thus taking away the key which will aid in making men 'wise unto salvation.' (2 Timothy 3:15–17.)

"Accordingly, Jesus is here heaping wo upon those who have contaminated and destroyed scriptures which would have guided and enlightened the Jews." (*Doctrinal New Testament Commentary,* 1:624–25.)

- How have the scriptures been a guide in your life?
- How can we demonstrate appreciation for the scriptures?

Luke 11:42–54
Find the woes

Ask family members to think of a person they highly respect. Ask how family members would feel if that person said the following statements about them:

- "I am very disappointed in you!"
- "Your actions frustrate me so much!"
- "I am so angry that you would act that way!"

Explain to your family that the word *woe* is an exclamation of grief. (See *Strong's Exhaustive Concordance,* Greek Dictionary of the New Testament, no. 3759.) It is used in scripture to show great disappointment, frustration, or anger. Ask family members to read Luke 11:42–54 and find and mark every time the word *woe* appears. Ask:

- To whom is the Savior speaking?
- What does this repetition of "woe" in these verses teach you about the Savior's feelings at this time?
- What was the Savior grieving over?

Assign each family member to look closer at the message associated with one of the woes. As they each study a different section, have them find these items and then report on them:

- What did the Savior specifically chastise that group of people for?
- Why is that problem so significant?
- What is a modern-day equivalent of that problem?
- How can we protect ourselves from doing this "woeful" thing?

Encourage family members to write in their journals a remedy for any woes that pertain to them and how they will resolve the problem. Share your desire for your family to live in such a way

that the Savior is not disappointed or grieving because of their actions.

LUKE 12: THE SERMON ON THE PLAINS

Luke 12:1–15, 22–34, 49–59
Gospel principles

Ask your family why they think scriptures were written and then share with them the following: "One cannot honestly study the scriptures without learning gospel principles because the scriptures have been written to preserve principles for our benefit." (Marion G. Romney, *Ensign,* Sept. 1980, 4.)

Explain that a principle is a main message, teaching, or idea contained in a scripture story.

Share Elder Richard G. Scott's statement: "Principles are concentrated truths, packaged for application to a wide variety of circumstances. A true principle makes decisions clear even under the most confusing and compelling circumstances. It is worth great effort to organize the truth we gather to simple statements of principle." (*Ensign,* Nov. 1993, 86.) It is helpful to put principles in "If . . . then . . ." statements, for example: *If* we keep the commandments, *then* the Lord will bless us.

Prepare pieces of paper with the following references on them:

Luke 12:1–3	Luke 12:13–15
Luke 12:4–5	Luke 12:22–31
Luke 12:6–7	Luke 12:32–34
Luke 12:8–9	Luke 12:49–53
Luke 12:10	Luke 12:54–57
Luke 12:11–12	Luke 12:58–59

Put the papers in a basket and have family members take turns drawing them out until they are all gone. Have everyone take turns reading their references aloud and then sharing one of the principles their verses teach.

When everyone has had a chance to share some important principles they have discovered, invite family members to share what principles they liked most from this chapter. Also ask them to choose a principle they can work on applying in their personal life and encourage them to do so.

Luke 12:16–21, 34–48
Christh teaches with parables

Ask your family what a parable is. Turn in your Bible Dictionary to the entry "Parables" on page 740 and read the first and second paragraphs aloud. Ask:

- According to the Bible Dictionary, what is a parable?
- Who frequently used parables in His teachings?
- Why did the Savior use parables?
- How do parables affect the spiritually strong, compared to how they affect the spiritually weak?

Divide your family into two groups. Assign one group to read and provide an application for the parable found in Luke 12:16–21 (see also D&C 58:27) and the other group to read and provide an application for the parable found in Luke 12:35–48 and Joseph Smith Translation, Luke 12:41–57.

Share the following from Elder James E. Talmage to help with verses 16–21: "The man's abundance had been accumulated through labor . . . ; neglected . . . fields do not yield plentifully. He is not represented as one in possession of wealth not rightfully his own. His plans for the proper care of his fruits and goods were not of themselves evil, though he might have considered better ways of distributing his surplus, as for the relief of the needy. His sin was twofold; first, he regarded his great store chiefly as the means of securing personal ease and sensuous indulgence; secondly, in his material prosperity he failed to acknowledge God. . . . In the hour of his selfish jubilation he was smitten. . . . The voice of God . . . spoke his doom: 'Thou fool, this night thy soul shall be required of thee.' He had used his time and his powers of body and mind to sow, reap and garner—all for himself." (*Jesus the Christ*, 439.)

The following information from Elder Bruce R. McConkie will be helpful for Luke 12:35–48: "All men shall not be alive at the day of his coming, but whenever they live, it will be as though the great and dreadful day of the Lord had come in their day. If his servants have served faithfully in his earthly house—the Church and kingdom of God on earth—his coming (to them) will be the year of his redeemed. If they have eaten and drunken with the wicked; if their lives have been overcharged with surfeiting and the cares of this life; if they have been proud and evil and prone to wickedness—his coming (to them) will be the day of vengeance which was in his heart." (*Mortal Messiah*, 3:461–62.)

You might ask some of these questions and share your testimony regarding the Lord's Second Coming:

- How does laying up treasure for ourselves make us "not rich toward God"? (See verses 12:21, 34.)
- What would you like to be doing at the time of His coming? (Verses 42–44.)
- Why do you think it would be important to be found serving faithfully when the Savior comes again?
- What can we do to be prepared for Christ's Second Coming?

LUKE 13: JESUS TEACHES PARABLES ON REPENTANCE AND HEALS ON THE SABBATH DAY

Luke 13:1–5
How can the righteous be protected?

Bring to family scripture study a newspaper account of someone who has suffered a tragedy of some sort. Ask:

- Do you suppose this person suffered because he or she was more wicked than others who did not suffer?
- Are righteous people spared all disasters?
- What does Matthew 5:45 teach about this?

Have your family read Luke 13:1–5 together. Ask:

- What did the Savior say about such personal tragedies?
- What do you think He meant by "except ye repent, ye shall likewise perish"?

Share the following explanation with your family: "True it is, as a general principle, that God sends disasters, calamities, plagues, and suffering upon the rebellious, and that he preserves and protects those who love and serve him. Such indeed were the very promises given to Israel—obedience would net them the preserving and protecting care of the Lord, disobedience would bring death, destruction, desolation, disaster, war, and a host of evils upon them.

"But to say that particular individuals slain in war, killed in accidents, smitten with disease, stricken with plagues, or shorn of their property by natural calamities, have been singled out from among their fellows as especially deserving of such supposed retribution is wholly unwarranted. It is not man's prerogative to conclude in individual cases of suffering or accident that such has befallen a person as a just retribution for an ungodly course." (McConkie, *Mortal Messiah,* 3:194–95.)

Have someone read Doctrine and Covenants 38:30. Ask:

- What does this verse suggest we do about the personal and world tragedies that will come in our future?
- What kinds of preparation help us meet the challenges and disasters that come our way?
- How would being prepared bring feelings of comfort?

Help your family understand that if we are prepared we need not fear disasters. Invite your family to come up with ways that they can be prepared both physically and spiritually for difficult challenges.

Luke 13:6–9
What's in a parable?

 Ask a family member to help you interpret the parable of the barren fig tree in Luke 13:6–9 by doing a side-by-side comparison.

Fold a sheet of paper in half lengthwise to create two columns out of the paper. Give the sheet of paper and a pencil to the family member and ask him or her to list each element or item in the parable in the left-hand column of the paper while another family member reads Luke 13:6–9 aloud. Other family members can also help identify the parts of the parable. Invite family members to give possible interpretations of each element and have the scribe write these in the right-hand column. Ask:

- What does this parable teach us about the way God deals with us?
- How might this parable apply to our family? (God is patient with all His children, even when they make mistakes.)

Share your testimony of God's long-suffering—that He gives us as much help as He can, but we must choose to "bear fruit" or we cannot dwell with Him. Invite family members to suggest "good fruit" they have seen growing in the family, or "good fruit" they think the family ought to try to cultivate, and talk about why this is an important parable for your family.

Luke 13:10–17
Doing good on the Sabbath

 As a family, take turns reading Luke 13:10–17. Ask:

- Where was Jesus in this story?
- What day of the week was it?
- What miracle did Jesus perform? (Verses 12–13.)
- Why was the leader of the synagogue so upset with Jesus? (Verse 14.)
- Why did Jesus call him a hypocrite? (Verses 15–16.)
- What did Jesus say about doing good on the Sabbath day? (See Matthew 12:9–15.)

As a family, talk about some of the good things they can do on the Sabbath. Encourage your family to concentrate on all the good things they can do to come closer to God on the Sabbath and to not spend time worrying about what they shouldn't do.

Luke 13:18–22
Can small things make a difference?

Have a family member read Luke 13:18–22. Ask:

- Why do you think Jesus chose a mustard seed and leaven (yeast) for this parable?

To help answer that question, show your family the picture of the mustard tree to help them see that from a small seed a large a tree can grow.

Pour warm water into the bowl of yeast and watch the activation take place, again noting that

the small amount of yeast causes a great effect. Ask:

- What examples can you think of where someone did a small thing that produced great results? (For example, Joseph Smith's first prayer.)
- What are some simple things we can do that will help or bless others and ourselves?

Share with your family some of the small things you have seen them do that have made a difference in your family or neighborhood. Have each one write in their journals one small thing they will do more consistently that can make a big difference in his or her life.

Luke 13:23–30

What are the steps required for admittance into the kingdom of God?

Have your family go to one of the interior doors in the house, such as a bedroom or bathroom. Shut the door with one person on either side. Whisper to one person not to let in the person knocking, no matter what. Whisper to the person on the outside of the door to try to get the person on the other side of the door to let him or her in but not to touch the doorknob. Let this go on for a few minutes, and then have everyone return to their seats. Ask the person trying to get in to the room the following questions:

- Why wouldn't the person behind the door let you in?
- Why was this a frustrating experience?

- What would it feel like if the door was the kingdom of heaven and the person behind the door was the Savior?

Read Luke 13:24–30. Ask:

- What does the person seeking admittance say to the Lord when they are not allowed into the kingdom? (Verse 26.)
- What did the Lord say would keep the person from entering the kingdom? (Verse 27.)
- What kinds of things does the Lord expect us to do to be admitted into the kingdom of heaven?

Divide your family into three groups. Assign one group 2 Nephi 9:23, 41–42; another group 2 Nephi 31:19–20; and the third group Articles of Faith 1:4. Have them study their assigned verses and report on the steps the Lord indicates will allow us into His kingdom. Make sure your family understands that this may not be everything that is expected of us, but it is a good start. Encourage family members to take these important steps in their personal lives.

Luke 13:31–35

Why did Jesus suffer for us?

Give the following list to your family and ask them what each of these animals may do to protect their young in times of danger:

- A mother bear and her cubs. (Sends the cubs up a tree.)
- A rabbit and her babies. (Stays perfectly still to avoid being noticed.)
- A lion and her cubs. (Puts herself between her cubs and the danger.)
- A hen and her chicks? (Read Luke 13:31–35 together to find the answer.)

Ask:

- Why do these animals act the way they do when protecting their young?
- In Luke 13:31–35, which one does Jesus say He is like? (Verse 34.)
- Who would be the chicks? (His people.)
- Why would Jesus put Himself between us and the powers and temptations of Satan? (As a family, turn to Doctrine and Covenants 18:10–13 and 19:16 to discover the answer.)

- What seems to be making Jesus sad in Luke 13:34?
- In what ways did they refuse His offer of protection? (They stoned and killed His representatives, and they did not listen to Him.)
- What can we do as a family to more fully gather under the Savior's protective "wings"?

LUKE 14: WHO ARE THE TRUE FOLLOWERS OF CHRIST?

Luke 14:1–6
A purpose of the Sabbath

Ask each family member to tell what they like best about the Sabbath day and how it has blessed them. Read together Luke 14:1–6, looking for what Jesus did on this Sabbath. Ask:

- What did Jesus seem to indicate was "lawful" to do on the Sabbath? (Verses 3–4.)
- What other example of this did He give in verse 5?
- In what ways might we need to be "healed" or "pulled out of a pit" today?
- How do you think this healing and deliverance can happen on the Sabbath? (See D&C 59:9–14.)

Ask your family to suggest other ways we could prepare to receive these healing blessings on the Sabbath. What kinds of things could we do to help bring healing to others on the Sabbath?

Luke 14:7–14
Figure out the meaning

Bring one or more dictionaries to family scripture study. Explain to your family that there are many key words that probably need to be defined in order to better understand what Jesus taught in Luke 14:7–14. Assign family members to write the definitions to the following words: *bidden, bade, exalteth, abased, recompence, maimed.*

After obtaining the definitions, read together Luke 14:7–11. Invite those with word definitions to share the meanings of their words when they appear. Ask:

- What point do you think Jesus is making? (The importance of being humble.)
- How might this apply to us at home?
- What about at school or at play?
- How do you think it applies to our attitude at all times?

Follow this same kind of discussion as you read aloud Luke 14:12–14, substituting definitions and discussing how it applies to today. As a family, discuss the personal characteristics Jesus emphasized that would make a person His disciple. Share with your family the following:

"I [agree with] the English author John Ruskin's memorable statement that 'the first test of a truly great man is his humility.' He continued: 'I do not mean, by humility, doubt of his own power. . . . [But really] great men . . . have a curious . . . feeling that . . . greatness is not *in* them, but *through* them. . . . And they see something Divine . . . in every other man . . . , and are endlessly, foolishly, incredibly merciful.'" (Marlin K. Jensen, *Ensign,* May 2001, 11.)

Invite family members to share ways they see examples of humility in Jesus' life. Ask them what they think helps a person to be more humble.

Luke 14:15–35
Excuses people make

Set a picture of Jesus in a prominent place for your scripture study. Set some barriers between the picture of Him and your family. Ask your family to name excuses that people give for not fully following the Savior. Write each of these excuses on a piece of paper and attach them to one of the barriers separating the family from the Savior. Discuss what these excuses have in common.

Tell your family that Jesus gave a parable about the excuses people make for not coming unto Christ. Read together Luke 14:15–24. If there are enough people, assign each member of the family to play a part and act out the story. (Someone can play the man, another person can play the servant, another "the first," and so on.) Afterward, ask your family the following:

- Although it seems crazy, what kinds of things did these people think were more important than following the Savior?

- What excuses do people give today that are like the ones in the parable? (For example, the piece of ground is like our possessions; the oxen are like our job or career; the new wife is like our social interests.)
- When do you think these people will realize they made a bad choice?
- What message do you think this parable has for members of the Lord's true Church?

Tell your family that the next few verses in Luke 14 may help answer this last question. Have a family member read Luke 14:25–26. Ask:

- What did Jesus say about what may stand between us and Him?
- Obviously, Jesus does not want us to hate our family or ourselves, so what is His point?

Share the following from President Ezra Taft Benson to help clarify the principle: "This, then, is the first and great commandment: 'Thou shalt love the Lord thy God with all thy heart, and with all thy soul, and with all thy mind, and with all thy strength' (Mark 12:30; see also Matt. 22:37; Deut. 6:5; Luke 10:27; Moro. 10:32; D&C 59:5). . . .

"To love God with all your heart, soul, mind, and strength is all-consuming and all-encompassing. It is no lukewarm endeavor. It is total commitment of our very being—physically, mentally, emotionally, and spiritually—to a love of the Lord." (*Ensign*, May 1988, 4.)

Have someone read Luke 14:34–35. Ask:

- How does salt losing its savor relate to the discussion of what we must do to truly become a disciple of Jesus? (Point out the object lesson you set up at the beginning.)
- What are the barriers that stand between you and becoming a true disciple of Jesus Christ?

Invite family members to consider how they will remove those barriers.

LUKE 15: LOST SHEEP, LOST COIN, LOST SON

Luke 15:1–7

How should we treat those who sin?

 If you have young children, hide the following items in the room before scripture study:

- A stuffed sheep. (Any stuffed animal that could be a pet will work.)
- A coin
- A boy action figure.

Ask your family if they have ever lost something that they loved. Invite them to share what it was and what they did to find it. Explain to your family that Luke 15 tells about three things that have been lost (a sheep, a coin, and a son). Tell your family that you have hidden three objects representing these three items somewhere in the room. Invite them to search for these three items and to bring them to you as they find them. Ask:

- If one of these objects was a favorite of yours, how would you feel when you finally found it?
- What would you have done if it hadn't been found?
- Can you think of a time when a child was either missing or lost? What effort was made to find and recover that child?

As you read together Luke 15:1–7, invite your family to watch for what was lost, how it got lost, and what it took to recover it. Ask:

- What were the Pharisees and scribes doing that led Jesus to teach them this parable? (Verse 2.)
- Who do you think the shepherd represents? (Jesus.)
- Who is represented by the lost sheep? (All who have sinned.)
- Who would be included in the ninety and nine who did not stray? (See Isaiah 53:6; there is really no one in this group because everyone has sinned.)
- Who thinks they are part of the ninety and nine? (The Pharisees.)
- How does this explain why the shepherd leaves the ninety and nine to go after the one?
- Have you ever tried to help someone who doesn't think they need the help? How hard is that?
- How does this explain why the heavens are happier about one sinner who repents than over ninety and nine?
- What is the Savior trying to teach the

Pharisees who criticized His work with sinners?

Discuss ways Church or family members are like sheep that wander and get lost. It might be helpful to ask some or all of the following questions:

- What are some things that tempt people away from the Church? (Wealth, fame, success, sins.)
- According to this parable, what should we do when a person wanders?
- How should we treat those that are found and return?
- What does the parable teach about the Savior's love for us?
- What does it teach about how we should love others?

Tell your family that not only do Church leaders, parents, and friends have concern for us but that there are also those in heaven who care for us. Share the following statements:

"The spirits of the just . . . are blessed in their departure to the world of spirits. Enveloped in flaming fire, they are not far from us, and know and understand our thoughts, feelings, and motions, and are often pained therewith." (Smith, *Teachings of the Prophet Joseph Smith,* 326.)

"I believe there is a strong familial pull as the influence of beloved ancestors continues with us from the other side of the veil." (James E. Faust, *Ensign,* May 2003, 62.)

Luke 15:8–10

How much is a lost coin worth?

Ask your family if they have ever seen a coin on the ground but didn't pick it up because they didn't think it was worth the trouble or because they would be embarrassed.

Read together Luke 15:8–10. Ask:

- How does a coin generally get lost? (Neglected, forgotten, misplaced.)
- How was this coin found?
- What happened when the coin was found?
- What does the coin represent? (Verse 10.)
- What does this parable teach about how the "angels of God" feel about each of us?
- How might keeping Church records and class

rolls help us "find" those who are lost? (See Moroni 6:4.)

Have your family write D&C 18:10–16 in the margin next to verses 8–10. Turn to this passage and read it. Share your feelings with your family about their worth to God.

Invite your family to think about people in their classes at Church or school who are often forgotten or neglected. Challenge them to make an effort to show kindness to them this week.

Luke 15:11–32

How much is a lost child worth?

Tell your family that you are going to study one of the most famous parables taught by Jesus. Take turns reading Luke 15:11–24. As you read, discuss some or all of the following questions:

- How did the prodigal son get lost? (The son willfully rebelled [verse 13].)
- Why do you think the father didn't go searching for his son? (To allow his son to suffer the consequences for his actions and to help him see what sin leads to.)
- How does verse 20 show that the father continued to love, pray for, and watch for his son's return?
- In what ways do you think the son has changed? (Verses 16, 19.)
- Why wasn't the father angry with his son?
- What did the father do to show his love for his lost son? (Verses 20–24.)
- What does this parable teach us about our Heavenly Father's love for us?
- How should we treat those who are trying to repent and make their way back?

Share the following statement by Elder Bruce C. Porter: "The parable of the prodigal son is a parable of us all. It reminds us that we are, in some measure, prodigal sons and daughters of our Father in Heaven. For, as the apostle Paul wrote, 'all have sinned, and come short of the glory of God' (Rom. 3:23)." (*Ensign,* Nov. 1995, 15.)

Ask:

- In what ways can each of us be considered "prodigal sons"?

- What can we learn from the prodigal son about repentance? (Verses 18–19, 21.)
- What has made it possible for us to return to our Father in Heaven and be reunited with Him?
- In what ways does the prodigal son's father represent the Savior? (Verses 20, 22, 24, 32.)

Have your family think of individuals who might be considered "prodigal sons" at this time in their lives. From what we've studied, what can we do to help those people? Challenge family members to pray for those individuals and continue to love them.

LUKE 16: THE PROPER USE OF WEALTH

Luke 16:1–18
The parable of the unjust steward

Ask your family why they feel some people are rich and others are poor. Then take turns reading Luke 16:1–8. Ask your family how they would describe the difference between "children of light" and "children of this world"? You may need to share the following statements to help them understand this parable:

"'Our Lord's purpose . . . was to show the contrast between the care, thoughtfulness, and devotion of men engaged in the moneymaking affairs of earth, and the halfhearted ways of many who are professedly striving after spiritual riches. Worldly-minded men do not neglect provision [financial plans] for their future years, and often are sinfully eager to amass [gather] plenty; while the "children of light," or those who believe spiritual wealth to be above all earthly possessions, are less energetic, prudent, or wise.' . . .

"The sense and meaning is: 'Ye saints of God, be as wise and prudent in spiritual things as the unjust steward was in worldly things. Use the things of this world—which are God's and with reference to which you are stewards—to feed the hungry, clothe the naked, and heal the sick, always remembering that when ye do any of these things unto the least of one of these my brethren, ye do it unto me. By such a course, when your money is

gone and your life is past, your friends in heaven will welcome you into eternal mansions of bliss.'" (McConkie, *Doctrinal New Testament Commentary,* 1:514–15.)

Ask:

- What does it mean to make friends of "the mammon of unrighteousness" (worldly wealth)? (It means to learn how to manage and use wealth wisely.)
- According to Luke 16:9 and Elder McConkie, why is that important?
- Why is it important to take as good care of your spiritual future as you do of your financial future?
- As you wisely gather wealth in this life, what are appropriate ways to use it?

Have family members search Luke 16:9–13 for answers to this last question. If someone notices the word *mammon* and wonders what it means, look up the word in the Bible Dictionary, page 728. Discuss ways family members can save their money and appropriately use it to help them gather treasures in heaven.

Luke 16:19–31
Which is greater: luxury in this life or the next?

Ask your family what they think is the purpose of this life. Invite a family member to read Alma 34:32–34. Ask, According to these verses, what is one of the purposes of this life? Tell your family that they are going to study a parable to see how it relates to Alma 34:32–34. Take turns reading Luke 16:19–31. Discuss some or all of the following questions:

- What did the beggar want from the rich man? (Verse 21.)
- If you invited the rich man to trade places with Lazarus, what do you think he would say?
- After they both died, what were their rewards? (Verses 22–23.)
- What do you think "Abraham's bosom" might be? (See Alma 40:11–12.)
- Why do you think the rich man went to hell? (See Alma 40:13–14.)

- What were the good things the rich man received in this life?
- If you were to ask the rich man if he would like to trade places with Lazarus now, what do you think he would say?
- What does this parable teach us we should do with the "good things" we have been given?

As a family, discuss how this story is a good example of how to live during our lives. Sing "Because I Have Been Given Much." (*Hymns,* no. 219.)

LUKE 17: JESUS SPEAKS OF OFFENSES, FORGIVENESS, FAITH, AND GRATITUDE

Luke 17:1–2
Sinking or swimming?

Show the picture of a millstone and ask if anyone knows what it is. Have a family member read aloud the "Millstone" entry in the Bible Dictionary, page 732. Explain that millstones often weighed between two hundred and three hundred pounds. Read together Luke 17:1–2. Ask:

- What do you think it would be like to swim with a millstone around your neck?
- According to these verses, how serious was it to offend "little ones"?
- In what ways do you think people can be guilty of offending children?
- Why do you think harming a little child is so serious?

Ask family members to think of how they have interacted with children during the past week and

ponder whether they have offended a child. If so, what could they have done differently?

Share this message from the First Presidency and the Quorum of the Twelve Apostles in "The Family: A Proclamation to the World":

"Husband and wife have a solemn responsibility to love and care for each other and for their children. . . . Parents have a sacred duty to rear their children in love and righteousness, to provide for their physical and spiritual needs, to teach them to love and serve one another, to observe the commandments of God and to be law-abiding citizens wherever they live. Husbands and wives—mothers and fathers—will be held accountable before God for the discharge of these obligations." (*Ensign,* Nov. 1995, 101; or see the appendix of this book.)

As a family, summarize the responsibilities parents have been given by the Lord.

Luke 17:3–10
"Lord, Increase our faith"

Invite your family to share what they think the following phrase means: "Faith moves mountains." Ask, How much faith would a person need to move a mountain? Read together Luke 17:5–6. Ask:

- What did the Apostles want of the Savior?
- What did Jesus say they could do if they had more faith?

Tell your family that in answer to the Apostles' request the Savior gave them the parable of the unprofitable servant. (You may need to use a dictionary to define *unprofitable.*) Take turns reading Luke 17:7–10 and then ask:

- What do you think this parable has to do with increasing faith? (Don't be surprised if you do not get any answers to this question.)
- How would you describe a servant of the Lord, like in verse 10, who does not expect to be praised for doing all that God commanded him to do? (Humble.)
- What might humility have to do with gaining more faith?

Tell your family how you feel about the Lord's blessings in your life and how humble obedience and service helps your faith to grow.

Luke 17:11–19
Are you the one?

⭐ Prior to teaching this lesson, write a short thank-you note to each family member expressing your gratitude for something they have done or what they mean to you. Give the thank-you notes to family members and allow time for them to read them. Ask family members how they feel when people express gratitude to them. Invite your family to share other experiences when someone made a special effort to show their appreciation and how it made them feel.

Read together Luke 17:11–19. Ask your family to describe what leprosy is. (See Bible Dictionary, "Leprosy," 724.) Ask the following questions:

- What did the lepers do when they saw Jesus? (Verse 13.)
- What do you think they meant by the phrase "have mercy on us"? (Verse 13.)
- What did Jesus tell the lepers to do to be healed? (Verse 14.)

Tell your family that just as these lepers went to a priest and were healed physically along the way, we can be healed spiritually as we visit with our priesthood leaders. Ask how that is so. Continue your discussion by asking the following questions:

- How many of the lepers returned to thank Jesus? (Verses 15–16.)
- How would you feel if you helped ten people and only one returned to thank you?
- What did Jesus say to the one who returned to give thanks? (Verse 19.)
- If you had been one of the lepers, do you think you would have returned to give thanks? Why or why not?
- What is the difference between being healed and being made whole?

To help answer that last question, share the following explanation from Bishop Merrill J. Bateman: "In becoming a whole person, the grateful leper was healed inside as well as on the outside. That day nine lepers were healed skin deep, but only one had the faith to be made whole." (*Ensign,* May 1995, 14.)

Have a family member read Doctrine and Covenants 59:7. Ask your family to answer the following question silently: How can we better express our gratitude to God?

Luke 17:20–37
The Second Coming

✂️ Have your family read the chapter heading to Luke 17 and ask what Jesus talked about at the end of the chapter. As a family, discuss the emotions they have when talking about the Second Coming of Jesus Christ. Ask:

- Why do you think the phrase "great and dreadful day of the Lord" is often used in scripture to explain the Second Coming of Christ?
- According to Doctrine and Covenants 38:30, how can we get ready for His return?

Have part of your family read Luke 17:20–25 and look for what Jesus said is a great way to prepare for His Second Coming. Have the rest of your family read Luke 17:26–30 and look for reasons we must always be prepared for the Second Coming. Invite each group to share what they learned. Ask, Why do you think Jesus doesn't give the exact time of His return?

Have family members share one thing they are doing to be ready for the Second Coming of Jesus Christ.

LUKE 18: THE SAVIOR TEACHES ABOUT PRAYER, CHILDREN, MIRACLES, AND MORE

Luke 18:1–8
What does it mean "always to pray, and not to faint"?

✂️ Have one member of your family dress up like a judge and another dress up like a poor widow. Have the widow, the judge, and a narrator read their parts in Luke 18:1–8 while the rest of your family follows along. Ask:

- Why do you think this judge is unjust?
- Why did the judge finally help the widow?
- From what you know about Heavenly Father, why do you think He pays attention to us?

- What would you say is the message of this parable?

Share this insight by James E. Talmage: "The judge was of wicked character; he denied justice to the widow. . . . Jesus did not indicate that as the wicked judge finally yielded to supplication [the woman's pleas] so would God do; but He pointed out that if even such a being as this judge, who 'feared not God, neither regarded man,' would at last hear and grant the widow's plea, no one should doubt that God, the Just and Merciful, will hear and answer. . . . The Lord's purpose in giving the parable is specifically stated; it was 'to this end, that men ought always to pray, and not to faint.'" (*Jesus the Christ*, 436.)

Ask:

- Why do you think Heavenly Father wants us "always to pray, and not to faint"?
- Since it is not possible to always be on your knees praying, what does it mean to "always pray"?
- How is it possible to pray even when you can't kneel down?
- What could we do as a family to remember to pray more regularly and faithfully?

Invite family members to share an experience when they "prayed always" and finally received an answer.

Luke 18:9–14

What attitude should we have when we pray?

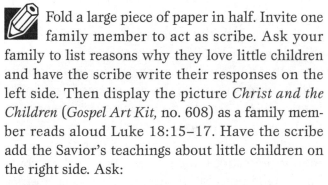 Ask for a volunteer to read from the Bible Dictionary about Pharisees (750) and another to read about publicans (755). Then read together Luke 18:9–13, but assign one family member to read the lines of the Pharisee (Luke 18:10–12) and another person read the lines of the publican (Luke 18:13). Ask:

- How did you feel about the two different prayers?
- What word would you use to describe the Pharisee?
- What word best describes the publican?
- Which prayer is the Lord most likely going to hear and answer? Why?

Invite everyone to read Luke 18:14 and find the Lord's comment about these two prayers. Ask:

- What consequence is there for the proud, boasting Pharisee?
- What promise is there for the humble publican?
- What are some ways we can learn to be more humble as we pray to our Heavenly Father?

Encourage family members to write in their journals what they will do to learn to be more humble before the Lord.

Luke 18:15–17

Why must we all be like little children?

Fold a large piece of paper in half. Invite one family member to act as scribe. Ask your family to list reasons why they love little children and have the scribe write their responses on the left side. Then display the picture *Christ and the Children* (*Gospel Art Kit,* no. 608) as a family member reads aloud Luke 18:15–17. Have the scribe add the Savior's teachings about little children on the right side. Ask:

- Why do you think the disciples tried to keep little children away from Jesus?
- What can we learn about little children from Jesus' response to them?

Invite your family to write in their journals a childlike quality that is missing from their lives and how they will better develop that quality.

Luke 18:18–30

How do we fall short?

Tell your family you need four volunteers to read the parts of the Savior, the rich young ruler, Peter, and a narrator. After they read their parts in Luke 18:18–30, it might be helpful to ask some or all of the following questions:

- Why is keeping the commandments necessary to inherit eternal life? (See Alma 11:37.)
- Which commandment does the rich young man choose not to keep? (Verse 22.)
- How will keeping the commandments help you have "treasure in heaven"?

- How might it help you to "follow" Jesus today?
- Why was the rich young ruler sorrowful? (Verse 23.)
- If he never repented, how sorrowful might he be now?
- How difficult do you think it would be for a camel to go through the eye of a needle? (Verses 25–27; see also footnote 27*a*.)
- Why do you think this troubled even Jesus' disciples? (Verse 26.)

It might be helpful to share the following insight by Elder James E. Talmage:

"At this statement the disciples were amazed. 'Who then can be saved?' they wondered. Jesus understood their perplexity [concern], and encouraged them with the assurance that with God all things are possible. Thus were they given to understand that while wealth is a means of temptation to which many succumb [give in], it is no insuperable [impossible] obstacle, no insurmountable barrier, in the way of entrance to the kingdom. Had the young ruler followed the advice called forth by his inquiry [question], his possession of riches would have made possible to him meritorious [praiseworthy] service such as few are able to render. Willingness to place the kingdom of God above all material possessions was the one thing he lacked." (*Jesus the Christ*, 478.)

Invite family members to think about the following question: Which commandment do you think Jesus would say you are finding it hard to obey? Have your family members write that commandment in their journals and list at least two things they can do to better live this commandment and "follow Jesus."

Luke 18:31–34
Prophecies of Christ fulfilled.

 Duplicate the matching exercise below and place it where all family members can see.

Have family members read Luke 18:31–33 and mark in their scriptures the prophecies listed in the left column. Then read aloud the references in the right column and match the fulfillment of these prophecies with those listed in the left column.

Read together Luke 18:34 and discuss reasons

Prophecies	Fulfillment
1. "go up to Jerusalem" (v. 31)	Matt. 27:26
2. "delivered unto the Gentiles" (v. 32)	Matt. 27:29
3. "mocked and spitefully entreated" (v. 32)	John 20:13–18
4. "spitted on" (v. 32)	Matt. 27:30
5. "scourge him" (v.33)	Mark 15:1
6. "put him to death" (v. 33)	Matt. 27:35
7. "the third day he shall rise again" (v. 33)	Matt. 21:8–10

(Answers: 1. Matthew 21:8–10; 2. Mark 15:1; 3. Matthew 27:29; 4. Matthew 27:30; 5. Matthew 27:26; 6. Matthew 27:35; 7. John 20:13–18.)

why the Savior's Apostles did not understand these very clear descriptions of what would happen to their Master. (One reason might be that no one in their day had any experience with resurrected beings.) Express your gratitude that the Savior willingly fulfilled the prophecies concerning Him and the hope we have for a glorious Resurrection because of it.

Luke 18:35–43
What is it that heals?

Have your family members close their eyes. Ask them to imagine what it would be like to be blind. While their eyes are still closed, read to them Luke 18:35–43. Ask:

- What do you think life was like for this blind man?
- Why do you think he continued to cry out even though he was told to keep quiet?
- What enabled the blind man to see again? (Have everyone open their eyes to look for the answer.)
- Why do you think faith is the basis for the Savior's miracles?
- How does learning more about Jesus Christ help you to have faith in Him?

Sing verses 1 and 2 of "I Know That My Redeemer Lives" with your family. (*Hymns*, no. 136.) Talk about other kinds of miraculous healings that can come into your life because of the Savior. Decide as a family on one thing you can do together to help develop the faith necessary to enjoy the Savior's healing touch.

LUKE 19: JESUS ENTERS JERUSALEM FOR THE LAST TIME

Luke 19:1–10
What we do for a living is less important than how we live

Tell your family you need three volunteers to act out Luke 19:1–10. You need the following roles to be played: Jesus, Zacchaeus, and a narrator. You will also need a chair or stool to represent the sycamore tree that Zacchaeus climbs into. Have the narrator begin reading and have those portraying Jesus and Zacchaeus act out and read their parts as they come to them. After acting out Luke 19:1–10, discuss the following questions:

- What kind of man was Zacchaeus? (Verses 2–4, 6–8.)
- If Zacchaeus was a good man, why did the crowd of people call him a sinner? (Verse 7.)
- What was Zacchaeus's occupation? (Verse 2; see Bible Dictionary "Publicans," 755.)
- How might his occupation have led people to believe he was a bad man?
- What lesson can we learn from what Jesus did? (It's not the occupation or job that is important but how we live our lives.)
- What did Jesus teach Zacchaeus?
- What can we learn from this story?
- Do you suppose there were some who thought Zacchaeus was foolish for being so honest?
- Why is honesty such an important quality?

Discuss how Zacchaeus's experience with Jesus might have been different if he hadn't had an honest character. Challenge your family to remember the phrase, "It's how you live." Attach that statement to the refrigerator as a reminder to your family.

Luke 19:11–27
The "Parable of the Pounds"

Take turns reading Luke 19:11–27. Because this is a difficult parable to understand, be sure to read the footnotes to such words as *occupy* (13*b*), *austere* (21*b*), and also be aware that the word *usury* means "interest," as in interest on a loan or savings account.

Discuss what each part of the parable might represent. After studying the parable, ask for a volunteer to summarize what they think it means. Then share the following statement as a summary:

"Christ is the nobleman; the far off country is heaven; the kingdom there to be given him is 'all power . . . in heaven and in earth' (Matt. 28:18); and his promised return is the glorious Second Coming. . . . The ten servants are the members of the Church to whom he has given physical, mental, and spiritual capacities (pounds) to be used in his service. Those designated as 'citizens' are the other people in the world, those who are subject to him because he is the God of the whole earth, but who have not accepted his gospel and come into his fold as servants. The servants are commanded to labor in the vineyard on their Lord's errand until he returns." (McConkie, *Doctrinal New Testament Commentary,* 1:572.) Ask:

- What does this parable teach about how to best prepare for the Lord's coming?
- How can we as a family better invest the pounds (talents and gifts) the Lord has given us so we can be ready to meet the Savior when He comes?
- Why do greater blessings come to those who are faithful?

Ask your family to record in their journals how they will make the best use of their gifts and talents so that they will find happiness in the celestial kingdom.

Luke 19:28–40, 45–48
Why did Jesus ride into Jerusalem on a donkey?

 Ask family members to close their eyes and imagine being at a special parade. Crowds of people are lining both sides of the road waiting to see a king. Finally, the king comes near to your location. Ask:

- What do you see?
- How is the king dressed?
- How is he traveling?
- Who is with him?

Have your family take turns reading a similar account in Luke 19:28–38. Ask:

- Who is the king in this story?
- Who is with Him?
- How do the people treat Him?
- What is he riding?

Show the picture *The Triumphal Entry* (*Gospel Art Kit*, no. 223) and share this statement from Elder James E. Talmage: "[Jesus] came riding on an ass [donkey], in token of peace, acclaimed by the Hosanna shouts of multitudes; not on a [horse] . . . and the accompaniment of bugle blasts and fanfare of trumpets. . . . The ass has been designated in literature as 'the ancient symbol of Jewish royalty.'" (*Jesus the Christ*, 516–17.) Ask:

- By entering Jerusalem in this way, what was Jesus announcing to the Jews about who He is? (This event is known as the triumphal entry and Jesus entered as the King of the Jews, the promised Messiah.)
- According to Luke 19:45–48, what did Jesus do when He entered Jerusalem?
- If we allow Jesus to have a "triumphal entry" in our hearts, what might be "cast out" of our lives?

Share your testimony regarding Jesus Christ and His power to triumphantly overcome sin through the Atonement.

Luke 19:41–44
What will happen to Jerusalem?

Invite a family member to read Luke 19:41 and ask:

- How would you describe Jesus' feelings as He looked over Jerusalem?
- Why do you think He wept?

Read together Luke 19:42–44. Ask:

- What does the Savior say will happen to Jerusalem?
- What and who will "compass" (surround) the city? (Verse 43.)
- What do you think it means to be laid "even with the ground"? (Verse 44.)

To help answer these questions, read the following to your family: In A.D. 66 the Jews rebelled against Rome. Soldiers were sent to put down the rebellion. Finally, in A.D. 70 a siege wall constructed around Jerusalem starved out its defenders

"'Pouring into the alleys, sword in hand, [the soldiers] massacred indiscriminately all whom they met, and burnt the houses with all who had taken refuge within. Often in the course of their raids, on entering the houses for loot, they would find whole families dead and the rooms filled with victims of the famine. . . .

"[Titus] gave orders that they should now demolish the entire city and temple. . . . [I]t was so thoroughly laid even with the ground by those that dug it up to the foundation, that there was left nothing to make those that came thither believe it had ever been inhabited." (Josephus, *Wars* 6.8–10, as cited in Galbraith et al., *Jerusalem, the Eternal City*, 215–16.) Ask:

- How does this information help you understand why Jesus wept over Jerusalem?
- Whom do you think the Savior might weep over today?
- How can our family help ensure that the Savior will weep tears of joy over us instead of tears of sorrow?

LUKE 20: CONFRONTATIONS WITH THE CHIEF PRIESTS AND SCRIBES

Luke 20:1–8, 19–47
Answering hard questions

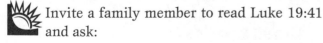 Tell about, or invite other family members to tell about, experiences when someone disagreed with or tried to prove your religion false. Especially explain how you felt about their motives and approach. Tell your family that Luke 20

contains several experiences where some chief priests and scribes sought to do a similar thing to Jesus.

Assign family members one of the following three incidents from Luke 20:

- Luke 20:1–8
- Luke 20:19–26
- Luke 20:27–38

For the passage they are assigned, have family members read it to themselves (and talk about it with their partner if more than one person is assigned to the passage), and be prepared to share the following:

- What the chief priests and scribes asked Jesus.
- What they wanted Him to believe was the reason they were asking the question.
- The real reason they were asking the question.
- What impresses you about the way Jesus responded.

After all three incidents have been reported on and discussed with the whole family, read aloud Luke 20:39–40 and ask:

- What was the response of the chief priests and scribes?
- Why do you think they responded in this way?

Read together Luke 20:45–47. Ask:

- What do we learn from these verses about the real desires and motives of the scribes?
- How can we avoid becoming like the scribes?
- What have you learned from, or about, Jesus in these incidents?
- How will you try to apply his example?

(Note: These incidents were also dealt with in this book with Matthew 21 and 22. You may want to refer to those sections of this book for additional helpful information.)

Luke 20:9–18, 41–44

Do you accept or reject Christ?

Assign a family member to be a scribe to write on a large piece of paper or whiteboard while the family takes turns reading Luke 20:9–15. Have the scribe write down the important elements of the parable (such as "a certain man," "vineyard," "servant," "son"). Have your family suggest what each element represents in the history of the Jews up to the time of Jesus (man = God; husbandmen = Jewish leaders; vineyard = Israel; servants = prophets; son = Jesus Christ). Ask:

- Why did the husbandmen want to kill the son?
- What sad truth will they learn when they carry out their plans? (Read Luke 20:16.)
- Who does "they" refer to in verse 16? (The chief priests and scribes.)
- Do you think "they" understood the real meaning of the parable? Why or why not?

Read together Luke 20:17–18. Tell your family that Jesus was quoting Psalm 118:22 in Luke 20:17. (They may want to write it in their scriptures because it is not referred to in the footnotes.) Ask:

- What is Jesus compared to in these verses? (A rock.)
- In what ways do you think this a good symbol for Jesus?
- How can this be a negative thing to people? (Verse 18.)
- How can this be a great strength to people? (See Helaman 5:12.)

Point out that Jesus is compared to a rock or a stone in both cases, but the effect on people is quite different. Ask, What is that difference?

Read together Luke 20:41–44. Invite family members to answer Jesus' question in verse 44. Help your family understand that although Jesus was a descendant of David because He was born of Mary, David knew that the Messiah (Jesus) would be his Lord because Jesus would also be the Son of God the Father in the flesh. Bear testimony to the fact that because Jesus truly is the Only Begotten Son of God in the flesh, He is also the only one who has power to work out the Atonement and bring us salvation. This knowledge that Jesus is the Christ, our Savior, can truly be a "rock" upon which we can build our lives and nothing can shake us.

LUKE 21: JESUS TEACHES ABOUT TROUBLES IN THE FUTURE

Luke 21
Can you imagine His return?

Accounts of Jesus' prophecies in Luke 21 are also found in Matthew 24 and Mark 13. If you have already studied those as a family, remind your family of this and tell them that you would like to review with an activity the things Jesus taught.

Assign a family member to one or more of the following groups of verses in Luke 21: 1–7, 9–19, 20–24, 25–28, 29–33, and 34–38. For each group of verses, the assigned family member is to come up with the following:

- A question that can be answered in those verses that draws attention to an idea they think is important
- A plan to act out (pantomime) one of the verses.

For each group of verses, invite all family members to read the verses to themselves. Have the person assigned to those verses pantomime their verse and have the family guess which verse is being acted out. Then have them ask their question. Allow each person to explain why they chose certain verses and ideas.

Ask your family if they think that the members of the Church will escape all problems associated with the Second Coming. To help answer that question, share the following statement by the Prophet Joseph Smith:

"Concerning the coming of the Son of Man . . . it is a false idea that the Saints will escape all the judgments, whilst the wicked suffer; for all flesh is subject to suffer, and 'the righteous shall hardly escape;' still many of the Saints will escape, for the just shall live by faith; yet many of the righteous shall fall a prey to disease, to pestilence, etc., by reason of the weakness of the flesh, and yet be saved in the Kingdom of God. So that it is an unhallowed principle to say that such and such have transgressed because they have been preyed upon by disease or death, for all flesh is subject to death; and

the Savior has said, 'Judge not, lest ye be judged.'" (*History of the Church,* 4:11.)

LUKE 22: THE FINAL 24 HOURS OF CHRIST'S MORTAL MINISTRY

Luke 22:7–20
When and why did the sacrament begin?

Ask your family what reminds them most about their best friends? Have your family read quietly Luke 22:7–20 to see what the Savior did to remind us of Him. Ask:

- What ordinance did the Lord begin? (The sacrament.)
- Why did He want His disciples to partake of it? (To remember Him. See verse 19.)
- What are the two main parts of the sacrament?
- When we take the sacrament, what is it that the Savior wants us to remember about Him?
- What are some things that you have done during the sacrament to remember Him or to show gratitude to Him?

Ask, How can we better remember Jesus Christ during the sacrament and each day of the week? Tell your family that there are also three promises we make when partaking of the sacrament. Read Moroni 4 with your family and discuss what those three promises are.

Luke 22:24–30
Is it better to serve or be served?

Ask your family to name all the kinds of people that live in a castle. (Answers could include a king, queen, prince, princess, servants, or peasants.) Ask: Which of all these people is the greatest? Is it the same in God's kingdom? Have your family read Luke 22:24. Ask someone what the disciples are arguing over. Invite another family member to read Luke 22:25–30. Ask, How did the Savior answer them? How have Heavenly Father and Jesus served more than anyone else in the kingdom? Read the following statement from President Gordon B. Hinckley:

"We are all in this great endeavor together. We

are here to assist our Father in His work and His glory, 'to bring to pass the immortality and eternal life of man' (Moses 1:39). Your obligation is as serious in your sphere of responsibility as is my obligation in my sphere. No calling in this church is small or of little consequence. All of us in the pursuit of our duty touch the lives of others." (*Ensign,* May 1995, 71.)

Ask:

- What does President Hinckley say we are all involved in?
- According to President Hinckley, how does our responsibility compare to his?
- When is a time you have served and how did it make you feel?

Luke 22:31–38, 54–62

All things can work for our good

Read Luke 22:31–32 to your family. Ask them who desires to have Peter? What did Jesus say Peter still needed to become? Have your family take turns reading Luke 22:33–38. Ask them what the Savior said would happen to Peter. Continue taking turns reading Luke 22:54–62. If it is available, show your family *Peter's Denial (Gospel Art Kit,* no. 229.) Ask:

- What two things happened right after Peter denied Christ the third time? (Verses 61–62.)
- How do you think Peter felt when the Savior turned and looked at him?
- How could this experience help Peter become more converted?
- Why do you think Peter denied he knew Christ three different times?

Tell your family that after this experience Peter became one of the great defenders of Christ and the faith. Ask them why they think he became so strong in the faith after this experience. Ask, What experiences have you had that have strengthened your testimony?

Luke 22:39–46, 63–71

Jesus Christ suffers in Gethsemane and is smitten by others

Show your family a picture of Christ kneeling in Gethsemane (*Gospel Art Kit,* no. 227), or have them imagine the scene. Have a family member read Luke 22:39–46, 63–71. Ask another family member to tell you what is happening. Ask:

- What verse shows Jesus' total submission to the will of the Father? (Verse 42.)
- Who appeared to strengthen Him? (Verse 43.)

Read the following from Elder Bruce C. Hafen:

"At selected moments in history, God has sent his holy angels to instruct, witness, comfort, and minister to his children. Think of the angel who visited Adam after the Fall to teach him about the Atonement; the angel who announced to Mary that she would conceive and bear the child, Jesus; the angels who sang glories to God and declared peace on earth at the moment of Christ's birth; the angel who comforted the Savior in his hour of anguish in the Garden of Gethsemane; the angels at Christ's tomb, who told the two Marys that he was risen; the angels who came to Joseph Smith with the Book of Mormon and the keys of the restored priesthood." (*Believing Heart,* 100.)

Ask your family to think about all those times mentioned by Elder Hafen. Ask: What does this teach us about our Father in Heaven's love for His children. Continue your discussion by asking the following questions:

- What did Jesus do "being in an agony"?
- What caused Him to bleed from every pore? (See D&C 19:18–19.)

Have your family write Alma 7:11–13 and D&C 19:16–19 next to Luke 22:42. Turn to those verses and read them. Ask a family member what additional insights we learn about the suffering of Jesus in Gethsemane. Share your feelings about the Savior and then invite your family to write or share their feelings about Him.

Luke 22:50–51

"Do good to those who hate you"

Have family members share a time when they have been hurt by someone. Ask, How did you feel toward that person? Read Luke 22:50–51 to your family and have them write Matthew 5:44 next to Luke 22:50–51. Turn to Matthew 5:44 and read it. Ask your family how

Jesus was an example of His teachings. Challenge your family to be more willing to forgive.

LUKE 23: JESUS IS CRUCIFIED

Luke 23:1–56
What would they say?

 Share with your family the following poem:

It was six men of Indostan
To learning much inclined,
Who went to see the elephant
(Though all of them were blind),
That each by observation
Might satisfy his mind.

The First approached the elephant,
And, happening to fall
Against his broad and sturdy side,
At once began to bawl:
"God bless me! but the elephant
Is nothing but a wall!"

The Second, feeling of the tusk,
Cried: "Ho! what have we here
So very round and smooth and sharp?
To me 'tis mighty clear
This wonder of an elephant
Is very like a spear!"

The Third approached the animal,
And, happening to take
The squirming trunk within his hands,
Thus boldly up and spake:
"I see," quoth he, "the elephant
Is very like a snake!"

The Fourth reached out his eager hand,
And felt about the knee:
"What most this wondrous beast is like
Is mighty plain," quoth he;
"'Tis clear enough the elephant
Is very like a tree."

The Fifth, who chanced to touch the ear,
Said: "E'en the blindest man
Can tell what this resembles most;
Deny the fact who can,

This marvel of an elephant
Is very like a fan!"

The Sixth no sooner had begun
About the beast to grope,
Than, seizing on the swinging tail
That fell within his scope,
"I see," quoth he, "the elephant
Is very like a rope!"

And so these men of Indostan
Disputed loud and long,
Each in his own opinion
Exceeding stiff and strong,
Though each was partly in the right,
And all were in the wrong!

So, oft in theologic wars
The disputants, I ween,
Rail on in utter ignorance
Of what each other mean,
And prate about an elephant
Not one of them has seen!

(John Godfrey Saxe, as quoted in Lyon et al., eds., *Best Loved Poems of the LDS People*, 196–98.)

Explain to your family that Luke 23 records the experience of many different people who witnessed Jesus' last hours. Like the "men of Indostan," however, they were generally unable to see the "big" picture of who Jesus really was. Assign each family member to represent one or more of the following witnesses of the last hours of Jesus: Pilate (verses 1–26, 50–53), Herod (verses 1–12), Simon (verses 13–33), a centurion, or Roman soldier (verses 13–53), women from Galilee (verses 13–56), Joseph of Arimathaea (verses 50–56). Have each person with an assignment do the following:

1. Read or scan the verses listed next to that witness.

2. Be prepared to share what they think that person might have felt and thought, or said to family and friends, or even recorded in their diary about the events of that day.

After each person reports, invite the rest of the family to tell what they would say about Jesus to help others understand the "big" picture of what happened that day.

Luke 23:32–47

Jesus' amazing character

Begin your scripture study by singing "I Stand All Amazed." (*Hymns,* no. 193.) Take turns reading the account of the Crucifixion of Jesus in Luke 23:32–47. Afterward, invite family members to tell what amazes them about Jesus in this account.

Ask your family what difference they think this understanding of the Savior ought to make in their lives.

Luke 23:39–43

What did Jesus promise the man on the cross?

Bring a dictionary to your scripture study and have someone report the meaning of *malefactor.* (A criminal; one who does evil.) Have your family find this word as they read Luke 23:39–43. Ask, Why would Jesus tell a malefactor that he would be in paradise?

Explain that some people have used this story as an excuse not to repent until just before they die. Share the following clarification from the Prophet Joseph Smith:

"I will say something about the spirits in prison. There has been much said by modern divines about the words of Jesus (when on the cross) to the thief, saying, 'This day shalt thou be with me in paradise.' King James' translators make it out to say paradise. But what is paradise? It is a modern word: it does not answer at all to the original word that Jesus made use of. Find the original of the word paradise. . . . There is nothing in the original word in Greek from which this was taken that signifies paradise; but it was—This day thou shalt be with me in the world of spirits: then I will teach you all about it and answer your inquiries. And Peter says he went and preached to the world of spirits (spirits in prison, 1 Peter, 3rd chap. 19th verse), so that they who would receive it could have it answered by proxy by those who live on the earth." (*Teachings of the Prophet Joseph Smith,* 309.)

LUKE 24: WITNESSES OF THE RESURRECTION

Luke 24:1–12

An empty tomb

Share the following story with your family: "Many years ago, about the turn of the century, a writer for a newspaper was asked an important question, 'What would be the most important news the world could receive?'"

Ask family members how they would answer that question. After their responses, continue with the rest of the story.

"He thought and thought about the question, he talked to many people, and read all he could in an effort to find an answer for himself. And finally, he printed his answer, 'To know that Jesus Christ lives today would be the most important news the world could receive. In fact, if He lives today, then we too will live eternally as He said.'" (James M. Paramore, *Ensign,* Nov. 1990, 64.)

Tell your family this chapter tells about witnesses to Jesus' Resurrection. Have a family member read Luke 24:1 aloud and find the witnesses "they" refers to in this verse. (See verse 10.) Have your family turn to the Appendix in the back of their Bibles, page 807, and read Joseph Smith Translation Luke 24:2–4. Ask:

- Whom did the women see when they went to the tomb? (Verse 2.)
- Why were the women "much perplexed"?
- What question did the angels ask? (Verse 4.)

Have family members turn back and read together Luke 24:6–12. Ask:

- What did the angels say to the women? (Verses 6–7.)
- What did the women do then? (Verses 8–10.)
- Why do you think the disciples had a difficult time believing the women's account?
- What do you think your reaction would have been if you had been there?
- How is the fact that Jesus lives today important to your life?

Ask someone to read Doctrine and Covenants 38:7. Ask, What does this verse have to do with the Resurrection of Christ? Testify to your family the importance of the role Christ is to play in our lives each day.

Luke 24:13–35
On the road to Emmaus

To help understand Luke 24:13–35, tell your family you would like them to do a reader's theater or a radio show. Ask one family member to be the narrator and three family members to portray the people in the story. You will need two to play the part of the disciples and one to play the part of Jesus. Have those playing parts read the lines spoken by the person they are portraying. After completing the dramatization, ask the following questions:

- Why were Cleopas and his companion sad as they walked along the road to Emmaus? (Verses 13–24.)
- What did the resurrected Christ teach them as they walked? (Verses 25–27.)
- What did it mean when the disciples said, "But we trusted that it had been he which should have redeemed Israel"? (Verse 21.)
- What did the two disciples feel in their hearts as Jesus taught them? (Verse 32.)
- What gave them this feeling?

Sing together or have someone read the verses of hymn 165, "Abide with Me; 'Tis Eventide." Invite family members to share experiences of when they have received a witness from the Spirit while studying the gospel or hearing someone teach it.

Luke 24:36–43
"Behold my hands and my feet"

Ask your family to look for information about resurrected beings as you read together Luke 24:36–43. To give clarification on why the disciples were meeting, have a family member read John 20:19. Ask:

- Why did the disciples have the door closed when Jesus appeared to them? (John 20:19.)

- How did the disciples react when they saw Jesus? (Verse 37.)
- What did Jesus do to prove He was resurrected? (Verses 39–43.)
- What can we learn about resurrected beings? (Possible answers include: they have a physical body that can be touched, move through walls, eat food.)
- Who will have resurrected bodies eventually? (See 1 Corinthians 15:20–22; Alma 11:40–44.)

Invite family members to share their gratitude for the Resurrection.

Luke 24:44–53
Instructions and assignments

Take turns reading Luke 24:44–53 and ask your family to look for instructions or assignments given to the disciples. Ask:

- What were they supposed to preach? (Verses 44–47.)
- Where was the gospel to be preached? (Verse 47.)
- What do you think it means to be a witness?

Share this insight from Elder Bruce R. McConkie: "A witness testifies; he has a testimony to bear; he tells what he knows. The gospel is not carried to the world by the teaching process only. Any minister or professor of religion can teach; whether his conclusions are true or false, he can present them and make them seem appealing to some. But only one who knows by personal revelation that certain things are true can testify with converting power." (*Doctrinal New Testament Commentary,* 1:855.)

- Can you qualify as a witness for Christ and His gospel although you may not have seen Him face to face? How?
- When are good times to witness to others and how?

Challenge your family to pray and look for opportunities to stand as witnesses of what the Lord Jesus Christ has done for them.

JOHN

John, the Apostle, was a faithful disciple throughout Jesus' mortal ministry and eventually became a member of the First Presidency. John was an eyewitness to the powerful teachings and miracles of Jesus. After the death of Jesus, John was banished to the Island of Patmos where he wrote the book of Revelation. John was translated allowing him to remain on the earth until the Second Coming. (See 3 Nephi 28:6.) In 1831 the Prophet Joseph Smith said that "John the Revelator was then among the Ten Tribes of Israel." (History of the Church 1:176.)

The Gospel of John was written to the Jews who speak Greek. His purpose in writing to them is outlined in John 20:31: "But these are written, that ye might believe that Jesus is the Christ, the Son of God; and that believing ye might have life through his name." John begins his Gospel with a statement concerning the premortal existence and takes us through the mortal ministry of Jesus and concludes with His death and Resurrection. You may want to have your family read under the heading "Gospels" in the Bible Dictionary, page 682, to see the differences among the writers of the Gospels. This will help your family understand why John wrote and to whom.

JOHN 1: JESUS BEGINS HIS MORTAL MINISTRY

John 1:1–14
How is Jesus our light?

 Bring a flashlight to family scripture study. Turn off all the lights and turn the flashlight on. Ask the following questions:

- What is the purpose of a flashlight?
- How is Jesus like a flashlight?

Turn the lights back on and take turns reading John 1:1–14 and notice each time a reference to Christ is made. Ask:

- Where did the Word dwell? (Verse 1.)
- What did the Word make? (Verses 3, 10.)
- Who was the Word? (Verse 14.)
- Who was the light? (Verse 4.)

Share the following insight: "Life abounds, all things exist, and the very planets roll on their course because of the light of Christ, 'The light which is in all things, which giveth life to all things, which is the law by which all things are governed.' It is the same light which enlightens men and quickens their understandings." (McConkie, *Doctrinal New Testament Commentary,* 1:71.)

- Who was the man that would bear witness of the light? (Verse 6.)
- If we receive Jesus, what can we become? (Verse 12.)

Share with your family how Jesus Christ has been a light in your life. Invite your family to tell of ways the Savior has taken darkness out of their lives.

John 1:15–34
John the Baptist testifies of Jesus Christ

 Show your family a picture of a place you have been but they have not. Ask:

- Have you ever been to this place?
- Do you know for yourself that this is a picture of this place?
- Could this picture be of some other place or

even a phony picture of a place that doesn't exist at all?

- How do you even know that this place really exists if you have never seen it?
- Would it make a difference if you knew somebody that has seen that place and can testify that it really exists?

Tell your family that you are such a witness and you can testify that it really exists. Then explain that this is an example of one way we also can know that God the Father and Jesus Christ really exist. Have a family member read John 1:15–17, 26–34. Ask:

- Who is John the Apostle quoting in these verses? (John the Baptist.)
- What is John the Baptist teaching us about Jesus Christ?
- Who did he say Jesus is? (Verse 34.)
- When did John receive a witness that Jesus is the Christ, the Son of God? (See verses 32–33 and Matthew 3:13–17.)

Ask your family if they know of any other people who are witnesses that Jesus lives and that He is the Son of God. (If they need help, see Genesis 32:30; Exodus 33:11; Acts 7:55–56; and Joseph Smith–History 1:17.)

Return to John 1:18 and reread the first phrase. Explain that since we know that Joseph Smith and others have seen the Father, there must be something missing in this verse. Turn to the Joseph Smith Translation in the Bible Appendix, page 808, and read verse 19. Ask how the changes the Lord gave Joseph Smith help clarify the verse. How does John 6:46 help explain how man can see God?

Add your own testimony that we can trust the testimonies of these eyewitnesses and that what the scriptures teach of Jesus Christ is true.

John 1:29–34
Why was Jesus baptized?

Ask family members what they remember most about their baptism. Have them share how it made them feel. Show them a picture of Jesus being baptized. (*Gospel Art Kit,* no. 208.) Have someone read John 1:29–34. Ask:

- What was John's main message? (Verse 29.)
- What is the purpose of baptism?
- Why did Jesus need baptism? As a family, turn to 2 Nephi 31:6–9. Read and mark the reasons Jesus was baptized.

In the margin next to John 1:29–34, write Mosiah 18:8–10, then have them turn to those verses. Have half of your family look for the reason we need to be baptized and the other half look for the promised blessings for those who enter the waters of baptism. As you find them, have your family mark them. Have each group share what they have discovered.

John 1:35–51
What's in a name?

 Invite family members to share the following:

- What their name means or what its origin is.
- Why that particular name was chosen for them.
- What they like most about their name.
- What names they may someday choose for their children.

Take turns reading John 1:35–51 and ask your family to look for the names of those whom Jesus chose and invited to follow Him. Use your Bible Dictionary to look up the names mentioned and identify their meanings. Ask:

- Why would Jesus call Peter Cephas? (Verse 42, footnote *a.*)
- What would Peter become?
- What changed Nathanael's opinion of Jesus from "Can there any good thing come out of Nazareth?" (verse 46) to "Thou art the Son of God"? (verse 49).
- What happened under the fig tree?
- What did Jesus mean when He told Nathanael that he was without guile? (Verse 47, footnote *b.*)

Invite your family to keep their names clean so that someday when they stand before their Maker, they will be like Nathanael, without guile.

JOHN 2: THE BEGINNING OF THE SAVIOR'S PUBLIC MINISTRY

John 2:1–11
Christ's first public miracle

 If you have a fifty-five gallon water storage container or a large trash can, have your family gather around it for scripture study.

Display a picture of a wedding reception, especially the refreshment table if one is available. Ask family members to imagine hosting a wedding reception and running out of refreshments before the reception was over. Ask, How would you feel? What would you do?

Invite one member of your family to read aloud John 2:1–11, paying particular attention to the Joseph Smith Translation in verse 4. To better understand the depth of this miracle, invite your family to turn to the Bible Dictionary, "Weights and Measures," 788–89, to find out how much a firkin is. Ask:

- Why was Jesus at the marriage? (Verse 2.)
- How many waterpots are mentioned? (Verse 6.)
- How many firkins of water did each pot hold? (Verse 6.)

Have someone do the math where all can see:

Firkin = 8.25 gallons

Each pot = 2–3 firkins

8.25 x 2 = 16.5 gallons x 6 pots = 99 gallons

8.25 x 3 = 24.75 gallons x 6 pots = 148.5 gallons

Compare your totals with the amount the water container or trash can would hold and talk about the majesty of this miracle.

Share the following insights about the following verses with your family:

John 2:5

"One of the most inspiring lines in all of the scripture was spoken by the mother of Jesus at the marriage feast at Cana. . . . 'Whatsoever he saith unto you, do it.' . . . What an inspiring motto that would make for our individual lives!" (Sterling W. Sill, Conference Report, Oct. 1959, 105.)

John 2:11

"We can well imagine the sense of reverential awe that came into the heart of the revelers as the servants let it be known what Mary's Son had done. . . . John says that by this act, Jesus 'manifested forth his glory, and his disciples believed on him.' Miracles follow faith, and miracles strengthen faith." (McConkie, *Mortal Messiah,* 1:453–54.)

Share an experience with your family when a miracle has strengthened your faith.

John 2:12–17
Why did the Savior drive people from the temple?

Give one of your children three strands of yarn, string, or rope. Ask them to braid a whip. If you have any small tables in the room where you hold scripture study, turn them over and toss coins on the floor. Begin scripture study with prayer and then ask the family how they feel about the mess and what they think the whip is for. Ask your family to read John 2:12–17 silently and find out what the whip and the mess have to do with these verses.

Display a picture of Jesus cleansing the temple (*Gospel Art Kit,* no. 224). Ask:

- Why do you think Jesus would be upset over such a scene and what did He do about His feelings? (Verses 14–16.)
- How does this experience help us understand the deep reverence and respect Jesus has for His Father?
- What would be wrong with buying and selling things in the temple courtyard?

Share this information from Elder Howard W. Hunter with your family: "In the process of moral decline, reverence is one of the first virtues to disappear. . . . Love of money had warped the hearts of many of Jesus' countrymen. They cared more for gain than they did for God. . . . Never did Jesus show a greater tempest of emotion than in the cleansing of the temple. Instantly he became avenging fury, and before the miscreants [evildoers, disbelievers] knew what was happening, their coins were rolling over the temple floor and their flocks and herds were in the street.

"The reason for the tempest lies in just three

words: 'My Father's house.' It was not an ordinary house; it was the house of God. It was erected for God's worship. It was a home for the reverent heart. It was intended to be a place of solace for men's woes and troubles, the very gate of heaven. 'Take these things hence' he said, 'make not my Father's house an house of merchandise.' . . . His devotion to the Most High kindled a fire in his soul and gave his words the force that pierced the offenders like a dagger." (*Ensign,* Nov. 1977, 52–53.)

Have family members follow along as you read Doctrine and Covenants 97:15 aloud. Ask:

- Why should no unclean thing enter God's house?
- What did Christ do at the temple to protect the dignity and integrity of His Father's house?

Have family members write in their journals what they can do to keep the temple a holy place.

John 2:18–25
Who gets signs and who does not?

 Ask your family members the following questions:

- Do people generally know when they are going to die or how?
- What might be some advantages and disadvantages of knowing when?

Remind your family that Jesus had just driven the money changers and sellers out of the temple. (John 2:12–17.) Read together John 2:18–25. Ask:

- What did the Jews want from Jesus? (Some sign to show why He had the authority to drive them out of the temple. Verse 18.)
- What answer did Jesus give them? (Verse 19.)
- What temple did the Jews think Jesus was talking about? (Herod's temple.)
- What temple was Jesus really talking about? (Verse 21.)
- How is our body like a temple?
- What does this tell us Jesus knew about His death and Resurrection?
- When did the disciples understand what He really meant? (Verse 22.)
- Why didn't Jesus give the Jews a sign they understood to help them believe?

To help answer that last question, read Doctrine and Covenants 63:7–12 and then ask:

- To whom did the Lord say He would give signs or proof?
- Why does the Lord not show signs to those with no faith? (See Alma 32:17–19. If they know but are not willing to obey, their punishment will be greater than if they did not know.)

Share your testimony of how the Lord shows us as much as we are ready to receive, but we won't receive more than we are prepared to live.

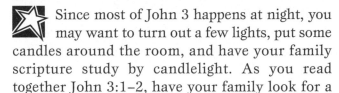

JOHN 3: NICODEMUS VISITS JESUS

John 3:1–2
Nicodemus takes a chance

 Since most of John 3 happens at night, you may want to turn out a few lights, put some candles around the room, and have your family scripture study by candlelight. As you read together John 3:1–2, have your family look for a reason you are reading by candlelight. Ask:

- What time of day was it when Nicodemus came to Jesus?
- What important religious group did Nicodemus belong to? (He was a "ruler of the Jews." See Bible Dictionary, "Sanhedrin," 769.)
- Why might a person belonging to the Sanhedrin come at night? (See John 9:22.)
- Why do you think Nicodemus would risk so much to visit Jesus?
- If you could talk to Nicodemus right now, whom do you think he would say it was more important to listen to, the Lord or other people?
- Why do some people fear what others might think when they participate in religious activities?

Challenge your family to care more about what God thinks about than what others may think.

John 3:3–7
What does it mean to be "born again"?

Show a birth certificate of a family member and ask if they know what it is. Can anyone have two of these? Then show a baptismal certificate and ask how it might be considered a second birth certificate. Invite a member of your family to read John 3:3–7 and ask your family to look for what might have been on Nicodemus's mind. Ask:

- What does it mean to be "born again"? (See Alma 5:14; Mosiah 27:24–29.)
- How can a person be born of the water (baptized) but not born of the Spirit?

Share the following by Elder Bruce R. McConkie: "Church members are not born again by the mere fact of baptism alone; rather, after baptism, they must so live as to experience a 'mighty change' in their hearts." (*Doctrinal New Testament Commentary*, 1:142.)

Show a kernel of unpopped popcorn and ask:

- How is this popcorn kernel like a person who has not been born again?
- How does this kernel change when heat is applied?
- What is the spiritual "heat" that is applied to people that creates a mighty change in them? (The Holy Ghost.)
- How does spiritual rebirth change a person's attitude? (See 1 John 5:3.)

Share an experience in your life when you felt a change of heart or spiritual rebirth. Explain that the process of spiritual rebirth happens over time. Testify that the sacrament allows a wonderful time to recommit one's self to following God. Encourage family members to always seek for a change of heart by becoming a little better each day. After scripture study you may want to make some popcorn to enjoy together.

John 3:8–13
How are the wind and the Spirit similar?

Divide your family into two groups, giving each group a paper and pencil. Read John 3:8 to them and explain that the word for "wind" and "spirit" are the same in Greek (*pneuma*). Have each group list as many similarities between the wind and the Spirit as they can. After each group has listed and shared the similarities they found, ask:

- What do you think Jesus was trying to teach about a person who has been born again?
- How does the Holy Spirit guide someone?
- What kinds of things might the Spirit direct someone to do?
- Why is it sometimes difficult to follow promptings from the Spirit?

As a family, read verses 9–13. Challenge your family to follow the promptings that come from the Holy Spirit.

John 3:14–17
Scriptures at sporting events?

Ask your family if they have ever noticed people holding up signs with scriptures on them during televised sporting events. If they have, ask if they remember what scripture it was. Explain that John 3 has one of the most commonly quoted scriptures. Have your family silently read John 3:14–17 and look for this famous scripture. Once someone identifies John 3:16, ask, "Why do you think someone would put that verse on a sign?"

Invite a family member to read John 3:16. Ask:

- What important truths do you find in this verse?
- What did God do to show that He loves us?
- What did Jesus Christ do so we would not perish?
- What does it mean to have "everlasting life"?
- What do we need to do to be "saved"? (See 2 Nephi 9:21–23.)

Share the following by Elder Bruce R. McConkie: "This is perhaps the most famous and powerful single verse of scripture ever uttered. It summarizes the whole plan of salvation, tying together the Father, the Son, his atoning sacrifice, that belief in him which presupposes righteous works, and ultimate eternal exaltation for the faithful." (*Doctrinal New Testament Commentary*, 1:144.)

John 3:18–21
What's the problem with this world?

Ask your family: What do you think is the biggest problem with this world? After they have discussed this thought, read together John

3:18–21 and look for what Jesus says is the problem with this world. Ask:

- Why would someone like darkness more than light?
- When can the darkness be an advantage? (When you are doing something you don't want others to see.)
- Why do some people seem to prefer hearing about other people's failures rather than their successes?
- Is most of the news on TV positive or negative? Why?
- Why do many people like to watch talk shows about people with bizarre problems?

Read Article of Faith 13 and challenge your family to look for and speak of the positive in others.

John 3:25–36
Happy for others

 Ask family members how they would feel if:

- You and a good friend both tried out for a part in the school play and your friend was chosen and you were not.
- You and a good friend both tried out for a spot on the basketball team and your friend was chosen and you were not.
- You and a good friend both ran for a student body office at school and your friend was elected and you were not.

Talk with your family about why it is not always easy to be happy about the success of others.

Then read together John 3:25–36 and discuss some of the following questions:

- What were John's disciples worried about? (Verse 26.)
- How did John feel about people following Jesus instead of him?
- What do you think John meant when he said, "He must increase, but I must decrease"?
- What part of John's testimony of Jesus in verses 28–36 impressed you the most?
- Why are people sometimes unwilling to compliment another? (Pride.)

- What does this teach us about John the Baptist's attitude toward Jesus?

Challenge your family to look for and compliment the good in others. To practice, have your family write in their journals a positive thing or two about every other member of the family. Invite them to share what they have written.

JOHN 4: JESUS TEACHES A WOMAN OF SAMARIA

John 4:5–42
How is Jesus Christ the living water?

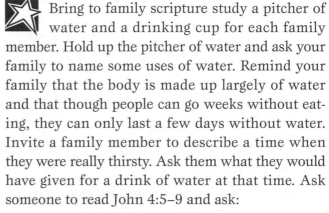 Bring to family scripture study a pitcher of water and a drinking cup for each family member. Hold up the pitcher of water and ask your family to name some uses of water. Remind your family that the body is made up largely of water and that though people can go weeks without eating, they can only last a few days without water. Invite a family member to describe a time when they were really thirsty. Ask them what they would have given for a drink of water at that time. Ask someone to read John 4:5–9 and ask:

- What area did Jesus travel to? (Samaria.)
- What time of the day did Jesus arrive at Jacob's well? (The "sixth hour" is noon.)
- What words in verse 6 indicate how Jesus felt following this journey?
- Why was the Samaritan woman surprised when Jesus asked her for a drink? (See Bible Dictionary, "Samaritans," 768.)

Pour a glass of water for each family member except for one. In that person's empty glass, place a piece of paper with John 4:10–14 written on it. Tell your family to drink the water and have the person with the empty glass read the verses. Ask your family:

- What did the woman think Jesus was offering her?
- What was He really offering her? ("Living water" represents the love God extends to his children through Jesus Christ; see also 1 Nephi 11:25.)

- In what way is the living water Jesus offers more desirable than what you just drank?
- How can someone obtain this living water?

Explain to your family that after Jesus taught the Samaritan woman about living water, He revealed His prophetic power. Take turns reading John 4:16–26. Discuss the following questions:

- What things did Jesus say to the woman that convinced her He was a prophet?
- How did Jesus teach the woman to worship God? (Verse 24.)
- How does the Joseph Smith Translation help us better understand what Jesus taught the woman about worshiping God? (See verse 24a.)
- What did Jesus reveal to the woman that told her He was more than a prophet? (Verses 25–26.)

Invite your family to silently read John 4:28–42 and look for how this Samaritan woman felt about Jesus' message and what she did about it. Ask:

- What came of this woman's excitement about the gospel message declared by Jesus?
- Who did she testify that He really was?
- What can we learn from her about our family's responsibility toward our friends and neighbors who are not of our faith?

Tell your family that water is life, especially in dry climates like Palestine. Testify that this is also true in a spiritual sense; people can die spiritually from the loss of "living water." Discuss ways your family can help quench the spiritual thirst of people you associate with.

John 4:43–54

"A prophet hath no honour in his own country"

 Ask your family the following questions:

- Have you ever known of a person who was more famous and respected in other places than in his own school, city, state, or country?
- In what ways might it be difficult for some members of a ward to accept a man who grew up in the ward from boyhood as a new bishop?

Read together John 4:43–45 and ask:

- What phrase describes how Jesus was accepted in His own country? (Verse 44.)
- How does this explain why Jesus visited other places in Galilee instead of His hometown? (Jesus was from Nazareth and was more accepted in Cana.)

Take turns reading John 4:46–54 and then ask:

- What happened in Cana that showed how the people there felt about the Savior?
- In what way did the "certain nobleman" show his faith in Jesus?
- How did Jesus reveal His power to perform miracles?

Discuss how your family can enjoy the Savior's power in their lives.

JOHN 5: HONORING THE FATHER

John 5:1–16

Headline news

Invite your family to imagine that they are a newspaper reporter covering an event described in the scriptures. Have them carefully read the events recorded in John 5:1–16 and gather information to prepare a "story" for the newspaper. This will require that they get all the facts and details correct and think about a possible headline for the editor to consider.

After each family member has had time to read and think about what they would write, have them share their ideas for a headline. Then have them close their scriptures and answer the following questions to see how well they recall the details of the story:

- What were the blind, halt, or withered folk on the porches waiting for? (Movement of the water.)
- What did the impotent man answer when Jesus asked him if he wanted to be made whole?
- What did Jesus then tell the man to do?
- How long had the man been sick?
- On what day was the man healed? (The Sabbath.)
- What did some of the Jews accuse the healed

man of doing wrong? (Carrying his bed on the Sabbath.)

- How did the healed man respond when he was asked who had told him to "Take up thy bed and walk"?
- What did certain Jews want to do to Jesus when they found out He was the one who "had done these things"? (Slay Him.)

When you have finished all the questions, have your family look in the verses to find any answers they couldn't remember. Ask, What is the real purpose of our Sabbath worship—or any other religious activity?

Share this insight from Elder Bruce R. McConkie: "Few things illustrate more pointedly the direful apostasy of the Jewish nation than their perverted concepts about Sabbath observance. What had once been a holy and sacred law, which stood as a sign identifying the Lord's own peculiar people, had been turned into a hollow mockery of the original divine intent." (*Doctrinal New Testament Commentary,* 1:188.)

Ask family members what they think was the original divine intent of the law of the Sabbath.

Discuss with your family ways they can better keep the Sabbath day holy.

John 5:17–47
The Father and Son relationship

 Ask your family:

- Have you ever been made fun of, or gotten into trouble for doing a good thing?
- What happened?
- How did you feel?

Read together John 5:16–18 and look for evidence that Jesus understood this kind of experience. Tell your family that Elder James E. Talmage said that Jesus' reply (John 5:17–47) to the Pharisees "stands as the most comprehensive sermon in scripture on the vital subject of the relationship between the Eternal Father and His Son, Jesus Christ" (*Jesus the Christ,* 208.)

Divide your family into three groups and assign one of the following sets of verses to each group: John 5:17–24; John 5:25–35; and John 5:36–47.

Have each group study their assigned verses and write what they learn about the relationship between God the Father and His Son, Jesus Christ. Allow each group to share their findings with the rest of the family. Ask, Why is it important to know this relationship between the Father and the Son?

Share the following by Elder Jeffrey R. Holland:

"Of the many magnificent purposes served in the life and ministry of the Lord Jesus Christ, one great aspect of that mission often goes uncelebrated. . . . It is the grand truth that in all that Jesus came to say and do, including and especially in His atoning suffering and sacrifice, He was showing us who and what God our Eternal Father is like, how completely devoted He is to His children in every age and nation. In word and in deed Jesus was trying to reveal and make personal to us the true nature of His Father, our Father in Heaven.

"He did this at least in part because then and now all of us need to know God more fully in order to love Him more deeply and obey Him more completely. . . .

". . . 'God does not look on sin with [the least degree of] allowance, but . . . the nearer we get to our heavenly Father, the more we are disposed to look with compassion on perishing souls; we feel that we want to take them upon our shoulders, and cast their sins behind our backs.'" (*Ensign,* Nov. 2003, 70–73.)

Encourage your family to think more about what they have learned about the Father as they pray in coming days.

John 5:28–29, 39
Searching the scriptures

 Have a family member read aloud John 5:39. Ask:

- Why does Jesus say we should "search the scriptures"?
- How can we make scripture study more meaningful?
- What is the difference between searching the scriptures and just reading them?
- What might the Jewish leaders have understood if they had searched and believed the scriptures?

Ask another family member to read aloud John 5:28–29 and explain it as best they can. Have another family member read Doctrine and Covenants 76:15–21. Ask, What knowledge and understanding have we been blessed with because Joseph Smith searched John 5:29? Invite family members to share how they have been strengthened by searching the scriptures.

JOHN 6: THE BREAD OF LIFE

John 6:1–21
The miraculous power of Jesus

Have someone read aloud John 5:39 and ask, In this verse, what did Jesus say the scriptures contain? (A testimony of Christ.) Tell your family that as they study John 6:1–21, you want them to look specifically for what these verses testify about Jesus Christ. Assign the following passages to various family members: John 6:1–4; John 6:5–11; John 6:12–15; John 6:16–20. For each passage, have family members respond to the following:

- What could we learn about Jesus from this passage? (There may be one or more correct answer in each passage.)
- What difference do you think it makes when a person believes and remembers this about Him?

Share the following application from Elder James E. Faust with your family regarding what we might learn from the story of how Jesus used the five loaves and two fishes:

"Some months ago, as Elder Spencer J. Condie and I were in the Salt Lake airport, we unexpectedly met a devoted and faithful couple who have been friends for long years. This couple has spent a lifetime of service, meekly, faithfully, and effectively trying to build up the Church in many places in the world. Elder Condie noted, 'Isn't it remarkable what people with five loaves and two fishes do to build up the kingdom of God.' . . .

"It has been said that this church does not necessarily attract great people but more often makes ordinary people great. Many nameless people with gifts equal only to five loaves and two small fishes magnify their callings and serve without attention or recognition, feeding literally thousands.

"What is the central characteristic of those having only five loaves and two fishes? What makes it possible, under the Master's touch, for them to serve, lift, and bless so that they touch for good the lives of hundreds, even thousands? After a lifetime of dealing in the affairs of men and women, I believe it is the ability to overcome personal ego and pride—both are enemies to the full enjoyment of the Spirit of God and walking humbly before him. The ego interferes with husbands and wives asking each other for forgiveness. It prevents the enjoyment of the full sweetness of a higher love. The ego often prevents parents and children from fully understanding each other. The ego enlarges our feelings of self-importance and worth. It blinds us to reality. Pride keeps us from confessing our sins and shortcomings to the Lord and working out our repentance.

"What of those who have talents equal only to two loaves and one fish? They do much of the hard, menial, unchallenging, poorly compensated work of the world. Life may not have been quite fair to them. They struggle to have enough to hold body and soul together. But they are not forgotten. If their talents are used to build the kingdom of God and serve others, they will fully enjoy the promises of the Savior. The great promise of the Savior is that they 'shall receive [their] reward, even peace in this world, and eternal life in the world to come' (D&C 59:23)." (*Ensign,* May 1994, 4–6.)

Ask your family the following questions:

- According to Elder Faust, who are those today with five loaves and two fishes?
- What quality in people allows the Lord to use them in miraculous ways?

Testify of the Lord's power to use us for things much greater than we imagine if we are humble, diligent, and have faith in His power.

John 6:22–58
"I am the bread of life"

 Take a loaf of bread to your family scripture study. Ask your family the following questions:

- What can this bread do for us?
- How long will its effects last in our bodies?
- How long can we go without it?
- When do you best enjoy eating bread?

Have a family member quickly tell in their own words the story of what happened with bread in John 6:5–14. Then read together John 6:22–26 and ask:

- Why were the people looking for Jesus?
- What could be wrong with these reasons for seeking Jesus?

Have someone read John 6:27 for Jesus' response. (You may want to tell your family that in these verses "meat" simply means food.) Ask, What should the people be seeking?

Before reading John 6:28–34 together, you may choose to review the story of God giving manna (bread from heaven) to the Israelites in the days of Moses. (See Exodus 16; see also Deuteronomy 8:1–3.) After reading John 6:28–34, ask:

- What do you think the people are asking of Jesus?
- What do you think Jesus is saying in response?
- When Jesus talks about bread in verse 33 and the people ask for bread in verse 34, do you think they are talking about the same thing? Why?

Read John 6:35 to your family. Draw attention to the loaf of bread you brought and the questions you asked about it. Ask, In what ways can Jesus be compared to bread? Have someone read John 6:47–51, and then ask your family: What specific comparisons to bread did Jesus make about Himself?

Read John 6:52 and ask: Do you think the Jews understood what Jesus was saying to them? Have family members read John 6:53–57 and invite one of them to tell in his own words what he thinks Jesus' message is. Ask:

- What ordinance of the gospel is designed to help us remember these teachings?
- How can the teachings of John 6 help make the sacrament more meaningful for you?
- If the sacrament is a commitment to "eat his flesh" and "drink his blood," how do we actually do these things on a daily basis?

Draw attention again to the loaf of bread. Share, or invite family members to share, ways that filling your life with the gospel of Jesus Christ has strengthened, nourished, sustained, and enriched your life—even as bread does your physical body—and invite them to make a commitment to strengthen their lives with a daily "feasting" on the things of Jesus Christ.

John 6:59–71
Rejecting or responding to the truth

Read John 6:59 to your family and invite them to give a summary of "these things" He taught in Capernaum. (See verses 22–58.) Have them include the entire background of what happened the day before He taught these things. (See verses 1–21.) Invite family members to read to themselves John 6:32–35, 48–51, 53–57 to remember specifically what Jesus taught. Have someone read aloud the response of "many" in John 6:60–61, 66. Ask:

- What do you think was so offensive in what Jesus taught?
- What do you think made Jesus' teachings "hard"?
- What do you think is the real problem?

Have a family member read the response of Simon Peter and the Twelve Apostles in John 6:67–69. Ask, Why do the Twelve choose to stay with Jesus and follow Him?

Share with your family the following statement:

"This thing which we call testimony is the great strength of the Church. It is the wellspring of faith and activity. It is difficult to explain. It is difficult to quantify. It is an elusive and mysterious thing, and yet it is as real and powerful as any force on the earth. . . .

"Personal testimony is the factor which turns people around in their living as they come into this Church. This is the element which motivates the membership to forsake all in the service of the Lord. This is the quiet, encouraging voice which sustains without pause those who walk in faith down to the last days of their lives." (Gordon B. Hinckley, *Ensign,* May 1998, 69–70.)

Invite family members to give examples of how their testimony has moved them to accept and do "hard" things. (See John 6:60.) Ask them how they think Peter and the Twelve became "sure." (See John 6:69.) Encourage your family to do the things that will daily keep their testimony strong and sure.

JOHN 7: OPINIONS OF MEN VS. A TESTIMONY OF CHRIST

John 7:1–13

Do you have an opinion or a testimony?

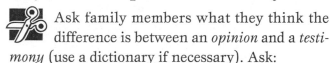 Ask family members what they think the difference is between an *opinion* and a *testimony* (use a dictionary if necessary). Ask:

- Why is a testimony of greater worth than an opinion?
- Why would you rather hear a testimony about Jesus than just an opinion?

Read together John 7:1–2 and ask:

- Why wouldn't Jesus "walk in Jewry"? (Jewry refers to the area around Jerusalem.)
- What was the "feast of tabernacles" and where was it held? (See Bible Dictionary, 673.)
- What problem might Jesus experience if He attended the "feast of tabernacles"?

Divide your family into two groups. Invite one group to read John 7:3–5 and the other group to read John 7:10–13. Have each group look for opinions or testimonies in the words expressed by the people in their assigned passage. Discuss the following questions:

- What do you learn about Jesus' "brethren" or brothers in verses 3–5? (Footnote 3*a* leads to references that clarify that these were His brothers, or half brothers, sons of Joseph.)
- How might a testimony spoken by the power of the Holy Ghost help people to know the truth?

Challenge your family to have more than an *opinion* about the Savior and to develop a deep and abiding testimony of Jesus Christ.

John 7:14–32

Jesus teaches in the temple at Jerusalem

Explain to your family that the "feast of tabernacles" took place almost six months before Jesus' last Passover and His death. Take turns reading John 7:14–19 and then ask:

- From whom did Jesus receive His education and doctrine? (James E. Talmage wrote, "His Teacher, greater even than Himself, was the Eternal Father, whose will He proclaimed." [*Jesus the Christ,* 400.])
- How did the people respond to the things Jesus taught?
- What did He accuse some of them of trying to do to Him? (Verse 19.)

Invite your family to silently read John 7:26–32 and compare the reactions of the Jews with the reactions of the leaders of the Jews. It may be helpful to discuss some or all of the following questions:

- How was Jesus' doctrine received by the Jews?
- How was it received by their religious leaders?
- Why did they find it so difficult to believe He was "the very Christ"?
- Why do some people living today find it difficult to really believe in the Savior?

Read together John 7:17. Ask:

- How can anyone know that Christ's doctrine is true? ("One learns the value of work by working, of play by playing, of food by eating; and one learns the value of faith by exercising faith, of love by trying to love fellow men. Even so, if one would have faith in God, he must at least say to himself, 'It could be that he lives. I shall give the idea a fair trial. I shall do his will. I shall read the scriptures, especially the life of Jesus, and I shall try to live as he says God would have me live.'" [Bennion, *Introduction to the Gospel,* 18.])
- What might have happened among the Jews had they practiced the principle in this verse?

Ask your family if they have ever tested a gospel principle by practicing it and discovering its truthfulness. Invite those who have to share their experience.

John 7:37–43

Why did the Jews have so much trouble believing in Jesus?

 Display a clear container of water. Have a family member read John 7:37–39. Ask:

- What did Jesus testify about Himself?
- Why do you think water is a good representation of the Savior? (Water is essential for life and was an important part of the "feast of tabernacles" celebration [see Bible Dictionary, 673].)
- How are Jesus' words like water to a spiritually thirsty person?

Explain to your family that even though Jesus bore a powerful testimony and invited the Jews to "come unto me," it had an interesting effect on the Jews. Read together John 7:40–43 to discover how the Jews reacted to this doctrine. Ask:

- Who did many of the people believe Jesus was? (A prophet or the Christ.)
- What was the question that caused a serious division among the people?
- How do you think such a seemingly minor issue became such a large cause for division among the people?

Share the following statement by Elder Bruce R. McConkie: "'Shall Christ come out of Galilee? Hath not our scripture said, That Christ cometh of the seed of David, and out of the town of Bethlehem . . . ?' How . . . adept Lucifer is at quoting scripture for his own purposes. . . . Now the evil one quotes holy writ by the mouths of his ministers. . . . as far as the record shows, there was none to refute their false assertions. Of course the Seed of David was to come from the City of David, from Bethlehem, as their scriptures said; but their scriptures also said that he was to come not only from Galilee, but from Nazareth in Galilee." (*Mortal Messiah*, 3:137.)

Ask your family if it would have helped the Jews if Jesus had simply told them where He was from. List the following references on a sheet of paper: John 7:16; John 7:18; John 7:28–29 and John 7:33–34. Have family members choose a reference and read it, looking for where Jesus said He was from. Ask:

- Where did Jesus say He was from or who had sent Him? (Father in Heaven.)
- Why do you think it was more important to Jesus that the Jews believe He was sent from His Father in Heaven than simply being from Nazareth or Bethlehem?

John 7:44–53

The Jews could not "take him"

 Read together John 7:44–53. Ask your family:

- How many times did the Pharisees determine to "take him"? (See also verses 30, 32.)
- Why did those sent to arrest Jesus fail to do so? (Verse 46.)
- What does this say about the power of teaching by the Holy Spirit?

Explain to your family that the religious leaders felt they had scriptural proof that Jesus was not the Christ because they knew He was from Galilee (John 7:50–52) and the Messiah was to be born in Bethlehem. The Pharisees did not want to believe and found reasons not to do so while those who wanted to believe were moved by the Spirit.

Discuss ways your family can avoid making the same mistake as the Pharisees (search the scriptures and act upon the Savior's words). Ask your family to share what they have learned that helps them believe in Jesus Christ.

JOHN 8: "THE TRUTH SHALL MAKE YOU FREE"

John 8:1–11

Between a "stone" and a hard place

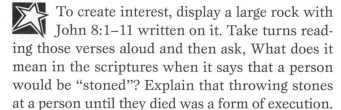 To create interest, display a large rock with John 8:1–11 written on it. Take turns reading those verses aloud and then ask, What does it mean in the scriptures when it says that a person would be "stoned"? Explain that throwing stones at a person until they died was a form of execution.

Read Deuteronomy 22:22 to your family and ask:

- What seems wrong with the situation in John 8:2–5 in light of the information in Deuteronomy 22:22? (There should be a man punished as well as a woman.)
- Why did they want to know Jesus' thoughts regarding this woman? (To trick Him so they could condemn Him.)
- If Jesus said she should be put to death, how would Jesus be condemned before the Romans? (The people were not allowed to put anyone to death without Roman consent. See John 18:31.)
- If Jesus said that she should not be put to death, how could Jesus be condemned before the Jews? (Jesus' decision would contradict the law of Moses.)
- What do we learn from Jesus' response in John 8:6–11?
- Why do you think people like to point out and condemn the mistakes of others?
- Why do you think the eldest left before the youngest?
- How do you think this event affected the woman's life?

Share with your family that the Joseph Smith Translation adds the following to verse 11: "And the woman glorified God from that hour, and believed on his name." (This passage is not included in the LDS edition of the Bible.)

Consider sharing your testimony of how much the Savior loves each of us and how much He wants to help us and not condemn us.

John 8:12–36

Are you free or in bondage?

Assign the groups of verses below to different family members. After they have had time to study their verses, discuss together the questions that accompany the verses.

1. John 8:12–18
- How is Jesus "the light of the world"?
- Why did they say His teaching wasn't true? (Verse 13.)
- Who else bears witness of Jesus? (Verse 18.)

2. John 8:19–30
- How does coming to know the Son help us come to know the Father?
- How does Jesus know what to say and do? (Verses 28–29.)
- According to 2 Nephi 32:2–3, how can we know what things we should do and say?
- What do we learn about Jesus from John 8:28–29?

3. John 8:31–36
- What do we need to do to become disciples of Jesus?
- How does committing sin make you a "servant of sin"?
- How does a sin such as using alcohol, drugs, or tobacco make us slaves socially, physically, and emotionally?
- According to the age of your family, you could also ask your family how other sins, such as cheating, fighting, and sexual activity outside of marriage, affect a person socially, physically, and emotionally?
- How does knowing and keeping commandments make us free socially, physically, and emotionally?

4. John 8:33
- What are a few nations the Jews had been in bondage to? (Egypt, Babylon, Persia, Greece, Rome.)
- Why do you think the Jews stated that they were never in bondage, in light of the fact that they were paying taxes to Rome and were under Roman law?

Ask family members to summarize what they have learned about bondage and freedom from these verses. Share your testimony of the freedom that comes from obedience.

John 8:37–50

The fruit does not fall far from the tree

Draw a simple picture of a fruit tree and under the tree write, "The fruit does not fall far from the tree." Show the picture to your family and ask them what they think it means. Tell your family that the saying is usually used to explain how children are often like their parents. Ask your family to tell of ways that the children in your family are like their parents (for example, how they look or the way they act).

Read together John 8:37–50 and have your family look for how Jesus uses that same sort of comparison with the Jews. Discuss the following questions as you read:

- Who did the Jews claim was their father? (Verse 39.)
- What did Jesus say they were doing that Abraham's children would not do? (Verses 39–40.)
- Who did the Jews then claim as their "Father"? (Verse 41.)
- If the fruit (the child) does not fall far from the tree (the parents), what would the Jews do if they were Heavenly Father's children? (Verse 42.)
- Who were the Jews acting like instead? (Verses 44–49.)

Set a goal as a family to continue to develop those qualities that will make them more like their Father in Heaven.

John 8:51–59
The Jews desire to stone the Savior

Read John 8:59 to your family. Pick up the large rock from the John 8:1–11 lesson idea and ask, What could have happened to make the religious leaders want to pick up rocks and stone Jesus? Have your family look for the answer to that question while you read John 8:51–58 together. Ask:

- What did Jesus teach them about death? (Verse 51.)
- What did Jesus teach them about Abraham? (Verse 56; that Abraham saw the coming of Jesus Christ.)
- Why did what Jesus said about being before Abraham make them want to stone Him?

To help answer that question, read Exodus 3:13–14 as a family and ask:

- What question did Moses ask the Lord?
- What was Moses told is one of the Lord's names? (I AM.)
- So what was Jesus really telling the Jews in

John 8:58? (That He was the Son of God who also is called I AM. See also the explanation by Elder Talmage below, if needed.)

- How does that help explain why the Jews got so angry?
- Why did the Jews seem to prefer a God who was far away in the Old Testament times but not one who was right there among them? (See John 8:45–47.)

"This was an unequivocal and unambiguous declaration of our Lord's eternal Godship. By the awful title I AM He had made Himself known to Moses and thereafter was so known in Israel. As already shown, it is the equivalent of 'Yahveh,' or 'Jahveh,' now rendered 'Jehovah,' and signifies 'The Self-existent One,' 'The Eternal,' 'The First and the Last.'" (*Jesus the Christ*, 382–83.)

JOHN 9: JESUS HEALS THE MAN BORN BLIND

John 9:1–7
How can clay heal?

 Bring a small amount of clay or mud to your scripture study. Ask your family:

- What is this?
- What can you do with it?
- What do you think the Son of God could do with it?

Invite your family to read John 9:1–7. Ask:

- How did Jesus make the clay and what did He do with it? (Verse 6.)
- What did the Savior tell the man to do after He applied the clay to His eyes? (Verse 7.)
- Do you think Jerusalem mud has special healing ability or did Jesus heal the blind man?
- Why do you think Jesus would choose to heal the man in this manner?

Tell your family that often there is a second or symbolic meaning besides the obvious one written on the page. Note that Jesus anointed the man's eyes with clay (material from this world) and then washed the clay (the things of this world) away. This is what helped the blind man to see. Ask:

- How can removing the things of this world help us to better see spiritually?
- What are some things you would like to change in yourself to improve your vision of what you ought to be doing?

Have your family describe some ways the Savior tries to strengthen our faith today. Share with your family a time when your faith was stretched and strengthened.

John 9:8–41
How does conversion take place?

Assign the following characters to your family members (you many need to assign more than one character per person): narrator, neighbors, Jesus, man born blind, mother and father of the man born blind, Jews, and the Pharisees.

Tell your family you are going to study how a man born blind was healed and converted and became a follower of Jesus Christ. Have the assigned characters read and act out their parts in John 9:8–34.

After your family has finished the reading, ask:

- What was the day of the week when this healing took place? (Verse 14.)
- Why would this matter? (See Bible Dictionary, "Sabbath," 764, third paragraph.)

Lead your family carefully through the following verses helping them see the change that came over the man born blind:

- Verse 11—The blind man called Jesus a "man."
- Verse 17—The blind man viewed Jesus as a "prophet."
- Verse 33—The blind man added further insight when he said that Jesus was a man of God.

As a family, discuss what these verses suggest happened to the man born blind as he learned more about Jesus Christ. Invite a member of your family to read John 9:34–41. Then ask:

- What did the Pharisees do to the man born blind? (Verse 34.)

- What does it mean that the Pharisees "cast him out"?
- According to verse 38, what was the final step in the conversion process for the man born blind?
- Why did Jesus heal the man born blind? (Verse 39.)
- What can we learn about the conversion *process* from the experience of the man born blind?

Testify of your conversion (whether as a new member or as a lifelong member). Let your family members know how important it is that they gain a testimony for themselves so that they can become converted.

JOHN 10: JESUS IS THE GOOD SHEPHERD

John 10:1–42
Why is Christ called the Good Shepherd?

Ask your family to close their eyes while they listen to some voices. Tell them they are going to try and guess to whom the voices belong. You might play a voice recording of some famous voices, or invite one or two family members to say a few words. Consider listening to a voice recording of the prophet or a member of the Quorum of the Twelve Apostles, if available. You could also play a recording of an often-watched movie or television show. When finished, ask:

- Whose voices did you hear?
- How were you able to recognize their voices?
- Why do you recognize some voices so easily while others are more difficult?
- In Palestine, where did the shepherd often walk when moving his sheep?
- How is the relationship of a "shepherd" to his sheep different from the relationship of a "sheepherder" to his sheep?

Take turns reading John 10:1–18 and discuss these questions:

- What is a "hireling" and how is he different from the shepherd?
- Who are Jesus' "sheep"? (See also 3 Nephi 15:21.)

- What did Jesus say He would do that would show His love for His sheep?
- According to John 10:27, how do we become Jesus' sheep?
- Why is Jesus called the Good Shepherd?

Ask a family member to read aloud John 10:28–33. Ask:

- What did Jesus teach that angered the Jews?
- How can you tell the Jews were not happy with Jesus? (Verse 31.)
- Why did the Jews want Jesus dead? (Verse 33.)

Have your family read John 10:34–42 to discover how Jesus answered the Jews' complaints against Him and how the Jews reacted at this point.

Tell your family that today there are many who act as shepherds over us. Ask them to name a few. (Example: parents, priesthood leaders.) Conclude by asking family members to share how they feel knowing that Christ knows each of us personally, by name, and that He has sent prophets to teach us in these latter days.

JOHN 11: JESUS RAISES LAZARUS FROM THE DEAD

John 11:1–57
Lazarus restored to life

Show your family a live flower, branch, or leaf and a dead flower, branch, or leaf. Ask if there is any way to make the dead flower, branch, or leaf look like the live one. Ask, Who has power to put life back into something that is dead? Tell your family that John chapter 11 gives an account that demonstrates Jesus' power over death. Read together John 11:1–10 and ask the following questions:

- How were Lazarus, Mary, and Martha related? (Verses 1–3.)
- What feelings did Jesus have for them? (Verse 5.)
- Where did Mary, Martha, and Lazarus live? (Verse 1.) Have your family find Bethany in the Bible Maps.

- Where was Jesus when He received word that Lazarus was ill? (John 10:40.)
- How long did Jesus delay His coming to Bethany after learning of Lazarus's sickness? (Verse 6.)
- Why would Jesus wait for two days? (See verse 4.)

Invite your family to look for the comparison Jesus used to describe what was wrong with Lazarus as you read together John 11:11–16. Ask:

- When Jesus said, "Our friend Lazarus sleepeth," what did His disciples think He meant? (Verses 11–12.)
- What did Jesus then "plainly" tell them? (Verse 14.)
- In what ways is sleep symbolic of death?

For verses 17–46, assign family members to portray the following characters: Jesus, Martha, Mary, and Lazarus. Depending on the age of family members, you may choose to have one reader, while those assigned portray their parts, or, you may choose to have a narrator with each assigned character reading their part as they act it out.

After reading, ask the following questions:

- How long is a furlong? (Verse 18, footnote *a*.)
- What did Martha think when Jesus told her Lazarus would rise again? (Verses 23–24.)
- What did Jesus teach her about Himself and the Resurrection? (Verse 25.)
- What was Martha's testimony? (Verse 27.)
- Why do you think Jesus wept?
- What was Martha's concern when Jesus told them to take away the stone? (Verse 39.)

Share this insight about Jewish beliefs: "To the Jews the term of four days had special significance; it was the popular belief among them that by the fourth day the spirit had finally and irrevocably departed from the vicinity of the corpse so that decompostion could go on apace." (McConkie, *Doctrinal New Testament Commentary*, 1:533.)

- Why did Jesus pray to Heavenly Father before He raised Lazarus? (Verses 41–42.)
- What did Jesus say to Lazarus? (Verse 43.)
- How was Lazarus clothed when he came forth? (Verse 44.)

- How do you think Mary and Martha felt as they witnessed this great miracle?
- How would you have felt if you had been there?
- How did the other people who witnessed this miracle respond? (Verses 45–46.)

Notice the reaction of the chief priests and Pharisees in verses 48 and 53.

- Why do you think the Pharisees and chief priests did not accept the miracle and follow Jesus?
- How does this miracle strengthen your knowledge that Jesus is the Son of God?

Share your testimony of the Savior's power over physical death and more importantly His power over spiritual death.

JOHN 12: JESUS PREPARES FOR AND PROPHESIES OF HIS DEATH

John 12:1–50
What do you think of Jesus?

Ask your family to list some of the different ways people might answer the question, What do you think of Jesus? Write some of the answers on a sheet of paper in a continuum similar to the one below.

Divide your family into three groups and assign one of the following passages to each group: John 12:1–9; John 12:10–19; and John 12:20–22, 42–43. Have each group search their scripture passage and identify those people (or groups of people) mentioned and determine where they would fit on the continuum of opinions about Jesus. Write the names of the people or groups on the continuum where they belong. As you talk about Mary, it

might be helpful to share the following information:

"Spikenard was a costly, scented ointment imported from the Himalayas. A pound of pure spikenard could be sold for over three hundred denarii, the better part of a year's wages." (Ogden, *Where Jesus Walked,* 133.) Ask:

- How does this quotation help explain what Mary thought of Jesus?
- What actions helped you see what others thought of Jesus?
- Why do you think they had such thoughts about Jesus?
- What similar things do some people do today that show what they think of Jesus?
- Where do you think someone watching your actions over the last couple of days would put you on the continuum of opinions about Jesus? Why?
- If we truly love Jesus, what will we do? (See John 14:15.)

Testify to your family that what we think of Christ will most truly be shown in our actions. Share the following by President Gordon B. Hinckley and invite family members to listen for ways we can show what we truly think of Jesus:

"What then shall we do with Jesus who is called Christ?

"Let us live with the certain knowledge that some day 'we shall be brought to stand before God, knowing even as we know now, and have a bright recollection of all our guilt' (Alma 11:43.) Let us live today knowing that we shall live forever. Let us live with the conviction that whatever principle of intelligence and beauty and truth and goodness we make a part of our life here, it will rise with us in the resurrection. . . .

"What shall we do then with Jesus who is called Christ? 'He hath shewed thee, O man, what is good; and what doth the Lord require of thee, but

Jesus is the Son of God and the Savior of the world.	Jesus seems like a good person and a good influence on people.	He's OK, but other things are more important to me.	I don't really know. He doesn't really matter to me.	It really bugs me that people actually believe that stuff.

to do justly, and to love mercy, and to walk humbly with thy God?' (Micah 6:8.). . . .

"What shall we do with Jesus who is called Christ?

"Learn of him. Search the scriptures for they are they which testify of him. Ponder the miracle of his life and mission. Try a little more diligently to follow his example and observe his teachings." (*Ensign,* Dec. 1983, 3–5.)

Invite family members to tell what they think they can do to show what the Savior really means to them.

John 12:23–41, 44–45
What do you see and hear?

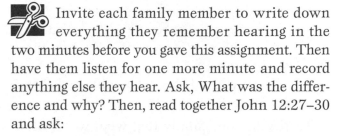 Invite each family member to write down everything they remember hearing in the two minutes before you gave this assignment. Then have them listen for one more minute and record anything else they hear. Ask, What was the difference and why? Then, read together John 12:27–30 and ask:

- What did some people hear?
- What did others hear?
- What do you think made the difference in what was heard?
- How does John 12:37–40 help you understand why people heard different things?

You may need to explain that John was quoting Isaiah in these verses. Isaiah prophesied that the Messiah's [Jesus'] ministry would happen in such a way that people would have to *choose* to see and believe by revelation or else they would remain blind and unconverted. Ask:

- How might John 12:44–45 explain why people didn't hear the voice described in John 12:27–30?
- What are some of the ways we can hear the voice of the Father and the Son?

To answer this last question, it might be helpful to have one family member read Doctrine and Covenants 18:34–36 and another read the following commentary on John 12:27–30 by Elder Harold B. Lee:

"Only the Master, apparently, knew that God had spoken. So often today, men and women are living so far apart from things spiritual that when the Lord is speaking to their physical hearing, to their minds with no audible sound, or to them through his authorized servants who, when directed by the Spirit, are as his own voice, they hear only a noise as did they at Jerusalem. Likewise, they receive no inspired wisdom, nor inward assurance, that the mind of the Lord has spoken through his prophet leaders." (Conference Report, Oct. 1966, 116.)

Invite family members to share examples of times when they have recognized God speaking to them through His servants or through the scriptures.

JOHN 13: THE LAST SUPPER

John 13:1–17
Why did Jesus wash the disciples' feet?

 Ask your family, Would you rather be served, or be the servant? Why?

Also ask them to describe some of the most significant acts of service they have known someone to do. Then, ask each family member to silently read John 13:1–17 to learn about one of the greatest acts of service the Savior performed. When they have finished, discuss the following questions:

- Why would some people be hesitant to wash the feet of another?
- In Bible times, who normally washed people's feet? (Usually the servant in the home.)
- What was Jesus showing the Apostles by washing their feet? (Verses 14–15.)
- Who is the greatest in the kingdom of God? (See Matthew 20:27.)
- Why do you think Peter did not want Jesus to wash his feet?
- Why do some have a difficult time letting others serve them?
- What can we learn from these verses about giving and receiving service?

Write the names of all your family members on slips of paper. Put the slips of paper in a bowl and allow everyone to draw a slip. Encourage them to render an act of anonymous service to that person sometime during the day.

John 13:18–30
Jesus identifies his betrayer

 Show your family a picture of the Last Supper in the upper room. (See *Gospel Art Kit,* no. 225.) Ask if they can identify where it is, or why that room is so special. If they cannot, ask your family to close their eyes and imagine being one of the Twelve Apostles in this room during the Last Supper. Imagine partaking of the Passover meal, having Jesus wash your feet, and enjoying a few quiet moments with Jesus. Read John 13:18–21 aloud to your family while they keep their eyes closed. Ask the following:

- What are you thinking?
- Could you possibly be the betrayer?
- Do you want to know who that betrayer is?
- What would you feel if you knew who the betrayer was?

Have everyone open their eyes and then take turns reading John 13:22–30. Ask:

- How did Jesus identify the betrayer? (Verse 26.)
- What were the Apostles wondering? (Verse 25.)
- What is a sop? (Use footnote 26*a.*)
- What did Judas do after receiving the sop? (Verse 30.)
- If Jesus knew who would betray Him, why didn't He do anything to stop Judas?
- What does this teach about agency?

Talk about ways a person might "betray" Jesus today. Discuss why those would be wrong and also discuss ways we can exercise our agency to support and sustain Jesus. Share your feelings about the importance of being true to one's testimony.

John 13:31–35
Love one another

As a family, sing or read the words to "Love One Another." (*Hymns,* no. 308.) Ask your family where these words came from. Read John 13:31–35 and have your family watch for the words they have just sung. Ask:

- How did Jesus exemplify these words?

- How will people know if we are disciples of Jesus Christ?
- What can we do to love each other in our home?
- If we show love to one another, what are we becoming? (Verse 35.)

Set a goal to have each family member memorize John 13:34–35. When all have accomplished that goal, plan a special activity the family will enjoy and that will allow all family members to feel each other's, and the Savior's, love.

JOHN 14: CHRIST TEACHES US OF THE GODHEAD

John 14:1–4
Jesus promises mansions for us

Show your family the following pictures of a heart and a mansion.

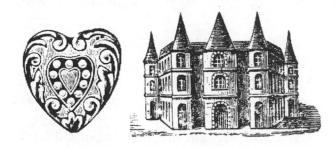

Have everyone read John 14:1–4. Ask what these pictures have to do with the verses. Ask:

- Why do you think the disciples' hearts were troubled (worried) as indicated in verse 1?
- How would the Savior's words in verses 2–3 help them "be not troubled"?
- How would you feel if the Savior promised you a mansion in heaven with Him?

Invite family members to think about times when they are worried and times when they are more confident about their lives and the future. Ask:

- What seems to be going on in your life during your worried times?
- What seems to be going on in your life during your confident times?
- During which of those times do you feel the closest to the Savior?

• Ask your family how they would feel if they built a large mansion for someone and then that person decided not to move into it?

Share your testimony that Jesus has truly done everything necessary for us to inherit a mansion in the presence of our Heavenly Father, but we must choose to receive this great gift by doing what is required to gain entrance to the place where that mansion is prepared.

John 14:2, 7–13, 16, 20–21, 24, 28, 30–31
Jesus teaches us of His Father

Share with your family the following statement by the Prophet Joseph Smith: "If men do not comprehend the character of God, they do not comprehend themselves." (*Teachings of the Prophet Joseph Smith,* 343.)

Ask one member of your family to act as scribe and record the truths shared by the family about Heavenly Father while you discuss the following questions:

• What do you think the Prophet Joseph Smith meant by this?
• What are some ways you have gained a greater understanding of who Heavenly Father is and what He is like?
• What are some of the more important truths you have learned about Heavenly Father?

Tell your family that John 14 contains many things that Jesus taught His disciples regarding our Father in Heaven. Divide your family into two groups. Give each group a sheet of paper and pencil. Ask one group to search John 14:2, 7–13, and the other group to search John 14:20–21, 24, 28, 30–31. Have both groups list on their papers what these verses teach about Heavenly Father. Have each group compare their list with the list compiled by the scribe and then share with the other group the new things they learned. Have the scribe add these things to the list. Ask your family to look at the list of things they know about Heavenly Father. Ask, Why does it matter that we know these things? Invite them to choose one thing on the list and tell how it could make a difference in a person's life if they truly believed it and remembered it each day.

Ask your family to find the witness that Jesus Christ bears of His Father in verses 10 and 28. Bear your testimony of Heavenly Father to your family. Have your family look at Jesus' feelings for His Father. Suggest that as family members pray, they express their love for Heavenly Father.

John 14:15–18, 25–27
The Comforter

Wrap one family member in a big, fluffy quilt and ask the person how it feels. Ask the rest of the family how they feel when they wake up in the middle of the night because they are cold and then pull a big, fluffy comforter over them.

Tell your family that there are two Comforters to comfort us. Read aloud John 14:16–18, 25–27. Ask:

• According to verse 16, footnote *a,* and verse 26, who are the two Comforters?
• What will the Comforters do for us? (Verse 18; see all of the footnotes.)

Teach your family that the comfort spoken of is the assurance that while Jesus is not present we still belong to Him, and that He has provided a way for us to be where He is. (See verses 2–6.) Furthermore, not only will we receive the assurance that we belong to Him, but this same gift of the Holy Ghost will "teach you all things, and bring all things to your remembrance" (verse 26) so we will know the way (verses 5–7).

Share with your family President Lorenzo Snow's description: "There is a way by which persons can keep their consciences clear before God and man, and that is to preserve within them the spirit of God, which is the spirit of revelation to every man and woman. It will reveal to them, even in the simplest of matters, what they shall do, by making suggestions to them. We should try to learn the nature of this spirit, that we may understand its suggestions, and then we will always be able to do right. This is the grand privilege of every Latter-day Saint. We know that it is our right to have the manifestations of the spirit every day of our lives. . . . The spirit is in every man and every woman . . . that knows just exactly what to say to them. From the time we receive the Gospel, go down into the waters of baptism and have hands laid upon us afterwards for the gift of the Holy Ghost, we have a friend, if we do not drive it from us by doing wrong. That friend is the Holy Spirit, the Holy Ghost, which partakes of the things of God and shows them unto us. This is a grand means that the Lord has provided for us, that we may know the light, and not be groveling continually in the dark." (Conference Report, Apr. 1899, 52.)

Teach your family that the Holy Ghost is a great blessing to us and that this chapter also teaches a great deal about the Second Comforter. Read verses 16–18, 21 and 23. Joseph Smith makes this Second Comforter very clear to us:

"Now what is this other Comforter? It is no more nor less than the Lord Jesus Christ Himself; . . . when any man obtains this last Comforter, he will have the personage of Jesus Christ to attend him, or appear unto him from time to time, and even He will manifest the Father unto him, and they will take up their abode with him, and the visions of the heavens will be opened unto him, and the Lord will teach him face to face, and he may have a perfect knowledge of the mysteries of the Kingdom of God." (*Teachings of the Prophet Joseph Smith*, 150–51.)

Have your family look through verses 16–18, 21 and 23 again and find what is needful in order to be blessed with the Second Comforter. Ask your family if there is anything in the verses that would discourage us from seeking the Second Comforter. Talk about what a great blessing it is to have the Holy Ghost in our lives. Ask:

- Should we not seek after that which has been promised to us?
- Would it not be an even greater blessing to have the Second Comforter? (Verse 27.)
- What can we do to work toward this greatest of all blessings? (Verse 15.)

Some Christians believe that the Father and the Son are one individual. Invite one member of your family to read aloud John 14:16 and then ask the family what evidence they can find in that verse that the Father and the Son are separate individuals. (Jesus would not pray to Himself.) Encourage family members to write the following in the margin of John 14:16: *Evidence that the Father and the Son are distinct and separate individuals.* Bear witness of this truth.

JOHN 15: JESUS CHRIST IS THE TRUE VINE

John 15:1–8
What is our relationship to the Lord?

Show your family a plant of some kind and ask what happens when a leaf or branch is cut off from the rest of the plant. How is our relationship to the Savior like this?

Tell your family that in John 15:1–8 the Savior compares Himself to a vine and His followers to the branches. Read those verses together and write on a sheet of paper the different symbols and what each symbol represents. Your list might look like the following:

- Vine = Jesus
- Husbandman (Gardener) = Heavenly Father
- Branches = Us
- Fruit = Good works

Discuss the following questions:

- What does Jesus teach us by this analogy?
- What do you think it means to "abide" with a person?
- What things help us "abide" in Christ?
- What things cut us off from the vine?
- What would happen to us if we were cut off from the Lord? (Our good works would dry up, and we would eventually die spiritually.)

Show your family some pruning shears and ask:

- What are these for?
- What is pruning? (Cutting out excessive or dead branches.)
- Which verse has to do with pruning? (You may need to explain that "purgeth" in verse 2 means "to prune.")
- What is the purpose of pruning? (So the tree or plant uses its energy to produce fruit or flowers, instead of other growth.)
- If you were a plant, what might you think as someone "pruned" your branches?
- Do people ever get angry or upset when they have trials?

- What does the story teach about God and trials?
- What are some cluttering activities that God may want to "prune" out of our lives?
- How does God do this with full-time missionaries?

Challenge your family to cut out things in life that get in the way of doing what is right.

John 15:9–15

Is it better to love or be loved?

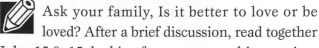 Ask your family, Is it better to love or be loved? After a brief discussion, read together John 15:9–15, looking for answers to this question. Ask:

- How can we "abide" in the Lord's love? (Verse 10.)
- What example does the Savior give for how we should love others? (Verse 12.)
- Do you think it would be more difficult to die for the Savior or live for Him? Why?
- How would a person live for the Savior?
- What does Jesus do (and has done) to show He is a friend to us?
- How can you be a friend to Jesus? (Verse 14.)

Share the following statement from Joseph Smith: "Sectarian priests cry out concerning me, and ask, 'Why is it this babbler gains so many followers, and retains them?' I answer, It is because I possess the principle of love. All I can offer the world is a good heart and a good hand.

"The Saints can testify whether I am willing to lay down my life for my brethren. If it has been demonstrated that I have been willing to die for a 'Mormon,' I am bold to declare before Heaven that I am just as ready to die in defending the rights of a Presbyterian, a Baptist, or a good man of any other denomination." (*Teachings of the Prophet Joseph Smith*, 313.)

Have your family write in their journals ways they can be better friends to others as Jesus has been a friend to them.

John 15:16

Who does the choosing?

 Ask your family:

- Who calls full-time missionaries?
- Who calls us to serve in Church callings?
- Why can't we call ourselves to serve in these callings?

Have your family read John 15:16. Ask, Which Article of Faith does this relate to? Have your family recite or read Articles of Faith 1:5.

John 15:17–27

What kinds of things does the world hate?

Share the following statement by the Prophet Joseph Smith: "The trials [the Saints] have had to pass through shall work together for their good and prepare them for the society [company] of those who have come up out of great tribulation, washed their robes, and made them white in the blood of the Lamb. Marvel not then if you are persecuted, but remember the words of the Savior, 'The servant is not above his Lord; if they have persecuted me, they will persecute you also.' . . . Afflictions, persecutions, imprisonments, and deaths we must expect according to the scriptures." (*Joseph Smith's Commentary on the Bible,* 139.) Ask:

- What would you say the Prophet is trying to teach?
- What kinds of persecutions have you seen or experienced?

Read John 15:17–27 as a family and ask:

- What kinds of things would a Latter-day Saint do that would cause the world to hate him or her? (Be different from the world.)
- If we are hated by the world, whose company are we in? (Verse 18.)
- If we are choosing the right, how can we expect the world to treat us?
- What comfort does the Lord give to those who are afflicted? (Verse 26.)

Testify to your family that choosing the right will not necessarily make life easy or that everyone will like you, but you will have peace, and it will be worth it. (See D&C 59:23.)

JOHN 16: JESUS TEACHES THE MISSION OF THE HOLY GHOST

John 16:1–13
Comfort from the Comforter

With your family, discuss the names and nicknames that have been given to family members and tell how or why those names were given. Read together John 16:7–13 and look for names that the Holy Ghost is known by. (Comforter, Spirit of Truth.) Discuss ways these other names appropriately describe the Holy Ghost.

Have a family member read John 16:1–6. Ask:

- What warnings did Jesus give His disciples?
- Why did Jesus give them these warnings? (See verses 4–5.)
- How might the Apostles have felt knowing that Christ would soon be leaving them? (See verse 6.)

Read John 16:7 to your family and have them listen for another reason why the Savior must leave His disciples. Ask:

- Whom did the Savior promise to send?
- What is a more familiar name than the "Comforter"? (Holy Ghost.)
- How does the name "Comforter" reassure us of what He will do for us?
- How might the Holy Ghost help the disciples face the trials described in verses 2–3?
- How might the Holy Ghost help them when the Savior leaves them alone?

Read the following from Elder James E. Faust:

"We find solace in Christ through the agency of the Comforter, and he extends this invitation to us: 'Come unto me, all ye that labour and are heavy laden, and I will give you rest.' (Matt. 11:23)." (*Ensign,* May 1992, 8.)

Remind your family that just as a righteous parent would never leave their children alone without someone watching over them, Christ never leaves

us alone. No matter how difficult life gets, the Holy Ghost can help us in our time of need. Ask your family to share times when the Holy Ghost has comforted them. Challenge them to work every day to be worthy of this important gift from God and thereby enjoy peace in a troubled world.

John 16:16–33
The Savior answers the disciples' questions with a parable

Ask your family to think of or relate a time when someone was separated or lost from the rest of the family or friends. Ask them what emotions or feelings they or the other person experienced. Invite a family member to read John 16:16–19. Ask:

- What were the disciples worried about and what did they not understand?
- What do you think the Savior was referring to? (His death and Resurrection.)

Tell your family that Jesus answered His disciples' questions with a parable. As you read together John 16:20–24, look for ways the parable relates to the question. Ask:

- How will the disciples respond when Jesus leaves them?
- How will the world respond?
- What experience from a woman's life does Jesus use to describe pain, sorrow, and joy?
- How will the death and Resurrection of Jesus Christ be filled with pain and sorrow but eventually overcome with joy?
- Can you name a time in your life when sorrow was turned into joy? If so, would you be willing to share it with our family?

Have a family member read aloud John 16:32–33. Ask:

- What promise did the Savior give His disciples? (Despite all the hard times, they would have peace.)
- Why was the Savior able to make this promise? (Because He has overcome the world.)
- In what ways have you found peace in your life because Jesus has "overcome the world"?

Testify of the peace that Jesus can bring, even though each day there is news of wars, natural disasters, terror, and crime. In spite of all this, Jesus has promised His followers that they may have peace in this world.

JOHN 17: JESUS OFFERS THE GREAT INTERCESSORY PRAYER

Before beginning your study of this chapter, tell your family that President David O. McKay said, in reference to John 17, "I know of no more important chapter in the Bible." (Conference Report, Oct. 1967, 5.) As you study John 17, invite family members to ponder why President McKay would feel this chapter is so important.

John 17:1–10

Do you "know" God?

 On a large piece of paper draw twelve dashes similar to the following:

— — — — — — — — — — — —

Invite your family to guess letters of the alphabet to fill in the blanks. Write correct letters in the appropriate spaces until you spell the word *intercessory*. If someone guesses the word correctly, ask if they know what it means. (You may want to have someone look up *intercessory* or *intercessor* in a dictionary.) The most common definition for *intercessor* is "a mediator," or "someone who speaks in behalf of another."

Tell your family that John 17 contains a prayer that is often called the Great Intercessory Prayer. Have your family read the chapter heading and find out who offers the prayer and for whom He prays. Read together John 17:1–10 and ask the following questions:

- As Jesus began His prayer, how did He describe what He came to earth to do? (Verses 1–2.)
- What is one of the requirements for eternal life? (Verse 3.)
- What do you think is the difference between *knowing* Heavenly Father and Jesus Christ and just knowing *about* them?

Ask:

- Who do you know that seems to know God the Father and Jesus Christ?
- How can we come to know God and His Beloved Son?

Assign the following passages to different family members: 1 John 4:7–8, Mosiah 5:13, and Alma 22:18. Have them read these references aloud and tell what they suggest we can do to better know God.

Quickly review John 17:4–6 and ask:

- What did Jesus say He had done to fulfill His earthly mission?
- In what way could we give a daily report to our Heavenly Father on how we are doing in our earthly mission? (Prayer.)
- How might it affect our lives if we told Heavenly Father each morning what we wanted to accomplish that day and then reported to Him each night on how well we had done?

Challenge your family to take time during the week to ponder how they might come to better "know" God.

John 17:11–19

"In the world but not of the world"

Have your family take turns reading John 17:11–19 and then discuss ways you can live in the world but not be of the world. Then share the following statement by Elder M. Russell Ballard:

"In the Church, we often state the couplet, 'Be in the world but not of the world.' As we observe television shows that make profanity, violence, and infidelity commonplace and even glamorous, we often wish we could lock out the world in some way and isolate our families from it all. . . .

"We should strive to change the corrupt and immoral tendencies in television and in society by keeping things that offend and debase out of our homes. In spite of all of the wickedness in the world, and in spite of all the opposition to good that we find on every hand, we should not try to take ourselves or our children *out* of the world." (*Ensign*, May 1989, 80.)

Ask your family:

- What did Jesus do in verses 12–19 that was helpful in keeping his Apostles from the influence of the world?
- What can we do with such things as media, fashions, etc., to avoid being "in the world"?

Make a list as a family of one or two things you could change to help yourselves be in the world but not of it. Place this list in a place that will help remind your family of the goal.

John 17:20–26
"One"

 Ask your family:

- Can three ever be one?
- Can twelve be one?
- Can (the number of members in your family) be one?

Have family members read John 17:20–26 and note the word *one* every time it is used. Discuss as a family ways Heavenly Father and Jesus Christ are one. Share the following by President Gordon B. Hinckley as he speaks of Heavenly Father, Jesus Christ, and the Holy Ghost:

"They are distinct beings, but they are one in purpose and effort. They are united as one in bringing to pass the grand, divine plan for the salvation and exaltation of the children of God. . . .

"It is that perfect unity between the Father, the Son, and the Holy Ghost that binds these three into the oneness of the divine Godhead." (*Ensign*, Mar. 1998, 7.) Ask:

- Who else did Jesus pray would be "one"? (Verses 20–21.)
- Why is it important for the Apostles to be united? (Verse 23.)
- What can we do to become "one" with Heavenly Father and Jesus?
- What can we do to become "one" as a family?
- When have you felt that our family was most united?
- How did that make you feel?

Have one family member read aloud John 17:26 and then another read aloud Mosiah 18:21. As the

verses are read, have the family listen for qualities that will increase unity. Choose a quality that might help your family become more "one."

Share the feelings of love and concern you have for your family and how much it means to you that your family be united.

JOHN 18: JESUS EXEMPLIFIES HOW TO HANDLE REJECTION

John 18:1–11
How does Jesus handle betrayal?

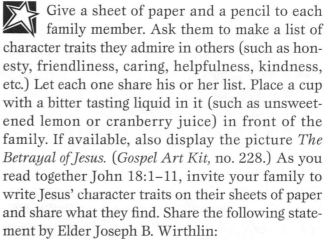 Give a sheet of paper and a pencil to each family member. Ask them to make a list of character traits they admire in others (such as honesty, friendliness, caring, helpfulness, kindness, etc.) Let each one share his or her list. Place a cup with a bitter tasting liquid in it (such as unsweetened lemon or cranberry juice) in front of the family. If available, also display the picture *The Betrayal of Jesus.* (*Gospel Art Kit*, no. 228.) As you read together John 18:1–11, invite your family to write Jesus' character traits on their sheets of paper and share what they find. Share the following statement by Elder Joseph B. Wirthlin:

"When the band of men and officers came to take [Jesus] prisoner and, ultimately, to his death, he faced them resolutely, asking, 'Whom seek ye?' The men answered that they sought Jesus of Nazareth.

"'I am he,' Jesus answered with such courage and power that many in the multitude moved back and fell to the ground.

"Then a second time Jesus asked them, 'Whom seek ye?' And when they named him, he said, 'I have told you that I am he: if therefore ye seek me, let these [his disciples] go their way' . . .

"This is the kind of courageous leader we would be willing to follow anywhere, anytime." (*Ensign*, Sept. 1995, 36.)

Ask some or all of the following questions:

- Who led this "band of men" to capture Jesus?
- How does it feel to be abandoned or betrayed by a close friend?
- Why do you think it would be hard to respond

the way Jesus did if dangerous men with weapons, torches, and lanterns came in the dark to take you away?

- According to verse 4, what did Jesus know that would have helped Him respond with courage?
- How could that help you have faith in following the Savior's advice for your life?
- What can you learn from Jesus about how to respond when your friends betray you?
- How did Jesus demonstrate that He always stands by His friends? (Verses 8–9.)
- What question did Jesus ask Peter? (Verses 10–11.)

Ask if there is a family member willing to drink from the bitter cup you have prepared. Invite them to share their feelings about its taste and then ask:

- What do you think Jesus was referring to when He said there was a "cup" he needed to drink? (The Atonement.)
- Who asked Him to drink the bitter cup? (Verse 11.)

Share with your family some of the different "cups" life has given you to drink. Explain what happened when you drank the cup and what happened when you did not. Relate to them that when we appropriately handle our trials, we gain insight and understanding into the Atonement.

John 18:12–14, 19–24, 28–32
Jesus is rejected by his own countrymen

Write the following words and numbers on small slips of paper and have family members draw one at a time out of a bowl until the slips are gone: (1) *Sanhedrin,* 769; (2) *Annas,* 609; (3) *Caiaphas,* 628; (4) *Pilate,* 751; (5) *Judgment hall,* 720. Explain that the number is the page in the Bible Dictionary where you can read more about the topic. Have each family member look up, read, and be prepared to report on what they learned.

After they have had time to prepare their report, explain that after being captured in the Garden of Gethsemane, Jesus was led to be questioned by members of the Sanhedrin. Invite your family to take turns reading aloud John 18:12–14, 19–24. Ask those prepared to report on the "Sanhedrin,"

"Annas," and "Caiaphas" to help answer the following questions:

- What was the Sanhedrin? (A council that ruled over the Jewish nation.)
- Who was Jesus led to first? (Annas.)
- Why was this not appropriate? (Annas was no longer the acting high priest.)
- Who was the acting high priest over the Sanhedrin and the Jews? (Caiaphas.)
- What counsel did he give to the Jews that year that was dangerous for Jesus? (Verse 14.)
- What did Annas ask Jesus about? (Verse 19.)
- Why do you think Jesus answered the way He did? (Verses 20–21.)
- What consequences did He suffer for His answer?
- Where did Annas finally send Him? (Verse 24.)

Read the following information by Elder James E. Talmage and have your family identify all illegal activities which happened to Jesus:

"When Jesus . . . was brought in . . . He was immediately put upon trial in contravention of [disobedience to] the law. . . . Such a preliminary inquiry was utterly unlawful; for the Hebrew code provided that the accusing witnesses in any cause before the court should define their charge against the accused, and that the latter should be protected from any effort to make him testify against himself. The Lord's reply should have been a sufficient protest to the high priest against further illegal procedure. . . . 'I spake openly to the world; . . . and in secret have I said nothing. Why askest thou me?— ask them which heard me. . . . ' This was a lawful objection against denying to a prisoner on trial his right to be confronted by his accusers. . . . One of the officers who stood by . . . actually struck Jesus a vicious blow, accompanied by the question, 'Answerest thou the high priest so?' To this cowardly assault the Lord replied with almost superhuman gentleness. 'If I have spoken evil, bear witness of the evil: but if well, why smitest thou me?' . . . this constituted another appeal to the principles of justice . . . what right had a police officer to judge, condemn, and punish." (*Jesus the Christ,* 621–23.)

Now read together John 18:28–32 and ask those

persons prepared to report on "Pilate" and the "Judgment hall" to help answer the following questions:

- Where did they take Jesus next? (The hall of judgment.)
- Why wouldn't the members of the Sanhedrin enter Pilate's judgment hall? (Elder Bruce R. McConkie explained: "To enter a Gentile home during the Passover . . . would render them ceremonially unclean according to their tradition—a horrible prospect for people with murder in their hearts!" [*Doctrinal New Testament Commentary,* 1:800.])
- What does it say about these Jewish leaders being more concerned with being ceremonially unclean than with condemning an innocent man to death?
- What is a malefactor? (A criminal. You could use a dictionary, if desired.)
- What evidence do you find in these verses that the Sanhedrin had already tried, convicted, and sentenced Jesus to death in their hearts prior to the trial? (Verses 31–32.)
- How would you have felt about being so severely rejected by your own people?
- What are some ways people reject the Savior today?
- What are some ways we can show Jesus that we accept Him?
- When have you felt most strongly that the Savior was pleased with you?

Invite family members to record in their journals things they will do to eliminate any behavior that would be like rejecting the Savior.

John 18:15–18, 25–27
Peter's denial of Jesus

Prior to family scripture study invite one family member to draw a picture of a rooster. Display next to it the picture *Peter's Denial* (*Gospel Art Kit,* no. 229). Ask your family what these two pictures have to do with each other. Read John 13:37–38 to your family and ask, What prophecy did Jesus make about Peter? Read together John 18:15–18, 25–27. Ask:

- What questions were asked of Peter and how did he answer them?
- How was Jesus' prophecy fulfilled?
- Looking at the picture of *Peter's Denial,* how does the artist portray Peter's feelings about what he had done?
- How do you think Peter felt when he heard the rooster crow the third time?

Invite your family to share ways people "deny" the Savior today. Discuss ways your family can avoid denying the Savior in their lives.

John 18:33–40
The Jews reject their King

 You might consider showing your family the Gospel Doctrine New Testament video *To This End Was I Born,* which portrays the events of John 18–20. Copies may be found in most ward libraries.

Have family members search John 18:33–40 and mark the questions Pilate asks Jesus and Jesus' answers. Ask:

- From the answers that Jesus gave Pilate, who did Jesus say He is? (Verses 36–37.)
- To what end was Jesus born?
- To what end are we born?
- Who hears the Lord's voice? (Verse 37.)
- Did Pilate find Jesus innocent or guilty? (Verse 38.)
- Why do you think Pilate referred to Jesus as "the King of the Jews"?
- Who was Barabbas? (See Bible Dictionary, 619.)
- How do you think the friends, disciples, and family of Jesus felt when Jewish religious leaders asked that a known murderer and robber be released rather than Jesus in whom there was no sin?

Testify that although Jesus was not released, through His sacrifice all of us can be released from the pain, suffering, and sins of this life.

JOHN 19: THE CRUCIFIXION OF CHRIST

John 19:1–5
A crown of thorns

 Discuss the following questions with your family:

- Was Jesus a king? (Read together John 18:36–37.)
- Did Jesus ever wear a crown? (Read together John 19:1–5.)
- Why do you think they put a crown of thorns on His head?
- What symbolic significance could a crown of thorns have? (See Genesis 3:17–18.)
- What are some of the "thorns" we have to deal with in this world? (Sickness, pain, suffering, sin, death, and so forth.)
- What did Jesus Christ do to help us with struggles and sorrows of this world? (Read Isaiah 53:4–5.)

Testify to your family that in Gethsemane and upon the cross, Jesus took upon Himself all the bad elements of this world so He could bless us and help us return to our Heavenly Father.

Speaking of all that Jesus suffered, Gerald N. Lund stated: "He showed condescension in his patience and restraint when brought before men for judgment. . . .

"When we think of what he could have done to these men who took him to judgment, we have a new and different sense of his condescension. When Judas led the soldiers and the high priests to the Garden of Gethsemane and betrayed him with a kiss, Jesus could have spoken a single word and leveled the entire city of Jerusalem. When the servant of the high priest stepped forward and slapped his face, Jesus could have lifted a finger and sent that man back to his original elements. When another man stepped forward and spit in his face, Jesus had only to blink and our entire solar system could have been annihilated. But he stood there, he endured, he suffered, he condescended." (*Doctrines of the Book of Mormon,* 85–86.)

Ask your family what impresses them most about the statement above. Share your gratitude for the Savior's suffering for you.

John 19:6–16
What would you do?

Ask family members to think about all the good things Jesus did for people and share one that they think is most memorable. Ask them why they think anyone would want to kill such a wonderful person. Read John 19:6–7 with your family and ask:

- Why did the Jews want Jesus crucified? (Verse 7.)
- Why do you think Heavenly Father let His Son, Jesus Christ, be crucified? (See 2 Nephi 9:5–7; 3 Nephi 27:14–17.)
- What would happen to us if Jesus had not sacrificed Himself for us?
- How do you feel towards our Father in Heaven in allowing this great act of love to occur?

Ask your family to try to imagine why Pilate did what he did, as you have them read John 19:6–16. Afterwards ask:

- Did Pilate want to have Jesus killed? Why or why not?
- Why did he allow Jesus to be crucified?
- In what verse did the Jews try to scare Pilate? (Verse 12.)
- How do people at school or work try to persuade others to do bad things?

Ask family members to share a time when either they or others they know have chosen the right even though some didn't want them to. Challenge your family to choose the right even when others want them to do bad things.

John 19:16–18
Excruciating pain

Ask your family to define the word *excruciating.* Read John 19:16–18 and ask your family what the verses and the word *excruciating* have to do with each other. Explain to your family that in the Latin form of the word (*excruciatus*) the main root is *crus,* which is Latin for "cross." The literal translation of *excruciating* in Latin is "out of the cross." Thus when a person says that their pain is excruciating, the connotation of what they are saying is that their pain is similar to crucifixion pain.

To better understand Christ's suffering read the following by Elder James E. Talmage:

"Death by crucifixion was at once the most lingering and most painful of all forms of execution. The victim lived in ever increasing torture, generally for many hours, sometimes for days. The spikes so cruelly driven through hands and feet penetrated and crushed sensitive nerves and quivering tendons, yet inflicted no mortal wound. The welcome relief of death came through the exhaustion caused by intense and unremitting pain, through localized inflammation and congestion of organs incident to the strained and unnatural posture of the body." (*Jesus the Christ*, 655.)

John 19:17–42
Concentration game

Before scripture study, cut some thick paper into 2-inch squares (You will need 16 pieces). Write one item from the list below on each of the 16 squares. Mix up the papers and spread them out face down on the floor in front of your family. While you are doing this, have your family study John 19:17–42 silently. Tell them you will play a "concentration" game with the information they learn from those verses. As you play the game, stop and take time to mark cross-references or answer questions.

- Name of the place where Jesus was crucified
- Golgotha
- Cast lots for His coat
- Psalm 22:18
- The name of the three women who stood at the foot of the cross
- Mary
- No bones broken
- Psalm 34:20
- "They shall look on him whom they pierced"
- Psalm 22:16
- Nicodemus and Joseph of Arimathaea
- Bury Jesus
- Given vinegar to drink
- Psalm 69:21
- Charged to take care of Jesus' mother
- The Apostle John the Beloved

To play the game, divide your family into two teams. Have one team select and turn over two pieces of the paper. If the information on the two pieces of paper is a match, then they remove those papers from the floor and get another turn. If the papers they turn over do not match, they turn them back over, and the other team gets a turn. The teams continue taking turns trying to find matches until all the papers have been taken.

Following the activity, remind your family of all that Christ did for them and testify of His great love for all mankind.

John 19:26–27
How do you feel about your mom?

Ask your family, If you were about to die, what would you be thinking about? After everyone has had a chance to respond, invite your family to look for what was on Jesus' mind as He was about to leave morality. (See John 19:26–27.) Ask:

- What does this teach us about Jesus?
- What lesson can we learn from Jesus' example?
- Who was the disciple Jesus referred to as the one whom He loved? (John.)
- Why do you think Jesus refers to John as the Beloved?

Challenge your family to do something nice for their mother. You may also want to discuss opportunities to help members of your family, especially grandparents or other aging members of your family.

JOHN 20: THE EMPTY TOMB

John 20:1–18
What was found in Jesus' tomb?

Ask your family to tell who they think was the first mortal person to see the resurrected Lord. Give each family member a sheet of paper and a pencil. Invite them to silently read John 20:1–9 and write questions that begin with each of the following words: *Who, What, When, Where, Why,* and *How.* When finished, have them ask their questions of each other, locating answers in the scriptures. You may want to discuss these questions:

- How did Mary, Peter, and John react when they discovered the empty tomb?
- According to verse 9, why would you say Mary, Peter, and John reacted this way?
- What do you think was so significant about the empty tomb?

Take turns reading John 20:10–18 as you discuss the following questions:

- What did Peter and John finally do? (Verse 10.)
- What did Mary do instead? (Verse 11.)
- How did Mary answer the angel's question? (Verses 12–13; she thought someone had "taken" Jesus' body.)
- Who did Mary think Jesus was at first? (Verses 14–15.)
- How did Mary finally recognize Jesus? (Verses 16–17.)
- What did Mary do after leaving the tomb? (Verse 18.)
- How do you think you might have felt if you had been there with Mary?

Show the picture *Mary and the Resurrected Lord.* (*Gospel Art Kit,* no. 233.) Tell your family that Mary was the first mortal person to bear witness of the resurrected Lord. Ask them to share what it might have been like for Mary to see the very first resurrected being. Testify of the blessing of empty tombs and the power and reality of the Resurrection.

John 20:19–31
Must we see to believe?

Bring an unshelled nut to family scripture study. Put the nut in your closed hand, making sure that no one can see it. Tell your family that you have something in your hand that has never been seen by the human eye. Allow them a minute to think about what you have told them. Ask:

- Do you believe me?
- What will it take for you to believe?

Take one family member away from the rest of the family and show him or her the nut. Explain that the nut inside the shell has never been seen by the human eye. Return to the rest of the family and have the person to whom you have shown the nut testify that there really is something in your hand that has never been seen by the human eye. Then ask:

- Do you believe me now?
- Why will you believe two people instead of just one?
- Why is it important to have more than one witness?

Do not show the nut to the rest of your family yet. As your family takes turns reading John 20:19–29 invite them to look for ways this scriptural account is like their experience with the nut. Show the nut to the rest of the family and ask:

- What was it that Thomas needed before he would believe? (Verse 25.)
- Did Thomas ever get what he needed to believe? (Verse 27.)
- What did the Lord say about those who believe but have not seen? (Verse 29.)
- Why do you think these people are "more blessed"?

Discuss as a family what you can do "to be not faithless, but believing." Testify to your family that as they believe in the Lord and live the gospel, their faith will increase and they will become like those described by the Savior: "Blessed are they that have not seen, and yet have believed."

JOHN 21: JESUS INVITES HIS DISCIPLES TO FEED HIS SHEEP

John 21:1–14
Experiences and symbols to remind us

 Read together John 21:1–7. Ask:

- Who recognized Jesus on the shore? (John, who is sometimes called the Beloved.)
- How do you think John recognized Him?

Have your family turn back to Luke 5 and read verses 1–11. Ask, How might that experience recorded in Luke have helped the disciples recognize the Lord in their experience recorded in John 21? Invite your family to write *Compare to Luke 5:1–11* in the margin next to John 21:6. Ask your family, Just as the Lord telling the disciples where to drop their nets brought them a multitude of fishes, in what ways has the Lord's direction to us brought a multitude of blessings? Read together John 21:9–13.

Point out to your family that on this occasion Jesus gave His disciples opportunities to recognize Him and remember things they had learned from Him through an activity they knew very well (fishing). Ask:

- Why do you think Peter went fishing in the beginning of John 21?
- After the experience we just read about, what do you think Jesus wants Peter to think about when he thinks of fish and fishing?
- What are some things in your life that you do on a regular basis that could remind you more of Jesus and the things He taught us? (Give your family some time to think and make suggestions—perhaps writing down the ideas and bringing them back in a week to see if it helped.)

John 21:15–19
Do we love Jesus?

Prior to your family scripture study, make a small stack of things that represent those things that can compete with the Lord for our time and love, or that distract us from doing the Lord's work. It might be computer software, sporting equipment, the TV listings for the week, or a number of other things.

Have someone read aloud John 21:15. Ask:

- What could "these" refer to in this verse? (The pile of fish the men had just brought to shore.)
- What are some things these fish represented to Peter? (His business; what he loved to do.)
- How are those fish like the things we stacked up today?

- What things in your life might compete with the Savior for your love?
- How could we show we love the Savior more than we love those items?
- What did the Savior say we would do if we loved Him more than "these"?

Read together John 21:16–17. Ask:

- Why do you think Jesus asked Peter this question two more times?
- How do you think Peter felt about being asked this question three times?
- Why is it easier to say "Yes, I love you" than it is to actually show that love in the way Jesus said we should?

Have someone read John 21:18–19 and ask your family what Jesus said about how total Peter's commitment would be. Share with them the following statement: "Eusebius's account of early Christian history [indicates that] Peter did indeed die in Rome, crucified upside down." (Thomas Mackay, "The Resurrected Lord and His Apostles," in *Studies in Scripture,* 5:467.)

Ask your family, Although we may not be asked to give our lives as Peter did, what can we do to more fully show the Lord we love Him—especially based on what we learn in John 21?

John 21:20–25
Did John ever die?

Ask your family, If you were given the opportunity to ask anything from the Savior, what would you ask of Him? Read together John 21:20–24 and ask:

- Who is being talked about here? (John.)
- What blessing was John apparently given?

Tell your family that latter-day revelation gives even more help concerning this event. Have your family read the heading (historical background) to Doctrine and Covenants 7. Ask:

- What led to this revelation?
- What is the original source of the revelation?

Take turns reading Doctrine and Covenants 7:1–8. Ask, What becomes more clear about what happened in John 21 because of what you read in Doctrine and Covenants 7?

Because some of your family is likely to want to know where John is, share with your family the additional revelation that came to the Prophet Joseph Smith, according to the historical record of a conference of the Church in June of 1831: "The Spirit of the Lord fell upon Joseph in an unusual manner, and he prophesied that John the Revelator was then among the Ten Tribes of Israel who had been led away by Shalmaneser, king of Assyria, to prepare them for their return from their long dispersion, to again possess the land of their fathers." (*History of the Church,* 1:176.)

Have your family look again at John 21:19, 22. Ask, What command is repeated? ("Follow me.") Point out that although John and Peter (and each of us) have different opportunities and missions, the message from Jesus is still the same: Follow Him. Since this is at the end of the four Gospels that teach us of the life and ministry of Jesus, you may want to take time to invite family members to share what they have learned from these four great testimonies that inspires them to more fully follow Him.

ACTS

"This book, as stated in its opening words, is the second of a two-part work written to Theophilus. The first part is known to us as the book of Luke." (Bible Dictionary, "Acts of the Apostles," 603.) While the Gospel of Luke is a testimony and history of Jesus' ministry, the book of Acts gives an account of the spreading of the gospel following Jesus' death, Resurrection, and Ascension. The first part of Acts records the missionary activities of the Twelve Apostles under the direction of Peter. The second half of the book records the missionary journeys of the Apostle Paul. "A brief outline of the book is foreshadowed by Jesus' words in Acts 1:8, 'Ye shall be witnesses unto me both in Jerusalem (chapters 1–5), and in all Judaea, and in Samaria (chapters 6–9), and unto the uttermost part of the earth (chapters 10–28).'" (Bible Dictionary, "Acts of the Apostles," 603.) The book of Acts, written by Luke, emphasizes the workings of the Holy Ghost and the power Jesus' Resurrection had on the people. The book concludes about A.D. 63 with an account of Paul's preaching at Rome while under house arrest.

ACTS 1: THE ASCENSION OF JESUS CHRIST

Acts 1:1–7
To whom did Jesus appear shortly after His Resurrection?

Ask your family if they have ever heard news, whether good or bad, that they just couldn't wait to tell someone. Invite some of your family members to share that news. Have your family members imagine living during the time of Christ and seeing Jesus shortly after His Resurrection. Talk about how excited they would be to share their experience with others. Read Acts 1:1–3 and ask:

- How many days did Christ visit among the people following His Resurrection?
- How would these visits help build the testimonies of the people?

Elder James E. Talmage lists at least eleven visits of the Savior recorded in the New Testament, to more than 500 people. (See *Jesus the Christ*, 699.)

Ask, What difference does it make to you that so many people saw the resurrected Savior?

Acts 1:8–11
The gospel is to be preached to the "uttermost part of the earth"

Hold up a flashlight. Turn the flashlight on and off a few times and ask your family how this is like those who have and those who don't have the gift of the Holy Ghost.

Refer to Acts 1:5 and ask your family what the disciples were promised. Read Acts 1:8 aloud and ask your family to tell what Christ's final commission was to the Apostles. (You might consider reading also Jesus' similar commission in Matthew 28:19–20 and John 21:15–17.) Tell your family that the book of Acts tells how the Apostles carried out this commandment: chapters 1–5 tells of missionary work in Jerusalem; chapters 6–9 tells of work in Judaea and Samaria, and chapters 10–28 tells of missionary work to the "uttermost part of the earth." Continue reading Acts 1:9–11 and ask:

- What occurred following Christ's final commission to His apostles?

- Who was there to witness the Ascension?
- What great future event did the angels who stood by foretell?

Show your family a map of the world and together identify all the places that you know of that have missionaries serving there, or have stakes organized there, or have temples built there. Share your testimony of how well the ancient Apostles and the modern Apostles have done at helping spread the gospel of Jesus Christ throughout the world.

Acts 1:12–26
A new Apostle is chosen

Have a family member read Acts 1:13 aloud while the rest count the number of men listed in that verse. Ask:

- Who are these men that met together following the Ascension of Christ?
- What was the total number present?
- Who of the original Twelve Apostles was missing? Why? (See Matthew 27:3–5.)

Ask your family what now needed to happen with the loss of Judas from the quorum. Have family members search Acts 1:21–22 for the qualifications Peter said the new replacement should have. Ask someone to share what they found.

Ask someone to read Acts 1:23. Ask:

- Who were the two that qualified to be the new Apostle?
- According to verse 24, how were they chosen?

Tell your family that casting lots was a method used in Old Testament times to determine the will of the Lord. (See Bible Dictionary, "Lots, Casting of," 726.) Ask who was chosen to be the new Apostle? (Verse 26.) Ask your family if they can name the Apostles named most recently to the current Quorum of the Twelve.

- How is the way of choosing an Apostle in the Lord's Church different from the way the world chooses its leaders?
- How do we show that we sustain our newly called leaders? (Uplifted hand, doing the work they call us to do, living the way they ask us to live.)

Ask a member of the family to tell how follow-ing our leaders has blessed his or her life. You may choose to conclude by singing "We Thank Thee, O God, for a Prophet." (Hymns, no. 19.)

ACTS 2: THE GIFT OF THE HOLY GHOST

Acts 2:1–4
An important gift

 Before beginning family scripture study, gift wrap an empty box. Show the gift box to your family and ask:

- How does it make you feel to receive a gift from someone?
- What are some of the favorite gifts you have received?
- According to Acts 1:4–5, what gift did Jesus promise His disciples they would soon receive?

Read together Acts 2:1–4 and ask:

- What was the day of Pentecost? (See Bible Dictionary, "Feasts," 673.)
- How did the Holy Ghost come upon the Apostles?

Have family members mark footnotes 2a and 3a in their scriptures. Have a family member read the Doctrine and Covenants 109 section heading and verses 36–37 aloud to find what Joseph Smith was requesting in the dedicatory prayer of the Kirtland Temple. Share the following statement:

At an evening meeting on the day the Kirtland Temple was dedicated, "Brother George A. Smith arose and began to prophesy, when a noise was heard like the sound of a rushing mighty wind, which filled the Temple, and all the congregation simultaneously arose, being moved upon by an invisible power; many began to speak in tongues and prophesy; others saw glorious visions; and I beheld that the Temple was filled with angels. . . . The people of the neighborhood came running together (hearing an unusual sound within, and seeing a bright light like a pillar of fire resting upon the Temple), and were astonished at what was tak-ing place." (History of the Church, 2:428.)

Explain that the gift of the Holy Ghost is not always so dramatic in our lives, but those two significant experiences in history can help us understand the great power and strength of the Holy Ghost. Invite family members to share experiences they have had feeling the Holy Ghost and testify how those feelings can be as helpful to us as the Pentecostal miracles were to those in the early Church.

Acts 2:4–13
What is the gift of tongues?

For this activity you will say "Holy Ghost" in several different languages. Do not tell what language you are using to begin with. Just say the words and ask your family if they know what it means. Here are the words in different languages:

Sung Sheen (Korean)   *Heiligen Geist* (German)

Espiritu Santo (Spanish)   *Banal na Espiritu* (Tagalog)

Ask your family why they do not understand what you are saying. Read together Acts 2:4–13 and ask:

- Can you count in these verses how many different languages or nationalities of people were in Jerusalem at this time?
- How many languages were being spoken by the Church leaders on this occasion? (One. They were all "Galilaeans.")
- How many people were able to understand the Apostles' language?
- How were these people who spoke other languages able to understand the Apostles?

Read this statement by the Prophet Joseph Smith: "The gift of tongues by the power of the Holy Ghost in the Church, is for the benefit of the servants of God, to preach to unbelievers, as on the day of Pentecost." (*Teachings of the Prophet Joseph Smith,* 195.)

Have a family member read aloud Doctrine and Covenants 90:11. Ask how the preaching of the gospel today is similar to that on the day of Pentecost. President Joseph Fielding Smith taught: "There has been no cessation of the gift of tongues. . . .

"The true gift of tongues is made manifest in the Church more abundantly, perhaps, than any other spiritual gift. Every missionary who goes forth to teach the gospel in a foreign language, if he is prayerful and faithful, receives this gift." (*Answers to Gospel Questions,* 2:26–29.)

If possible, share examples from your own family or extended family of missionaries who have felt this gift in their missionary assignments.

Acts 2:14–36
God will pour out His Spirit

Have a family member read aloud Acts 2:7–8, 12–13. Ask, What two different reactions did the people have to this great miracle? As you read together Acts 2:14–21, have your family look for Peter's response to those who were mocking the Apostles' ability to speak in tongues.

Ask which Old Testament prophet Peter quoted. (Verse 16.) Tell your family that President Gordon B. Hinckley, speaking in October 2001 general conference, said:

"The vision of Joel has been fulfilled wherein he declared: 'And it shall come to pass afterward, that I will pour out my spirit upon all flesh; and your sons and your daughters shall prophesy, your old men shall dream dreams, your young men shall see visions:

"'And also upon the servants and upon the handmaids in those days will I pour out my spirit.' (Joel 2:28–29)." (*Ensign,* Nov. 2001, 4–5.)

Take turns reading Acts 2:22–36 and ask your family what part of Peter's response impresses them the most. Testify of the value of having living prophets today to give us our Father in Heaven's words.

Acts 2:37–47
"Pricked in their heart"

When your family is gathered around, cut a heart shape out of a piece of paper and then prick the heart with a pin. Ask:

- What does that have to do with Acts 2:37?
- What do you think it means to be pricked in your heart? (One meaning is to be touched or to feel guilty.)
- What caused the hearts of the people to be pricked?
- What question did the people ask as a result of being pricked in their hearts?

Have your family members read Acts 2:38–40 to see how Peter answered their question. Ask:

- What did Peter tell the people they needed to do to receive the gift of the Holy Ghost?
- Which Article of Faith is similar to verse 38? (Articles of Faith 1:4.)

Ask a family member to recite or read Article of Faith 4. Ask:

- What do you think you need to do to receive guidance from the Holy Ghost?

Read Acts 2:41–47. Ask:

- How many people were baptized on the day of Pentecost? (Verse 41.)
- What did these people do after they were baptized to show they were converted to the gospel of Jesus Christ? (Verses 42–47.)
- What can we learn from their example?

Invite your family to share an experience when they felt the promptings of the Holy Ghost.

ACTS 3: HEALING AND PROPHECIES

Acts 3:1–18
Focus!

If you have a pair of binoculars in your home, take turns looking at an object, which is out of focus. Teach your family how to focus the binoculars and then have them look at the object again. Allow everyone to share feelings about the difference it makes to see an object in focus. (You could also have family members look through a pair of eyeglasses that were prescribed for another person.)

Ask your family to keep that demonstration in mind as they read the following scripture story. Take turns reading Acts 3:1–17 aloud. Have family members look for all the action words they find in the story. Discuss the following:

- Who did Peter ask the lame man to focus on? (Verses 4 and 6.)
- Why do you think the lame man was to focus on Jesus Christ instead of on Peter?
- After the man was healed, where was his focus? (Verse 8.)

- Who were the people focused on? (Verse 12.)
- Who did Peter tell the people they should be focused on? (Verse 13.)
- What did Peter say that he and John were witnesses to? (Verse 15–16.)
- To what and to whom did Peter give credit for the healing of the lame man? (Verse 16.)

Ask your family why it is important to focus on the Savior. What blessings has faith brought in your life? Share your testimony regarding faith in the power of Jesus Christ to heal.

Invite your family to mark all of the names they can find in Acts 3:13–15 that are used for Jesus and talk about their meaning and significance.

Acts 3:18–26
Prophecy regarding restoration

Show your family an item that could be restored, such as a broken piece of furniture, an old fading photograph, or a broken toy.

Briefly talk about ways the item could be fixed, or restored. Discuss what the word *restoration* means. Explain that to restore something means to put it back to its original state.

Read Acts 3:19–21 and ask your family to mark the word in verse 21 that means the same thing as restoration (restitution). Discuss the following questions:

- What coming of Jesus Christ do these verses generally refer to? (The Second Coming.)
- What did Peter describe would need to happen before that event? (A restoration.)
- How many things need to be restored before the Savior's coming? (All things; see verse 21.)

Explain that as part of the Restoration in the last days, many prophecies are to be fulfilled. Assign the verses below to individual family members and have them research the accompanying footnote or Topical Guide references to find details about its fulfillment. When they have finished, have family members report on their findings.

Acts 3:18
Acts 3:20
Acts 3:21
Acts 3:22–23
Acts 3:25

ACTS 4: PETER'S EXAMPLE OF COURAGE

Acts 4:1–22

Why is Jesus called a "stone"?

 Ask your family:

- Can you think of a time when you were accused of doing wrong when you were really doing right?
- How did it make you feel?
- What happened when the truth came out?
- What role does the court system play in finding the truth in difficult cases?

Invite someone to read Acts 4:1–4 and ask your family to find something good that Peter and John were doing and something bad that happened to them. (They were imprisoned for preaching about Jesus.)

Have your family act out Acts 4:5–22 as if you are in a courtroom. Have family members take the following roles: narrator, one or more members of the Sanhedrin (the court of the day), and Peter.

Have the remaining family members be the "jury." Ask them to watch this story unfold and when it is finished their job will be to give their feelings on these questions:

- Were Peter and John treated fairly? Why or why not.
- What is your opinion of Jesus Christ after hearing the testimonies?
- What decision would you make if you were a juror at that council about Peter and John healing the lame man?

Acts 4:23–31

Heavenly Father can give us courage

Review with your family what had just happened to Peter and John when they were arrested for healing and preaching about Jesus. (See Acts 4:1–22.) Ask your family to think about these questions:

- How would you feel if a law was passed in your city making it illegal to be a Latter-day Saint?

- Would you still go to Church?
- Would you be willing to move somewhere else?

Take turns reading Acts 4:23–31 together as a family and discuss the following questions as you read:

- Why do you think they praised God instead of being angry about their sufferings? (See verses 23–24.)
- Why do Peter and John and the others not seem surprised that they were persecuted for teaching about Jesus Christ? (See verses 24–26.)
- What do you find interesting about the blessings they asked for in verses 29–30?
- What answer did the Lord give them? (See verse 31.)

Invite your family to talk about times when they have been made to feel uncomfortable or even afraid because they are members of the Church and they believe in Jesus Christ. If they have not had such an experience, explain that the time may come when they will. Ask:

- Who was more powerful, Heavenly Father or the Jewish leaders?
- What principle can we learn from Peter and John about how and where to find courage when we are persecuted for our belief in Jesus Christ?

Invite your family to share how they would complete the following statement:

"When I am afraid, I can receive courage and strength if I _____."

Acts 4:32–37

What does it mean "they had all things common"?

Show your family the following scrambled letters and ask them to unscramble the letters to form a word: *NTOOCSAERINC.* If they cannot guess the word, have them look at Doctrine and Covenants 42:30–31 for a clue. (The word is *consecration.*) Ask if anyone can explain what *consecration* means.

If they need help, share the following statement: "Righteous saints in all ages have consecrated [dedicated] their time, talents, strength, properties, and monies to the establishment of the Lord's work and kingdom in their respective days." (McConkie, *Mormon Doctrine,* 157.)

Have your family look in Acts 4:32 and mark the phrase "had all things common." Explain that this phrase is often used in scripture for the principle of consecration. Take turns reading Acts 4:32–37, stopping each time you come to a phrase that describes how these Saints lived that is different from how most people live today.

Tell your family that in the Book of Mormon we find another example of a people who lived this way. Read together 4 Nephi 1:2–5, 15–17 and mark phrases that describe how they lived. Ask:

- What would motivate a person to share his or her possessions with others?
- How would life be different if we all lived that way today?
- How would the world be better if we all lived that way?
- What do you think would be the hardest part having "all things common"?
- What would be the best part?

Share the following statement:

"We tend to think of consecration only as yielding up, when divinely directed, our material possessions. But ultimate consecration is the yielding up of oneself to God. . . .

"Spiritual submissiveness is not accomplished in an instant, but by the incremental improvements and by the successive use of stepping-stones. Stepping-stones are meant to be taken one at a time anyway." (Neal A. Maxwell, *Ensign,* May 2002, 36.)

ACTS 5: THE APOSTLES CONTINUE THE WORK IN BOLDNESS AND POWER

Acts 5:1–11
What are the consequences of breaking covenants?

Have a family member report on what Acts 4:32–37 says Church members were doing with their worldly possessions and why they did it. (See teaching idea for Acts 4:32–37.) Emphasize to

your family that when people consecrate things to the Lord and His Church they do so willingly. Consecration can never be forced—it must be freely given or it really isn't consecration.

Take turns reading Acts 5:1–11. Ask:

- What truth did Peter remind Ananias of in verse 4? (That he decided to freely give the full price of his property.)
- According to verse 4, what did Peter say was the real sin? (Lying to God.)
- What else did Peter say about this couple's sin in verse 9? (They "agreed together" to "tempt the Spirit of the Lord," or, sought to receive God's blessings without living His laws.)
- In what ways are some people today tempted to pretend to live certain laws of God in order to try to receive certain privileges or blessings?

Share with your family the following application from President Gordon B. Hinckley: "In our time those found in dishonesty do not die as did Ananias and Sapphira, but something within them dies. Conscience chokes, character withers, self-respect vanishes, integrity dies." (*Ensign,* May 1976, 61.)

Ask, How would your reaction to this event compare to the reaction of the people of that time, as described in verses 5 and 11?

Assure your family that there is no need to fear if we keep our covenants and are honest with the Lord. Remind them that "if we will keep our covenants, the covenants will keep us spiritually safe." (Neal A. Maxwell, *Ensign,* May 1987, 71.)

Acts 5:12–16
The fulfillment of prophecy

Have a family member read aloud John 14:12–13 and identify what Jesus promised the Apostles the night before He gave His life.

Point out the Joseph Smith Translation in footnote 13a of Acts 5. Have someone read Acts 5:13–14, inserting the Joseph Smith Translation change. Ask:

- Why do you think the "rulers" would not join themselves to the Church while "multitudes" of others did?
- What does this teach us about the role of

miracles and the fulfillment of prophecy in converting people to the truth? (People can deny miracles if they choose.)

- What is the most significant factor in whether miracles and the fulfillment of prophecy lead us to a stronger testimony? (See 1 Corinthians 2:10–11, 15; Alma 12:9–11.)

Encourage your family to keep a soft heart, looking for miracles and fulfillment of prophecy occurring all the time in this last dispensation.

Acts 5:17–42

Jewish leaders' reactions to the Apostles

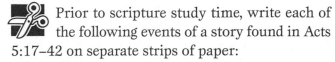 Prior to scripture study time, write each of the following events of a story found in Acts 5:17–42 on separate strips of paper:

- The high priest has the Apostles put in a prison.
- An angel comes at night and opens the prison doors.
- The Apostles teach in the temple.
- The officers find the Apostles missing from prison.
- The Apostles are arrested at the temple and brought before the council.
- Peter testifies that he ought to obey God rather than man.
- Some of the council wants to kill the Apostles.
- Gamaliel says to leave the Apostles alone, for if their work is not of God, it will fail.
- The Apostles are beaten and sent away.

Mix up the strips of paper. Give them to your family and ask them to put them together in the order they think they would find them in Acts 5. As you read together Acts 5:17–42, make corrections to the order of the strips of paper, if needed. After reading, ask:

- Why were certain Jews so opposed to the Apostles and why did they want them killed?
- How was Gamaliel's speech more accurate than he probably thought?
- What things impressed you about the actions and words of the Apostles? Why?
- What do we learn from this story and how can we put it into practice in our lives?

ACTS 6: STEPHEN IS CALLED TO MINISTER

Acts 6:1–7

How can Church leaders take care of *all* the members?

Ask your family: What advice would you give to a bishop who is discouraged because he can't seem to help all his ward members with their needs? After giving them a chance to share a few suggestions, have someone read Acts 6:1 and ask:

- Who was not being taken care of?
- Why couldn't the Twelve Apostles continue to take care of all of the needs of each Church member? (Church membership was quickly growing.)

Have family members read Acts 6:2–6 and ask:

- What was the solution to the challenge faced by Church leaders? (Verses 2–4.)
- Why don't the Twelve Apostles today visit and take care of all the needs of each Church member?
- Who was called and set apart to help the Apostles better take care of all the members? (Verses 5–6.)
- Who is responsible to help take care of the needs of individual Church members today? (Families, bishops and other priesthood leaders, Relief Society sisters, etc.)

Share with your family the following statement by President Gordon B. Hinckley: "The Church is becoming a very large and complex organization. . . . We are becoming a great global society. But our interest and concern must always be with the individual. Every member of this church is an individual man or woman, boy or girl. Our great responsibility is to see that each is 'remembered and nourished by the good word of God.'" (*Ensign,* May 1995, 52.)

Ask the following questions and share the quotation that follows:

- Why would it be difficult for the bishop to do all those things mentioned by President Hinckley?

- What can Church members do to help the bishop attend to all these duties?

"To lighten the load of the bishopric, auxiliary presidencies and Melchizedek Priesthood quorum presidencies and group leaders need to exercise initiative and fully function in the great responsibilities of their callings. Bishops are responsible to call; they should not be required to beg or push. All of us should accept the callings we are given and serve in all diligence." (Dallin H. Oaks, *Ensign,* May 1997, 23.)

Invite a family member to read Acts 6:7 and ask:

- What effect did delegating responsibility to others have on the Church in Jerusalem?
- In what ways have you noticed similar blessing in the Church today?

You may want to conclude by sharing these encouraging words of President Gordon B. Hinckley:

"We are all in this great endeavor together. We are here to assist our Father in His work and His glory, 'to bring to pass the immortality and eternal life of man' (Moses 1:39). Your obligation is as serious in your sphere of responsibility as is my obligation in my sphere. No calling in this church is small or of little consequence. All of us in the pursuit of our duty touch the lives of others." (*Ensign,* May 1995, 71.)

Acts 6:8–15
That "celestial glow"

Invite family members to think about a Church leader who has had a great influence in their life. Ask them to share the most important qualities of this person. Read together Acts 6:8–11, 15 and look for qualities that made Stephen an influential leader. Ask:

- What words or phrases describe Stephen and his influence on others?
- What kind of a Church leader do you suppose he was?
- In what ways do some Church leaders or members appear to be different from others today?
- What influence does the Holy Spirit have on the way faithful followers of Christ appear before others? (Verse 15.)

Explain that Stephen did not always have a positive influence on others. Have your family silently read Acts 6:9, 11–14 and look for how others reacted to Stephen's ministry among the Jews. Ask:

- Why do you suppose some people tried to oppose such a man as Stephen?
- What did his enemies do to cause trouble for Stephen? (Verses 11–14.)
- What lies or twisted truths do people tell about the Church or its leaders today?
- What can we do to help people know what we really believe?

Tell your family that just being good is no guarantee that others will treat us fairly. Testify that, like Stephen, we can still know that we are right with God and be sanctified despite the persecution of others. Challenge your family to live each day so the Spirit of God can shine in their faces (see Alma 5:14) and be a positive influence on others.

ACTS 7: THE DEATH OF STEPHEN

Acts 7:1–36
The history of Israel is retold

Tell your family that in these verses Stephen is retelling the history of Israel and how they rejected Moses and many other prophets. Divide your family into two groups. Assign one group to silently read Acts 7:1–8 and the other group to silently read Acts 7:9–16. When finished, invite members of each group to share what they learned about Abraham and Joseph.

Now take turns reading together Acts 7:17–36 and then ask some or all of the following questions:

- What was the situation like for the Israelites living in Egypt when Moses was born? (Verses 17–19.)
- Who raised Moses and how was he taught? (Verses 21–22.)
- What did Moses do at the age of 40? (Verse 23.)
- What did Moses do in verse 24 that indicates he knew he was of Hebrew lineage? (Smote an Egyptian.)
- According to verse 25, what did Moses know

concerning his destiny? (He would be a deliverer of the people.)

- Why did Moses flee out of Egypt? (Verses 26–29.)
- What happened to him at age 80? (Verse 30.)
- How might Moses have learned of his calling to deliver Israel out of bondage? (See JST Genesis 50:24–38, which relates Joseph's prophecy of a deliverer. Also remind your family that Moses' real mother was asked to help raise Moses—perhaps she taught him of his lineage.)
- What did God send Moses to do for Israel? (Verses 34–36.)

Tell your family that Moses gave up the luxuries of Egypt to be with his people. Discuss what your family should be willing to give up for The Church of Jesus Christ of Latter-day Saints. Testify to your family that whatever we give up to belong to God's family is well worth it.

Acts 7:37–54
Israel's apostasy

Ask your family members to tell as many reasons as they can think of why people get angry.

Read the following statement by President John Taylor: "Truth has always been opposed by the children of men, it comes in contact with the corrupt hearts and wicked practices. The Prophets have always been persecuted; and why? because they dared to tell the word of the Lord to the people." (*Teachings of Presidents of the Church: John Taylor,* 214.)

Tell your family that Stephen had a similar experience when he told the truth to the Jewish leaders. Invite your family to quickly scan Acts 7:37–50. Ask:

- Why do you think the Jews became so upset with Stephen? (See verses 51–53.)
- What wicked things did Stephen accuse them of? (They resisted the Holy Ghost; they rejected the prophets whom Jesus [the Just One] sent; they murdered Jesus; and they received the gospel but "have not kept it.")
- What would be the wisest thing to do when

our Church leaders tell us the truth about what we are doing wrong?
- What good does it do to get angry when we are corrected and pretend we are not wrong?

Share your testimony of the value of repentance and always giving heed to the words of the Lord's servants.

Acts 7:54–60
Stephen's testimony rejected

Remind your family that in Acts 6 Stephen was arrested on the false charge of blasphemy, and in this chapter he tells the Jewish council (the Sanhedrin) that they are like ancient Israel, always in a state of apostasy and refusing to obey the words of the prophets in the scriptures. (See Acts 7:9–53.) Ask:

- What is blasphemy? (See Bible Dictionary, "Blasphemy," 625.)
- Why do you think Stephen reminded the Jews of Israel's frequent forgetfulness and disobedience to God?
- According to Acts 7:54, how did the Sanhedrin respond to Stephens's remarks? (To *gnash* means to "grind." These Jews were grinding their teeth together in anger.)
- Why do you think they were so angry?

Tell your family that while these angry Jewish religious leaders "gnashed on him with their teeth," Stephen had a remarkable experience. Read together Acts 7:55–60 and ask:

- What vision did Stephen see?
- What did the people do to Stephen for testifying that he saw God?
- Before Stephen's death, what Christlike attribute did he show? (See verse 60.)
- What do Stephen's last words reveal about his faith in Jesus Christ? (See verses 59–60.)
- What do we know about Heavenly Father and Jesus from Stephen's experience? (The Father and the Son are separate and distinct from each other.)
- Why do you think Stephen was given this vision at that particular time?

Read the following by President James E. Faust: "In recent times the price of oil, gold, and other precious minerals has greatly increased. These treasures are all obtained by looking down. They are useful and necessary, but they are tangible riches. What of the treasures that are to be found by raising our vision? What of the intangible riches which come from the pursuit of holiness? Stephen looked upward: 'Being full of the Holy Ghost, [he] looked up steadfastly into heaven, and saw the glory of God, and Jesus standing on the right hand of God.' (Acts 7:55.) Like Stephen, those who pursue holiness see the glory of God. (See Acts 7:55.)." (*Ensign,* May 1981, 8.)

Discuss as a family the blessings you might receive from looking up toward the Lord. Let your family know of your belief in the separate nature of each member of the Godhead and of your love for those who stand for truth like Stephen.

ACTS 8: PHILIP'S MINISTRY

Acts 8:1–4
Saul persecutes the Church

 Ask family members if they have ever made "havock" (spelled *havoc* today) or done any "haling." (You may need to spell out H-A-L-I-N-G as opposed to H-A-I-L-I-N-G). Tell them they may get some help as to what "havock" and "haling" mean in Acts 8. Read together Acts 8:1–4 and ask someone to tell what they think those words mean. If they need help, have someone look up *havoc* and *hale* in a dictionary. Ask:

- Who was trying to make "havock" or destroy the Church?
- What was Saul doing to the members? (Dragging them to prison.)
- Why do you think Saul was persecuting the Church members so?
- In spite of the persecution, what did Church members continue to do? (See verse 4.)
- How did the persecution help the disciples fulfill Jesus' command in Matthew 28:19?

Ask your family to think about how the Church in the days of the Prophet Joseph was like what we just read about in Acts 8. Ask:

- What similarities do you see between what

happened to the Church in Peter's day and what happened to the Church in the days of the Prophet Joseph Smith? (Both endured persecution by those in authority.)
- What did the Church in Joseph Smith's day do about the persecution?

Ask your family members if they have ever faced persecution for their beliefs. Discuss ways your family can help fulfill the destiny of The Church of Jesus Christ of Latter-day Saints in this day.

Acts 8:5–25
Can priesthood power be purchased?

Before beginning this lesson, write the following on a strip of paper:

Priesthood power	is not	for sale!
fold back ↑	fold ↑	

Fold the strip of paper where the arrows indicate so "is not" will be covered up and it will look like this:

Priesthood power	for sale!

Hold the strip at the fold as you show it to your family and ask what they would think if they saw a sign like this displayed. How much would you be willing to pay for priesthood power? Tell your family to look for principles about priesthood power as you study Acts 8:5–25.

Read Acts 8:5 to your family and ask:

- What do you remember about Philip? (Philip was one of the seven men chosen to assist the Apostles [see Acts 6:1–6].)
- What do you remember about Samaria?

As you take turns reading Acts 8:6–25, ask some or all of the following questions:

- How did the people of Samaria respond to Philip's preaching? (Verses 6–8.)
- How did the people receive the gift of the Holy Ghost? (Verses 14–17.)
- Who was Simon and what had he been doing? (Verses 9–11.)
- How did Simon try to get the priesthood? (Verses 18–19.)

- What answer did Simon receive from Peter? (Verses 20–23.)
- What is the right way for a man to obtain the priesthood?

Show your family again the word strip that says:

Priesthood power	for sale!

Ask what it should say and then pull the ends so it unfolds and reads:

Priesthood power	is not	for sale!

Share this statement from President James E. Faust: "This greatest of all powers, the priesthood power, is not accessed the way power is used in the world. It cannot be bought or sold. . . . Worldly power often is employed ruthlessly. However, priesthood power is invoked only through those principles of righteousness by which the priesthood is governed." (*Ensign*, May 1997, 43.)

If you have a priesthood holder in your family, invite him to share his feelings about being a priesthood holder.

Acts 8:26–40
A model of good missionary work

Indicate to your family that Acts 8:26–40 gives an account of another missionary experience of Philip's. Write the four questions listed below on a sheet of paper and tell your family to search Acts 8:26–40 for answers:

- How was Philip guided to the Ethiopian eunuch? (Verses 26–29; for a definition of *eunuch*, see Bible Dictionary, 667.)
- What was the Ethiopian reading? (Verses 30–33; *Esaias* means Isaiah.)
- How did the Ethiopian demonstrate humility?
- What blessings came as a result of his humility?

Allow time for family members to study Acts 8:26–40 as individuals or pairs and then review each question.

Ask your family what principles they have learned from these verses that could apply in their lives.

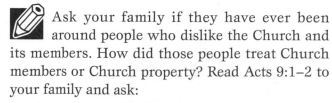

ACTS 9: THE CONVERSION OF SAUL

Acts 9:1–9
Who appeared to Saul on the road to Damascus?

Ask your family if they have ever been around people who dislike the Church and its members. How did those people treat Church members or Church property? Read Acts 9:1–2 to your family and ask:

- How did Saul feel about members of Christ's Church in his day?
- What did he want to do with the Christians?

Invite your family to share how they might feel if the Savior appeared to them. How might your feelings change if you knew you were not worthy? Read together Acts 9:3–9 and ask:

- Whom did Saul see?
- What did Jesus ask Saul? (Verse 4.)
- How would you describe Saul's feelings on this occasion?
- What does Saul's question in verse 6 teach us about his character?
- Considering Saul's destructive mission, in what way do you think this experience changed his life? (See verse 20.)

Invite family members to write the following references in the margin beside Acts 3:6–8: 1 Samuel 3:10; 1 Nephi 3:7; Luke 1:38. Ask for volunteers to look up the references and report how others responded to the Lord in a similar experience.

Explain to your family that even though the Savior may not appear to them, He also has things for them to do. Have them write in their journals the question Saul asked: "Lord, what wilt thou have me to do?" Challenge them to ponder this question often and when they receive an answer to write it in their journal and act upon it.

Acts 9:10–19
Chosen vessels

As you begin family scripture study, consider offering a prayer in behalf of individuals who are suffering or have gone astray. At the conclusion of the prayer, ask family members if they pray for those who struggle spiritually and/or physically. If so, invite them to share how their prayers have been answered.

Invite three family members to read the parts of Ananias, Jesus, and the narration found in Acts 9:9–19. Once they have read their parts, discuss some of the following questions:

- How long was Saul blind and how long did he fast? (Verse 9.)
- What were Ananias's concerns about Saul? (Verses 13–14.)
- Why were prayers, offered in behalf of Saul in verses 11 and 17, answered so quickly? (Verse 15.)
- Why do you think Saul was considered a "chosen vessel"?
- In what way can we be considered "chosen vessels"?
- What will be required of Saul as a result of answered prayers? (Verse 16.)
- What would you be willing to suffer for the Savior?
- In addition to being healed from blindness, what great gift was Saul given? (Verse 17.)
- In what way was Saul healed of both physical and spiritual blindness?

Explain to your family that Saul's experience (which is similar to Alma the Younger's in Mosiah 27:8–37) was unusual. Most people come unto the Savior in less dramatic ways. Discuss as a family how each family member might also be considered a "chosen vessel."

Acts 9:20–31

What goes around, comes around

Ask your family if they understand the meaning of the saying: "What goes around, comes around." If they do not, take time to explain it.

Remind your family what Saul had done to the Christians (see Acts 9:1–2) and then take turns reading Acts 9:21–31. As you read, have your family look for things that Saul had sent around that were now coming back around to him. Ask:

- According to verse 20, how would you describe the difference in Saul's life?

- What did Saul teach that caused people to want to kill him?
- What did the disciples do to protect Saul?
- Why were some disciples still afraid of Saul?
- Have you ever been hurt by someone who later became a friend? How long did it take for you to trust that person?
- What finally happened that allowed the churches to have "rest" concerning Saul?

Testify to your family that just as Saul's testimony of the Savior helped convince Christians that he really did have a mighty change of heart, so can their testimony of the Savior help assure that good things will go around from them so that good things will come back around to them.

Acts 9:32–43

Peter performs similar miracles to those of Jesus

Write Acts 9:32–35 on one sheet of paper and Acts 9:36–43 on another. Divide your family into two groups and give each group one of the two sheets of paper. Assign each group to either act out or retell the drama found in their verses and give them time to prepare their presentation. When the presentations are finished, ask them if they can think of similar miracles performed by the Savior. (See John 5:5–9; Mark 5:35–43.) Ask:

- What is significant about the fact that Peter, through the power of the Holy Ghost, performed miracles similar to the Savior's?
- To whom did Peter give the credit for his miraculous power? (Verse 34.)
- What does the fact that Peter was able to do these miracles teach us about some of the people living in Joppa and Lydda? (See Mark 16:17–18; Mormon 9:24.)
- What can happen in our lives as our faith increases?

Sing together or read the words to "God Moves in a Mysterious Way." (*Hymns,* no. 285.) Talk about the message of each verse with your family.

ACTS 10: THE GOSPEL GOES TO THE GENTILES

Acts 10:1–33

Cornelius, Peter, and two visions

Bring the following to scripture study: a sheet, several stuffed animals, a bathrobe, a bath towel, and a broom.

To better understand this chapter it will be helpful for your family to know about the two main characters, Simon Peter and Cornelius. Remind your family that Peter was the head of the Church and was the chief Apostle while Jesus was on the earth. To learn about Cornelius, take turns reading the following verses: Acts 10:1, 2, 22, 24, and 30 and ask:

- What did Cornelius do for a living? (Verse 1; see also Bible Dictionary, "Centurion," 632, and the first paragraph for "Cornelius," 650.)
- What does it mean that Cornelius "feared God"? (Used this way, *fear* means to have great reverence and respect.)
- What are alms? (See the first few sentences in Bible Dictionary, "Almsgiving," 606.)
- How did the Jews feel about Cornelius? (Verse 22.)
- Who appeared to Cornelius after he had fasted and prayed much? (Verse 30.)

With a better understanding of who Cornelius was, have your family act out Acts 10. Put the stuffed animals in the sheet and gather the four corners of the sheet together, covering the stuffed animals. Dress one person in a bathrobe to play the part of Cornelius. Drape the towel over the right shoulder of another family member to play Peter. Finally, give the broom (which represents a spear) to another family member to play a Roman soldier. Take turns reading Acts 10:1–33 and act out the verses. Explain that this revelation given to Peter was the beginning of the missionary work to the Gentiles, or people not of the house of Israel. Ask:

- Why do you think it was so hard for Peter to believe it was time to teach the gospel to the Gentiles? (See Matthew 10:5–6.)
- How was the vision of the clean and unclean animals a good way to teach Peter that it was now time to teach the gospel to the Gentiles?
- How do we know that Peter learned this important doctrine? (See verses 34–35.)

Discuss as a family ways that the Church continues to teach the gospel to all people who will listen. If there is a returned missionary in the family, invite him/her to share his/her testimony about people he/she taught.

Acts 10:34–43

What is a testimony?

Ask your family to share how they would explain to a friend what a testimony is. Read, or have someone else read, the following statement by Elder M. Russell Ballard:

"Although we can have testimonies of many things as members of the Church, there are basic truths we need to constantly teach one another and share with those not of our faith. Testify God is our Father and Jesus is the Christ. The plan of salvation is centered on the Savior's Atonement. Joseph Smith restored the fulness of the everlasting gospel of Jesus Christ, and the Book of Mormon is evidence that our testimony is true." (*Ensign,* Nov. 2004, 41.) Ask:

- According to Elder Ballard, what should our testimony be focused on?
- What can we do to build our testimonies in these areas?
- Who are some of our neighbors or friends with whom we could be sharing our testimonies?

Read together Acts 10:34–43 and look for what Peter included in his testimony. Ask:

- What similarities do you see between Peter's testimony and Elder Ballard's counsel on what a testimony should include?
- Why do you think it is important to have a testimony of Jesus Christ both then and now?
- How might Joseph Smith and the Book of Mormon help build our testimonies of Jesus Christ?

Ask:

- What happens when a person bears testimony of a true principle?

• Who benefits when the Spirit comes to bear witness of a truth?

Share your testimony and then encourage family members to share their testimonies with someone in the next few days.

ACTS 11: THE CHURCH BEGINS TO GO ABROAD

Acts 11:1–18
Reviewing the revelation

This chapter reviews the story in Acts 10. Understanding that story is essential to understanding this chapter. You may wish to study Acts 10 if you have not already done so as a family.

• What was the importance of the revelation Peter had in Acts 10 that led to the conversion of Cornelius? (Gentiles could be baptized into the Church.)

• Do you think the Jews would have reacted positively or negatively toward this revelation? Why?

Have a family member read Acts 11:1–3 aloud to the family to see exactly what the Jews' reaction was. Tell your family that in response to their concerns, Peter related his experience again. Since this is a repeat of the story found in Acts 10, have your family close their scriptures for the following review quiz over details of Peter's experience. Before beginning the quiz, show them a word strip like the following:

___ ___ ___ ___ ___ ___ ___ ___ ___ ___ ___ ___

___ ___ ___ ___ ___ ___ ___ ___

i n e t o c r g u v a l

Tell your family that the blanks on the word strip represent the letters of a two-word idea that is an important part of the Lord's true Church. This idea explains why practices can and will change in the Church from time to time. (The words are *continuing revelation*.) Tell them that the letters shown are all the letters used in these two words (although some of the letters are used more than one time). For each question your family answers correctly, let them choose a letter, and then you write that letter in its correct blank (or blanks). Don't give them the correct answer if they

get it wrong. As they fill in letters on the word strip, let them guess what the two words are. If they still can't figure out the words because they didn't get some of the questions correct, let them go back and look up answers in Acts 11 and then choose a letter for each they find. When you have completed the activity, you might also note that this is often the way revelation comes—both individually and to the Church—a little piece at a time until we get the whole picture or idea.

Quiz

• What city was Peter in when he had the revelation that led him to eventually baptize Cornelius and open the gospel to the Gentiles? (Joppa; see Acts 11:5.)

• What was on the sheet that came down from heaven that Peter saw in his vision? (Beasts, creeping things, fowls; see Acts 11:6.)

• What was Peter told to do with the things on the sheet? (Kill and eat them; see Acts 11:7.)

• Why didn't he want to? (Because they were "unclean" according to the law of Moses; see Acts 11:8.)

• What did the voice say about why it was now OK? (God had "cleansed" these things; see Acts 11:9.)

• How many times did Peter have this vision? (Three; see Acts 11:10.)

• What was Peter told to do as the vision closed? (Go down to meet three men sent from Caesarea to see him; see Acts 11:11–12.)

• What remarkable experience did Cornelius tell Peter about? (He had seen an angel who told him to send for Peter; see Acts 11:13.)

• What remarkable thing happened to Cornelius and the people who were with him when Peter proclaimed the gospel to them? (The Holy Ghost fell upon them; see Acts 11:15.)

Have a family member read aloud Acts 11:18. Ask: What was the reaction of Church leaders and members to Peter's account of what he experienced? Challenge your family to always live in a way that when Church leaders explain their revelations, we can be quickly convinced of their truthfulness.

Acts 11:27–30

"Because I have been given much . . ."

Share with your family the following statement of the Prophet Joseph Smith: "A man filled with the love of God, is not content with blessing his family alone, but ranges through the whole world, anxious to bless the whole human race." (*History of the Church,* 4:227.)

Have your family read Acts 11:27–30 and look for examples showing that Joseph Smith's statement was true in the early Church, and then share what they find.

Tell your family some of the ways we send relief to others today by sharing an article in a recent *Church News* or Church magazine about the humanitarian work of the Church. Remind them that the humanitarian work of the Church is funded by contributions of Saints all over the world who want to help. Encourage your family members to give to this great effort regularly .

Sing as a family "Because I Have Been Given Much." (*Hymns,* no. 219.)

ACTS 12: PETER IS FREED FROM PRISON

Acts 12:1–25

One Apostle is killed; the other escapes

Explain to your family that you will be playing a game in connection with this chapter. Have your family read the chapter together and listen carefully for details that they might be asked about later. Encourage family members to mark key points and ideas in the chapter to help them remember the information.

After the reading, give family members a piece of scratch paper and have them write numbers 1 through 11. Read each question from the list below and have them write the letter they think provides the best answer.

At the end of the game, ask each question again. Invite family members to share their answers and identify the verse(s) the answer comes from. When you read Acts 12:4, use footnote *b* to determine what a "quaternion" is.

1. Who killed James? (Verses 1–2.)
   A. An angry Pharisee.
   B. An angry mob of Jews.
   C. An apostate.
   D. Herod.

2. How many soldiers where guarding Peter? (Verse 4.)
   A. 4.
   B. 8.
   C. 16.
   D. More than enough.

3. Who was chained next to Peter? (Verse 6.)
   A. John.
   B. Two guards.
   C. Some smelly guy.
   D. No one.

4. Who hit Peter on the side? (Verse 7.)
   A. John.
   B. A guard.
   C. An angel.
   D. The smelly guy.

5. How did Peter get the chains off? (Verse 7.)
   A. They just fell off.
   B. An angel smote the chains.
   C. The guard helped him.
   D. Peter had skinny hands and slipped them off.

6. Why had so many Church members come to Mary's house? (Verse 12.)
   A. To play board games.
   B. To enjoy a casserole Mary had made.
   C. To plan a way to break Peter out of prison.
   D. To pray for Peter.

7. What did the young girl do when she saw it was Peter at the door? (Verse 14.)
   A. She warmly greeted the Apostle.
   B. She left him standing at the door.
   C. She thought it was a ghost and ran away screaming.
   D. She went to have another helping of that wonderful casserole.

8. Who did the members think Peter was at first? (Verse 15.)
   A. The angel of Peter.
   B. John.
   C. A door-to-door salesman.
   D. A child playing a prank.

9. What did Herod do with the soldiers? (Verses 18–19.)
   A. Promoted them to a higher rank.
   B. Kicked them out of the army.
   C. Invited them to play board games.
   D. Put them to death.

10. What did the people say Herod was? (Verse 22.)
    A. A pretty good leader.
    B. A big jerk.
    C. A god.
    D. An angel.

11. How did Herod die? (Verse 23.)
    A. He ate some bad food.
    B. Some Jews killed him for blasphemy.
    C. A servant betrayed him.
    D. Something was eating him up inside.

In conclusion, ask family members to tell what they think is the most significant thing they learned from this chapter. (If you have the time, consider using the next teaching idea instead of this conclusion.)

Have your family review Acts 12 again and choose the teachings or principles that most impressed them.

Elder Richard G. Scott said: "Principles are concentrated truth, packaged for application to a wide variety of circumstances. A true principle makes decisions clear even under the most confusing and compelling circumstances. It is worth great effort to organize the truth we gather to simple statements of principle." (*Ensign,* Nov. 1993, 86.)

After your family has had a chance to share, you could ask the following questions to assist in leading them to discover some additional teachings.

1. Read Doctrine and Covenants 42:46–47 and ask: How do these verses comfort us about the death of the Apostle James? Why would these verses *not* be a comfort to Herod?

2. Why did God prevent Peter's death but not James's death? Why, many years later, did God allow Peter to be put to death?

3. Why were the Church members gathered together to pray? How did prayer make a difference? (See James 5:16.)

4. For what specific sin did God have the angel kill Herod? (Verse 23.) What is an example today of someone not giving "God the glory"? When should we give "God the glory" today?

ACTS 13: PAUL AND BARNABAS'S FIRST MISSION

Acts 13:1–13
How are missionaries called?

 If available, place a map or globe of the world where the whole family can see it. Ask them to identify places where family members or friends have served missions and locate those places on the map or globe. If anyone present has served a mission, invite him/her to share the experience of receiving his/her call. If not, ask family members to imagine what feelings or emotions might accompany receiving a mission call from the Lord. Read together Acts 13:1–4 and ask:

- Who is receiving a mission call and to where?
- According to Acts 13:1–2, where did this call come from?
- What occurred before they were sent on their mission? (See verse 3.)
- Who sets missionaries apart today? (Stake presidents, as authorized by the First Presidency.)
- Because they were set apart by proper authority, what does Acts 13:4 say about how these missionaries were directed?
- How will this help them in their service?
- How is this story in Acts 13 an example of Articles of Faith 1:5?
- What experiences have helped you know that Church callings are inspired by the Lord?

Read Acts 13:5–13. Ask:

- Where did Paul and Barnabas go to find people to teach? (Verse 5.)
- If you were currently serving a mission, how might you find people to teach?

THE MISSIONARY JOURNEYS OF PAUL

Event	Scripture references	Time period	Sites traveled in order	Companions	Significant events	Epistles written
First Mission	Acts 13–14	A.D. 47–49 A.D. 49–50	Antioch and Seleucia in Syria; Salamis and Paphos on Isle of Cyprus; Perga in Pamphylia; Antioch, Iconium, Lystra, and Derbe in Galatia. Total: 1,400 miles	Barnabas, John Mark (Acts 13:2, 5, 13)	Confronted by Elymas, a sorcerer; preached and healed on Sabbath; was persecuted and expelled from Antioch; stoned and thought to be dead; revived and preached again	Unknown
Jerusalem Conference	Acts 15; Galatians 2:1–10	A.D. 49–50	Jerusalem	Barnabas, Titus (Acts 15:2; Galatians 2:3)	Honored by Church leaders as a champion of the Gentiles in the gospel cause. Gentile converts do not need to become converted to Judaism first	Unknown
Second Mission	Acts 15:36–18:22	A.D. 50–53	Antioch in Syria; Tarsus, Derbe, Lystra, Iconium, and Antioch in Galatia; Troas; Philippi, Thessalonica, and Berea in Macedonia; Athens and Corinth in Greece; Ephesus in Lydia; Jerusalem. Total: 3,000 miles	Silas (Acts 15:40), Timothy (Acts 16:1–3), Luke (Acts 16:10)	Directed in vision to teach in Macedonia; cast evil spirit out of damsel in Philippi; beaten and imprisoned with Silas; converted jailor; preached at Mars Hill	1 Thessalonians (A.D. 50–51); 2 Thessalonians (A.D. 50–51); both epistles written from Corinth
Third Mission	Acts 18:23–21:15	A.D. 54–58	Antioch in Syria; Tarsus, Iconium, and Antioch in Galatia; Ephesus, Troas; Philippi, Thessalonica, and Berea in Macedonia; Corinth; Miletus, Patara; Tyre, Caesarea, and Jerusalem. Total: 3,500 miles	Timothy, Erastus (Acts 19:22); Gaius of Macedonia, Aristarchus (Acts 19:29); Sopater, Secundus, Gaius of Derbe, Tychicus, Trophimus (Acts 20:4); Luke (Acts 20:5–6)	It appears by Paul's third mission that he is now an Apostle (1 Corinthians 1:1). Conferred gift of Holy Ghost by laying on of hands; special miracles wrought of God through Paul; confronted worshippers of Diana; raised Eutychus from dead; foretold his own arrest and death	A lost epistle to Corinth (see 1 Corinthians 5:9); 1 Corinthians (A.D. 55 from Ephesus); 2 Corinthians (A.D. 56 from Macedonia); Galatians (A.D. 56 from Macedonia); Romans (A.D. 57 from Corinth)

Event	Scripture references	Time period	Sites traveled in order	Companions	Significant events	Epistles written
Arrest at Jerusalem and Imprisonment at Caesarea	Acts 21:16–26:32	A.D. 58–59	Jerusalem and Caesarea	Unknown	Persecuted, arrested, bound; recounted story of his conversion; was tried before Ananias and Sanhedrin; the Lord appeared to him; brought before Felix, Festus, and King Agrippa; appealed to Caesar	Unknown
Journey to Rome	Acts 27:1–28:16	A.D. 59–60	Caesarea and Sidon; Islands of Crete, Malta, and Sicily; Puteoli to Rome along the Appian Way. Total: 1,400 miles	Aristarchus, Luke (Acts 27:2)	Perilous voyage to Rome; comforted by an angel; prophesied of danger; shipwrecked at Malta; bitten by viper but unharmed	Unknown
First Roman Imprisonment (House Arrest)	Acts 28:16–31	A.D. 60–62	Rome	Epaphroditus (Philippians 4:18), Epaphras (Philemon 1:23), Timothy (Philippians 1:1), Tychicus (Ephesians 6:21), Justus (Colossians 4:11	Guarded daily by Roman soldiers; preached to many visitors	Philippians; Colossians; Ephesians; Philemon; Hebrews (all written from Rome between A.D. 60–62)
Roman Imprisonments	None	A.D. 62–65	Asia, Macedonia, Crete, and perhaps Spain	Unknown	Sent counsel to priesthood leaders in letters	1 Timothy (A.D. 64 from Macedonia); Titus (A.D. 65 from Ephesus)
Second Roman Imprisonment	None	A.D. 65	Rome	Luke (2 Timothy 4:11)	Wrote final testimony in 2 Timothy; beheaded and died a martyr's death	2 Timothy (A.D. 65 from Rome)

- What was one of their first spiritual experiences in the area? (Verses 6 and 11.)
- What effect did that experience have upon others?

Ask your family to share a spiritual experience they have had doing missionary work or that they know about. Discuss how a missionary and his family are blessed by missionary service. Testify of how missionaries are truly called by inspiration and why we need to share the gospel message.

Acts 13:14–43

Paul sets a pattern for his missionary service

Tell your family that Paul was one of the greatest missionaries in history and that we can learn much from his experiences. Ask someone to be a scribe and have him or her write the following headings on a chart: *Finding People to Teach What to Teach? Reactions to the Teaching.* Read aloud Acts 13:5–52, verse by verse. Pause after each verse is read and have each family member choose an item or event that could be listed under any of the three headings. Have the scribe record the responses.

When you have completed the chapter, the following model may be of help as you talk about the things your family listed for each topic.

Finding People to Teach

- What do you think we can learn from where and how Paul found people to teach?
- Why do you think Sergius Paulus called for the missionaries? (Verse 7.)
- What causes people to be interested in the Church today? How do they know who to ask when they have questions?
- Do you think the people you associate with know how important the gospel is to you?

What to Teach?

- Why do you think Paul talked to the people in the synagogue about their history?
- What did Paul especially want to emphasize in verses 27–39?
- What did Paul call the message of Jesus in verse 32?
- What difference does it make when you see your message as "the glad tidings" or "the

good news"? (Both of these phrases are literal translations of the word *gospel;* see Bible Dictionary, "Gospels," 682.)

Reactions to the Teaching

- What do you think we can learn from the different ways people reacted to the teachings of these missionaries?
- How are the reactions of the people in Acts 13 like the reactions of people today when they hear the gospel preached?
- Why do you think the Jews were so upset in verse 45? Have you ever seen people act like that toward the Church today?

Give each family member a chance to share at least one thing they are going to do because of what they learned about missionary work in Acts 13.

ACTS 14: MISSION EXPERIENCES OF SAUL AND BARNABAS

Acts 14:1–28

Mission experiences

 Ask your family:

- What do you think are the hardest things about being a full-time missionary?
- What do you think are the best or most rewarding things about being a full-time missionary?

Tell your family that they will find both hard and rewarding parts of missionary work as they read about the mission of Paul and Barnabas in Acts 14. Write in large letters on a piece of paper the word *Rewarding,* and on another piece of paper write in large letters the word *Hard.* Put them up where your family can see them while you study Acts 14.

As a family, take turns reading aloud Acts 14:1–28. As you do, display the papers with the words *Rewarding* and *Hard* on them. Invite them to say "Stop" anytime someone reads something in Acts 14 that they believe demonstrates something about Paul's mission that would fit in either of those categories. When a person says "Stop," invite him or her to explain what he or she found. Ask your family to describe ways this experience might be like things missionaries experience today. If you have a returned missionary in your family, you may want to have him or her share some of his or her mission experiences that are similar to those of Paul and Barnabas.

The following questions might help you sum up what you read:

- What did the returning missionaries "rehearse" to the Saints in Antioch who had sent them? (Verse 27.)
- What is impressive about the way they viewed "their" mission? (They saw it as things that "*God* had done with them.")
- What does that tell you about why they were willing to go through the hard things as well as the rewarding things?
- What things from Acts 14 do you want to put into practice in your life?

ACTS 15: APOSTLES DECLARE DOCTRINE AND POLICY

Acts 15:1–34
How is Church policy decided?

Tell this story to your family: "Spencer W. Kimball was baptized in Thatcher, Arizona, . . . in the hog-scalding tub that was also used as the family's bathtub. His father stood outside the tub."

Ask family members to vote on whether the baptism was performed properly or not.

Ask your family what we should do when we have a question about Church doctrine or policy?

Explain to your family that, in New Testament times, Jewish converts to Christianity thought that Gentile converts should first submit to the requirements of the law of Moses and be circumcised before they could be part of Christ's Church. Depending on your family's curiosity and maturity level you may want to explain more about circumcision by referring to the Bible Dictionary, 646. While reading Acts 15:1–12 together with your family, ask them to look for how early Church leaders answered some difficult questions. Ask:

- How did Church leaders settle questions of doctrine? (Verse 2.)
- Who felt that Gentiles needed to keep the law of Moses? (Verse 5.)
- What did Peter say that ended their dispute? (Verses 7–12.)
- Who was the Church president in Acts 15? (Peter.)
- Who states doctrine and policy for the Church today?

Have your family give examples of Church policy and procedure changes they can remember. (For example, Official Declaration 2; "The Family: A Proclamation to the World" [*Ensign,* Nov. 1995, 101; or see the Appendix of this book.])

Finish the story about President Kimball's baptism: "His father stood outside the tub, which some people felt was not a correct way to baptize. To be sure that Spencer was properly baptized, he was baptized again, when he was twelve years old, in the Union Canal just a block away from his home." (William Hartley and Rebecca Todd, *Friend,* Aug. 1997, 43.)

We learn from the *Family Guidebook* (19) that the person performing the baptism "stands in the water with the person who will be baptized."

Read Acts 15:13–22 aloud. Give each member of your family a piece of paper and a pencil and ask them to write a letter explaining the policy which the Church leaders pronounced from Acts 15:19–20. Have family members share their letters with each other.

Invite one family member to read the letter written by the Apostles to the Gentiles in Acts 15:23–32 and then ask if all points of the letter from the brethren were covered in your family's letters.

Ask:

- What was it that assisted the brethren in resolving the conflict regarding the Gentiles and circumcision? (Acts 15:8, 28.)
- What does Peter say that purified the hearts of the Gentiles? (Verse 9.)
- According to Peter, what is it that will save the Gentiles rather than the law of Moses? (Verse 11.)

Bear testimony to your family of one of these principles.

ACTS 16: PAUL'S SECOND MISSION

Acts 16:1–11
Paul's missionary work

Ask your family to list some locations where they have had friends or family serve missions. Explain that Acts 16 describes part of Paul's second mission. In this chapter there are many places listed where Paul visited, and some of those places have unusual names. To understand this part of Paul's mission, read Acts 15:40–41 together and find the name of Paul's companion for this mission. Have everyone turn to the maps in the back of the Bible and find the map of Paul's missionary journeys (Map 13 in post-1999 copies of the Bible; Map 20 in pre-1999 copies; see also the chart "The Missionary Journeys of Paul" on pages 162–63 of this volume). Invite one family member to read aloud the first twelve verses of Acts 16 while the others look at their maps to find the places listed there. Follow the line on the map charting Paul's second mission though Asia Minor.

Invite your family to suggest ways that Paul's missionary travels would have been different from a missionary today.

Acts 16:12–40
What must I do to be saved?

Bring a piece of purple cloth, a hymnbook, your baptismal certificate, and a chain to scripture study. Display these items and explain they all relate to Acts 16:12–40. Invite family members to look for these items as you study this story. When someone has an idea of how one of these items relates to the story, ask him or her to share the ideas with the others.

Invite someone to read Acts 16:12–15 and ask:

- What city were Paul and Silas in?
- Who was the convert?
- Where was she from?
- What was her occupation? (A seller of purple; see verse 14.)
- Who else was converted at the same time? (Verse 15.)

Take turns reading Acts 16:16–40. The following are the verses where the rest of the items could be pointed out: verse 24—chains; verse 25—hymnbook; verse 33—baptismal certificate. After you have finished the reading, ask:

- What gave Paul and Silas added strength to endure the terrible conditions they were in? (Verse 25.)
- When has prayer and powerful spiritual music helped you in your life?
- What was the guard ready to do when he thought the prisoners were gone? (Verse 27.)
- When the guard realized that the prisoners were still there, what life-changing question did he ask? (Verse 30.)
- What answer did Paul give him? (Verse 31.)
- What did the jailer do to show he really did "believe on the Lord Jesus Christ"? (Verse 33.)

To help your family better understand Acts 16:35–40, share the following: Paul and Silas were asked to leave quietly, but they refused on the ground that they were Roman citizens. Roman citizens had rights that non-Romans did not enjoy. Elder Bruce R. McConkie said: "Two Romans, citizens of the mightiest empire on earth—entitled thereby to an impartial trial; to an appeal to the emperor; to freedom from degrading punishments, including bonds, scourging, and crucifixion—are here condemned without a trial, scourged without mercy, imprisoned in bonds in a damp and pestilential cell, all for the testimony of Jesus and the hope of a better resurrection." (*Doctrinal New Testament Commentary*, 2:151.)

Discuss the following:

- According to what Elder McConkie said, why was it that those who jailed them "feared, when they heard that they were Romans"?
- What does this teach us about the courage and testimony of those missionaries?

Help your family understand the importance of being obedient, no matter the cost, just as Paul and Silas were.

ACTS 17: IN ATHENS PAUL TESTIFIES OF A LIVING GOD

Acts 17:1–15
What is the question?

Tell your family that you are going to give them a "backwards" quiz on Acts 17:1–15. You will give them the *answers,* and they will come up with the *questions.* Give family members a copy of the following "answers" listed below. Have them read Acts 17:1–15 and write a question for each answer. When everyone is finished, let each family member ask the question(s) they wrote and see if the others can answer it. (Younger children may need help from an older family member.)

Answers:

- Thessalonica
- Jesus Christ suffered and rose from the dead
- Devout Greeks and chief women
- The house of Jason
- Say that there is another king besides Caesar
- Berea
- Synagogue of the Jews
- Received the word of God with readiness of mind
- Silas and Timotheus
- Athens

After reviewing questions and answers, ask your family what role the scriptures played in Paul's preaching and in the conversion of those Paul preached to. (See Acts 17:2–3, 11.) Read together the promise about the scriptures in 1 Nephi 15:23–24. Ask:

- How does this passage help explain why it was so important that Paul teach from the scriptures?
- Why do you think it was important for those Paul taught to search the scriptures in the process of their conversion?
- What do you think we should do to strengthen our testimonies?

Testify of the importance of "holding fast" to the word of God so that we might recognize truth in our lives and be better able to teach it to others.

Have a family member share the following promise from President Ezra Taft Benson:

"When individual members and families immerse themselves in the scriptures regularly and consistently, . . . other areas of activity will automatically come. Testimonies will increase. Commitment will be strengthened. Families will be fortified. Personal revelation will flow." (*Ensign,* May 1986, 81.)

Acts 17:16–34
Who is God?

If family members have a copy of the Bible printed since 1999, have them turn in the Bible Maps and Photographs section to the photo of Athens (photo no. 29). Tell them that for many centuries Athens was the center of learning in the ancient world, the place where Plato, Socrates, Homer, and many other philosophers, writers, and learned men had lived. Invite two family members to read the following quotations about Athens:

It also "was the world center of idol worship. Temples, statues, and altars were everywhere. 'Petronius, a contemporary writer at Nero's court, says satirically that it was easier to find a god at Athens than a man.' (Jamieson, p. 201.)" (Dummelow, p. 842.) (McConkie, *Doctrinal New Testament Commentary,* 2:155.)

Tell your family that in some ways, being in Athens in those days would be like being on the campus of the most prestigious university you can think of today, where there are many intelligent people and many competing ideas of what is right.

Read together Acts 17:16–23 and ask:

- Why was Paul's "spirit stirred" to want to teach in Athens? (Verse 16.)
- What doctrine seemed "strange" to the learned men of Athens? (Verse 18.)
- Where did they want to take Paul? Why? (Verses 19–21; note that photo no. 29 in post-1999 copies of the Bible is of the Areopagus.)
- What did Paul notice when he got there and what did he want to do about it? (Verses 22–23; note footnotes 22*a* and 23*a.*)

Assign a family member to be a scribe and list what Paul taught the Athenians about the true and living God as you read together Acts 17:24–31.

Stop after each verse and ask the question: What truth (or truths) did Paul teach in this verse about the God he knew? When you finish, invite all to look and/or listen to the list of teachings written by the scribe. Invite family members to choose one thing on the list and tell why they think it is important to know this about God. Share your own testimony of how a true understanding of the reality of God has made a difference in your life.

ACTS 18: PAUL ENDS HIS SECOND AND BEGINS HIS THIRD MISSIONARY JOURNEY

Acts 18:1–6
What have prophets done for a living before becoming prophets?

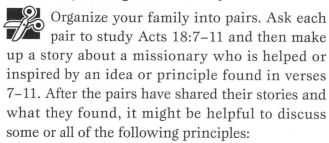 Write on a piece of paper in two columns the lists shown below so you can play a matching game. Ask individual family members to match the occupations in Column 2 with the people listed in Column 1.

Peter	Tax collector
Jesus	U.S. Secretary of Agriculture
Joseph Smith	Tentmaker
Matthew	Fisherman
Moses	Carpenter
Paul	Shepherd
Ezra Taft Benson	Farmer

If your family is unsure of their answers, review the following references: Peter (Matthew 4:18–19), Jesus (Mark 6:3), Joseph Smith (Joseph Smith–History 1:58), Matthew (Matthew 9:9, footnote *b*), Moses (Exodus 3:1), Ezra Taft Benson (he served as U.S. Secretary of Agriculture for President Dwight D. Eisenhower for 8 years). For Paul, have your family read together Acts 18:1–6 and ask:

- What was Paul's career before his call as an Apostle? (Verse 3.)
- What responsibilities came to Paul as an Apostle? (Verse 4.)
- What verse shows that Paul listened to and followed the promptings of the Spirit? (Verse 5.)

Testify to your family that they should listen to the promptings of the Spirit, study and work hard so later they can also have an honorable profession to support their family.

Acts 18:7–17
How can you help a missionary?

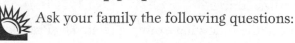 Organize your family into pairs. Ask each pair to study Acts 18:7–11 and then make up a story about a missionary who is helped or inspired by an idea or principle found in verses 7–11. After the pairs have shared their stories and what they found, it might be helpful to discuss some or all of the following principles:

- We should not be afraid to share the gospel with others.
- The Lord will be with us as we do missionary work.
- The Lord prepares people to hear the gospel.

Give each family member a sheet of paper and have them imagine they have recently received a letter from a missionary they know (a friend or sibling) who has expressed fear of doing missionary work. Invite them to write a letter that might help their friend or sibling, based on what they have learned from the Apostle Paul.

Acts 18:24–28
How can we help people not of our faith?

Ask your family the following questions:

- Are there good people in the world who read the scriptures and love the Savior but are not members of our Church?
- What is our responsibility for these people?

Have your family look for the answer to the last question as you read together Acts 18:24–28. Ask, How was Apollos's life changed by the help of Aquila and Priscilla? (Verses 27–28.)

Ask one family member to read Doctrine and Covenants 123:12 and another to read Doctrine and Covenants 88:81. Ask your family how these scriptures relate to the story of Apollos. Challenge your family to seek to become a friend to, and share the gospel with, those around them.

ACTS 19: PAUL'S THIRD MISSIONARY JOURNEY

Acts 19:1–12

Paul and priesthood power

Display pictures of a person being baptized and a child receiving the gift of the Holy Ghost. (See *Gospel Art Kit*, nos. 601 and 602). Invite your family to tell what these ordinances are and why they are so important. Read together Acts 19:1–9 and ask:

- What seems unusual about the kind of disciples Paul found in Ephesus? (They had not heard about the Holy Ghost; verse 2.)
- What did John the Baptist tell those he baptized? (See Matthew 3:11.)
- So, how did Paul know they had not really been baptized by John the Baptist?
- What did Paul do when he recognized they had not been baptized by the proper authority? (Verses 5–6.)
- How can you tell they really received the gift of the Holy Ghost after they were baptized properly? (Verse 6.)

Have a family member read Acts 19:11–12. Ask:

- How would you describe the other blessings that came from the Lord through Paul?
- By what power do you think he was able to do these things?

Read the following example related by President Joseph Fielding Smith about Joseph Smith and the Saints in the Nauvoo area:

"In this manner the Prophet and the brethren passed from house to house, healing the sick and recalling them from the mouth of the tomb. It was on this occasion that a man, not a member of the Church, seeing the mighty miracles which were performed, begged the Prophet to go with him and heal two of his children who were very sick. The Prophet could not go, but said he would send some one to heal them. Taking from his pocket a silk handkerchief he handed it to Elder Wilford Woodruff and requested him to go and heal the children. He told Elder Woodruff to wipe the faces of the children with the handkerchief, and they should be healed. This he did and they were healed." (*Essentials in Church History,* 224)

Ask the following questions:

- What was it that healed the person mentioned in the story above? (Faith and priesthood.)
- So in the story above, what part did the handkerchief play in the healing? (Obedience and faith.)

Testify to your family that miracles follow true believers of Jesus Christ. Remind them that faith precedes these great miracles.

Acts 19:13–20

How are miracles performed?

Invite a family member who holds the priesthood to share his priesthood line of authority back to Jesus Christ. Ask:

- How does that make you feel to know that there are men on earth who can trace their priesthood all the way back to the Savior?
- Why is it important that our authority comes from the Savior?

Take turns reading Acts 19:13–20. Ask:

- Why do you think this evil spirit refused to obey the command of these Jews?
- Why did even using the name of Jesus fail? (They lacked true authority.)
- What was the result in trying to use authority they did not have? (Verse 16.)
- What effect did this have on others who witnessed this event? (Verses 19–20.)

Read the following statement by Elder John H. Taylor: "You remember the occasion when the seven sons of Sceva [tried] to do the things that Paul had been doing. . . . God has always limited the power and the right to speak in his name to the men who hold his Holy Priesthood. Because of this priesthood we have a number of blessings that no one else can have. Others may wish them; they may desire them, but the only way they can have them is by becoming members of his Church." (Conference Report, Apr. 1945, 84–85.)

Ask your family to list some of the blessings that come from holding the priesthood or from having the priesthood in your home.

Acts 19:21–41
What is idol worship?

Take the following items to family scripture study: a picture of a ski boat, a picture of a fancy house, a statue, and a picture of a sports star. Display these items in front of your family and ask:

- What do all these things have in common? (Let them struggle with the question.)
- Is it possible for people to worship these kinds of things?
- How could you tell if these things were more important to a person than God?
- What would you call it if someone worshipped one of these items? (Idolatry.)

Invite your family to take turns reading Acts 19:21–30, searching for difficulties Paul encountered among those who worshipped idols. Invite your family to share what they discovered. Ask:

- Why were certain people upset with Paul's teachings? (They would lose money from their business of selling little statues.)
- What did the silversmith tell the people to get them angry with Paul? (Told them Paul was against their goddess Diana; see verse 27.)
- What types of idols do some people worship today?
- What effect can idol worship have on a person?

Read the following statement by President Spencer W. Kimball: "Modern idols or false gods can take such forms as clothes, homes, businesses, machines, automobiles, pleasure boats, and numerous other material deflectors from the path to godhood. What difference does it make that the item concerned is not shaped like an idol? Brigham Young said: 'I would as soon see a man worshipping a little god made of brass or of wood as to see him worshipping his property.' . . .

"Many worship the hunt, the fishing trip, the vacation, the weekend picnics and outings. Others have as their idols the games of sport, baseball, football, the bullfight, or golf. These pursuits more often than not interfere with the worship of the Lord and with giving service to the building up of the kingdom of God. To the participants this emphasis may not seem serious, yet it indicates where their allegiance and loyalty are." (*Miracle of Forgiveness,* 40–41.)

Ask if there are any modern idols that sometimes get in the way of your family really serving the Lord. Discuss ways your family can eliminate false gods and idols and more readily worship the Lord.

ACTS 20: A MIRACLE AND A WARNING

Acts 20:1–12
Paul raises Eutychus from the dead

Ask the following questions:

- When was the last time you saw someone fall asleep in Church?
- Why do you think people sometimes fall asleep in Church?

Tell your family they are now going to read an account of a young man who fell asleep in Church and learn what happened to him as a result. Read together Acts 20:1–12. Ask:

- What is the name of the young man who fell asleep? (Verse 9.)
- Why might it have been hard for you to stay awake during this meeting?
- What happened as a result of his fall? (Verse 9.)
- What miracle did Paul perform? (Verse 10.)
- Why do you think he saved that boy?
- What was the reaction of the people? (Verse 12.)
- What does this miracle teach us about Heavenly Father's love for His children, even the sleepy ones?

Encourage your family to try their best to stay awake in Church by paying attention to what the speakers are teaching.

Acts 20:13–27
"Pure from the blood of all men"

If you have a Scout in the family, invite him to share the Scout Oath. If no one knows it, share the following part of that oath: "On my honor, I will do my best to do my duty to God and to my country." Read together Acts 20:17–27 and ask:

- In what way would you say that Paul had done his duty to God? (Verses 19–22.)
- What had Paul suffered in order to teach the gospel? (Verses 23–24.)
- What do you think Paul meant by saying he was "pure from the blood of all men"? (Verses 26–27.)

Share this insight from Elder Bruce R. McConkie: "God's servants must, at the peril of their own salvation, deliver the message entrusted to them. (D. & C. 4:2.) If they raise the warning voice as directed by the Lord (D. & C. 88:81), they are free from the blood and sins of those to whom they are sent. If they fail to warn the wicked, the Lord holds them accountable for the sins of the unrepentant. (Ezek. 3:17–21; 33:7–9.) Paul here announces that he has been true to the trust imposed upon him and is thus free from personal responsibility for the sins of those to whom he was sent to minister." (*Doctrinal New Testament Commentary*, 2:177.)

Ask family members if they feel they have been "true to the trust" given them.

Tell them President John Taylor taught: "If you do not magnify your callings, God will hold you responsible for those you might have saved, had you done your duty." (*Ensign*, Nov. 2002, 55.)

Ask your family what things they should do that would be considered doing our duty?

Acts 20:28–30
Wolves and sheep

Imagine a flock of sheep with wolves prowling around it. Ask your family what wolves would do to a flock of sheep. Read together Acts 20:28–30. Ask:

- Who is the flock Paul is referring to? (Members of the Church.)
- Who are the "grievous wolves" Paul warned about? (Enemies of the Church.)
- Who else did Paul warn about in verse 30? (Church members who apostatize and try to lead others away.)

- How can we protect ourselves and others from those who want to destroy our faith?

Give each family member a pencil and a sheet of paper or have them write in their journals. Invite each of them to write the following incomplete sentence: "I will keep myself and others from being led away by 'grievous wolves' by _____" Have them thoughtfully finish the sentence and then share their thoughts if they choose to.

ACTS 21: PAUL REPORTS HIS MISSION AND IS CAPTURED IN JERUSALEM

Acts 21:8–14
Paul is warned

Display a long piece of fabric, a belt, or a bathrobe tie before your family. Invite your family to silently read Acts 21:8–14 and be the first to demonstrate what needs to be done with the object. Ask:

- What warning did Agabus give Paul? (Verse 11.)
- How was that warning similar to one given earlier by other disciples? (See verse 4.)
- What was the source of these warnings? (The Spirit.)

1	2	3	4	5	6	7	8	9	10

I'm going!   Do you think it's safe?   Don't go!

Draw a scale from 1–10 similar to the one above and ask your family to mark in blue on the scale how the disciples, Agabus, and Philip's household feel about Paul going to Jerusalem (see verses 11–12) and then mark in red how Paul feels about going to Jerusalem (see verse 13). Ask:

- How did the disciples and Agabus know to warn Paul? (Verses 4 and 11.)
- Why is Paul still confident to go to Jerusalem in spite of knowing by the power of the Holy Ghost that he will be bound and delivered to the Gentiles? (Verse 13.)

Share the following insight from Elder Bruce R. McConkie:

"Should Paul have gone to Jerusalem? Did the journey accord with the will and purposes of the Lord?

"Whatever the answers to these questions may be, it is clear that Paul was forewarned of the persecutions and trials that would attend such a journey. . . . He is told flatly . . . by the Holy Ghost, that he should not go up, although the meaning of the warning may have been that he should not go unless he was prepared to face the promised trials. . . .

" . . . out of his journey to Jerusalem came the arrest which enabled him, while in Roman custody, to testify before the Jews of Jerusalem, before Festus and then Agrippa . . . and in Rome itself. To take the witness of Christ to kings and rulers, it oftentimes seems to require the arrest and trial of the Lord's servants. Surely Paul's trip to Jerusalem tested his mettle and ennobled his soul, and because of it, he gained opportunities to stand in defense of truth and righteousness which otherwise would have been denied him." (*Doctrinal New Testament Commentary,* 2:181.)

Discuss as a family how Paul's warnings from the Spirit actually helped to strengthen his character and prepared him to fulfill his foreordained mission. (See Acts 9:15.) You may want to sing "I'll Go Where You Want Me to Go." (*Hymns,* no. 270.) Give family members time to record in their journals what they think the will of the Lord is in their lives and what character traits they need to develop in order to accomplish it.

Acts 21:15–26
Why is unity so important?

If you have a member of your family who has reported a mission to the stake presidency and high council, ask them to share how the brethren responded to their report. Read Acts 21:15–19 to your family. Ask:

- How is Paul's report to James and other elders of the Church similar?
- What do you think it would be like to report your mission to the First Presidency and the Twelve?

Remind your family that Paul was warned about going to Jerusalem. Explain that Acts 21:20–26

give clues about a possible danger to Paul. As you read together these verses, you may find it helpful to discuss the following questions:

- How did the Church leadership feel about Paul's report on his mission?
- What law did Christian Jews seem to insist on living? (Verse 20; the law of Moses.)
- What was Paul teaching the Jews among the Gentiles about this law? (Verse 21; to forsake it.)
- How might this be a sore spot among the Jews living in Jerusalem who still really believed in the law?
- What compromise did the brethren suggest to help keep the Jews from being angry with Paul? (Verses 22–24; Paul is to participate in a law of Moses purifying rite.)
- According to verse 25, how do the elders of the Church make it plain that the Gentiles do not have to live the law of Moses?
- What did Paul do about this counsel? (Verse 26.)

Share this insight from Sidney B. Sperry: "It is a curious fact that the brethren, knowing Paul's attitude toward the Law, should ask him to give the appearance that he himself obeyed the Law. But the Apostle, realizing the gravity of the problem and knowing that it was important to hold the Jewish and Gentile groups of the Church together, readily agreed to assume the role of peacemaker." (*Paul's Life and Letters,* 208.)

Invite someone to read aloud Matthew 5:9, 25. Ask family members how these scriptures apply to what Paul did and what principle Paul is teaching by his example. Invite family members to share how they will be peacemakers.

Acts 21:27–40
Will they kill Paul?

Assign the following groups of verses to three members of your family. Have them read the verses aloud and then discuss the questions that follow:

1. Acts 21:27–30
2. Acts 21:31–34
3. Acts 21:35–40

- In what way does this event fulfill warnings given to Paul in verses 4 and 11?
- If you were Paul, what do you think you would feel, think, and do?
- How do you feel about what is happening to Paul?

Following this activity, ask family members:

- What character trait does Paul demonstrate?
- Where did Paul gain the courage he showed in this story?
- What do you think Paul might do once he gains the crowd's attention? (Verse 40.)

Have the family share ideas of how they can demonstrate courage in the difficult circumstances of their lives. Tell them that this exciting experience in the life of Paul, Apostle and missionary, is to be continued in Acts 22.

ACTS 22: PAUL TEACHES ON THE TEMPLE MOUNT

Acts 22:1–30
Paul testifies of his conversion

 Invite someone to read Acts 22:1–2 and ask:

- Who was Paul speaking to?
- Why did they stop and listen?
- What did he ask them to listen to? (His "defence.")

Explain that for his defense Paul tells his conversion story. Give each family member a pencil and a sheet of paper and explain that you are going to give them a test to see how much they remember of Paul's story. Have them write the numbers 1–10 in a single column and then ask the questions below. After you have given them the test, review Acts 22:2–21 to check their answers.

1. What language did Paul speak? (Verse 2.)
2. Where was Paul born? (Verse 3.)
3. Who was Paul's teacher? (Verse 3.)
4. What did Paul do to the Christians before his conversion to Christianity? (Verses 4 and 19.)
5. What was the name of the city that Paul was headed to when he was miraculously converted? (Verse 6.)

6. What happened to Paul that led to his conversion? (Verses 7–8.)
7. What did Paul's traveling companions see at the time of Paul's conversion? (Verse 9.)
8. Paul was told to go the city and find a man by the name of Ananias. What did Ananias do for Paul? (Verse 13.)
9. What was Paul told to do after his visit with Ananias? (Verse 16.)
10. How did Paul participate in Stephen's stoning? (Verse 20.)

After you have checked the answers to the quiz, discuss with your family how this story explains why Paul, once a persecutor of Christians, had become a Christian. Ask:

- What impresses you most about Paul's conversion story?
- Why do you think Paul shares this story with the Jews?
- What do you see in the way Paul is treated by the Jews here in Acts 21 and 22 that reminds you of the experiences of the Prophet Joseph Smith after the First Vision? (See Joseph Smith–History 1:21–26.)

As a family, talk about how being a witness for the truth of the gospel will not always be popular and sometimes others might even be unkind. Discuss what we can do today if that happens. Share examples from your own experience of how to best make friends of those who are unkind without giving up what we know to be true.

Take turns reading Acts 22:22–30 and ask:

- What did the Jews want to do with Paul? (Verses 22–23.)
- What were the Roman soldiers going to do to him? (Verses 24–25.)
- How did the Roman centurion and chief captain react when they found out Paul was a Roman citizen?
- How did Paul's rights as a Roman citizen provide a way for him to preach the gospel of Jesus Christ?
- In what ways do our own rights as citizens allow us to share the truth of the Restoration with people we know?

Commit your family to be more aware of their

nonmember friends and opportunities to share the truth with them. Challenge them during the next week to ask for Heavenly Father's help to have missionary opportunities. Bear testimony of the importance of sharing the message of truth.

ACTS 23: PAUL ESCAPES THOSE WHO WOULD KILL HIM

Acts 23:1–35

Who played what role?

 Tell your family that Acts 23 tells the continuing story of Paul's arrest in Jerusalem and that several individuals and groups of people play a role in what ultimately happens to Paul. To help learn more about them and to better keep the story straight, invite your family to participate in the following activity:

Assign family members one or more of the following individuals or groups of people: Ananias; the Pharisees; the Sadducees; the chief captain; certain of the Jews ("more than 40"); chief priests and elders; Paul's sister's son; one of the centurions; Felix. Tell them not to let other family members know which group or individual they are assigned to. Have them read Acts 23:1–35 to themselves and find out what role these individuals and groups played in the story. Remind them to read the whole chapter so they can learn about the people assigned to other family members.

When family members have read the chapter, invite them to write two clues, in the form of sentence-long statements, to help the rest of the family guess which individual or group in Acts 23 he or she is representing. For example, if you were assigned Ananias, you might write: "I commanded that Paul be smitten on the mouth. I am the high priest."

When everyone has finished writing their statements, take turns sharing them and seeing if the rest of the family can guess the person or persons each family member represents in the story. After all have taken their turn, tell them you have one more individual who played a role. Read the following to them: "Be of good cheer, Paul: for as thou hast testified of me in Jerusalem, so must thou bear witness also at Rome." (Acts 23:11.) Ask your family:

- Who said this in the story? (The Lord.)
- What important role did He play?
- What did Paul experience in Acts 23 that would make you think he would need this message?
- How do you suppose this message from the Lord helped Paul?

Share with your family the following statement from an Apostle in this dispensation: "The Lord is always able and always willing to sustain His servants in the performance of all the labors and duties which He assigns unto them. He does not leave men to themselves when He calls them to office; but He gives them gifts and graces and qualifications [they need]. . . . In the midst of trials, and the difficulties that we have to contend with, and the afflictions we have to bear, the testimony constantly is that this is God's work, that He is caring for it, that it does not depend upon us to manage it with our short-sighted wisdom; but that He, with His supreme wisdom and with His Almighty power, and with His eternal providence, is caring for all its interests, is watching over every detail, and is controlling all the labors of His people, the counsels and instructions of His servants, and even the acts of the wicked themselves, for the accomplishment of His purposes and the fulfilling of His great designs. This is a constant consolation which God gives unto His people. And how comforting and sustaining it is!" (George Q. Cannon, in Stuy, *Collected Discourses,* 2:10.)

Share your own testimony that the Lord is watching over us and that if we are faithful, He can help our trials become blessings to us and use our trials to help accomplish His work. (See D&C 90:24.)

ACTS 24: PAUL TESTIFIES BEFORE FELIX

Acts 24:1–27

Covering the story

One fun way of studying Acts 24 is to do a reader's theater. Assign the parts of

Tertullus, Paul, Felix, and the narrator to members of your family. As everyone follows along, have these four people read the parts of the chapter that belong to them. Ask them each to use a dramatic voice as they read.

After your family has read the chapter, have everyone pretend they are news reporters in Jerusalem working together to cover the story of Paul being arrested and imprisoned for two years. Explain that when good reporters cover a story, they often make sure they have answered questions that start with the following words: *What, Why, Where, When,* and *How.* Ask each family member to create a question beginning with one of those words. Take turns letting each person ask their question and discuss the answers as a family. Review Acts 24 as needed to discover the answers.

To further your investigation, you could also discuss the following questions:

- What three things did Paul teach Felix about in verse 25? (See also footnote 25*a*.)
- Would it be difficult to stand up for your beliefs if you were Paul?
- What did Felix also want from Paul in verses 25–27? (See also footnote 26*a*.)
- When have you had to stand up for your beliefs in difficult circumstances?

Acts 24:16

How can we have a clear conscience?

Ask a family member to read Acts 24:16 and ask if it seems familiar to them. Have them write D&C 135:4 beside it and explain that it was also something Joseph Smith said as he rode to Carthage Jail where he was murdered. Ask:

- What must we do to have a clear conscience?
- Why should having a clear conscience be important to us? President David O. McKay taught, "The first condition of happiness is a clear conscience." (*Gospel Ideals,* 498.)

Challenge your family to repent of anything that would prevent them from having a clear conscience before God.

ACTS 25: PAUL APPEALS TO CAESAR

Acts 25:1–27
No man is taken before his time

Tell your family that the better we understand the people and places mentioned in scriptures, the better we will understand the principles and doctrines taught in the scriptures. Invite your family to match the following names and places with the appropriate answers. This can be done individually or in groups using the Bible Dictionary or other Bible helps. (The answers are 1-e; 2-d; 3-b; 4-f; 5-c; 6-a.)

Name or Place	Answers
1. Festus	a. The first Roman emperor
2. Caesarea	b. Apostle of Jesus Christ
3. Paul	c. Sister to Agrippa
4. King Agrippa	d. Important seacoast city
5. Bernice	e. Procurator [Governor] of Judea
6. Augustus	f. Brother of Bernice and son of Herod

Tell your family that now that they understand who these people and places are, you are going to study Acts 25 together to see why they are important to the chapter. Have a family member read Acts 25:1–3. Discuss what the high priest was plotting against Paul. Read Acts 25:4–12 and ask:

- Was the high priest successful in his plot?
- Why didn't Festus allow Paul to go at this point? (Verse 9.)
- How is knowledge of the law helpful to Paul and to us?
- To whom did Paul appeal for help? (Verse 11.)
- How did Festus respond to Paul's appeal? (Verse 12.)

Tell your family that under Roman law, each citizen accused of a crime had the right and privilege of being heard before Caesar and that local authorities, such as Festus, could decide if the case warranted such a privilege. Read Acts 25:13 and ask your family who came to visit Festus. Tell your family that Festus retells everything again that was mentioned in the previous verses of Acts 25. Read Acts 25:14–27 and then ask: Why do you think

Festus tells Agrippa everything he has previously experienced with Paul? (See verse 26.) Read Acts 25:22 and ask what King Agrippa desires. Remind your family that the Jewish leaders wanted to stop Paul from preaching the gospel. Tell your family that something similar happened to the Prophet Joseph Smith. Read the following prophecy by the Prophet Joseph directed to his accusers who wanted to kill him:

"The Standard of Truth has been erected; no unhallowed hand can stop the work from progressing; persecutions may rage, mobs may combine, armies may assemble, . . . but the truth of God will go forth boldly, nobly, and independent, till it has penetrated every continent, visited every clime, swept every country, and sounded in every ear, till the purposes of God shall be accomplished, and the Great Jehovah shall say the work is done." (*History of the Church,* 4:540.)

Testify to your family that no servant of the Lord will be taken from the earth before his time. To help your family understand this, you could read the following statement given by President Ezra Taft Benson at President Spencer W. Kimball's funeral:

"It has been said that the death of a righteous man is never untimely because our Father sets the time. I believe that with all my soul." (*Ensign,* Dec. 1985, 33.) Invite your family to share the names of people they know in scripture who were allowed to be spared until their work was finished. (For example: Paul, Abinadi, Jesus Christ, Joseph Smith, Nephi, Alma.)

ACTS 26: PAUL BEFORE AGRIPPA

Acts 26:1–21

Paul is permitted to speak for himself

Explain to your family that they are going to learn about the trial of the Apostle Paul before King Agrippa. Write the odd-numbered statements (1, 3, 5, 7) and the even-numbered statements (2, 4, 6, 8) below on two separate pieces of paper. Divide your family into two groups and give a paper to each group. Tell both groups they are to read Acts 26:1–21 and determine whether the statements they have been given are true or false. If they determine a statement is false, they are to cross out the word that makes it false and write in the word that makes it a true statement.

1. Paul was happy for the opportunity to present his case before King Philip.

2. Paul said that he had been a Sadducee, the "most straitest" sect among the Jews.

3. Paul once thought he should "do many things contrary to the name of Jesus of Nazareth."

4. Paul put many Saints in prison.

5. One night, on his way to Damascus, Paul had a vision.

6. Paul heard a voice saying, "Saul, Saul, why lovest thou me?"

7. The reason the Lord appeared to Paul was to make him both "a minister and a witness."

8. The Jews caught Paul in the wilderness and sought to kill him.

When both groups have finished their assignments, go through each statement in numerical order and have each group take turns telling about their statement and answering any questions. Below are examples of the corrected statements and the verse they came from.

1. Paul was happy for the opportunity to present his case before King ~~Philip~~ Agrippa. (Verse 2.)

2. Paul said that he had been a ~~Sadducee~~ Pharisee, the "most straitest" sect among the Jews. (Verse 5.)

3. True. (Verse 9.)

4. True. (Verse 10.)

5. One night (At midday), on his way to Damascus, Paul had a vision. (Verse 13.)

6. Paul heard a voice saying, "Saul, Saul, why ~~lovest~~ persecutest thou me?" (Verse 14.)

7. True. (Verse 16.)

8. The Jews caught Paul in the ~~wilderness~~ temple and sought to kill him. (Verse 21.)

When you have finished correcting the statements, discuss with your family what this story teaches about Paul. What does it teach about courage? What does it teach about the power of a testimony?

Acts 26:22–32

"Almost thou persuadest me"

Tell your family that as Paul continued his defense before King Agrippa and Festus, he taught important doctrine. Have a family member read Acts 26:22–23 aloud and explain what Paul taught them. Invite family members to look for how Festus and King Agrippa each reacted to Paul's testimony as you read together Acts 26:24–32. Ask:

- How did Festus's and Agrippa's reactions to Paul's testimony differ?
- How were they similar?
- What reasons might King Agrippa have had for not fully accepting Paul's testimony and becoming a Christian?

Tell your family President Harold B. Lee wrote of a bishop who referred to King Agrippa's reply of "Almost thou persuadest me to be a Christian" (Acts 26:28) as "the saddest words that he knows of a man in high station. . . . The bishop said, 'The king knew the truth but he lacked the courage to do that which would be required. . . .'

"And then [the bishop] characterized some things that he discovered in his own ward in a short but powerful sermon: 'In response to the Master, "Come . . . follow me" (Mark 10:21), some members almost, but not quite, say, "thou persuadest me almost to be honest but I need extra help to pass a test."

"'Almost thou persuadest me to keep the Sabbath day holy, but it's fun to play ball on Sunday.

"'Almost thou persuadest me to love my neighbor, but he is a rascal; to be tolerant of others' views, but they are dead wrong; to be kind to sister, but she hit me first; to go home teaching, but it's too cold and damp outside tonight; to pay tithes and offerings, but we do need a new color TV set; . . . almost thou persuadest me to attend stake leadership meeting, but I know more than the leader on that subject, so why should I go? Thou persuadest me almost to go to sacrament meeting, but there is going to be such an uninteresting speaker. . . . Almost! Almost! Almost! but not quite, not able quite to reach.'" (*Teachings of Harold B. Lee,* 147.)

Invite family members to consider what good things they are almost persuaded to do and if they will now commit to do them.

ACTS 27: PAUL IS SHIPWRECKED

Acts 27:1–44

A lesson about prophets from a story of a shipwreck

Tell family members this chapter contains the story of Paul's shipwreck while he traveled to Rome. Make a worksheet for each family member containing the following six questions. Invite family members to study Acts 27:1–44 on their own. As they do, have them each complete the worksheet.

1. Who are the main participants in this story?

2. Why was Paul on this boat traveling to Rome?

3. How many people were on the boat during this journey? (276; see verse 37.)

4. What did Paul warn the others about and how many times did he warn them? (He warned them four times about the danger of making the journey and how they could be safe; see verses 10, 21–26, 31, 33–34.)

5. How did Paul know what to warn the people about? (An angel of God revealed it to him; see verse 23.)

6. How did the people respond to Paul's warnings and what was the result? (They ignored him, for the most part, and suffered the consequences.)

Apply this story to modern times. Tell your family that Paul's journey to Rome could be compared to our journey through life. We often face "storms" along the way. Ask:

- What kinds of "storms" do we face in our lives? (Temptations, trials, or challenges; see Helaman 5:12.)
- What is a difficult "storm" you have faced recently?

Explain to your family that God gives us prophets like Paul to help guide us through our difficulties and challenges. Ask:

- What does Doctrine and Covenants 1:17–18 teach you about the role of prophets?

- How do prophets know what counsel to give us? (Revelation.)
- Why should we have faith in the prophets' words when we face the "storms" of life?

Conclude your discussion by singing "Follow the Prophet" (*Children's Songbook*, no. 110), or "We Thank Thee, O God, for a Prophet" (*Hymns*, no. 19).

ACTS 28: PAUL IS SHIPWRECKED WHILE TRAVELING TO ROME

Acts 28:1–10
Paul on the island of Melita

 Show your family a toy snake or a picture of a snake.

Ask:

- Why are some people afraid of snakes?
- What is dangerous about some snakes?
- What can happen to someone bitten by a poisonous snake?

Tell your family the Savior made His ancient and modern disciples some specific promises, including a promise regarding snakes. Have family members read Mark 16:17–20 and Doctrine and Covenants 84:64–72 and identify these promises. Then take turns reading Acts 28:1–10 to find out more about Paul's experiences, particularly the one regarding the snake. Discuss the following questions:

- Which promises of the Savior did Paul specifically experience?
- How did Paul's experience with the snake help the people he served?
- What does this teach you about Paul's faith?
- What most impresses you about this story?

Remind your family that Christ's disciples today can enjoy many miracles and gifts of the Spirit (for example, see D&C 46:11–26.) Have someone read Doctrine and Covenants 46:8–9 aloud and ask: To whom does the Lord give these gifts? Help your family understand that when necessary to move forward the Lord's work for His people, these various gifts are enjoyed by those who exercise faith and whose eyes are single to His glory.

Acts 28:11–31
Paul teaches in Rome

Show your family a picture of a missionary and ask each family member to imagine being a missionary today. Invite your family to think about the following question: What are some effective ways a missionary could find people to teach? Get responses from each family member and compile a list of their responses. (Some answers may include tracting, or going from door to door; getting referrals [names of people] from Church members; talking to people on the street in public places; and speaking in gatherings and meetings.)

Ask your family to rank their responses in order from most effective to least effective and talk about why some approaches to finding people are better than other approaches.

Take turns reading Acts 28:17–24. Ask:

- What method of missionary work did Paul use?
- Why did Paul need to have the people come to him? (Verse 16. Paul was under house arrest.)
- Which group of people did Paul invite to listen to his message? (Verse 17.)
- What is the message of Paul and missionaries today? (Verse 23.)

Invite someone to read Acts 28:24–31 and have your family look for ways people responded to Paul's message and why they responded the way they did. Ask:

- How did the people respond to Paul's message? (Verses 24–25, 29.)
- According to verse 27, what is one reason people responded as they did?
- How do you feel when people you share the gospel with do not receive it? Why?

Read Doctrine and Covenants 20:59 and ask which phrase in that verse describes the duty of all Church members. (To invite all to come unto Christ.) Help your family understand that it is our obligation to share the gospel and invite others to come unto Christ. It is not our duty to convert them. That is the role of the Spirit. People still have the agency to choose to accept or reject that invitation. Encourage your family to continue to share the message of truth with others.

ROMANS

This epistle, or letter, from Paul to Church members in Rome begins a new section of the New Testament containing messages from priesthood leaders to members in the early Christian Church. The letters of Paul come first, followed by epistles of other Apostles. Paul's letters are not placed in chronological order but according to size— Romans is the largest and Philemon is the smallest. Hebrews "was placed last because some have questioned whether or not it was written by Paul." (Bible Dictionary, "Pauline Epistles," 743.)

Rome was the center of western civilization and the capital city of the Roman Empire. While it is unclear how the Christian Church began in Rome, many Jews had apparently lived there for some time. Paul had not yet visited Rome when he wrote this epistle, but he apparently planned to. (See Romans 1:10–12; 15:30–32.)

The main subject of this letter deals with the relationship between the law of Moses and the gospel of Jesus Christ.

Romans can be challenging for the average reader. However, with the help of the Holy Ghost, Romans can be a "highly edifying and instructive document, one that portrays gospel doctrines in such a way as to expand the mind and to enlighten the understanding. From it those with spiritual insight will gain gospel views which will add peace to their lot here and open the door to higher spiritual attainment hereafter." (McConkie, Doctrinal New Testament Commentary, 2:211.)

ROMANS 1: "I AM NOT ASHAMED OF THE GOSPEL OF CHRIST"

Romans 1:1–16

What can we learn about Paul?

Invite your family to imagine that they are one of the Saints in Rome. Have them read Romans 1:1–16, looking for clues that might help them learn more about this man they've never met. When everyone is finished, choose one person to be a scribe. Invite family members to share what they learned about Paul from their reading and have the scribe make a list of characteristics. Review the list and ask your family which of the characteristics most impressed them and why.

Ask, What does Paul say about the gospel in Romans 1:1–16? In what ways can you tell he really believes he has "good news" for people? How can we convey to others that we believe we have "good news" for them in the message of Jesus Christ?

Romans 1:16–32

All men are held accountable before God

Divide your family into two groups. Have one group read Alma 30:43–44 and the other group read Moroni 7:15–17. Have each group find answers to their assigned questions listed below:

Group 1

- What did Alma say to Korihor about ways people can recognize that there is a God?
- What are some ways you know there is a God?

Group 2

- What is given to *every* man to know good from evil?
- How can this help you know the difference between right and wrong?

Have each group help answer these questions as you read together Romans 1:16–21:

- What did Paul teach in Romans 1:20 that is like the truth Alma taught Korihor?
- What did Paul teach in Romans 1:19 that is like the truth Mormon taught in Moroni 7?
- According to Romans 1:21, what happens to those who refuse to listen to the spirit within and believe in God?
- In contrast to this, what does Doctrine and Covenants 50:24 say happens when we do accept, acknowledge, and obey God?

Share the following insight from President Boyd K. Packer about this gift that is given to every person: "Regardless of whether this inner light, this knowledge of right and wrong, is called the Light of Christ, moral sense, or conscience, it can direct us to moderate our actions—unless, that is, we subdue it or silence it. . . .

"The Light of Christ is as universal as sunlight itself. Wherever there is human life, there is the Spirit of Christ. Every living soul is possessed of it. It is the sponsor of everything that is good. It is the inspirer of everything that will bless and benefit mankind. It nourishes goodness itself." (*Ensign*, Apr. 2005, 9, 13.)

Help your family see that the light of Christ has influenced them in various ways by asking these questions:

- How do you feel when you give service to another?
- What feelings do you have when you are involved in contention?

Testify to your family that these feelings are evidence of the light of Christ. Remind them that just as Paul taught, we are accountable for what we learn through this gift. In addition, because all people receive this gift, we can encourage those around us to be true to this inner light, which will lead them closer to God.

ROMANS 2: THOSE HAVING THE GOSPEL SHOULD LIVE THE GOSPEL

Romans 2:1–16
How are we judged?

Assign half of your family to read 2 Nephi 9:15 and the other half to read Mormon 3:20. Have them report what important truth is taught in their verse. (Everyone will appear before God to be judged.) Ask, When you think about this event, what thoughts and feelings do you have?

Explain that Paul taught the Romans some truths that help us know a little more about the final judgment. To help identify these truths, write the following statements on strips of paper and distribute them among family members:

1. "God's judgment is based on truth—things as they really are."

2. "God will judge each person based on what they truly seek and what they do."

3. "People of certain religions and backgrounds are more favored at the judgment."

4. "We are judged by the amount of law and light we were given in this life."

5. "All people are given a conscience—the light of Christ—for which they are accountable in the day of judgment."

Have family members carefully read Romans 2:1–16 and look for what Paul taught that would demonstrate each statement to be either true or false and then share with the rest of the family what they found. (No. 1 is true—verses 1–3; no. 2 is true—verses 6–8; no. 3 is false—verses 9–13; no. 4 is true—verses 11–16; no. 5 is true—verses 13–16.) As each truth is shared, invite family members to tell why they think it is important that we know that particular truth.

Romans 2:17–29
Who is a Jew (or a Latter-day Saint)?

Ask your family if one of them has been with a group of people at some gathering and had the impression that certain people were members of the Church—even though your family member didn't know it before. How did your family member identify them as Church members? What are some of the ways you hope that others identify you as a Latter-day Saint?

Read together Romans 2:17–23 and list what Paul said about how the Jews wanted to, and should be, identified. (They should believe in and rely on the law [of Moses] they should live what they teach, thereby honoring God.)

Explain to your family that the term *circumcision* came to represent all of what it means to be a Jew—circumcision representing a covenant with God. Have someone read Romans 2:25 and ask, What does Paul say about why it is of real value to call yourself of the circumcision, or the people of the covenant? (That you keep the laws and covenants. If you don't keep the laws and covenants, it is as if you were not circumcised.) Have someone read Romans 2:26 and ask, How does this principle apply to those who were not of the circumcision? What point do you think Paul is making in verses 25–26 about what is truly important?

Invite a family member to read aloud Romans 2:28–29 and replace "Jew" with "Latter-day Saint;" and "circumcision" with "baptism," and ask your family how you think it teaches an important lesson to us today.

Share with your family the counsel of President Gordon B. Hinckley on this subject: "It is not enough to simply be known as a member of this Church. A solemn obligation rests upon us. Let us face it and work at it.

"We must live as true followers of the Christ, with charity toward all, returning good for evil, teaching by example the ways of the Lord, and accomplishing the vast service He has outlined for us." (*Ensign*, May 2004, 84.)

Ask your family what President Hinckley said about how we can truly be Latter-day Saints.

To help remember this principle, you may want to have a family member make a poster with President Hinckley's words: "It is not enough to simply be known as a member of this Church. . . . We must live as true followers of the Christ." Put this poster in a prominent place in your home to remind everyone of this important lesson.

ROMANS 3: RIGHTEOUSNESS COMES THROUGH FAITH

Romans 3:9–26

Am I righteous enough to go to heaven?

Ask your family if they think they are righteous enough to make it to heaven. Read together Romans 3:10–12 and ask:

- According to Paul, how many people in his day were righteous enough to go to heaven? (None.)
- Why do you think he would say that "there is none that doeth good"?

Have your family silently read Romans 3:13–18 for answers to this last question. After your family has shared what they found, read 1 Nephi 10:21. Ask:

- According to this verse, how does one become "unclean"? (By seeking to do wicked things.)
- What kinds of people are unable to dwell with God? (Unclean.)
- What did Paul teach in Romans 3:23 about being able to dwell with God? ("All have sinned, and come short of the glory of God.")
- Is there no hope for anyone?

Read together Romans 3:24–26 and ask:

- How can we become righteous enough to dwell in God's presence? (Through Jesus Christ.)
- What did the Savior do that gives us all hope?
- What can we do to be worthy of the Savior's offering for each of us? (Have faith in Christ, repent of our sins, and follow His example.)

Read Moroni 10:32 together as a family and list other things you can do to have hope in Christ.

Romans 3:27–31

Works or faith or both?

Ask your family to imagine they want to be a great mountain climber. Ask:

- What is one of the most important tools used by mountain climbers? (A good rope.)

- Why would it be more dangerous to climb a mountain without a rope?
- If you compared life to mountain climbing, what might the rope represent? (The gospel of Jesus Christ, the Atonement, etc.)
- In what ways do some try to make it through life by their own power and without God's help?

Tell your family that one of Paul's greatest challenges was teaching Jews who still insisted on living the rituals of the law of Moses even though Jesus fulfilled this law and brought the gospel instead. (See Matthew 5:17–19.) Read Romans 3:27–31 together and ask:

- Can doing the deeds of the law of Moses save us? Why not?
- To whom does God choose to give salvation? (Verse 28: Those with true faith.)
- How can you tell if a person has real faith in God? (His good works; see verse 31.)
- Instead of faith canceling out "works" or the commandments, what does faith do according to verse 31? (Faith in Christ helps followers live the commandments better than ever before.)

Challenge your family to try as hard as they can to be like the Savior, knowing that He will help them even though they will make some mistakes.

ROMANS 4: WE ARE JUSTIFIED BY FAITH, RIGHTEOUS WORKS, AND GRACE

Romans 4:1–12
Abraham's faith

Invite a family member to read Doctrine and Covenants 132:32 and ask:

- Whose works are we commanded to do? (Abraham's.)
- What blessing comes to those who do Abraham's works? (They are saved.)
- What does this tell you about the kind of person Abraham was?

Tell your family that Abraham was called the "Father of the Faithful," but even he was not

perfect and fell short of what was needed to return to Heavenly Father's presence. Review with your family Romans 4:1–8 looking for the "works" of Abraham that make him an excellent example for us to follow. Ask:

- What do you think the word *justified* means? (Declared clean, not guilty.)
- How does believing we are "justified" by our own effort deny God's power and glory? (Verse 2.)
- Why was Abraham counted righteous? (Verse 3.)
- Why is "grace" essential for any of us to return to our Father in Heaven's presence? (Verse 4; see also the first paragraph of "Grace," in the Bible Dictionary, 697.)
- What part does repentance play in our ability to enjoy God's grace? (Verse 7; we can be forgiven.)

Tell your family that Paul used Abraham as an example of one who obtained grace through great faith and then gave evidence of his great faith in the way he lived his life. Ask: What "works" can we do that shows our faith in Jesus Christ and helps us obtain God's grace and blessings? Testify to your family of God's love for all of us and His desire for us to be clean.

Romans 4:13–16
Who are Abraham's seed?

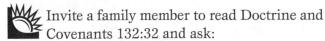 Invite your family to name the "fathers" they have. (Father, grandfather, Father in Heaven, etc.) Ask your family to turn to Abraham 2:10 and explain that in this passage the Lord is speaking directly to Abraham. Have someone read verse 10 and ask:

- Who is considered one of your "fathers"? (Abraham.)
- How do people become the seed or children of Abraham? (Those who receive the gospel shall be called after Abraham's name and considered his seed.)

Read together Romans 4:13 and footnote 16*a* and invite your family to mark the words *promise, faith, grace,* and *seed.* Ask:

- How does the faith of Abraham and his seed [children] allow them to enjoy God's grace?
- How are God's promises a demonstration of His grace towards us?
- What kinds of blessings do you think are promised to Abraham's children?
- What kinds of "works" will Abraham's seed or children do? (See James 2:14–16.)

Read to your family the following statement by Elder Bruce R. McConkie: "*God's grace* consists in his love, mercy, and condescension [coming down to earth] toward his children. . . .

"Grace is granted to men . . . as they conform to the standards of personal righteousness that are part of the gospel plan." (*Mormon Doctrine,* 338–39.)

Testify to your family how you feel about the Atonement of Jesus Christ and how grateful you are for His grace that saves all people who come unto Him. You may want to conclude by reading 2 Nephi 25:23 that teaches that we are saved by grace after all we can do.

Romans 4:17–25.
The works and faith of Abraham

Ask your family to list three things that are necessary for a fire to burn. Then show your family the drawing below and ask:

Fire Triangle

Oxygen

Heat

Fuel

- Why do you think this drawing is called the fire triangle?
- What would happen to the fire if any one of the three elements were missing?

Have your family silently scan Romans 4:17–20, looking for three spiritual elements that helped Abraham live righteously throughout his life. Ask:

- What three elements did you find? 1. He "believed" in God. 2. He had "hope" in God's promises to him. 3. He had "strong" faith.
- In what way do you think belief in God, hope, and strong faith is similar to the elements that allow a fire to burn? (You need all of them to be saved.)

Read with your family Romans 4:23–25:

- Who else, besides Abraham, can also have God's promises "imputed" [counted] to them? (We can; see verses 23–24.)
- What must we do to obtain God's promises? (Believe in Heavenly Father and His Son Jesus Christ; see verse 24.)

Encourage your family to follow Abraham's example and live a life of faith and good works.

ROMANS 5: BECOMING RECONCILED TO GOD

Romans 5:1–5
Patience—do you have it?

Ask your family members if they have ever heard the phrases "hold your horses" or "keep your shirt on." Ask, What quality is being requested by those phrases? (Patience.)

Read this insight from Elder Joseph B. Wirthlin: "I believe that a lack of patience is a major cause of the difficulties and unhappiness in the world today. Too often, we are impatient with ourselves, with our family members and friends, and even with the Lord. We seem to demand what we want right now, regardless of whether we have earned it, whether it would be good for us, or whether it is right. Some seek immediate gratification or numbing of every impulse by turning to alcohol and drugs, while others seek instant material wealth by questionable investments or by dishonesty, with little or no regard for the consequences. Perhaps the practice of patience is more difficult, yet more necessary, now than at any previous time." (*Ensign,* May 1987, 30.)

Ask, Why do you think Elder Wirthlin would

say that having "patience is more difficult, yet more necessary, now than at any previous time"?

Have family members read Romans 5:1–5 and look for what Paul taught about patience. Ask:

- How can we have "peace with God"?
- What did Paul say helps us learn patience?
- Whom should we learn to rely on when faced with tribulation?
- What blessing comes to us through the Holy Ghost?

Read the following by Elder Neal A. Maxwell: "Patience is tied very closely to faith in our Heavenly Father. Actually, when we are unduly impatient, we are suggesting that we know what is best—better than does God. Or, at least, we are asserting that our timetable is better than his. Either way we are questioning the reality of God's omniscience [knowledge]." (*Ensign,* Oct. 1980, 28.) Ask:

- How can we show our faith in Heavenly Father?
- Why is it important to recognize that God knows what is best for us?
- How might this knowledge help us get through trials?

Testify to your family that patience is one way we come to be more Christlike. Remind your family that patience gives us the hope that Christ's Atonement will save us.

Romans 5:6–11
Justified and reconciled

Have family members read Romans 5:6–11 and underline or note any words they do not understand. Two words they might have difficulty understanding are *justified* and *reconciled*. To help them understand these words, share the following:

Justified: refers to the action by which a person is 'accounted or made righteous by God.'" (S. Michael Wilcox, *Ensign,* June 1991, 51.)

Reconciled: Elder Bruce R. McConkie taught: "Reconciliation is the process of ransoming [saving] man from his state of sin and spiritual darkness and of restoring him to a state of harmony and

unity with Deity." (*Doctrinal New Testament Commentary,* 2:422.)

Tell your family that the important thing to know is what actually makes a person "justified" or "reconciled." To aid in this, have a family member read Romans 5:11 aloud. Ask:

- What is it that allows us to be brought back into a state of "harmony and unity" with God? (See 2 Nephi 25:23.)
- We may be "reconciled" to God through the death of Jesus Christ, but how are we saved?
- How can the life that Jesus lived help save us? (As we follow Christ's example and become more like Him, we become worthy to enter God's presence.)
- How can we show our appreciation for the Atonement?

Discuss how baptism helps a person become "justified" before God. Remind your family that obeying our Heavenly Father's commandments following baptism helps to keep us "reconciled" or righteous.

Romans 5:12–21
The Fall and the Atonement

Ask for a volunteer to recite the second Article of Faith. Ask for another volunteer to recite the third Article of Faith. Tell your family that these two Articles of Faith summarize Paul's message to the Roman Saints in Romans 5:12–21. Take turns reading those verses and then ask the following questions:

- Who is the "one man" spoken of in verse 12?
- What are two things that entered the world because of Adam's transgression? (Verse 12.)
- Who provides the "free gift" spoken of in verses 15, 16 and 18?
- What is the "free gift"? (Resurrection from physical death.)
- According to verses 19 and 21, who makes it possible for us to be "made righteous" and to obtain "eternal life"?

Discuss as a family what you can do to enjoy the greatest power of Christ's Atonement.

ROMANS 6: LIFE THROUGH CHRIST

Romans 6:1–11
"Walk in newness of life"

 Draw the following symbols on a paper large enough for your family to see: $ % & :) Show them to your family and discuss what each means. Discuss the meaning of the words *symbol*, *symbolic*, and *symbolism*. Then, ask family members to think of the day they were baptized. Ask:

- What unique symbols do you see when someone is baptized? (People are dressed in white, stand in a font of water, are immersed in the water, etc.)
- What are some symbolic messages of baptism by immersion?

Read Romans 6:1–11 and have your family identify the symbol of baptism Paul taught about. Have family members mark footnote 7a and note the correction the Joseph Smith Translation makes to Romans 6:7. If possible, display pictures of Jesus' burial and Resurrection, such as *Gospel Art Kit*, nos. 231 and 233. Then ask how the ordinance of baptism is symbolic of death, burial, and resurrection. Share this insight from President Brigham Young:

"Has water, in itself, any virtue to wash away sin? Certainly not; but the Lord says, 'If the sinner will repent of his sins, and go down into the waters of baptism, and there be buried in the likeness of being put into the earth and buried, and again be delivered from the water, in the likeness of being born—if in the sincerity of his heart he will do this, his sins shall be washed away.' [See D&C 128:12–13.] Will the water of itself wash them away? No; but keeping the commandments of God will cleanse away the stain of sin." (*Discourses of Brigham Young*, 159.)

Ask family members who have been baptized to describe how they felt as they came out of the waters of baptism. Have family members reread Romans 6:4 and underline the phrase they think best describes the feeling. Ask how we can maintain the "newness of life" we experienced at baptism.

Romans 6:12–23
Sin brings death; Christ brings life

 Show this yield sign or draw a larger one of your own.

Ask, If you saw a sign similar to this while driving, what would it mean? Tell them Paul also taught the Roman Saints about yielding. Have them read Romans 6:12–23 and mark each time the word *yield* or *yielded* occurs. Ask:

- What does Paul warn us not to yield to?
- To whom and to what should we yield ourselves?

Ask a family member who is currently working or who recently had a job to answer the following questions:

- What is your current wage?
- Are you satisfied with your wage?
- Who signs your paychecks?
- What two wages are spoken of in Romans 6:23?
- Which of those two wages would you rather have and why?
- What are some things we must do to receive the "wage," or reward, of eternal life?

ROMANS 7: LAW OF MOSES IS FULFILLED IN CHRIST

Romans 7:1–4
To which law are we bound?

 Prepare six strips of paper with one of the following phrases written on each strip:

- Wife
- First husband
- Second husband
- House of Israel
- Law of Moses
- Law of the gospel of Christ

Place them in random order on the floor or table so your family can see them. Tell your family that this is a pairing activity, and they need to pair the strips correctly. Have everyone silently read Romans 7:1–4 and then call on a family member to pair the word strips correctly. Ask if everyone agrees. They should be paired as follows:

Wife—House of Israel

First husband—Law of Moses

Second husband—Law of the gospel of Christ

Once everyone agrees with the pairings, ask:

- What point do you think Paul was trying to make with this illustration?
- To which law are we bound today, the law of Moses or the law of the gospel of Christ?
- In what ways can people today be unfaithful to the law by which they are bound?

If the illustration is difficult for your family to understand, you might share the following statement from Elder Bruce R. McConkie:

"Paul was an absolute genius at devising illustrations to drive home his gospel teachings. Here he compares Israel's allegiance to the law of Moses with that of a wife to her husband. As long as her husband lives, a wife is bound to him, must obey his laws, and if she be with another, she is an adulteress. But when the husband dies, he can no longer direct her actions, and she is free to marry another; she can no longer be subject to him that is dead.

"So with Israel and the law. As long as the law lived, and was therefore in force, Israel was married to it and required to obey its provisions. If she went after other gods, or followed other religions, it was as adultery. But now the law is fulfilled; it no longer lives; it has become dead in Christ; and Israel is married to another, even to Christ, whose gospel law must now be obeyed." (*Doctrinal New Testament Commentary*, 2:253–54.)

As a family, list ways that you are blessed or receive strength as a result of being faithful to the law of the gospel of Christ.

Romans 7:5–25
Paul: Before and after

Have family members mark Romans 7:5 footnote *a* in their scriptures. Remind them that excerpts from the Joseph Smith Translation are in the Appendix of their copy of the Bible. Have

them turn to Joseph Smith Translation Romans 7:5–27, in the Appendix (809–10). Point out that the *italicized* words represent the Prophet's inspired changes.

Have your family count how many verses in Joseph Smith Translation Romans 7:5–27 were not changed. (Only two, verses 7–8; verse 27 has no added words, some words from the King James Version have been omitted.) Ask which version will be most helpful in understanding the message Paul is trying to teach. Invite your family to see if they can discover that message as you read together Joseph Smith Translation Romans 7:5–27. After reading, have family members share any insights they gleaned and then share this summary:

"The whole tenor of this chapter as presented in the Inspired Version [Joseph Smith Translation] is that when Paul obtained the gospel he became a changed man and had a power over sin that he did not have before. This is Paul's dynamic testimony that the gospel can have a powerful influence on a human life and that Christ is the enabling power to attain righteousness." (Robert J. Matthews, *Ensign*, Sept. 1975, 11.)

Invite family members to share how the gospel of Jesus Christ has changed their lives.

ROMANS 8

Romans 8:1–13
"Carnally minded" vs. "spiritually minded"

 Draw the following on a piece of paper large enough for all to see:

_____ vs. _____

Ask what vs. means. (It is the abbreviation for *versus,* which means "against, contrasted with, or considered as an alternative to.") Tell your family that Paul presents such a contest in Romans chapter 8. Have them read Romans 8:1–13 and determine what should go in the blanks. (Possible answers may include "*flesh*" vs. "*Spirit*" or "*carnally minded*" vs. "*spiritually minded.*") Ask family members to browse through the verses again and choose the one verse they think gives the most impressive message about the contest between flesh and Spirit. Have family members share which verse they chose and why and then discuss the following questions:

- What does it mean to be "carnally minded"? (Desires of the flesh dominate our spirit.)
- What are the consequences of being "carnally minded"?
- How does being "carnally minded" lead to death?
- What do you think it means to be "spiritually minded"?
- What are the blessings promised for being "spiritually minded"?

Share the following insight from Elder Joseph B. Wirthlin: "In the scriptures, peace means either freedom from conflict or war, or an inner calm and comfort born of the Spirit.

"The value of peace in our hearts cannot be measured. When we are at peace, we can be free of worry and fear, knowing that with the Lord's help, we can do all that is expected or required of us. Few, if any, blessings from God are more valuable to our spiritual health than the reward of peace within. . . .

"Despite dismal conditions in the world and the personal challenges that come into every life, peace within can be a reality. . . .

"Attaining harmony within ourselves depends upon our relationship with our Savior and Redeemer, Jesus Christ, and our willingness to emulate Him by living the principles He has given us.

"President David O. McKay (1873–1970) said, 'The peace of Christ does not come by seeking the superficial things of life.' This peace is 'conditioned upon obedience to the principles of the Gospel of Jesus Christ.'" (*New Era,* Feb. 2005, 4.)

Discuss as a family how to eliminate the carnal from our minds and hearts and focus more on the spiritual. Make a list of five things your family can do to be more "spiritually minded" in the upcoming week.

Romans 8:14–34
Children of God and joint-heirs with Christ

 Ask the following questions:

- What is an heir? (A person who is entitled to inherit another's property, rank, title, or office.)
- What things would you most like to inherit from parents or grandparents?
- If you could choose to inherit the possessions of any one person, who would you choose? Why?

Have someone read Romans 8:16 aloud and ask what Paul taught. Share the following statement from Elder Dallin H. Oaks: "Consider the power of the idea taught in our beloved song 'I Am a Child of God' (*Hymns,* 1985, no. 301). . . . Here is the answer to one of life's great questions, 'Who am I?' I am a child of God with a spirit lineage to heavenly parents. That parentage defines our eternal potential. That powerful idea is a potent antidepressant. It can strengthen each of us to make righteous choices and to seek the best that is within us. Establish in the mind of a young person the powerful idea that he or she is a child of God, and you have given self-respect and motivation to move against the problems of life." (*Ensign,* Nov. 1995, 25.)

Sing together as a family "I Am a Child of God." (*Hymns,* no. 301.) Ask:

- "How does it make you feel to know you are a child of God?
- What does the fact that we are children of God imply about our potential?

Have family members read Romans 8:17 and look for the great promise we receive as children of God. Ask:

- What kind of heirs do we become?
- What do you think it means to be a "joint-heir" with Christ?

Share the following definition from Elder Bruce R. McConkie: "A joint-heir is one who inherits equally with all other heirs including the Chief Heir who is the Son. Each joint-heir has an equal and an undivided portion of the whole of everything." (*Mormon Doctrine,* 395.)

Read Doctrine and Covenants 6:37 together as a family and discuss the following questions, inviting family members to share their testimonies as part of their answers:

- What must we do to qualify for this grand inheritance?
- How does it make you feel to know that you can inherit the kingdom of heaven?

Romans 8:35–39
The love of Christ

Ask family members to close their eyes. Tell them you are going to tell them a word and you want them to pay attention to what they envision or imagine as they think of that word. The word is LOVE.

After giving them a few seconds to ponder, ask them to share what they envisioned. Read together Romans 8:35–39 and ask:

- What does Paul teach about the love of Jesus Christ?
- Since it lists many things that cannot separate us from the love of God, is there anything that can? Can we separate ourselves? How?

Sing together or read the words of "I Feel My Savior's Love." (*Children's Songbook,* 74.) Invite family members to share how they have felt the Savior's love in their lives and what difference it makes in facing life's challenges.

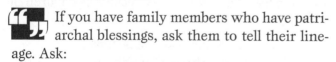

ROMANS 9: GOD'S LAW OF ELECTION

Romans 9:1–8
"Who are Israelites?"

If you have family members who have patriarchal blessings, ask them to tell their lineage. Ask:

- What do you think it means to be of one of the tribes of Israel? (See Bible Dictionary, "Israel," 708.)
- What blessings come to those of the house of Israel?

Invite your family to read Romans 9:6–8 and look for ways the children of Israel can lose the blessings of being of Israel. Ask:

- What do you think the following phrase means: "For they are not all Israel, which are of Israel"? (See footnotes 6*a* and *b.*)

- How would you describe the difference between being "children of the flesh" and "children of God"?

Share this statement by Elder Bruce R. McConkie with your family: "The house of Israel was a distinct people in pre-existence; that is, by obedience and devotion, certain of the spirit children of the Father earned the right to be born in the lineage of Abraham, of Isaac, and of Jacob, and of being natural heirs to the blessings of the gospel. But some of them, after such a favored birth, after being numbered with the chosen seed, turn from the course of righteousness and become children of the flesh; that is, they walk after the manner of the world, rejecting the spiritual blessings held in store for Israel." (*Doctrinal New Testament Commentary,* 2:276.) Ask:

- How do some who are of Israel end up rejecting their spiritual blessings?
- What do we need to do to continue to be of Israel?
- How can obedience and devotion assure that you remain of Israel?

Encourage family members to write and finish the following sentence in their journals: "Today I will keep my place in the house of Israel by _____."

Romans 9:9–29
God's election

Prior to family scripture study, prepare enough ballots, each containing a list of different family positions similar to the ones below, for each family member. Adjust the positions available to fit your family.

- Official Lawn Mower _____
- Chief Chef _____
- Lovely Laundry Lady _____
- Terrific Trash Collector _____
- Wonderful Weed Whacker _____

Give each person a ballot and a pencil. Have them write on each blank space the name of the family member they feel would do the best job in that position. Collect the ballots, tally the votes, and congratulate the winners. Make sure that everyone is elected to a position.

Explain that God also chooses those who have positions in His house. This is called the doctrine of election. Divide your family into four individuals or pairs and give each person or pair a slip of paper and a pencil. Invite them to look up "Election" in the Bible Dictionary, 662–63, and assign one of the four paragraphs to each individual or pair. Have them silently read their paragraph and write a question about the doctrine of election on their slip of paper. (If you have more than four individuals or pairs, paragraph 3 is the largest and could be divided.) Place the finished questions in a bowl and mix them up. Take out one question at a time and read it. Refer to the Bible Dictionary as needed.

Paul gives examples of the law of election in Acts 9:9–29. As you study this passage, you will notice that some of the verses are difficult to understand. Select the passages and questions below that you feel comfortable teaching.

- Why does God elect some over others? (Verses 9–13 and footnote 13a.)
- Why might some think God unfairly chooses one child over another? (Verses 14–18 and footnote 18b.)
- Why is it improper to blame God for our failures or weakness? (Verses 19–20.)
- How can Gentiles also be "elected" of God? (Verses 24–26; see 2 Nephi 30:2.)
- What word is used to describe how many members of the house of Israel will be saved? (Verse 27.)
- What gospel principle must the Gentiles, or anyone else, live by in order to be righteous? (See verse 30.)
- How might focusing on "the works of the law" have caused the Israelites to stumble over the more important principle of faith? (See verse 32.)
- Who was the "stumblingstone" mentioned in verse 33? (See footnote 33a.)
- How can faith in the "stumblingstone" save us?

ROMANS 10: TEACHINGS ABOUT FAITH

Romans 10:1–21
What is the duty of those who believe in Jesus Christ?

Invite one family member to stand up and give him or her a bag of treats. Discuss the following questions:

- What would be the value of keeping all of these treats for yourself?
- How would you feel if you shared these treats with one or two other family members?
- How do you think those family members would feel who did not get any treats?
- How do you think you would feel if you shared the treats with everyone in the family?
- Would you rather be a person who is selfish, shares with some, or shares with all? Why?

Ask that family member to imagine that instead of a lot of candy, they were blessed with a testimony of Jesus Christ, and discuss the following questions:

- Would you rather keep that to yourself, share it with a few, or share it with everyone?
- According to Romans 10:1, who did Paul seem to be concerned with, himself or others?
- How many did he want to help save?

Divide your family into two groups. Ask each group to study Romans 10:1–21. Have each group focus on one of the following areas, learning all they can about it. When they have finished, have one member of each group report what they discovered.

- Group 1: Look for messages about what a person can do to gain a testimony, develop stronger faith, or be saved in the kingdom of God.
- Group 2: Look for the verses about sharing the message of the gospel with others, and what we can learn about the importance of telling others about what you know for yourself.

Share your testimony of missionary work, the gospel message, or faith. You may also enjoy singing "Called to Serve" (*Hymns,* no. 249), and talking about ways your family could better share the gospel with other people.

ROMANS 11: GOD'S GRACE TO THE JEWS AND THE GENTILES

Romans 11:13–15

The gospel is for the house of Israel and the Gentiles

Give family members paper and pencils and explain that there will be a short quiz following their silent reading of Romans 11:13–15. When they have read, give the following quiz:

1. Who was the "apostle of the Gentiles"? (Paul.)

2. What word did Paul use to describe his service? (Magnify; see verse 13.)

3. What did Paul want to provoke those of his "flesh" (house of Israel) to do in verse 14? (To emulate his example by accepting the gospel of Jesus Christ.)

4. What do you think *emulation* means? (To imitate.)

5. To what did Paul compare the "receiving" or return of the house of Israel to God? (To "life from the dead"; see verse 15.)

Explain to your family that you are part of Latter-day Israel. Discuss how you might "magnify" your calling and lead others to a spiritual life in the gospel of Jesus Christ.

Romans 11:16–32

Why does God have an olive tree?

To clearly understand what Paul is saying about the tame and wild olives trees, it would be helpful for your family to read the chapter headings for Romans 11 and Jacob 5. You might also review the Book of Mormon Gospel Doctrine video for Jacob 5 from your ward library.

Before beginning, obtain a nice-sized tree branch. Break off some of its branches. Put it in a pot so it looks like a tree.

If this is not possible, make drawings of a tree and two branches. Label the tree the Olive Tree.

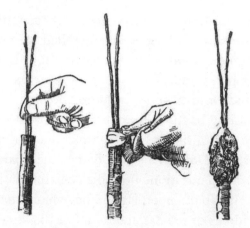

Label one branch Wild Olive Branch and the other Natural Olive Branch.

Invite one member of your family to read aloud Romans 11:16–24 while you demonstrate grafting the Wild Olive Branch and the Natural Branch into the Olive Tree. (Cut a place for the branch to go on the tree and then wrap it with fabric or tape; see illustration above.) Ask:

- What do you think the olive tree represents? (House of Israel.)
- What does the natural branch represent? (Jews of Paul's day.)
- What does the wild branch represent? (Gentiles.)
- Following grafting, what benefit does the wild olive branch (Gentiles) now have? (It can be nourished by the "root and fatness" of the house of Israel; see verse 17.)
- Why should the wild branch (Gentiles) not boast that they have taken the place of the natural branch (apostate Israelites)? (Verses 18, 20–21.)
- Why was the natural branch (house of Israel) broken off? (Verse 20.)
- Why was the wild branch (Gentiles) grafted in? (Because of their faith; see verse 20.)
- How is God's love for the house of Israel expressed in verse 24?

Give all family members a tree branch, so they all have an opportunity to graft their branches onto the tree. Sing verse 2 of "Israel, Israel God is Calling" (*Hymns,* no. 7) with your family and ask how they are part of the "people of his choice."

As a family scan Romans 11:25–32 and look for key words or phrases that show how God will save all His children, including the Gentiles. Then testify that God's mercy will be extended to His children through the Lord Jesus Christ.

ROMANS 12: A LIVING SACRIFICE

Romans 12:1–21

What does it mean to be a living sacrifice?

Have your family bring one of their favorite possessions, or a representation of that possession, to family scripture study. Ask them why they chose that particular item. Collect the items and ask:

- How would you feel if we were to give these favorite things to a local charity?
- What word do you think best describes giving up something you value? (Sacrifice.)
- What do you think the phrase "a living sacrifice" might mean?

Ask a family member to read Romans 12:1–2 aloud while the rest of your family looks for what Paul suggests a living sacrifice is. Have them share what they have discovered. Discuss what kinds of things a person might need to give up to become a living sacrifice.

Give a piece of paper and pencil to someone who will act as scribe for the rest of the family. Explain to your family that Romans 12:3–21 lists things that need to be sacrificed or accumulated in order to become living sacrifices. As you take turns reading the passage, have them report their findings to the scribe who will record the information.

When the verses are read and the list is compiled, invite each member of your family to choose one thing from the list they would like to rid from their lives and one thing they would like to develop. Have them write their choices in their journals and create an action plan on how they will be able to accomplish their goals. Ask:

- If you were able to master each of the items on this list, what kind of a person would you be? (A Saint; see Romans 12, headnote.)
- How is Jesus Christ a good example of being "a living sacrifice"?

To help them understand one way a person can become a Saint, share a story recounted by President Ezra Taft Benson:

"'There was a little crippled boy who ran a small newsstand in a crowded railroad station. He must have been about twelve years old. Every day he would sell papers, candy, gum, and magazines to the thousands of commuters passing through the terminal.

"'One night two men were rushing through the crowded station to catch a train. One was fifteen or twenty yards in front of the other. It was Christmas eve. Their train was scheduled to depart in a matter of minutes.

"'The first man turned a corner and in his haste to get home to a Christmas cocktail party plowed right into the little crippled boy. He knocked him off his stool, and candy, newspapers, and gum were scattered everywhere. Without so much as stopping, he cursed the little fellow for being there and rushed on to catch the train that would take him to celebrate Christmas in the way he had chosen for himself.

"'It was only a matter of seconds before the second commuter arrived on the scene. He stopped, knelt, and gently picked up the boy. After making sure the child was unhurt, the man gathered up the scattered newspapers, sweets, and magazines. Then he took his wallet and gave the boy a five dollar bill. "Son," he said, "I think this will take care of what was lost or soiled. Merry Christmas!"

"'Without waiting for a reply the commuter now picked up his briefcase and started to hurry away. As he did, the little crippled boy cupped his hands together and called out, "Mister, Mister!"

"'The man stopped as the boy asked, "Are you Jesus Christ?"

"'By the look on his face, it was obvious the commuter was embarrassed by the question. But he smiled and said, "No, son. I am not Jesus Christ, but I am trying hard to do what He would do if He were here."' (*American Opinion,* December 1971, pp. 13–14.)" (*Ensign,* Apr. 1984, 11–12.)

Discuss ways your family can "do what [Jesus] would do." Share your testimony on the importance of becoming a saint, or being "a living sacrifice."

ROMANS 13: PAUL'S COUNSEL CONTINUES

Romans 13:1–14
How do we become a living sacrifice?

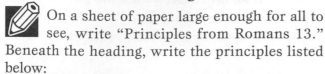 On a sheet of paper large enough for all to see, write "Principles from Romans 13." Beneath the heading, write the principles listed below:

If we resist the power of God, we will receive damnation.

If we do good, we will be blessed.

If we do evil, we have need to fear, for God's wrath will be upon us.

To fulfill God's law, we must love one another.

As we cast off the works of darkness, we can put on the armor of light.

Explain to your family that Romans 13 is a continuation of Romans 12 and contains more of Paul's teachings about becoming living sacrifices. Take turns reading verses from Romans 13 aloud, and ask family members to raise their hand when they identify a principle. Have them show the principle.

When you have finished, discuss the following questions:

- How can these principles better help us to become living sacrifices?
- Which of these principles do you need to work on most and why?

Read aloud Romans 13:14 and ask what family members think it means to "put ye on the Lord Jesus Christ." Share your ideas of how we can have the Lord's Spirit with us more consistently.

You could invite your family to think of Jesus as much as possible during the next twenty-four hours and to report on their experience during your next scripture study.

ROMANS 14: EVERYONE SHALL GIVE ACCOUNT OF HIMSELF UNTO GOD

Romans 14:1–6, 12–15, 20–21
Arguing or helping?

 Discuss the following questions with your family:

- What things in the Word of Wisdom, if used, could keep a person from having a temple recommend?
- What are some things people sometimes associate with the Word of Wisdom that would not keep a person from having a temple recommend? (Eating meat or drinking some soft drinks.)
- Have you ever heard someone argue about those things?

Explain to your family that just as some people today argue about aspects of the Word of Wisdom, in Paul's day many argued about dietary aspects of the law of Moses and what parts of it they were to continue observing. Have your family look for the contention it caused as they read Romans 14:1–6. Ask:

- What does it mean to receive a person "to doubtful disputations"? (Get into an argument with someone.)
- Why shouldn't we get into an argument about the finer details of the Word of Wisdom?
- What counsel does Paul give us concerning judging each other? (Verse 4.)
- Who is our master?

Read together verses 12–15 and ask:

- Who will we have to give an account of ourselves to? (Verse 12.)
- How can judging others put a stumbling block in a person's way?

Have your family read verses 20–21 and ask:

- If we do feel it is okay to eat or drink some things that others feel break the Word of Wisdom, why is it good not to do it in front of them? (Verse 21.)

You may want to read the following statement by President Gordon B. Hinckley: "It is not an easy thing to become a member of this Church. In most cases it involves setting aside old habits, leaving old friends and associations, and stepping into a new society which is different and somewhat demanding.

"With the ever increasing number of converts, we must make an increasingly substantial effort to assist them as they find their way. Every one of them needs three things: a friend, a responsibility, and nurturing with 'the good word of God' (Moro. 6:4). It is our duty and opportunity to provide these things." (*Ensign,* May 1997, 47.)

Challenge your family to avoid contention and not do things that would lead others to become offended.

ROMANS 15: TRUE SAINTS HELP EACH OTHER

Romans 15:1–7
Do as Jesus does

Have your family divide into pairs and sit closely, facing each other. Explain that you want them to play a game called Mirror. Pick one person to be the leader and the other to be the mirror. Tell the leader to slowly move his hands, body and face. The person acting as a mirror will try to do the exact same thing as the leader. As the two move slowly enough and in unison, it will become difficult for an observer to tell the difference between the leader and the mirror. After a time have them switch roles.

Have your family silently read Romans 15:1–7 and look for similarities to the game. Ask:

- What reason did Paul give that we should help each other? (Verses 1–2.)
- How did Christ help others instead of just looking out for Himself? (Verse 3.)
- What does it mean, "Receive ye one another, as Christ also received us to the glory of God"? (We should be kind to others as Christ was kind to us.)

Challenge your family to try to "mirror" Jesus by serving others.

Romans 15:23–29
Spiritual needs versus temporal needs

Have your family look for the reason Paul is going to Jerusalem, as they read Romans 15:23–29. Ask:

- In what two ways did Paul desire to minister to Church members in Jerusalem? (Verse 27; in "spiritual things" and "carnal things.")

- What are some examples of spiritual things?
- What are some examples of carnal things? (Footnote 27c; "carnal things" are temporal things, such as living conditions, economic conditions, feeding the poor, etc.)
- What kind of temporal things does the Church deal with today?
- Why does the Church concern itself with things that seem to go beyond spiritual matters?

Share the following statement from President Joseph F. Smith: "'It has always been a cardinal [central] teaching with the Latter-day Saints, that a religion which has not the power to save the people temporally and make them prosperous and happy here cannot be depended upon to save them spiritually, and exalt them in the life to come' (quoted in L. Arrington, *Great Basin Kingdom,* 1958, p. 425, n. 16)." (Ludlow et al., *Encyclopedia of Mormonism,* 4:1554.)

Ask:

- From what region of the world did Church members want to help the poor in Jerusalem? (Verse 26; the Saints in these countries were mostly non-Jewish converts.)
- As a Church, what are some of the different ways we help the less fortunate in the world?

Explain that it is through our fast offerings and other humanitarian contributions that we as members of the Church can help those in need around the world. Challenge each family member to earn and give something extra (as appropriate) to fast offerings or Church humanitarian aid this month.

Romans 15:30–33
Why do we need to pray for Church leaders?

Give everyone in your family a piece of paper and have them list three things they always seem to mention in their prayers. Invite some to share what they have written. Invite someone to read Romans 15:30–33 and look for what Paul asked the Roman Saints to always include in their prayers. Ask:

- Who did Paul want them to pray for?
- Why is it so important to pray for Church leaders?

Share the following statement from President Spencer W. Kimball: "The children will learn to honor and revere the Lord's anointed leaders as they are taught to pray for their local and general authorities; they will love the Lord as they pray for his work; they will love their fellowmen as they pray for the sick, the mourners, the distressed. They will anticipate with gladness their own missions as they pray for the missionaries out preaching the gospel." (*Teachings of Spencer W. Kimball,* 117.)

Challenge your family to always include Church leaders in their prayers.

ROMANS 16: PAUL COUNSELS THE SAINTS

Romans 16:1–23

Do Church leaders know and care about me personally?

As your lesson begins, call each of your family members by name and welcome them to your family scripture study. Ask:

- How do you feel whenever someone calls you by your name?
- What differences do you feel when someone calls you by name instead of just saying, "Hey, you"?

Read Romans 16:1–15, 21–23, looking for the names of the many different people Paul addresses. Tell your family that in Romans 16 Paul addresses greetings to at least thirty individuals in Rome. Invite your family to find out how many of the names belong to women. (About one-fourth.) Invite your family to describe the value and responsibilities of women in the Church. You may want to read the following statement from Sister Sheri Dew:

"As daughters of our Heavenly Father, and as daughters of Eve, we are all mothers and we have always been mothers. And we each have the responsibility to love and help lead the rising generation. How will our young women learn to live as women of God unless they see what women of God look like, meaning what we wear, watch, and read; how we fill our time and our minds; how we

face temptation and uncertainty; where we find true joy; and why modesty and femininity are hallmarks of righteous women? How will our young men learn to value women of God if we don't show them the virtue of our virtues?" (*Ensign,* Nov. 2001, 97.)

Tell your family that these letters (Romans 16) were written to many leaders of the Church who were serving faithfully. Invite your family to now look through Romans 16:1–16, looking for what impresses them most about what Paul said to these early Church members and leaders. Call each of your family members by name again and let them know of your love for them and the service they render. Remind them that our Father in Heaven knows each of them by name and desires to bless them.

Romans 16:17–27

How can we protect ourselves from the deceptions of anti-Christs?

If anyone in your family knows a magic trick, have them demonstrate it for the others. If not, perhaps the following would suffice:

What you need:

A glass that's nearly full of clear soda pop
A pushpin

What you do:

This is a fun and easy trick that really *looks* like magic.

1. While telling your audience about an ancient "water purification ritual" you learned, drop the pushpin in the soda.

2. Tell them that in ancient times, the people did not have water filters. When they came to rivers or lakes they would first bless the water so that all of the dangerous things would rise out.

3. Begin to chant. Just sound mystical and mysterious as you moan. While you do this, watch the pin closely.

4. *By itself* the pin will start to stand up. (Try to pretend it is because you are a good dancer, but really it's because the pin is so light that the tiny bubbles in the soda make it float when they stick to the plastic.

5. Gesture with your hands as if you are drawing

the pin out magically. It will float all the way to the surface, where you can pull it out!

Tip: The flatter the soda is (when the carbonation is gone), the longer it will take the pin to rise. But if the soda is fresh, the pin may float to the top so fast that you can't do a dance. Practice until you find the right amount of time to let the soda sit.

Invite a family member to read Romans 16:17–20 aloud. Ask:

- What did Paul say about people who teach false doctrines?
- How could the deceptions of a magic trick possibly be compared to the deceptions of Satan?

- How is Satan trying to deceive people today?

Have family members write 2 Nephi 28:12–15 in the margin next to verses 17–20 and then ask someone to read it aloud. Ask, What caused many of the people in the Book of Mormon to be deceived? Read with your family Matthew 7:15–20 and Doctrine and Covenants 46:7–9. Ask, How can we "mark" (watch out for) and "avoid" people who teach false doctrine? Testify to your family that Satan desires to deceive the Saints and weaken their faith. Encourage them to be found in holy places that will protect them from deception.

1 CORINTHIANS

"Corinth, the capital of the Roman province of Achaia, was one of the richest and most immoral cities in the world." (Ogden and Skinner, Acts through Revelation, *128.) Paul's first visit to Corinth lasted nearly two years during his second missionary journey. (See Bible Dictionary, "Pauline Epistles," 743; see also Acts 18:1–18.)*

"First Corinthians is actually Paul's second letter to the Corinthian Saints (see 1 Corinthians 5:9). The first has not survived, and their reply (see 1 Corinthians 7:1) is also lost. The Corinthian members may have sent oral [spoken] communications to Paul as well (see 1 Corinthians 1:11; 16:17). Thus, 1 and 2 Corinthians represent part of a continuing dialogue between Paul and the Corinthian Saints. . . . It deals with spiritual gifts, resurrection, degrees of glory, baptism for the dead, Jehovah as Christ, charity, unity, moral cleanliness, personal revelation, and the sacrament" among other teachings and counsel. (See Ogden and Skinner, Acts through Revelation, *128–29.)*

1 CORINTHIANS 1: THERE IS STRENGTH THROUGH UNITY

1 Corinthians 1:1–16
How do we become unified in Christ's Church?

Hold up a single toothpick and invite a family member to break it in two. Hold up a large number of toothpicks bound together, and invite the same person to attempt breaking the bundle in two. (You can do the same thing with tearing sheets of paper.) Ask your family what made it much more difficult the second time. Ask:

- What lessons can we learn from this object lesson?
- How can we apply it to an individual and a family? (When we are bound together as one we're much stronger.)

Take turns reading 1 Corinthians 1:10–16, stopping after each verse to identify the problems that existed among the Corinthian Saints. (For example, divisions, contentions, lack of unity.) Ask:

- How do you think the problems of Corinth relate to the object lesson?
- What do you think it means that some of the Saints claimed to be "of Paul," some "of Apollos," some "of Cephas [Peter]," and some "of Christ"? (Instead of following Jesus Christ as one, some Saints divided into groups according to leaders they liked best.)
- How do some make this same mistake today?
- Why do you think Paul wanted to correct this problem?
- What blessings might be enjoyed if divisions and contentions were eliminated? (See Mosiah 18:21–22; 4 Nephi 1:15–16.)

Invite family members to write 3 Nephi 11:28–30 next to 1 Corinthians 1:10. Ask someone to read aloud 3 Nephi 11:28–30. Then discuss how your family can avoid contention. Share the following statement:

"A house divided against itself cannot stand.

(See Mark 3:25.) Unity is basic and essential. Declared the Lord, 'If ye are not one ye are not mine.' (D&C 38:27.)" (Gordon B. Hinckley, *Ensign,* May 1990, 51.)

Ask your family what message President Hinckley is trying to communicate to us. Bear testimony of what can happen when a family, team, community, or nation come together as one. Encourage your family to work together as one so that Satan can have no power over them.

1 Corinthians 1:17–31

God hath chosen the foolish things of the world to confound the wise

 Read together 1 Corinthians 1:18–25 and ask:

- What did Paul teach about the wisdom of God and the foolishness of men?
- How is God's wisdom different from the world's wisdom? (See Isaiah 55:8–9; D&C 38:1–2.)
- What are some examples of God's wisdom making foolish the wisdom of the world?
- In what ways can worldly wisdom and learning be a blessing to us?
- In what ways can it be a serious problem? (See 2 Nephi 9:28–29.)
- Why is it important to take time to know the "things of God"?

Read aloud 1 Corinthians 1:25–27. Ask:

- What did Paul mean when he said that God had chosen "the foolish things of the world to confound the wise" and "the weak things of the world to confound the . . . mighty"? (Verse 27.)
- Why does God often choose the "weak things of the world" to fulfill his purposes?
- In what ways are missionaries good examples of "foolish things of the world" who will "confound the wise"?

Share the following statement by President Gordon B. Hinckley: "I had been interviewed by a representative of the BBC Radio Worldwide Service. He had seen the missionaries and noted their youthful appearance. He asked me, 'How do you expect people to listen to these callow youth?'

"In case some of you do not know the meaning of *callow,* it means immature, inexperienced, lacking sophistication.

"I replied to the reporter with a smile, 'Callow youth?' Yes, they are lacking in sophistication. What a great blessing this is. They carry no element of deception. They speak with no element of sophistry. They speak out of their hearts, with personal conviction. Each is a servant of the living God, an ambassador of the Lord Jesus Christ. Their power comes not of their learning in the things of the world. Their power comes of faith, and prayer, and humility." (*Ensign,* Nov. 1995, 51.)

Ask your family what they now think it means that the foolish would confound the wise. Conclude by reading Doctrine and Covenants 1:17–19 to your family. Ask your family why they think Joseph Smith was referred to as a weak thing in this verse. Testify to your family that it is our testimonies that make us strong and able to confound the wise.

1 CORINTHIANS 2: GOD'S WISDOM IS GREATER THAN MAN'S WISDOM

1 Corinthians 2:1–8

What is the best way to preach the gospel of Christ?

Invite a family member to stand up while the other family members take turns asking him or her questions that might be asked by someone not of our faith. (Example: Why do you believe Joseph Smith was a prophet, or why don't Mormons smoke or drink alcohol?) Ask the person standing to answer the questions and then discuss the following as a family:

- What is the difference between preaching and teaching the gospel? (Preach: To proclaim; to publish in religious discourses. Teach: To give instruction.)

Show your family a copy of the newest missionary manual entitled *Preach My Gospel* and talk about why that title may have been chosen. Read the following statement by Elder Bruce R. McConkie:

"There was of old, there is now, and to all eternity there shall be only one approved and proper way to preach the gospel—Preach by the power of the Spirit. Anything short of this is not of God and has neither converting nor saving power. All the religious learning, of all the professors of religion, of all the ages is as nothing compared to the Spirit-born testimony of one legal administrator." (*Doctrinal New Testament Commentary,* 2:318.)

Invite your family to read 1 Corinthians 2:1–9, looking for how Paul instructs us to preach the gospel. Ask:

- What words and phrases show how and why Paul preached the gospel?
- How can those words and phrases help you as you preach the gospel to your friends and neighbors?

Invite your family to share times when the Lord helped them when they felt inadequate to do His work. Testify of the blessings God has prepared for those who love Him and keep His commandments.

1 Corinthians 2:9–16
The Spirit reveals all things

Invite your family to explain how they would make the following decisions or where they would go for help and answers regarding those decisions:

- Which vegetables to buy at the grocery store.
- What type or style of car to buy.
- Which brand of soup to buy.

Invite your family to explain the kind of information they ask Heavenly Father about, what questions they look for His guidance on, and how those questions and information differ from the three items listed above. Read the following statement by Elder Dallin H. Oaks:

"No answer is likely to come to a person who seeks guidance in choosing between two alternatives that are equally acceptable to the Lord. Thus, there are times when we can serve productively in two different fields of labor. Either answer is right. Similarly, the Spirit of the Lord is not likely to give us revelations on matters that are trivial. I once heard a young woman in a testimony meeting praise the spirituality of her husband, indicating that he submitted every question to the Lord. She told how he accompanied her shopping and would

not even choose between different brands of canned vegetables without making his selection a matter of prayer. I think that is improper. I believe the Lord expects us to make most of our decisions by using the intelligence and experience he has given us." (*The Lord's Way,* 37.)

Invite your family to silently read 1 Corinthians 2:9–16. Tell your family that the Joseph Smith Translation changes the last part of 1 Corinthians 2:11 to read, "the things of God knoweth no man, except he has the Spirit of God." Ask: What did Paul teach in verses 9–16 about the things of God, the Spirit, and the "natural man"? (Also see D&C 76:5–10; Mosiah 3:19 for additional help.) Ask your family to turn again to 1 Corinthians 2:10–13 and ask:

- According to Paul, how can we know the "things of God"?
- Why do we sometimes rely more on our own wisdom and intellect than on revelation through the Spirit?

Ask a family member to read aloud 1 Corinthians 2:14. Ask them:

- What does Paul say keeps a person from the Spirit of God? (The tendencies and desires of the "natural man.")
- Why do you think this is so?
- What must we do to overcome the natural man? (See Mosiah 3:19.)
- According to 1 Corinthians 2:16, what happens to us as we put off the natural man?

Testify to your family the value of taking upon themselves the "mind of Christ." Ask them what it might be like to think and act as Jesus would. Invite them to think about how the world would be different if all people took upon themselves the mind of Christ.

1 CORINTHIANS 3: OUR BODIES ARE TEMPLES OF GOD

1 Corinthians 3:1–15
Milk comes before meat in the Church

 Prior to scripture study, place the following items in two separate bags, keeping them hidden from your family: In bag no. 1 place some things used by a baby, such as a baby bottle full of milk, baby food, a pacifier, a diaper, etc. (If these items are not available, consider drawing or obtaining pictures of these items.) In bag no. 2 place items used or eaten by adults. (Example: meat, chips, athletic glove, pair of pants, etc.) After gathering for scripture study, pull the items from bag no. 1 and place them in front of your family. Ask:

- Who are these items intended for?
- Why do you feed milk to a baby and not steak?
- What action might you take if you saw a little baby being fed pizza by a brother or sister?

Pull the items from bag no. 2 and ask:

- Who are these items used by?
- Would an adult generally prefer meat to baby food? Why?
- Why can't babies eat what adults eat?

Ask a family member to read aloud 1 Corinthians 3:1–2. Ask:

- What did Paul compare the Corinthian Saints to?
- Why had the Corinthian Saints received only the "milk" of the gospel?
- How can we prepare ourselves to be fed the "meat" of the gospel?

Read together 1 Corinthians 3:6–11 and look for ways people can mature in the gospel. Ask:

- Who gives "the increase" as we work and grow in the gospel? (Verse 6.)
- What do we become as we labor in the gospel? (God's building; verse 9.)
- What is the foundation upon which we must build in order to prepare for the meat of the gospel? (Verse 11.)
- What do we learn from Helaman 5:12 about why it is important that we have the Savior as the foundation of our faith?

Invite a family member to recite or read Article of Faith 1:4. Discuss ways the first principles of the gospel help your family build upon the foundation of Christ. Also discuss why it is important to have a basic knowledge of the gospel (milk/first principles) prior to being taught the meat (more advanced part) of the gospel. Testify of how impor-

tant it is to grow "line upon line, precept upon precept" after being built upon the foundation of Christ.

1 Corinthians 3:16–23
"Know ye not that ye are the temple of God"

Prior to family scripture study, obtain a picture of a family member. Show your family a picture of a temple (such as *Gospel Art Kit,* no. 502) and have one of them read aloud 1 Corinthians 3:16–17. Hold a picture of a family member next to the temple and ask:

- What did Paul compare our bodies to?
- What do you think he was trying to teach us by this comparison?
- What would defile a temple and make it unholy?
- What things can defile our bodies or make them unclean or unworthy?
- How can we treat our bodies as temples?
- How can you treat others' bodies as temples?

Discuss with your family what the Lord has said about how we should treat our bodies. (See *For the Strength of Youth* pamphlet, 14, 22, 26, 29.) Ask them how this is different from what the world believes is acceptable behavior.

Read 1 Corinthians 3:18–21 aloud. Ask:

- What did Paul teach about the world's wisdom? (Verse 19.)
- Why is it more important to listen to God than to the wisdom of the world?
- According to verse 23, who do we really belong to?
- How might this understanding influence how we dress and act?

Discussing the following questions and referring to the quotes below might aid in your discussion:

- Why do you think sexual sins are so serious?
- What are the blessings of being morally clean?

"Any sexual intimacy outside of the bonds of marriage—I mean any intentional contact with the sacred, private parts of another's body, with or without clothing—is a sin and is forbidden by God. It is also a transgression to intentionally stimulate these emotions within your own body." (Richard G. Scott, *Ensign,* Nov. 1994, 38.)

"He [Satan] knows that this power of creation is not just an incident to the plan, but the key to it. He knows that if he can entice you to use this power prematurely, to use it too soon, or to misuse it in any way, you may well lose your opportunities for eternal progression." (Boyd K. Packer, *Ensign,* July 1972, 112.)

Share with your family the value of keeping yourself clean. Ask them to testify of the blessings of obeying Paul's counsel about treating our bodies as a temple.

1 CORINTHIANS 4: CHURCH LEADERS TO REMAIN FAITHFUL TO THE END

1 Corinthians 4:1–8
What are the mysteries of God?

Invite your family to define the word *mystery*. Read aloud 1 Corinthians 4:1 and ask what they think the mysteries of God are. Read the following statement by President Joseph Fielding Smith:

"There are in the gospel such things as mysteries. A mystery is, of course, some truth which is not understood. All the principles of the gospel and all truth pertaining to the salvation of men are simple when understood. Until it is understood, however, a simple truth may be a great mystery" (*Doctrines of Salvation,* 1:296.)

Ask, According to Paul in 1 Corinthians 4:2, what does the Lord require of His servants in order to understand the mysteries of God? Read to your family the following statement by Elder Neal A. Maxwell:

"Speaking to His disciples, Jesus said, 'It is given unto you to know the mysteries of the kingdom of heaven, but to them [the unbelieving multitude] it is not given' (Matthew 13:11; Luke 8:3). Jesus was able to teach his Apostles things that were kept from the world, including information about sacred ordinances. It is noteworthy that Paul saw Church leaders as 'stewards of the mysteries of God' (1 Corinthians 4:1)." (*Not My Will, but Thine,* 130.)

Discuss the following questions with your family:

- What are some sacred things the Lord may want kept from wicked people in the world today?
- Why do you think the Lord wants some things to continue as mysteries? (See also D&C 82:3.)
- What is your duty regarding those sacred and important things?

Testify to your family how following the Lord's leaders allows us to better understand the mysteries of God and qualify for His redeeming love.

1 Corinthians 4:9–21
The righteous are persecuted for righteousness' sake

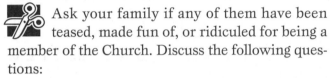 Ask your family if any of them have been teased, made fun of, or ridiculed for being a member of the Church. Discuss the following questions:

- Why do you think some people do that?
- How does it make you feel?
- How do you think the Lord expects us to react toward those people?

Invite a family member to read aloud 1 Corinthians 4:8–14 and ask:

- What are some of the trials that Paul and other Apostles endured?
- What things did he do to endure each trial? (Verses 12–13.)
- Why did Paul share these experiences with the Corinthians? (Verse 14.)

Ask a family member to read aloud verses 15–16 and discuss the following questions:

- Whose example did Paul want the people to follow?
- Why would Paul be a good person to follow? (Because he follows Christ; see verse 16.)
- How does following our righteous Church leaders bring us closer to Christ and our Father in Heaven? (Verse 17 indicates that their example is Christ's way.)

Read the following statement by President Ezra Taft Benson:

"The gospel of Jesus Christ certainly offers

incentives to achieve and accomplish challenges which develop a person's inner powers. Only by daily applying its principles and teachings in our lives may the power which is inherent within us be released and made manifest among men. Thus may we achieve the ideal spoken of by Paul when he explained to the Corinthian Saints that 'the kingdom of God is not in word, but in power' (1 Corinthians 4:20)." (*Teachings of Ezra Taft Benson,* 341.)

You may also choose to read the following scripture:

Turn to James 1:22 and have a family member read it aloud. Ask, What are some ways that people know we believe in our Father in Heaven and His Son? Read 1 Corinthians 4:20–21 and ask your family where the kingdom of God is found. Invite your family to share, after reading verse 21, how they would prefer that Paul "come" to them.

1 CORINTHIANS 5: KEEPING THE CHURCH PURE

1 Corinthians 5:1–13
The purpose of Church discipline

Show your family, or describe for them, a piece of fruit that has a bruise or has started to go bad in some part of it. Ask:

- What would you do with this fruit?
- Is the whole thing bad or ruined?
- What would happen ultimately if you did not do something with the part that went bad?

Invite someone read aloud 1 Corinthians 5:1–2. Ask:

- What was one serious problem among the Corinthian Saints?
- What did Paul say in verse 2 that helps reveal the apparent attitude of Church leaders about this problem? (They had not taken the problem seriously.)

Have your family silently read 1 Corinthians 5:3–7. Ask:

- What did Paul say these Church leaders needed to do about this problem, and why?
- How does Paul's counsel relate to the fruit we talked about before? (Purge or cut it out.)

Share the following commentary with your family to help them understand Paul's counsel:

"Apparently a member of the Church in Corinth had married his stepmother, either because she was a widow or had been separated from her prior husband. . . . Paul . . . describes the intimacies resulting from such unions as fornication, condemns his Corinthian brethren for winking at the offense, and directs the excommunication of the offender. If the sinner were left in the Church, Paul reasons, his influence . . . would spread throughout the whole Church. The Church must, therefore, purge out this . . . wickedness and replace it with . . . righteousness." (McConkie, *Doctrinal New Testament Commentary,* 2:335.)

Tell them that Elder M. Russell Ballard taught that there are three purposes for Church discipline: "to save the soul of the transgressor, to protect the innocent, and to safeguard the Church's purity, integrity, and good name." (*Ensign,* Sept. 1990, 15.)

As you read together 1 Corinthians 5:9–13, ask your family to look for ways that Paul's counsel relates to what Elder Ballard said about Church discipline. (You may have to clarify that when Paul asks the Saints not to "company with" those in serious sin, or "not to eat" with them, and to "put them away," he is asking Church leaders to take away Church privileges from those who are guilty—including the "eating" of the sacrament—and to make sure these people know that their conduct is unacceptable.)

Read together the counsel Jesus gave to the Nephites in 3 Nephi 18:31–32 about dealing with those who need Church discipline. Ask:

- What does this passage teach about the Lord's desire for all who sin?
- What is our responsibility to those in sin?

Share the following quote by Elder M. Russell Ballard: "When members need to have certain blessings withheld, the Lord's object is to *teach* as well as to discipline. So probation, disfellowshipment, and excommunication, when they become necessary, are ideally accompanied by eventual reinstatement and restoration of blessings." (*Ensign,* Sept. 1990, 12.)

Read Doctrine and Covenants 18:10–13, noting and bearing testimony of the following:

1. Why the Lord performed the Atonement.

2. How He feels about us using this great gift.

3. What the eventual results will be if we do use this gift.

1 CORINTHIANS 6: OUR BODIES ARE TEMPLES

1 Corinthians 6:9–20
The importance of our bodies

" Have your family imagine that a wealthy couple comes to you and asks your family to stay in their home for three years while they serve in a foreign land. After you agree, they instruct you to make yourself at home while you live there but that they expect to return to that same home and live there for the rest of their lives. Ask:

- How would you feel about remodeling the house while they are gone to make it fit some specific need you believe you have?

- Why do you feel this way?

- How would you feel about painting and repairing things that become worn or broken through use? Why?

Invite your family to read 1 Corinthians 6:19–20 to themselves. Ask:

- Who "owns" our bodies, and when did He "buy" them? (You may want to cross-reference 1 Corinthians 6:19–20 to D&C 18:10–13 and 19:16–19, where we learn more about the price He paid, why He paid it, and how He feels about paying it.)

- Knowing this to be true, what do you think of the saying, "It's my body and I can do what I want with it"?

Invite your family to suggest some of the commandments the Lord has given us concerning our bodies. You may want to consult the booklet *For the Strength of Youth*. Read also the sins Paul listed in 1 Corinthians 6:9–10, with the help of the footnotes to give the meanings of some words and phrases. Ask, Why do you think there are so many commandments from the Lord regarding our bodies?

Share with your family the following quotation:

"In the premortal realm we learned that the body was a part of God's great plan of happiness for us. . . .

"We knew that our bodies would be in the image of God. We knew that our bodies would house our spirits. We also understood that our bodies would be subject to pain, illness, disabilities, and temptation. But we were willing, even eager, to accept these challenges because we knew that only with spirit and element inseparably connected could we progress to become like our Heavenly Father (see D&C 130:22) and 'receive a fullness of joy' (D&C 93:33). . . .

"Satan learned these same eternal truths about the body, and yet his punishment is that he does not have one. Therefore he tries to do everything he can to get us to abuse or misuse this precious gift. He has filled the world with lies and deceptions about the body. He tempts many to defile this great gift of the body through unchastity, immodesty, self-indulgence, and addictions. He seduces some to despise their bodies; others he tempts to worship their bodies. In either case, he entices the world to regard the body merely as an object.

"What would happen if we truly treated our bodies as temples? The result would be a dramatic increase in chastity, modesty, observance of the Word of Wisdom, and a similar decrease in the problems of pornography and abuse, for we would regard the body, like the temple, as a sacred sanctuary of the Spirit. Just as no unclean thing may enter the temple, we would be vigilant to keep impurity of any sort from entering the temple of our bodies.

"Likewise, we would keep the outside of our bodily temples looking clean and beautiful to reflect the sacred and holy nature of what is inside, just as the Church does with its temples. We should dress and act in ways that reflect the sacred spirit inside us." (Susan W. Tanner, *Ensign*, Nov. 2005, 13–14.)

Ask:

- What did Sister Tanner say that helps us realize why the Lord gives so many commandments about our bodies?

- How will these truths affect choices we make every day?

1 CORINTHIANS 7: MARRIAGE IS ORDAINED OF GOD

1 Corinthians 7:1–40

Paul counsels the Corinthians about marriage

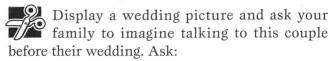 Display a wedding picture and ask your family to imagine talking to this couple before their wedding. Ask:

- What would you say to them if they were Church members?
- What would you say if they were not members of the Church?
- What would you say if only one was a member?
- What would you say if one was a currently serving full-time missionary?

Explain that in 1 Corinthians 7:1–19 Paul is responding to serious questions written to him by the Saints in Corinth. Many of the Saints in Corinth were in situations similar to those referred to in the questions above. Some of the material in this chapter is difficult to understand; however, Elder Bruce R. McConkie provided the following helpful insights about the Saints in Corinth:

"1. They knew about the law of eternal marriage and understood full well its relationship to eternal life.

"2. They knew Paul had the theoretical knowledge, the practical experience, and the heaven-bequeathed inspiration to guide others who had marital questions and problems.

"3. Further, they had asked him to comment on several specific and difficult problems involving members of their congregation. And unfortunately—we do not know what those problems were. In other words, we have some guarded and carefully phrased answers." (*Doctrinal New Testament Commentary,* 2:343.)

Divide your family into five groups or individuals. Assign each group or individual to study the scripture references as shown in the accompanying chart.

Group or Individual	Scripture Reference	Topic
1	1 Corinthians 7:1–3	Husbands and wives
2	1 Corinthians 7:7–9	The unmarried and widows
3	1 Corinthians 7:10–11	Divorce
4	1 Corinthians 7:12–14 (see also D&C 74:2–7)	Unbelieving spouse
5	Joseph Smith Translation 1 Corinthians 7:29–33 (in Bible Appendix, 810)	Missionaries

Have each group or individual study their scripture reference and see if they can write a question that Paul seems to be answering in his letter to the Corinthian Saints. Tell your family to carefully read the footnotes for important insights. When they are finished have them share their question and a summary of Paul's answer. It may be helpful to discuss the following questions:

- What important counsel did Paul give to husbands and wives?
- What insights did he give about "unbelievers"?
- What were Paul's feelings about divorce?
- What counsel did he give to widows and those who were single?
- What important counsel did Paul give to missionaries?
- From what you have studied in this chapter, how important was marriage to Paul?

Conclude by reading the following statement to your family: "The family is ordained of God. Marriage between man and woman is essential to His eternal plan." ("The Family: A Proclamation to the World," *Ensign,* Nov. 1995, 102; or see the Appendix of this book.) Share your testimony on the importance of family and express your love for your family.

1 CORINTHIANS 8: TRUE WORSHIP OF OUR HEAVENLY FATHER

1 Corinthians 8:4–13
Is it bad to eat meat?

Discuss the following questions as a family and ask them to give examples to support their answers:

- Do you believe your example can help another person to become interested in the gospel?
- Do you believe someone's bad example could cause another to lose interest in the gospel?
- Do you believe you could be participating in an acceptable activity but another person could misunderstand what you are doing and see your actions as a bad example?
- Why do you think it is important to avoid even the "appearance of evil"? (1 Thessalonians 5:22.)

Explain that in Paul's day some Church members were eating meat that had been sacrificed to idols. Many Church members asked Paul if this was acceptable. Share the following statement:

"The Corinthians had asked Paul for counsel about eating meat sacrificed by pagan people to their idols. He replies that in theory it is completely immaterial whether the Saints eat such meat or not, because idols are not true gods, and there is actually no religious significance to the pseudo-sacrifices one way or the other. But, he reasons, in practice it may be wise not to eat this meat, since such a course might cause those who are weak in the faith to assume there was virtue and benefit in the sacrifices themselves and therefore to be led astray." (McConkie, *Doctrinal New Testament Commentary,* 2:348.)

Read together 1 Corinthians 8:4–13 and ask:

- Why did Paul state it was admissible to eat the meat that had been offered to an idol? (See verses 4 and 8.)
- Why might some become offended if they saw Church members eat that meat? (See verses 9–10.)
- What did Paul teach he would do if in the presence of a Church member who could become offended? (See verse 13.)
- How might Paul's teachings apply to the activities we participate in today?

Testify of the importance of making good choices, and encourage family members to avoid anything that may cause others to see us as hypocrites.

1 CORINTHIANS 9: PAUL'S EFFORTS TO FURTHER THE GOSPEL

1 Corinthians 9:1–18
Financial support and sharing the gospel

Tell your family that in the Apostle Paul's day some tried to stop the Lord's work by criticizing Church leaders. Read together 1 Corinthians 9:1–6 and look for ways people were critical of Paul. Ask:

- What did Paul give as proof of his apostleship? (Verses 1–2; see footnote 2a.)
- How did Paul answer those who questioned his authority? (Verses 3–6; see footnote 3a.)
- What do you think Paul meant by asking, "Have not we power to forbear working" (verse 6 to "forbear" means to abstain or keep from.)

Explain to your family that Paul could have had Church members support him because he was engaged full time in missionary service. Invite your family to scan 1 Corinthians 9:7–18 and look for reasons Paul chose to support himself financially. Ask:

- Why did Paul choose not to take financial support from those he served?
- How could a person abuse receiving financial support?
- How could this stop or hinder the ministry?
- Who do you know today that serves in the Church with no financial reward?

Challenge your family to thank someone this week who serves them in the Church.

1 Corinthians 9:19–27
"All things to all men"

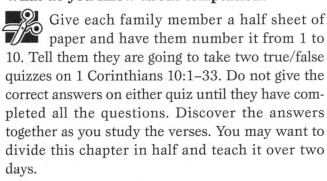 Explain that Paul is considered one of the greatest missionaries who ever lived. Read 1 Corinthians 9:22 and ask: What is one thing Paul tried to do to help spread the gospel? ("I am made all things to all men.")

Ask your family to look for ways Paul was "all things to all men" as they study 1 Corinthians 9:19–27. Draw a chart on a sheet of paper. As you take turns reading 1 Corinthians 9:19–23, match Paul's characteristics in the left column that allowed him to influence the groups of people listed in the right column.

Characteristics of Paul	People Paul Taught
Spoke Hebrew	• Verse 20. Those under the law (Jews)
Struggled with some physical aliment	
Spoke Greek	• Verse 21. Those without the law (Gentiles)
Was a former Pharisee	
Was a tentmaker by trade	• Verse 22. To the weak (Those who suffer or are sinners)
Was a great sinner in that he persecuted the Church	

It might be helpful to discuss the following questions:

- How can the things you learn or trials you face help you share the gospel with others?
- Why is it important to be able to adapt how you teach to the level of your investigator?

Tell your family that Paul also taught in this chapter a powerful key to succeed in the gospel cause. Read together 1 Corinthians 9:24–27 and ask:

- To what did Paul compare succeeding in the gospel cause? (Running a race.)
- Why is self-mastery and self-control so important to following the Savior?

Share the following quote by Gordon B. Hinckley: "Mental control must be stronger than physical appetites or desires of the flesh. . . .

"The timeless proverb is as true now as when it was first spoken: 'For as he thinketh in his heart, so is he' (Proverbs 23:7).

"Each of us, with discipline and effort, has the capacity to control our thoughts and our actions. This is part of the process of developing spiritual, physical, and emotional maturity." (*Ensign,* May, 1987, 47.)

Challenge your family to better prepare themselves so they can share the gospel in a variety of ways with those around them.

1 CORINTHIANS 10: PAUL COUNSELS NEW CHURCH MEMBERS

1 Corinthians 10:1–33
What do you know about temptation?

Give each family member a half sheet of paper and have them number it from 1 to 10. Tell them they are going to take two true/false quizzes on 1 Corinthians 10:1–33. Do not give the correct answers on either quiz until they have completed all the questions. Discover the answers together as you study the verses. You may want to divide this chapter in half and teach it over two days.

True/False Quiz for 1 Corinthians 10:1–13

1. When the Israelites followed Moses through the Red Sea, it represented their baptism. (True; see verse 2.)

2. What the Israelites experienced in the wilderness was to point them to Jesus Christ. (True; see verse 4.)

3. We are given examples like these in the scriptures so we will do what they did. (False; see verses 6–11.)

4. Everyone faces very different types of temptations. (False; see verse 13.)

5. You can never put yourself in a situation in which the temptation will be too great to resist. (False; see verse 13.)

As you review 1 Corinthians 10:1–13, give the correct answers to your quiz. Once you have read verse 13, ask your family to name some situations in which temptation might become so great that you cannot overcome it. Have your family write Alma 13:28 in their scriptures next to

1 Corinthians 10:13 and then read it. Discuss the additional insight gained from Alma 13:28.

True/False Quiz for 1 Corinthians 10:14–33

6. The sacrament represents the body and blood of Christ. (True; see verse 16.)

7. We should never expect to stay worthy if we participate in activities related to the devil. (True; see verses 21–22.)

8. All things were lawful for Paul to do. (False; see verse 23 footnote *a*.)

9. "Shambles" are rundown houses. (False; see verse 25 footnote *a*.)

10. If we are invited to dinner by someone of a different religion, we should not worry if the food was dedicated to false gods unless we are told. (True; see verses 27–28.)

After the quiz, ask your family the following questions:

- What are some spiritual activities that God wants us to participate in? (The sacrament, prayer, scripture study, etc.)

- What are some activities that relate to evil that we should not participate in? (Witchcraft, Ouija boards, fortune telling, immorality, stealing, etc.)

- Why can't we participate in a little bit of both?

Read again verse 21 and testify of the importance of staying on the Lord's side and away from evil activities.

1 CORINTHIANS 11: PAUL'S COUNSEL TO NEW CHURCH MEMBERS

1 Corinthians 11:3–16

How do we become one?

Divide a piece of paper in half with two columns and headings as shown below. Have family members read 1 Corinthians 11:3–15 and write what they can find that belongs either in the Customs or the Doctrines column. When you are finished, your paper should look something like the accompanying chart:

After completing the chart, discuss as a family how these teachings might lead some to believe

Customs in Paul's Day	Doctrines
When men pray or prophesy, they should not cover their heads.	God is the head of Jesus Christ.
When women pray or prophesy, they should cover their heads.*	Christ is the head of man.
If a woman's head is shaved, she should cover it.*	Man is the head of woman.
If a man have long hair, it is a shame unto him.	Man is created in God's image and is His glory.
If a woman have long hair, it is a glory to her.	Woman is the glory of her husband.
There is no custom for men to be contentious.	

*"A Woman should have her head covered when she prays or prophesies, lest she be as though her head was shaven, which according to local custom would identify her as an adulteress." (McConkie, *Doctrinal New Testament Commentary,* 2:361.)

that Heavenly Father loves men more than woman or that He thinks men are better than women. Share this statement by Elder Bruce R. McConkie: "Women are not one whit behind men in spiritual things; perhaps, on the whole, they are ahead of them. . . . Women . . . are as much entitled to revelation, visions, and gifts of the Spirit as are men." (*Doctrinal New Testament Commentary,* 2:361.)

Have everyone look at 1 Corinthians 11:11 and circle the word "nevertheless" and underline "in the Lord." Explain that Paul concluded his teachings in verse 11 with the most important doctrine regarding the husband-wife relationship. Ask:

- Why do you think it is important in any organization, business, or family to have someone at the head?

- Why is it important that there be only one "head" even when two people are good, talented, or capable? (See D&C 132:8.)

- What does a man or a woman need in order to inherit the celestial kingdom? (An eternal partner; see D&C 132:19.)

Ask the parents in your family to share their feelings about the importance of the marital relationship and what a magnificent thing it is to be "in the Lord" as a couple.

1 Corinthians 11:17–34
Paul points out a problem

 Invite your family to compare 1 Corinthians 11:2 and 17. Ask:

- What difference did you find in these two verses?
- Why did Paul praise the Saints in Corinth?
- How does Paul suggest that they are still not perfect?

Explain that even though the Corinthians deserved praise in one area, Paul discovered an area where they needed correction. Read together 1 Corinthians 11:18–22 and find what needed correcting. Be sure to check footnote 20a for a correct reading of that verse and then share the following:

"When Jesus instituted the ordinance of the sacrament, he and his apostles were celebrating the Feast of the Passover. . . . With this pattern before them, the early saints apparently adopted the practice of eating together a meal or supper and of then partaking of the sacrament." (McConkie, *Doctrinal New Testament Commentary*, 2:364.)

Ask:

- What resulted when the Corinthians combined the sacred sacrament with a festive feast? (See verses 21–22.)
- How would you solve this problem?

Invite your family to scan 1 Corinthians 11:23–34, looking for things Paul taught that might help solve this problem. Have them underline words or phrases that give specific instruction on partaking of the sacrament. Ask:

- Why is the sacrament considered to be so sacred? (Verses 23–27.)
- How can we ensure that we partake of it worthily? (Verse 28.)
- What are the consequences of taking the sacrament unworthily? (Verses 29–30.)
- How might judging ourselves help keep us from being judged by God? (See footnote 31a.)
- When and where should our festive feasts be eaten? (Verses 33–34.)

Sing verse 2 of "As Now We Take the Sacrament." (*Hymns,* no. 169.) Ask family members what they think it means to "examine" ourselves with regards to the sacrament and then have them write a personal examination of themselves in their journals.

1 CORINTHIANS 12: GIFTS OF THE SPIRIT

1 Corinthians 12:1–11
The Holy Ghost and spiritual gifts

Wrap the bottom part of a box (like a shoe box) to look like a gift. Give each person a pencil and as many pieces of paper as there are family members. Give the box to one family member and invite everyone else to write on a piece of paper a spiritual gift or quality (such as faith, kindness, service, knowledge, or wisdom) they feel that person has been given and deposit it in the box. Then ask the person with the box to read aloud what is written on each paper. Pass the box around the room and repeat this process for each family member. Then read together 1 Corinthians 12:1–3 and ask:

- Why do you think Paul wanted the Corinthian Saints to know about spiritual gifts?
- What spiritual gift is required to know that Jesus is the Christ? (Verse 3.)

Assign the following scriptures to three different family members: 1 Corinthians 12:4–7, 11; Moroni 10:8; Doctrine and Covenants 46:8–10. Have them read their verses out loud and then discuss the following questions:

- What is the purpose of spiritual gifts?
- Who gets them?
- Who decides who gets them?

Write the following spiritual gifts as listed in 1 Corinthians 12:8–10 separately on small boxes or gift bags: wisdom, knowledge, faith, healing, miracles, prophecy, discerning of spirits, tongues, interpretation of tongues. (If you do not have boxes or bags, 3 x 5 cards will do.) Place the bags or boxes on the table and have your family take turns drawing them. Once all of the gifts have been taken, have everyone turn to the Bible Dictionary or the

Book of Mormon Index and spend five minutes preparing to share information they learn about their chosen gift. (See the spiritual gifts and page numbers listed below.)

Bible Dictionary	Book of Mormon Index
Gift of knowledge, 721	Gift of wisdom, 401
Gift of faith, 669	Gift of healing, 146
Gift of miracles, 732	Gift of prophecy, 282–83
Gift to behold angels and ministering spirits, 608	Gift to teach words of wisdom, 401, and knowledge, 360
	Gift of tongues, 370
	Gift of interpretation of tongues, 166
	Gift to discern spirits, 83

When they have finished their search, ask for volunteers to share what they have learned about their assigned spiritual gift. Be sure to cover all of the gifts mentioned. Have everyone select a gift of the spirit they do not yet have and devise a plan of how they can develop it. Bear testimony that the Holy Spirit will help them develop certain gifts. You might also sing or read verse 1 of "Let the Holy Spirit Guide." (*Hymns*, no. 143.)

1 Corinthians 12:12–31
What does a body have to do with spiritual gifts?

Give everyone paper and crayons or colored pencils. Ask them to try and draw a picture of a whole body using only one of the following things:

1. feet	3. ears	5. noses
2. hands	4. eyes	6. heads

When the drawings are finished, display them for all to see. Be sure to enjoy and comment on the creativity. As you study 1 Corinthians 12:12–27, ask some or all of the following questions:

- What do these verses have to do with the drawings?
- Why are all body parts important and necessary?

- How does footnote 13a help us understand what the "body" is in verse 14?
- How could verses 15–17, 21 help us explain to individuals who feel unimportant that they are needed in Christ's Church?
- How does God feel about each individual in His Church? (Verse 18.)
- What does Christ's Atonement do for those who lack "honour"? (Verse 24.)
- What does *schism* mean in verse 25? (A split or a division.)
- Why are schisms destructive to God's Church?
- Why is it significant that we care for, suffer with, and honor all the members of the Church? (See Mosiah 18:8–9.) How will doing these things help us be members of the "body of Christ"? (Verse 27.)

Testify to your family that the Lord loves and wants all of us in the kingdom. As a family, choose someone in the ward who might need to be recognized for their less noticed accomplishments.

1 CORINTHIANS 13: CHARITY IS THE PURE LOVE OF CHRIST

1 Corinthians 13:1–13
"Charity never faileth"

As your family gathers for scripture study, play music that has full orchestral background. Following the opening prayer, have members of your family play such things as a toy xylophone, a chime (wind chimes will work), a whistle, or toy cymbals. Ask them how these toy instruments compare in quality with the orchestra music they just heard.

Read 1 Corinthians 13:1–3 and ask:

- Why is charity more imortant than any other gift?
- Why would an individual lacking in charity sound like a "tinkling cymbal" rather than a full orchestra?

Divide your family into teams. Invite them to take turns listing as many synonyms (words having the same or nearly the same meaning) for the word *charity* as they can. If one team is unable to list a word, the opportunity reverts to the other team until both teams' ability is exhausted. Write these synonyms in the margins. Be sure to add the definition found in Moroni 7:47.

Read 1 Corinthians 13:8–10 aloud to your family and ask:

- Why do you think Paul says that prophecies will fail, tongues will cease, and knowledge will pass away? (See verses 9–10.)
- When other gifts of the spirit will fail, cease and pass away, why will charity never fail? (See verse 8.)

Place a pair of the darkest sunglasses you have on your youngest reader. Dim the lights in the room. Ask them to read aloud 1 Corinthians 13:11–13 and ask what the dark glasses have to do with those verses. Ask:

- When did Paul act like a child? (See Acts 7:58–59; 8:1, 3; 9:1–2.)
- When did Paul become a man? (See Acts 9:3–9, 17–22.)
- What does Paul mean by the image "now we see through a glass, darkly"? (See footnotes 12*a* and *b*. Presently we cannot see and know all things because of the veil that has been drawn over our memories of our premortal life.)

Have someone read aloud 1 Corinthians 13:13. Ask:

- Why would charity, the pure love of Christ, be the greatest gift of the spirit we could possibly possess?
- What are some things required of us in order to love others as Jesus Christ loves them?
- What kinds of experiences do we need in order to learn charity?
- How easy is it to have charity for those who are unkind and even cruel to us?
- Whose life can we emulate as the greatest example of charity? (Jesus Christ.)

Encourage family members as they study the life, example, and teachings of Jesus Christ to notice His charitable acts and pattern their lives after His. Continue your study by having a family member read the following story:

"During the waning years of the depression, I used to stop by Brother Miller's roadside stand for farm-fresh produce.

"On one particular day, I noticed a small boy, ragged but clean, hungrily appraising a basket of freshly picked green peas. Pondering the peas, I couldn't help overhearing the conversation between Brother Miller and the ragged boy.

"'H'lo, Mr. Miller. Jus'admirin' them peas—sure look good.'

"'How's your Ma?'

"'Fine. Gittin' stronger alla'time.'

"'Good. Anything I can help you with?'

"'Nosir, jus' admirin' them peas.'

"'Would you like to take some home?'

"'Nosir, got nuthin' to pay for 'em with.'

"'Well, what have you to trade me for . . . ?'

"'All I got's my prize marble–best marble around here.'

"'This one is blue. I sort of go for red. Do you have a red one like this at home?'

"'Not zackley—but almost.'

"'Take this sack of peas home, and next trip, let me look at that red marble.'

"'Sure will. Thanks, Mr. Miller.'

"Mrs. Miller came over to help me. She said: 'There are two other boys like him in our community—all three are in very poor circumstances. Jim just loves to bargain with them for peas, apples, tomatoes. . . . When they come back with their red marbles, he decides he doesn't like red, and he sends them home with a bag of produce for a green marble.'

"I left the stand, impressed with this man.

"Several years went by and then I learned that Brother Miller had died.

"Upon arrival at the mortuary we fell into line. Ahead of us in the line were three young men. One was in an army uniform and the other two wore short haircuts, dark suits, and white shirts, obviously potential or returned missionaries. They approached Sister Miller by her husband's casket. Each of the young men hugged her, kissed her on the cheek, spoke briefly with her and moved on to the casket. Her misty, light blue eyes followed them as each young man stopped briefly, placed his hand over the cold pale hand in the casket, and left the mortuary awkwardly wiping his eyes.

"As our turn came to meet Sister Miller, I told her who I was, and mentioned the story she had told me about the marbles. Eyes glistening, she took my hand and led me to the casket.

"'This is an amazing coincidence. Those three boys that just left were the boys I told you about. They just told me how they appreciated the things Jim 'traded' them. Now, at last, when Jim could not change his mind about color or size, they came to pay their debt. We've never had a great deal of the wealth of this world . . . but right now Jim would consider himself the richest man in Idaho.'

"With loving gentleness she lifted the lifeless fingers of her deceased husband. Resting underneath were three magnificent shiny red marbles." (Adapted from William E. Petersen, *Ensign,* Oct. 1975, 39.)

Invite your family to look again at the list of synonyms they marked in their scriptures for *charity*. Ask them which of those synonyms would describe Brother Miller in the story above.

Encourage all family members to choose a stranger or an enemy to pray for and anonymously serve. Encourage them to pay close attention to how their feelings for that person change over time. Ask each family member to report on their experience in a future family home evening.

1 CORINTHIANS 14: GIFTS OF THE SPIRIT

1 Corinthians 14:1–28
Would it be better to speak in tongues or to prophesy?

Ask your family to tell which of the following three spiritual gifts the Apostle Paul said was greatest: hope, faith, and charity. (See 1 Corinthians 13:13, if they need a reminder.) Invite family members who experimented with charity according to the lesson in 1 Corinthians 13 to share their experience. Read together 1 Corinthians 14:1 and find what Paul believed was an even greater desire. Share the following statement by Elder Bruce R. McConkie:

"Prophecy is greater than charity, because in order to prophesy a man must first have the pure love of Christ in his soul (which is charity), and

then he must attune himself to the Holy Spirit so as to receive the spirit of revelation and of prophecy. Chiefly the gift of prophecy is to know by revelation from the Holy Ghost of the divine Sonship of our Lord. (See Rev. 19:9b–10.)" (*Doctrinal New Testament Commentary,* 2:384.)

Tell your family that in this chapter Paul compares the gift of prophecy to another spiritual gift. Have them silently read 1 Corinthians 14:2–3 and then tell which other gift Paul taught about. Ask your family to tell which gift they would desire the most and why.

Divide your family into two groups. Have one group search 1 Corinthians 14:4–28 and mark those reasons Paul gave for feeling that prophecy is the greater gift. Have the other group search the same verses and mark reasons Paul gave that show that the gift of tongues is a lesser gift. Have each group share their findings. Ask:

- What would you say is the main purpose for spiritual gifts? (See verses 12 and 26.)
- According to 1 Corinthians 14:22–25, what benefits come with the gift of prophecy over the gift of tongues?
- In what situations might it be important to have the gift of tongues?

Read (or have someone else read) the following quotation from President Joseph F. Smith:

"I believe in the gifts of the Holy Spirit unto men, but I do not want the gift of tongues, except when I need it. I needed the gift of tongues once, and the Lord gave it to me. I was in a foreign land, sent to preach the gospel to a people whose language I could not understand. . . . There was a purpose in it. There was something in it to strengthen my faith, to encourage me and help me in my ministry. If you have need of this gift of tongues, seek for it and God will help you in it." (*Gospel Doctrine,* 201.)

Encourage family members to increase their testimony of Jesus so they can invite the gift of prophecy in their personal lives.

1 Corinthians 14:29–33, 36–40
Who can have the gift of prophecy?

 Ask your family to tell what it might be like to be students in a classroom with several teachers teaching at the same time. Read aloud 1 Corinthians 14:30–33 and ask:

- Why do you think Paul gave counsel for some to "hold his peace" or, in other words, remain silent?
- How might having several prophesy at the same time result in confusion?
- Who can have the gift of prophecy?

Invite family members to read the following quote by Elder Bruce R. McConkie:

"Who may prophesy? Who can receive revelation? To whom are visions and heavenly manifestations vouchsafed [granted]? Not to members of the Council of the Twelve only, not to bishops and stake presidents alone, not just to the leaders of the Church. Rather, that God who is no respecter of persons and who loves all his children, speaks to every person who will heed his voice. Prophecy is for all: men, women, and children, every member of the true Church." (*Doctrinal New Testament Commentary*, 2:387.)

Read together 1 Corinthians 14:37–40. Ask:

- What did Paul tell the Corinthian Saints to do to obtain the gift of prophecy? (Verse 39.)
- What did he mean by "covet"? (See verse 39*a*; to covet is to desire.)
- If all members of the Church sought and obtained this gift, how might our families, wards, communities, and even the world be better?

Invite your family to share ways they think a person can develop the gift of prophecy. Read together 2 Nephi 32:4 and Alma 17:2–3 and make a list of things a person can do to develop this gift. Invite family members to write goals in their journals of what they can do to work toward having the gift of prophecy.

1 CORINTHIANS 15: PAUL TEACHES ABOUT THE PLAN OF SALVATION

1 Corinthians 15:1–11
Many have witnessed the resurrected Lord

 Ask your family the following questions:

- Have you ever seen Chicago (or some other city you have been to but they have not)?
- How do you know Chicago really exists? (Explain that you are a witness that it exists.)
- Do you think it is possible to believe something exists that you have never personally seen before?
- What does Alma 32:21 teach about this question, and how does this question relate to Jesus Christ?
- What witnesses do we have who have seen and know for certain that Jesus Christ lives?
- How does their testimony help strengthen you?

Ask your family to search 1 Corinthians 15:1–11 and find the number of people Paul listed who were witnesses of Jesus Christ's Resurrection. Explain that Paul did not list every person who ever saw the resurrected Lord, but there are many who are listed in the scriptures. Invite your family to find other references listing additional witnesses of the Savior's Resurrection. (For example, you could refer to D&C 76:22–24; 3 Nephi 11:8–10; and Acts 7:55–56.) Share the following testimony of Elder Bruce R. McConkie, which he gave in his final address before he died in 1985:

"And now, as pertaining to this perfect atonement, wrought by the shedding of the blood of God—I testify that it took place in Gethsemane and at Golgotha, and as pertaining to Jesus Christ, I testify that he is the Son of the Living God and was crucified for the sins of the world. He is our Lord, our God, and our King. This I know of myself independent of any other person.

"I am one of his witnesses, and in a coming day I shall feel the nail marks in his hands and in his feet and shall wet his feet with my tears.

"But I shall not know any better then than I know now that he is God's Almighty Son, that he is our Savior and Redeemer, and that salvation comes in and through his atoning blood and in no other way.

"God grant that all of us may walk in the light as God our Father is in the light so that, according to the promises, the blood of Jesus Christ his Son will cleanse us from all sin.

"In the name of the Lord Jesus Christ, amen." (*Ensign,* May 1985, 11.)

Express your feelings and share your testimony of Jesus Christ, His Resurrection, and His power to bless our lives. Read 1 Corinthians 15:12–19 aloud and ask your family to identify the logic Paul used to support his testimony of the Resurrection. Talk about the power of witnesses and how the number of ancient and modern witnesses adds to our understanding and testimony of the resurrected Lord.

1 Corinthians 15:20–23
Paul testifies of the Resurrection

Show your family a ballpoint pen (one that you can unscrew and remove the ink cartridge from). Without saying a word, take the pen apart and put the two halves of the pen together without putting the ink cartridge inside. Lay the pen and the ink cartridge side by side and ask:

- How are these items like 1 Corinthians 15:20–23? (Explain that the pen can represent the body and the ink cartridge can represent the spirit.)
- What happens to the body at death? (Set the pen aside and help them see that the body is placed in the grave.)
- What happens to our spirit when we die? (Hold up the ink cartridge and explain that the spirit, which can never die, will go to the spirit world and await the Resurrection.)
- What will happen to our bodies and our spirits at the Resurrection? (Put the pen and the cartridge back together and write with it. Explain that when our bodies are resurrected, they will work better than before, for they will be perfect.)

Testify of the wonders of the Resurrection and how you look forward to having a perfect body.

Ask your family to look again at verses 20–23. Discuss the following questions to better help your family understand the doctrine of Resurrection:

- Who was the first person to be resurrected?
- Whose death brought death to all people?
- Because of Jesus Christ's Atonement and Resurrection, how many people will be resurrected?
- What additional information can you learn about the Resurrection from Alma 11:42–44 and Alma 40:21–24?

Show a picture of a loved one who is elderly or perhaps one who has passed away. Ask your family to tell why the doctrine of the Resurrection is such a comfort.

1 Corinthians 15:24–58
Paul testifies of the plan of salvation

Explain that 1 Corinthians 15:24–58 deals with the plan of salvation. To help your family understand the different parts of the plan, draw the accompanying diagram (see next page), on a sheet of paper without including the labels or verses. Ask family members to label each item in the drawing from their memory. When they have concluded, label the parts of the drawing they could not remember.

Now read 1 Corinthians 15:24–58 together as a family. As you do, look for different parts of the plan of salvation Paul discusses. Each time a family member identifies a verse describing part of the plan of salvation ask them to add those verses in the appropriate place in the diagram.

Explain that there are many very important doctrines explained in these verses. Assign each family member one of the sections of the plan of salvation. (For example, the premortal life, earth life, resurrection, etc.) Ask them to spend a few minutes and do the following activities:

- Think about all you know concerning that part of the plan of salvation.
- Look for additional scriptures that give more help in understanding that part of the plan.
- Read in the Bible Dictionary or other resource book about that part of the plan of salvation.
- Ponder what difference knowing about your Heavenly Father's plan makes to you.

When all have had opportunity to finish their assignment, invite each person to share what they have found.

Consider how your life would be different if you did not know about or understand this plan, and

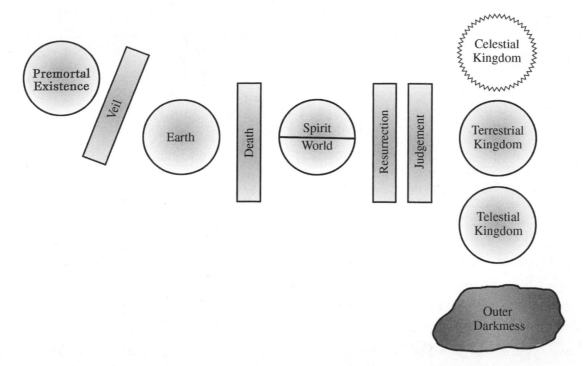

share your testimony and the love you have for Heavenly Father and for this glorious plan of salvation.

1 CORINTHIANS 16: FINAL INSTRUCTIONS AND DETAILS

1 Corinthians 16:1–24
Reading between the lines

Bring a copy of a letter you have recently received from a friend or relative. Read it to your family. Invite them to imagine someone many years from now reading this same note. Ask:

- What are some things they would not understand if they did not know the people or the situations written about in the letter?
- Why would it be important to have such information?

Remind your family that 1 Corinthians is a letter written by Paul to people who knew him or have been told about him by people who knew him. Also, there was a Church organization in Corinth that Paul knew and understood. Invite your family to read 1 Corinthians 16:1–24 and look for clues that might help them answer the

following questions about Paul and the Church of that day and be prepared to share what they found.

- When did they hold their Church meetings? (A clue is in verse 2.)
- Where did they hold their Church meetings? (An example is in verse 19.)
- Who are some of the leaders of the Church in those days?
- How does Paul feel about other Church leaders?
- What has Paul planned for his future and what do you think he based his decisions on? (See verses 6–9.)
- How did Paul feel about the Saints in Corinth?

After family members share their clues that they think help answer the questions above, discuss the following questions:

- What important counsel did Paul give in verses 13–14?
- What difference could it make if we followed this counsel in our family? In our Church? In our neighborhood?

Especially considering what was learned from 1 Corinthians 13, you may want to make a small poster out of 1 Corinthians 16:14 to be hung where family members can see it on a regular basis.

2 CORINTHIANS

It is clear from the title that this letter from Paul to the Saints in Corinth was written as a follow-up to his earlier epistle. In First Corinthians, Paul appeals for unity in the Church and sharply reproves the Saints for many wrong beliefs and practices. After being driven from Ephesus, and while continuing his missionary efforts in Macedonia, Paul met Titus (2 Corinthians. 7:5–6, 13), "who brought him news from Corinth that his letter had been well received and had produced the desired effect." (Bible Dictionary, 744.) In this epistle Paul expresses gratitude for the progress made but continues to encourage faithfulness in keeping the commandments and fulfilling their duties. "Second Corinthians is not a definitive epistle; it does not analyze and summarize gospel doctrines as such. Instead it applies already known doctrines to the circumstances of the Corinthians, much as an inspired sermon applies the gospel to the congregation in which it is preached." (McConkie, Doctrinal New Testament Commentary, 2:407.)

2 CORINTHIANS 1: GOD COMFORTETH AND CARETH FOR HIS SAINTS

2 Corinthians 1:1–10
Receiving and giving comfort

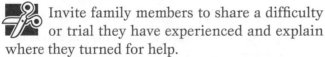 Invite family members to share a difficulty or trial they have experienced and explain where they turned for help.

Have them read together 2 Corinthians 1:1–10 and look for insights Paul gave regarding adversity. Ask:

- In whom should we place our trust? (Verse 9.)
- Who can we always count on for help? (Verses 3–4.)
- What are some purposes of affliction according to verses 6 and 7?
- What is "consolation"? (Have someone find the word in a dictionary if they need help.)
- What did Paul say he knew of tribulation? (See verses 8–10.)

Share this teaching from President George Q. Cannon: "'No matter how serious the trial, how deep the distress, how great the affliction, [God] will never desert us. He never has, and He never will. He cannot do it. It is not His character [to do so]. . . . We have found that God. We have made Him our friend, by obeying His Gospel; and He will stand by us.' ("Freedom of the Saints," in *Collected Discourses,* comp. Brian H. Stuy, 5 vols. [1987–92], 2:185; emphasis added)." (Jeffrey R. Holland, *Ensign,* Apr. 1998, 19–20.)

Ask, According to verse 4, what obligation do we have once "we ourselves are comforted of God"?

Invite someone to read this message from Elder Jeffrey R. Holland: "Once we have come unto Christ and found the miracle of his 'covenant of peace,' I think we are under obligation to help others do so, just as Paul said in that verse to the Corinthians—to live as much like he lived as we possibly can and to do as much of what he did in order that others may walk in this same peace and have this same reassurance. . . . I ask you to be a healer, be a helper, be someone who joins in the work of Christ in lifting burdens, in making the load lighter, in making things better. As children, when we had a bump or a bruise, didn't we say to Mom or Dad, 'Make it better'? Well, lots of people on your right hand and on your left are carrying bumps and bruises that they hope will be healed and made whole. Someone you know is carrying a spiritual or physical or emotional burden of some sort, or some other affliction drawn from life's catalog of a thousand kinds of sorrow. In the spirit of Christ's first invitation to his twelve Apostles, jump into this work. Help people. Heal old wounds and try to make things better." (*Ensign,* Apr. 1998, 20–21.)

Discuss ways you can help others in their times of adversity. If your family enjoys singing you may want to sing "Lord, I Would Follow Thee." (*Hymns,* no. 220.)

2 Corinthians 1:12–24
Reciprocate

Invite a family member to look up the word *reciprocate* in a dictionary and read it to the family. Then ask them what they think a reciprocal relationship might be.

Have them scan 2 Corinthians 1:12–24 and find evidence of a reciprocal relationship between the Corinthians and Paul and Timothy. Ask:

- Why do you think Paul and Timothy rejoice in the people of Corinth and the people of Corinth rejoice in Paul and Timothy? (Verse 14.)
- What has God done for Paul and Timothy? (Verses 21–22.) "What Paul suggests is that we have been given the Holy Ghost, an initial payment of blessedness which serves as a guarantee of a much fuller payment in the future if we continue faithful." (*Life and Teachings of Jesus and His Apostles,* 302.)
- What have Paul and Timothy done for the Corinthians? (Verses 23–24.)

Talk to your family about reciprocal relationships they enjoy in their lives and encourage them to reciprocate to someone who has done something for them recently, especially family members. Discuss why it is important or beneficial to treat others as kindly as they have treated us.

2 CORINTHIANS 2: LOVING AND FORGIVING ONE ANOTHER

2 Corinthians 2:1–17
Do I have to forgive someone if . . . ?

 Choose some of the following questions to ask your family:

- How would you feel toward someone who broke one of your new toys?
- How would you feel toward someone who made fun of you or called you names?
- How would you feel toward someone who spread false rumors about you?
- How would you feel toward someone who hurt you physically or stole from you?

Read the following news story related by President Gordon B. Hinckley:

"'How would you feel toward a teenager who decided to toss a 20-pound frozen turkey from a speeding car headlong into the windshield of the car you were driving? How would you feel after enduring six hours of surgery using metal plates and other hardware to piece your face together, and after learning you still face years of therapy before returning to normal—and that you ought to feel lucky you didn't die or suffer permanent brain damage?

"'And how would you feel after learning that your assailant and his buddies had the turkey in the first place because they had stolen a credit card and gone on a senseless shopping spree, just for kicks?'" (*Ensign,* Nov. 2005, 83–84.)

After allowing time for family members to share how they would feel if this happened to them, tell your family you want them to look for how Paul's counsel to the Saints in 2 Corinthians could relate to such experiences. Take turns reading 2 Corinthians 2:1–17. Ask someone to summarize, in a sentence or two, what they think is the main message. Have family members write D&C 64:8–10 in the margin by 2 Corinthians 2:7. Ask one family member to then read Doctrine and Covenants 64:8–10 aloud. Ask:

- What does it say is required of us?

- How difficult would it be to forgive those who offended us in the examples we shared earlier?
- Why does Jesus require us to forgive "all men?"(See 3 Nephi 13:14–15.)
- What advice would you have for someone trying to learn to be more forgiving?

Share your testimony of the Atonement, and of the special gift of forgiveness Jesus has extended to us. Share your desires for your family to follow His example and forgive others at all times.

Continue telling the rest of the story shared by President Hinckley:

"'This is the kind of hideous crime that propels politicians to office on promises of getting tough on crime. It's the kind of thing that prompts legislators to climb all over each other in a struggle to be the first to introduce a bill that would add enhanced penalties for the use of frozen fowl in the commission of a crime.

"'The New York Times quoted the district attorney as saying this is the sort of crime for which victims feel no punishment is harsh enough. "Death doesn't even satisfy them," he said.

"'Which is what makes what really happened so unusual. The victim, Victoria Ruvolo, a 44-year-old former manager of a collections agency, was more interested in salvaging the life of her 19-year-old assailant, Ryan Cushing, than in exacting any sort of revenge. She pestered prosecutors for information about him, his life, how he was raised, etc. Then she insisted on offering him a plea deal. Cushing could serve six months in the county jail and be on probation for 5 years if he pleaded guilty to second-degree assault.

"'Had he been convicted of first-degree assault—the charge most fitting for the crime—he could have served 25 years in prison, finally thrown back into society as a middle-aged man with no skills or prospects.

"'But this is only half the story. The rest of it, what happened the day this all played out in court, is the truly remarkable part.

"'According to an account in the New York Post, Cushing carefully and tentatively made his way to where Ruvolo sat in the courtroom and tearfully whispered an apology. "I'm so sorry for what I did to you."

"'Ruvolo then stood, and the victim and her assailant embraced, weeping. She stroked his head and patted his back as he sobbed, and witnesses, including a Times reporter, heard her say, "It's OK. I just want you to make your life the best it can be." According to accounts, hardened prosecutors, and even reporters, were choking back tears' ("Forgiveness Has Power to Change Future," Deseret Morning News, Aug. 21, 2005, AA3).

"'What a great story that is, greater because it actually happened, and that it happened in tough old New York. Who can feel anything but admiration for this woman who forgave the young man who might have taken her life?" (Ensign, Nov. 2005, 84.)

Challenge family members to demonstrate more love and to try and be more forgiving of others. You could close by singing or reading the words to "Help Me, Dear Father." (Children's Songbook, 99.)

2 CORINTHIANS 3: TABLES OF THE HEART

2 Corinthians 3:1–18
What kind of heart should ours be?

Bring to scripture study a rock (about the size of your fist) and a soft sponge or wadded-up hand towel similar in size to the rock. Place the rock and the sponge on the table for your family to see. Ask the following questions to help your family make some contrasts and comparisons between the two:

- Which is more pliable?
- Which can be more easily penetrated?
- Which do you think is more like our heart?
- What problems would it cause if our hearts were like the rock?

Ask someone to read 2 Corinthians 3:1–3. Hold up the rock and explain that our life's experiences are not written on stone tablets but in our hearts. Tell your family that for today's lesson, the rock (which is stiff and dead) represents the law of Moses and the soft pliable sponge represents the gospel of Jesus Christ.

Divide your family into two groups and give each a sheet of paper and something to write with.

Give the rock to one group and the sponge to the other. Assign each group to search 2 Corinthians 3:3–17. Have the group with the rock look for things that pertain to the law of Moses and the group with the sponge look for things pertaining to the gospel of Jesus Christ. Their lists may look something like the following:

Rock (Law of Moses)	Sponge (Gospel of Jesus Christ)
Written not with ink (Verse 3.)	But with the spirit of the living God (Verse 3.)
Tables of stone (Verse 3.)	Fleshy tables of the heart (Verse 3.)
	Our sufficiency is of God (Verse 5.)
The letter, for it killeth (Verse 6.)	The Spirit, giveth life (Verse 6.)
The ministration of death (Verse 7.)	Ministration of the spirit (Verse 8.)
Written and engraved in stones (Verse 7.)	
Ministration of condemnation (Verse 9.)	Ministration of righteousness exceed in glory (Verse 9.)
Done away (Verse 11.)	That which remaineth is glorious (Verse 11.)
Vail over our faces (Verse 13.)	Plainness of speech (Verse 12.)
Minds were blinded (Verse 14.)	Vail is done away in Christ (Verse 14.)
Vail is upon their heart (Verse 15.)	Vail shall be taken way (Verse 15.)
	Where the Spirit of the Lord is there is liberty (Verse 17.)

When they have finished compiling their lists, have each group share what they learned. Hopefully they will clearly see that the law of Moses is dead while the gospel of Christ is alive and glorious. Invite someone to read verse 18 then share the following:

"As a mirror reflects the likeness of a person, so the saints should reflect the image of Christ, and as they progress in obedience and personal righteousness, they attain this image; by the power of the Spirit, they become like Christ." (McConkie, *Doctrinal New Testament Commentary,* 2:416.)

Share your testimony of the importance of the gospel of Jesus Christ in your life and encourage your family to live in such a way that Jesus can be seen in their countenance, and be able to touch their hearts.

2 CORINTHIANS 4: THE LIGHT OF THE GLORIOUS GOSPEL

2 Corinthians 4:1–16
We should look toward Christ's light

 Bring a flashlight to scripture study, but do not show it to your family. Turn out the lights and ask:

- What could we use to help us see in the dark? (When someone mentions a flashlight, turn it on.)
- What does the flashlight do to the darkness?
- What is the difference between physical darkness (when the lights are out) and spiritual darkness? (See Matthew 6:23.)
- What is a person missing when they are in spiritual darkness?

To help answer those questions, invite someone to read 2 Corinthians 4:1–6. Ask:

- What things in verse 2 can bring spiritual darkness into our lives?
- Who wants us to be spiritually blind? (See verse 4.)
- Who is the "god of this world"? (See footnote 4*a*.)
- Who is it that brings the gospel light into our lives? (Verse 6.)
- What does verse 5 suggest we should do with the light we receive?

Take turns reading 2 Corinthians 4:7–16 and look for how the light brought Paul and others out of the darkness (verses 8–9) and what it is that they bore witness of (verses 10, 11, 14).

Encourage your family to share the gospel with their friends and then watch the light in both of you grow.

2 Corinthians 4:17–18
Our afflictions are "but for a moment"

Ask family members to talk about the last time they each felt discouraged, disappointed, or depressed. Talk about the following questions:

- What caused these discouraged feelings?
- How did you deal with this difficulty?
- How long did the discouragement last?
- What did you do to overcome those feelings?

Read 2 Corinthians 4:17–18 and ask:

- How long does Paul indicate that afflictions last?
- Why is it that some feel that discouragement lasts for a long time and others feel that they last, "but for a moment"?

To help answer that last question, share the following statement from Elder Dallin H. Oaks: "As faithful members of The Church of Jesus Christ of Latter-day Saints, we have a distinctive way of looking at life. We view our experiences in terms of eternity. As we draw farther from worldliness, we feel closer to our Father in Heaven and more able to be guided by his Spirit. We call this quality of life *spirituality*. To the faithful, spirituality is a lens through which we view life and a gauge by which we evaluate it." (*Ensign,* Nov. 1985, p. 61.)

Help your family understand that the way we look at things makes a great difference in how long the affliction lasts in our lives. Explain to them that whenever they are discouraged they can take Paul's advice, put that particular affliction in its proper perspective in the eternal scheme of things, and thereby realize just how insignificant their affliction really is.

2 CORINTHIANS 5: "WE WALK BY FAITH, NOT BY SIGHT"

2 Corinthians 5:1–11
Earthly and heavenly tabernacles

Show your family a picture of the Salt Lake City Tabernacle. (*Gospel Art Kit,* no. 503.) Ask them to identify the building. Then ask:

- What kinds of things has the Church done in the tabernacle over the years? (General Conferences, Mormon Tabernacle Choir broadcasts, etc.)
- In what ways might we consider the tabernacle sacred?
- If you have ever been to the tabernacle, have you felt the Spirit there?

Take turns reading 2 Corinthians 5:1–4 and have your family to watch for a different tabernacle. Ask:

- What "tabernacle" was Paul referring to in these verses? (Our "earthly house" or physical body.)
- In what way is our "earthly house" or body similar to the tabernacle in Salt Lake City?
- What do you think is the "house which is from heaven" in verse 2? (Our spirits "clothed upon" with a resurrected body.)

Explain that Paul's message to the Corinthians was one of hope. Everyone will die, but the gospel declares that all spirits will be "clothed" again with a resurrected body. Have your family silently read 2 Corinthians 5:5–10 and identify at least two things we need to know about living in mortality. Ask:

- What help has God given us to live out our days in mortality? (See verse 5, the "earnest," meaning a pledge or promise, of help of the Spirit.)
- Since we are no longer in God's presence and do not remember our association with Him, what principle must we live by now? (Verses 6–7.)
- What will we be judged by when we stand before the judgment seat of Christ? (Verse 10.)
- If part of our judgment has to do with our "earthly house," why must we make sure our bodies are worthy to have the Spirit with us?

Discuss ways you can develop "tabernacles" worthy of the Spirit.

2 Corinthians 5:12–21
Reconciliation

 Have someone in the family who does the finances explain in a simple way what it means to reconcile a checking account. (Reconciling a bank account means that the individual and the bank agree on how much is in the bank after money has been spent. Sometimes the bank makes mistakes in their records but most often people do.) Invite your family to scan 2 Corinthians 5:18–21, looking for the word *reconcile* (or a form of the word) that is repeated five times. Ask your family what they think *reconcile* means the way Paul used it. Then share this definition:

"Reconciliation is the process of ransoming [saving] man from his state of sin and spiritual darkness and of restoring him to a state of harmony and unity with Deity. Through it God and man are no longer enemies. Man, who was once carnal and evil, who lived after the manner of the flesh, becomes a new creature of the Holy Ghost; he is born again; and, even as a little child, he is alive in Christ." (McConkie, *Doctrinal New Testament Commentary*, 2:422–23.)

Ask:

- How is being reconciled with God similar to being reconciled with the bank?
- What is one way we get into spiritual debt? (We sin.)
- Who helps us pay our spiritual debt so we can agree or become one with God? (See verses 18–19.)
- How does it make you feel to know that Jesus suffered for your sins even though He was sinless?

It is important to explain that the Savior will not do all of the work to get us out of spiritual debt. Read 2 Nephi 10:24 and talk about our part in becoming reconciled to God. List ways your family can more fully do "the will of God" and not "the will of the devil and the flesh."

2 CORINTHIANS 6: MINISTERS OF CHRIST

2 Corinthians 6:1–13
How should ministers of Christ act?

Ask a family member to be a scribe for today's study. Give him or her a piece of paper and something to write with. Have your

family think of a church leader they really admire, and ask: "What is it about this leader that you admire?" Have your family list as many qualities about this leader as they can while the scribe records their responses. Take turns reading 2 Corinthians 6:1–10 and compare your list with Paul's list about God's ministers. Ask:

- Which of the attributes Paul mentioned do you like the best? Why?
- Why do you think it is so important for Church leaders to have these attributes?
- Do you think others should also possess these same attributes? Why or why not?

Read 2 Corinthians 6:11–13 as if it were a letter from your ward bishopric but substitute your last name for the word "Corinthians" in verse 11. The following translation of these verses may be helpful: "We have spoken freely to you, Corinthians, and opened wide our hearts to you. We are not withholding our affections from you, but you are withholding yours from us. As a fair exchange—I speak as to my children—open wide your hearts also." (*NIV Study Bible*, 2 Corinthians 6:11–13, 1769–70.) Discuss the following:

- How would you feel receiving such counsel from your bishop?
- Why do you think it is important to show love for your Church leaders?
- What can we do as a family to demonstrate our gratitude for our leaders?

Make a family plan to show an expression of thanks to a Church leader.

2 Corinthians 6:14–18
Marriage within the covenant

Show your family the image of a yoke (see next page). Ask what it is and how it works.

Read 2 Corinthians 6:14–18 together and talk about these questions:

- Who did Paul warn us against being yoked with?
- What dangers could exist if we were to be yoked with unbelievers?
- Why do you think it is important to "touch not" unclean things?

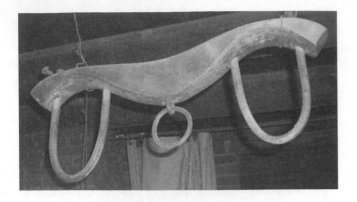

- What are some things in the world that you believe we should separate ourselves from?
- According to footnote 14*a*, what is one way we could yoke ourselves with unbelievers?
- What is the danger of marrying outside the covenant?

Read the following insight from President Ezra Taft Benson:

"If someone wants to marry you outside the temple, whom will you strive to please—God or a mortal? If you insist on a temple marriage, you will be pleasing the Lord and blessing the other party. Why? Because that person will either become worthy to go to the temple—which would be a blessing—or will leave—which could also be a blessing—because neither of you should want to be unequally yoked (see 2 Corinthians 6:14).

"You should qualify for the temple. Then you will know that there is no one good enough for you to marry outside the temple. If such individuals are that good, they will get themselves in a condition so that they too can be married in the temple." (*Teachings of Ezra Taft Benson,* 351.)

Bear your testimony of the importance of temple marriage.

2 CORINTHIANS 7: THE CORINTHIANS REPENT

2 Corinthians 7:1–16
How can sorrow be good?

Ask your family: If I told you that a certain person was happy because another person was sad, what would you generally think of that situation or relationship? Read together 2 Corinthians 7:2–16 looking for who was happy because another was sad, and why. After reading, use the following questions to guide your discussion of what you read:

- What words and phrases throughout these verses describe how Paul feels about the Corinthians? (See especially verses 3–4, 7, 9, 12–14, 16.)
- What reasons does Paul give for why he feels as he does?
- How do you think the Corinthians felt as they read these expressions of Paul for them?
- What seemed to be the biggest reason Paul was happy and rejoiced over the Corinthians? (See verse 9.)
- According to verse 10, what are two kinds of sorrow? How are they different?

Read together Mosiah 23:9–10 and Mormon 2:11–13, and ask your family how Alma the elder and the Nephites in Mormon's army represent these two different kinds of sorrow. Invite your family to write these two cross-references next to 2 Corinthians 7:10 in their scriptures.

Share with your family the following from President Spencer W. Kimball:

"The felon in the penitentiary, coming to realize the high price he must pay for his folly, may wish he had not committed the crime. That is not repentance.

"The truly repentant man is sorry before he is apprehended. He is sorry even if his secret is never known. He desires to make voluntary amends. The culprit has not 'godly sorrow' who must be found out by being reported or by chains of circumstances which finally bring the offense to light. The thief is not repentant who continues in grave offenses until he is caught. Repentance of the godly type means that one comes to recognize the sin and voluntarily and without pressure from outside sources begins his transformation." (*Teachings of Spencer W. Kimball,* 89.)

Ask your family how they think a person becomes sorry in a "godly manner," or in other words, what experiences have led them to be sorry in a way that leads to change or repentance?

2 CORINTHIANS 8–9: "GOD LOVETH A CHEERFUL GIVER"

2 Corinthians 8:1—9:15

"Because I Have Been Given Much"

Sing as a family (or read the words to) the hymn "Because I Have Been Given Much." (*Hymns,* no. 219.) Ask:

- What do you think of when you sing this hymn?
- Can you think of times when you have been willing to give or serve and other times when you have not?
- How does it make you feel when you freely serve or give to others?
- How are your feelings different when you have not freely served or given?

Tell your family that the message of this hymn is similar to the message of Paul in 2 Corinthians 8–9. Share the following background with them:

"Years earlier, probably around A.D. 44, the council in Jerusalem had decided that a collection would be made from the church to send to the impoverished [poor] saints in Palestine, and Paul and Barnabas were put in charge of the project. (Acts 11:29–30.) Now, thirteen years later, Paul is still carrying out his assignment. . . . [I]n chapters 8 and 9 in 2 Corinthians, he gives an extended exposition [explanation] on the subject." (David R. Seely, "Is Christ Divided? Unity of the Saints through Charity," in *Studies in Scripture,* 6:77.)

Explain that in 2 Corinthians 8:1–5, Paul talked about the Saints in Macedonia as an example of the spirit of giving he hoped the Corinthians Saints would seek. Read these verses aloud, and invite your family to look for why the Macedonian Saints were such great "givers." Because they are challenging verses to understand, use the helps for each verse listed below to help your family understand what they are reading:

- Verse 1—Read footnote 1a.
- Verse 2—In other words, in a time of trial and poverty they still found a way to be very generous. See also footnotes 2a and 2c.
- Verse 3—The Macedonian Saints gave what was in their power to give and then chose to give even beyond that.
- Verse 4—Another way of saying this is: They pleaded for the privilege to help other Saints.
- Verse 5—Paul is saying: What they did was beyond our expectation, but it was because of their commitment to the Lord.

Write the questions listed below on a sheet of paper for each family member (without the scripture references). Have your family answer these questions from their own experience and knowledge. Then have them scan 2 Corinthians 8 and 9, looking for answers to these questions. Invite them to note the verses where they found their answers and be prepared to share what they found.

- Who is the greatest example of what it means to be a giver? (See 2 Corinthians 8:9; 9:15.)
- Who should give? (See 2 Corinthians 8:7.)
- What should be our attitude about giving? (See 2 Corinthians 8:8, 12; 9:7.)
- How much should we give? (See 2 Corinthians 8:7; 9:6.)
- How should offerings be handled? (See 2 Corinthians 8:16–23.)
- Why is giving so important? (See 2 Corinthians 8:7–8, 24.)
- What are the likely results of our giving? (See 2 Corinthians 8:14–15; 9:8–12.)

Explain to your family that while Paul was specifically talking about gifts of money to take care of less-fortunate Saints, there are other ways to give. Share the following suggestions given by President Howard W. Hunter in a Christmas message:

"This Christmas, 'Mend a quarrel. Seek out a forgotten friend. Dismiss suspicion and replace it with trust. Write a letter. Give a soft answer. Encourage youth. Manifest your loyalty in word and deed. Keep a promise. Forego a grudge. Forgive an enemy. Apologize. Try to understand. Examine your demands on others. Think first of someone else. Be kind. Be gentle. Laugh a little more. Express your gratitude. Welcome a stranger. Gladden the heart of a child. Take pleasure in the beauty and wonder of the earth. Speak your love and then speak it again.' (Adapted from an unknown author.)" (*Teachings of Howard W. Hunter*, 270–71.)

Give your family a moment of silence to determine ways they can apply what they've learned here in the coming week. Invite them to write it down (without showing anyone), and put it in a place where they can be reminded until they accomplish their commitment to be a "cheerful giver."

2 CORINTHIANS 10: WALKING AS A DISCIPLE OF CHRIST

2 Corinthians 10:1–18
Where did you get that idea?

Study 2 Corinthians 10 by playing the game: "Where did you get that idea?" To do this, write the bolded statements below where all can see them. Then as you read together 2 Corinthians 10, have your family look for verses where each of these statements might have come from. Write the verse number next to the bolded statement. Also, discuss any additional information or questions that are listed with each bolded statement.

____ **Disciples of Jesus do not use physical weapons to change the world but spiritual ones.** (Verses 3–4.)

____ **We must learn to control our thoughts.** (Verse 5.)

- Why is it so important to learn to control our thoughts? (Sin usually starts in our hearts and thoughts.)
- Read together Proverbs 23:7.
- President Ezra Taft Benson taught, "The mind has been likened to a stage on which only one act at a time can be performed. . . .

  "We are the stage managers; we are the ones who decide which thought will occupy the stage. Remember, the Lord wants us to have a fulness of joy like His, while the devil wants all men to be miserable like unto himself (see 2 Nephi 2:18, 27). We are the ones who must decide whose thought will prevail. We are free to choose, but we are not free to alter the consequences of those choices. We will be

what we think about—what we consistently allow to occupy the stage of our minds." (*Teachings of Ezra Taft Benson*, 382.)

____ **We should not always judge by how things look on the outside.** (Verse 7.)

- Why is it not a good idea to judge according to how things look on the outside?
- Read together 1 Samuel 16:7.

____ **It is not wise to compare ourselves with others.** (Verse 12.)

- Why should we not compare ourselves to others?
- C. S. Lewis stated: "Pride gets no pleasure out of having something, only out of having more of it than the next man. . . . It is the comparison that makes you proud: the pleasure of being above the rest. Once the element of competition has gone, pride has gone." (*Mere Christianity*, 109–10.)

____ **We should not seek to praise ourselves but seek that praise which comes from God.** (Verses 14–18.)

- How can we seek to please God more than man?

After the activity, challenge your family to try to live better in one of the three areas talked about:

- Refraining from comparing ourselves with others.
- Controlling our thoughts.
- Refraining from judging by outward appearances.

2 CORINTHIANS 11: CONFLICTS WITH FALSE APOSTLES

2 Corinthians 11:1–15
Conflicts with false apostles

 Ask your family to imagine being part of a battle, and ask:

- Why would it be important to know who your enemy is?
- How would it help if you knew the enemy's tactics?

- Why would knowing nothing about your enemy be a big problem?
- What war are we actually engaged in here in mortality and who is our enemy? (See D&C 76:28–29.)

Help your family understand we need not be unduly fearful of Satan because he is under God's control, but it is helpful to understand his tactics. Invite your family to quickly look over the Bible Dictionary references for "Devil" and "Lucifer." Ask:

- What did you learn about him?
- What do we learn from the meanings of the name Lucifer? ("The Shining One," "Lightbringer," or "The Son of the Morning.")
- According to 2 Corinthians 11:14 and 2 Nephi 9:9, how does Satan sometimes appear to others?
- Why would Satan want to appear as an angel of light?
- Why might that be dangerous for someone who did not know who he really was?
- What was a similar way that some of Satan's servants were tricking people in 2 Corinthians 11:13?

Explain that as verse 13 suggests, the Church in Corinth was having difficult problems from people who claimed to be leaders of the Church but were false apostles, leaders, or teachers. Read 2 Corinthians 11:1–15 together as a family and ask:

- How do Paul's works testify of his calling as an Apostle?
- How can we be able to identify false apostles, leaders, or teachers? (By their works; verses 13–15.)

Bear your testimony of the calling and service of the Lord's chosen servants in this day. Encourage your family to pray for them and follow their counsel.

2 Corinthians 11:16–33
Paul's resumé

Ask your family to describe what a resumé is, and show them one of yours if it is available. Talk about the following questions:

- How can a resumé help a person seeking a job?
- Why do you want to put as many positive things about yourself as possible on your resumé?
- How does the information you put on a resumé compare to just boasting or bragging about yourself?
- When are some other times you would want to tell someone about your abilities or qualifications?

Explain to your family that because of false apostles saying bad things about him, Paul felt the need to give some credentials and qualifications in the last half of 2 Corinthians 11. Have your family look for how Paul felt about the idea of boasting as they read 2 Corinthians 11:16–20.

Get out a pad of paper and write "Resumé" at the top. Have a family member act as a scribe for the family. As you read verses 21–33 stop after every three verses and write down any qualifications or challenges Paul had endured that show his faithfulness as an Apostle. Afterward ask your family if they have ever suffered challenges for the gospel's sake. Challenge your family to follow Paul's example and remain faithful no matter the difficulty.

2 CORINTHIANS 12: PAUL'S THORN IN THE FLESH

2 Corinthians 12:1–21
God strengthens us in our times of trials

Invite your family to imagine that a friend came to them with some serious gospel questions. What would you say if you were asked some of the following?

- Why doesn't life just go smoothly; why do there always have to be trials?
- How does adversity make me a better person?
- Why, after having a spiritual experience, do my life seem to drift back into the things of the world?

Invite a family member to read aloud 2 Corinthians 12:1–3. Ask:

- What spiritual experience did Paul tell the

Corinthian Saints about? (Being caught up to the third heaven.)

- What do you think Paul was referring to as "the third heaven"? (Elder Bruce R. McConkie indicated that Paul was speaking of the celestial kingdom; see *Mortal Messiah*, 4:394.)

Have your family turn to Doctrine and Covenants 137:1–5 and read the description of the celestial kingdom. Ask your family to imagine what Paul would have felt like while viewing the celestial kingdom. Then take turns reading 2 Corinthians 12:7–10 and ask:

- What spiritual danger did Paul say he struggled with after having wonderful revelations? (A "thorn in the flesh.")
- Why did the Lord give Paul this adversity? (Verse 7.)
- What did Paul learn when the Lord did not take away his "thorn in the flesh" as he had asked? (Verses 8–10.)
- How can our weaknesses help us receive strength from Jesus Christ? (See Ether 12:27.)
- How have you experienced the truth of Paul's statement that "when I am weak, then am I strong"?

Remind your family that neither the scriptures nor modern revelation tell us what "thorn in the flesh" afflicted Paul though many believe it was a physical disability that hindered his missionary labors.

Testify to your family that Paul grew spiritually as he overcame physical trials. Remind your family that there is strength in living the commandments in spite of the trials and challenges we face.

2 CORINTHIANS 13: PAUL'S CONCERN FOR THE CORINTHIANS

2 Corinthians 13:1–14
What does the Lord want us to do?

 Tell your family that this chapter, though short, has good counsel from Paul to the Saints at Corinth. Divide the verses in this chapter evenly between your family members. Invite each person to read his or her verses and find one teaching or principle that impresses them. Give everyone a chance to share what teaching or principle they selected, what verse it came from, and why he or she thinks that teaching is important.

Reread 2 Corinthians 13:1 with your family, and explain that while studying this chapter your family has shared several "witnesses" or testimonies of truth. Ask:

- How many witnesses did God say He would use to establish His word?
- Why do you think it is important to have two or three witnesses when seeking to establish truth?
- How does the Lord's law of witnesses apply to priesthood ordinances today? (There are at least two witnesses of each ordinance.)
- How does it help our family when more than one of us believe, testify, and follow the truth?

Encourage your family members to support one another with their testimonies and witnesses of the gospel and its true doctrines.

GALATIANS

Although the Apostle Paul addressed this epistle, or letter, to the Galatian Saints, it is not certain when it was written. It was probably written while Paul was traveling through Macedonia and received news of apostasy among the Galatian Saints. (See Map 13, "The Missionary Journeys of the Apostle Paul" in the post-1999 Bible maps; Map 20 in pre-1999 maps, and locate the regions of Galatia and Macedonia. Galatia is in the region known today as Turkey.)

"These Galatians are Gentile converts. They are now being contaminated by Jewish-Christians who tell them they must ... live the law of Moses to be saved. Paul's purpose is to call them back to Christ and his gospel."

"Galatians is thus written to people ... who are adopting false doctrines and ordinances, who are being overcome by the world. ...

"Consequently we read in it what the Galatians and the sectarians alike must believe and do to be saved." (McConkie, Doctrinal New Testament Commentary, 2:455.)

GALATIANS 1: THE PROBLEM OF APOSTASY

Galatians 1:1–24

True gospel vs. false gospels

Duplicate the following numbers and lines on a large sheet of paper and post it where all can see it.

1. __ __ __ __ __
2. __ __ __ __ __ __ __
3. __ __ __ __ __ __ __ __ __
4. __ __ __ __ __ __ __ __ __ __ __
5. __ __ __ __ __ __ __
6. __ __ __ __ __ __
7. __ __ __ __ __
8. __ __ __ __ __

Tell your family that this is the answer sheet to eight questions you will ask. Their task is to discover the answers by searching Galatians 1:1–24. Each blank represents a letter in the correct answer. (Notice that one blank in each answer is in **bold** print.) Assign one family member to be the scribe and fill in the blanks as the correct answers are discovered. Ask the questions one at a time. Do not to go on to the next question until a correct answer has been found. Ask:

1. What word describes Paul's reaction at finding out that many Galatians had already removed themselves from the true gospel? (Verse 6; MARVEL.)

2. What word describes what happens to anyone who preaches any other gospel than the true one? (Verses 8–9; ACCURSED.)

3. By what method had Paul been taught the gospel? (Verse 12; REVELATION.)

4. What phrase describes how much Paul persecuted the Church of God before his conversion? (Verse 13; BEYOND MEASURE.)

5. Who was Paul called to preach among? (Verse 16; HEATHEN [note footnote 16a].)

6. Where did Paul go after Jesus appeared to him on the road to Damascus? (Verse 17; ARABIA.)

7. Who did Paul go to see in Jerusalem? (Verse 18; PETER.)

8. What is the name of the other Apostle whom Paul saw? (Verse 19; JAMES.)

After all the answers have been filled in, tell

your family their next challenge is to take the letters from the **bold-faced** blanks and unscramble them to spell a word. If your family has a hard time coming up with the word, have a family member read the introduction to the book of Galatians in this book. (The word is APOSTASY.) Ask:

- How would you define the word *apostasy*?
- What led to apostasy among the Galatians?
- What might lead to apostasy among Saints today?
- What can we do to avoid falling into apostasy?

Share the following counsel:

"When individuals or groups of people turn away from the principles of the gospel, they are in a state of apostasy. . . .

"We must each guard against personal apostasy. You can safeguard yourself against personal apostasy by keeping your covenants, obeying the commandments, following Church leaders, partaking of the sacrament, and constantly strengthening your testimony through daily scripture study, prayer, and service." ("Apostasy," *True to the Faith,* 13–14.)

As a family, repeat aloud the things we can do to safeguard ourselves against personal apostasy. Invite family members to write these safeguards in their journals and challenge each one to live them.

GALATIANS 2: SALVATION COMES THROUGH JESUS CHRIST

Galatians 2:11–21

How are we justified?

Ask your family if any of them have ever had a difference of opinion with a good friend. Just because you disagreed with your friend, did that mean your friend was a bad person? Tell them if they have ever had such an experience they will understand what happened between Paul and Peter in these verses.

Read Galatians 2:11–14 with your family and use the following questions and insights to help them understand those verses.

- What did Paul mean by "I withstood [Peter] to the face"? (Verse 11.)
- What did Peter do that Paul disagreed with? (Verses 12–13. See footnote 13a for help with "dissimulation.")
- Can two righteous men have a difference of opinion?
- Was Paul right or was Peter?

Share the following insight to help explain these verses. "Peter and Paul—both of whom were apostles, both of whom received revelations, saw angels, and were approved of the Lord, and both of whom shall inherit the fulness of the Father's kingdom—these same righteous and mighty preachers disagreed on a basic matter of church policy. Peter was the President of the Church; Paul, an apostle and Peter's junior in the church hierarchy, was subject to the direction of the chief apostle. But Paul was right and Peter was wrong. Paul stood firm, determined that they should walk 'uprightly according to the truth of the gospel'; Peter [wavered] for fear of offending Jewish semiconverts who still kept the law of Moses.

"The issue was not whether the Gentiles should receive the gospel. Peter himself had received the revelation that God was no respecter of persons, and that those of all lineages were now to be heirs of salvation along with the Jews. (Acts 10:21–35.) Further, the heads of the Church, in council assembled, with the Holy Ghost guiding their minds and directing their decisions, had determined that the Gentiles who received the gospel should not be subject to the law of Moses. (Acts 15:1–35.) The Jewish members of the Church, however, had not been able to accept this decision without reservation. They themselves continued to conform to Mosaic performances, and they expected Gentile converts to do likewise. Peter sided with them; Paul publicly withstood the chief apostle and won the debate, as could not otherwise have been the case. Without question, if we had the full account, we would find Peter reversing himself and doing all in his power to get the Jewish saints to believe that the law of Moses was fulfilled in Christ and no longer applied to anyone either Jew or Gentile." (McConkie, *Doctrinal New Testament Commentary,* 2:463–64.)

Read together Galatians 2:15–17. Ask:

- What does it mean to be "justified"? (See footnote 16f. You might also share this definition with your family. "To 'justify' is to award forgiveness through Christ's sacrifice. One is justified when his sins are canceled through Christ's atonement." (Anderson, *Understanding Paul,* 159.)
- Why could a person not be justified or guiltless by obeying the law of Moses? (No one could live the law perfectly; see Romans 3:23.)

Invite family members to choose one thing they could do this week to develop more faith in Jesus Christ.

GALATIANS 3: PAUL CHASTENS THE SAINTS AND REMINDS THEM OF THE NEED FOR FAITH

Galatians 3:1–18
Paul scolds the Galatians for rejecting Christ's saving grace for the law of Moses

Ask family members to think of times they were scolded. Ask them how they knew they were being scolded. Ask everyone to scan Galatians 3:1–5. Ask:

- What words indicate Paul is scolding the Saints in Galatia?
- How many of those verses contain question marks? (All of them.)
- What is Paul basically questioning the Galatian Saints about? (Whether we receive the Spirit by the law of Moses or by faith. Note that Paul had just given them the answer in Galatians 2:16.)
- Why does Paul feel the Galatians are foolish? (They have reverted to the law of Moses after having received the gospel. See Bible Dictionary, "Epistle to the Galatians," 744, first paragraph.)

Explain to your family that after Paul scolded the Galatians he then taught them true doctrine that would bless their lives.

Read Galatians 3:6–9 aloud and ask your family:

- How can we become "children of Abraham"

and therefore be entitled to his blessings? (Be "of faith" or, in other words, partakers of the covenants of the gospel. See verses 6 and 9.)
- How will Abraham be a blessing to heathens (Gentiles)? (See Bible Dictionary, paragraph 2, 602 and D&C 132:30–31.)
- What is our responsibility as the seed of Abraham? (See Abraham 2:9.)
- Why are Abraham's covenant blessings so wonderful?

Share the following statement: "What does it mean to be the seed of Abraham? . . . The Lord made a covenant with Abraham . . . that all nations would be blessed through him. . . . Any man or woman can claim the blessings of Abraham. They become his seed and heirs to the promised blessings by accepting the gospel, being baptized, entering into temple marriage, being faithful in keeping their covenants, and helping to carry the gospel to all the nations of the earth." (James E. Faust, *Ensign,* Nov., 2004, 54.)

Give one family member an 8½ x 11 sheet of paper and a pair of scissors—no rulers allowed. Ask the person to cut ¼-inch strips across the entire length of the paper so that every strip is **exactly** the same. As he/she cuts, stack the paper strips together so it becomes obvious the person cutting is not doing a perfect job and continue to point out that the performance is not perfect. (The family member may complain about the impossibility of the task.) Discuss the following questions:

- Are we required to never make a mistake and be absolutely perfect in order to become exalted? (Yes. See 1 Nephi 10:21; Matthew 5:48.)
- According to Galatians 3:10 and Romans 3:23, how many people make mistakes and are not perfect? (Everyone.)
- What hope do we have then to gain exaltation? (Repentance through Jesus Christ's Atonement is our only hope.)
- How does the message in Galatians 3:11 and 3 Nephi 27:19 help us better understand this doctrine?

Read Galatians 3:12–18 aloud and ask:

- Why is faith in Christ's atoning sacrifice so crucial for us? (See verses 15–19.)
- What did Christ do to redeem us from the "curse of the law"? (See verses 12–13; see also Deuteronomy 21:23.)
- What are the blessings promised to Abraham? (See 3 Nephi 20:25–27.) Explain that from 3 Nephi 20:27 we see that part of the blessing is the Holy Ghost.

Remind your family members of the great price the Savior paid for them through the Atonement and encourage everyone to share ideas of what they can do to be faithful to the covenants they have made with God.

Galatians 3:19–29
The law of Moses, faith, and the gospel of Jesus Christ

Read Galatians 3:19–20 to your family while everyone follows along. Ask someone to explain what Paul has said. If they find this material difficult, have them mark footnote 19a and then read the Joseph Smith Translation of these verses in the Appendix of your Bible on page 810. Share this information:

"The JST helps us understand the Apostle Paul's points: the law of Moses was not designed to stand for all time but until the coming of the promised seed (the Messiah); the law did contain the promises given to Abraham, including that of the coming Messiah; Moses was not the mediator of the covenant God made with Abraham; Christ alone mediated that covenant because it dealt with eternal life. It was this higher covenant that the Messiah instituted when He came." (Richard D. Draper, *Ensign,* Sept. 1999, 28.)

Have one family member read Galatians 3:21–29 aloud and then ask:

- What is a schoolmaster? (Verses 24b–25; it is another word for schoolteacher.)
- Did God intend for the law of Moses to last forever? (No. It was only to prepare the people for a higher law.)

Explain to your family that the law of Moses was temporary to prepare the people for something better—the gospel of Jesus Christ. Bear testimony

to your family of the blessings that have come to you as a result of the fulness of the gospel in your life. Express gratitude that the Savior came as promised and fulfilled the law of Moses, providing us with covenants and ordinances that will chart a course for us to return to His presence.

GALATIANS 4: FREEDOM OR BONDAGE

Galatians 4:1–31
Christ's covenants bring freedom

Explain to your family that in his letter to the Galatians, Paul teaches Jewish converts how living under the law of Moses is like bondage and living the gospel of Jesus Christ is freedom.

Prior to scripture study, cut 20 strips of paper and write the following words or phrases on them: Heir, Bondage, Son, Servant, Weak, Beggarly, Abraham, Bondmaid, Freewoman, Born after the flesh, By promise, Mount Sinai, Agar or Hagar, Jerusalem, Jerusalem which is above, Free, Isaac, Children of promise, After the spirit, Bondwoman. Make two additional strips and write the following headings: LAW OF MOSES and GOSPEL OF CHRIST.

Mix up the word strips in a bowl and dump them in front of your family. Have them take turns drawing a word strip and deciding whether it fits best under LAW OF MOSES or GOSPEL OF CHRIST. When the sorting is complete, the word strips should be as follows:

Law of Moses	Gospel of Christ
Bondage	Heir
Servant	Son
Weak	Abraham
Beggarly	Freewoman
Bondmaid	By promise
Born after the flesh	Jerusalem which is above
Mount Sinai	Free
Agar or Hagar	Isaac
Jerusalem	After the spirit
Bondwoman	Children of promise

Evenly divide up the verses in Galatians 4 among family members and have them look for evidence that the word strips are under the correct headings. If someone suggests that a word strip should be moved to a different heading, have that person read the verse and explain why.

Ask:

- In what way did the gospel of Jesus Christ bring a new life to the Galatians over the law of Moses that was now dead?
- In what way does the gospel of Jesus Christ bring life to us today?

Bear testimony that saving ordinances are only found in the gospel of Jesus Christ. After Jesus established His gospel and kingdom on earth, the lesser law of Moses was no longer needed. The old law was therefore dead, and the new law of the gospel brought life, even eternal life. Challenge your family to be ready to share the message of the restored truth to their friends and neighbors.

GALATIANS 5: FRUITS OF THE SPIRIT VERSUS WORKS OF THE FLESH

Galatians 5:1–12
Freedom or bondage?

 Have your family read together Galatians 5:1. Ask:

- From what has Christ made us free? (The "yoke of bondage.")
- What is a yoke? (Show your family the picture of a yoke on page 220.)
- How would you like to be forced to carry heavy burdens like that?
- How would it feel to be made free?
- How would you feel about being in bondage again after being made free?

Explain to your family that the bondage Paul is talking about in these verses involved false beliefs and traditions. Some false teachers were telling Paul's new converts that in order to be saved they had to accept the Jewish rite of circumcision according to the law of Moses. (See Bible Dictionary, "Circumcision," paragraphs 1, 5 and 6,

646.) Read together Galatians 5:2–12 and learn how Paul felt about this teaching. Ask:

- Why did Paul consider circumcision to be like a yoke of bondage? (It is trusting in the law of Moses instead of Christ; see verses 3–4.)
- What really matters in the life of a convert, according to verse 6?

Ask your family to think about how these verses might apply to our day. Ask:

- What are some activities or ideas that the world thinks are acceptable but that the Lord has said are wrong? (See *For the Strength of Youth* pamphlet for examples.)
- How is becoming involved in these sins like a yoke of bondage? (See D&C 88:86.)

Share your testimony of how much better and freer a person feels when he puts off the burden of sin and follows the Savior. Read or sing, "How Gentle God's Commands." (*Hymns*, no. 125.)

Galatians 5:13–15
Pecking each other to death

Ask your family if they know what a flock of chickens will do when one chicken is hurt and bleeding. Explain that unless the injured chicken is removed and allowed to heal, the other chickens will peck at it until it dies. Ask your family to look for this same idea as you read together Galatians 5:13–15. Ask:

- How can Church members sometimes be enemies to other members?
- What counsel did Paul give in verse 13 that would help avoid having enemies among the Saints? (Love and serve one another.)
- How are gossiping, faultfinding, criticizing, and backbiting similar to Paul's description of "biting," "devouring," and "consuming" among the Galatian Saints?
- How can you sum up the whole law of the gospel? (Verse 14.)

Have your family think about the last time they gossiped or talked negatively about another person. Ask them how they feel when others find fault with them. Ask your family to make a conscious effort to remove gossiping, faultfinding, criticizing, and backbiting from their lives. Sing all five verses of "Truth Reflects upon Our Senses" (*Hymns,* no. 273) and ask family members to share their feelings about the hymn.

Galatians 5:16–26
The flesh vs. the Spirit

 Ask your family:

- Have you ever felt like doing wrong but knew you shouldn't?
- Have you ever been prompted to do something good but part of you didn't want to because it would be hard?
- Do you ever feel like there is a struggle between good and evil going on inside you?
- What do you think are the two conflicting parts that are fighting within you?

Have your family look for these two conflicting parts inside each of us as you read Galatians 5:16–18. Ask:

- What did Paul call these two conflicting parts in each of us? (Spirit and flesh.)
- According to verse 16, how do we overcome the temptations of the flesh?
- How does a person "walk in the Spirit"? (Pray always, study scriptures, surround oneself with good influences.)

Explain that Paul entitled these two warring parts within each of us the "Works of the Flesh" and the "Fruit of the spirit." Write these two phrases as titles at the top of two columns on a sheet of paper or poster. Divide your family into two groups. Have one group study Galatians 5:19–21 and list the "works of the flesh" and the other group study Galatians 5:22–23 and list the "fruit of the Spirit." (Use the footnotes and a dictionary to understand difficult words.) Have each group report their lists and what each word means.

Challenge your family to notice when they are feeling the "fruits" of the Spirit.

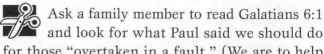

GALATIANS 6: THE LAW OF THE HARVEST

Galatians 6:1–6
How do we help those struggling in sin?

 Ask a family member to read Galatians 6:1 and look for what Paul said we should do for those "overtaken in a fault." (We are to help "restore" them.) Ask:

- What do you think it means to restore a person? (To restore is to bring back.)
- How did Paul say to restore one who has fallen away from the truth? (In the spirit of meekness.)
- How do you use meekness to help those who have strayed from the Church?
- What warning did Paul give? (Be careful not to fall into temptation yourself as you help others.)

Galatians 6:7–10
What is the law of the harvest?

Show your family a handful of seeds and ask them what they think they will grow after they are planted and why. Give each family member a cup with soil in it. Have them plant their seed and water it. Ask your family the following questions:

- If this is a watermelon seed, can it grow into a carrot? Why?
- What amount of time is necessary for a seed to mature?
- What are some things that are needed to help the seed grow?
- Why do you think some seeds take longer than others?
- If we compare our lives to the seeds, what do we need that will help us grow?

Invite your family to turn to Galatians 6:7–10 and write Alma 41:10–15 in the margin. Have one family member read aloud Galatians 6:7–10 and another person Alma 41:10–15. Ask:

- The principle described in these verses is sometimes called the Law of the Harvest. How would you describe this law in your own words?

Ask your family what counsel they would give in the following situation: James, a faithful member of the Church, pays his tithing and serves faithfully in his calling but struggles in school and does well to get "B" grades on his report card. Yet he sees Todd, who cheats on exams, doesn't attend Church meetings, and doesn't pay his tithing get "A" grades.

After your family has had a chance to comment on the story, read the following statement by President Spencer W. Kimball:

"The wicked may prosper for a time, the rebellious may seem to profit by their transgressions, but the time is coming when, at the bar of justice, all men will be judged, 'every man according to their works.' (Rev. 20:13.) No one will 'get by' with anything. On that day no one will escape the penalty of his deeds, no one will fail to receive the blessings he has earned. . . . There will be total justice." (*Miracle of Forgiveness,* 305.)

Remind your family that just as it takes time for seeds to grow and mature, the Lord will eventually reward or punish those who've planted righteousness or wickedness in their lives. Discuss with your family how they can plant or sow and help to produce good fruit in their lives.

Place your cups with newly planted seeds on a window sill where the sun will shine on them and watch them grow for the next couple of weeks. From time to time during the next month, have your family bring in their plants and ask if they can tell what seed was planted by looking at the plant as it grows.

EPHESIANS

Paul most likely wrote his epistle to the Saints in Ephesus around 61 A.D. while in prison at Rome. Ephesus was a key city in the Asian province of the Roman Empire, sitting comfortably at the crossroads of important trade routes. (See Map 21 in the pre-1999 Bible maps; Map 9 in post-1999 maps.) Paul recognized this unique position and used Ephesus as his base of operations for two years during his third mission. (See Acts 19:1, 19.) With all of the exports and goods that traveled through this city, none were as important as the good news heard throughout Asia because of Paul and others who spread the Word so faithfully.

As Paul departed from Ephesus, he warned the Saints that "grievous wolves" would enter their congregation and lead many astray by "speaking perverse things." (Acts 20:29–30.) As was his practice, Paul wrote epistles to help strengthen those he loved and longed to see stay faithful. Here is Paul's writing at its best as he develops doctrines such as foreordination, restoration, the Holy Spirit of Promise, grace, Church leadership, Christ's love, unity of faith, righteous living, spousal love, honoring of parents, and the armor of God.

EPHESIANS 1: PAUL CLARIFIES IMPORTANT DOCTRINES

Ephesians 1:1–8
Predestination vs. foreordination

Have your family silently read Ephesians 1:1–8, noting words they do not understand. Ask family members to share what they found. If anyone identifies the word "predestinated," read together Ephesians 1:4–5 and invite someone to read footnote 5a. Ask:

- What is a simple definition of the word *predestinated*? (Predetermined.)
- Why is predestination considered a false doctrine? (Elder Bruce R. McConkie wrote: "Predestination is the false doctrine that from all eternity God has ordered whatever comes to pass. . . . Some souls . . . are . . . chosen for salvation, others for damnation; and there is said to be nothing any individual can do to escape his predestined inheritance in heaven or in hell." [*Mormon Doctrine*, 588].)

- What Greek word is recommended instead of predestination?
- Why do you think foreordination is considered a true doctrine? (It allows God's children to use their agency.)

Invite family members to read the following quotation: "To carry forward his own purposes among men and nations, the Lord foreordained chosen spirit children in pre-existence and assigned them to come to earth at particular times and places so that they might aid in furthering the divine will. These pre-existence appointments made 'according to the foreknowledge of God the Father' (1 Pet. 1:2), simply designated certain individuals to perform missions which the Lord in his wisdom knew they had the talents and capacities to do." (McConkie, *Mormon Doctrine*, 290.)

Ask:

- How do you feel about having a foreordained calling?
- What can you do to find out what it is?
- How might a patriarchal blessing help identify such a calling?

If appropriate, invite a family member who has a patriarchal blessing to share an example of a fore-ordained mission. Encourage those family members who have a patriarchal blessing to read it often and do all they can to fulfill their missions. For those who do not yet have a patriarchal blessing, remind them that they were also "foreordained to receive . . . the companionship of the Holy Ghost . . . eternal life . . . the everlasting gospel . . . baptism . . . Membership in the Church . . . remission of sins . . . adoption into the family of God . . . joint-heirs with Christ." (McConkie, *Doctrinal New Testament Commentary* 2:490.)

Ephesians 1:9–14
"The dispensation of the fulness of times"

Ask your family if they can tell what a "dispensation" is. (A dispensation is a period of time when God reveals again the gospel to His children on earth.) Explain that there have been several dispensations throughout history. (For example, the dispensations of Adam, Enoch, Noah, Moses, etc.). Choose one family member to read aloud Ephesians 1:10–12. Ask:

- What dispensation does Paul refer to in this verse? (Dispensation of the fulness of times.)
- What do you think is meant by the "dispensation of the fulness of times"? (See footnote 10a.)

Share the following statement: "The work of the Lord in these last days is one of vast magnitude and almost beyond the comprehensions of mortals. . . . And it is truly the dispensation of the fullness of times, . . . when all things shall be restored, as spoken of by all the holy prophets since the world began." (Smith, *Joseph Smith's Commentary on the Bible,* 175.) Ask:

- What does it mean to you to have been one in the premortal existence who "first trusted in Christ" and was foreordained to live in the dispensation of the fulness of times?
- How can you show your gratitude for the blessings of living in this dispensation?

Ephesians 1:15–23
God the Father and His Son

Ask your family to think of individuals they pray for and the reasons why they pray for them. Invite some to share their reasons. Have someone read Ephesians 1:15–18 while the rest of the family follows along. Ask:

- Why does Paul pray for the Ephesian Saints?
- What blessings does he ask God to give them?
- Why would Paul want the Saints to have "the spirit of wisdom and revelation"?

Give colored pencils to each family member. Have them scan Ephesians 1:19–23 and mark words Paul uses to describe God's power and attributes and also how He feels about His Only Begotten Son.

Invite family members to share what impressed them most about God's power and attributes. Then have them share what impressed them most about the Only Begotten Son. Finally, sing verse 1 of "I Am a Child of God" (*Hymns,* no. 301) and talk about Heavenly Father's love for His children. Bear testimony of the Father and the Son and your relationship with them.

EPHESIANS 2: THE GRACE OF JESUS CHRIST

Ephesians 2:1–10
Are we saved by Christ's grace or by our own works?

 Ask family members to read Ephesians 2:9 and discuss the following questions:

- What do you think it means to be saved by grace?
- Do you believe that because of God's grace we do not need to worry about the commandments? Why or why not?
- According to 2 Nephi 9:6–7 and 10, what two obstacles does the "infinite atonement" help us overcome? (The Atonement helps us overcome sin and death. We overcome sin through the power of repentance, and we overcome death through the power of the Resurrection.)
- What does 2 Nephi 25:23 add to your

understanding about the relationship between grace and good works?

Show your family the following diagram and discuss the following questions:

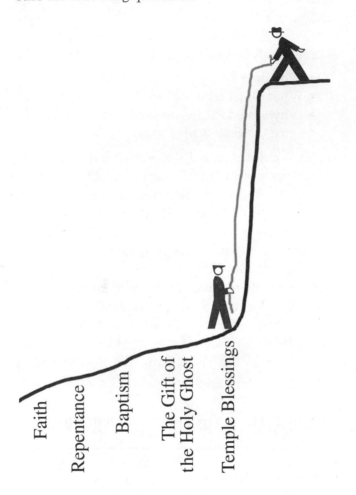

Faith
Repentance
Baptism
The Gift of the Holy Ghost
Temple Blessings

- Would it be possible for the man to make it to the top of the cliff without using the rope? (No.)
- If the top of the cliff represents exaltation, what would the man with the rope represent? (Jesus Christ and His Atonement.)
- How does this diagram relate to the doctrine of grace and works we have been studying? (We must do our part by climbing to the base of the cliff by keeping God's commandments and receiving the necessary ordinances. However, we can go no farther without the saving grace of Jesus Christ.)

Sing verse 2 of "Rock of Ages," *Hymns,* no. 111, with your family. Express your feelings about the saving grace of our Savior and Redeemer, Jesus Christ.

Ephesians 2:11–19
Christ spilled His precious blood for His people

Divide the room you are studying in into two distinct areas by putting up some sort of barrier, partition, or wall. Have half of your family sit in one area and the other half sit in the opposite side. Ask your family to imagine that one part of the room represents The Church of Jesus Christ of Latter-day Saints and the other half represents other religions. Discuss the following:

- Would you like people who are not Church members to join our Church? Why?
- What are some ways they might need to change in order to become Church members?
- What kind of help could you give to those who are converted to the Church? Why?

Read Ephesians 2:11–12 and see if your family can identify the two groups being discussed. (The children of the covenant and the Gentiles.)

Read aloud Ephesians 2:13–19 and then ask:

- How do you feel when there is a partition or division between you and others—physically, emotionally, socially, and religiously?
- Who abolished the partition between the Jews and the Gentiles? (Jesus Christ. See verse 13.)
- How was He able to accomplish this? (Verse 16.)
- How does Christ make us one? (Numbers 15:15; Matthew 18:20; Romans 12:5; Galatians 3:28–29; Hebrews 2:11; 2 Nephi 31:21; D&C 35:2.)
- How would breaking down a partition or a barrier bring peace? (Verse 14.)
- How did abolishing the law of commandments (Mosaic law) make new men of the Gentiles and thereby bring peace? (Verse 15a.)
- How do you feel about your great blessing to participate in the covenant?

Sing "I Stand All Amazed" (*Hymns,* no 193) with your family and then express gratitude for Christ's redeeming Atonement so that we need not be aliens and strangers without God. Encourage your family to help others find the gospel and to accept and welcome new converts who join the Church.

Ephesians 2:19–22
Foundations and cornerstones

Ask one of the children in your family to construct a building out of blocks. Explain that Paul used an analogy of a building to discuss the Church of Christ.

Invite everyone to follow along and mark their scriptures as you read Ephesians 2:19–22 aloud. Discuss the following questions:

- What do you think of when you think of "strangers" or "foreigners"?
- According to verse 19, what invitation did Paul give to those who are strangers or foreigners to the Church? (To be fellowcitizens with the Saints and join the Church.)
- Why would it be better to be a fellowcitizen rather than a stranger?

Remove the cornerstone from the building your child has constructed and ask:

- What happened, or would eventually happen, to a building without a cornerstone or foundation?
- In Paul's analogy, what is the foundation of the Church?
- Why are the Apostles and prophets the foundation? (Without the priesthood keys they hold and the revelation they receive, we would be left to our own interpretation, resulting in confusion which would cause the downfall of the building or the Church organization.)
- What is the cornerstone of the building?
- Without the cornerstone, how long will the foundation last?
- What does this teach you about the importance of Jesus Christ?

Talk to your family about the great blessing it is to be members of the Church of Jesus Christ restored in these latter days with the exact same foundation and cornerstone that existed for the Saints at the time of Jesus.

EPHESIANS 3: THE LOVE OF CHRIST IS FOR ALL GOD'S CHILDREN

Ephesians 3:1–13
Paul, the "prisoner of Jesus Christ"

Share the following story: "'In January of 1975, on a dark, rainy night in Tasmania, a 7,300-ton barge smashed into two piers of the Tasman Bridge, which connects Hobart, Tasmania, with its eastern suburbs across the bay. Three spans of the bridge collapsed. An Australian family by the name of Ling were driving across the bridge when suddenly the bridge lights went out. Just then a speeding car passed them and disappeared before their very eyes. Murray Ling slammed on his brakes and skidded to a stop, one yard from the edge of a black void' (Stephen Johnson, "Over the Edge!" *Reader's Digest,* Nov. 1977, p. 128).

"Murray got his family out of the car and then began warning oncoming traffic of the disaster ahead. As he frantically waved his arms, to his horror, a car swerved around him and plummeted into the abyss. A second car barely stopped in time, but a third car showed no sign of slowing down and crashed into the Lings' car at the edge of the bridge.

"Suddenly a loaded bus headed toward Murray, ignoring his waving arms. In desperation, risking his very life, he ran alongside the driver's window. 'There's a span missing,' he yelled. The bus swerved just in time and came to a halt against the railing. Dozens of lives had been saved.

"I am grateful for these Brethren whom we sustain as prophets, seers, and revelators who forewarn us of bridges not to be crossed. . . . Their motives are pure as they strive to build the kingdom of God and to uplift and edify the Saints of God. In the words of the Apostle Paul, they have become 'prisoners of Christ' (see Eph. 3:1; Eph. 4:1; Philem. 1:1, 9; 2 Tim. 1:8), whose only desire is to do the Lord's will. Nothing more. Nothing less. And nothing else. These are men of God! May we heed their warning voices." (Spencer J. Condie, *Ensign,* Nov. 1993, 17.)

Ask:

- According to Elder Condie, how are the prophets, seers, and revelators like Mr. Ling?
- What kinds of dangers do they warn us about today?
- Are there people who refuse to listen?
- What happens to those who refuse to heed their warnings?

Tell your family that when Paul wrote to the Ephesians, he was under house arrest in Rome. (See Acts 28:30.) Read together Ephesians 3:1–8, 13 as you discuss the following questions:

- Why would you say Paul described himself as a "prisoner of Jesus Christ" for the Gentiles? (Paul was called to preach the gospel specifically to the Gentiles and was jailed while fulfilling his mission.)
- What was the mystery Paul spoke about in verses 3–6? (Elder Bruce R. McConkie explained that "the gospel in former ages was reserved primarily for the members of certain families, but that now it is to go to all the world." [*Doctrinal New Testament Commentary,* 2:505.])
- What do you think it meant to the Gentiles to know that they were worthy to receive the "unsearchable riches of Christ" or the blessings of the gospel?

Explain to your family that many of God's children are totally unaware of the "riches of Christ." Discuss ways your family can make others aware of these "riches."

Ephesians 3:14–21
Rooted and grounded in God's love

Give your family time to write in their journals what kinds of things they pray for when they pray for others. When everyone has finished, tell them that Paul loved the Saints in Ephesus and prayed for them. Choose someone to read aloud Paul's prayer in Ephesians 3:14–21 and have the others make a list of the things Paul prayed for. Ask:

- What blessing did Paul ask for first? (Verse 16; see also 3 Nephi 19:8–9; D&C 76:114, 116.)

- How can a person be "rooted and grounded" in the love of Christ? (See verse 17.)
- How might it affect a person's life to be so "grounded"?
- How might being "rooted and grounded in [Christ's] love" help us "be filled with all the fulness of God"?

Share the following thought by Neal A. Maxwell: "The very process of daily living makes and breaks followers. Life's stern seasons and storms overturn those not grounded and rooted. . . . However, those who 'believe and are sure' (John 6:69) about Jesus' divinity do not panic, for instance, at the arrival of a new volley of fiery darts; they merely hold aloft the quenching shield of faith." (*Ensign,* Nov. 1988, 32.)

Explain to your family how the Spirit has blessed your life. Perhaps you have had an experience with the Spirit that has caused you to be "rooted and grounded" in Christ's love. Encourage family members to be valiant in keeping commandments and in their search for knowledge of Heavenly Father and His Son Jesus Christ so that they can experience the "fulness of God."

EPHESIANS 4: HOW CHRIST'S TRUE CHURCH IS ORGANIZED

Ephesians 4:1–6
Is there more than one true church?

Bring a copy of your local telephone book and have a family member look up the listings under "Churches." Have them read the names of some of the churches and estimate how many different churches are listed. Ask another family member to read aloud Ephesians 4:4–6. Ask:

- From what Paul taught in these verses how many churches should there be?
- Why do you think there are so many different churches?
- How many true churches are there in the world?

Share these comments from Elder Bruce R. McConkie: "There is no more self-evident truth in this world, there is nothing in all eternity more obvious than that there is and can be only one true Church. . . . All churches may be false, but only one can be true, simply because religion comes from God, and God is not the author of confusion." (*Doctrinal New Testament Commentary,* 2:506–7.)

Have family members look at footnote 5a and mark Doctrine and Covenants 1:30. Read together Doctrine and Covenants 1:30 and find what the Lord declared about The Church of Jesus Christ of Latter-day Saints. Bear testimony of the truths we have in the Church and the need we have to live those truths and share them with others.

Ephesians 4:7–16
How is Christ's Church organized?

 On a large piece of paper, draw a diagram similar to the one below, only larger and without the words in the boxes. Show the diagram to your family and tell them it represents the Church.

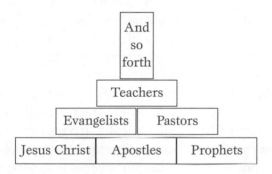

Ask family members if they can remember from their study of Ephesians 2 what words would go in the bottom layer of boxes, which represents the foundation of the church. If someone can remember, have him or her write the correct words in the boxes. If no one can come up with the correct answer, invite someone to read Ephesians 2:20. Tell your family to look in Ephesians 4:11 to find the words that go in the next three boxes and have someone write the correct responses as they are found. Ask:

- Which Article of Faith is very similar to Ephesians 4:11?
- Can anyone recite Articles of Faith 6 from memory? (If needed, see page 60 in the Pearl of Great Price.)

- Do we have evangelists and pastors in the Church today? (See Ephesians 4:11, footnotes *d* and *e,* or Articles of Faith 1:6, footnotes *c* and *e,* to discover that evangelists are patriarchs and pastors are bishops.)
- What do you think "and so forth" refers to at the end of the sixth Article of Faith? (Write "and so forth" in the last box in the diagram.)

Tell your family that in the next few verses Paul gives reasons for having the Church and some of the duties of its officers. Read together Ephesians 4:12–16 and have family members identify as many reasons as they can find for having a church organization.

Ephesians 4:17–32
Putting off the old, putting on the new

Show this sign or draw one similar to it and ask:

DANGER

- What does this sign mean?
- What human emotion can you find in this word by erasing one letter? (If you need to, cross out the D, making it "ANGER.")
- What kinds of things make you angry?
- Is there danger in anger? Why?
- What is the Lord's attitude toward anger?

To help answer that question, have a family member read Ephesians 4:26. (Note the JST correction in footnote 26a.) Have another family member read 3 Nephi 11:29–30 and someone else read Ephesians 4:31–32. Ask:

- In what ways can anger lead to sins?
- What does the Lord say we should do with anger? (It should be "put away.")

Read Ephesians 4:22–24. Make two columns on a piece of paper and at the top of one column write "Put off" and at the top of the other write "Put on." Have family members scan Ephesians 4:17–32, looking for things to add to each list. After you have made the two lists, invite family members to choose one item from each list to work on this week.

EPHESIANS 5: WALKING IN THE LIGHT OF HIS LOVE

Ephesians 5:1–18
Walking in love and light

Make a small obstacle course for your family by scattering pieces of paper on the floor. Ask for a volunteer to walk from one side of the room to the other without touching any of the pieces of paper. Blindfold the volunteer and let him or her attempt it. Ask what can be learned from the object lesson. Sing together "Teach Me to Walk in the Light." (*Hymns,* no. 304.) Tell your family that in Ephesians 5:1–18 the Apostle Paul teaches about walking in the light. Have them read those verses, looking for what Paul teaches, and then discuss their findings. Ask:

- What are some of the keys to walking in the light?
- What attributes found in verses 3–6, 11–12, 15, 17–18 lead us away from light?
- Why is having the Spirit with us essential to walking in the light?

Invite family members to choose one thing they can work on to bring more light in their lives.

Ephesians 5:22–33
The marriage triangle

Prior to beginning this session of family scripture study, cut a sheet of paper in the shape of a triangle and then cut a heart-shaped section out of the middle of the triangle. (Later, you will also need a wedding picture, preferably of the parents, to put behind the paper so the picture shows through the heart-shaped cutout.)

Show the paper to your family and ask if they know what it is. Tell them it is a "Love Triangle" and its explanation and meaning can be found in Ephesians 5:22–33. Read the verses together and then put the wedding picture behind the paper as mentioned earlier. Ask:

- What comparison did Paul use when he described the marriage relationship? (He compared it to Christ and the Church.)
- What kinds of things does Christ do for the Church?
- What can we learn from this to help strengthen marriages?
- What is the significance of the triangle? (It has three sides.)
- Who are the three parties that should be involved in a marriage? (Verses 22–23.)
- Why is it essential to have God be an important part of a marriage relationship?

Share the following with your family: "The family is ordained of God. Marriage between man and woman is essential to His eternal plan. Children are entitled to birth within the bonds of matrimony, and to be reared by a father and a mother who honor marital vows with complete fidelity. Happiness in family life is most likely to be achieved when founded upon the teachings of the Lord Jesus Christ. Successful marriages and families are established and maintained on principles of faith, prayer, repentance, forgiveness, respect, love, compassion, work, and wholesome recreational activities." ("The Family: A Proclamation to the World," *Ensign,* Nov. 1995, 102; or see the Appendix of this book.)

Share your feelings of the importance of husbands and wives loving each other and making God an integral part of that relationship.

EPHESIANS 6: THE WHOLE ARMOUR OF GOD

Ephesians 6:1–9
Children should honor their parents

Share a story from your childhood of a time when you disobeyed your parents' instructions and things went badly because of it.

Read Ephesians 6:1–3 and ask:

- What similar message did Paul teach?
- What are some ways children can honor their parents?

Ask a family member to read the quote below and then ask the questions that follow: "Young people, if you honor your parents, you will love them, respect them, confide in them, be considerate of them, express appreciation for them, and demonstrate all of these things by following their counsel in righteousness and by obeying the commandments of God." (Dallin H. Oaks, *Ensign,* May 1991, 14.)

- What do you think it means to follow your parents' counsel in righteousness?
- According to Ephesians 6:4, what responsibility does the Lord place on parents?
- How can we encourage greater love and harmony in our home?

Ephesians 6:10–24
"Put on the whole armour of God"

Prepare eight strips of paper, leaving four strips blank and writing one of the following phrases (one per strip) on the four remaining strips: thoughts, feelings or attitudes, virtue and chastity, goals and objectives. Also, on a large sheet of paper, draw a stick figure with several darts or arrows pointing at it from many directions.

Show the drawing to your family and ask if they can tell what it represents. Have them find a clue to what the arrows represent in Ephesians 6:16. When they discover that the arrows represent "fiery darts," ask if they know what "fiery darts" are. Explain that the scriptures sometimes refer to temptations as "the fiery darts of the adversary." (D&C 3:8; see 1 Nephi 15:24; D&C 27:17.) The Apostle Paul taught the Ephesians how they could protect themselves from the devil's influence. Read together Ephesians 6:10–13. Ask:

- What kind of war are we involved in?
- What are wiles? (Sly tricks or deceit.)
- What do we need to do to withstand the evil day? (Put on the whole armor of God.)

Have family members read Ephesians 6:14–17 and look for the four main parts of the body Paul suggests we need to protect. (Loins, heart, feet, and head.) Write the words *loins, heart, feet,* and *head* on the four remaining blank strips of paper and place them on the floor along with the four strips you prepared previously and have your family match them appropriately. When finished, the strips should be matched as follows:

Loins	Virtue and chastity
Heart	Feelings or attitudes
Feet	Goals and objectives
Head	Thoughts

Discuss each body part protected by armor by asking the following questions and having family members draw the corresponding piece of armor on the stick figure as you discuss each one:

Loins

- According to verse 14, how are we to protect the loins?
- What do you think it means to "gird your loins with truth"? ("Now the loins is that part of the body between the lower rib and the hip in which you will recognize are the vital organs which have to do with reproduction . . . he was saying that that part of the body was one of the most vulnerable. . . . We should have our loins girt about with truth. What is truth? . . . What is going to guide us along the path of proper morals or proper choices? It will be the knowledge of truth." [Lee, *Feet Shod with the Preparation of the Gospel of Peace,* 2–4, 6–7].)

Heart

- How are we supposed to protect the heart? (With the breastplate of righteousness.)
- How does one put on the breastplate of righteousness? ("What kind of a breastplate shall protect our conduct in life? We shall have over our hearts a breastplate of righteousness. Well, having learned truth we have a measure by which we can judge between right and wrong and so our conduct will always be gauged by that thing which we know to be true." [Lee, *Feet Shod with the Preparation of the Gospel of Peace,* 2–4, 6–7].)

Feet

- What did Paul teach about protecting our feet?

Head

- What piece of armor should we use to protect our head? (Helmet.)

Have a family member read aloud Doctrine and Covenants 121:45 and ask what it teaches concerning our thoughts. Have another family member reread Ephesians 6:16. Ask:

- What type of armor will help protect us from the fiery darts of the wicked? (Shield.)
- Spiritually speaking, what is the shield made of?

Share this message from Elder Boyd K. Packer: "[The] shield of faith is not produced in a factory but at home. . . .

"The ultimate purpose of all we teach is to unite parents and children in faith in the Lord Jesus Christ, that they are happy at home, sealed in an eternal marriage, linked to their generations, and assured of exaltation in the presence of our Heavenly Father. . . .

"The plan designed by the Father [is] that man and woman, husband and wife, working together, fit each child individually with a shield of faith made to buckle on so firmly that it can neither be pulled off nor penetrated by those fiery darts. . . .

"In the Church we can teach about the materials from which a shield of faith is made: reverence, courage, chastity, repentance, forgiveness, compassion. In church we can learn how to assemble and fit them together. But the actual making of and fitting on of the shield of faith belongs in the family circle." (*Friend,* July 2003, 39.)

Discuss things you could do as a family to strengthen and properly make and fit your shields.

Explain to your family that all the pieces of armor you have talked about so far are used defensively to protect against the adversary. Ask if they noticed in their reading any weapons that could be used offensively as well. Have someone reread Ephesians 6:17 aloud. Ask:

- What weapon is mentioned in this verse? (Sword.)
- What is the sword of the Spirit?
- How could you increase your knowledge of the word of God? ("I can't think of any more powerful weapons than faith and a knowledge of the scriptures in which are contained the Word of God. One so armoured and one so prepared with those weapons is prepared to go out against the enemy." [Lee, *Feet Shod with the Preparation of the Gospel of Peace,* 7.])

Remind your family that Paul stressed the importance of putting on "the whole armor of God" and ask what might happen if only part of the armor is worn or if we fail to put it on each day. Tell your family that Elder Joseph B. Wirthlin of the Quorum of the Twelve warned that Satan "seeks to find any chink in the armor of each person. He knows our weaknesses and knows how to exploit them if we allow him to do so. We can defend ourselves against his attacks and deceptions only by understanding the commandments and by fortifying ourselves each day through praying, studying the scriptures, and following the counsel of the Lord's anointed." (*Ensign,* Nov. 1988, 35.)

Invite family members to examine their armor and determine what they need to do to cover any chinks. Bear testimony of the importance of doing the seemingly small things each day to properly protect us from the onslaught of evil.

PHILIPPIANS

Philippians was written by Paul to the Saints who lived in Philippi around 61 A.D. Paul was living under house arrest in Rome at this time.

Philippi was "a prominent city of the gold-producing region of Macedonia.... Named originally after Philip II, the father of Alexander the Great." (NIV Study Bible, 1801.) It was in Philippi where Paul cast an evil spirit out of a woman and converted a jailor to the gospel of Jesus Christ. (See Acts 16:12–40.)

To learn more about the book of Philippians, see Bible Dictionary, 745.

PHILIPPIANS 1: A LETTER OF THANKS

Philippians 1:1–11
A message of gratitude and counsel

Begin by giving each family member a chance to make a list of some of the things they are grateful for. Explain that the first eleven verses of Paul's epistle to the people of Philippi is an expression of thanksgiving and counsel. Take turns reading Philippians 1:1–11 and have your family make one list of the things Paul expressed thanks for and another list of the things Paul counseled them to do. Ask:

- How are the things Paul was thankful for like our list?
- What did Paul want the Philippians to do that would also be good for our family to do?
- How did Paul show his love for the Saints in Philippi?
- How can we show more love and appreciation in our family?

Ask each family member to choose one of the things from the lists that he or she could do to increase the love in the family. Share your love and gratitude for your family and the Savior.

Philippians 1:12–30
Paul councils the Saints at Philippi

Write the seven situations or questions listed below on separate pieces of paper. Give each member of your family one or more of these pieces of paper until all seven situations have been assigned. Have them read their situation and the accompanying verse(s) and determine what counsel Paul would give according to the teachings in Philippians 1:15–30.

1. The other day at school I was made fun of because I would not smoke a cigarette. (Verse 29.)

2. When life gets really hard, I can't help but think it would be easier to live in heaven with Jesus Christ instead of enduring things here on earth. (Verses 23–24.)

3. My friends tell me I need Christ in my life. I wonder why. (Verse 21.)

4. Why do I have to suffer so many trials? What good are they? (Verse 19.)

5. What can I do when I am talking with another and they try and sway me from what I know is right? (Verse 27.)

6. I hear both good things and bad thing about Jesus Christ. What should I believe? (Verse 15.)

Have each family member take turns reading their situation(s) and then share what they learned from the Apostle Paul. Encourage them to mark scriptures that impress them. Express your gratitude for Christ and the blessings He gives, as we are obedient.

PHILIPPIANS 2: PAUL CHALLENGES THE SAINTS TO BE UNIFIED

Philippians 2:1–11
"Let this mind be in you"

Show your family a paper with the following written large enough for them to see: "Be _____; and if ye are not _____, ye are not _____." Ask them to guess what words go in the blanks and who is speaking. ("One," "one," and "mine" are the words the Lord is speaking.) Invite them to find and mark this phrase in Doctrine and Covenants 38:27. Ask them why they think unity is such an important description of the Lord's people.

Read together Philippians 2:1–4 and ask:

• What does Paul want the Saints to do?
• What specific things does he say they should do to achieve this unity?

Invite family members to try to state verse 4 in their own words. Then ask:

• What things might change in our family or community if people worried more about others than about themselves?
• According to verse 5, whose "mind" or attitude did Paul say we should emulate?
• Who is the greatest example you know of selflessness?
• How does the Savior's great love for us make you feel about Him?
• Would you like other people to feel that way about you?

Take turns reading aloud the verses in Philippians 2:6–11. Ask:

• What do these verses teach us about what Christ was willing to do to help bring about unity among God's children?
• What happened to Jesus because of His completely selfless attitude?

Ask your family, What is the most selfless act ever performed on the earth? (The Atonement.) Point out that some people have noted that the word *Atonement* can be broken down to "at-one-ment." In other words, the purpose of the Atonement is to unify us or make us "one" with God. As an example of this desire of Jesus, read together John 17:20–23. Testify that when we seek for righteous unity we are following the example of the Savior and inviting the spirit of the Atonement into our relationships.

Philippians 2:12–30
Who is a trusted representative?

Have your family imagine that they had to leave everything behind for the next 2–4 years and serve in a foreign land. As part of this service, you would be required to choose someone to take care of your belongings, to represent you in your work, and to represent you in important interviews or business decisions. Ask, Who would you want to be your official representative and why?

As a family, take turns reading the verses in Philippians 2:19–30 and identify the following:

• Who Paul wanted to represent him to the Philippians.
• What qualities these individuals had that Paul wanted them to represent him.

Read together Philippians 2:12–18 and ask:

• What phrase in verse 15 identifies what Paul says we ought to be as Church members? ("Lights to the world.")
• What counsel does he give in verses 12–18 concerning how they could "shine as lights in the world"?
• What did Paul say he had done and was willing to do to fulfill his role?

Have someone read in 3 Nephi 27:27 what Jesus said to those who represent Him concerning what they should be like. Ask:

• What do you think are the biggest challenges in accepting this responsibility from the Lord?
• What are some of the ways you have recognized that the Lord's servants truly represent Him?

PHILIPPIANS 3: SELF-RIGHTEOUSNESS VERSUS CHRIST'S RIGHTEOUSNESS

Philippians 3:1–12

How can we be righteous enough for heaven?

Ask your family how obedient they have to be to get to heaven. Explain to your family that there are actually two ways to become obedient and righteous enough to get to heaven. The first is to be perfectly righteous all the time by never making a mistake. The second is to be *made* righteous through faith in Jesus Christ.

Have your family follow along in their scriptures as you read the next two scriptures aloud. Emphasize with your voice the words in italics:

- "These are they who are just men *made perfect* through Jesus the mediator of the new covenant, who wrought out this perfect atonement through the shedding of his own blood." (D&C 76:69.)
- "Yea, come unto Christ, and be *perfected in him,* and deny yourselves of all ungodliness; and if ye shall deny yourselves of all ungodliness and love God with all your might, mind and strength, then is his grace sufficient for you, that by his grace ye may *be perfect in Christ;* and if by the grace of God ye are *perfect in Christ,* ye can in nowise deny the power of God." (Moroni 10:32.)

Ask your family:

- Which of these two ways (living perfectly or relying on Jesus Christ) will work for us to become righteous enough to make it to heaven? (The second. Only Christ was able to be righteous enough on His own merits.)
- Which way did the Jews trust who rejected Jesus Christ and instead followed the law of Moses?

Explain to your family that Paul referred to this type of righteousness as being through the flesh rather than by faith. Read together Philippians 3:1–12 looking for what Paul learned about righteousness. Discuss the following questions as you read:

- Why did Paul think that if anyone could boast of personal righteousness, he could more? (Verses 4–6.)
- What did Paul say it had cost him to follow Christ? (Verse 8.)
- What words or phrases in verses 8–10 show that Paul thought the price he had to pay to know Jesus Christ was worth it?
- What does the Lord ask us to give up to know Him?
- How do we show our faith in Christ?

Challenge your family to show their faith in the Lord by always remembering Him and keeping the commandments to the best of their abilities.

Philippians 3:12–21

Paul's advice for reaching heaven

Remind your family that in the first part of Philippians 3 Paul taught that we are saved by having faith in Jesus Christ and doing our best to be obedient, not in depending on our own righteousness to save us. To illustrate this idea, read together the parable of the Pharisee and the publican in Luke 18:9–14. Ask:

- Why did the Pharisee think he was better than the publican?
- What did the Pharisee think was going to get him into heaven?
- Who was the publican depending on to save him?
- Which of the two did Jesus approve of?
- How is this parable like what Paul taught in Philippians?

Invite someone to review what Paul (then called Saul) was doing before the Lord appeared to him. (See Acts 8:1–3; 9:1–6; and Philippians 3:6 for help if needed.) Then discuss the following questions:

- How do you suppose Paul felt when he discovered that he had been persecuting the very God he thought he was serving?
- How easy would it have been for Paul to feel that God would never forgive him?
- Have you ever heard of someone feeling that their past was so bad that they could never be forgiven?

Read together Philippians 3:12–21 and look for

what Paul might say to a person like that. Discuss the following questions as you read:

- Where does Paul say he is on the road to perfection? (Verses 12–14.)
- Whose example does he say we can follow? (His example and others who are trying to follow Christ; verses 16–17.)
- What does he say about those who do not follow Christ? (Verses 18–19.)
- What does he say the Savior will do for those who trust in Him and not themselves? (Verses 20–21.)

Share your testimony of the power and willingness of the Lord to forgive us and help us to change. Encourage your family to look to Jesus Christ in all they do.

PHILIPPIANS 4: HOW TO HAVE A HAPPY LIFE

Philippians 4:1–13
The secrets to happiness

Explain to your family members that Philippians 4 is about happiness and that they will be the ones to teach it. Depending on the ages and size of your family, divide them into two to four groups. Listed below are scripture blocks, and ideas for each group to help prepare them to teach. Assign them to read the verses, identify secrets to happiness, and then share them with the family.

Group 1: Verses 1–5

- How does the service in verse 3 bring happiness?
- Give an example of when serving brought you joy.
- What hymn does verse 4 remind you of? (See "Rejoice, the Lord Is King," *Hymns*, no. 66. You might even sing it together.)
- What difference does footnote 5a make to the meaning of the verse?
- How does gentleness bring happiness?

Group 2: Verses 6–7

- What insights do footnotes 6a and 6b add to these verses?

- How might making requests to God be better than worrying?
- In what ways does the peace of God "surpass all understanding"?
- Describe a time when God gave you peace in the midst of difficulties.

Group 3: Verse 8–10

- What Article of Faith does verse 8 remind you of? (You might want to write Articles of Faith 1:13 next to verse 8.)
- How does thinking about the kinds of things mentioned in verse 8 bring happiness?
- How does exposure to evil influences take away our happiness?

Group 4: Verses 11–13

- How did Paul learn to be content in every situation? (Verse 12; Paul's personal experiences.)
- What is the opposite of "content"? (Dissatisfied.)
- How does contentment bring happiness?
- How would trusting in God's strength help? (Verse 13.)
- When is a time that the Lord strengthened you?

Have your family list ways the gospel of Jesus Christ brings happiness to them.

Philippians 4:14–23
The spirit of service

Take turns reading Philippians 4:14–23 and have your family look for and mark every reference to service they can find. After your family has pointed out what they found, share the following story:

"On reaching Kirtland, the family with whom Lydia [Knight] had traveled set at once to make arrangements to settle down. Leaving his wife and Lydia at the hotel, Mr. Knight went out, soon returning with his brother Vincent Knight, who was a resident of Kirtland. On being introduced to Lydia, Vincent Knight said: 'Sister, the Prophet is in bondage and has been brought into distress by the persecutions of the wicked, and if you have any means to give, it will be a benefit to him.'

"'Oh yes, sir,' she replied, 'here is all I have. I only wish it was more,' emptying her purse, containing perhaps fifty dollars, in his hand as she spoke.

"He looked at it and counted it and fervently exclaimed: 'Thank God, this will release and set the Prophet free!'

"The young girl was without means now, even to procure a meal or a night's lodging. Still that sweet spirit that rested upon her whispered 'all will be well.'

"As evening drew on, Vincent Knight returned and brought the welcome news that Joseph was at liberty, and Lydia's joy to think that she had been the humble means of helping the Prophet was unbounded." (Gates, *Lydia Knight's History,* p. 25, as quoted in Hartshorn, *Remarkable Stories from the Lives of Latter-day Saint Women,* 1:55–56.)

Invite a family member to share how they felt following the act of being of service to someone. Testify to your family that the good feeling that accompanies service is the Holy Ghost witnessing of the value and importance of that act.

COLOSSIANS

Colossae was a city about 110 miles east of Ephesus. Paul probably wrote his epistle to the Colossians while he was imprisoned in Rome. Epaphras, a fellow missionary, visited Paul and reported that the Colossians were falling into serious error. These Saints were now preoccupied in mystical experiences, worship of angels, and other false teachings. Paul wrote to these Saints, encouraging them to believe in Christ and His teachings.

COLOSSIANS 1: PAUL WARNS AGAINST FALSE TEACHINGS

Colossians 1:1–12

A time of prayer and thanksgiving

Ask your family members to name their favorite holiday and why. Following their responses, invite them to tell you how they feel about Thanksgiving. Ask:

- According to Doctrine and Covenants 59:21, how does Heavenly Father feel about those who don't express thanks?
- When was the last time you sincerely expressed gratitude?

- How does it make you feel when you sincerely tell someone "thank you"?
- What does that do for your relationship with that person?

Invite your family to silently read Colossians 1:1–12, looking for what Paul says we should be grateful for and pray for. Following their study of these verses, ask them to name what they found.

Read the following statement to your family by Elder Neal A. Maxwell: "Let our gratitude . . . be expressed by striving to become, attribute by attribute, more and more as Jesus is (see 3 Nephi 27:27). By so living, ours will not then be a mere appreciation of Jesus, nor a modest admiration of Him. Rather, ours will be an adoration of Jesus expressed by our emulation of Him!" (*Ensign,* Nov. 1993, 20.)

Share with your family those things for which you are grateful. Let them know of your gratitude for the Atonement of Jesus Christ and His many blessings given to you. You could sing "For the Beauty of the Earth" (*Hymns,* no. 92) to conclude your scripture study.

Colossians 1:19–29

What is the "mystery which hath been hid from the ages"?

Ask your family to define the word *mystery.* Following their definitions, tell them that the dictionary defines a mystery as "a religious truth that one can know of only by revelation and cannot fully understand." (*Webster's Ninth New Collegiate Dictionary,* "Mystery," 785.) Invite your family to read Colossians 1:19–23, looking for what the mystery mentioned in verse 26 might be. Following their reading of the verses ask them what the mystery might be. Ask:

- How can the Atonement, Resurrection, and birth of Christ be called mysteries?
- Why are many of these not mysteries to members of the Church?
- How are members able to testify of the truth and reality of these events? (Revelation.)
- According to verses 27–29, what is our responsibility once we know these things are true?

Testify to your family of the reality of the birth, death, Atonement, and Resurrection of Jesus Christ. Remind them that with revelation given through our prophets, the "mysteries" are often unlocked for our understanding.

COLOSSIANS 2: PAUL TEACHES THE ATTRIBUTES OF GOD

Colossians 2:1–12

How can we increase our testimony of the Savior?

 Invite your family to silently read Colossians 2:6–7, 10. Ask:

- What do you think it means to "walk" in Christ? (Verse 6.)
- How can being "rooted and built up" in Christ help us in times of trial? (Deep roots withstand strong winds.)
- In what ways might being "stablished in the faith" help us become "complete" in Christ? (Verse 10.)
- What does Paul teach we should be thankful for? (Jesus Christ and His Atonement.)
- How can walking in Christ show our gratitude for Him?

Read to your family the following statement by Elder Neal A. Maxwell: "When we take Jesus' yoke upon us, this admits us eventually to what Paul called the 'fellowship of [Christ's] sufferings'

(Philip. 3:10). Whether illness or aloneness, injustice or rejection, etc., our comparatively small-scale sufferings, if we are meek, will sink into the very marrow of the soul. We then better appreciate not only Jesus' sufferings for us, but also His matchless character, moving us to greater adoration and even emulation." (*Ensign,* May 1997, 12.)

Ask your family what it means to "emulate" (imitate or follow) someone. Discuss as a family ways you can better "emulate" the Savior. Ask, How would emulating the Savior helps us increase our testimony and combat false teachings?

Colossians 2:13–23

Christ fulfilled the law of Moses

Ask your family if they would rather have the prophet tell them which movies they can attend, books they can read, clothes they can wear (or not wear), or let them choose their own movies, books, and clothing. Tell your family that anciently the children of Israel lived under the law of Moses that told them specifically what they could do or could not do. In contrast, Jesus Christ revealed the law of the gospel that taught people correct principles and then allowed them to choose for themselves. Ask:

- What would be good about living under the law of Moses?
- What would be difficult?
- Why would you prefer to live under the law of the gospel?
- What is the hardest part about living under the law of the gospel?

Read together Colossians 2:13–17 and look for words or phrases that show that Jesus Christ fulfilled the law of Moses when He came into the world to introduce the higher law. To help you understand these difficult verses, write the following statements by Elder Bruce R. McConkie on separate pieces of paper and give them to family members to read when the corresponding verses are read:

Verses 14–15. "Christ fulfilled the law of Moses, thereby blotting out its ordinances and performances, symbolically nailing them to his cross.

Verse 16. "Accordingly, do not be misled by

following the rituals and restrictions of the law of Moses.

Verse 17. "These performances were only a type and a shadow of Christ and his gospel, and we now have the substance itself rather then the shadow." (*Doctrinal New Testament Commentary,* 3:33.)

After discussing these verses, invite a family member to read the following statement by Elder Jeffrey R. Holland:

"The *For the Strength of Youth* pamphlet is very clear in its call for young women to avoid clothing that is too tight, too short, or improperly revealing in any manner, including bare midriffs. Parents, . . . Second only to your love, they need your limits. Young women, choose your clothing the way you would choose your friends—in both cases choose that which improves you and would give you confidence standing in the presence of God. Good friends would never embarrass you, demean you, or exploit you. Neither should your clothing.

"I make a special appeal regarding how young women might dress for Church services and Sabbath worship. We used to speak of 'best dress' or 'Sunday dress,' and maybe we should do so again. In any case, from ancient times to modern we have always been invited to present our best selves inside and out when entering the house of the Lord—and a dedicated LDS chapel is a 'house of the Lord.' Our clothing or footwear need never be expensive, indeed should *not* be expensive, but neither should it appear that we are on our way to the beach. When we come to worship the God and Father of us all and to partake of the sacrament symbolizing the Atonement of Jesus Christ, we should be as comely and respectful, as dignified and appropriate as we can be. We should be recognizable in appearance as well as in behavior that we truly are disciples of Christ, that in a spirit of worship we are meek and lowly of heart, that we truly desire the Savior's Spirit to be with us always." (*Ensign,* Nov. 2005, 29.)

Ask:

- Do you feel that Elder Holland is teaching young women correct principles and allowing them to govern themselves, or is he specifically telling them what to do?
- If you had the responsibility for the youth of

the Church, how would you teach them to act and dress?

Invite your family to share how following the Spirit and making their own choices can be a great blessing in their lives. Discuss how living a lesser law sometimes helps prepare people for a higher law. (For example, the law of tithing prepares the Saints for the law of consecration.) Explain to your family that the law of Moses was a "schoolmaster" to bring the children of Israel to Christ. Testify that we are privileged to live in a day when the law of the gospel has been revealed and that we enjoy great blessings because of it.

COLOSSIANS 3: BECOMING BETTER INDIVIDUALS AND FAMILIES

Colossians 3:1–15
What must I do to become a "new man" or woman?

⭐ Bring twelve articles of summer clothing and many sets of winter clothes to scripture study. Dress one family member like a mannequin by putting the twelve summer clothing items on him or her. Tell your family that in the first fifteen verses of Colossians 3, Paul tells of attributes that we need to gain or lose in order to become a "new man" or woman in Christ. Ask family members to read Colossians 3:8, 12, 14 and find the phrases which mean the same thing as "gaining" or "losing." ("Put on" and "put off.")

Divide your family into two groups and give each group paper and a pencil. Have each group study Colossians 3:1–15 with one group making a list of the things we are to "put on" and the other group making a list of the things we are to "put off." When they are finished, ask each group to read their list aloud, starting with the list of things to "put off." Each time an item is listed that should be "put off," have the family member dressed like a mannequin take off one item of summer clothing. While the list is read of what should be "put on," have that same family member then put on an item of winter clothing. When this activity is finished, discuss the following questions:

- What kind of things did the summer clothes represent? (Negative or evil characteristics.)
- What could eliminating the summer clothes be likened to? (Repentance.)
- What does each piece of winter clothing represent?
- Why is it important that we eliminate sinful things in our lives, before we put on the attributes of godliness?

Explain that if we are to become new men and women in Christ we must prepare. The attributes described by Paul are important for this preparation. Ask family members to identify one item from Paul's list they could "put off," and one item they need to strive to "put on." Have them devise a plan to accomplish these goals.

Colossians 3:18–25

How to be a Christlike family

Bring a photograph of your family to scripture study. Show your family the photograph and tell your family that Paul gives some great council for specific family members in Colossians 3:18–25. Take turns reading verses 18–24 and have your family watch for the counsel for the different family members. Ask:

- What should wives do? (Verse 18.)
- What should husbands do? (Verse 19.)
- What should children do? (Verse 20.)
- How should fathers deal with their children? (Verse 21.)

Read verse 25 to your family and ask them how they feel when someone in the family is mean to them. According to verse 25, what is the reward for those who are mean? Encourage them to be kind to each other and build family unity thus becoming a Christlike family.

COLOSSIANS 4: PAUL BIDS FAREWELL

Colossians 4:1–6

Paul's final counsel to the Colossians

 Have your family imagine that this is their last day on earth. Ask:

- What do you want to do?
- Who would you like to see?
- What message would you like to leave with your friends and family?

Explain that although it wasn't Paul's last day on earth, his letter to the Colossian Saints was his last communication with them. Take turns reading Colossians 4:1–6 and invite your family to look for some of Paul's final words of counsel to them. Ask:

- In what way do we all have a "Master"? (Verse 1.)
- How might our prayers help missionary work? (Verses 2–4.)
- How should we treat those not of our faith? (Verse 5.)
- How should we spend our time? (Verse 5.)
- How should we speak with others? (Verse 6.)

Compare Paul's counsel to the Colossians with the things your family listed while answering the questions at the beginning. Discuss as a family how to best live as if this were their last day on earth.

1 THESSALONIANS

Thessalonica was a prominent city in ancient Macedonia, which was part of Greece. The Apostle Paul visited Thessalonica on his second missionary journey. (See Map 20 in pre-1999 copies of the Bible; Map 13 in post-1999 copies; see also the chart "The Missionary Journeys of Paul" on p. 161–62 of this book.) Paul's experience as described in Acts 17:1–10 records that after severe persecution at the hands of local Jews who opposed the work, Paul and Silas fled the city. He wanted to return and meet with these Saints whose faithfulness he spoke of in other letters (see 2 Corinthians 8:1–5; 11:9), but was unable to do so. (See 1 Thessalonians 2:18.) He sent Timothy in his place. (See 1 Thessalonians 3:1–6.) The First Epistle to the Thessalonians appears to be Paul's response to these Saints after Timothy returned and gave his report.

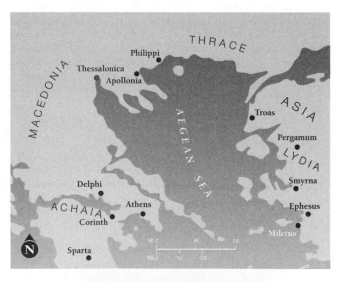

1 THESSALONIANS 1: THE FAITHFULNESS OF THE THESSALONIAN SAINTS

1 Thessalonians 1:1–10
Learning from new converts

Invite family members to think about people they know who converted to the Church. Ask, What things impressed you about their conversion?

As you read together 1 Thessalonians 1:1–10,

have family members look for words or phrases that show why Paul felt the converts in Thessalonica were "ensamples [examples] to all that believe." (Verse 7.) Ask:

- Which of the qualities you found apply to our family and why?
- What clues do you find in these verses about why the Saints became converted and showed such a great example to others?

Share with your family the following explanations of what happens to new converts: "As new converts receive the Holy Ghost, they experience 'a mighty change.' . . . Answering a reporter in a press interview, President Hinckley said: 'The most satisfying experience I have is to see what this gospel does for people. It gives them a new outlook on life. It gives them a perspective that they have never felt before. It raises their sights to things noble and divine. Something happens to them that is miraculous to behold. They look to Christ and come alive.'" (Joseph B. Wirthlin, *Ensign*, Nov. 1997, 33.)

"Upon receiving a testimony of the truth of the restored gospel, [new converts] have unhesitatingly sacrificed all that was required to assure that its blessings will be available to their children and to generations unborn. Some have sold all their property to travel to a temple. Some have lost employment. Many have lost friends. Some have even lost parents and extended family, as new converts have been disowned for their faith. This must be the greatest sacrifice of all. . . .

" . . . We should also assure that these same qualities are guiding principles for each of us as we have opportunities to sacrifice for our nations, our families, our quorums, our members, and our Church." (Dallin H. Oaks, *Ensign,* Nov. 1997, 72–73.)

Ask your family: From these statements by Elder Wirthlin and Elder Oaks, what can we learn from new converts to apply in our lives?

1 THESSALONIANS 2: THE EFFORTS AND JOYS OF GOSPEL TEACHERS

1 Thessalonians 2:1–20
Learning from a great missionary

Share the following from Elder David A. Bednar: "The single most important thing you can do to prepare for a call to serve [a full-time mission] is to *become* a missionary long before you *go* on a mission. . . .

" . . . The issue is not going on a mission; rather, the issue is becoming a missionary and serving throughout our entire life with all of our heart, might, mind, and strength. . . .

"My earnest hope . . . is that you will not simply go on a mission—but that you will become missionaries long before you submit your mission papers. . . .

" . . . You can increase in your desire to serve God (see D&C 4:3), and you can begin to think as missionaries think, to read what missionaries read, to pray as missionaries pray, and to feel what missionaries feel. You can avoid the worldly influences that cause the Holy Ghost to withdraw, and you can grow in confidence in recognizing and responding to spiritual promptings. Line upon line and precept upon precept, here a little and there a little, you can gradually become the missionary you hope to be and the missionary the Savior expects." (*Ensign,* Nov. 2005, 45–46.)

Paul was a tremendous missionary, and because many of his writings have been preserved, we can learn great things from him. For example, though 1 Thessalonians 2 wasn't necessarily written to teach about missionary work, there are many insights into what great missionaries do, think, feel, know, and experience.

Appoint a family member to be a scribe. Have the scribe make three columns on a sheet of paper or poster and write the following three titles at the top: (1) Things Missionaries Experience; (2) Attitudes and Motives of Great Missionaries; (3) Things Missionaries Do.

As you take turns reading 1 Thessalonians 2:1–20, invite family members to look for things that they think belongs in one of these three categories. As each idea is identified, do the following:

1. Have the scribe record it in the appropriate column.

2. Have the person who found it tell why it helped Paul be a successful missionary.

3. Have the family tell how it applies to us today.

Have your family members look over the lists and choose one thing they would like to work on in their own lives. Invite them to tell why they chose it.

1 THESSALONIANS 3: ENCOURAGEMENT TO "STAND FAST"

1 Thessalonians 3:1–13
Agree or Disagree?

Write the following statements on strips of paper and put them where family members can see them:

- When we fully accept the gospel, trials and afflictions will be eliminated from our lives.
- Our faith can lift others who have affliction.
- God can help us feel more love for others.

Ask your family if they agree or disagree with these statements and give reasons why. As you read 1 Thessalonians 3:1–13, have family members identify when they read something that gives them reason to agree or disagree with one of the statements above. The following questions may help as you talk about each idea:

When we fully accept the gospel, trials and afflictions will be eliminated from our lives.

- What does Paul say about this in verses 3–4?
- How does this compare with the revelation to Joseph Smith in Doctrine and Covenants 24:8?
- How does it help to know that we should *expect* trials and afflictions?
- What does Paul say we should do in the midst of afflictions? (Verse 8.)
- What information do you learn from Joseph Smith's experience in Liberty Jail, in Doctrine and Covenants 121:7–8; 122:9?

Tell your family that Elder Joseph B. Wirthlin reminded us that "affliction is not necessarily a sign of God's anger and a punishment for sin," but that it "may be for discipline, experience, and instruction." (*Ensign,* Nov. 1987, 8.) Invite family members to tell how trials have blessed them.

Our faith can lift others who are in affliction.

Share with your family the following insights from Joseph Smith, written while in Liberty Jail: "Those who have not been enclosed in the walls of prison without cause or provocation, can have but little idea how sweet the voice of a friend is; one token of friendship from any source whatever awakens and calls into action every sympathetic feeling; it brings up in an instant everything that is passed; it seizes the present with the avidity of lightning; it grasps after the future with the fierceness of a tiger; it moves the mind backward and forward, from one thing to another, until finally all enmity, malice and hatred, and past differences, misunderstandings and mismanagements are slain victorious at the feet of hope; and when the heart is sufficiently contrite, then the voice of inspiration steals along and whispers, My son, peace be unto thy soul; thine adversity and thine afflictions shall be but a small moment; and then if thou endure it well, God shall exalt thee on high." (*History of the Church,* 3:293.)

Invite family members to tell how others' words, faith, and example have helped them in a time of trial or affliction.

God can help us feel more love for others.

- What evidence do you find in 1 Thessalonians 3 of Paul's love for the Saints?
- What role do you think the Holy Ghost plays in our ability to love others?

Read together John 13:34–35 and Moroni 7:46–48, looking for why this love for others is so important and how we obtain it. Compare what Moroni said in Moroni 7:48 about what the result of having charity will be with what Paul said in 1 Thessalonians 3:13 will be the results.

Tell your family that while we all have trials and afflictions, when we "stand fast" in those trials and extend love to each other in word and action we will strengthen and help each other. Help them know that while this is certainly true in our wards and stakes and communities, it is even truer in our family.

1 THESSALONIANS 4: "CAUGHT UP ... TO MEET THE LORD IN THE AIR"

1 Thessalonians 4:13–18
The Second Coming

Take your family outside to study these verses. Have them look into the sky and imagine that today is the day the Savior returns to the earth for the Second Coming. Ask:

- What do you imagine that day will be like?
- What have you learned about His coming?
- What else would you like to know?

Ask your family the following question: When the Savior returns at the Second Coming, will we
A. be looking up at Him as he comes down?
B. be caught up in the air and meet Him in the clouds?

Have your family look for the answer as they read 1 Thessalonians 4:13–18. Ask:

- What does it mean when the verses refer to those who are "asleep"? (Those who die before the Second Coming.)
- What will happen to them when He comes again?
- What will happen to those who are alive?

- How does the Joseph Smith Translation in footnote 17*a* clarify the meaning of the verse?

Have your family write D&C 88:96–98 in the margin next to 1 Thessalonians 4:17 and then read together both sets of verses. Discuss with your family what is taught there. Share the following statement by Elder Bruce R. McConkie:

"Salvation is given the saints—all of them, both the living and the dead—at the Second Coming. The living are caught up to meet their returning Lord, and with him they shall return to live on this earth, which will then be changed and receive its paradisiacal glory. (Tenth Article of Faith.) When the living arrive at the age of a tree, 100 years, they shall be changed from mortality to immortality in the twinkling of an eye and shall then reign as kings and priests in exalted glory. (D. & C. 101:23–31.)

"Also at our Lord's return, the righteous dead shall come forth from their graves with celestial bodies to meet their God. They, then, as kings and priests, shall live and reign with Christ on earth in resurrected glory for a thousand years." (*Doctrinal New Testament Commentary,* 3:51–52.)

Challenge your family to be worthy to meet the Lord at the Second Coming.

1 THESSALONIANS 5: HOW TO PREPARE FOR THE SECOND COMING

1 Thessalonians 5:1–13
Will the Church be surprised when Jesus comes?

Hide a small, soft object before scripture study. Call a family member's name and throw the soft object at him or her. Ask:

- Did you expect me to throw something at you?
- Were you surprised? Why?
- How was this like the Second Coming?
- Why will the Second Coming be a surprise to some?

Take turns reading 1 Thessalonians 5:1–13, looking for answers to the following questions:

- Why would you be surprised to find a thief breaking into your house?
- Why will most of the world be surprised at the Lord's return?
- According to verse 6, why will the Church be different than the rest of the world?
- How will we know when He is coming? (We will recognize the signs as they appear.)

Share the following statement by Elder Bruce R. McConkie:

"We do not know the day nor the hour, and for that matter neither do the angels of God in heaven (Matt. 24:36), but we do know the time and the season; that is, we know the approximate time, shall we say, the generation of his return.

"But his coming shall not overtake the saints as a thief, for they know and understand the signs of the times." (*Doctrinal New Testament Commentary,* 3:53–54.)

Read again 1 Thessalonians 5:9 and ask:

- What do you think the phrase "For God hath not appointed us to wrath" means?
- How does this suggest Church members will escape the tribulations prior to Christ's coming?

Share the following statement by President Wilford Woodruff: "Can you tell me where the people are who will be shielded and protected from these great calamities and judgments which are even now at our doors? I'll tell you. The priesthood of God who honor their priesthood and who are worthy of their blessings are the only ones who shall have this safety and protection. They are the only mortal beings. No other people have a right to be shielded from these judgments. They are at our doors; not even this people will escape them entirely." (*Young Women's Journal* 5 [August 1894]: 512.)

Challenge your family to be prepared for the Lord's coming.

1 Thessalonians 5:14–28
How should we prepare for Christ's coming?

Ask your family the two questions below and have them tell which question is most important:

- When is the Second Coming?
- How do I prepare for the Second Coming?

Ask your family why it is more important to be prepared for the Second Coming than to know when it will happen. Explain that 1 Thessalonians 5:14–28 gives ways to prepare for the Second Coming. Divide all verses among family members. (Give short verses to the youngest children.) Have them rewrite their assigned verse(s) into their own words and be ready to teach the rest of the family how they can prepare for the Second Coming.

2 THESSALONIANS

Paul's second letter to the recent converts in Thessalonica was written shortly after his first letter and demonstrates his love and concern for these new members. These Saints had suffered from persecution and apparently had the mistaken belief that Christ would soon return. This belief came from a misunderstanding of Paul's teachings and resulted in undue idleness on the Saints' part. Paul sought to correct their misunderstandings and help inspire them to better works.

2 THESSALONIANS 1: THE LORD WILL TAKE VENGEANCE ON THE UNGODLY

2 Thessalonians 1:1–12
Glorious or terrible?

 What is a typical way to begin a letter?

Have your family look for three good qualities of the Saints in Thessalonica that Paul mentions as you read together 2 Thessalonians 1:1–6. Ask, What qualities did you find? Draw a chart similar to the one below on a piece of paper. Show it to your family members and have them rate themselves in each area by mentally placing a dot somewhere between the two extremes on the scale.

"I have great faith"_____"My faith is poor."

"I am very charitable to others" _____ "I am not very charitable."

"I am very patient with people" _____ "I lack patience with others."

Have each family member determine one thing they could do to improve in each area.

Ask someone to read 2 Thessalonians 1:7 and ask what day or event is being referred to in this verse. Have another family member read Doctrine and Covenants 2:1 and ask if the Second Coming will be great or dreadful. Share this message from President Ezra Taft Benson: "[The Savior's] coming will be both glorious and terrible, depending on the spiritual condition of those who remain" (*New Era*, May 1982, 49.) Ask, What does President Benson say will determine whether the Second Coming will be glorious or terrible?

Invite each family member to read 2 Thessalonians 1:8–12 to themselves and choose the phrase they like best which describes the positive aspects of the Second Coming and one phrase they think best describes the negative aspects. Have everyone share their selected phrases. Ask, What must we do to qualify for the promised blessings and avoid the punishments?

2 THESSALONIANS 2: APOSTASY PRECEDES THE SECOND COMING OF CHRIST

2 Thessalonians 2:1–17
Did the early Apostles know there would be an apostasy?

Relate the following story to your family and then discuss why Satan is often present just before or just after a significant spiritual experience:

"Joseph Smith, Jun., prophesied the day previous that the man of sin would be revealed. While the Lord poured out His Spirit upon His servants, the devil took a notion to make known his power. He bound Harvey Whitlock and John Murdock so that they could not speak, and others were affected but the Lord showed to Joseph, the seer, the design of the thing; he commanded the devil in the name of Christ, and he departed, to our joy and comfort." (*History of the Church,* 1:195.)

Ask your family to silently read 2 Thessalonians 2:1–3. Ask:

- According to verse 3, what will men attempt to do prior to Christ's Second Coming?
- What does Paul say in verse 3 will happen prior to Christ's return?
- What word is used that describes a person or group that falls away from the Church and its teachings?
- What is the Apostasy? (See *True to the Faith,* "Apostasy," 13; or *Preach My Gospel,* 33–36 for additional help, if needed.)
- Who is the "man of sin"? (Satan.)

Have your family read verses 4–12 and ask:

- According to verses 4–12, what tactics does Satan use to deceive us?
- Whose responsibility is it to reveal or point out Satan and his tactics? (Prophets, parents, priesthood leaders.)

Read to your family the following statement by President Harold B. Lee: "Now the only safety we have as members of this Church is to do exactly what the Lord said to the Church in that day when the Church was organized. We must learn to give heed to the words and commandments that the Lord shall give through his prophet. . . . You may not like what comes from the authority of the Church. It may contradict your political views. It may contradict your social views. It may interfere with some of your social life. But if you listen to these things, as if from the mouth of the Lord himself . . . 'the gates of hell shall not prevail against you.'" (Conference Report, Oct. 1970, 152.)

Ask your family to silently read Joseph Smith History 1:15. Ask:

- According to verse 15, what did Satan attempt to do to discourage Joseph?
- By overcoming Satan's tactics, what blessing came to the boy prophet?

Ask your family to silently read to themselves 2 Thessalonians 2:15–17, looking for ways a person can keep from being deceived. Take time to list and discuss your families' findings. Let your family know of your feelings for those leaders who continue to protect us from Satan's deception.

2 THESSALONIANS 3: BE NOT WEARY IN WELL DOING

2 Thessalonians 3:3–15
Paul's counsel for today

 Write the following questions where all can see them. Omit the references.

- What if I sometimes have a hard time doing all I am supposed to do? (Verses 3–5.)
- What if a ward member is causing trouble in the ward and is saying things that don't agree with Church teachings? (Verses 6–7.)
- What if one of our ward friends borrows money but never pays us back? (Verses 8–12.)
- What if one of our ward friends needs our help, but it takes a lot of our time? (Verse 13.)
- What if one of our friends is breaking the commandments and getting into trouble? (Verses 14–15.)

Invite your family to divide into pairs and study 2 Thessalonians 3:3–15 and find verses that help answer the questions. Tell them to be prepared to explain their answers and show which verses they used. Have each pair in turn share what they found until all the questions have been reported on. Discuss together Paul's counsel as you review the questions, their answers, and additional scriptural insights.

- What if I have a hard time doing all I am supposed to do? (Verses 3–5.)

Read together Philippians 4:13 and 1 Nephi 3:7 and talk about how relying on Christ can help us do anything the Lord expects.

- What if a ward member is causing trouble in the ward and saying things that don't agree with Church teachings? (Verses 6–7.)

Read together 3 Nephi 11:29 and Alma 4:19 and

discuss what these passages add to Paul's counsel. Discuss the importance of keeping a safe distance from those who teach falsehoods.

- What if one of our ward friends borrows money but never pays us back? (Verses 8–12.)

Read together the following passages: Genesis 3:19 and Doctrine and Covenants 42:42 and discuss why we feel so much better about life and ourselves when we earn our own way. Then read Mosiah 4:16–23 and discuss how we should treat those who may not be able to support themselves.

- What if one of our ward friends needs our help but it takes a lot of our time? (Verse 13.)

Invite your family to share experiences of helping someone in need, especially when it was inconvenient, and how it made them feel. Read Mosiah 2:17–18 and talk about what our service means to our Heavenly Father.

- What if one of our friends is breaking the commandments and getting into trouble? (Verses 14–15.)

Discuss what it means to be a true friend. Share the following counsel: "Choose your friends carefully. They will greatly influence how you think and act, and even help determine the person you will become. Choose friends who share your values so you can strengthen and encourage each other in living high standards. A true friend will encourage you to be your best self." (*For the Strength of Youth,* 12.)

1 TIMOTHY

Unlike many of Paul's letters, which were written to congregations in a certain location, this epistle is written to a former missionary companion named Timothy. Elder Bruce R. McConkie asked, "Could he have been the equivalent of a stake president, or at least the presiding officer over a number of wards or their equivalents?" (Doctrinal New Testament Commentary, 3:69.) To learn more about Timothy, read the entry for "Timothy" in the Bible Dictionary, page 784.

1 TIMOTHY 1: PAUL COUNSELS TIMOTHY

1 Timothy 1:12–20
Jesus Christ is our Savior

 Ask family members to write answers to the following questions:

- What are five words that best describe what it feels like when you sin?
- What are five words that best describe how it feels when you repent?

Have family members share the words they wrote. Explain that the Bible and Book of Mormon give accounts of people's experiences with repentance. Read together 1 Timothy 1:12–17 and discuss the following questions as you read:

- What did Paul do wrong? (Verse 13.)
- To whom did he give the credit for being saved? (Verses 14–15.)
- What does that teach us about Christ? (Verse 16.)

Read Alma 36:12–21 with your family and compare Alma's experience to Paul's.

- What words or phrases describe how Alma's sins made him feel? (Verses 12–18.)
- What words describe how it felt to be forgiven? (Verses 19–21.)
- What do these experiences teach us about the power of the Atonement of Jesus Christ?

Sing the hymn "God Loved Us, So He Sent His Son." (*Hymns,* no. 187.) Share your testimony of the Atonement and your gratitude for the gift of repentance.

1 TIMOTHY 2: SPECIFIC COUNSEL FOR CHURCH MEMBERS

1 Timothy 2:1–10
How and for what should I pray?

Display a sheet of paper with the word *Prayer* on it. Have each family member suggest a different word to replace *prayer.* For example, *plead, cry unto the Lord, ask, call upon His name,* and so forth. Add their words to the paper. Ask your family:

- Why do you think there are so many different words and phrases that refer to prayer?
- What are some reasons we pray?
- According to Doctrine and Covenants 19:28, what kinds of prayer does God command?
- Give examples of each.

Have family members silently read 1 Timothy 2:1 and mark the different words Paul uses for prayer. Using your own knowledge and a dictionary, determine as a family the differences in these four kinds of prayer and how we would use them.

Have a family member read 1 Timothy 2:2–4. Ask:

- What did Paul specifically request the Saints to pray for?
- What reasons did he give that we should pray for these people?
- In addition to what Paul said, why do you think we should pray for these people?

Share with your family the following counsel on praying for government leaders: "I know of no better way to inculcate love for country than for parents to pray before their children for the land in which they live, invoking the blessings of the Almighty upon it that it may be preserved in liberty and peace. I know of no better way to build within the hearts of our children a much-needed respect for authority than remembering in the daily supplications of the family the leaders of our respective countries who carry the burdens of government." (Gordon B. Hinckley, *Ensign*, Feb. 1991, 4–5.)

Have family members silently read 1 Timothy 2:3–7. Ask, Is there anything in these verses that is a little confusing or different from what you think is true? Point out footnote 4*a*, which references a change made in the Joseph Smith Translation found in the Bible Appendix, page 810. Have a family member read the Joseph Smith Translation for 1 Timothy 2:4 and ask: How does this clarify what could be misunderstood in the King James Translation?

Assign someone to be a scribe. List together as a family all the things you learn about the Godhead from 1 Timothy 2:5–8. (Include the JST.) Ask:

- Why do you think it is important to know these things about the Father and the Son?
- Which of these truths is the least understood or the least thought about?
- What would happen if we knew, believed, and thought more often about these things?
- What do you think Paul is trying to tell the people about prayer in these verses?

Ask your family the following question and give them about 30 seconds to think of answers and write them in their journals: In what ways am I going to improve in prayer because of what we have discussed?

1 Timothy 2:11–15

What does Paul teach about women?

As you study 1 Timothy 2:11–15, your family may be troubled by some of the things taught regarding women. If so, share the following clarifications and commentary:

"The Greek word translated [in verse 11] as 'silence' means quietness, tranquility. . . . The intent of this passage [1 Timothy 2:11–15] is to counsel that women should support their leaders and not try to dominate or usurp [take] authority over those who are called of God as priesthood leaders." (Ogden and Skinner, *Acts through Revelation,* 215.)

Remind your family that in this letter Paul gave Timothy specific counsel regarding specific traditions practiced in that time and place. For example, Paul could also have counseled the men to support their leaders and not try to usurp authority, but apparently a different situation existed that specifically involved women.

The Lord's servants warn about trends, teachings, or doctrines that tend to pull men or women away from their God-given opportunities and responsibilities. Notice what Paul taught in 1 Timothy 2:15. What God-given blessing is given to women that men can never have?

Share the following quotations: "Nowhere does the doctrine of this Church declare that men are superior to women." (James E. Faust, *Ensign*, May 1988, 36.)

"Elder James E. Talmage (1862–1933) of the Quorum of the Twelve Apostles stated . . .

"'There are those who suggest that males are favored of the Lord because they are ordained to hold the priesthood. Anyone who believes this does not understand the great plan of happiness. The premortal and mortal natures of men and women were specified by God Himself, and it is simply not within His character to diminish the roles and responsibilities of any of His children.'" (M. Russell Ballard, *Ensign*, Apr. 2002, 66.)

1 TIMOTHY 3: THE QUALIFICATIONS OF A BISHOP

1 Timothy 3:1–7
How does a priesthood bearer become a bishop in the Church?

Invite your family members to tell who the bishop (or branch president) is and how they think he got that office. Have them read 1 Timothy 3:1. Ask:

- Why do you think Paul described the calling of a bishop as a good work?
- What are the blessings of being a bishop?

Ask your family to read 1 Timothy 3:2–7 and list what Paul says a bishop must be. (See also Titus 1:6–9). After your family has listed the qualifications for a bishop, ask if there are any words or phrases they do not understand. (Use the cross-references or a dictionary to help with words not understood. For example, look at footnote 6a to understand what the word *novice* means.) Ask:

- Why would the Lord prefer an experienced priesthood holder to be a bishop, over a new convert?
- Why do you think bishops should have the characteristics described by Paul?
- How have bishops been a blessing to us?

Discuss what you can do to prepare to be future Church leaders.

Read the following statement by Elder M. Russell Ballard: "No young man should aspire to a calling, but as surely as you are sitting in this priesthood meeting tonight, many of you will preside over wards, stakes, missions, quorums, and, of course, your own families. Priesthood training, my brethren, starts when a young man is ordained a deacon in the Aaronic Priesthood. You Aaronic Priesthood bearers need to understand that you are in training." (*Ensign*, May 1985, 41.)

Tell your family that bishops are called by inspiration and revelation. Explain that the stake president submits the bishop's name to the First Presidency and Quorum of the Twelve, who in turn approve and then invite the stake president to extend the call. Thus, the call comes from the Lord. Ask:

- How would you feel about receiving a call to serve as a bishop/branch president over your ward/branch?
- How should we approach every call we receive in this Church?
- How can we support and sustain Church leaders?

1 TIMOTHY 4: PAUL DESCRIBES LATTER-DAY APOSTASY

1 Timothy 4:1–6
Meat and marriage

Prior to the lesson, gather a branding iron (or a clothes iron or soldering iron), a wedding ring, and some meat. Show the objects to your family and ask what they think these items have in common. As you read together 1 Timothy 4:1–6, have your family look for how these objects relate to Paul's teachings. Ask:

- What time period is Paul referring to? (See verse 1.)
- What word is often used to describe "departing from the faith"? (See chapter heading.)
- What signs of apostasy does Paul describe in this letter to Timothy? (Verses 1–3.)

Hold up the iron and ask, What does it mean to have your "conscience seared with a hot iron"? Share the following insight: "There is a defense mechanism to discern between good and evil. It is called conscience. It is our spirit's natural response to the pain of sin, just like pain in our flesh is our body's natural response to a wound—even a small sliver. Conscience strengthens through use. . . . Those who have not exercised their conscience have their conscience seared with a hot iron. (1 Tim. 4:2.) A sensitive conscience is a sign of a healthy spirit." (James E. Faust, *Ensign*, May 1991, 68.) Ask: What can we do to keep our conscience from being seared?

Hold up the wedding ring and ask: What false doctrine does Paul say would be taught concerning marriage? Have family members write D&C 49:15–19 in the margin next to 1 Timothy 4:3 and then read together those verses. Ask, What is the correct doctrine for marriage?

Hold up the meat and ask, What is the correct doctrine for the eating of meat? (See D&C 89:12.)

Read 1 Timothy 4:6 and ask how you can keep from being deceived by false doctrines. Testify of the importance of following living prophets and being nourished by the good word of God.

1 Timothy 4:12–16
"Be thou an example"

 Invite a youth to stand and read aloud 1 Timothy 4:12. Ask:

- What do you think Paul meant when he said, "Let no man despise thy youth"?
- Have you had an experience where you were ignored because of your age?
- How does Paul suggest we can be examples of believers? (Verse 12.)

Share the following story from President N. Eldon Tanner: "The example we set before the world will determine, in large measure, whether we gain friends or enemies. It is most important that each of us live according to the standards of the Church, adhering to the precepts of the gospel and keeping the commandments of our Lord and Savior Jesus Christ, which have been so well defined for us.

"It is always impressive to read the stirring stories of what can be accomplished through the power of good example. I recently read a story which I would like to repeat. A nonmember relates that about ten years ago he was assistant manager of a discount store where they hired high school students to work the night shift. He stated:

"'I don't remember how I hired the first Mormon girl, who was about 16 or 17, and I don't even remember her name. But I'll never forget her example. She was unusually honest, dependable and clean-cut, yet those words can't fully describe her the way I'd like. Compared to the other kids, she really stood out.'

"Soon he hired one of her friends and found that she, too, was an exemplary employee. Both were friendly and helpful in their attitudes toward the other employees and the customers.

"'Pretty soon I tried to hire any more of their Mormon friends that I could find. Individually and collectively, they were the best kids I ever had work for me,' he said. 'Never was there a single occasion when any of them let me down or proved to be untrustworthy. They were the finest employees and fellow workers that anyone could want.'

"One night he wanted a pizza for dinner but was unable to leave the store, so one of the Mormon girls went to get it for him. When she returned he found she had been in a minor accident. He offered to pay for the damages to her car because she was on his errand, but she refused, saying it was her responsibility. He said: 'I didn't think many young people that age would have that kind of character and I've never forgotten it.'

"This man recently met some LDS missionaries through his son, has had some of the discussions, and has attended some meetings. 'I have found that the things I admired in those girls ten years ago hold true among the Mormon adults I have met,' he said. 'I like their emphasis on the family and they seem to me like the happiest group of people I have ever met.' (*Church News,* 9 May 1981, p. 7.)

"How wonderful . . . if all of us could make that kind of impression on those with whom we come in contact!" (*Ensign,* Dec. 1981, 2.)

Invite family members to share times when they have been influenced for good or when they have influenced another person for good.

After reading 1 Timothy 4:12, invite family members to think how they would respond to the following questions raised by Sister Elaine S. Dalton :

"Now the call to each of you is the same as the call the Apostle Paul made to his young friend Timothy: Be thou an example of the believers (1 Tim. 4:12). Will you do that? Will you show the world and the Lord that you believe by the way you dress, by the way you speak, by the way you respect your body, by the very purity of your lives?" (*Ensign,* May 2004, 112.)

Let your family know the value of being an example of a believer. Testify of those in your life who have influenced you for good.

1 TIMOTHY 5: CHURCH POLICY

1 Timothy 5:1–18
What is our responsibility to the poor?

 Ask your family:

- Have you ever been approached by someone asking for money?
- How did you feel? What did you do?
- Has there ever been a time in your life when you were in need of something and had to ask for help?
- How do you think Heavenly Father feels about His children who are poor?
- What do you think He would have us do for the poor?

Take turns reading 1 Timothy 5:1–18 and have your family look for, list, and mark principles concerning the poor. When you have finished, ask family members to report their findings. Make sure the following principles are discussed:

1. When the poor or widows need help, the family is to assist them. If the family is unable, then the Church will assist. (Verses 3–8, 16.)

2. In order to qualify for help from the Church, widows must
    a. be three score [60] years old. (Verse 9.)
    b. do "good works." (Verse 10, footnote *c*.)

3. Young widows are encouraged to marry and raise families. (Verses 13–14.)

4. Families with husbands in full-time missionary service can receive help. (Verses 17–18; see D&C 75:24.)

Ask:

- What are some other ways people are poor?
- How can people be poor physically, spiritually, emotionally, socially, or mentally?

Share this story by President Thomas S. Monson with your family: "I yearned as only a boy can yearn for an electric train. My desire was not to receive the economical and everywhere-to-be-found wind-up model train, but rather one that operated through the miracle of electricity.

"The times were those of economic depression, yet Mother and Dad, through some sacrifice . . .

presented to me on Christmas morning a beautiful electric train. For hours I operated the transformer, watching the engine first pull its cars forward, then push them backward around the track.

"Mother entered the living room and said to me that she had purchased a wind-up train for Widow Hansen's boy, Mark, who lived down the lane. I asked if I could see the train. The engine was short and blocky—not long and sleek like the expensive model I had received.

"However, I did take notice of an oil tanker car which was part of his inexpensive set. My train had no such car, and pangs of envy began to be felt. I put up such a fuss that Mother succumbed to my pleadings and handed me the oil tanker car. She said, 'If you need it more than Mark, you take it.' I put it with my train set and felt pleased with the result.

"Mother and I took the remaining cars and the engine down to Mark Hansen. The young boy was a year or two older than I. He had never anticipated such a gift and was thrilled beyond words. He wound the key in his engine, it not being electric like mine, and was overjoyed as the engine and two cars, plus a caboose, went around the track.

"Mother wisely asked, 'What do you think of Mark's train, Tommy?'

"I felt a keen sense of guilt and became very much aware of my selfishness. I said to Mother, 'Wait just a moment—I'll be right back.' . . .

"I ran to our home, picked up the oil tanker car plus an additional car of my own, ran back down the lane to the Hansen home, and said joyfully to Mark, 'We forgot to bring two cars which belong to your train.'

"Mark coupled the two extra cars to his set. I watched the engine make its labored way around the track and felt a supreme joy difficult to describe and impossible to forget." (*Ensign,* May 1977, 2–4.)

Ask:

- Why do you think Elder Monson felt guilty?
- How did he respond to his guilt?
- What can we do to follow his example?
- Why does the Church give humanitarian service?
- Why will we be more successful as missionaries when the people we teach are not starving?

• What can we do to help people who are "poor" mentally, spiritually, emotionally, or socially?

1 TIMOTHY 6: INSTRUCTIONS TO SAINT-SLAVES IN EPHESUS

1 Timothy 6:1–8
Be content

Ask family members if they have ever read a book about slavery or studied that issue. Have them share what they know about slavery. Explain that Paul sent instructions to Timothy who was then in Ephesus, concerning certain converts to Christianity who were slaves. Elder Bruce R. McConkie explained, "The social structure which kept them in bondage was outside the power of the Ephesian Saints to change, . . . Paul thus has no alternative but to recognize their state and counsel them how to live under it. Slavery as such is in fact abhorrent to gospel standards [D&C 101:79]." (*Doctrinal New Testament Commentary,* 2:522.)

Have someone read 1 Timothy 6:1–3 and ask:

• What four guidelines does Paul want Timothy to teach the Saints who are "under the yoke" (in bondage) in Ephesus?
• What is the reason Paul gives in verse 1 for this counsel?

Ask half your family to imagine being slaves and the other half to imagine being Apostles speaking to slaves, while you read 1 Timothy 6:4–6, 8 aloud. Have your family mark in one color all of the attributes Paul encourages Saints to acquire (verses 6, 8) and with another color all of the attributes Paul warns against (verses 4–5). Ask:

• Why do you think Paul encourages these Saints in bondage to be content with their situation? (See verses 6, 8 and Elder McConkie's statement above.)
• Where does contentment, for any situation or circumstance, come from? (Verse 6.)
• Could you be content in bondage?
• How would it help if an Apostle asked you to be content?

• Why are the attributes in verses 6 and 8 worth more than silver and gold?
• How would obtaining these attributes help you?

Read together Alma 29:1–3 and talk about what Alma says we should do with righteous desires. Share Elder Neal Maxwell's comments: "Nevertheless, we are to do what we can within our allotted 'acreage,' while still using whatever stretch there may be in any tethers. Within what is allotted to us, we can have spiritual contentment . . . signifying the adequate presence of attributes such as love, hope, meekness, patience, and submissiveness." (*Ensign,* May 2000, 72.)

Ask family members what they see as restrictions in the "acreage" of their lives and what they can do to "stretch" themselves and behave with "spiritual contentment" in a godly manner.

Ask the half of your family who imagined themselves as slaves to share their feelings about Paul's counsel. Ask the half of your family who imagined themselves as Apostles why they think Paul gave this particular counsel and if there is any additional counsel they would offer.

1 Timothy 6:7–19
The love of money

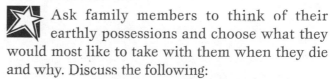

Ask family members to think of their earthly possessions and choose what they would most like to take with them when they die and why. Discuss the following:

• What can we take with us when we leave this earth? (D&C 130:18–19.)
• Since we can take knowledge and intelligence with us, what should we be doing?

Empty all the money in your wallet or purse onto the floor or table. Ask someone to read 1 Timothy 6:7, 9–12, 17–21 aloud and then ask:

• Why is the "love of money" evil? (Verse 10.)

Share President Gordon B. Hinckley's statement: "It is the love of money and the love of those things which money can buy which destroys us. We all need money to supply our needs. But it is the love of it which hurts us, which warps our values, which leads us away from spiritual things and fosters selfishness and greed." (*Ensign,* May 1997, 49.)

- How can we stay focused on the Lord rather than on temptations, snares, and foolish, hurtful lusts which can accompany wealth? (See verses 11–12, 17–19; see Matthew 6:19–21.)
- Whom does Paul say we can trust? (Verse 17.)
- What does Paul suggest we be rich in? (Verse 18; see D&C 42:29–31.)

- How does providing for the poor build a "good foundation . . . on eternal life"?
- What should we do with our riches?

Make a plan to contribute to Church humanitarian efforts or in some other specific way bless those who are less fortunate.

2 TIMOTHY

The Bible Dictionary tells us that "2 Timothy was written during Paul's second imprisonment, shortly before his martyrdom" ("2 Timothy," 748.) Realizing that his ministry was about to end, the Apostle Paul gives some last counsel to his faithful companion, Timothy. The letter encourages Timothy to be diligent in his work at Ephesus and shows Paul's trust in this devoted disciple. The theme of the letter seems to be one of faithfully enduring present trials and those tests that lie ahead. Writing about 2 Timothy, Elder Bruce R. McConkie said:

"In the four short chapters of Second Timothy, our friend Paul—literary craftsman and master theologian that he is—teaches, exhorts, prophesies and testifies as few but he have ever done.

"Here we find him making the announcement that He who is the Resurrection and the Life hath abolished death and brought life and immortality to light through the gospel.

"Here we read the comforting assurances that Christ hath called his saints with an holy calling, and shall yet call them to reign with him in eternal glory.

"Here we find persuasive pleas to be strong in the faith, to keep the commandments, to shun contention, to seek godliness, to come off victorious in the war with the world. . . .

"Plain words are also found as to the need and purpose of holy writ, together with a solemn charge that God's ministers teach there from.

"And then the Apostle testifies that he himself shall have eternal life, as well as all saints who believe and obey." (Doctrinal New Testament Commentary, 3:97.)

2 TIMOTHY 1: BE FAITHFUL TO THE END

2 Timothy 1:1–7
Faith is the opposite of fear and doubt

Tell your family you are going to play the opposites game. Explain that you will say a single word and the rest of the family must say an opposite for it. Use the following words:

Words		Opposites
Black	-	(White)
Hot	-	(Cold)
Male	-	(Female)
Wet	-	(Dry)
Good	-	(Evil or bad)
Obedience	-	(Disobedience)
Faith	-	(????)

To help your family better understand the opposite of faith, take turns reading Paul's words to Timothy in 2 Timothy 1:1–7. Ask:

- What words describe how Paul felt about Timothy? (Verses 1–4.)
- How did Timothy acquire his great faith in the gospel? (Verses 5–6.)
- What influence can parents, grandparents, and priesthood leaders have upon our faith?
- According to verse 7, what word did Paul use that would be the opposite of faith?

It might be helpful to share the following thoughts: "Where doubt and uncertainty are there faith is not, nor can it be. For doubt and faith do not exist in the same person at the same time; so that persons whose minds are under doubts and fears cannot have unshaken confidence; and where unshaken confidence is not there faith is weak; and where faith is weak the persons will not be able to contend against all the opposition, tribulations, and afflictions which they will have to encounter in order to be heirs of God, and joint heirs with Christ Jesus; and they will grow weary in their minds, and the adversary will have power over them and destroy them." (Smith, *Lectures on Faith*, 6:12.)

Give each family member a sheet of paper and a pencil. Invite them to silently read Mormon 9:27 and Doctrine and Covenants 6:36 and then write a sentence that teaches a doctrine about faith and fear. Discuss the following questions:

- What message did you find in these verses about fear and faith?
- According to 2 Timothy 1:5, who did Timothy look to for an example of faith?
- Who do you look to?

Discuss as a family how you might develop the faith necessary so others can look to you as an example of faith.

2 Timothy 1:12–18
Let us continue in sound doctrine

 List on a sheet of paper the following references in order (leaving out the answers):

- 1 Timothy 1:12 (Be not ashamed of the gospel)
- 1 Timothy 1:13 (Hold fast to sound words and doctrine)
- 1 Timothy 1:14 (Be worthy of the Holy Ghost)
- 1 Timothy 1:15 (Beware of being "turned away" into apostasy)
- 1 Timothy 1:16–18 (Be obedient and endure to the end)

Show the list to your family and tell them that in each passage Paul teaches a single point of doctrine. Assign each of the passages to family members and have them read their passage and find that doctrine. Explain that they will also need to share how they can apply that doctrine in their lives. When

they are finished, have them share what they learned.

Testify that the more good we fill our lives with the fewer chances there will be for evil to creep in.

2 TIMOTHY 2: COUNSEL FOR ENDURING FAITHFULLY

2 Timothy 2:7–13
Why do we endure?

Share the following story with your family: "In the early days of the Church, Stillman Pond was a member of the second quorum of the seventy in Nauvoo. He was an early convert to the Church, having come from Hubbardston, Massachusetts. Like others, he and his wife, Maria, and their children were harassed and driven out of Nauvoo. In September 1846 they became part of the great western migration. The early winter that year brought extreme hardships, including malaria, cholera, and consumption. The family was visited by all three of these diseases.

"Maria contracted consumption, and all of the children were stricken with malaria. Three of the children died while moving through the early snows. Stillman buried them on the plains. Maria's condition worsened because of the grief, pain, and the fever of malaria. She could no longer walk. Weakened and sickly, she gave birth to twins. They were named Joseph and Hyrum, and both died within a few days.

"The Stillman Pond family arrived at Winter Quarters, and like many other families, they suffered bitterly while living in a tent. The death of five children coming across the plains to Winter Quarters was but a beginning.

"The journal of Horace K. and Helen Mar Whitney verifies the following regarding four more of the children of Stillman Pond who perished:

"'On Wednesday, the 2nd of December 1846, Laura Jane Pond, age 14 years, . . . died of chills and fever.' Two days later on 'Friday, the 4th of December 1846, Harriet M. Pond, age 11 years, . . . died with chills.' Three days later, 'Monday, the 7th of December, 1846, Abigail A. Pond, age 18 years,

. . . died with chills.' Just five weeks later, 'Friday, the 15th of January, 1847, Lyman Pond, age 6 years, . . . died with chills and fever.'

"Four months later, on May 17, 1847, his wife, Maria Davis Pond, also died. Crossing the plains, Stillman Pond lost nine children and a wife. He became an outstanding colonizer in Utah and later became a leader in the quorums of the seventy. Having lost these nine children and his wife in crossing the plains, Stillman Pond did not lose his faith. He did not quit. He went forward." (James E. Faust, *Ensign,* Feb. 2006, 6–7.)

Ask your family: What do you think motivated Stillman Pond to endure so faithfully?

Remind your family that the Apostle Paul endured many difficulties. In addition, he was writing this epistle to Timothy at a time of persecution and false teachings when many Church members were finding it difficult to stay true to the faith. Read together 2 Timothy 2:7–13 and consider what he says about enduring. After reading the verses, together make a list of truths that motivated Paul to faithfully endure. Begin each item on the list with, "He believed that . . ." Look at the list together and ask: Which one of these truths has helped you to faithfully endure challenges and how?

2 Timothy 2:14–26
What kind of vessel?

Show your family a variety of bowls, cups, or other containers that could hold and carry water. Some should be big, some small, and some damaged so they will leak. Ask:

- Which of these vessels do you think is the most useful?
- What makes a useful vessel?

Have your family read 2 Timothy 2:20–21. (See footnotes.) Ask:

- What does Paul say about vessels?
- What is he comparing vessels to?
- Which of the vessels placed before us would you compare yourself to?
- Which of these vessels would you like to be? Why?

Have family members read 2 Timothy 2:14–16, 19, 22–26 to themselves, and make a note of everything Paul says would make a person a useful vessel "for the master's use." (Verse 21.) Appoint one person to be a scribe. Have family members share something from their lists and have the scribe record it on a "Useful Vessel" list for the family. For each idea shared, have the person explain how it might apply to the family (such as, "We could be more patient with each other's weaknesses").

2 TIMOTHY 3: GODLY LIVING IN THE LAST DAYS

2 Timothy 3:1–9
Are we in the "last days" yet?

 Ask your family:

- Have you ever been on a trip and asked, "Are we there yet?"
- Why is it nice to know how close you are to a particular destination?
- What destination or time period is Paul prophesying about in 2 Timothy 3:1?
- How would you answer the question "Are we in the last days yet?"
- How do you know?

Have a family member read 2 Timothy 3:2–9 aloud. Stop them every time they read a word or phrase describing conditions in the last days and ask, Are we there yet? Ask family members to give examples they have seen of modern people or events that remind them of the word or phrase you saw in those verses. (You may need to use the footnotes for clarification on difficult words. Also note that according to Jewish tradition, the two men mentioned in verse 8 were two priests of Pharaoh who contended with Moses.) Ask:

- Which of those aspects of our day seem to be the biggest problem and what can we do to overcome them?
- Which one does our family need to work on?

Have everyone set a goal to improve in one area and write about it in their journals. Challenge your family to be especially faithful, knowing we are living in the last days.

2 Timothy 3:10–12
Do righteous people ever have any problems?

Ask your family to pretend they have a family friend who has recently joined the Church and that the following excerpt is part of a letter from that person:

"Things have not been easy lately. It seems the harder I try to do what is right, the more trials and persecution I have. I thought that if I did what was right, things would work out and life would be easier. I just don't understand."

Have your family share different responses they would give this friend. Ask them to look for further ideas as they read 2 Timothy 3:10–12. Ask:

- Although the Apostle Paul was trying to serve God, what did he say about his life?
- What had Paul's challenges taught him? (See verse 10.)
- What have you learned from your challenges?
- How did Paul's character traits compare with the character traits in verses 2–7?
- What did the Lord do for Paul? (See Verse 11.)
- How has the Lord done the same for you?
- How do you feel about what Paul said in verse 12? Why?
- Who are some of the best and most righteous people who ever lived on the earth and what kinds of trials did they experience?
- How did their trials help them become the great people they are?

Share the following statement from the Prophet Joseph Smith: "I am like a huge, rough stone rolling down from a high mountain; and the only polishing I get is when some corner gets rubbed off by coming in contact with something else . . . all hell knocking off a corner here and a corner there. Thus I will become a smooth and polished shaft in the quiver of the Almighty." (*Teachings of the Prophet Joseph Smith*, 304.)

2 Timothy 3:13–17
Where can you get the strength to withstand the world?

Bring to family scripture study some newspaper headlines about the sins and wickedness in the world. Talk to your family about how the world has changed in the last fifty years. Have your family read 2 Timothy 3:13 and ask:

- Do you think the Lord knew that the world would get more wicked?
- Do you think the Lord has an idea how best to get through difficult times?

Have your family read verses 14–15 to find what Paul told Timothy to do to be strong in hard times. Ask:

- How do the scriptures give us the strength we need to overcome evil influences?
- Why should children study the scriptures?
- What advantage does scripture study bring?

Read verse 16 and ask:

- How does the Joseph Smith Translation footnote change the verse?
- What makes something scripture according to this verse?

Have your family read 2 Timothy 3:16–17 and Doctrine and Covenants 68:3–4. Discuss these questions:

- How can the scriptures make us "thoroughly furnished"?
- What are the verses saying we should do if we want to be ready to answer someone's questions or concerns about the Church?

2 TIMOTHY 4: PAUL'S LAST WORDS

2 Timothy 4:1–5
Do we have "itching ears"?

Invite a family member to read the first sentence of the chapter heading of 2 Timothy 4. Have your family read 2 Timothy 4:1–5 to discover more about Paul's challenge to preach the gospel and the day of apostasy. Discuss the following questions:

- What did Paul encourage Timothy to do?
- What words and phrases help you understand what an "apostasy" is? (Verses 3–4.)
- What did Paul say Church members would start to do with the doctrine? (Verses 3–4.)
- What does it means to have "itching ears"?

- In what ways do some Church members today have "itching ears"?
- Why don't Church leaders just tell us what we want to hear?

Discuss as a family what you can do to avoid turning away from the truth into apostasy.

2 Timothy 4:6–8
Have you "fought a good fight"?

 Invite family members to bring their journals to scripture study. Have them imagine they are nearing the end of their life. Ask them to write in their journals a message they would want to leave for those they love.

Explain to your family that 2 Timothy 4 is believed to be Paul's last written words as he sat in a prison in Rome awaiting execution. Read 2 Timothy 4:6–8 and ask:

- If you were Paul, what do you think would be your feelings at this time?
- How can you tell that Paul knew he would soon die?
- How do you think Paul felt about his service to God?
- What words show that Paul did not fear death?
- What can we do to have a similar confidence when we are near death?

Share the following statement on these verses from the Prophet Joseph Smith: "No one, we presume, will doubt the faithfulness of Paul to the end. None will say that he did not keep the faith, that he did not fight the good fight, that he did not preach and persuade to the last. And what was he to receive? A crown of righteousness. And what shall others receive who do not labor faithfully and continue to the end? . . . Reflect for a moment, brethren, and enquire whether you would consider yourselves worthy [for] a seat at the marriage feast with Paul and others like him if you had been unfaithful. Had you not fought the good fight and

kept the faith, could you expect to receive? . . . Here, then, we understand that Paul rested his hope in Christ, because he had kept the faith and loved his appearing; and from his hand he had a promise of receiving a crown of righteousness." (*History of the Church,* 2:19–20.)

Have your family members look at what they wrote in their journals. Invite them to make any changes or additions to their message if they would like to.

2 Timothy 4:9–22
Some principles for living

Ask your family:

- How hard would it be to do what is right if your friends say they will leave you because of it?
- Why would it be so hard?
- How would you feel about a friend who stood by you?

Have your family scan 2 Timothy 4:9–22 for the names of Paul's friends. Determine which ones supported him and which ones betrayed him. Ask: Who was Paul's greatest friend?

Write the four statements listed below on a large sheet of paper. (Leave out the answers.) Invite family members to search these verses again and then write which verses contain the principles.

1. We should leave judgment in God's hands. (Verses 14–15.)

2. Even when others choose not to stand with us in time of need, the Lord will always be with us. (Verses 16–17.)

3. We should love the things of God rather than the things of the world. (Verses 9–10.)

4. The Lord delivers His faithful children from evil and saves them. (Verse 18.)

Discuss the following questions:

- How can I be a faithful friend?
- Why is the Lord our greatest friend?

TITUS

Paul wrote this letter to Titus, one of his converts and missionary companions. Titus had been left to care for the churches on the island of Crete. The letter gives him instructions concerning his ministry in dealing with opposition, warnings of false teachings, and counsel on how the Saints should live following baptism. Elder Bruce R. McConkie explained: "Titus is the epistle of obedience. Paul seems increasingly impressed by the Spirit to counsel his beloved Titus, . . . of the overpowering need to walk in paths of truth and righteousness." (Doctrinal New Testament Commentary, 3:119.)

TITUS 1: LIVING IN THE WORLD WITHOUT BEING OF THE WORLD

Titus 1:5–16
Living righteously following baptism

Have family members turn to Map 13 (in both pre-1999 and post-1999 printings) in the map section of their Bibles and find the island of Crete. Explain that this is where Titus was assigned as a Church leader. Invite your family to search Titus 1:5–16, looking for what Paul counseled Titus to do and why.

As in Paul's previous letters, you may need to look up definitions of words that you do not understand. Use the footnotes or Bible Dictionary to do this activity. Close by letting your family know of the value of living the commandments following baptism.

Titus 1:7–9
Your bishop

Ask your family to make a list of as many wonderful qualities they can think of that your bishop possesses. Read Titus 1:7–9 aloud and have your family identify and share what they have learned. Ask:

- How would these qualities allow a bishop to better serve others?
- How do you think the Lord feels about those who serve as bishops?

Invite each family member to write a short note of gratitude to your bishop. Help them develop a greater love and appreciation for him by sharing stories of how your bishop has helped your family.

TITUS 2: SAINTS SHOULD LIVE RIGHTEOUSLY

Titus 2:1–15
Qualities for young and old

Divide a large piece of paper into four columns. Write the following headings: Old men, Old women, Young men, and Young women. Tell your family that in a letter to Titus, the Apostle Paul describes qualities that these different groups of people should possess. Assign family members to read and research each of the groups in Titus 2:1–8 and then list on the paper what they find. Compare lists and discuss the different qualities. Tell your family the footnotes in the scriptures can be helpful in understanding the meaning of some of the words. In addition, the following definitions may be helpful:

Sober—"characterized by reason, sanity, or self-control; showing mental and emotional balance."

Grave or Gravity—"requiring serious thought," "solemnity . . . of manner or character; earnestness."

Temperate—"moderate in one's actions, speech, etc; self-restrained."

Tell your family that Titus 2:12–14 combines the groups and describes attributes that all Saints, old and young, should possess. Have family members identify those attributes and add them to the bottom of the paper. Ask:

- What kind of people does Christ want us to be?
- What does Paul mean when he says we should be "a peculiar people"?
- How can we be a peculiar people?
- What does to be "zealous of good works" mean?

Have a family member read Titus 2:1 aloud and ask what Paul calls these teachings in this chapter. (Sound doctrine.) Share the following statement from Elder Boyd K. Packer: "True doctrine, understood, changes attitudes and behavior. The study of the doctrines of the gospel will improve behavior quicker than a study of behavior will improve behavior." (*Ensign,* May 2004, 79.)

Bear testimony of the importance of developing Christlike attributes and invite family members to review the list in their own category. Have everyone choose one of the qualities Paul mentions in this chapter and improve it.

TITUS 3: SALVATION THROUGH GRACE AND WORKS

Titus 3:1–11
Are we saved by grace?

 Explain to your family that in the William Shakespeare play *Hamlet,* we find Hamlet, who is concerned about death, saying, "To be, or not to be, that is the question." In Titus 3 we will ask the same question but with a slight twist: "To do, or not to do, that is the question." Take turns reading Titus 3:1–11 with your family members and make a list of things Paul said we should do and should not do in order to gain salvation. After discussing what they find, invite someone to reread verse 5 and discuss these questions:

- Do our righteous works bring us salvation?
- What role do righteous works have in our salvation?
- How important do you think it is to do the things Paul taught in this chapter? Why?

Share the following quotation:

"There is no salvation in good works as such. That is: There are no good works which men may do which—standing alone—will cause them to be resurrected or to gain eternal life. Immortality and eternal life come through the atonement of Christ, the one being a free gift, the other being offered freely to all who will be baptized and who then keep the commandments." (McConkie, *Doctrinal New Testament Commentary,* 3:126–27.)

Have your family look again at the end of verse 5 for what Paul said we must do in order for Christ to accept our "works of righteousness." Make sure they find what "washing of regeneration" and "renewing of the Holy Ghost" means. (See footnotes 5*c* and *d*.) Share the following insight from Elder Bruce R. McConkie:

"Baptism in water, so named to signify that baptized converts are regenerated; that is, they become new again spiritually; they become like little children, alive in Christ and without sin." (*Doctrinal New Testament Commentary,* 3:127.)

Help your family understand that the only way we can be saved is through the grace of God after all we can do. (See 2 Nephi 25:23.)

PHILEMON

Like the epistles to Timothy and Titus, the epistle to Philemon is a letter from Paul to a specific individual. "Philemon was apparently a rich and faithful member of the Church, a resident of Colossae." He had a slave, named Onesimus (Greek, "useful"), who had run away and perhaps even taken things from his master. (Philemon 1:18.) Though Paul was under house arrest in Rome, he somehow met Onesimus and converted him to Christ and the Church. Paul wrote this letter to Philemon and asked Onesimus to carry it to his master. It should be noted that "slavery, or servitude, was not viewed as evil by the Judaeo-Christian culture at the time of Christ; it was an institution supported by Roman law. Slaves actually constituted twenty to thirty percent of the population of the empire. Onesimus had done something illegal in running away, and the punishment for runaway slaves was usually death." (Ogden and Skinner, Acts through Revelation, *197–98.) This understanding makes this letter all the more impressive as Paul encourages Philemon to grant Onesimus his freedom.*

PHILEMON 1: FROM SERVANT TO BROTHER

Philemon 1:1–25
Receiving and extending mercy

Share with your family the background to this epistle. Explain to them that since slavery was accepted and common in that day, Paul could be in even more legal trouble if he did not encourage Onesimus to return to his master. Only a slave's master could lawfully provide freedom. Ask:

- What kind of feelings do you suppose Onesimus had at this time—both as a slave who had done wrong and as a new convert to Christ?
- Why do think that Paul's request might have been hard for Philemon to accept?

Read together Philemon 1:1–7, and ask:

- What do you learn about Philemon from these verses?
- Knowing what Paul is going to ask of Philemon, which words or phrases used by Paul might help prepare Philemon's heart to consider Paul's request? (Verses 5–7.)
- In what ways do you think Paul can relate to Onesimus's slavery? (Hint: In what ways was Paul a slave before his conversion to Christ?)

Have your family silently read Philemon 1:8–14. Ask:

- According to verses 8–9, what could Paul have done but chose not to do?
- How does verse 14 further show Paul's respect for Philemon's agency? (Footnote 14a.)

Remind your family that Onesimus means "useful" or "profitable." Invite them to scan Philemon 1:15–21 and look for ways Onesimus represents each of us, Paul, and the Savior. Discuss the following questions:

- In what way does Paul try to convince Philemon that extending mercy and freedom to Onesimus would be "profitable"?
- How might Paul be compared to the Savior? (Compare Paul's pleading for Onesimus to Jesus' pleading for us; see D&C 45:3–5.)

- How would you feel if you were Onesimus and read what Paul said about you?
- If tradition is correct, and Onesimus later became the bishop in Ephesus (see David R. Seely, "Unprofitable Servant to Beloved Brother," in *Studies in Scripture,* 6:174), how do you think the things he learned from this experience helped him in that calling?

Invite your family to quietly consider how they can apply the example of the Apostle Paul in their relationships with others.

HEBREWS

The Apostle Paul wrote this epistle about 60 A.D. to the Hebrew members of the Church probably living around Jerusalem. Jewish converts were then having a difficult time understanding how Christ and His gospel superseded the teachings contained in the law of Moses. Paul uses a well-composed outline in this book to show the superiority of Christ over angels (see chapters 1–2), over Moses (see chapters 3–4), over the high priests (see chapters 5–6), over Melchizedek and Abraham (see chapters 7–8), and over the temple and its burnt offerings (see chapters 9–10). The last chapters of Hebrews show that faithful living brings God's blessings.

HEBREWS 1: "SO MUCH BETTER THAN THE ANGELS"

Hebrews 1:1–4
What are some incredible characteristics about the Savior?

Show your family members a picture of a beloved relative or friend. Ask them to share what they think of when they see a picture of this special person.

Next show your family a picture of the Savior. Ask them to identify their favorite character traits of Jesus. Talk about why they perceive the Savior that way and what stories from the Savior's life illustrate that trait.

Ask a family member to read the introductory paragraph above. Ask what it teaches about Paul's purpose for writing this book. Have your family read Hebrews 1:1–3 and identify as many attributes of the Savior as they can find in those verses. Ask them to mark their findings. You may want to make sure they note the following:

- The Father speaks to us through his Son.
- Jesus has or will receive all that the Father has.
- Jesus created the world.
- Christ's life and appearance teach us what the Father is like in every way.
- Christ's power keeps all things going.
- It is through Christ that our sins are removed.

- Jesus is next to God in glory.

Share the following statement by Elder Bruce R. McConkie:

"So the Son appears and is in all respects like his Father; and conversely, the Father looks and acts and is in all respects like the Son. Their physical appearance is the same, both possess the attributes of godliness in their fulness and perfection; each would do and say precisely the same thing under the same circumstances. (*Mormon Doctrine,* 294–95.) Hence the . . . statement: 'He that hath seen me hath seen the Father.'

"Thus, God was in Christ manifesting himself to the world—a gracious and condescending thing for the Eternal Father to do, for thereby men could come to know him and to gain that eternal life which such knowledge brings." (*Doctrinal New Testament Commentary,* 1:731.)

Share with your family your feelings or testimony of the power and greatness of Jesus Christ.

HEBREWS 2: CHRIST IS GREATER THAN THE ANGELS

Hebrews 2:1–18
Christ's preeminence over the angels

 Play a game together called "Stump or Be Stumped." To play this game you will need some treats for rewards. Have family members silently read the chapter. Pair young children with older family members. Family members can win a treat by either

A. Asking a question you can't answer correctly.

or

B. Correctly answering a question you ask.

Here are questions you can ask your family:

- What should we be careful not to let "slip"?
- "How shall we escape, if we neglect so great _____" (Salvation; verse 3.)
- How does God bear witness? (Verse 4.)
- What was man made a little lower than? (Angels; see footnote 7*a*.)
- What did Jesus do for us? (Verse 9.)
- Who is the captain of our salvation?
- How was Jesus made perfect? (Verse 10.)
- How can we become "one" with Jesus? (Verses 11–13.)
- How does Christ destroy the devil? (Verses 14–15.)
- Who had the power of death? (The devil; verse 14.)
- Because Jesus suffered and was tempted, what can He do for us? (Verses 17–18.)

Invite each family member to ask additional questions from the chapter. Share your testimony of the divinity of Christ.

HEBREWS 3: JESUS CHRIST IS GREATER THAN ANY PROPHET

Hebrews 3:1–19
What is God's rest?

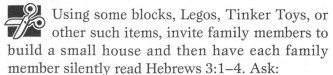 Using some blocks, Legos, Tinker Toys, or other such items, invite family members to build a small house and then have each family member silently read Hebrews 3:1–4. Ask:

- Why do people build houses?
- Which deserves more honor, the house or the builder?
- How is a house built by God greater than one built by men?
- To the Jews, Moses was a great builder, but who was greater than he?

- How is Jesus Christ greater than all men?

Read together Hebrews 3:5–11 and discuss the following questions:

- What great prophet was faithful "in all his house"? (Moses.)
- What can we do to rest safely in God's house?
- Why were the ancient children of Israel not allowed to enter into God's rest? (Verses 8–11.)
- What does it mean to "enter into my rest"? (Verse 11.)

Share the following explanation by President Joseph F. Smith: "The ancient prophets speak of 'entering into God's rest'; what does it mean? To my mind, it means entering into the knowledge and love of God, having faith in his purpose and in his plan, to such an extent that we know we are right, and that we are not hunting for something else, we are not disturbed by every wind of doctrine, or by the cunning and craftiness of men who lie in wait to deceive. . . . The man who has reached that degree of faith in God that all doubt and fear have been cast from him, he has entered into 'God's rest.'" (*Gospel Doctrine*, 58.)

Invite your family to silently read Hebrews 3:12–19, looking for ways we can avoid living in a modern-day wilderness. Ask:

- What counsel or commandments are given to help us be at "rest" with Heavenly Father?
- What part can "unbelief" play in our inability to enjoy God's rest?
- According to Mosiah 2:41, what blessings does God offer His children for obedience? (Have your family write Mosiah 2:41 in the margin next to Hebrews 3:12.)

Share how Father in Heaven has blessed you as you've lived his commandments.

HEBREWS 4: ENTERING INTO THE REST OF THE LORD

Hebrews 4:1–11
How do we enter His rest?

 With quiet music playing in the background, have everyone lie down and rest for a few moments and then share how it feels. Have family members scan Hebrews 4:1–11 and mark the word *rest* each time they find it. Ask how many times *rest* appears in those verses.

Remind your family that you talked about what God's rest is when you discussed Hebrews 3. Now, as you read together Hebrews 4:1–11, have your family look for insights about how we can enter into the Lord's rest. Tell your family to write D&C 84:23–24 in the margin of their scriptures and then have someone turn to that reference and read it aloud. Ask:

- How do these verses define "rest"?
- Why didn't the children of Israel enter God's rest in Moses' day? (See D&C 84:24.)
- According to what you have read, how can a person "enter into the Lord's rest" in this life? Share this insight: Our knowledge of the truth of the gospel of Jesus Christ is one way mortals can enter the Lord's rest. "From the Prophet Joseph Smith we . . . learn that 'God has . . . a time . . . appointed . . . when He will bring all His subjects, who have obeyed His voice and kept His commandments, into His celestial rest. This rest is of such perfection and glory, that man has need of a preparation before he can, according to the law of that kingdom, enter it and enjoy its blessings. . . . God has given certain laws to the human family, which, if observed, are sufficient to prepare them to inherit this rest.' [*Teachings of the Prophet Joseph Smith*, sel. Joseph Fielding Smith (1976), 54.]" (*Ensign*, May 2005, 16.)

  Elder Nelson added: "[God's] hope for us is eternal life. We qualify for it by obedience to covenants and ordinances of the temple—for ourselves, our families, and our ancestors. We cannot be made perfect without them. We cannot *wish* our way into the presence of God. We are to obey the laws upon which those blessings are predicated. [See D&C 128:15, 18; 130:20–21.]" (*Ensign*, May 2005, 18.)

- What does it mean to enter into the Lord's rest in the life to come? (Elder Bruce R. McConkie also taught: "The rest of the Lord, in eternity, is to inherit eternal life, to gain the fulness of the Lord's glory." (*Mormon Doctrine*, 633.)

Have family members mark footnote 3a in Hebrews 4:3 and then read the Joseph Smith Translation of Hebrews 4:3 in the Bible Appendix, 811. Ask:

- What keeps a person from entering into God's rest?
- What do we need to do to be worthy to enter God's rest? (See 3 Nephi 27:19; see also Alma 13:12–13.)

Hebrews 4:14–16

Where can we turn for peace?

Ask family members to think of times of trial and difficulty when they felt that no one could understand what they were going through. Tell your family you are going to read the words of a hymn that asks questions and then gives answers. Read the first two verses of "Where Can I Turn for Peace?" (*Hymns*, no. 129.)

1. *Where can I turn for peace?*
   Where is my solace
   When other sources cease to make me whole?
   When with a wounded heart, anger, or malice,
   I draw myself apart,
   Searching my soul?

2. *Where, when my aching grows,*
   Where, when I languish,
   Where, in my need to know, where can I run?
   Where is the quiet hand to calm my anguish?
   Who, who can understand? [Have a family
       member give an answer.]
   He, only One.

Ask who "He, only One" refers to. As you read together Hebrews 4:14–16, have your family look for why He can understand our sorrows and our grief. Ask:

- Are there any trials we face that the Savior does not understand?
- Are there any sorrows for which the Lord cannot give comfort? Why?
- What do we need to do to take full advantage of what "He" offers?

Share an experience when the Savior brought you peace, comfort, or understanding.

HEBREWS 5: PRIESTHOOD AUTHORITY

Hebrews 5:1–4
Priesthood authority comes from God

Ask family members if they have ever played a game where they pretended to be a policeman, a judge, or a fireman. Ask:

- What would happen if someone actually impersonated a police officer, a military officer, or a judge?
- Why would it be wrong or even dangerous for us to impersonate one of these people?
- What is the difference between a real police officer and someone who just pretends to be? (Authority.)

Invite a priesthood holder in your family to find and share their priesthood line of authority. If you do not have access to one, use this example:

Melvin Jay Wilcox was ordained a high priest by E. LeGrand Bindrup—Jan. 30, 1972

E. LeGrand Bindrup was ordained a high priest by LeGrand Richards—Feb. 24, 1962

LeGrand Richards was ordained an Apostle by David O. McKay—Apr. 10, 1952

David O. McKay was ordained an Apostle by Joseph F. Smith—Apr. 9, 1906

Joseph F. Smith was ordained an Apostle by Brigham Young—Jul. 1, 1866

Brigham Young was ordained an Apostle by "the Three Witnesses, viz., Oliver Cowdery, David Whitmer, and Martin Harris . . .

"These Three Witnesses were then blessed by the laying on of the hands of the Presidency." (Smith, *History of the Church,* 2:187–88.)

Joseph Smith, Jr. and Oliver Cowdery were ordained to the Melchizedek Priesthood in 1829 (D&C 27:12–13) by

Peter, James, and John, who were ordained by the Lord Jesus Christ (John 15:16).

Ask:

- What is "priesthood"? ("The eternal power and authority of God." [*True to the Faith,* 124].)

- As you look at this priesthood lineage, where did Melvin Jay Wilcox get priesthood authority? (Ultimately from Jesus Christ.)
- Why would you want someone to have authority from Jesus Christ when performing ordinances for you or giving you blessings?

Read together Hebrews 5:1, 4 and ask:

- What did the Apostle Paul say about how a man must get the priesthood?
- How did Aaron receive the priesthood? (Footnote 4c; see Exodus 28:1.)
- How did Moses know Aaron should receive the priesthood? (By revelation.)

Ask a family member to recite Articles of Faith 1:5 or turn to page 60 in the Pearl of Great Price and read it aloud. Ask:

- How did Joseph Smith summarize the steps necessary to receive the priesthood?
- What qualifies a man to be called? (Worthiness.)

Invite family members to share experiences when priesthood authority blessed their lives.

Hebrews 5:5–10
Jesus Christ, the great high priest

Ask your family members if they believe Jesus Christ held the priesthood, and if so, what office he held. Have someone read aloud Hebrews 5:5–6. Ask:

- Why do you think the Savior needed to be ordained to the priesthood? Elder Bruce R. McConkie taught, "Christ our Lord received the Melchizedek Priesthood here on earth, and was ordained to the office of high priest . . . setting an example for others." (*Doctrinal New Testament Commentary,* 3:157.)
- According to Doctrine and Covenants 107:1–4, what was the original name of the Melchizedek Priesthood? Why was it changed?
- Who was Melchizedek? (See Bible Dictionary, "Melchizedek" and "Melchizedek Priesthood," 730–31.)

Invite half of your family to study Hebrews 5:7–8 to learn more about Melchizedek (tell them to read footnote 7a) and the other half to read

Hebrews 5:9–10 to learn more about the Savior. Invite both groups to tell what they have learned. You might share the following quotations from Elder Bruce R. McConkie to clarify Paul's teachings:

- Hebrews 5:7–8: "Verses 7 and 8 apply to both Melchizedek and to Christ, because Melchizedek was a prototype [example] of Christ and that prophet's ministry typified and foreshadowed that of our Lord." (*Doctrinal New Testament Commentary,* 3:157.)
- Hebrews 5:9–10: "Christ was always perfect in that he obeyed the whole law of the Father at all times and was everlastingly the Sinless One . . . on the other hand he was made perfect, through the sufferings and experiences of mortality, in the sense that he thereby died and was resurrected in glorious immortality." (*Doctrinal New Testament Commentary,* 158.)

Discuss as a family how Jesus learned obedience through suffering. How can we learn obedience through suffering? Sing "There Is a Green Hill Far Away" (*Hymns,* no. 194), pointing out how the Savior suffered.

HEBREWS 6: PRINCIPLES OF THE GOSPEL AND THE DOCTRINE OF CHRIST

Hebrews 6:9–12
How do we show our love for God?

Write the following words on separate slips of paper: *look after; care for; wait on; comfort; attend to.* Divide the slips of paper among family members. Have them silently read Hebrews 6:10–12 and find a word that their word could replace. Invite each person to share both the word in the scriptures they could replace and the word on their slip of paper. (It is intended that each of them will find the word *minister* in verse 10.) Ask:

- How do these new words help you better understand how to "minister" to others?
- How can this kind of ministering be considered a "labor of love"? (Verse 10.)

- How might ministering in this way show your love for your Father in Heaven?
- How long should we be willing to minister?

Hebrews 6:13–20
Swearing with an Oath

 Ask your family members the following questions:

- Have you ever broken a promise?
- How did it make you feel?
- Have you ever experienced someone making a promise to you and then breaking it?
- How did you feel about that?

Explain that in ancient times a promise was often accompanied by an "oath." Share the following insight from Elder Bruce R. McConkie: "In ancient dispensations . . . the taking of oaths was an approved and formal part of the religious lives of the people. These oaths were solemn appeals to Deity [God] . . . usually made in the name of the Lord, by people who valued their religion and their word above their lives." (*Doctrinal New Testament Commentary,* 3:163.)

Read together Hebrews 6:13–16 and then discuss these questions:

- Who did God swear by when He made promises to Abraham?
- What did Abraham do to receive God's promised blessings? (Verse 15.)
- According to verse 16, how did men make an "end of all strife," or argument, about whether an oath was of any value or not?
- What difference would it make if everyone valued promises as did the ancient Saints?
- What must we do today to make our promises sure? (See Matthew 5:33–37.)

Encourage family members to remember how important it is to make promises only when you fully intend to keep them. Explain that our Heavenly Father wanted His children to be able to have hope and confidence in His most important promise. Have your family silently read Hebrews 6:17–20 and find this most important promise. Ask:

- What is Father in Heaven's most important promise to us? (Verse 20.)
- How does God convince us that He is true to His promises? (Verse 17.)
- How can the promise of Jesus as our Savior be considered "the hope set before us"?
- In what way can our hope in Christ become "an anchor of the soul"? (Verse 19.)

Share this information by Elder Bruce R. McConkie: "As the high priest in Israel passed through the veil into the holy of holies on the day of atonement, as part of the cleansing rites which freed Israel from sin . . . so Jesus has entered into heaven to prepare the way for those who through obedience to his laws become clean and pure." (*Doctrinal New Testament Commentary*, 3:165.)

HEBREWS 7: THE AARONIC AND MELCHIZEDEK PRIESTHOOD

Hebrews 7:1–10
Who is Melchizedek?

Prior to teaching this lesson, assign one family member to make a paper crown and write *King of Righteousness* on it. Place it, along with a tithing envelope and receipt, in front of everyone. Ask family members to guess which scripture person could be identified by these symbols. Read the entry for "Melchizedek" in the Bible Dictionary (page 730) and ask:

- What is Melchizedek's title?
- What seems impressive to you about him?

List what they mention on a large sheet of paper for everyone to see. Then write on that paper the following references: Genesis 14:18–20; Hebrews 5:6; Joseph Smith Translation Genesis 14:17–40; Alma 13:14–19; Doctrine and Covenants 84:14; 107:1–4. Assign each reference to a different family member. Have them study those verses and share what else they learn about Melchizedek and list those on the paper also.

Read together Hebrews 7:1–10 and have family members find everything else they can about Melchizedek and list it on the paper. Ask:

- What do the tithing envelope and receipt have to do with Melchizedek? (Verses 1, 4.)
- How does it help your testimony to know that even the ancients paid tithing?
- Who else is known as King of Righteousness?
- Why is Melchizedek also called the King of Righteousness and how does that help you know what he was like? (See Alma 13:14, 18–19.)
- Why do you think his name is appropriate to use when we identify the higher priesthood?
- What does this passage in verse 3 mean: "Without father, without mother, without descent"? (See JST, Bible Appendix, 811.)

Share this explanation by Elder Bruce R. McConkie: "The right to this higher priesthood was not inherited in the same way as was the case with the Levites and sons of Aaron. Righteousness was an absolute requisite for the conferral of the higher priesthood." (*Mormon Doctrine*, 478.)

Ask your family what the relationship between the priesthood and righteousness should mean to one who holds the Melchizedek Priesthood. What should it mean to a young man who does not yet hold the Melchizedek Priesthood? Have all your family members who hold the priesthood record in their journals what they can do to better follow Melchizedek's example. Ask all other family members to list in their journals those things they can do to assist and support priesthood holders in their righteous endeavors.

Hebrews 7:11–19
The Aaronic and Melchizedek Priesthood

Give everyone paper and pencils. Have them number their papers from 1–7 and give them the following true/false quiz. When the quiz is finished, have family members trade papers and correct them using Hebrews 7:11–19, as well as the following scripture references:

1. The Aaronic Priesthood is sometimes called the lesser or the Levitical Priesthood. (True; see D&C 107:1, 13–14.)

2. The Aaronic Priesthood is the authority to administer in outward ordinances. (True; see D&C 84:26; 107:14.)

3. The Melchizedek Priesthood is the authority

used to administer the ordinances necessary for exaltation. (True; see D&C 84:19–21.)

Elder Bruce R. McConkie wrote: "Without the Melchizedek Priesthood salvation in the kingdom of God would not be available for men on earth, for the ordinances of salvation . . . could not be authoritatively performed." (*Mormon Doctrine,* 479.)

4. Melchizedek held the Aaronic Priesthood and administered in the outward ordinances under the law of Moses. (False; see verse 13.)

5. Melchizedek is a high priest similar to, or a type of, Jesus Christ. (True; see verse 15.)

6. Jesus Christ is a descendant of the tribe of Ephraim. (False; He was of the tribe of Judah. See verse 14.)

7. The priesthood power of Jesus Christ enables us to have "endless life" that is not attainable through the "weakness and unprofitableness" of the law of Moses. (True; verses 16, 18.)

Elder McConkie taught: "The Melchizedek Priesthood is the power by which men gain eternal life. Where this priesthood is, there men can work out their own salvation and gain a celestial fullness; and where this priesthood is not, there can be no full inheritance in the kingdom of God." (*Doctrinal New Testament Commentary,* 3:171.)

Ask if there are any questions as a result of the quiz.

Hebrews 7:19–21
The oath and covenant of the priesthood

Before scripture study, ask a family member to review the Old Testament story of Eli and his two sons, Hophni and Phinehas, and prepare to briefly share it during scripture study. The story is found in 1 Samuel 2:22–25, 27–36; 3:1, 11–18; 4:4–22.

After this story is shared, ask another family member to read aloud the Joseph Smith Translation of Hebrews 7:19–21 (Bible Appendix, 811) and another to read the following statements by Joseph Smith:

"The Levitical [Aaronic] Priesthood is forever hereditary [passed from father to son]—fixed on the head of Aaron and his sons forever." (*Teachings of the Prophet Joseph Smith,* 319.)

"The Levitical Priesthood, consisting of priests to administer in outward ordinance, made without an oath; but the Priesthood of Melchizedek is by an oath and covenant." (*Teachings of the Prophet Joseph Smith,* 323.)

Ask:

- How did ancient members of the Aaronic Priesthood receive their right to the priesthood? (It was passed from father to son.)
- What problems occurred with Eli's sons and the priesthood?
- Why do you think those problems occurred?
- Why do you think that today it would be more important to give the priesthood to faithful and righteous men instead of just to those who are sons of priesthood holders?
- How do Aaronic and Melchizedek Priesthood holders today receive their right to the priesthood? (See Hebrews 5:4; D&C 84:39.)

Ask your family to name things that would constitute worthiness to hold the priesthood and why priesthood holders should be worthy.

Hebrews 7:22–28
Jesus Christ is our only Savior

Fold a large piece of paper in half lengthwise. List all of the synonyms you can think of for *sure,* as in "It is a *sure* thing." Then write all of the definitions you can think of for *testament.*

Have someone act as a scribe and record everyone's answers under the appropriate columns.

At the bottom of the paper, write: "By so much was Jesus made a _____ of a better _____."

Ask family members to read Hebrews 7:22 and find words to fill in the blanks.

Share President James E. Faust's insights: "The Savior as a surety is a guarantor of a better covenant with God. . . .

"The New Testament is a 'better testament' [covenant] because the intent of a person alone becomes part of the rightness or wrongness of human action." (*Ensign,* Sept. 2003, 3.)

Turn over the piece of paper you used above and this time label the columns "Jesus" and "Other Priests." As a family, take turns reading Hebrews 7:24–28. Stop after each verse and insert information you find in the verses that applies to Jesus or to the other priests. Read this quotation from Elder

Bruce R. McConkie regarding Hebrews 7:28: "The Lord swore that his Son would have the higher priesthood, which administers the gospel and therefore supplants the law." (*Doctrinal New Testament Commentary,* 3:175.)

Bear your testimony of the Savior's role in Heavenly Father's plan regarding some of the things mentioned in these verses.

HEBREWS 8: A NEW COVENANT

Hebrews 8:1–5
Earthly things are shadows of heavenly things

Show your family an illustration of the tabernacle built anciently by Moses. (See *Gospel Art Kit,* no. 108.) Tell your family what it is and ask:

- What do you think the tabernacle meant to the children of Israel?
- What similar buildings do we worship in today? (Temples.)
- How do these buildings help remind us of heaven?

Explain to your family that in Hebrews 8 Paul taught the people about heavenly things by comparing them with earthly things. Have your family scan and compare Hebrews 8:1, 3–4, and then verses 2, 5. Ask them to identify at least two earthly things Paul compares to heavenly things. To help your family find these comparisons, ask the following questions:

- What does Paul compare in verses 1, 3–4?
- When did God have priests who offered sacrifices?
- Who is the high priest in heaven? (Footnote 1*a*.)
- What was Jesus' "sacrifice"? (See footnote 4*a*.)
- What does Paul compare in verses 2 and 5?
- Where do you think the "true" tabernacle built by the Lord exists? (In heaven.)
- How were ancient priests and the tabernacle a "shadow of heavenly things?"

To help explain how the tabernacle is a "shadow of heavenly things," draw the following simple top view of the tabernacle on a piece of paper. Show

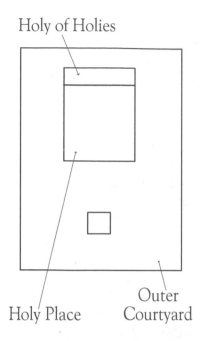

Holy of Holies

Holy Place

Outer Courtyard

this drawing to your family and ask the questions below. As answers are given, write them on your drawing. Ask:

- If you compared the tabernacle built by Moses to the three degrees of glory, what might types of the Holy of Holies, the Holy Place, and the outer courtyard represent? (The celestial, terrestrial, and telestial kingdoms.)
- How might this have reminded the children of Israel about God's plan of salvation?

Discuss how modern temples help teach us about God's plan of salvation and how it also is a "shadow of heavenly things."

HEBREWS 9: CHRIST IS THE MEDIATOR OF THE NEW COVENANT

Hebrews 9:1–10
Becoming clean through the blood of the Lamb

Having very briefly overviewed the tabernacle in Hebrews 8, your family is prepared for a more in-depth study in Hebrews 9.

Draw once more a top view of the tabernacle as you did for Hebrews 8. Take turns reading

Hebrews 9:1–7 and label the furnishings inside the tabernacle.

- Ark of the Covenant (Verses 4–5.)
- Veil and Golden Censor (Verses 3–4.)
- Candlestick and Table of Shewbread (Verse 2.)

Ask:

- What was kept inside the Ark of the Covenant? (Verse 4.)
- Why would these things be important to keep?
- Who could go into the first room, the Holy Place of the tabernacle? (Verse 6.)
- Who could enter the second room or the Holy of Holies? (Verse 7.)
- How often could the High Priest enter the Holy of Holies? (Verse 7.)
- What was he to take with him into the Holy of Holies? (Verse 7.)
- Who did the high priest represent? (Verses 11–12.)

Since Paul's reference to the Day of Atonement is probably not familiar, see Bible Dictionary, "Fasts," 671, third paragraph.

Express your gratitude for the Savior's sacrifice and the cleansing power of the Atonement in your life.

Hebrews 9:11–28

Jesus had to die

Ask your family what the following phrase means: "It is better that one man should perish than a whole nation should perish." Ask:

- How was this true in the case of Laban in the Book of Mormon? (See 1 Nephi 4:10–18.)
- Share other situations where this is true.

Invite your family to look for another situation as you study Hebrews 9:11–28. Remind your family that Paul wrote Hebrews to help Jewish Christians understand how Christ brought a *new covenant* to replace the *old* one established anciently through Moses. Many Jews still tried to live according to the law of Moses. In Hebrews 9 Paul continued to show how the ancient tabernacle and priests were merely symbols of what was to come through the Savior. Take turns reading Hebrews 9:11–17, 22, 24–26 and look for what was

necessary for the new covenant to have power to save. Ask:

- Who is the high priest in the new covenant?
- Why does Jesus not need to offer the blood of animals, as the priest did, in order to enter into the Holy Place? (Verse 12.)
- What is the title given to our new high priest in verse 15? (Mediator.)
- According to footnote 15c, what is the definition of *testament*?
- What must happen to the testator, Jesus Christ?
- Why must the testator die? (Verses 17, 22; Jesus had to die in order for God's children to have a remission of their sins.)
- Anciently, the high priest entered the Holy of Holies once a year "with the blood of others," but according to verses 24–26, where was Jesus Christ, the new high priest, to enter?
- What does Jesus' "sacrifice of himself" promise to "put away"? (Verse 26.)
- Why can you have hope in Christ?

HEBREWS 10: CHRIST'S SACRIFICE BRINGS FORGIVENESS AND POWER

Hebrews 10:1–4

Shadows and realities

Have a family member stand in a light so everyone can see the shadow. Have the person move so the shadow moves, and point out to everyone that a shadow is a real, moving thing. Ask:

- Can you recognize a person from the shadow?
- Can you tell what the person is doing by looking only at the shadow?

Ask the person casting the shadow if they would like a treat of some kind. When they say, "Yes," put the treat on their shadow and ask, "How does that taste?" Ask:

- How many treats would I need to put on this shadow before his/her hunger is satisfied?
- How does this example relate to what Paul was

saying about the sacrifices of the law of Moses compared to Christ in Hebrews 10:1–4?

Read together Alma 34:9–14 and ask:

- What was the purpose of sacrifices under the law of Moses? (To help people look forward to the great and last sacrifice of Jesus Christ.)
- In what way was the law of Moses a shadow for the gospel of Jesus Christ?
- Because Christ's sacrifice has been offered and accomplished, we do not need to look forward to it, but instead we do things to always keep it in remembrance. What ordinance helps us remember that His sacrifice is now available to forgive, bless, strengthen, and perfect us?

Testify to your family that Christ's sacrifice is no longer a shadow.

Hebrews 10:5–17

What is Paul quoting? What does it mean?

Have your family find the words "he saith" in Hebrews 10:5–7. Tell them that Paul is quoting Psalm 40:6–8. Have them put opening quotation marks before the word *Sacrifice* in verse 5 and ending quotation marks after the word *God* in verse 7. They could also write a cross-reference, Psalm 40:6–8, by verse 7. Have a family member read aloud Hebrews 10:8–9, and point out that Paul quotes again from that same passage in Psalm 40 to make his point. Ask:

- What do you think his point is?
- How does 3 Nephi 9:19–20 clarify his point?

Have a family member read Hebrews 10:15–17. Tell them that Paul is again quoting from the Old Testament, and have them put quotation marks at the beginning of verse 16 and the end of verse 17. In the space at the end of verse 16, have them write Jeremiah 31:33, and in the space at the end of verse 17, have them write Jeremiah 31:34. Ask:

- What do these quotations say about the effects of the sacrifice, or Atonement, of Christ?
- What does Doctrine and Covenants 58:42–43 say about what we must do in order to receive this blessing of the Atonement? (Have your family write this reference in the margin next to Hebrews 10:17.)

Ask, How does the law of sacrifice apply to us today?

Hebrews 10:18–39

Therefore, what?

 Show a picture of Christ in Gethsemane, or a video clip that depicts His suffering. (See *The Lamb of God* video produced by the Church.) Ask, When you ponder Christ's sacrifice, what do you want to do as a result?

Explain to your family that in the preceding chapters of Hebrews, the Apostle Paul wrote to help Hebrew Church members better understand the significance of Christ's Atonement for all and that by Hebrews 10 he is beginning to make some conclusions about what that should mean for them. Have family members read Hebrews 10:18–25, 34–38, looking for the things Paul says we should do because of what we understand about Christ's Atonement. Have them mark in their scriptures or make notes of what they find.

Appoint one person to be a scribe and record what is said as the family shares what they find. The list should look something like this:

- Draw near to God with a full assurance of faith. (Verse 22.)
- Hold fast to our faith without wavering. (Verse 23.)
- Consider one another and encourage each other to love and good works. (Verses 24–25.)
- Have compassion on those in adversity. (Verse 34.)
- Be joyful in enduring adversity. (Verse 34.)
- Cast not away our confidence in God and the rewards that will come. (Verse 35.)
- Have more patience in God's blessings. (Verse 36–37.)
- Have more faith. (Verse 38.)

Hold up the picture of Christ again. Ask:

- How did Jesus exemplify these qualities as He lived in mortality and performed the Atonement?
- What does thinking about what He did for us do for our desire to live the things on our list?

HEBREWS 11: FAITH IN JESUS CHRIST PRODUCES POWER

Hebrews 11:1–3
A definition of faith

 Place a set of keys in your pocket. Tell your family that you have a set of keys in your pocket. Ask:

- How many of you believe I have a set of keys in my pocket? Why?
- Are you able to see the keys?
- How do you know they are there?
- What would be a way I could increase your faith that there are keys in my pocket?

Shake the pocket containing the keys. Ask, Now, how many of you believe I have a set of keys in my pocket? Why? Invite your family to silently read Hebrews 11:1–3. Ask them how Paul defines the word *faith*. Ask your family to check Hebrews 11:1, footnote *b*. Ask, What is the word that the Joseph Smith Translation uses instead of *substance*? (*Assurance.*) Read the following statement by Elder Howard W. Hunter:

"Faith makes us confident of what we hope for and convinced of what we do not see. The scientist does not see molecules, atoms, or electrons, yet he knows they exist. He does not see electricity, radiation, or magnetism, but he knows these are unseen realities. In like manner, those who earnestly seek for God do not see him, but they know of his reality by faith. It is more than hope. Faith makes it a conviction—an evidence of things not seen." (*Ensign*, Nov. 1974, 97.)

Invite your family to write Alma 32:21 and Ether 12:6 next to Hebrews 11:1. Turn first to the Alma reference and have your family silently read it. Turn to the Ether reference and silently read it. Ask, What have you now learned about faith?

Continue by asking what it then means to have faith in Jesus Christ. Testify to your family of the need for exercising faith in Jesus Christ. Tell them that even though we do not now see Him, you know He exists.

Hebrews 11:4–40
Great examples of faith

 Tell your family that Hebrews contains examples of people with great faith. Invite your family to read verses 3–40, looking for and marking the phrases "through faith" and "by faith." After the scriptures are marked, invite everyone to tell about the people Paul used as examples of faith, and then discuss what they did "by faith." Ask family members to tell what they could do to become more like these people.

Ask your family to focus on verses 10, 13, 16, and 39, looking for the words "city," "promises," and "country." Ask, What do you think these words are referring to? (See Moses 7:16–21.) Write D&C 45:11–14 next to one of the verses. Ask your family to turn to Doctrine and Covenants 45:11–14 and read those verses. Ask:

- What was "sought for by all holy men"? (Zion; verse 12.)
- Why did they not find it? (Verse 12.)
- How does faith help to establish a holy city? (See Moses 7:18.)

Let your family know of your feelings about the power of faith in Jesus Christ. Help them see how through faith all things are possible.

HEBREWS 12: STAYING STRONG IN THE FAITH

Hebrews 12:1–11
"Whom the Lord loveth he chasteneth"

Ask family members to share any experiences they have had with racing. Invite a family member to read Hebrews 12:1 and discuss the following questions:

- What kind of a race do you think Paul was referring to? (The race of life.)
- Is the race of life like a sprint or a marathon?
- What "weights" should we set aside to enable us to run better?

Read together Hebrews 12:2–4 and ask:

- Who should we look to as an example of how to run the race?
- What did Jesus endure to finish His race?

• What helped Him endure His race of life? (The joy that was set before Him.)

Ask family members what *chastening* means. Refer your family to footnote *7b*. Have family members quickly scan and mark Hebrews 12:5–11 and notice how many times the word "chastening" or a form of it occurs. Then have them silently read Hebrews 12:5–6, 11. Ask:

• How and why does the Lord chasten us?

Share the following insight: "President Howard W. Hunter once said, 'God knows what we do not know and sees what we do not see.' None of us knows the wisdom of the Lord. We do not know in advance exactly how He would get us from where we are to where we need to be. . . . We encounter many bumps, bends, and forks in the road of life that leads to the eternities. There is so much teaching and correction as we travel on that road. Said the Lord, 'He that will not bear chastisement is not worthy of my kingdom.' 'For whom the Lord loveth he chasteneth.'" (James E. Faust, *Ensign,* Nov. 2004, 21.)

Invite family members to tell about times when they have been chastened and what they learned.

Hebrews 12:9
"Fathers of our flesh . . . Father of spirits"

 Have a family member read aloud Hebrews 12:9. Ask:

• Who is the father of your flesh?
• Who else are you a son or daughter of?
• How do you feel knowing you are a child of God?
• Why is it important to honor both our earthly father and our Heavenly Father?

Read the following statement from President Boyd K. Packer: "Before we came into mortal life, we lived as spirit children of our Father in Heaven. All human beings—male and female—are created in the image of God. Each is a beloved spirit son or daughter of heavenly parents, and, as such, [you have] a divine nature and destiny. Gender [male and female] is an essential characteristic of individual premortal, mortal, and eternal identity and purpose." (*Ensign,* Nov. 2003, 24–25.)

Talk about situations in which it would be extremely important to remember who our earthly parents are and that we are children of God.

Hebrews 12:12–17
"Lift up the hands which hang down"

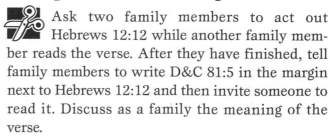 Ask two family members to act out Hebrews 12:12 while another family member reads the verse. After they have finished, tell family members to write D&C 81:5 in the margin next to Hebrews 12:12 and then invite someone to read it. Discuss as a family the meaning of the verse.

As you read together Hebrews 12:13–17, have family members look for ways Paul suggests the strong can strengthen the weak. Ask, What ideas did you find?

Share the following from President Spencer W. Kimball: "God does notice us, and he watches over us. But it is usually through another person that he meets our needs. Therefore, it is vital that we serve each other. . . . In the Doctrine and Covenants we read about how important it is to 'succor the weak, lift up the hands which hang down, and strengthen the feeble knees.' (D&C 81:5.) So often our acts of service consist of simple encouragement or of giving mundane help with mundane tasks—but what glorious consequences can flow from mundane acts and from small but deliberate deeds." (*New Era,* Sept. 1974, 5.)

HEBREWS 13: CONCLUDING COUNSEL

Hebrews 13:1–25
Identify the verse

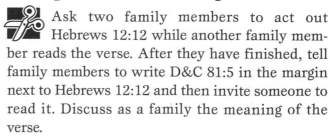 Tell your family you are going to play a game called "Identify the Verse." The object is to be the first one to identify the verse that the phrase of counsel or doctrine comes from in Hebrews 13:1–25. Divide the family into two teams. Tell your family you will read a phrase and the first person to raise his or her hand and correctly identify the verse it comes from will score a point. (To add more interest, you may want to also give each team that answers correctly a chance to

earn more points by showing their skill at a game such as bean bag toss, shooting a small ball in a basket, dropping a bean in a bottle, or putting a golf ball, etc.) The team with the most points after all the phrases have been identified is the winner. The phrases, with the verse they come from, are given below:

1. Be content with things you have. (Verse 5.)
2. Pray for Church leaders. (Verse 18.)
3. Love others. (Verse 1.)
4. Don't get carried away with strange doctrines. (Verse 9.)

5. If we are righteous, we do not need to fear what men can do to us. (Verse 6.)
6. Give thanks to God. (Verse 15.)
7. Marriage is a good thing. (Verse 4.)
8. Be helpful to strangers in need. (Verse 2.)
9. Obey leaders in the gospel. (Verse 7 or 17.)
10. Remember to do good. (Verse 16.)
11. God will help us improve in our good works. (Verses 20–21.)
12. Receive words of Church leaders. (Verse 22.)

Ask family members to share at least one important idea they learned from this chapter.

JAMES

The Epistle of James is the first of a small number of epistles in the New Testament not written by Paul. It is addressed to "the twelve tribes which are scattered abroad" (James 1:1), which most likely refers to members of the Church who accepted Christ by covenant. (Galatians 3:27–29.)

Three men named James are mentioned in the New Testament. One is the brother of John, the son of Zebedee, who was one of the original twelve chosen by Jesus as Apostles. (See Matthew 10:1–4; Luke 6:13–16.) Herod killed this James sometime after the Savior's Resurrection. (See Acts 12:1–2.) Another of the original Twelve Apostles is named "James the son of Alphaeus" (Luke 6:15), but nothing else is ever said about him in the New Testament—unless he is the author of this epistle. The more likely author, however, is a man named James who is noted in Matthew 13:55 as the brother of Jesus. (See also Galatians 1:19.) This seems to be the same James to whom Paul refers in 1 Corinthians 15:7 as one of the witnesses of the risen Lord and a leader of the Church in Jerusalem. (See Acts 15; 21:18.)

More than any other epistle in the New Testament, James emphasizes answers to the questions: If we know the truth, how should we live? Does the way we practice our religion really matter?

JAMES 1: BE YE DOERS OF THE WORD, AND NOT HEARERS ONLY

James 1:1–4, 8–16
Dealing with trials and temptation

 Have your family read James 1:2. Ask:

- Is there anything that seems strange about this verse?
- How does the Joseph Smith Translation change this verse? (See footnote 2a.)
- How is it still strange even with the Joseph Smith Translation?
- In what ways might a person "count it joy" because he/she has "many afflictions"? (James 1:3–4.)

Invite someone to share how they have seen James's explanation in verses 3–4 to be true.

Have a family member read James 1:12. Ask:

- What does James say is an additional affliction?
- What happens to you, and to the temptation, the more you resist it?
- What is the source of most temptation?
- What are the consequences of giving in to temptation?
- How can afflictions and temptations bless us?

Share the following insight from Rulon G. Craven: "Temptation is a necessary part of our earthly experience. The Lord through the Prophet Joseph Smith explains the reason why we are tempted: 'It must needs be that the devil should tempt the children of men, or they could not be agents unto themselves; for if they never should have bitter they could not know the sweet' (D&C 29:39). . . .

"As eternal beings living this earthly experience, we will not be free from temptation. Temptation implies an inner struggle to do that which is right. . . .

"Elder George Q. Cannon said: 'Unless they [individuals] were exposed to temptation they never could know themselves, their own powers, their own weaknesses nor the power of God. If Satan had no power to tempt mankind, they would be in a state where they could neither know good nor evil; they could not know happiness nor misery' . . .

"Through obedience to gospel principles, the enticements of the world lessen in our lives. With each right choice we make, we spiritually empower ourselves. The accumulation of right choices builds inner spiritual strength and divine character. We should expect temptation, for without temptations there would be little education and little character improvement." (*Ensign*, May 1996, 76–77.) Ask:

- How can temptation be a blessing to us?
- When is temptation not a blessing?
- What must we do so that temptation will help us grow rather than bring us to misery?

Conclude with the promise in 1 Corinthians 10:13, and your testimony of this principle.

James 1:5–7
What can be the impact of a single verse?

Ask your family what scripture they think has had more impact on them than any other. After some discussion, share the following:

"This single verse of scripture has had a greater impact and a more far reaching effect upon mankind than any other single sentence ever recorded by any prophet in any age." (Bruce R. McConkie, *Doctrinal New Testament Commentary,* 3:246–47.)

Ask your family: What verse of scripture do you think Elder McConkie was referring to? (James 1:5.) Have everyone read that verse silently, and re-read the statement from Elder McConkie. Ask, Why you think he said that about this verse? (Because of the impact it had on the Prophet Joseph Smith and then the impact Joseph Smith has had on the world.)

Remind your family of the confusion young Joseph Smith had about which church he should join. Read together Joseph Smith–History 1:11–14.

Have someone tell in his or her own words what happened as Joseph Smith applied James 1:5. Have another person read aloud James 1:6. Ask, What are some ways we see this verse to be true in the story of the Prophet Joseph Smith? (Although we don't know all the ways, JS–H 1:13–16 describes several ways in which he exercised "faith, nothing wavering." He determined to "do as James directs," he acted on a specific plan, he did things he "had never as yet" tried, and he persevered amid great opposition.)

Have a family member read the Prophet Joseph's concluding testimony in Joseph Smith–History 1:26. Share your own testimony that among all the wonderful things we learn from the Prophet Joseph Smith's First Vision, one of the important truths is that God will hear and answer the prayers of those who ask in faith.

James 1:17–27
What is true religion?

Ask your family: How can you tell if someone is truly religious? After giving each family member a chance to give their opinion, tell them that answering this question seems to be a main topic in James's epistle.

Have each family member write at the top of a page in their scripture notebook (or a piece of paper): "A truly religious person is one who . . ." Then have them carefully read James 1:17–27 and make a list of everything James says in these verses that describes a truly religious person.

Invite each person to share one thing from his or her list. Also ask each family member to describe how each item on their list might help your family become more religious. The following may help as you emphasize some points James makes:

Verse 19. What does James say every person should "be"? What difference would it make just in our own home if we lived these three principles? You may want to put these three simple statements in large letters on a piece of paper and hang them in a prominent place in the home.

Verses 23–25. Show your family members a small mirror and have them look in it. (This is the "glass" referred to in verse 23.) Ask, Do you recognize who is in the mirror? What do we "look into" that helps us see who we really are? What helps you remember who you are? What difference does it make when you remember who you are? How could looking at the list you made when you read these verses in James be like looking in the mirror?

Verse 26. Explain what a bridle is. How do we bridle our tongue? What advice would you suggest to someone who is trying to better control his or her language?

Verse 27. What do you think it means to be "unspotted from the world"? What are some of the ways you get "spotted" by the world? What helps you become "unspotted"? Who are the fatherless and widows we know that we might be of service to? You may want to take the time to make specific plans to help one of the widows or widowers in your ward or neighborhood.

Encourage everyone to keep their list on a mirror, as a reminder to be "doers of the word, and not hearers only." (Verse 22.)

JAMES 2: FAITH WITHOUT WORKS IS DEAD

James 2:1–13
What should we do with the "royal law"?

Have your family imagine that the next time they go to church all the seats are assigned according to the amount of tithes and offerings they have paid. Those who paid the most sit in the front benches, and those who paid the least sit in the very back. Ask your family how they would feel about that practice. What would be wrong with it? Read together James 2:1–4 (including footnotes 1*a* and 4*a*), and ask:

- How is this passage from James similar to the situation imagined above?
- How does the Joseph Smith Translation clarify the doctrine taught by James?

Continue reading together James 2:5–13. When finished, discuss the following:

- What reasons did James give for why it is wrong to favor the rich over others?
- What is the "royal law"?
- In what ways are we tempted to love some of

our neighbors more or less than others? (Note that President Gordon B. Hinckley taught: "I remind you that no man who makes disparaging [belittling] remarks concerning those of another race can consider himself a true disciple of Christ. Nor can he consider himself to be in harmony with the teachings of the Church of Christ. How can any man holding the Melchizedek Priesthood arrogantly assume that he is eligible for the priesthood whereas another who lives a righteous life but whose skin is of a different color is ineligible?" (*Ensign,* May 2006, 58.)

- According to verse 9, what did James say about those who show favoritism to one group of people over another?
- According to verse 12–13, what does the "royal law" have to do with the way we are judged at the last day?

Invite your family to write the cross-reference Alma 41:14 next to James 2:13–14. Read Alma 41:14 and discuss how it clarifies and adds a second witness to what James taught.

James 2:14–26
Faith without works is dead

 Prior to family scripture study, ask three family members to do the following:

- Person 1. Lie on the floor and groan, "I am so hungry and cold."
- Person 2. Go to the person on the floor and say (with feeling), "I'm so sorry you're hungry or cold. I have faith that God can help you."
- Person 3. Run to the kitchen and bring back something for the hungry person to eat and a blanket to cover the person with and say, "I'm sorry you're so hungry and cold. Here are some things to help."

Have your family read James 2:14–17. Ask:

- What important truth did James want us to understand by this little example?
- What additional example of this truth does he give in James 2:19?

Share the following additional example from Elder James E. Talmage:

"It is said that during an epidemic of cholera in a great city, a scientific man proved to his own satisfaction, by chemical and microscopic tests, that the water supply was infected, and that through it contagion [unsafe germs] was being spread. He proclaimed the fact throughout the city, and warned all against the use of unboiled water.

"Many of the people, although incapable of comprehending his methods of investigation, far less of repeating such for themselves, had faith in his warning words, followed his instructions, and escaped the death to which their careless and unbelieving fellows succumbed. Their faith was a saving one.

"To the man himself, the truth by which so many lives had been spared was a matter of knowledge. He had actually perceived, under the microscope, proof of the existence of death-dealing germs in the water; he had demonstrated their virulence [destructive power]; he knew of what he spoke.

"Nevertheless, in a moment of forgetfulness he drank of the unsterilized water, and soon thereafter died, a victim to the plague. His knowledge did not save him, convincing though it was; yet others, whose reliance was only that of confidence or faith in the truth that he declared, escaped the threatening destruction." (*Articles of Faith*, 90; paragraphing altered.)

Have your family look through James 2:20–26 and identify two examples James uses from the scriptures that show that only when we act upon our faith does it bring power and blessings. Ask:

- What would have been different if Abraham had said, "Yes, I have faith in God, so I don't think I really need to prove it by offering up Isaac?" What would Abraham have missed? What would we have missed?
- What would have been different if Rahab had said, "I believe the servants of the Lord, but I might get in some kind of trouble with the other people in town if I help?"
- What other examples show how "faith without works is dead, being alone"? (See James 2:17.)

JAMES 3: WE WILL BE JUDGED BY WHAT WE SAY

James 3:1–18
By governing the tongue we gain perfection

Before teaching this chapter, write the following statement on a piece of paper: "James Wilson was a scholar. He read his scriptures every night for three months and followed that with a meaningful prayer each night as well."

Tell your family that you're going to begin scripture study with an activity. Let them know you have written a message on a piece of paper and you are going to whisper that message to the person next to you. Ask each person in turn to then whisper the message to the person seated next to him or her and so on until everyone has heard the whispered message. Invite the last person to repeat aloud the message that was whispered to them. Compare what the last person said with what was written. Ask family members to notice how the message was changed from the original. Ask your family:

- What sometimes happens to stories and events after a series of people tell them to one another?
- What is it called when we purposefully spread rumors, stories, and events?

Ask your family to read James 3:1–18 and look for what James taught about our "tongues," (the words we use). Invite family members to share what they found. Ask:

- What does a bit do for a horse? (See verse 3.)
- What is the most difficult part of the body to control? (The tongue.)
- Why is it difficult to control our tongues?
- Why would learning how to control the tongue lead to greater happiness?
- How is saying rude things like lighting things on fire? (Fires are easy to start but difficult to put out.)
- How is the tongue like deadly poisons?
- When is a time you have been poisoned by what someone has said?

- According to verses 9–11, what are good things our tongues can do?
- How "sweet" is the language the young people use at the school you attend?
- Do you feel that gossiping, swearing, or telling off-colored jokes or stories happens less at church than at school? Why or why not?
- What are some ways a person can overcome bad language, thoughts, or gossiping?

Show a match and ask:

- How much do you think this single match costs?
- How much damage, in dollars, could one match cause?
- How is this analogy similar to gossip, evil speaking, or using bad words?

Cross reference Mosiah 4:29–30 to this chapter and have someone read it aloud. Ask, Why do you think we will be judged by what we say and by what we do? Read *For the Strength of Youth* pamphlet, page 22.

Reread James 3:17–18 and ask how our words should edify others. Share the following event from the life of President Spencer W. Kimball:

"In the hospital one day I was wheeled out of the operating room by an attendant who stumbled, and there issued from his angry lips vicious cursing with a combination of the names of the Savior. Even half-conscious, I recoiled and implored: 'Please! Please! That is my Lord whose names you revile.' There was a deathly silence, then a subdued voice whispered: 'I am sorry.'" (*Teachings of Spencer W. Kimball,* 198.)

Ask your family how they feel about President Kimball's action in the story.

JAMES 4: RESIST EVIL AND COME UNTO CHRIST

James 4:1–17
You cannot serve two masters

Invite a family member to read aloud Matthew 6:24. Ask your family to define *mammon.* (See the Bible Dictionary, "Mammon," 728.) Then have your family search James 4:1–4

and name symptoms of spiritual sickness among people who love things of the world.

Explain that the Lord has provided a way for us to overcome the things of the world. Have your family silently read James 4:7–12, looking for ways we can overcome the world. Ask:

- How might James's counsel help us to overcome the things of the world?
- What is our responsibility?
- Do you want to know what the Lord expects of you or do you want to stay in ignorance of His laws and commandments? Why?
- How can we be blessed by following the commandments of the Lord?
- Why is it important for us to learn all we can about the gospel?

Have someone read James 4:13–17. Ask:

- What is our responsibility as members of Christ's Church?
- Why is it important for those who "knoweth to do good" to make sure that they are good?
- How might our life be better if we learn to say, "If the Lord wills"?

Read the following statement by Elder Gene R. Cook: "What a glorious principle to understand: the Lord's assistance to us—whether we have strong faith or weak faith; whether a man, a woman, or a child—is not based just on what we know, how strong we are, or who we are, but more upon our giving all that we can give and doing all that we can do in our present circumstance. Once one has given all he can, then the Lord, through His grace, will assist him (see D&C 123:17)." (*Ensign,* May 1993, 81.)

JAMES 5: "IS ANY SICK AMONG YOU?"

James 5:1–6
What did James teach about riches?

 Set the following items in front of your family: scriptures, money, treats, and toys. Ask:

- Which of these items would you choose? Why?

- Which of the items do you think would bring you the most happiness right now?
- How long would the happiness last?
- Which of the items do you think would bring you the most happiness forever? Why?
- Why do you think so many people have developed a love of money?

Have each family member silently read James 5:1–6 looking for what James taught about those who love riches. Invite your family to share what they found. Encourage your family to write 2 Nephi 9:30 and Jacob 2:17–19 in the margin next to James 5:1–6. Turn with your family to 2 Nephi 9:30 and ask a family member to read aloud that verse. Continue by going to Jacob 2:17–19 and doing the same. Ask:

- What counsel does the Lord give us in these verses concerning riches?
- What good can be done with riches?
- How do members of the Church share the wealth they have with those less fortunate? (Show your family a donation slip that is used for contributions to the Church. If needed, explain what the donations are and what they are used for.)
- According to Jacob 2:19, why does the Lord bless many with the wealth of this world?

Ask your family to share a time when they gave something to another person and the feelings that accompanied that act. Let your family know that by giving to someone less fortunate than ourselves, we also lift and bless ourselves.

James 5:14–16
What are priesthood blessings?

Share the following story about Elder Neal A. Maxwell: "As a 14-year-old boy, he came home from work one night to find his six-week-old sister desperately ill. 'She was lying on the round dining room table and had stopped breathing,' Elder Maxwell recalled. 'I watched my father, after the manner of the New Testament, bless her by the power of the priesthood, and I saw her begin to breathe again. I knew then the power of the priesthood was real.'" (*Ensign,* Nov. 1996, 109.)

Invite someone to read James 5:14–16. Ask:

- What did James teach about administering to the sick?
- How have you been blessed or seen others be blessed by the healing power of the priesthood?

Turn to Doctrine and Covenants 42:43–52 and ask your family to look through these verses for information about when to administer to the sick, how to administer, and the conditions upon which healings take place. Invite your family to share what they learned from these latter-day verses. Ask, How does it make you feel to know that the power of God is available through a priesthood blessing when there is a need?

Testify of the power of the priesthood and of its ability to heal a person. You could conclude with a personal experience to this effect or sharing one from scripture or another person's life.

1 PETER

Peter, whose name in Greek means "rock," was one of the first Apostles called by our Lord Jesus Christ. (See Matthew 4:18.) He was also known as Simeon (Acts 15:14) or Simon, and Cephas. (John 1:40–42.) He and his brother Andrew (who was also an Apostle) earned their living as fishermen on the Sea of Galilee. Peter had a home in the city of Capernaum. (See Matthew 8:14.) Peter, James, and John were with the Lord on several very important occasions. (Matthew 16:15–19; 17:1; 26:37; Acts 1:2.) In May or June of 1829, under the Lord's direction, Peter, James, and John visited Joseph Smith and Oliver Cowdery and conferred upon them the Melchizedek Priesthood. (D&C 27:12–13.) (See also "Peter," Bible Dictionary, 749.)

The First Epistle of Peter was written from Babylon (1 Peter 5:13) and is addressed to the Christians of Pontus, Galatia, Cappadocia, Asia, and Bithynia. (1 Peter 1:1.) These are cities in Asia Minor. "Its objective is to encourage . . . men who were in danger of being terrified into a denial of their Lord, but it also contains valuable teaching about the incarnation and atonement . . . , and the doctrine of regeneration." (Bible Dictionary, 749.) Of Peter's writings, Joseph Smith said, "Peter penned the most sublime [inspiring] language of any of the apostles." (Teachings of the Prophet Joseph Smith, 301.)

1 PETER 1: BECOMING MORE LIKE CHRIST

1 Peter 1:1–12
Working toward exaltation

Explain to your family that you are going to read the definitions for three words that are found in the first 12 verses of 1 Peter 1. These words will help clarify the meaning of this passage of scripture. Read the word and definition of each of the words.

Sanctification. "To be sanctified is to become clean, pure, and spotless; to be free from the blood and sins of the world." (McConkie, *Mormon Doctrine*, 675.)

Election. "The elect are foreordained to be sanctified, by virtue of the blood of Christ, on conditions of gospel obedience." (McConkie, *Doctrinal New Testament Commentary*, 3:284.)

Mercy. "In the gospel sense, mercy consists in

our Lord's forbearance [restraint], on certain specified conditions, from imposing punishments that, except for his grace and goodness, would be the just reward of man." (McConkie, *Mormon Doctrine*, 483.)

Take turns reading 1 Peter 1:1–12 and have your family review the definition each time they find one of these words.

After having gone though the helps provided, return to verse 2 and point out there is a sequence of ideas that builds to a climax in verse 9. Use the following to assist your family in finding the sequence as they revisit 1 Peter 1:1–12.

Verse 2: We become *sanctified* through *obedience* and the blood of Jesus Christ.

Verse 3: *Mercy* is extended through a lively *hope* of the Resurrection.

Verse 4: We will receive an *inheritance incorruptible and undefiled.*

Verse 6–7: Our *faith* will be tried through temptation.

Verse 9: Until the *end of our faith,* even the *salvation of your soul.*

If all these things are building to the salvation of our souls, salvation must be very important. Ask, What is salvation? Read the definition:

Salvation. "The gospel is a gospel of eternal life, of exaltation, of glory and honor, and so the Lord chooses to have his prophets equate salvation with the type and kind of life he lives, rather than with the ultimate inheritance of some lesser being." (McConkie, *Doctrinal New Testament Commentary,* 3:285.)

Help your family understand that as we are obedient we become clean and the Lord's mercy will be extended to us.

1 Peter 1:18–25
How can we become more like Christ?

 Bring the following to scripture study:

- A red spot
- Something silver (or silver-colored)
- Something gold (or gold-colored)
- A picture of someone being baptized
- A drawing of a heart
- A blade of grass

Place these items in front of your family and have them each choose one. Explain that these items are found in 1 Peter 1:18–25. Ask everyone to silently read the verses and find the verse that mentions the item they chose. Have them prepare to report on the following when they have finished:

- What did Paul compare that item with?
- What was Paul trying to teach by using that item?

(Note: The following examples may help members of your family as they prepare their reports.)

Silver and gold: verse 18—Silver and gold are corruptible. We must not center our lives on money or worldly things.

Red spot: verse 19—Red is the color of blood, and blood is a representation of the Atonement. It is through the atoning blood of Jesus Christ that we can be saved.

Heart: verse 22—Our heart must be purified though the Spirit.

Baptism: verse 23—Baptism is symbolic of being born again. We must all be born again to enter the kingdom of God. (See John 3:5.)

Blade of grass: verses 24–25—We, like the grass and flowers of the earth, will die. On the other hand the word of God will endure forever.

Help your family understand the importance of being Christlike.

1 PETER 2: ALL MUST COME TO CHRIST

1 Peter 2:1–3
Milk before meat

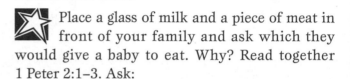 Place a glass of milk and a piece of meat in front of your family and ask which they would give a baby to eat. Why? Read together 1 Peter 2:1–3. Ask:

- Who does Peter refer to as "newborn babes"? (See the chapter heading.)
- What might be considered the milk of the gospel?
- What might be considered the meat of the gospel?
- Why would you want to give a new member "the sincere milk of the word" before the meat?

Share the following from President Gordon B. Hinckley: "With the ever-increasing number of converts, we must make an increasingly substantial effort to assist them as they find their way. Every one of them needs three things: a friend, a responsibility, and nurturing with 'the good word of God' (Moro. 6:4). It is our duty and opportunity to provide these things." (*Ensign,* May 1997, 47.)

Discuss ways your family can share the milk of the gospel with their friends.

1 Peter 2:4–10
Where should we build our foundation?

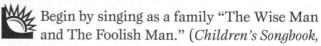 Begin by singing as a family "The Wise Man and The Foolish Man." (*Children's Songbook,* 281.) Ask:

- Why was the man wise to build his house on a rock?

- Why was the other man foolish to build his house on the sand?
- In the gospel, what does our "house" represent? (See Helaman 5:12.)
- What does the rock represent?

As they take turns reading 1 Peter 2:4–10, ask your family to keep in mind that the sure foundation (rock or stone) we should build on is Jesus Christ. Then ask your family:

- What is the "chief corner stone"?
- How could Jesus become "a stone of stumbling and a rock of offence"? (See JST 1 Peter 2:7.)
- What is Christ to those who believe? (He is precious.)
- How does Paul describe those who accept Jesus as the chief cornerstone? (Verse 9.)
- In what ways are we peculiar today?

Read the following statement by President Joseph Fielding Smith: "The saints are peculiar. This is true of them both regarding their habits and their religious belief. If they are true to their faith, they cannot help being different from other peoples. Their religion requires it of them." (*Doctrines of Salvation,* 1:234.)

Testify to your family the value of being "peculiar" and how building upon the foundation of Jesus Christ has made a difference in your life.

1 Peter 2:11–25
What counsel does Peter give Church members?

Tell your family they are going to identify what Peter taught the ancient Saints about their relationship with the Savior. Invite family members to choose (until all are selected) verses to study from the following list: 11, 12, 13, 14–15, 16–17, 18–20, 21–25. Give each family member a piece of paper and something to write with. Then have them silently read their assigned verse/verses and write a one-line description of what Peter taught. Have them share what they learned. Their findings may reflect what is listed below:

- Verse 11. Abstain from fleshly lusts.
- Verse 12. Be honest in word.
- Verse 13. Submit yourselves to all ordinances.
- Verses 14–15. Submit your will to the governors.
- Verses 16–17. Be people of honour, love the brotherhood, fear God, honour the king.
- Verses 18–20. To servants: subject yourselves to your masters both those who are good and those who are wicked.
- Verses 21–25. Look to Christ our examplar.

Ask:

- How might this counsel lead a person to "come unto the Savior"?
- How is the counsel similar to counsel given to Saints today?

Turn to the page of a conference report in a May or November *Ensign* which lists the titles of the talks, who gave them, and the topics covered. Read through the topics and compare them with Peter's message.

1 PETER 3: LIVING IN HARMONY WITH FAMILY AND FELLOWMEN

1 Peter 3:1–13
Love at home

After reading together 1 Peter 3:1–10, read the statements below one by one and have your family identify which verse(s) matches it best.

A. "In my family, we should stick together and be unified." (Verse 8.)

B. "I should be kind, even when someone is rude to me." (Verse 9.)

C. "I've learned that having the Spirit makes a person more beautiful than following the latest fashion trend." (Verses 3–4.)

D. "I should honor and take care of my wife as I would a delicate and precious object." (Verse 7.)

E. "I've learned that one secret to happiness is to never speak evil or negatively of anyone." (Verse 10.)

F. "I should be compassionate and courteous to family members." (Verse 8.)

Decide which verses add more harmony to your family. Conclude by having someone read verses

11–13 and then ask each family member to write their own statements similar to the list above.

1 Peter 3:14–17
"What's different about you?"

Have your family imagine they are at school or work, and a person says to them, "I've noticed that you are usually happy and have a quiet confidence about you? Why is that?" Invite family members to share how they would respond to this person's question. Have them read 1 Peter 3:14–17 and ask:

- According to verse 15, what will people see in us as we are living the gospel? (Hope.)
- What should we always be prepared to do?
- What would be the best reason we could give for why we have that hope about us?
- Which verse tells us what to do if people are speaking negatively about us? (Verse 16.)
- What might a person be tempted to do if someone is speaking negatively about him or her?
- How does the Joseph Smith Translation change verse 16?
- How might this cause people to become more interested in the Church?
- Which verse best teaches about missionary work?

Encourage your family to be prepared to share their good example even when people are not being nice to them.

1 Peter 3:18–22
Preaching of the gospel in the spirit world

Ask your family the following:

- Where does a person immediately go after they die? (The spirit world.)
- Where do many nonmembers believe the dead go? (Heaven or hell.)
- What happens to those in the spirit world who did not have a chance to hear the gospel on earth? (See D&C 138:29–30 for more on how the work for the dead went forth.)

Have your family read and mark 1 Peter 3:18–19 and 1 Peter 4:6 (including the JST in footnote 6a). Have them write D&C 138:29–30 next to 1 Peter

3:18–19. Discuss as a family how the Savior's work in the spirit world gives evidence of God's love for His children. Testify of God's great mercy in having the gospel preached to the spirits in the spirit world.

1 PETER 4: THE CHALLENGES OF CHRISTIAN LIVING

1 Peter 4:1–19
How strong are you?

Take turns reading the verses indicated below from 1 Peter 4. Read the following "fill in the blank" sentences to your family and see if they remember the correct words from the verses. After you read each group of verses, discuss the accompanying questions, talk about insights your family learns, and share ideas of how you can apply these teachings into your life.

Verses 1–3. "That he no longer should live the rest of his time in the flesh to the lusts of men, but to _____ of God"

- Why is it important to "cease from sin"?
- What are some "lusts of the flesh" people struggle with today?
- Why does obeying God's will bring more happiness than following our own desires?

Verse 4. "Wherein they think it ____ that ye run not with them . . ."

- What do you think it might mean to "not run with" some people involved in wickedness?
- What are some experiences you (or others) have had of needing to change the group of people you "ran with"?
- How did the change of friends bless your life?

Verses 5–7. "For for this cause was the gospel preached also to them that are _____,"

- Why is it important that the gospel is preached to those in the spirit world?
- What does that teach you about God's love for His children?

Verses 8–9. "Charity shall _____ the multitude of sins." (See footnote 8a.)

• Why do you think charity can cover or prevent sin?

Verses 10–11. "Jesus Christ, to whom be _____ and _____ for ever and ever."

• Why does Jesus deserve all praise and blessings?

Verses 12–13. "Think it not strange concerning the _____ _____ which is to try you"

• Why should we not be surprised by trials?
• What are some ways your trials have strengthened or helped you?

Verses 14–16. "If any man suffer as a _____, let him not be ashamed;"

• What are some bad reasons to suffer?
• What would be a good reason to suffer?

Verses 17–19. "Wherefore let them that suffer according to the will of God commit the _____ _____ _____ _____ to him"

• How could you commit your soul to God?
• Why do you think this would bless your life?

1 PETER 5: PETER COUNSELS LEADERS IN THE CHURCH

1 Peter 5:6–14

What is the principle?

Show your family how to write principles by explaining that many principles are written as "If—then" statements. On top of a sheet of paper, write: "If I _____, then _____." Have your family study 1 Peter 5:6–11 and find as many "If—then" principle statements as they can in the teachings found there. When finished, discuss what they found and write the principles on the paper. Your statements may be similar to the following:

• *If* I humble myself, *then* eventually I will be exalted. (Verse 6.)
• *If* I cast my burdens upon the Lord, *then* He will help me. (Verse 7.)
• *If* I am watchful, *then* I will be able to escape the temptations of Satan. (Verse 8.)
• *If* I am patient in suffering, *then* God will strengthen me. (Verse 10.)

Ask your family which of these principles they think applies most to them and why.

2 PETER

The second epistle of Peter, which was written near the time of his death (2 Peter 1:14), is an example of his straightforward, powerful way of expressing the doctrines about which he felt so strongly. (See Bible Dictionary, "Peter, Epistles of," 750.)

2 PETER 1: "PARTAKERS OF THE DIVINE NATURE"

2 Peter 1:1–9

Steps to becoming Christlike

 Before scripture study, place a blank sheet of paper on the floor across the room.

Draw four sets of footprints as large as the paper on other sheets of paper and set them on the floor as steps leading to the blank paper.

Read together 2 Peter 1:1–4 and see if your family can find what Peter wanted the ancient Saints to obtain. (Hint: it is something that we should be "partakers of.") When someone answers, have them write "Divine Nature" on the blank sheet of paper on the floor. Discuss what it means to "be partakers of divine nature." Share the following from President Ezra Taft Benson:

"The Apostle Peter spoke of the process by which a person can be made a partaker 'of the divine nature'. This is important, for if we truly become partakers of the divine nature, we shall become like [the Savior]." (*Ensign,* Nov. 1986, 45.)

Tell your family the process of becoming Christlike is a step-by-step process. Have your family look for these steps in Peter's teachings in 2 Peter 1:5–9. Ask:

- What is the first quality or principle we must develop? (Share this added insight: "Faith is the foundation upon which a godlike character is built. It is a prerequisite for all other

virtues." [Ezra Taft Benson, *Ensign,* Nov. 1986, 45.])
- How can we demonstrate our faith in Christ?
- What other characteristics does Peter say we must add to our faith?

As family members identify each step, have them write them on the footprints. Take turns reading the quotations as each attribute is written on one of the footprints.

A list of these attributes is given below, with a quotation about each one.

Virtue. "Virtuous behavior implies that he has pure thoughts and clean actions. He will not lust in his heart, for to do so is to 'deny the faith' and to lose the Spirit (D&C 42:23)—and there is nothing more important in this work than the Spirit. . . . A priesthood holder should actively seek for that which is virtuous and lovely and not that which is debasing or sordid. . . . How can any man indulge himself in the evils of pornography, profanity, or vulgarity and consider himself totally virtuous?" (Ezra Taft Benson, *Ensign,* Nov. 1986, 46.)

Knowledge. "Every priesthood holder should make learning a lifetime pursuit. While any study of truth is of value, the truths of salvation are the most important truths any person can learn."

Temperance. "This means he is restrained in his emotions and verbal expressions. He does things in moderation and is not given to overindulgence . . . he has self-control. He is the master of his emotions." (Ezra Taft Benson, *Ensign,* Nov. 1986, 47.)

Patience. "Patience is another form of self-control.

It is the ability to postpone gratification and to bridle one's passions. In his relationships with loved ones, a patient man does not engage in impetuous behavior that he will later regret. Patience is composure under stress. A patient man is understanding of others' faults.

"A patient man also waits on the Lord. We sometimes read or hear of people who seek a blessing from the Lord, then grow impatient when it does not come swiftly. Part of the divine nature is to trust in the Lord enough to 'be still and know that [he is] God' (D&C 101:16)." (Ezra Taft Benson, *Ensign,* Nov. 1986, 47.)

Godliness. "Godliness characterizes each of you who truly loves the Lord. You are constantly mindful of the Savior's atonement and rejoice in His unconditional love. Meanwhile you vanquish [conquer] personal pride and vain ambition. You consider your accomplishments important only if they help establish His kingdom on earth." (Russell M. Nelson, *Ensign,* Nov. 1991, 61.)

Brotherly kindness. "One who is kind is sympathetic and gentle with others. He is considerate of others' feelings and courteous in his behavior. He has a helpful nature. Kindness pardons others' weaknesses and faults. Kindness is extended to all—to the aged and the young, to animals, to those low of station as well as the high." (Ezra Taft Benson, *Ensign,* Nov. 1986, 47.)

Charity. "The final and crowning virtue of the divine character is charity, or the pure love of Christ (see Moro. 7:47). If we would truly seek to be more like our Savior and Master, then learning to love as He loves should be our highest goal. . . .

"The world today speaks a great deal about love, . . . the pure love of Christ differs greatly from what the world thinks of love. Charity never seeks selfish gratification. The pure love of Christ seeks only the eternal growth and joy of others." (Ezra Taft Benson, *Ensign,* Nov. 1986, 47.)

Ask your family to ponder which of these attributes they lack. Invite them to improve in that area.

2 Peter 1:16–18
"Eyewitnesses of His majesty"

Ask your family members to each imagine that he or she has done some incredible thing. How hard do you think it would be to get neighbors and friends to believe you if no one saw you do it? How valuable would an "eyewitness" be in establishing the truth?

Invite someone to read 2 Peter 1:16–18 and look for who the "eyewitnesses" were in those verses. Ask:

- What were Peter and the other Apostles "eyewitnesses" of? (The majesty of Christ.)
- Whose voice did they hear?
- What did He say?

Tell your family that the "holy mount" referred to is the Mount of Transfiguration. (See Matthew 17:1–6.) Ask your family to share other instances where the Father introduces the Son in similar fashion. (Matthew 3:16–17; see 3 Nephi 11:7; see Joseph Smith–History 1:17.) Ask:

- How does it help your testimony to know that there have been many eyewitnesses to who Jesus Christ really is?
- How can you know what the witnesses say is true? (See D&C 8:1–3; Moroni 10:4–5.)

Share your testimony of how you know that Jesus is the Son of God.

2 Peter 1:19–21
Prophecy comes by the power of the Holy Ghost

 Read aloud 2 Peter 1:20–21. Ask:

- What did Peter teach regarding the source of the scriptures?
- What did Peter teach about interpreting scriptures?
- Why can't just anybody explain what the scriptures mean?

Share the following from Elder Bruce R. McConkie: "Let it be known—in all places, among every people, in all ages, from creation's morn to all eternity—that all scripture comes from God, by the power of the Holy Ghost, and means only what He who knows all things intended it to mean! There are no private interpretations! This is a basic law of scriptural interpretation!

"Unless and until a scripture means to a man what it means to God, man has not caught the vision of the truth taught, or comprehended the doctrine being revealed. Two persons, . . . or two churches cannot reach divergent [different] conclusions as to the meaning of any scripture and both of them be right. . . .

"All scripture comes by the power of the Holy Ghost, no matter what age of the earth is involved, and must and can be interpreted only by the same power." (*Doctrinal New Testament Commentary,* 3:356.)

2 PETER 2: A WARNING AGAINST FALSE TEACHERS AND WICKEDNESS

2 Peter 2:1–9
False teachers

 Ask your family to think about this scenario:

- A teacher explains to his class that 2 plus 2 equals 5.
- A student thinks that explanation must be correct because the teacher said so.
- That student tells others that 2 plus 2 equals 5.

Discuss the following questions:

- Was the teacher correct?
- How did the teacher's mistake affect the student?
- Should the student be accountable for the correct answer even if he was taught improperly? Why or why not?
- How does this scenario apply to gospel teachers who may teach false doctrine?

Ask your family, "What is a heresy?" Tell them Elder Bruce R. McConkie taught:

"In the true gospel sense, any opinion or doctrine in opposition to the revealed word of the Lord as recorded in the standard works of the Church and as taught by The Church of Jesus Christ of Latter-day Saints is an heresy. The issue is not how many people may believe a teaching; it is whether the doctrine is true or false." (*Mormon Doctrine,* 352.)

Have your family read 2 Peter 2:1 and ask:

- What was a damning heresy taught in Peter's day?
- What are some heresies in the world today? (God does not have a body, revelation has ceased, Satan is not real.)
- What is meant by the phrase "denying the Lord that bought them"?

Share this insight: "Our Lord pays the price for the sins of all those who believe in him and obey his laws (D.&.C. 19:16–20), thus saving them from spiritual death. Accordingly, those who belong to the Church have been 'purchased with his own blood' (Acts 20:28); they have been bought with a price—the life blood of the Lamb. And what more abominable heresy is there than for them to deny the atoning sacrifice of their Lord?" (McConkie, *Doctrinal New Testament Commentary,* 3:358.)

Study 2 Peter 2:2–9 together and have your family look for the following:

- What are characteristics of false teachers?
- Who were deceived by false teachers?
- What are some effects upon the followers of false teachings?

Discuss ways your family members can avoid being led away by false teachers today.

2 PETER 3: THE SECOND COMING

2 Peter 3:1–18
Scoffers versus the faithful

 Get a bowl and a spoon and pretend to be stirring something. Have your family read 1 Peter 3:1–2 and ask:

- How does this relate to what you just read?
- Of what did Peter want them to be mindful?

Have family members mark footnote 3a and turn to Joseph Smith Translation 2 Peter 3:1–13 (Bible Appendix, 811–12). Invite family members to note the changes as you read together Joseph Smith Translation 2 Peter 3:3–4. Ask:

- What important phrase was left out of verse 4? (Denying the Lord Jesus Christ.)
- What will some scoff at in the last days?

Divide your family into two groups. Have the first group study Joseph Smith Translation 2 Peter 3:5–13 and the other group study 2 Peter 3:14–18 from the King James Bible. Have the first group look for signs or events concerning the Second Coming and the second group look for what we can do to remain faithful and prepare for the Second Coming. Have each group report their findings.

1 JOHN

Traditional beliefs credit John as author of this epistle because the language is very close to that of his Gospel. The First Epistle General of John was probably written after John's Gospel, some sixty years following the Crucifixion and Resurrection of Jesus Christ. (See Bible Dictionary, 715.) This first epistle of John testifies of Christ's mortality and His effect on all mankind. It also explains many of the truths found in John's Gospel, testifies of Christ's light and love, and identifies His followers as children of light.

1 JOHN 1: JOHN TESTIFIES OF CHRIST

1 John 1:1–4

John is an eyewitness

 Ask family members to name their five senses. (Touch, sight, smell, taste, and hearing.) Discuss these questions:

- Which of your five senses do you use most? Why?
- How does each of your senses help you learn or discover truth?
- Why does your confidence in something grow if you use more than one of the five senses to understand or know about something?

Explain that John, like several others, had the opportunity to be in the presence of the glorified, resurrected Lord. Ask your family to study 1 John 1:1–4 and look for which of John's five senses he used during his interaction with Jesus. Ask:

- What do you think about John's witness?
- What do you imagine it would be like to see and hear the voice of the resurrected Lord?
- How do you think it increased John's witness to be able to "handle" or touch the Lord?
- Can you think of other people who have had similar experiences?

Have everyone compare John's witness in his Gospel, John 1:1–2, 14 with his witness in 1 John 1:1–4 and find all of the words that John duplicates in both testimonies. Ask:

- Why do you think John repeats words like "beginning" and "Word"?
- Why is "Word" capitalized in these verses?
- Who is the "Word"? (See John 5:7.)
- What reason does John give in verse 3 for sharing this very intimate witness with us?
- What can we do to have this kind of witness?
- What is *fellowship*? (One of the definitions of *fellowship* in the *Noah Webster 1828 American Dictionary of the English Language* is: "Communion; intimate familiarity.")
- With whom does John wish us to fellowship?
- What reason does he give that makes this fellowship desirable?

Ask your family what they think it would be like to have fellowship with the Father and His Son and what we can do to obtain it.

1 John 1:5–10

John testifies of Christ's message

Turn out all of the lights and allow your family to sit in darkness. Then light a candle or turn on your brightest flashlight. Invite family members to share their feelings about darkness and light. Have them name some individuals whose countenances reflect light, as described in Alma 5:14. Ask if they have ever noticed anyone whose countenance seemed dark and how they felt around that individual. Turn the lights on and have them look in 1 John 1:5 and find someone who is total light with no darkness. Read Doctrine and Covenants 50:24; 88:49–50, and talk about what those verses teach about the light.

Give everyone a white piece of paper, and a dark piece of paper (like a brown grocery bag). Have them write **LIGHT** on the white sheet of paper and **DARK** on the dark paper. Have family members silently read 1 John 1:6–10 and write everything they can find that pertains to light on the white paper and everything that pertains to darkness or sin on the dark sheet of paper. Have family members share what they wrote on their papers. Encourage your family to do those things that will bring light into their lives.

1 John 1:6–10
"If—then" principles

Remind your family that the scriptures and scripture stories contain gospel principles, or in other words, they contain important messages of truth. Sometimes these truths are written in an "If—then" format. To help your family understand this style, write the following statement where all can see them and ask family members to fill in the blanks:

- If I go to bed early, then _____.
- If I obey my parents' rules, then _____.
- If I am unkind to others, then _____.
- If I don't do my homework, then _____.
- If I read my scriptures each day, then _____.

Ask:

- Which part of the "If—then" statements above could be considered the rule?
- Which part could be considered the result (either a blessing or a punishment)?

Tell your family that 1 John 1:6–10 teaches very clear principles of truth in an "If—then" format. Write the following sentences where your family can see them:

1. If we say we follow Christ but walk in darkness, then _____.

2. If we walk in the light, then the blood of Jesus Christ will _____.

3. If we say we have no sin, then _____.
4. If we confess our sins, then _____.
5. If we say we have never sinned, then _____.

Have your family search 1 John 1:6–10 and mark each time the word "if" appears. Have them notice that these verses do not have the word "then" in them, but each verse does contain an associated blessing or curse as a result. Have them complete each principle statement from what they find in those verses. Ask:

- How is each blessing or curse a result of the "rule" part of the statement?
- Which of these "If—then" verses do you think is most powerful? Why?
- How does understanding the "If—then" relationship make it easier to obey the rule?
- How might you apply these teachings?

1 JOHN 2: FOLLOW CHRIST, NOT THE WORLD

1 John 2:1–2
Is Christ our advocate or propitiator?

Prior to family scripture study, prepare enough 3x5 cards, one for each person, as follows. For team A, write the first word and definition below on one 3x5 card and write just the word but not the definition on the other cards. For team B, write the second word and definition on one 3x5 card and just the word on the others.

1. *Advocate:* "To plead in favor of; to defend by argument . . . to support or vindicate"

2. *Propitiation:* "The act of appeasing [soothing] wrath and gaining the favor of an offended person." (See Noah Webster's 1828 *American Dictionary of the English Language.*)

Divide your family into teams as planned and give them their cards. Explain that the object of the game is to trick the other team into believing that you are giving an accurate definition of the word. Have each member of team A make up a believable definition for *advocate*. The person with the real definition should give it using their own words. Have them take turns sharing their definitions. Team B will vote on whose definition is the real one. Team B will then share their definitions with team A. Team A will then vote on who is telling the truth. After the voting takes place, the person with the real definition should stand up.

Read aloud 1 John 2:1–2. (See footnotes 1*a* and 2*b*.) Have your family mark the words *advocate* and *propitiation* and then ask how the definitions given above help them understand Christ's role in Heavenly Father's plan. Invite two family members to read aloud Doctrine and Covenants 45:3–5 and Alma 42:13–15. When finished, discuss as a family how Christ is our *advocate* and *propitiator*. Ask:

- For whom did Christ propitiate? (Verse 2.)
- What must we do to gain the benefit of our Advocate? (1 John 2*a*.)

Invite family members to share their feelings about how our Savior bridges the gap between our sins and forgiveness.

1 John 2:3–14
How can we know God?

 Write the following words or phrases on strips of paper and place them in a basket: keep His commandments (verse 4); liars (verse 4); love of God (verse 5); walk as Christ (verse 6); darkness blinds our eyes (verse 11); hatred (verse 11); darkness is past (verse 8); the true light now shines (verse 8); abideth in Christ (verse 6); no stumbling (verse 10).

Read aloud 1 John 2:12–14 and ask your family, To whom Paul is writing? Invite family members to draw word strips from the basket until they are all taken. Have family members look up their word or phrase in the verse provided and then explain why they think John's counsel would be helpful to those he was writing to. (Fathers, young men, and little children.) When each family member has talked about their word strips, it might be helpful to discuss the following:

- What do you know about Jesus because you keep His commandments?
- How can we walk as He walks?
- What do you do to demonstrate that you have brotherly love?
- How is hatred like darkness and blindness and love like light?

- Why can you not hate your brother and be in the light? (See Luke 6:37; Ephesians 4:32.)
- How does lack of love for our fellow beings cause us to stumble?
- How can these messages help us today?

1 John 2:15–17
Love or love not

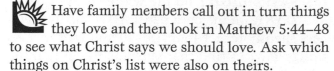 Have family members call out in turn things they love and then look in Matthew 5:44–48 to see what Christ says we should love. Ask which things on Christ's list were also on theirs.

Then have them call out things they do not love. Have them look in 1 John 2:15–17 for things that God asks us not to love. Ask them if anything on their list is similar to the things on God's list. Read together 1 John 2:15–17 and find reasons why God does not want us to love the things of the world. (Exodus 20:1–5; Matthew 6:24.) Ask:

- What worldly things would be very hard for some to give up?
- How might worldly things endanger our salvation?

Encourage family members to consider worldly habits they have and how to rid their lives of them.

1 JOHN 3: WHO ARE THE CHILDREN OF GOD?

1 John 3:1–3
Sons of God purify themselves and become like Him

 Display pictures of animals, birds, and fish. Point to each picture and ask:

- What kind of offspring or babies do these different kinds of animals have?
- In what ways are the offspring like the parents?
- In what ways are you like your parents?

Have a family member read 1 John 3:1–3 and ask the following questions:

- What does it say in verses 1 and 2 that we should be called? (Sons of God.)
- What does this title imply about Heavenly Father's relationship to you?

- As "children of God," whom can we be like?
- How can "sons of God" become like God?
- How can the Savior help us do this?

Invite one family member to read Paul's insight in Philippians 2:5–6 and then another to read the following quote by the Prophet Joseph Smith:

"God himself was once as we are now, and is an exalted man, and sits enthroned in yonder heavens . . . [men] have got to learn how to be Gods . . . the same as all Gods have done before." (*Teachings of the Prophet Joseph Smith,* 345–46.)

Invite everyone to write the following headings on a sheet of paper or in their scripture journals:

> *Physical   Social*
> *Mental   Spiritual*
> *Emotional*

Have them write under each heading how they are like Heavenly Father and Jesus. For example:

Physical

> I have a body like my heavenly parents.
> I am now a mortal being as God once was.

Explain to your family that just as the off-spring, or babies, of animals grow up to be like their parents, so we also have the potential to grow to be like our Heavenly Parents.

1 John 3:4–10
Jesus Christ and the devil

 Refer to *Gospel Art Kit,* no. 316 or 240. Have one of the children draw a picture of a devil and then set it next to the picture of the Savior. Invite someone to read aloud 1 John 3:4–10, stopping after each verse and asking whether what was read refers to the Savior or to the devil. (Some verses may apply to both.) Ask:

- Who has never sinned and takes "away our sins"? (The Savior; see verse 5.)
- Why do you think John teaches us that if we sin we do not know Christ? (Bruce R. McConkie taught that "those saints who strive to keep the commandments, and are continually repenting and returning to the Lord, no longer continue in that course of sinful rebellion against God and his laws. . . . Members who . . . continue to sin are members in name

only." (*Doctrinal New Testament Commentary* 3:386.)

- How does Joseph Smith's translation in 1 John 3:9*b* clarify the meaning?
- How does the Spirit help you avoid sin? (See Mosiah 5:2.)
- According to verse 10, how can we tell if we are children of God or children of the devil?

Give each family member a sheet of paper and have them tear it in half. On one piece have them list things people do that indicates they follow God and on the other sheet list things people do that indicates they follow Satan. Have one member of the family read the lists aloud and then put the lists next to the appropriate picture.

Discuss as a family what you can do to be on the Lord's side.

1 JOHN 4: GOD IS LOVE

1 John 4:1–6, 14–15
The truth about Jesus

Ask your family:

- What are some views you think other people have of Jesus?
- Who might they say He is, or what might they think He is like?
- What do you think is the hardest thing for nonbelievers to accept about Jesus Christ?
- How can you know the truth about and develop a strong testimony of the Savior?

Ask someone to read 1 John 4:1 and explain what John's concern was. (Footnote *b*.)

Have another family member read aloud 1 John 4:2–3. Ask your family:

- What false teaching about Jesus does John seem worried about?
- Why do you think it is important that we have a true understanding of this doctrine?
- Why is it hard for some people to believe Jesus really was the Son of God?
- What are some ways you can know this truth?

Read together 1 John 4:14–15, and ask:

- How has the testimony of others strengthened your testimony of what Jesus did?

- Whose testimony is shared in 1 John 4:14–15?
- How does he know the truth?
- Who bears this testimony today? (D&C 107:23.)

Have someone read aloud 1 John 4:4–6. Ask:

- What does John say about knowing truth from error when talking about God?
- How has your life been affected because you know the truth about God?

Share the following from Elder Dieter F. Uchtdorf concerning the difference knowing truth can make: "Faith in Jesus Christ and a testimony of Him and His universal Atonement is not just a doctrine with great theological value. Such faith is a universal gift, glorious for all cultural regions of this earth, irrespective of language, race, color, nationality, or socioeconomic circumstance. The powers of reason may be used to try to understand this gift, but those who feel its effects most deeply are those who are willing to accept its blessings, which come from a pure and clean life of following the path of true repentance and living the commandments of God." (*Ensign,* May 2005, 38.)

1 John 4:7–21
The importance of love

Have your family members look through 1 John 4:7–21 and see if they can guess what topic John was writing about. Have them count how many times the word *love,* in some form, is found in these verses. (27 times.)

Share the following from Elder John H. Groberg, and invite them to answer his questions:

"What is it about true love that touches every heart? Why does the simple phrase "I love you" evoke such universal joy?"

After your family has offered answers to his questions, share with them his answer:

"Men give various reasons, but the real reason is that every person who comes to earth is a spirit son or daughter of God. Since all love emanates from God, we are born with the capacity and the desire to love and to be loved. One of the strongest connections we have with our premortal life is how much our Father and Jesus loved us and how much we loved them. Even though a veil was drawn over our memory, whenever we sense true love, it awakens a longing that cannot be denied.

"Responding to true love is part of our very being. We innately desire to reconnect here with the love we felt there. Only as we feel God's love and fill our hearts with His love can we be truly happy." (*Ensign,* Nov. 2004, 9.)

Give each family member a piece of paper and pen. Have them write and share as many truths involving the principle of love as they can find in 1 John 4:7–21.

Share the following from President Howard W. Hunter:

"In ancient times, one test of the purity of gold was performed with a smooth, black, siliceous stone called a touchstone. When rubbed across the touchstone, the gold produced a streak or mark on its surface. The goldsmith matched this mark to a color on his chart of graded colors. The mark was redder as the amount of copper or alloy increased or yellower as the percentage of gold increased. This process showed quite accurately the purity of the gold. . . .

"I suggest to you that the Lord has prepared a touchstone for you and me, an outward measurement of inward discipleship that marks our faithfulness. . . .

"Eternal life, God's life, the life we are seeking, is rooted in two commandments. . . . Love God and love your neighbor. The two work together; they are inseparable. In the highest sense they may be considered as synonymous. And they are commandments that each of us can live. . . . [and] might be considered as the Lord's touchstone." (*Ensign,* Nov. 1986, 34.)

Ask, How would I measure up if my life were tested against the "touchstone?"

1 JOHN 5: JOHN CONCLUDES HIS LETTER

1 John 5:1–21
Who is born of God?

Remind your family of the recent birth of a baby they might all be familiar with. Discuss the following questions:

- How did the parents prepare for the baby?
- How could you tell they were excited?
- How important is birth in the plan of salvation?
- According to Mosiah 27:25, what other kind of birth does the Lord teach Alma?
- How would you describe what happens to those who are "born of God"?

Have your family take turns reading 1 John 5:1–5, 18–21. Have them look for answers to the following two questions as they read:

- According to John, what does it mean to be born again, or born of God?
- What must people do to be born again?

Share the following account by President Ezra Taft Benson:

"President David O. McKay tells of a singular event that happened to him. After falling asleep, he said he 'beheld in vision something infinitely sublime.' He saw a beautiful city, a great concourse of people dressed in white, and the Savior.

"'The city, I understood, was his. It was the City Eternal; and the people following him were to abide there in peace and eternal happiness.

"'But who were they?

"'As if the Savior read my thoughts, he answered by pointing to a semicircle that then appeared above them, and on which were written in gold the words:

"'These are They Who Have Overcome the World—Who Have Truly Been Born Again!

"'When I awoke, it was breaking day.' (*Cherished Experiences from the Writings of President David O. McKay,* comp. Clare Middlemiss, Salt Lake City: Deseret Book Co., 1976, pp. 59–60.)

"When we awake and are born of God, a new day will break and Zion will be redeemed." (*Ensign,* Nov. 1985, 7.)

Invite your family to close their eyes and imagine being in the City Eternal. Ask them to share how the Savior makes such a magnificent blessing available. Have one family member read 1 John 5:6–8 and another read Moses 6:58–60. Ask:

- What do you think John was trying to say about water, blood, and the spirit?
- How does Moses 6:58–60 clarify or explain this doctrine?
- What do the water, blood, and spirit represent in the process of becoming born again?

Invite your family to silently read 1 John 5:11–13 and then have them complete the following sentence: I love Jesus Christ because _____.

2 JOHN

Although the author of this epistle does not identify himself, he is believed to be the author of the Gospel of John, or John the Beloved. In this book John condemns false teachings, especially those who did not believe Christ actually had a physical body. This epistle was probably written around the same time as 1 John, between 85 and 95 A.D.

2 JOHN 1: WARNINGS AGAINST FALSE DOCTRINE

2 John 1:1–6

The elder unto the elect lady

Hand someone a piece of paper and a pen. Tell them to start a letter to a close friend. Stop them after they have finished the first few lines. Ask how would your letter be different if it were written to the Bishop, to your mother or father, to the President of the United States? Explain that John wrote a letter and their job is to decide to whom it was written and how formal or informal the letter is. Read 2 John 1:1–6. Ask:

- Who was doing the writing?
- Who was he writing to?
- What was John's main message? (Verses 4, 6.)
- How formal or informal was his tone?

To help your family better understand the answers to these questions, share the following definitions from Elder Bruce R. McConkie:

"'The elder' refers to John, the apostle. 'An apostle is an elder.' (D. & C. 20:38 .) . . .

"'The elect lady' 'An elect lady is a female member of the Church who has already received, or who through obedience is qualified to receive, the fulness of gospel blessings. This includes temple endowments, celestial marriage, and the fulness of the sealing power. She is one who has been elected or chosen by faithfulness as a daughter of God in this life, an heir of God, a member of his household. Her position is comparable to that of the elders who magnify their callings in the priesthood and thereby receive all that the Father hath. (D. & C. 84:38.)" (*Doctrinal New Testament Commentary*, 3:410.)

Encourage your family to develop qualities of an elect lady or an Apostle.

3 JOHN

John writes to Gaius to give thanks and encourage his work. He also names Demetrius as one who has done well, and warns Diotrephes. This epistle was written about the same time period as 1 and 2 John.

3 JOHN: ENCOURAGEMENT AND WARNINGS

3 John 1:1–14
To be in favor with the Lord

Divide your family into three groups. Explain that three men are mentioned in 3 John 1 and that each group is to represent one of these men. Their names are Gaius, Diotrephes, and Demetrius. Give each group a piece of paper and pen. Explain that each group will be responsible for finding information about their assigned person. Have each group study 3 John 1:1–14 and write the information they find, both the praises and the warnings. When they have finished, have each group share the information they have found. Ask:

- How would it make you feel if you were Gaius, Demetrius, or Diotrephes? (It is believed that Diotrephes was an apostate bishop who so desperately wanted to be in charge that he did not want John to visit.)
- What problems would it create in the Church today if there were a bishop who would not allow an Apostle to visit his ward?

Encourage your family to always live their lives so that they might be in favor with the leaders of the Church, and thus in favor with Heavenly Father.

Reread verse 4 and ask what it means to walk in truth.

JUDE

Jude was a brother of James and, like James, a half brother to Jesus. Jude was of the "brethren of the Lord." (See "Jude," Bible Dictionary, 719.) He used scripture stories and examples to warn the Saints about the apostasy seeping into the Church. He told them that "ungodly" and false men had "crept in unawares." (Jude 1:4, 15.) Elder Bruce R. McConkie taught:

"In the whole Bible, it is Jude only who preserves for us the concept that preexistence was our first estate and that certain angels failed to pass its tests.

"It is to him that we turn for our meager knowledge of the disputation between Michael and Lucifer about the body of Moses.

"He alone records Enoch's glorious prophecy about the Second Coming of the Son of Man." (Doctrinal New Testament Commentary, 3:415.)

JUDE 1: THE POWER OF THE WORD

Jude 1:1–25
A voice of warning

Have a family member read the following statement from President Harold B. Lee: "There are some as wolves among us. . . . some who profess membership in this church who are not sparing the flock. And among our own membership, men are arising speaking perverse things. Now perverse means diverting from the right or correct, and being obstinate in the wrong, willfully, in order to draw the weak and unwary members of the Church after them." (*Ensign*, Jan. 1973, 105.)

Ask:

- Do you know of persons who try to lead "weak and unwary members" to do wrong?
- Why would anyone want to do that?

Tell your family that the book of Jude warned Church members anciently about false teachings that had crept into the Church and also taught how to avoid them. Divide the verses in Jude 1:1–19 equally among your family. Ask them to read their assigned verses, looking for false teachings in the Church. When all have finished, ask them to share what they found.

Ask:

- What does Jude compare sinners to?
- Why are clouds without water, trees without fruit, raging sea, and darkened stars of little use or help?
- What consequence will come upon such sinners?
- What does Jude want us to remember in verses 17 and 18?

Invite your family to read Jude 1:20–25 looking for Jude's teachings on how to avoid false teachings. Invite them to comment on what they found.

Ask:

- What are some things that might keep us strong in the faith?
- In what way do you think Christ's Atonement keeps us from falling?

Read the following by President Ezra Taft Benson:

"The word of God, as found in the scriptures, in the words of living prophets, and in personal revelation, has the power to fortify the Saints and arm them with the Spirit so they can resist evil, hold fast to the good, and find joy in this life. . . .

" . . . When individual members and families immerse themselves in the scriptures regularly and consistently, these other areas of activity will automatically come. Testimonies will increase. Commitment will be strengthened. Families will be fortified. Personal revelation will flow. . . .

"Success in righteousness, the power to avoid deception and resist temptation, guidance in our daily lives, healing of the soul . . . are but a few of the promises the Lord has given to those who will come to His word." (*Ensign,* May 1986, 80–82.)

Discuss as a family how your study of the New Testament has strengthened your testimonies.

REVELATION

The revelation in this book was revealed to the Apostle John during his exile on the Isle of Patmos. Many believe he wrote this revelation around 95 A.D. The word revelation *(apocalypse in Greek) means to uncover and unveil. Most of Revelation uncovers, or speaks about, the events just prior to Christ's Second Coming. This book is written in a style that uses much imagery and symbolism; however, Joseph Smith taught that Revelation is "one of the plainest books God ever caused to be written" (Teachings of the Prophet Joseph Smith, 290.) Although the symbols and details of the book can be difficult to understand, the general message is simply that God will eventually triumph over Satan and all evil on earth. If you will read this precious book, looking for that general message, with a "little study," you will be able to perceive that theme "even if the details are not completely identified." (See Bible Dictionary, "Revelation of John," 762.)*

REVELATION 1: THE WORD OF THE LORD TO THE SEVEN CHURCHES

Revelation 1:1–11

The who, what, where, when, and why

Explain that news reporters often ask questions like, who, what, where, when, and why to make certain they have full details of a story. Invite your family members to pretend to be news reporters and assign each of them one of the questions below. Have them read the verses and information that go with their assignment and then share with other family members what answers they find.

- *Who* gave this revelation and to whom is it written? (Verses 1–4, 8–11.)
- *What* is this revelation primarily about?
- *Where* was John when he received this revelation and what is the location of the seven churches to which he wrote? (See verses 9, 11 and the map accompanying this chapter.)
- *When* was this revelation given? (See verse 10 and book summary above.)
- *Why* was this revelation given? (Verses 5–7.)

Read aloud the entire book summary of Revelation above and share your excitement for learning more about this important book.

Revelation 1:12–20

Symbols in the book of Revelation

Ask your family if they know what the words symbol or symbolic means. Ask each one to give an example of a symbol and what that symbol represents.

Discuss the following questions:

- Why can symbols convey more meaning than words alone? (The dollar sign can mean dollars, riches, expensive, greed, wealth, etc.)
- What does God communicate in symbols?
- What are some symbols in scripture that have helped you better learn the gospel?

Have your family silently study Revelation 1:12–16 and identify the symbols. Ask:

- What do the seven candlesticks around Jesus represent? (Read verse 20.)
- Why are candlesticks good symbols for our churches? (Read Matthew 5:14–17.)
- What does this description of the Lord teach you about Him? (See D&C 110:2–3.)
- What is in the Lord's right hand? (Verse 16.)
- What do the stars represent? (Verse 20b.)
- Why are stars good symbols for those who serve in the church? (They give us light.)
- What can Jesus holding those servants in His hand teach us? (Jesus upholds and cares for those who serve Him. We are in His hands.)
- What does the sword out of the Lord's mouth represent? (Read Ephesians 6:17.)
- Why could a sword symbolize the word of God? (Read Hebrews 4:12 and Alma 31:5.)

Have your family look for symbols as someone reads Revelation 1:17–19. Show your family the accompanying graphic and explanation of "Alpha" and "Omega" and ask:

Alpha and Omega are the first and last letters in the Greek alphabet.

- What does the phrase, "I am the first and the last," mean? (This shows that He has been there from the beginning, is always there, and will always be there for us.)
- What does it mean that Jesus has the keys of hell and death? (Because of Jesus' Atonement, He has the power to save us from hell and the powers of death.)

REVELATION 2: JOHN COUNSELS THE CHURCHES IN ASIA MINOR

Revelation 2:1–29
Different counsel to different churches

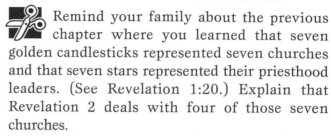 Remind your family about the previous chapter where you learned that seven golden candlesticks represented seven churches and that seven stars represented their priesthood leaders. (See Revelation 1:20.) Explain that Revelation 2 deals with four of those seven churches.

Have your family scan Revelation 2:1, 8, 12, and 18 and identify these four churches.

Study John's counsel to these churches by assigning a family member to each of the four cities. Give them a sheet of paper and have them create a chart for their assigned city like the one on page 315 by reading the verses and writing the appropriate information for each verse designated.

Share the following quotations from Elder Bruce R. McConkie (*Doctrinal New Testament Commentary*, 3:446–52):

Verses 6, 15: Nicolaitans. "Members of the Church who were trying to maintain their church standing while continuing to live after the manner of the world. . . . Whatever their particular deeds and doctrines were, the designation has come to be used to identify those who want their names on the records of the Church, but do not want to devote themselves to the gospel cause with full purpose of heart."

Verses 7, 11, 17, 29: "He that hath an ear, let him hear". "In the sense of believing and understanding, only those whose souls are enlightened by the power of the Holy Spirit can hear the word of God. The hearing ear is the ear of faith."

Verse 13: Where Satan's seat is. " . . . Satan dwells in every place and among every people where he, as the author of sin and the advocate of unrighteousness, finds those who open their hearts to him, who believe his doctrines, and who follow his ways."

Verse 14: The doctrine of Balaam. "To divine [prophesy] for hire; to give counsel contrary to the divine will; to pervert the right way of the Lord—

Cities	Positive Praise	Negative Information	Closing words
Ephesus Verses 1–7	Verse 2 Verse 3	Verse 4 Verse 5 Verse 6	Verse 7
Smyrna Verses 8–11	Verse 9 Verse 10		Verse 11
Pergamos Verses 12–17		Verse 13 Verse 14 Verse 15 Verse 16	Verse 17
Thyatira Verses 18–29	Verse 19	Verse 20 Verse 21 Verse 22 Verse 23	Verse 25 Verse 26 Verse 27 Verse 28 Verse 29

all with a view to gaining wealth and the honors of men. In effect, to preach for money, or to gain personal power and influence."

Verses 14, 20: "Eat things sacrificed unto idols". "If this is merely eating such meats without attaching religious significance to the act, it is of little moment one way or the other. . . . But if, as here, it is eating such meat as a religious performance, as an act of worship to an idol, it is an abomination before the Lord."

Verse 20: Jezebel. "As Ahab's wife led Israel to sacrifice to Baal and to worship false gods (i. e. to commit fornication), so another self-styled prophetess was leading many in Thyatira in an almost identical course; and the sin of the faithful members of the congregation was that they permitted her to teach her false doctrines."

After filling in the chart ask:

- Which of the churches had only negative things said about it?
- Which of the churches had only positive things said about it?
- What made the difference between the two?

Read verse 26 to your family to help them see the reason for the differences. For further clarification, have someone read the Joseph Smith Translation for Revelation 2:26–27 (Bible Appendix, 812). Discuss how the Prophet's translation helps clarify why there was such a difference in the counsel given to these churches.

REVELATION 3: COUNSEL FOR THE BRANCHES OF THE CHURCH CONTINUES

Revelation 3:1–6
Death in the city of Sardis

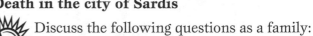 Discuss the following questions as a family:

- Is it possible to attend Church regularly but not really be converted? Why?
- Could a person seem very spiritual to others but not really be very spiritual?
- What would cause someone to be different on the inside than they appear on the outside?
- What do 1 Samuel 16:7, Matthew 23:27–28 and Alma 5:14–16 teach about this idea?

Invite your family to read Revelation 3:1–6, looking for how these verses apply to this principle.

To help your family understand these verses, share the following statement from President Spencer W. Kimball: "There are many people in this Church today who think they live, but they are dead to the spiritual things. . . . Their service is much of the letter and less of the spirit." (Conference Report, Apr. 1951, 105.) Ask:

- What does it mean when someone is "just going through the motions"?
- What advice does the Lord give to this group?
- What additional insight do Matthew 5:5–8 and 2 Corinthians 3:6 give?
- What do we need to do in our lives so we can stay spiritually strong in a wicked society?
- What blessings are promised in Revelation 3:5 to those who heed the counsel of Jesus Christ?
- What is the Lord encouraging us to do in Revelation 3:6?

Challenge your family to do the right things, for the right reason.

Revelation 3:7–13
Would you like to live in Philadelphia?

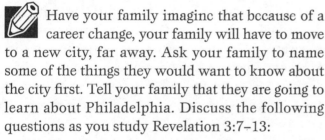 Have your family imagine that because of a career change, your family will have to move to a new city, far away. Ask your family to name some of the things they would want to know about the city first. Tell your family that they are going to learn about Philadelphia. Discuss the following questions as you study Revelation 3:7–13:

- What is a good thing the Saints of Philadelphia did in verse 8?
- How can we show the Lord that we do not deny His name today?
- How is the Lord going to show the wicked that He loves the Saints in Philadelphia?
- How would you feel if the Lord said that about you?
- When have you felt that the Lord loves our family like that?
- What could we do better in our family so that the Lord could show His love more?
- What is the Lord going to do for these Saints because they have been faithful? (Verse 10.)
- What are some ways that the Lord keeps us from temptation?

- What counsel does the Lord give these Saints in verse 11?
- What promise does the Lord make in verse 12 to those who overcome?

Revelation 3:14–22
A city of bad beverages and closed doors

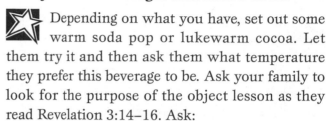 Depending on what you have, set out some warm soda pop or lukewarm cocoa. Let them try it and then ask them what temperature they prefer this beverage to be. Ask your family to look for the purpose of the object lesson as they read Revelation 3:14–16. Ask:

- What is compared to beverages in this chapter? (People's works.)
- What is a person like who is spiritually hot?
- What is a person like who is spiritually cold?
- What is a person like who is lukewarm?
- Why do you think God prefers a "hot or cold" person rather than a "lukewarm" person?

Have your family read verses 17–19. Ask:

- What does it say the Lord does to those He loves?
- What does chastening mean?
- Why is God's chastening a sign of love?
- How is a parent's chastening similar?

Have your family look for the reward of taking correction as they read verses 21–22.

Without warning, exit the room through the nearest door. Knock on the door till someone opens it. Show a picture of Jesus standing at the door and knocking. (*Gospel Art Kit,* no. 237.)

Have someone read verse 20. Ask:

- What does the door represent? (The door to our souls or hearts.)
- In what ways does Jesus knock on the door to our hearts? (Promptings of the Spirit.)
- Under what circumstances is it difficult to hear Him knocking?
- Why would someone not want to let Jesus in?
- What does it mean to "sup" with him?

Encourage your family to follow the promptings of the Spirit.

REVELATION 4: JOHN SEES THE FUTURE OF THIS EARTH

Revelation 4:1–11

A symbolic representation of the celestial kingdom

Remind your family that sometimes the scriptures are symbolic, visual images to help us better understand God's teachings. For example, we learned in Romans 6:4 that baptism by immersion can represent or symbolize the death and burial of our old way of life, and the coming forth or resurrection of our new self. Have your family briefly practice thinking about symbolism by completing the following sentences. When they have finished, ask them to explain why they chose the words they did.

- God is powerful like a _____.
- Prayers are like _____.
- The Holy Ghost could be compared to _____.
- Repentance is like _____.

Tell your family that Revelation 4 contains many symbolic representations. Ask each family member to read Revelation 4:1–11 and draw a picture of what is represented. After the family has had time to draw what they think John is describing, ask them to show and explain their drawings. Share some of the following information with your family about the items John saw, also paying close attention to the Bible footnotes:

The earth is a "sea of glass" (Revelation 4:6)

Have a family member read Doctrine and Covenants 130:6–9. Ask, Why do you think the Lord compares this earth to a sea of glass? (It becomes a great Urim and Thummim.) To better understand how the Urim and Thummim is like a sea of glass, read the following statement to your family: "With the records was found a curious instrument, which the ancients called 'Urim and Thummim,' which consisted of two transparent [see-through] stones set in the rim of a bow fastened to a breast plate. Through the medium of the Urim and Thummim I translated the record by the gift and power of God." (Joseph Smith, *Discourses*

of the Prophet Joseph Smith, compiled by Alma P. Burton, 217.)

Winged beasts (Revelation 4:4–8)

Invite your family to turn to Doctrine and Covenants 77:1–5 and read aloud the questions asked by the Prophet Joseph about Revelation 4 and the answers from the Lord. Ask:

- According to Doctrine and Covenants 77:4, what do the eyes of the beasts represent?
- Why is the eye an appropriate symbol for light and knowledge?
- What do the beast's wings represent?
- What are some means we use today to move quickly from one place to another?

Four classes of beasts (Revelation 4:7)

Ask a family member to read aloud Revelation 4:7. Ask, What are the four beasts mentioned in this verse? What does Doctrine and Covenants 77:3 teach us about these four beasts?

Encourage your family to identify other important symbols mentioned in this chapter. Have them pay close attention to the words describing the throne of God, the feelings of those who are described as being in God's presence, and the descriptions of glory associated with the celestial kingdom. Encourage your family to remain faithful so they may enjoy the full blessings of exaltation in the Celestial Kingdom, surrounding the throne of God.

REVELATION 5: "WORTHY IS THE LAMB"

Revelation 5:1–14

Who can open the book?

If you have a family picture album or personal journal, bind it with string or ribbon so it cannot be opened. If family members do not recognize the album let them know what it contains. Show the album to your family and ask:

- Why might you want to look at what is inside?
- How would you feel if you could only open it if you have never made a mistake?

Read together Revelation 5:1–4 and look for

how this is like John's description in these verses. Ask:

- Who held the book? (Verse 1.) Tell your family that Elder Bruce R. McConkie said that "him that sat on the throne" refers to "God the Father." (*Doctrinal New Testament Commentary*, 3:471.)
- What kind of book was he holding? (Verse 1.) Have your family mark footnote 1*b* which refers them to Doctrine and Covenants 77:6. Remind them that the Prophet Joseph Smith had questions about some things in the book of Revelation and the Lord provided answers in Doctrine and Covenants 77. Have someone read Doctrine and Covenants 77:6.
- What do the seven seals represent? (D&C 77:7.)
- Why did John weep? (Verse 4.)

Explain to your family that now you know what is in the book that John has seen, what would you be willing to do to take a look?

Read together Revelation 5:5. Ask:

- Why was John told not to weep?
- Who is "the Lion of the tribe of Juda, the Root of David"? Share the following explanation: "Christ is the Lion of the Tribe of Judah. (Rev. 5:5.)" (McConkie, *Mormon Doctrine*, 449.)
- What could Christ do that no one else could do? If you look symbolically, what could Christ do that no one else could do?

Tell your family to look for what John saw next, as you read together Revelation 5:6–14. Ask:

- What was the response of every creature in heaven as the Lamb of God (Jesus Christ) took the book and prepared to open the seals?
- What are some of the words and phrases they used as they sang their hymns of praise? Tell your family that Elder Bruce R. McConkie wrote of these passages: "There are no words to describe, no language to use, no rhetoric to employ, which can begin to praise and glorify the Son for all that he has done for us. The words here sung by the myriads of myriads who praise his holy name perhaps come as close as anything in holy writ." (*Doctrinal New Testament Commentary*, 3:472–73.)

Hymn no. 67, "Glory to God on High," is based on these verses. You may want to conclude by singing or reading the words. Ask, How can we honor Jesus Christ today?

REVELATION 6: SIX SEALS

Revelation 6:1–17
Unlocking the mystery of the seals

Prior to scripture study, write the questions from the list below on six sheets of paper, one for each seal. Put the papers in six separate envelopes. Seal the envelopes, and label each envelope with the correct number seal and the corresponding verses from Revelation 6. (The information to put on the envelopes is in italic in the list below.)

Pass out all of the envelopes to family members. Read Doctrine and Covenants 77:6–7 together and explain that you will be studying about the six seals explained in those verses. Tell your family you will open the envelopes one a time (beginning with number one and ending with number six.) Ask the person holding envelope one to open it and do the following:

- Read the question aloud.
- Show family members the scripture reference listed.
- Study the corresponding verses from Revelation 6 to discover the answer.

When you have completed answering the questions in envelope one, continue this pattern until answers in all six envelopes have been found.

Envelope 1 *first seal—*
Revelation 6:1–2

- What kind of noise is made?
- What color is the horse?
- What does the rider have?

Envelope 2 *second seal—*
Revelation 6:3–4

- What color is the horse?
- What power does the rider have?
- What does the rider hold?

Envelope 3 *third seal—*
Revelation 6:5–6

- What color is the horse?
- What does the rider have?
- What does the voice say?

Envelope 4 *fourth seal—*
Revelation 6:7–8

- What color is the horse?
- What is the name of the rider?
- What followed along with the rider?
- What power did they have?

Envelope 5 *fifth seal—*
Revelation 6:9–11

- What is under the altar?
- What do the souls of men say, and what are they given?

Envelope 6 *sixth seal—*
Revelation 6:12–17

- What happened when the sixth seal was opened?
- What do the people do and say?

Share the information below. The information all comes from *Doctrinal New Testament Commentary,* 476–88 by Elder Bruce R. McConkie.

First Seal: 4000 B.C. to 3000 B.C., . . . John saw . . . someone on a white horse (the emblem of victory); who had a bow (weapons of war); wore a crown (the garland or wreath of a conqueror); and who went forth conquering and to conquer (that is, was victorious in war). . . .

"It is clear that the most transcendent happenings involved Enoch and his ministry. John saw . . . the unparalleled wars in which Enoch, as a general over the armies of the saints, 'went forth conquering and to conquer.' . . .

"Truly, never was there a ministry such as Enoch's, and never a conqueror and general who was his equal! How appropriate that he should ride the white horse of victory . . . !"

Second Seal: "Who rode the red horse . . . of war and bloodshed and a sword, during the second seal? Perhaps it was the devil himself, for surely that was the great day of his power, a day of such gross wickedness that every living soul (save eight

only) was found worthy of death by drowning, which wickedness caused the Lord God of Heaven to bring in the floods upon them. . . .

"Suffice it to say that the era from 3000 B.C. to 2000 B.C., was one of war and destruction . . .

"Of the wickedness and abominations of Noah's day [see] (Moses 8:22, 28–29.)"

Third Seal: "As famine follows the sword, so the pangs of hunger gnawed in the bellies of the Lord's people during the third seal. From 2000 B.C. to 1000 B.C., as never in any other age of the earth's history, the black horse of hunger influenced the whole history of God's dealings with his people.

"In the beginning years of this seal, the famine in Ur of the Chaldees was so severe that Abraham's brother, Haran, starved to death, while the father of the faithful was commanded by God to take his family to Canaan. (Abra. 1:29–30; 2:15.) Of his struggle to gain sufficient food to keep alive, Abraham said: [see] (Abra. 2:17, 21.) [see] (Gen. 41:53–57; 42; 43; 44.)

"Abraham's tenure in mortality was from 1996 to 1822 B. C.; the seven years of famine foretold in Pharaoh's dream commenced in 1709 B. C.; and the exodus from Egypt was in 1491 B. C. Truly the third seal was a millennium in which hunger among men affected the whole course of God's dealings with his people."

Fourth Seal: "During the fourth seal, from 1000 B. C. to the coming of our Lord, death rode roughshod through the nations of men, and hell was at his heels. . . . the slain among the ungodly in this age of bloodshed—whether by sword or by famine or by pestilence or by wild beasts—were, at their death, cast down to hell. This is the millennium of those great kingdoms and nations whose wars and treacheries tormented and overran, again and again, the people whom Jehovah had chosen to bear his name. This is also the general era in which the Lord's own people warred among themselves and sent countless numbers of their own brethren to untimely graves."

Fifth Seal: "Where the Lord's people are concerned, the events of the fifth seal, that period from our Lord's birth down to 1000 A.D., . . . :

"1. The birth into mortality of God's only Son; his ministry among men; and the atoning sacrifice which he wrought by the shedding of his own blood.

"2. The spread and perfection of the Church which was set up by Him whose Church it is, and the unbelievable fanaticism among unbelievers that made acceptance of martyrdom almost synonymous with acceptance of the gospel.

"3. . . . the complete falling away from true and perfect Christianity, which sad 'eventuality ushered in the long night of apostate darkness' . . .

"The Lord revealing here, that portion of the sealed book which deals with the doctrine of martyrdom. Among the ancient saints martyrdom was an ever present possibility, one which completely occupied their thoughts and feelings. They knew that by forsaking all to follow Christ, they might, if fate so decreed, be called to lay down their lives for Him who had laid down his life for them. In an almost death-inviting sense, the meridian of time was the dispensation of martyrdom."

Sixth Seal: "We are now living during the final years of the sixth seal, that thousand year period which began in 1000 A.D. and will continue through the Saturday night of time and until just before the Sabbatical era when Christ shall reign personally on earth, when all of the blessings of the Great Millennium shall be poured out upon this planet. This, accordingly, is the era when the signs of the times shall be shown forth, and they are in fact everywhere to be seen. Speaking of events destined to occur near the close of the sixth seal, the Lord, on December 27, 1832, said to Joseph Smith: [see] (D. & C. 88:87.)"

REVELATION 7: THE EXALTED STAND BEFORE THE THRONE OF GOD

Revelation 7:1–8
Who are the 144,000?

Tell your family to multiply 12,000 x 12. Explain that Revelation 7:1–8 gives the answer to the problem in two different ways. Have them scan verses 1–8, looking for the answer represented in two different ways. Ask:

• Which verse tells the total number?

• Where do these 144,000 come from? (Verse 4.)
• How do verses 5–8 give the other way 144,000 is stated?

Help your family better understand who these 144,000 are by reading Doctrine and Covenants 77:9, 11 and sharing the following quotation from the Prophet Joseph Smith:

"The servants of God are sealed in their foreheads, which signifies sealing the blessing upon their heads, meaning the everlasting covenant, thereby making their calling and election sure." (*Teachings of the Prophet Joseph Smith*, 321.)

Discuss the following questions:

• According to Doctrine and Covenants 77:11, what are these 144,000 to do?
• Why does Heavenly Father want us to share the gospel with others?
• What can you do to help?
• Who is one person you could share the gospel with this week?
• What might you do to help that person?

Revelation 7:9–17
What will it be like to stand in the presence of God?

Read Joseph Smith History—1:17 to your family, emphasizing the phrase: "whose brightness and glory defy all description." Ask, What do you think Joseph Smith meant?

Read Doctrine and Covenants 76:113–16 and explain that these verses were written just after Joseph Smith and Sidney Rigdon had a vision of the celestial kingdom. Ask:

• What might it be like to gaze into heaven?
• What words or phrases show how difficult it is to explain heavenly visions?

Share the following statement:

"Could you gaze into heaven five minutes, you would know more than you would by reading all that ever was written on the subject." (*Teachings of the Prophet Joseph Smith*, 324.)

Explain that John the Revelator also had a chance to see the celestial kingdom. He described it in Revelation 7. Remind your family of two things: 1) that as you study his vision, you will sense how difficult it might have been for him to describe the beauty and glory of that sacred place; 2) the book of Revelation is filled with symbolism.

Have your family read Revelation 7:9–17, looking for answers to the following questions. When they have finished, ask everyone to report:

- What evidence do you see of people worshipping God?
- What type of people are privileged to stand in God's presence?
- What evidence do you see that the celestial kingdom is a place of joy and happiness?

Following your discussion, read verse 14. Ask:

- How did their robes become white?
- How can a robe become white in blood?

Explain that the blood of the Lamb (Jesus Christ) is the only way in which we can become clean from the stains of this world. As a family, read Isaiah 1:18. Share your testimony regarding the power of the Atonement.

Have someone read Revelation 7:16–17. Explain that this is a fulfillment of prophesy given by Jesus while He was on the earth. Read to your family John 4:14 and 6:35, and ask if they can understand how Revelation 7:16–17 fulfills the earlier prophecy of never hungering and thirsting?

Share your testimony of Jesus Christ and how He is the "Living Water" and the "Bread of Life."

REVELATION 8: THE SEVENTH SEAL OPENS

Revelation 8:5–13
Guess what it is

Read Revelation 8:5–6 to your family and explain that as each trumpet sounds, another plague comes upon the earth. The first four of seven plagues are in chapter 8 and the rest are in chapter 9. Divide your family into four groups and secretly give them one of the references below. Instruct them to draw a picture representing the information in their verses:

1. Verse 7
2. Verses 8–9
3. Verses 10–11
4. Verses 12–13

After they have illustrated their verses, have each group show their picture with an explanation of what it represents. Then read together Revelation 8:7–13 and have family members guess which illustration goes with which verses. Ask:

- What do you think each plague is describing? (Volcano, asteroid, pollution, etc.)
- What warning is there in verse 13?
- What plagues did Moses bring upon the Egyptians? (See Exodus 7–12.)
- While the plagues punished the Egyptians, what good did they do for Israel?

Remind your family that the judgments are to punish the wicked, not the Lord's followers.

REVELATION 9: LAST GREAT WAR

Revelation 9:1–21
Who will survive that last great war before Christ comes?

Explain to your family that Revelation 9 describes events of the last great war before Jesus Christ returns to the earth. Ask your family to begin reading Revelation 9. When they become confused, read the following commentary by Elder Bruce R. McConkie:

"Influenced by the temptations of the devil wicked men (locusts) began their warfare.

"During this particular period of the war and desolation the evil forces will be directed against all men, save those sealed up unto eternal life, for those in Zion shall be preserved. The plagues and torments of this era shall so afflict men that they shall desire to die rather than to suffer more. Perhaps John is seeing such things as the effects of poisonous gas, or bacteriological warfare, or atomic fallout, which disable but do not kill.

"In prophetic imagery John here seeks to describe a war fought with weapons and under circumstances entirely foreign to any experience of his own or of the people of that day. . . .

"It is not improbable that these ancient prophets were seeing such things as men wearing or protected by strong armor; as troops of cavalry and companies of tanks and flame throwers; as airplanes and airborne missiles which explode, fire shells and drop bombs; and even other weapons yet to be devised in an age when warfare is the desire and love of wicked men. . . .

"Satan [Abaddon or Apollyon] is the unseen head of the armies of men as they fight in the last great battles of earth." (*Doctrinal New Testament Commentary,* 3:501–3.)

Read together Revelation 9:1–19 and have your family identify and write in their scriptures words or ideas from Elder McConkie's commentary that help explain each verse. Discuss the following:

- Who was the head over the wicked army?
- Who will be saved or preserved?
- What might we do to have God's "seal"? (See Revelation 3:12; 22:4; D&C 109:22–28.)

Read together verses 20–21 and ask why the wicked refuse to repent even after all the calamities. Have your family scan Mormon 2:12–15 and Mormon 4:10–11, looking for similar people in the Book of Mormon. Share your gratitude that one day the Lord will cleanse the earth of all wickedness and preserve His people.

REVELATION 10: JOHN THE BELOVED'S MISSION

Revelation 10:1–11
What is the "little book" that John eats?

Invite your family to recall or imagine a mission call coming to a family member. Ask them what they think it would be like for a person to open a mission call from the Lord. Silently read Revelation 10:1–11 to see what it was like for the Apostle John to receive a mission call. Ask:

- What does John see in verses 1–2?
- What do you think the angel meant by saying "there should be time no longer?" (Verse 6; Bruce R. McConkie wrote: "That there should be no more delay—not that time as such should end and eternity begin, for the Millennial Era is still ahead—but, . . . that 'Satan shall be bound,' thus ending the 'time' (it 'shall be no longer'!) when persecution prevails. . . . The appointed season or time of delay is at an end." (*Doctrinal New Testament Commentary,* 3:506.)

- What was John asked to do with the "little book"? (Verses 8–9.)
- What two words describe what John tasted as he ate the book? (Verse 9.)
- How can a mission be both sweet and bitter?
- What does the bitter belly represent?
- How might preaching the gospel be "sweet"?
- What was John's mission?

Have one family member read Doctrine and Covenants 77:14. Ask:

- What does the book seem to represent?
- Whom is John called to minister to?
- How is John to help the lost ten tribes?
- How could John do all that in his lifetime? (Remind them that John was a translated being [see D&C 7] and allowed to live without aging so he could accomplish his mission.)
- Do you think John fulfilled his mission?

Read the following statement to your family:

"The Spirit of the Lord fell upon Joseph in an unusual manner, and he prophesied that John the Revelator was then among the Ten Tribes of Israel . . . to prepare them for their return . . . to again possess the land of their fathers." (Smith, *History of the Church,* 1:176.)

Encourage your family to prepare now to serve however and wherever the Lord calls. Testify of the blessings that have come from accepting calls.

REVELATION 11: "MY TWO WITNESSES"

Revelation 11:1–19
Two prophets shall be slain in Jerusalem

Write the following numbers on small slips of paper and place them face down (so the numbers cannot be seen) in front of family members: 42, 1260, 2, 3½, ⅒, 7,000. Tell them to take turns turning over the slips of paper to reveal a number. When a number is revealed, have them search Revelation 11:1–14 and find how that number pertains to the chapter. Have them discuss their findings before turning the next one over. You will find information and questions on the following page to help in your discussion.

(42) "Forty and two months" (Verse 2.) The time the holy city shall be trodden down by the Gentiles.

(1260) "A thousand two hundred and threescore days" (Verse 3.) The time two witnesses shall prophesy.

(2) "Two witnesses" (Verse 3.) Have family members write D&C 77:15 in the margin next to Revelation 11:3. Have someone read Doctrine and Covenants 77:15 aloud. Share the following insight: Bruce R. McConkie said, "No doubt they [the two witnesses] will be members of the Council of the Twelve or of the First Presidency of the Church. Their prophetic ministry to rebellious Jewry shall be the same in length as was our Lord's personal ministry among their rebellious forebears." (*Doctrinal New Testament Commentary,* 3:509–10.) Ask:

- What powers will these two witnesses have?
- What will happen to these two witnesses?
- What will they finish before they are killed?
- What does that tell us about who is really in control?

"Two olive trees and the two candlesticks" (Verse 4.) These are symbols of the two witnesses.

(3½) "Three days and a half" (Verses 9, 11.) How long the bodies of the slain witnesses shall lie in the streets before they are resurrected. Ask:

- How will many of the people react to the death of these two witnesses? (Verse 10.)
- What will they feel when they see these same two witnesses resurrect? (Verse 11.)

(¹⁄₁₀) "The tenth part of the city" (Verse 13.) Part of the city that falls with the great earthquake.

(7,000) "Seven thousand" (Verse 13.) This is the number of men slain in the earthquake.

Read together Revelation 11:15–19. Ask:

- What great event is being spoken of when the kingdoms of this world become the kingdoms of our Lord, and He reigns personally upon the earth? (Verse 15.)
- What will the righteous receive? (Verse 18.)
- What will happen to the wicked? (Verse 18.)

Testify about the importance of living righteously as you watch for the signs or events described in this chapter.

REVELATION 12: SATAN WAGES WAR WITH THE WOMAN

Revelation 12:1–17
The war in heaven rages on today

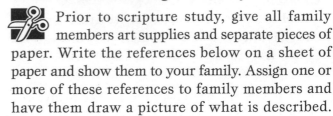 Prior to scripture study, give all family members art supplies and separate pieces of paper. Write the references below on a sheet of paper and show them to your family. Assign one or more of these references to family members and have them draw a picture of what is described. Joseph Smith Translation Revelation 12:1–17 is found in Bible Appendix, 812–13.

1. JST Revelation 12:1–2
2. JST Revelation 12:3–4
3. JST Revelation 12:5
4. JST Revelation 12:6
5. JST Revelation 12:7
6. JST Revelation 12:8–9
7. JST Revelation 12:10–12
8. JST Revelation 12:13–14
9. JST Revelation 12:15
10. JST Revelation 12:16
11. JST Revelation 12:17

When the drawings are finished, have each person read their references, show their drawings, and explain what they represent. Display the drawings in chronological order on a wall. If any references were not illustrated, study those verses together as a family.

Discuss the following questions:

- Who is the woman? (JST Revelation 12:7.)
- Who is the child? (JST Revelation 12:7.)
- Who is the dragon? (See Moses 4:1–4; D&C 29:36–38.)
- Who are the stars of heaven? (See Job 38:4–7.)
- Who is Michael in Joseph Smith Translation Revelation 12:7*b*?
- What else do we know about the dragon (Satan)? (See D&C 76:25–26; 93:25.)
- Why could salvation only come after Satan was cast to the earth? (Elder Bruce R. McConkie wrote: "It is only by resisting his [Satan's] wiles and rising above his carnal way of life that men can pass the test of mortality

which assures them of salvation. Without opposition there could be no salvation." [*Doctrinal New Testament Commentary,* 3:518.])

- What else is required for salvation, according to JST Revelation 12:11? (See D&C 76:40–42.)
- What might it mean in verse 14 that the woman (the Church) fled "into the wilderness"? (See D&C 86:3*c*; Bruce R. McConkie also wrote: "[Satan] prevails; the Church is taken from the earth—for a specified period, for the age of spiritual darkness and universal apostasy." [*Doctrinal New Testament Commentary,* 3:519.])
- Who else besides the woman (the Church) does the dragon wage war with? (Verse 17.)

Ask family members to silently read JST Revelation 12:11, 17. Ask them why Satan desires to war against those who have testimonies of Christ. Remind them that the war that Satan began in heaven continues to rage on earth today. Share the statement below:

"What kind of war? The same kind that prevails on earth; the only kind Satan and spirit beings can wage—a war of words, a tumult of opinions, a conflict of ideologies; a war between truth and error, between light and darkness, between the gospel of Jesus Christ, with all its saving power, and the false religions of the world. . . . the battle lines are still drawn. It is now on earth as it was then in heaven; every man must choose which general he will follow." (McConkie, *Doctrinal New Testament Commentary,* 3:518.)

Ask family members to record on the chart below where they are in the battle:

Faithful	Wavering	Falling	Overcome by Satan

Then have them record what they can do to continue faithful and strong.

REVELATION 13: SATAN CONTROLS EARTHLY KINGDOMS

Revelation 13:1–18

What are we to understand regarding the beasts in John's vision?

 Ask your family to define the word "counterfeit" and give examples. Tell your family that as they learn about the beasts John the Revelator saw and described in Revelation 13, have them look for a counterfeit. Divide your family into two groups and give each a sheet of paper and a pen. Assign the first group verses 1–10 and the second group verses 11–18. Encourage them to use footnotes, the chapter heading, and the Bible Dictionary. Have each group record the following:

- How would you describe the beast?
- What is the beast doing?
- Who inspires the beast?
- Who will follow and worship this beast?

Allow your family time to read and prepare the required information. Have both groups share what they found. Discuss the following questions:

- What did Joseph Smith say the two beasts in this chapter represented? (Footnote 13:1*a*.)
- Who gave these beasts their power? (Elder Bruce R. McConkie wrote: "The devil gives power, positions of influence, and great authority to those kingdoms which follow him. 'There is a mistranslation of the word dragon' in this verse, the Prophet says. 'It ought to be translated devil in this case and not dragon.' [*Teachings,* p. 293.]" [*Doctrinal New Testament Commentary,* 3:521.])
- What is the beast's desire? (Verses 7, 14.)
- What might the second beast be a counterfeit of? (Verse 11; trying to seem harmless as a lamb. Bruce R. McConkie wrote: "The Great Imitator is able to blind the eyes and deceive the hearts of men." [*Doctrinal New Testament Commentary,* 3:524].)
- How were the followers of the beast identified? ("All" refers to the wicked [Revelation 20:4].)
- Why was a mark placed on their foreheads or hands? ("Figuratively, this means they receive blessings—if his rewards lawfully may be so named—from under his hands. . . ." [McConkie, *Doctrinal New Testament Commentary,* 3:524.])

Explain that in Revelation 13 we see Satan trying to impersonate the truth. Ask:

- Why do you think Satan tries to impersonate the truth?

- How can we recognize the counterfeits and stay on the Lord's side?

Encourage your family to watch out for life's imposters and to lay hold upon the Lamb of God.

Tell your family that even though it is difficult to understand everything represented in the scriptures, we do have a great promise from the Lord. Read Doctrine and Covenants 101:32–33.

REVELATION 14: THE RESTORATION COMES THROUGH ANGELIC MINISTRY

Revelation 14:6–7
The angel of the Restoration

Show your family a picture of the angel Moroni atop one of our latter-day temples. (*Gospel Art Kit,* no. 502—*Salt Lake Temple.*)

Talk about who is represented by this statue and share ideas about why a Moroni statue is atop some of our temples. Read Revelation 14:6–7 aloud and ask family members to guess who the angel is referred to here. Sing or read the words of verses 1 and 4 from "An Angel from on High." (*Hymns,* no. 13.) Share the following information by Elder Bruce R. McConkie:

"Moroni brought the word . . . found in the Book of Mormon. . . . Also . . . John the Baptist, and Peter, James and John . . . had brought keys and powers . . . other angels were yet to come—Moses, Elias, Elijah, Gabriel, Raphael . . . (D&C 128:21.)

"Thus . . . Moroni brought the message, that is, the word; but other angels brought the keys and priesthood, the power. . . . The fullness of the everlasting gospel consists of all of the truths and powers needed to enable men to gain a fullness of salvation. . . .

"One of the most interesting things about John's record of his vision is that it is one of those great prophetic utterances destined to have dual fulfillment. . . . One is past, the other is future. The gospel has been restored. . . . there is a future day when the angel of the restoration shall fly again. . . . (D&C 88:103–104.)" (*Doctrinal New Testament Commentary,* 3:530.)

Ask your family what they can do to demonstrate their appreciation for the blessings of the Restoration.

Revelation 14:8–20
The destruction of the wicked and the gathering of the righteous

Have family members scan through Revelation 14:8–20 and mark each time they find the word "angel." Explain that these angels prepare the earth for the Savior's Second Coming. Assign each family member to one of the angels they found and look for the following information about that angel:

- What was the angel doing?
- What items was the angel holding or using?
- Does this angel seem to be working for the righteous or against the wicked?
- What do this angel's actions teach you about God's preparations for the Second Coming?

Invite family members to share how they answered their questions. The following questions and statements may help you in a follow-up discussion:

- What is meant by fornication? "Literally, sex immorality; figuratively, the worship of false gods." (McConkie, *Doctrinal New Testament Commentary,* 3:532.)
- What do you think the "wine of the wrath of God . . . poured without mixture into the cup of his indignation" means? "'This wine of God's wrath is undiluted; there is no drop of water to cool its heat.' (*Jamieson,* p. 586.) It is justice, not mercy which the Lord will pour out upon the ungodly." (McConkie, *Doctrinal New Testament Commentary,* 3:533.)
- When someone worships the beast (Satan), what are the consequences in wrath and torment "for ever and ever"? "*Eternal damnation* is also used to specify the punishment of those who come forth in the *resurrection of damnation* (John 5:29) meaning those who are destined to inherit the telestial kingdom and those who will be cast out to reign with the devil and his angels as sons of perdition. (D&C 76:30–49, 81–112; 88:100–102.)" (McConkie, *Mormon Doctrine,* 234.)

• What does it mean that the "torment ascendeth up forever and ever"? " . . . they are damned, and cannot go where God and Christ are (D&C 76:112), are never completely free from the lingering remorse that always follows the loss of opportunity." (McConkie, *Mormon Doctrine*, 235.)

REVELATION 15: CELESTIAL GLORY

Revelation 15:1–8
Heaven and angels

Ask a family member to read the chapter heading for Revelation 15 to discover two main themes in this chapter. Have everyone scan Revelation 15:1–8 and ask:

• Which verses focus on the celestial kingdom?
• How do you think it might feel to enter into the presence of God?
• How will the exalted children of Heavenly Father treat Him?
• Why would you want to glorify His name and worship Him eternally?
• What feelings of love do you possess for God?

To help your family better understand the "sea of glass" mentioned in Revelation 15:2, have them read Doctrine and Covenants 130:7–11. Ask:

• What can be seen by those who dwell on a globe of molten sea of glass?
• What is another name for the molten sea?
• What will become of this earth?
• What will be given to all who dwell there?
• What is written on the white stone?

REVELATION 16: SEVEN ANGELS POUR OUT PLAGUES UPON THE WICKED

Revelation 16:1–12
Pouring out plagues upon the wicked

 Set six glasses or cups in front of your family. Inside each container, place a piece of paper with one of the scripture references written on it listed below:

Verses	Where	Contents of Vial
2	Earth	Noisome, grievous sore
3	Sea	Blood
4–7	Rivers, fountains	Blood
8–9	Sun	Fire, heat
10–11	Seat of beast	Darkness, pain
12	Euphrates	Drought

Ask your family members to silently read Revelation 16:1. Tell them that a vial is a small container that holds liquid. Ask:

• What do the vials contain?
• What does the word wrath mean?
• What are the angels asked to do with the contents of each vial?

Invite family members to take a slip of paper from one of the vials. Explain that each piece of paper has written upon it a verse describing a plague that God will pour out upon the earth. Ask each person to read the verse(s) and explain what is in the vial and where it will be poured out. (See the six references in the chart above for additional help.) Ask:

• What happened after each vial was poured?
• What emotions do you feel as you read about these events?
• Why should the righteous not be afraid of these plagues? (See 1 Nephi 22:14–19, 28.)

Ask your family to think about why God will pour out these plagues. Read aloud Doctrine and Covenants 19:15 and ask:

• What does our Father in Heaven desire that all His children do?
• If we don't repent, what will God do?
• Why do you think it is best to choose humility rather than suffer God's punishments?
• Why do you think these plagues will be poured out upon the wicked?

Tell your family that we can either be humble and repent on our own, or our Father in Heaven will humble us.

Revelation 16:13–21
The battle of Armageddon and the Second Coming of Christ

 Ask your family to silently read Revelation 16:13–14. Ask:

- What images are mentioned in verse 13?
- What fallen angel do you think of when hearing: dragon, beast, false prophet?
- What is their purpose? (Verse 14; see also Mathew 24:24.)

Read aloud Revelation 16:14–15. Ask your family what they think it means to "[keep] your garments?" Read the following:

"To keep one's garments is to be ready for any eventuality. (Specifically, here, the coming of the Lord.)" (Parry and Parry, *Understanding the Book of Revelation*, 210.)

Ask, What great battle do soldiers need to be prepared for? (Armageddon; verse 16.) Explain to your family that Satan will do his best to show false signs and try to deceive the very elect as he leads kings into this great last battle.

Remind your family that earlier you read about what was in the six vials being poured out upon the earth. Read aloud Revelation 16:17–21. Ask:

- Where does the seventh angel pour his vial? Remind your family that six angels had already poured their vials upon the earth.
- What events can be caused in the air or atmosphere of this earth? (Verse 18.)
- What great city will be destroyed? (Babylon; verse 19.) Remind your family that Babylon is symbolic of wickedness upon the earth.
- What does verse 20 teach about the power of the great earthquake poured out upon the earth?
- How can we tell that the atmosphere is also in great commotion? (Bible Dictionary, "Weights and Measures," 789, for the weight of a talent.)

Ask your family how we can find peace even when the world is in commotion. (See John 14:27.)

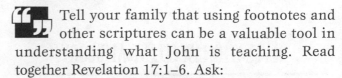

Revelation 17:1–18
"The church of the devil"

Tell your family that using footnotes and other scriptures can be a valuable tool in understanding what John is teaching. Read together Revelation 17:1–6. Ask:

- What does the "great whore" symbolize? (Footnote 1*b*.)
- What do the "many waters" symbolize?

Tell your family that the prophet Nephi was shown similar things in vision some six hundred years before the Apostle John's revelation. Fortunately, we can read his account in the Book of Mormon. Have family members study Revelation 17:51 and 1 Nephi 14:9–12 and discuss why they think the Lord said there were really only two churches, even though we see many different churches all around us.

Share the following from Elder Bruce R. McConkie: "The titles church of the devil and great and abominable church are used to identify all churches or organizations of whatever name or nature—whether political, philosophical, educational, economic, social, fraternal, civic or religious—which are designed to take men on a course that leads away from God and his laws and thus from salvation in the kingdom of God." (*Mormon Doctrine*, 137–38.)

"The church of the devil . . . is all the forces of evil linked together. . . . All men are in one camp or the other; those who are not for the Lord are against him. In other words, the church of the devil is the world; it is all the carnality and evil to which fallen man is heir; it is every unholy and wicked practice." (*Doctrinal New Testament Commentary*, 3:551.)

Take turns reading Revelation 17:7–18 and share the following statement: "These passages dealing with the beast upon which the woman sat, and of the relationship of various kingdoms to the events seen, is a perfect illustration of what the Prophet [Joseph Smith] had in mind when he said:

'Whenever God gives a vision of an image, or beast, or figure of any kind, he always holds himself responsible to give a revelation or interpretation of the meaning thereof, otherwise we are not responsible or accountable for our belief in it. Don't be afraid of being damned for not knowing the meaning of a vision or figure, if God has not given a revelation or interpretation of the subject.' (*Teachings,* p. 291.)" (McConkie, *Doctrinal New Testament Commentary,* 3:553–54.)

Have family members write 1 Nephi 14:13–17 at the end of Revelation 17:14 and study both those passages. Ask:

- Who is going to win the war?
- How important then, is the decision about which side we're on?

Bear testimony that no matter how numerous the wicked become, the Lord is more powerful.

REVELATION 18: BABYLON FALLS

Revelation 18:1–8
The end of wickedness

Sing verses 1 and 3 of "Israel, Israel, God is Calling," (*Hymns,* no. 7) together with your family. Have a family member read Revelation 18:1–2 aloud. Ask your family what similarities they see between these verses in Revelation and that hymn. Also consider reading the information regarding Babylon in the Bible Dictionary, p. 618, especially the last phrase which states: "In D&C 1:16, Babylon means the world."

Invite family members to list some of the wicked things they see in the world today. Read Revelation 18:3 and find what this verse could add to your list.

Set a measuring cup full of water in a pie tin. Ask family members to read Revelation 18:6–8 and tell how much more water you would have to pour into the cup to match the punishments God has promised to pour out on the wicked.

Read together Doctrine and Covenants 1:9; 64:24; 86:7. List what else the Lord has promised would come upon Babylon because of her wickedness. Ask your family members how it makes them feel to hear of these dreadful sins and what they

think they can do to avoid becoming entangled in the sins and plagues of this world. Have family members look in Revelation 18:4, 1 Nephi 14:14, and Doctrine and Covenants 133:14 for recommendations. Make a list of ways your family can avoid the wickedness of this world.

Share this statement by Elder M. Russell Ballard: "In the Church, we often state the couplet, 'Be in the world but not of the world.' As we observe television shows that make profanity, violence, and infidelity commonplace and even glamorous, we often wish we could lock out the world in some ways and isolate our families from it all. . . .

"Perhaps we should state the couplet previously mentioned as two separate admonitions. First, *'Be in the world.'* Be involved; be informed. Try to be understanding and tolerant and to appreciate diversity. Make meaningful contributions to society through service and involvement. Second, *'Be not of the world.'* Do not follow wrong paths or bend to accommodate or accept what is not right. . . .

"Members of the Church need to influence more than we are influenced. We should work to stem the tide of sin and evil instead of passively being swept along by it. We each need to help solve the problem rather than avoid or ignore it." (*Ensign,* May 1989, 80.)

REVELATION 19: THE SECOND COMING

Revelation 19:1–9
Marriage supper of the Lamb

Show your family wedding pictures of someone they know. Tell stories about that day and discuss the excitement and nervousness associated with a wedding. Ask everyone:

- Who will you invite to your wedding?
- What will the bride and groom wear?
- Where will your wedding take place?

Explain that Revelation 19:1–9 describes a wedding. Have family members take turns reading those verses looking for whose wedding is described and what the bride and groom are wearing. Also discuss the following questions:

- Who is the bride? (Verse 8.)

- Why is it important for the bride to be "clean and white"? (See verse 8; Psalms 24:3–4.)
- According to Psalms 24:3–4, how do we qualify to stand in holy places?
- In what ways is the temple a holy place?
- Who is the groom? (Verse 9; footnote *c*.)
- If Jesus is the groom and the bride represents the Saints, why are they marrying? (Couples make covenants with one another in the temple. This can bind or seal them together forever as a family. Similarly, we can make covenants with Jesus Christ to be bound eternally to God and His kingdom. The marriage of the Saints to Jesus is a way of signifying that eternal, binding covenant.)
- What can you do to prepare yourself for "the marriage supper of the Lamb"?

Share the following insight:

"'In this dispensation the Bridegroom, who is the Lamb of God, shall come to claim his bride, which is the Church composed of the faithful saints who have watched for his return. . . . ' (*Mormon Doctrine*, 2nd ed., 469.) The elders of Israel are now issuing the invitations to the marriage supper of the Lord; those who believe and obey the gospel thereby accept the invitation and shall sit in due course with the King's Son at the marriage feast." (McConkie, *Doctrinal New Testament Commentary*, 5:563–64.)

As we share the Gospel message with others, we are helping Christ invite others to His marriage feast.

Revelation 19:11–21
Armageddon

Ask your family to imagine a flesh-eating bird, a white horse, the Savior, and a scene from a battle or war. Tell them that all of these images are discussed in Revelation 19:11–21. Invite family members to read the entry under "Armageddon" in the Bible Dictionary, 614. Ask:

- Where will the last great battle, prior to the Second Coming, take place? Use map 10 (map 5 in pre-1999 copies of the Bible) in the King James Version of the Bible to locate Megiddo and read the short paragraph that accompanies it.

- What is the name of the valley where the great last battle will commence? (Explain that a terrible battle will take place in the Jezreel Valley. It will move south and encircle Jerusalem. After a long and terrible battle, Jerusalem will be close to falling. The Savior will come, stopping the battle and saving the inhabitants.)

Read Revelation 19:11–21 with the understanding that the battle of Armageddon is being described in these verses. The following information will be helpful:

- Verse 11, the white horse. (White is a representation of purity. The horse is a representation of war, power, and strength.)
- Verses 12–16, the horse's rider. (Read footnote 11*a* to discover who the rider is, and then have your family read Doctrine and Covenants 110:2–3 for another description of that same rider.)
- Verses 17–18, "the supper of the great God." (This is a description of what will happen after the war has been stopped and Jesus has destroyed the wicked. The birds will come and devour the flesh of the dead.)
- Verses 19–21, those who fight against the Savior. (The beast [Satan], the false prophets and all those who received the mark of the beast [Satan's followers] will be cast into their place by the "sword, which proceeded out of his mouth" [by the word of Jesus Christ]. [See footnote 15*a*.])

Testify to your family that while there will be war preceding the Second Coming, it will also be a time of rejoicing and great hope.

REVELATION 20: BINDING OF SATAN, MILLENNIUM, RESURRECTION, AND JUDGMENT

Revelation 20:1–3, 7–10
How is Satan to be bound?

Bring a set of keys to scripture study. Show your family the keys and ask them to explain some of the ways we use keys. Have someone read Revelation 20:1–3 and discuss the following questions:

- What does the key in verse 1 open?
- What is another name for the bottomless pit?
- Who will be bound and cast into the pit?
- How long will Satan be confined to the bottomless pit?
- How will Satan be bound? (1 Nephi 22:26.) Elder Bruce R. McConkie wrote: "When we speak of the binding of Satan in connection with the millennium, we mean that he will be bound during that era, that his powers will be limited after that day commences." (*Doctrinal New Testament Commentary,* 3:570.)
- What is the result of Satan's binding?
- What would life be like if Satan were bound today? (See Doctrine and Covenants 45:58.)
- How could we, as a family, begin a type of Millennium in our home? (We can bind Satan through obedience. For example, read 3 Nephi 11:29 and discuss how eliminating contention can bind Satan.)

Ask your family what they think happens at the end of the Millennium. Read together Revelation 20:7–10. Ask:

- According to these verses what happens at the end of a thousand years?
- How long might a "little season" be? "President Joseph Fielding Smith suggests it [a little season] may last about 1000 years. His reasoning is that Christ came in the meridian or midday of time; that from the fall to his coming was 4000 years; that from then until now is another 2000; that the millennium itself will be 1000; and that to make the time of his coming the actual meridian of earth's temporal continuance needs the added 1000 years of postmillennial existence. (See *Doctrines of Salvation,* vol. 1, p. 81.)" (McConkie, *Doctrinal New Testament Commentary,* 3:572.)
- According to verse 8, what does Satan do when he is loosed? ("Gog and Magog" is a name given to the war that comes after Satan is loosed and deceives the nations after the Millennium.)
- Who will participate in the war known as Gog and Magog? ("This final great battle, in which

evil spirits, mortal men, and resurrected personages all participate, will be the end of war as far as this earth is concerned." [Bruce R. McConkie, *Mormon Doctrine,* 75.])

Talk to your family about the consequences of following Satan and what they can do to avoid such a fate.

Revelation 20:11–15
Judgment

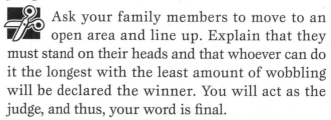 Ask your family members to move to an open area and line up. Explain that they must stand on their heads and that whoever can do it the longest with the least amount of wobbling will be declared the winner. You will act as the judge, and thus, your word is final.

After the activity is over, discuss what you saw and declare a winner. Ask:

- What role did I play? (Judge.)
- Why was it important to have a judge?
- What could not have happened without a judge?

Take turns reading Revelation 20:11–15. Ask:

- Who will be the final judge? (God.)
- What will we be judged by? (Our works.)
- In what book is kept the record of our works?
- What will happen to those whose names are not recorded in the book of life?
- How can we ensure our names are written in the book of life?

Remind your family of the activity at the beginning of the lesson and that there was only one winner declared. Explain that in God's plan all that are obedient will be winners; thus the whole family can win through obedience.

REVELATION 21: CELESTIAL GLORY

Revelation 21:1–8, 22–27
How wonderful will celestial glory be?

Ask your family to imagine being in heaven. List their ideas of what they think heaven will be like on a sheet of paper. Divide your family into two groups. Have one group read Revelation

21:1–8 and the other Revelation 21:22–27. Have each group find more things to add to the list. These additional things might include:

Group One

1. A holy city. (Verse 2.)
2. God will dwell with man. (Verse 3.)
3. God will comfort His people and remove all sorrow, pain and death. (Verse 4.)
4. Everything will be new. (Verse 5.)
5. We will drink from the "fountain of the water of life freely." (Verse 6.)
6. We will "inherit all things" and be Christ's children. (Verse 7; see also Romans 8:17.)
7. We will dwell with people with similar values. (Verse 8.)

Group Two

1. God and the Savior will be our temple.
2. Light will come from "God and the Lamb."
3. Kings and nations will honor God.
4. The gates will always be open. (Verse 25.)
5. There shall be no night or darkness there.
6. Nothing unclean will come into God's glory.
7. Everyone whose name is written in the Lamb's book will be there. (Verse 27.)

Ask your family what things on these lists appeal to them most and why.

Revelation 21:9–21
Characteristics of the New Jerusalem coming down from heaven

Tell your family that when the Apostle John saw the celestial kingdom, he saw a holy city. Read aloud Revelation 21:2. Ask:

* What is the name of John's holy city?
* Where does it come from?

Read together Revelation 21:9–17 and look for characteristics that describe this New Jerusalem.

Have your family note everything of worldly value in verses 18–21. Ask:

* What do you think the most precious metal is?
* What are our roads made of?
* What are the streets made of in heaven?
* What does that show us about the material things people value in this life?
* Knowing this, what should our treasures be? (See Matthew 6:19.)

Ask your family what they think it will be like to live in this heavenly city and whether or not they would like to live there. Challenge your family to seek God's kingdom first and then they will have all things added unto them.

REVELATION 22: THE FAITHFUL SAINTS INHERIT A CELESTIAL EARTH

Revelation 22:1–7
John sees the throne of God

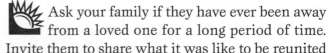 Ask your family if they have ever been away from a loved one for a long period of time. Invite them to share what it was like to be reunited with that loved one. Ask:

* How long have you been away from your Father in Heaven?
* What do you imagine it will be like when you return to His presence?

To find out what it might be like to return to God's presence, take turns reading Revelation 22:1–7 as you discuss the following questions:

* What did John see flowing from God's throne? (Verse 1.)
* What do you think this "water of life" represents? (See John 4:10, 14.)
* What grew along the bank of the river?
* Who saw the tree of life? (See Genesis 2:8–9; 1 Nephi 8:10–11; 1 Nephi 11:25.)
* In Lehi and Nephi's dream, what did the tree of life represent? (See 1 Nephi 11:25.)
* What was the source of light in God's kingdom according to John's vision? (Verse 5.)
* What does verse 7 tell us about the Savior's coming?

Read together 1 John 3:2 and find out what we will be like when we return to be with our Father in Heaven and His Son. Testify to your family that we will be like them; we will be one with them.

Revelation 22:8–11
"I am thy fellow servant"

 Tell your family you'd like to play a game called, "Who or what am I?" Explain that as you read clues revealing the identity of a person or thing, they are to raise their hand and tell the answer as soon as they think they know it. If they have answered correctly, give them the number of points listed next to that clue. If they answer incorrectly, subtract that number of points from their total. At the end, total each person's points and reward them.

First set of clues (Answer: The book of Revelation)

- I wasn't written last. (5 points)
- Sometimes they call me Apocalypse. (4 points)
- I'm not a person. (3 points)
- Though I wasn't written last, I appear last. (2 points)
- What am I? (1 point)

Second set of clues (Answer: John)

- I wrote a book in the New Testament. (6 points)
- Four other books bear my name. (5 points)
- I am an Apostle. (4 points)
- I was often found with Peter. (3 points)
- I am called the "Beloved." (2 points)
- Who am I? (1 point)

Third set of clues (Answer: An angel sent from God)

- I appeared to the Apostle John in the book of Revelation. (5 points)
- I told John, "I come quickly." (4 points)
- John fell down and worshipped me. (3 points)
- I told John "I am thy fellowservant." (2 points)
- Who am I? (1 point)

Have your family silently read Revelation 22:8–11. After reading these verses, ask:

- Who is speaking? (An angel.)
- Why do you think John fell down to worship the angel of the Lord?
- Who does the angel tell John to worship? (Verse 9.)
- Though we have prophets, seers, and revelators in the Church, who do we worship? (Jesus Christ and the Father.)

Let your family know that our goal is to introduce Jesus Christ to others. Tell your family that like the angel who appeared to John, we too are fellow servants and should hold up the light of Christ for others to see.

Revelation 22:12–17
"I come quickly"

 Invite a family member to share from memory the parable of the ten virgins. (Matthew 25:1–13.) Have another family member read aloud Doctrine and Covenants 45:56–59. Ask:

- How does the passage in the Doctrine and Covenants help explain the parable?
- What do you think the Lord is asking His people to prepare for? (His Second Coming.)

Read together Revelation 22:12–17. Ask:

- How does the Savior describe His coming?
- What are other names for Christ?
- What must we do to be able to enter the gates of the eternal city? (Verse 14.)
- What word is spoken three times in verse 17 and what do you think it means?

Share the following account of a vision of a beautiful city seen by President David O. McKay:

"The city, I understood, was [the Savior's]. It was the City Eternal; and the people following him were to abide there in peace and eternal happiness.

"But who were they?

"As if the Savior read my thoughts, he answered by pointing to a semicircle that then appeared above them, and on which were written in gold the words: *These Are They Who Have Overcome the World—Who Have Truly Been Born Again!*" (*Cherished Experiences,* 102.)

Ask:

- Who will dwell with the Savior when He comes again?
- What are some terms used to describe those who are not worthy to dwell in His presence?
- What do you think it means to "take the water of life freely?" (See John 7:37–38.)

Discuss with your family the need to prepare for Christ's return.

Revelation 22:18–22
John closes the book of Revelation

Invite someone to read aloud Revelation 22:18–22. Tell your family that these verses of scripture are sometimes used by those trying to discredit the Book of Mormon. They claim that these verses mean that God's revelation to man is finished; nothing more is to be added and nothing is to be taken away. They say that the Book of Mormon is an attempt to add to the words of the Bible. Hand a piece of paper to each family member and have them pretend that someone they know, who is not a member of the Church, says that the Book of Mormon cannot be a true record since it adds to the Bible. To prove their point, they quote to you Revelation 22:18–19. Look up these verses and compare them to Deuteronomy 4:2. Read the following by President Howard W. Hunter:

"The answer to this query is really very simple. A careful reading of the words makes it clear that the warning against adding to or taking away does not refer to the whole Bible or even to the New Testament, but to use John's words, only to the words of 'the book of this prophecy.' That is, the prophecy contained in the book of Revelation. This is substantiated by the fact that some of the books of the New Testament had not yet been written when John wrote the book of Revelation, and even those that had been written and were in existence at that time had not yet been gathered into one compilation." (*Ensign,* May, 1981, 64.)

Tell your family that this concludes our study of the New Testament. Ask them to read silently Revelation 22:20 and decide why John might have ended this verse with "come, Lord, Jesus." Ask your family if there are times you wish Jesus would hurry up and come. Why?

Bear testimony of the blessings that the righteous will receive at Christ's coming. Let your family know that righteousness will triumph over wickedness and that there is hope for all of us who live upon this earth. You may want to provide time for other family members to share how they feel about the New Testament, the Savior, and His teachings.

APPENDIX

"The Family, a Proclamation to the World," was written by the First Presidency and Council of the Twelve Apostles of The Church of Jesus Christ of Latter-day Saints. It was read by President Gordon B. Hinckley as part of his message at the General Relief Society meeting held September 23, 1995, in the Tabernacle in Salt Lake City, Utah.

A PROCLAMATION TO THE WORLD

THE FIRST PRESIDENCY AND COUNCIL OF THE TWELVE APOSTLES OF THE CHURCH OF JESUS CHRIST OF LATTER-DAY SAINTS

WE, THE FIRST PRESIDENCY and the Council of the Twelve Apostles of The Church of Jesus Christ of Latter-day Saints, solemnly proclaim that marriage between a man and a woman is ordained of God and that the family is central to the Creator's plan for the eternal destiny of His children.

ALL HUMAN BEINGS—male and female—are created in the image of God. Each is a beloved spirit son or daughter of heavenly parents, and, as such, each has a divine nature and destiny. Gender is an essential characteristic of individual premortal, mortal, and eternal identity and purpose.

IN THE PREMORTAL REALM, spirit sons and daughters knew and worshiped God as their Eternal Father and accepted His plan by which His children could obtain a physical body and gain earthly experience to progress toward perfection and ultimately realize his or her divine destiny as an heir of eternal life. The divine plan of happiness enables family relationships to be perpetuated beyond the grave. Sacred ordinances and covenants available in holy temples make it possible for individuals to return to the presence of God and for families to be united eternally.

THE FIRST COMMANDMENT that God gave to Adam and Eve pertained to their potential for parenthood as husband and wife. We declare that God's commandment for His children to multiply and replenish the earth remains in force. We further declare that God has commanded that the sacred powers of procreation are to be employed only between man and woman, lawfully wedded as husband and wife.

WE DECLARE the means by which mortal life is created to be divinely appointed. We affirm the sanctity of life and of its importance in God's eternal plan.

HUSBAND AND WIFE have a solemn responsibility to love and care for each other and for their children. "Children are an heritage of the Lord" (Psalms 127:3). Parents have a sacred duty to rear their children in love and righteousness, to provide for their physical and spiritual needs, to teach them to love and serve one another, to observe the commandments of God and to be law-abiding citizens wherever they live. Husbands and wives—mothers and fathers—will be held accountable before God for the discharge of these obligations.

THE FAMILY is ordained of God. Marriage between man and woman is essential to His eternal plan. Children are entitled to birth within the bonds of matrimony, and to be reared by a father and a mother who honor marital vows with complete fidelity. Happiness in family life is most likely to be achieved when founded upon the teachings of the Lord Jesus Christ. Successful marriages and families are established and maintained on principles of faith, prayer, repentance, forgiveness, respect, love, compassion, work, and wholesome recreational activities. By divine design, fathers are to preside over their families in love and righteousness and are responsible to provide the necessities of life and protection for their families. Mothers are primarily responsible for the nurture of their children. In these sacred responsibilities, fathers and mothers are obligated to help one another as equal partners. Disability, death, or other circumstances may necessitate individual adaptation. Extended families should lend support when needed.

WE WARN that individuals who violate covenants of chastity, who abuse spouse or offspring, or who fail to fulfill family responsibilities will one day stand accountable before God. Further, we warn that the disintegration of the family will bring upon individuals, communities, and nations the calamities foretold by ancient and modern prophets.

WE CALL UPON responsible citizens and officers of government everywhere to promote those measures designed to maintain and strengthen the family as the fundamental unit of society.

This proclamation was read by President Gordon B. Hinckley as part of his message at the General Relief Society Meeting held September 23, 1995, in Salt Lake City, Utah.

BIBLIOGRAPHY

Anderson, Richard Lloyd. *Understanding Paul.* Salt Lake City: Deseret Book, 1983.

Avigad, Nahman. *Discovering Jerusalem.* Nashville: T. Nelson, 1983.

Bennion, Lowell L. *An Introduction to the Gospel.* Salt Lake City: Deseret Sunday School Union Board, 1959.

Benson, Ezra Taft. *The Teachings of Ezra Taft Benson.* Salt Lake City: Bookcraft, 1988.

Brewster, Hoyt W., Jr. *Doctrine and Covenants Encyclopedia.* Salt Lake City: Bookcraft, 1988.

Children's Songbook of The Church of Jesus Christ of Latter-day Saints. Salt Lake City: The Church of Jesus Christ of Latter-day Saints, 1989.

Church News. Salt Lake City: Deseret News, 1980–1995.

Conference Report. Salt Lake City: The Church of Jesus Christ of Latter-day Saints, 1899–1970.

Cowley, Matthias F. *Talks on Doctrine.* Chattanooga, Tenn.: Ben. E. Rich, 1902.

Duties and Blessings of the Priesthood. Part A: A Basic Manual for Priesthood Holders. Salt Lake City: The Church of Jesus Christ of Latter-day Saints, 1993. Revised 2000.

Encyclopedia of Mormonism. Edited by Daniel H. Ludlow, et al. New York: Macmillan, 1992.

Family Guidebook. Salt Lake City: The Church of Jesus Christ of Latter-day Saints, 1999.

For the Strength of Youth [pamphlet]. Salt Lake City: The Church of Jesus Christ of Latter-day Saints, 1990.

Galbraith, David B., D. Kelly Ogden, and Andrew C. Skinner. *Jerusalem, the Eternal City.* Salt Lake City: Deseret Book, 1996.

Hafen, Bruce C. *The Believing Heart.* Salt Lake City: Deseret Book, 1986.

Hartshorn, Leon R. *Remarkable Stories from the Lives of Latter-day Saint Women.* 2 vols. Salt Lake City: Deseret Book, 1973.

Hinckley, Gordon B. *Teachings of Gordon B. Hinckley.* Salt Lake City: Deseret Book, 1997.

Hunter, Howard W. *The Teachings of Howard W. Hunter.* Edited by Clyde J. Williams. Salt Lake City: Bookcraft, 1997.

Hymns of The Church of Jesus Christ of Latter-day Saints. Salt Lake City: The Church of Jesus Christ of Latter-day Saints, 1985.

Joseph Smith's "New Translation" of the Bible. Independence, Mo.: Herald House, 1970.

Journal of Discourses. 26 vols. London: Latter-day Saints' Book Depot, 1854–86.

Kimball, Spencer W. *Faith Precedes the Miracle.* Salt Lake City: Deseret Book, 1972.

———. *The Miracle of Forgiveness,* Salt Lake City: Bookcraft, 1969.

———. *The Teachings of Spencer W. Kimball.* Edited by Edward L. Kimball. Salt Lake City: Bookcraft, 1982.

Lee, Harold B. *Feet Shod with the Preparation of the Gospel of Peace.* Brigham Young University Speeches of the Year. Provo, 1954.

———. *Stand Ye in Holy Places.* Salt Lake City: Deseret Book, 1974.

———. *The Teachings of Harold B. Lee.* Edited by Clyde J. Williams, Salt Lake City: Bookcraft, 1996.

Lewis, C. S. *Mere Christianity.* New York: Macmillan, 1960.

Life and Teachings of Jesus and His Apostles. Salt Lake City: The Church of Jesus Christ of Latter-day Saints, 1979.

Lund, Gerald N. In *Doctrines of the Book of Mormon: 1991 Sperry Symposium on the Book of Mormon.* Edited by Bruce A. Van Orden and Brent L. Top. Salt Lake City: Deseret Book, 1992.

Lyon, Jack M., Linda Ririe Gundry, and Jay A. Parry, eds. *Best-Loved Poems of the LDS People.* Salt Lake City: Deseret Book, 1997.

Maxwell, Neal A. *Even As I Am.* Salt Lake City: Deseret Book, 1982.

———. *Not My Will, but Thine.* Salt Lake City: Bookcraft, 1998.

———. *That Ye May Believe.* Salt Lake City: Bookcraft, 1992.

McConkie, Bruce R. *Doctrinal New Testament Commentary.* 3 vols. Salt Lake City: Bookcraft, 1965–73.

————. *Mormon Doctrine*. 2d ed. Salt Lake City: Book-craft, 1966.

————. *The Mortal Messiah: From Bethlehem to Calvary*. 4 vols. Salt Lake City: Deseret Book, 1979–91.

————. *A New Witness for the Articles of Faith*. Salt Lake City: Deseret Book, 1985.

McConkie, Joseph Fielding. *Gospel Symbolism*. Salt Lake City: Bookcraft, 1999.

McKay, David O. *Cherished Experiences from the Writings of President David O. McKay*. Compiled by Clare Middlemiss. Salt Lake City: Deseret Book, 1976.

————. *Gospel Ideals: Selections from the Discourses of David O. McKay*. Salt Lake City: Improvement Era, 1953.

The NIV Study Bible: New International Version. Edited by Kenneth Barker. Grand Rapids, Mich.: Zondervan, 1985.

Oaks, Dallin H. *The Lord's Way*. Salt Lake City: Deseret Book, 1991.

Ogden, D. Kelly. *Where Jesus Walked: The Land and Culture of New Testament Times*. Salt Lake City: Deseret Book, 1991.

Ogden, D. Kelly, and Andrew C. Skinner. *Verse by Verse, Acts through Revelation*. Salt Lake City: Deseret Book, 2006.

Parry, Jay A., and Donald W. Parry. *Understanding the Book of Revelation*. Salt Lake City: Deseret Book, 1998.

Preach My Gospel. Salt Lake City: The Church of Jesus Christ of Latter-day Saints, 2004.

The Savior, the Priesthood, and You. Salt Lake City: The Church of Jesus Christ of Latter-day Saints, 1973.

Smith, Joseph. *Discourses of the Prophet Joseph Smith*. Compiled by Alma P. Burton. Salt Lake City: Deseret Book, 1977.

————. *History of The Church of Jesus Christ of Latter-day Saints*. Edited by B. H. Roberts. 7 vols. Salt Lake City: The Church of Jesus Christ of Latter-day Saints, 1932–51.

————. *Joseph Smith's Commentary on the Bible*. Salt Lake City: Deseret Book, 1994.

————. *Lectures on Faith*. Compiled by N. B. Lundwall. Salt Lake City: Bookcraft, n.d.

————. *Teachings of the Prophet Joseph Smith*. Selected by Joseph Fielding Smith. Salt Lake City: Deseret Book, 1976.

Smith, Joseph F. *Gospel Doctrine*. Compiled by John A. Widtsoe. Salt Lake City: Deseret Book, 1939.

Smith, Joseph Fielding. *Answers to Gospel Questions*. 5 vols. Salt Lake City: Deseret Book, 1957–66.

————. *Doctrines of Salvation*. Compiled by Bruce R. McConkie. Salt Lake City: Bookcraft, 1954–56.

————. *Essentials in Church History*. Salt Lake City: Deseret Book, 1950.

Sperry, Sidney B. *Paul's Life and Letters*. Salt Lake City: Bookcraft, 1955.

Strong, James. *Strong's Exhaustive Concordance of the Bible*. Nashville: Abingdon, 1986.

Studies in Scripture. 8 vols. Edited by Kent P. Jackson and Robert L. Millet. Salt Lake City: Deseret Book, 2004.

Stuy, Brian H., comp. *Collected Discourses*. 5 vols. Sandy, Utah: BHS Publishing, 1987–92.

Talmage, James E. *Articles of Faith*. Salt Lake City: Deseret Book, 1981.

————. *Jesus the Christ*. Salt Lake City: Deseret Book, 1983.

Teachings of Presidents of the Church: John Taylor. Salt Lake City: The Church of Jesus Christ of Latter-day Saints, 2002.

True to the Faith, a Gospel Reference. Salt Lake City: The Church of Jesus Christ of Latter-day Saints, 2004.

Unger, Merrill F. *The New Unger's Bible Dictionary*. Edited by R. K. Harrison. Chicago: Moody Press, 1988.

Webster, Noah. *American Dictionary of the English Language*. 1828. Reprint, San Francisco: Foundation for American Christian Education, 1980.

Young, Brigham. *Discourses of Brigham Young*. Selected by John A. Widtsoe. Salt Lake City: Deseret Book, 1954.

TOPICAL INDEX

Adversity: 2 Corinthians 1:1–10; 4:17–18;
    1 Thessalonians 3:1–13
Advocate: 1 John 2:1–2
Agency: Philemon 1:1–25
Angels: Luke 1:1–38; Hebrews 2:1–18; Revelation
    14:6–20; 22:8–11
Anger: Acts 7:37–54; Ephesians 4:17–32
Apostasy: Acts 7:37–54; 20:28–30; Romans 11:16–32;
    2 Corinthians 11:1–15; Galatians 1:1–24;
    2 Thessalonians 2:1–17; 1 Timothy 4:1–6;
    2 Timothy 4:1–5; 2 Peter 2:1–9; Revelation
    12:1–17
Apostles: Matthew 10:1–4; Mark 3:7–21; Luke
    6:12–16; John 1:35–51; Acts 1:8–11; 1:12–26; Acts
    15:1–34; Romans 1:1–16; Ephesians 2:19–22
Armageddon: Revelation 16:13–21; 19:11–21
Armor of God: Ephesians 6:10–24
Atonement. *See* Jesus Christ, Atonement of
Authority: Matthew 21:23–27

Baptism: Matthew 3:13–17; Mark 1:1–45; 1:1–11; John
    1:29–34; Acts 19:1–12; Romans 5:12–21;
    1 Corinthians 12:12–31; Titus 3:1–11
Baptism for the dead: 1 Corinthians 15:24–58
Barabbas: Matthew 27:15–25; John 18:33–40
Beatitudes: Matthew 5:1–12
Bishops: Titus 1:7–9
Blessings. Matthew 4:11–12; 20:1–19, 20:29–34; John
    14:1–4; Romans 9:1–8; 1 John 1:6–10
Boasting: Luke 18:9–14
Born again: 1 John 5:1–21

Celestial kingdom: Revelation 4:1–11; 7:9–17; 15:1–8;
    21:1–8, 22–27; 22: 1–7
Charity: Matthew 7:1–5; 26:1–13; Luke 6:20–49;
    19:1–10; Acts 11:27–30; 20:31–38; Romans
    15:23–29; 1 Corinthians 13:1–13; 16:1–24;
    2 Corinthians 8:1–9:15; 2 Thessalonians 1:1–12;
    1 Peter 4:1–19; 2 Peter 1:1–9
Chastening: Hebrews 12:1–11
Childlike: Mark 10:13–16
Children: Matthew 18:1–10; 22:15–22; Luke 17:1–2;
    18:15–17

Church: Romans 15:30–33; Ephesians 2:19–22; 4:1–16
Church discipline: 1 Corinthians 5:1–13
Church service: John 15:16; 1 Corinthians 9:1–18;
    16:1–24; 2 Corinthians 6:1–13
Cleanliness: Matthew 21:12–16; Mark 7:14–23; Luke
    11:1–41, 52–54
Comfort: Matthew 4:11–12; Luke 20:1–8, 19–47
Commandments: Matthew 11:28–30; 22:34–40; Luke
    18:18–30; John 8:12–36
Commitment: Matthew 22:1–14; John 3:8–13;
    21:15–19; Acts 26:22–32
Compassion: Matthew 12:14–21; Mark 8:1–9; Luke
    7:11–18
Consequences: Luke 15:11–32
Contention: Romans 14:1–6, 12–15, 20–21;
    1 Corinthians 1:1–16; 2 Thessalonians 3:3–15
Contentment: 1 Timothy 6:1–8
Conversion: Matthew 5:1–12; Mark 4: 3–9, 14–20;
    Luke 15:1–7; John 3:3–7; 9:8–41; Acts 17:1–15;
    2 Corinthians 3:1–18; 1 Peter 2:1–3
Courage: Mark 15:1–15; Acts 4:23–31; 5:17–42; 8:1–4;
    21:27–40
Covenants: Mark 2:18–22; Acts 5:1–11; Romans 9:1–8;
    2 Corinthians 6:14–18; Galatians 3:1–18
Criticism: Galatians 5:13–15
Crucifixion: Matthew 27:34–66; Mark 15:16–47; Luke
    23:1–56; 23:32–47; John 2:18–25; 19:16–18;
    19:17–42

Death: Luke 13:1–5; 1 Corinthians 15:20–23
Deception: 2 Peter 2:1–9
Diligence: 2 Timothy 4:6–8; Hebrews 6:9–12; Acts
    20:13–27; 22:1–30
Discipleship: Matthew 4:17–22; 5:13–16; 8:23–27;
    16:21–28; 23:1–35; Mark 1:1–45; Luke 5:27–39;
    8:1–56; 14:15–35; 18:18–30; John 3:8–13;
    3:14–17; 13:31–35; 15:17–27; Acts 6:1–7; 7:54–60;
    Revelation 3:1–6, 14–22
Dispensation: Ephesians 1:9–14
Divorce: Matthew 19:1–12; Mark 10:1–12;
    1 Corinthians 7:1–40
Doctrine: Acts 15:1–34; Galatians 5:1–12; 2 Timothy
    1:12–18

Jesus Christ

Atonement of:
Matthew 5:20, 48; 26:17–29; 26:31–46; Mark 5:1–20; 14:32–42; 15:16–47; Like 13:31–35; 19:28–40, 45–58; 22:39–46 63–71; John 18:1–11; 19:1–5; 19:6–16; 19:16–18; Acts 26:22–32; Romans 3:9–26; 5:6–11; 5:12–21; 1 Corinthians 12:12–31; 2 Corinthians 5:12–21; Galatians 3:1–18; Ephesians 2:1–19; Philippians 2:1–11; 1 Timothy 1:12–20; Hebrews 7:22–28; 9:1–10; 10:5–39; Revelation 7:9–17

Betrayal of:
Matthew 26:47–75; 27:1–14; John 18:1–11; 18:33–40

Birth of:
Matthew 1:18–25; 2:1–11; Luke 1:1–20; John 7:37–43

Childhood of:
Luke 2:40–52

Suffering of:
Matthew 27:26–33; Luke 18:31–34
John the Baptist: Matthew 3:1–6; 3:7–12; 3:13–17; 11:1–6; 14:1–12; Luke 1:1–38; Luke 1:76–80; John 3:25–36
Jonah: Matthew 12:38–42; 16:1–12
Joy: John 16:16–33
Judas: Matthew 27:1–14
Judging: Matthew 7:1–5; 12:22–30; 23:25–26; Romans 14:1–6, 12–15, 20–21; 2 Corinthians 10:1–18
Judgment: Matthew 25:14–30; 25:31–46; Luke 6:20–49; John 7:1–13; 8:1–11; 14:1–4; Romans 2:1–16; 1 Corinthians 11:17–34; Revelation 20:11–15
Justification: Romans 4:1–12; 5:6–11; Galatians 2:11–21

Keys: Matthew 17:1–13; Mark 9:1–10
Kindness: 2 Corinthians 1:12–24; 2 Peter 1:1–9
Kingdom of God: Matthew 6:24–33; 13:31–33, 44–50; Mark 4:26–32; Luke 13:23–30; Luke 13:23–30

Language: James 3:1–18
Last days: 2 Timothy 3:1–17; Revelation 6:1–17; 8:5–13; 9:1–21; 11:1–19; 16:13–21
Last Supper: John 13:1–17; 13:18–30
Law of Moses: Matthew 5:17–20; 5:21–48; John 7:1–13; Acts 7:1–36; 21:15–26; Romans 3:27–31; 7:1–4; 2 Corinthians 3:1–18; Galatians 2:11–21; 3:1–18; 3:19–29; 4:1–31; Colossians 2:13–23; Hebrews 10:1–4
Leadership: Luke 8:1–56; Acts 6:1–7; 15:1–34; 1 Corinthians 4:9–21; 16:1–24; 2 Corinthians 6:1–13; 11:1–15

Leaven: Mark 8:14–21
Light: Matthew 4:13–16; Mark 4:21–25; Luke 11:1–41, 52–54; John 1:1–14; 3:18–21
Light of Christ: Romans 1:16–32; Ephesians 5:1–18; 1 John 1:5–10
Love: Matthew 7:12; 26:1–13; Mark 12:28–34; Luke 6:20–49; 9:57–62; 13:31–35; John 3:14–17; 13:31–35; John 15:9–15; 21:15–19; Acts 11:27–30; James 2:1–13; 1 Peter 3:1–13; 1 John 2:15–17; 4:7–21
Love of God: Mark 14:32–42; Luke 9:51–56; 15:1–7; 15:11–32; Romans 8:35–39; 13:1–14; Ephesians 3:14–21; 1 John 4:1–15; Revelation 15:1–8

Marriage: Matthew 19:1–12; 22:23–33; Mark 10:1–12; 1 Corinthians 7:1–40; 11:3–16; 2 Corinthians 6:14–18 Ephesians 5:22–33; 1 Timothy 4:1–6
Martyr: Mark 6:14–32; Acts 7:54–60; 12:1–25
Mary and Joseph: Luke 2:21–39; John 12:1–50
Melchizedek: Hebrews 5:5–10; 7:1–19
Mercy: Matthew 12:14–21; Luke 6:20–49; Romans 11:16–32; Philemon 1:1–25; 1 Peter 1:1–12
Millennium: Revelation 11:1–19; 20:1–10; 21:1–21
Miracles: Matthew 8:1–33; 8:28–34; 9:1–38; 14:14–21; 14:22–33; 15:21–28; 17:24–27; 20:29–34; Mark 1:1–45; 6:1–6; 6:33–44; 6:45–56; 7:31–37; 8:1–9; 8:22–33; Luke 1:1–38; 4:33–44; 5:12–26; 7:1–10; 9:1–62; 13:10–17; 18:35–43; John 2:1–11; 4:43–54; 9:1–7; 11:1–57; 21:1–14; Acts 5:12–16; 5:17–42; 9:10–19; 9:32–43; 12:1–25; 19:1–12; 19:13–20; 20:1–12; 28:1–10; Hebrews 11:4–40
Missionary work: Matthew 3:1–6; 7:6; 10:5–42; 13:3–8, 18–23; 13:31–33, 44–50; 18:11–14; 28:19–20; Mark 4:3–9, 14–20; 6:7–13; 16:9–20; Luke 2:1–20; 4:14–32; 5:1–11; 24:44–53; John 4:5–42; Acts 1:8–11; 6:8–15; 8:1–4; 10:1–33; 13:1–13; 13:14–43; 14:1–28; 16:1–12; 18:7–17; 18:24–28; 22:1–30; 28:11–31; Romans 10:1–21; 11:13–15; 1 Corinthians 1:17–31; 2:1–8; 9:19–27; 2 Corinthians 4:1–16; 1 Thessalonians 2:1–20; 1 Peter 2:1–3; 3:14–17; Revelation 7:1–8
Modesty: Colossians 2:13–23
Money: 1 Timothy 6:7–19; James 5:1–6
Morality: 1 Corinthians 3:16–23; 6:9–20

Oaths: Hebrews 6:13–20; 7:19–21
Obedience: Matthew 4:17–22; 5:20, 48; 7:13–14, 21–23; 7:15–20; 7:24–29; 9:1–38; 11:28–30; 19:16–30; 21:28–32; 22:34–40; Mark 3:28–30; 4:21–25; 7:14–23; 10:17–31; 12:28–34; Luke 10:1–20; 13:18–22; 13:23–30; 18:18–30; John 1:35–51; 8:51–59; 13:31–35; 14:1–4; 19:6–16; 20:19–31; Acts 7:37–54; 16:13–40; Romans 6:12–23; 13:1–14; 1 Corinthians 4:1–8;

1:1–12; 2 Peter 3:1–18; Revelation 6:1–17; 8:5–13; 9:1–21; 11:1–19; 14:8–20; 16:13–21; 19:1–21; 22:12–17

Self-control: Acts 24:1–27; 1 Corinthians 9:19–27; 2 Corinthians 10:1–18

Selfishness: Luke 12:16–21, 35–48

Service: Matthew 4:17–22; 5:13–16; 6:1–18; 7:12; 7:13–14, 21–23; 11:28–30; 14:14–21; 20:1–19; 20:20–28; 25:31–46; Mark 8:34–38; 10:32–45; 12:16–21, 35–48; 12:28–34; Luke 10:25–37; 22:24–30; John 6:1–21; 13:1–17; Acts 20:31–38; Romans 15:1–7; 1 Corinthians 12:12–31; 2 Corinthians 1:12–24; 8:1–9:15; Galatians 5:13–15; 6:1–6, 18; Philippians 4:14–23; Hebrews 12:12–17; James 1:17–27; 4:1–17

Seventy: Luke 10:1–20

Sharing: Matthew 7:12; Acts 11:27–30

Sheep, and goats: Matthew 25:31–46

Sign of the dove: Matthew 3:13–17

Sign-seeking: Matthew 12:38–42; 16:1–12

Sin: Matthew 12:31–32; 14:1–12; Mark 3:28–30; 5:1–20; 7:14–23; 9:38–50; Acts 7:37–54; Romans 6:12–23; 8:1–13; 1 Corinthians 10:1–33; Galatians 5:1–12; 5:16–26; James 4:1–17; 1 John 1:5–10; 3:4–10

Slavery: 1 Timothy 6:1–8

Sons of God: 1 John 3:1–3

Sorrow: John 16:16–33; 2 Corinthians 7:1–17

Spirit world: Luke 23:39–43; 1 Peter 3:18–22; 4:1–19

Standards: Mark 7:1–13; 1 Corinthians 8:4–13; James 3:1–18

Symbolism: Revelation 1:12–20; 4:1–11

Tabernacle: Hebrews 8:1–5; 9:1–10

Talents: Matthew 25:14–30; Mark 8:1–9; Luke 19:11–27

Teaching: 1 Corinthians 2:1–8

Temples: Matthew 21:12–16; Mark 11:15–19; John 2:12–17; 1 Corinthians 3:16–23; Hebrews 8:1–5

Temptation: Matthew 4:1–11; Mark 1:1–45; Luk4:1–13; Romans 16:17–27; 1 Corinthians 10:1–33; 2 Corinthians 11:1–15; Galatians 5:16–26; 6:1–6, 18; James 1:1–4, 8–16

Testimony: Matthew 8:28–34; 11:1–6; 13:3–8, 18–23; 16:13–20; Mark 8:14–21; Luke 1:39–75; 4:14–32;

24:44–53; John 1:1–14; 1:15–34; 6:59–71; 7:14–32; 7:44–53; 8:12–36; 9:8–41; Acts 4:1–22; 9:20–31; 10:34–43; 17:1–15; Romans 1:1–16; 1:16–32; 1 Corinthians 1:17–31; 15:1–11; Colossians 2:1–12; Hebrews 9:11–28; 2 Peter 1:16–18; 1 John 4:1–15

Tithing: Mark 12:41–44

Traditions: Mark 7:1–13

Transfigured: Mark 9:1–10

Translated beings: Matthew 17:1–13; John 21:20–25

Trials: Matthew 11:28–30; 15:21–28; Mark 14:12–72; Luke 22:31–38; 54–62; John 15:1–8; 15:17–27; 16:1–13; Acts 16:13–40; 21:8–14; 21:27–40; 23:1–35; 27:1–44; Romans 5:1–5; 1 Corinthians 4:9–21; 2 Corinthians 11:16–33; 12:1–21; Galatians 6:1–6, 18; 1 Thessalonians 3:1–13; 2 Timothy 2:7–13; 3:10–12; 1 Peter 5:6–14

Triumphal entry: Matthew 21:1–11; Mark 11:1–10; Luke 19:28–40, 45–48

Trust: Matthew 14:22–33

Truth: Matthew 15:1–20; Mark 4:21–25; John 18:33–40; 1 Corinthians 1:17–31

Unity: Luke 11:1–41, 52–54; John 17:20–26; 1 Corinthians 1:1–16; 12:12–31; Philippians 2:1–11

War: Revelation 12:1–17

Wealth: Matthew 19:23–26; Luke 5:27–39; 16:1–18; 16:19–31; 18:18–30; 1 Timothy 6:7–19; James 5:1–6

Welfare: Romans 15:23–29

Wickedness: Revelation 18:1–8

Wise men: Matthew 2:1, 11

Witness: Mark 16:9–20; Luke 23:1–56; John 20:19–31; 2 Corinthians 13:1–14; 1 John 1:1–4

Women, role of: 1 Timothy 2:11–15

Word of Wisdom: Romans 14:1–6, 12–15, 20–21; 1 Corinthians 8:4–13

Work: Acts 18:1–6

Work for the dead: 1 Peter 3:18–22

Works: Romans 3:27–31; 4:13–16; 4:17–25; James 2:14–26

Worldliness: John 17:11–19

Worthiness: 1 Corinthians 11:17–34; Hebrews 7:19–21